The Principles of Constitutional Government

The Principles of Constitutional Government
Political Sovereignty

by
Warren L. McFerran

PELICAN PUBLISHING COMPANY
GRETNA 2009

To my daughter, Lisa

ISBN: 9781589807280

Printed in the United States of America
Published by Pelican Publishing Company, Inc.
1000 Burmaster Street, Gretna, Louisiana 70053

Contents

"The Government of the United States derives its existence from the same source, and exercises its functions by the will of the same sovereignty that creates and confers authority upon the State governments. The people of each State are, in either case, the source. The only difference is that, in the creation of the State governments, each sovereign acted alone; in that of the Federal Government, they acted in cooperation with the others. Neither the whole nor any part of their sovereignty has been surrendered to either Government."

– Jefferson Davis

"*Sovereignty*, the ultimate and supreme power within a body politic, is not to be confused with governmental powers. The one is the source for the others. Governmental powers, which are derived from sovereignty, may be delegated and divided; sovereignty itself cannot be. In the United States, sovereignty resides in the people of each of the separate States."

– Richard N. Current

"Asking one of the States to surrender part of her sovereignty is like asking a lady to surrender part of her chastity."

– John Randolph of Roanoke

"It is...objected..., against the doctrine of State Rights,..., that, if it should prevail, the peace of the country would be destroyed. But what if it should not prevail? Would there be peace? Yes, the peace of despotism; that peace which is enforced by the bayonet and the sword; the peace of death, where all the vital functions of liberty have ceased. It is this peace which the doctrine of State Sovereignty may disturb by that conflict, which, in every free State, if properly organized, necessarily exists between liberty and power; but which, if restrained within proper limits, gives a salutary exercise to our moral and intellectual faculties...."

– John C. Calhoun

Some Key Contributors to the States' Rights School of Thought
During the Ante-Bellum and Civil War Periods

First Row: Thomas Jefferson, John Taylor of Caroline, and James Madison. *Second Row:* John Randolph of Roanoke, Robert Y. Hayne, and John C. Calhoun. *Third Row:* Jefferson Davis and Alexander H. Stephens.

Some Key Contributors to the Consolidating School of Thought
During the Ante-Bellum and Civil War Periods

First Row: Alexander Hamilton, George McDuffie, and John Marshall. *Second Row:* Joseph Story, Henry Clay, and Daniel Webster. *Third Row:* Edward Everett and Abraham Lincoln.

Chapter One

The Significance of Sovereignty

There is perhaps no other word in the English language that has been more misunderstood, misused, distorted, and perverted than the word sovereignty. In modern times, the word has virtually disappeared from the vocabulary routinely utilized by the general public, and rare indeed is the American who is able to properly define the term, let alone comprehend the crucial significance of sovereignty within our system of constitutionally limited government. Even among those who ought to be readily familiar with the term and the concepts associated with it, and whose responsibility is to teach others, its meaning has been so distorted that it is cited to destroy precisely what its true meaning was intended to preserve.

Over the course of modern world history, the term "sovereignty" and its derivative, "sovereign," have been employed to describe everything from Almighty God, to governments, to kings, to nations, to delegated powers, to people, and even to coins. The word *sovereignty* has been utilized to justify the unlimited despotism and "divine rights" of kings, as well as to provide the basis for government-by-the-consent-of-the-governed. In bygone ages, kings often proclaimed themselves to be sovereign in order to acquire a supremacy over their subject peoples. During the Age of Reason, sovereignty was proclaimed to be invested in the people in order to give them a supremacy over kings. And in more modern times, clever and cunning theorists have managed to once again bestow sovereignty upon government by proclaiming that the people and their government are one and the same and by promulgating such heresies as "partial" sovereignty, "divided" sovereignty, and even "delegated" sovereignty.

To set aside any confusion that may exist as to the true meaning of sovereignty, it would be prudent to offer, at the very start of our treatise on the subject, a definition of the term sovereignty and to differentiate between the main types of authority encompassed by that concept. *Webster's II New Riverside University Dictionary* gives four definitions of the term *sovereignty*, three of which apply to a republican form of government, and one of which applies only to a monarchical government: "1. Supremacy of authority or rule as exercised by a sovereign or a sovereign state. 2. Royal rank, power, or authority. 3. Total independence and self-government. 4. A territory existing as an independent state." The term *sovereign* is defined by this same dictionary as meaning "paramount: supreme," "having supreme rank or power," and "self-governing: independent." [1]

The New Lexicon Webster's Dictionary of the English Language defines sovereignty as "undisputed political power," and defines the word sovereign as "having undisputed right to make decisions and act accordingly," "unlimited, absolute, *sovereign power,*" and "a person or body of persons supreme in a state." [2] This same dictionary defines *supreme* as "being the highest authority," "highest in quality," and "highest in degree." It defines *supremacy* as "the quality or state of being supreme" and "the position of being superior to all others in something." [3] And this dictionary defines *power* as "controlling influence, political power" and as "authority." [4]

Word associations are also conducive to ascertaining the meaning of words. The third edition of *Roget's International Thesaurus* categorizes the term sovereignty under the general heading of "authority." Under this general heading, the thesaurus associates the concepts of *authority* and *sovereignty* with the concepts of *legal or rightful power, right, jurisdiction, command, control, rule, supremacy*, and *seat of authority.* [5]

Let us now combine these dictionary definitions and word associations to arrive at a concise, accurate definition of the term in question. Sovereignty may be defined as the supreme power or highest authority on earth, a power that can only be derived from God. The Creator of the Universe, needless to say, must be the originator of all earthly sovereignty, for He is the Supreme Authority in the Universe. Since all men are created equal, they can rightfully exercise authority over themselves and over one another only because God has granted such authority to mankind.

Just as mankind finds anarchy distasteful, so does God abhor chaos, as is evidenced by the existence of the *Laws of Nature*, which God has decreed to govern and create order in the natural world. For this reason, He has granted to mankind authority to control and regulate man's relationship with his fellow man. Mankind is thus rightfully entitled to exercise sovereignty or supreme authority in those areas and for such purposes that God has granted to the human race. Specifically, there are four distinct types of sovereignty that have been bestowed by our Creator, one of which is entirely personal, two of which relate to the family, and the last of which concerns civil society.

---

[1] *Webster's II New Riverside University Dictionary*, The Riverside Publishing Company, Boston, 1984, p. 1112.
[2] *The New Lexicon Webster's Dictionary of the English Language*, Lexicon Publications, Inc., New York, 1990, p. 950.
[3] *Ibid.*, p. 995.
[4] *Ibid.*, p. 787.
[5] Peter Mark Roget, *Roget's International Thesaurus*, Third Edition, Thomas Y. Crowell Company, New York, 1962, p. 490.

A man may thus assume *Personal Sovereignty* over his own welfare, because God has granted to all men individually the rights to life, liberty, and property. Likewise, a man may rule over or govern his own wife because God has granted *Patriarchal Sovereignty* to husbands. And a mother and father may rightfully exercise *Parental Sovereignty* over their own children because God has granted that authority to them. Finally, mankind may exercise *Political Sovereignty* by instituting government to enforce justice and an observance of the laws of nature because God has granted such authority to the human race.

To repeat what has been said, Holy Writ reveals to us that all men are made in the image of God and are therefore created equal. This is the principle, incidentally, asserted within our Declaration of Independence as being the foundation of a just system of government. Because all men are created equal, no one could legitimately exercise any authority over others unless such authority has been granted by God to promote order, avoid anarchy, and fulfill the will of God. Such authority, which we may term sovereignty, has been granted in four distinct forms. Although our focus within this treatise is on only one type of sovereignty – *Political Sovereignty* – it may prove beneficial to briefly examine the other types of supreme authority.

Personal Sovereignty

Since all men are created equally, it naturally follows that all men are endowed by their Creator with certain inalienable rights, which may be summarized as *life*, *liberty*, and *property*. The purpose of such rights is to allow each man to determine his own destiny and utilize his wealth and freedom to serve God. For this reason, God has granted to every man a natural right to be his own master, a concept that can be best described by the term Personal Sovereignty.

Because every human being possesses Personal Sovereignty over his own life, liberty, and property, we find that the Bible is quite clear in forbidding violations of these rights. The Ten Commandments, for example, state emphatically that murder is wrong, that stealing is wrong, and that even the desire to steal is wrong. Likewise, the Bible reveals that liberty is the blessing of God upon mankind. The inscription on the Liberty Bell, in fact, was derived from the Scriptures, as a reading of Leviticus 25:10 will reveal. Personal Sovereignty over life, liberty, and property has clearly been invested by God in each man. As a consequence, every man may be said to possess a natural, supreme dominion over himself.

The reason why every man possesses Personal Sovereignty is not difficult to discern. In addition to allowing every individual freedom to worship God, such authority is required for the preservation and advancement of the human race. It takes little imagination to picture what a tragic state the human race would be in if all men refused to assume authority over their own lives and to exercise responsibility to care for themselves. Common sense, as well as Holy Writ, dictate the necessity of Personal Sovereignty.

While it is undeniably true that all men possess Personal Sovereignty over themselves on an individual basis, this means only that each man has supreme authority over himself in respect to all other men. It does not mean that any man is supreme over, or even equal to, God Himself. Although every man possesses the right to control his own life, liberty, and property as he sees fit, without having to answer to any other man, he is held accountable by his Creator.

As with all forms of authority wielded by man, Personal Sovereignty can be used for purposes not intended by the Creator. Yet, the natural laws of *right and wrong* have been written in the hearts of all men, and each man needs only to consult his own conscience to know the difference between the two. And should any individual maliciously exercise his Personal Sovereignty to harm another, then Political Sovereignty, as we shall discover, gives to mankind the right of self-defense and punishment.

Patriarchal Sovereignty

Two types of sovereignty – Patriarchal and Parental – are associated with the God-ordained institution of *Holy Matrimony*. As revealed in the Book of Genesis, God took one of Adam's ribs and created Eve to be his wife. While in the Garden of Eden, and prior to the advent of sin, the man and the woman were equal partners within marriage. Then sin was introduced to the world when Eve yielded to the temptation offered by Satan, and Adam yielded to that offered by Eve. As a consequence, Adam and Eve were expelled from the Garden of Eden.

As further punishment for their sinful natures, Adam was forced to toil for food and Eve was commanded to be in subjugation to Adam. As Genesis 3:16 informs us, "Unto the woman he said, I will greatly multiply thy sorrow and thy conception; in sorrow thou shalt bring forth children; and thy desire shall be to thy husband, and he shall rule over thee." [6] Other revelations in the Bible make it evident that God's statement to Eve was a permanent subjugation of all wives to their respective husbands. In Ephesians 5:22, for example, we read the following: "Wives, submit yourselves unto your own husbands, as

[6] C.I. Scofield (ed.), *The New Scofield Reference Bible*, Oxford University Press, New York, 1967, p. 8.

unto the Lord." [7] Such God-ordained masculine supremacy of a husband over his own wife is the authority encompassed within the concept of Patriarchal Sovereignty.

The Creator has granted this authority to the husband for a specific purpose, and that objective is to fulfill God's will. The supremacy God has granted to all husbands over their own wives is the means by which each husband may guide his marital union in the pursuit of godly ends. As we have before observed, no man possesses a supremacy over God, and all must answer to Him for the manner in which they have exercised the authority that He has given to them.

All types of authority wielded by the human race are subject to abuse whenever the wielder of power substitutes illegitimate ends for the godly ends for which such authority was granted. This is as true for Patriarchal Sovereignty as it is for any other type of authority, and our modern feminists have attempted to cite examples of misuse of Patriarchal Sovereignty in an attempt to deny that any such authority rightfully exists. But their real quarrel is with God, whose revelations in the Bible clearly indicate that Patriarchal Sovereignty does indeed exist and that it exists for a very good and practical reason.

As the Bible states in Ephesians 5:23, Patriarchal Sovereignty provides a very practical benefit for the wife, in that it serves to protect her from the harsh realities of the material world: "For the husband is the head of the wife, even as Christ is the head of the church; and he is the savior of the body." [8] While Christ is the savior of the soul, the husband is the *savior* of the wife in materialistic considerations. God's grant of this authority to the husband is truly a blessing for the wife, although there will always be a few malcontents who will ever attempt to falsely proclaim that that blessing is a curse upon women.

Parental Sovereignty

From the bonds of Holy Matrimony springs another type of natural dominion and rightful authority of one human being over another. Since time immemorial, it has been universally acknowledged that children of a minor age should obey and be under the control, guidance, and rule of their parents. This type of authority – a dominion of parents over their own children – is encompassed within the concept of Parental Sovereignty.

This proper and natural parent-child relationship is in accordance with the Laws of Nature and rests upon a biblical foundation. From the Old Testa-

---

[7] *Ibid.*, p. 1277.
[8] *Ibid.*, p. 1277.

ment to the New Testament, we find references to this type of authority. In the twenty-first chapter of Deuteronomy, in verses 18 through 23, for example, is presented the punishment for a disobedient son. These passages begin with the words, "If a man have a stubborn and rebellious son, who will not obey the voice of his father or the voice of his mother, and *that,* when they have chastened him, will not harken unto them...." [9]

According to the Law of Moses, the parents of such a son could seize him, bring him before the elders of the city, and "all the men of his city shall stone him with stones, that he die." The harsh punishment was required due to the evil nature of rebellion against Parental Sovereignty: "So shalt thou put evil away from among you, and all Israel shall hear, and fear." [10]

The existence and importance of Parental Sovereignty is stressed in Ephesians 6:1, which states, "Children obey your parents in the Lord; for this is right." [11] And in Colossians 3:20, we read, "Children, obey *your* parents in all things; for this is well-pleasing unto the Lord." [12]

Like the other two types of sovereignty we have thus far considered, this type of sovereignty provides a practical blessing for children and society in general, for it serves to protect children from the cruelties of a harsh world. This truth is so readily apparent that it needs only to be stated. In fact, so basic and fundamental is the need of the young for protection by their parents, that we observe the exercise of this type of sovereignty even among the many species of animals found in the world.

In addition to the obvious benefits of Parental Sovereignty for the care, well-being, and security of children, such supreme authority is beneficial to the well-being and advancement of civil society. Children who are improperly reared grow up to become irresponsible, disrespectful, and disorderly adults. Such improperly reared children become, at best, a drain upon society, and at worst, a menace to the existing social order.

Although parents possess supreme authority over their own children, this supremacy is in relation to other human beings, and is clearly not a supremacy over God. A man may therefore rightfully raise his children as he sees fit, although he is accountable to God for his exercise of this authority.

Political Sovereignty

The final type of supreme authority that God in His infinite wisdom has

[9] *Ibid.*, p. 241.
[10] *Ibid.*, p. 241.
[11] *Ibid.*, p. 1278.
[12] *Ibid.*, p. 1288.

granted to mankind is Political Sovereignty. This is the authority that governs man's relationship with his fellow man in civil society. It has long been a recognized fact that Political Sovereignty originates from mankind's God-ordained *power of life and death* over those who violate the Laws of Nature. From this type of sovereignty emanates the power to form civil society, institute government, and establish rules for the punishment of criminals. Such authority can only originate in the form of divine authorization to administer *capital punishment* to criminals. Not only is the practical necessity of government apparent to all who possess common sense, but Political Sovereignty rests upon a biblical foundation.

In the Book of Genesis, we are told that Cain murdered his brother Abel. While Cain feared, afterwards, that others would kill him for revenge and punishment, God put a mark upon him so that no man would harm him. At that point in time, mankind had not yet been granted Political Sovereignty, and no man possessed the authority to punish a murderer.

Following the Great Flood, however, one of the Dispensations in the Noahic Covenant granted to mankind the power to enforce the laws of nature. From that moment onward, mankind possessed Political Sovereignty. This divine authorization for Political Sovereignty is found in Genesis 9:6: "Whoso sheddeth man's blood, by man shall his blood be shed; for in the image of God made he man." [13]

With respect to this profound Dispensation, the editors of *The New Scofield Reference Bible* have noted:

> *The Third Dispensation: Human Government.* This dispensation began when Noah and his family left the ark. As Noah went into a new situation, God (in the Noahic Covenant) subjected humanity to a new test. Heretofore no man had the right to take another man's life (cp. Gen. 4:10-11, 14-15, 23-24). In this new dispensation, although man's direct moral responsibility to God continued ("Render...unto God the things that are God's," Mt. 22:21), God delegated to him certain areas of His authority, in which he was to obey God through submission to his fellow man ("Render therefore unto Caesar the things which are Caesar's," Mt. 22:21). So God instituted a corporate relationship of man to man in human government.
>
> The highest function of government is the protection of human life, out of which arises the responsibility of capital punishment...."The powers that be are ordained of God," and to resist the power is to resist God. Whereas in the preceding dispensation restraint upon men was internal (Gen. 6:3), God's Spirit working through moral responsibility, now a new and external restraint was added, i.e. the power of civil government.
>
> Man failed to rule righteously. That both Jew and Gentile have governed for self, not for God, is sadly apparent....However, man's responsibil-

[13] *Ibid.*, p. 14.

> ity for government did not cease but will continue until Christ sets up His kingdom. [14]

As with the other types of sovereignty we have considered, Political Sovereignty is a great blessing to mankind, in that it provides a powerful means of protecting the lives, liberties, and properties of the innocent from the invasions of criminals. Like other forms of sovereignty, this type of supreme authority is susceptible to abuse, although its necessity and usefulness – when properly exercised – can never be denied.

Definition of a Sovereign State

Now that we have a basic understanding of what constitutes Political Sovereignty, we should briefly consider what constitutes a *sovereign State* or *Nation*. As our guide, we may turn to what is undoubtedly the most influential book on the subject of *International Law* ever written.

In 1758, a brilliant book penned by the distinguished Swiss theorist, Emmerich de Vattel, was published under the title of *The Law of Nations or the Principles of Natural Law Applied to the Conduct and to the Affairs of Nations and of Sovereigns*. This book, widely referred to as simply Vattel's *Law of Nations*, had a profound effect on how the world, especially the United States and Great Britain, understood the concept of sovereign Nations and the *Natural Laws* that rightfully governed their conduct.

In his introduction to the re-publication of Vattel's work in 1916, Albert de Lapradelle wrote that, "From 1776 to 1783, the more the United States progressed, the greater became Vattel's influence. In 1780 his *Law of Nations* was a classic, a *text book* in the universities." [15] "Of all the authors, even the English who have written upon the Law of Nations," Mr. Lapradelle noted, "not one is more often nor more copiously quoted than Vattel." [16]

The impact of Vattel's *Law of Nations* in the United States of America was summarized by Charles G. Fenwick in the August, 1913 issue of *American Political Science Review*:

> Vattel's treatise on the Law of Nations is quoted by judicial tribunals, in speeches before legislative assemblies, and in the decrees and correspondence of executive officials. It is the manual of the student, the reference

---

[14] *Ibid.*, pp. 13-14.

[15] Emmerich de Vattel, *The Law of Nations or the Principles of Natural Law Applied to the Conduct and to the Affairs of Nations and of Sovereigns*, Translation of the Edition of 1758, Carnegie Institution of Washington, Washington, 1916, p. xxx.

[16] *Ibid.*, p. xxxiv.

> work of the statesman, and the text from which the political philosopher draws inspiration. Publicists consider it sufficient to cite the authority of Vattel to justify and give conclusiveness and force to statements as to the proper conduct of a State in its international relations. [17]

Although newer views of International Law arose in the latter part of the Twentieth Century, in an effort to supposedly justify the quest for a New World Order, Vattel's *Law of Nations* will forever remain the "bible" of International Law to those who value truth, cherish justice, and respect the natural rights of mankind. And now that we have examined Mr. Vattel's vast influence on the world, let us turn to him for an answer to the question: What constitutes a sovereign State? At the very beginning of his book, Mr. Vattel stated:

> Nations or States are political bodies, societies of men who have united together and combined their forces, in order to procure their mutual welfare and security.
>
> Such a society has its own affairs and interests; it deliberates and takes resolutions in common, and it thus becomes a *moral person* having an understanding and a will peculiar to itself, and susceptible at once of obligations and of rights. [emphasis added] [18]

Because a sovereign State is a *moral person*, all Nations must possess the same natural rights and must be regarded as *equal* to one another in regard to such rights, regardless of their differences in size, strength, and population. As Mr. Vattel noted:

> Since men are by nature equal, and their individual rights and obligations the same, as coming equally from nature, Nations, which are composed of men and may be regarded as so many free persons living together in a state of nature, are by nature equal and hold from nature the same obligations and the same rights. Strength or weakness, in this case, counts for nothing. A dwarf is as much a man as a giant is; a small Republic is no less a sovereign State than the most powerful Kingdom. [19]

For this reason, the Golden Rule, which asserts that we should treat others as we want them to treat us, applies to sovereign States as well as to individuals. Commenting on this principle, Mr. Vattel wrote:

> Since Nations are free and independent of one another as men are by nature, the second general law of their society is that each Nation should be left to the peaceable enjoyment of that liberty which belongs to it by nature.

---

[17] *Ibid.*, quoted on p. xxxviii.
[18] *Ibid.*, p. 3.
[19] *Ibid.*, p. 7.

> The natural society of nations can not continue unless the rights which belong to each by nature are respected. No Nation is willing to give up its liberty; it will rather choose to break off all intercourse with those who attempt to encroach upon it. [20]

As Mr. Vattel noted, there are Natural Laws, deduced by reason and logic from the moral rule of God over the affairs of men, which govern the conduct of sovereign States:

> We must therefore apply to nations the rules of the natural law to discover what are their obligations and their rights; hence the Law of Nations is in its origin merely the Law of Nature applied to Nations....
>
> Since, therefore, the necessary Law of Nations consists in applying natural law to States, and since the natural law is not subject to change, being founded on the nature of things and particularly upon the nature of man, it follows that the necessary Law of Nations is not subject to change.
>
> Since this law is not subject to change and the obligations which it imposes are necessary and indispensable, Nations can not alter it by agreement, not individually or mutually release themselves from it. [21]

Let us cite one more passage from Vattel's *Law of Nations*:

> A Nation or a State, as we have already said in the introduction, is a political body, a society of men who have united together and combined their forces in order to procure their mutual welfare and security.
>
> From the fact that this group of men forms a society in which they have common interests and must act in concert it is necessary that a public authority be set up, which shall regulate and prescribe the duties of each member with respect to the object of the association. This public authority constitutes the sovereignty; and he, or they, in whom it is vested is the sovereign. [22]

These passages from Vattel's *Law of Nations* should suffice to provide an adequate understanding of the definition of a sovereign State or Nation. To summarize, a sovereign State is a self-governing, independent Nation that can be considered a moral person, having rights and obligations in accordance with the Laws of Nature. All sovereign Nations have equal rights, regardless of size, population, and martial power. Even the most powerful Nation is morally obliged to respect the freedom, independence, and equality of rights of the weakest State. And whoever is the supreme authority – having the ultimate political power – within a State or Nation is the *sovereign power*, in whom Politi-

[20] *Ibid.*, p. 6.
[21] *Ibid.*, p. 4.
[22] *Ibid.*, p. 11.

cal Sovereignty is vested.

Who Is Sovereign?

Although Vattel's *Law of Nations* clearly and logically presents the obligations and rights of sovereign States in regard to their affairs with one another, it does not address the vitally crucial question of *who*, within a sovereign State, can or should possess Political Sovereignty. The key to answering this question is to determine what *elements* constitute a sovereign State or Nation. Condensed to its most basic elements, a State or Nation consists of three entities: *people*, *government*, and *territory*. Inasmuch as Political Sovereignty is the supreme or ultimate political power within the State, and there can be only one supreme authority, one and only one of these entities *should* possess that supreme authority. We may also assert that only one of these entities *can* possess Political Sovereignty, inasmuch as supremacy is an attribute that cannot be divided or shared.

Immediately we can eliminate territory from our consideration. No one would seriously assert that rocks, rivers, trees, mountains, and valleys could possibly possess political supremacy. And if Political Sovereignty can never be an attribute of geography, then it can only reside in either people or government. Lest there be any doubt as to who should possess that supreme authority within a Nation, then we should reflect upon a crucial concept. *A sovereign people is the foundation of a free society, while a sovereign government is the cornerstone of tyranny.*

Political Sovereignty, as we have already observed, is a gift from God, granted to mankind to enable man to enforce an observance of Natural Law, secure the rights of the innocent, and punish criminals. In making this grant to the human race, God Himself did not create civil societies, establish human governments, and select the rulers of nations. Rather, He granted Political Sovereignty to mankind as *individual human beings*.

That this is true may be deduced from the biblical verse cited previously, that God made man in His own image. Thus, all men are created *equal* by God, a principle acknowledged by the American Declaration of Independence and deduced by common sense. And if all men are equal in the eyes of God, then God's grant of Political Sovereignty must, of necessity, have been a grant *to all men equally as individuals*. Having received this grant from the Creator, men were then empowered to proceed on their own to establish civil societies, constitute governments, and select their own rulers by a process known as *agreement*, *compact*, or *consent*. It is from this principle that the concept of *gov-*

ernment-by-the-consent-of-the-governed may be derived.

By definition, Political Sovereignty is the supreme power or highest political authority within a body politic or civil society. It is this authority that may rightfully constitute a government, describe its objectives, delegate powers to it, and prescribe the limits to its powers. It is this supreme authority that can alter, amend, or abolish a government. Whoever possesses this authority within a state or nation is clearly the sovereign.

It may perhaps facilitate our understanding of the significance of Political Sovereignty by considering the relationship between *creator* and *creature.* God created people, and people created government. Thus, God is naturally supreme over people, and people are naturally supreme over government. People possess endowed rights that are bestowed upon them by their Creator, while government possesses delegated powers that are entrusted to it by the people. The will of God is expressed in the Bible, while the political will of the people is expressed in a constitution.

If another analogy is required, then we may cite the relationship between a *master* and a *servant.* In a Nation where Political Sovereignty resides in the people, they are the masters and their government is their servant. But should the government come to possess the supreme authority, then it becomes the master and the people become its slaves. It is this consideration of the relationship between the people of a civil society and their government that underscores the true significance of Political Sovereignty.

As is apparent from what has been presented thus far, government may be either a blessing or a curse to mankind, depending on whether the people of a civil society possess sovereignty and a government of constitutionally limited powers, or whether the government has stolen sovereignty from the people and usurped tyrannical powers. Government, by its very nature, is merely concentrated *power* – it is *force* – with access to the pockets of the people and sufficient strength to command obedience. Should this instrument of coercion and power fall into the wrong hands, the servant could easily be transformed into the master of an enslaved population.

Such thoughts motivated George Washington to liken government to fire, a useful servant to mankind, but also a fearful master. As the Father of His Country so eloquently stated this fundamental concept, "Government is not reason; it is not eloquence; it is force! Like fire, it is a dangerous servant and a fearful master." [23]

Although Political Sovereignty rightfully belongs to the people within any civil society, such a natural right has rarely been respected in actual prac-

---

[23] G. Edward Griffin, *The Fearful Master: A Second Look at the United Nations*, Western Islands, Boston, 1964, p. ii.

tice. All too often, governments, once established, have usurped power and have stolen the supreme authority from the people to enslave a Nation. And history is replete with illustrations of one Nation waging war upon another State to subdue it and rob it of its independence and sovereignty. Adding insult to injury, there have arisen a number of philosophers throughout the ages who have attempted to justify the grand theft of Political Sovereignty from its rightful owners. Since the dawn of human government, an epic battle has taken place within one Nation after another, between the forces of liberty and those of tyranny. Invariably, the advocates of despotism have sought to rob the people of a Nation of their supremacy by promoting the supremacy of government, for only a sovereign government has the capacity to enslave a Nation. Such efforts, we must sadly observe, have been all too effective.

In time, the human race descended into a period known as the Dark Ages, in which kings were proclaimed sovereign, and their subject peoples were forced to bow before them. Corrupt philosophers attempted to justify this form of despotic rule by proclaiming the concept of the *Divine Rights of Kings*, asserting that the rulers derived their powers directly from God. By such a concept, the natural order was turned upside down – the people became the servants, and their government became their master. That such a perversion of nature should be promulgated in the name of God was one of the greatest ironies in human history.

The political darkness was lifted from the world by the dawn of the Age of Reason, when honest philosophers – most notably John Locke – once again derived their inspiration from Natural Law and reasserted the supremacy of the people over government. So thoroughly did they expose the fallacies of the Divine Rights of Kings, that no one would ever again dare to assert such foolishness. And so great was this new awakening throughout the civilized world, that the Founding Fathers of the United States justified their revolution against Great Britain on the principle of the supremacy of people over government and stated that those principles would guide them in establishing the United States of America. But the conspiracy to enslave mankind, although suffering a setback due to the Age of Reason, was not eliminated. Although it was no longer possible to justify efforts to steal Political Sovereignty from the people by advocating the Divine Rights of Kings, over time even more clever – yet equally foolish and absurd – justifications were conjured up to accomplish that goal.

It is necessary, therefore, for all who cherish freedom to better understand Political Sovereignty and the schemes and excuses put forth to supposedly justify the theft of such supremacy from the people. Since we will confine the remainder of our inquiry to that species of sovereignty known as Political Sovereignty, we will no longer utilize the qualifying adjective – *Political* Sovereignty –and will refer to this type of supremacy in subsequent chapters simply as *sovereignty*.

Our inquiry will begin with an examination of the rise of the Age of Reason, and particularly with John Locke's great contribution to the concept of the sovereignty of the people. Then we will direct our attention to the concept of a social contract or compact in the creation of civil society. Of course, our chief interest lies in the concept of sovereignty within the United States of America, and we will therefore examine the foundations of what may be termed the *American Theory of Government*, as defined by those who established our Federal Republic. Afterwards, we will examine the rise of the two great opposing schools in the United States – the Consolidating School of Thought and the States' Rights School of Thought – during the ante-bellum period of our history. As we shall discover, it was the former school that posed the primary threat to the sovereignty of the people, by advocating an unconstitutional centralization of all powers in the Government of the United States and the transfer of sovereignty to that government. The latter school, as we shall discover, championed the cause of the sovereignty of the people by defending the rights of the States and the constitutionally prescribed limits to the powers of the Federal Government. Particular attention will be focused on the historically famous Webster-Hayne Debate in 1830 and the equally significant Webster-Calhoun Debate of 1833. Those debates, perhaps more than any other debate in American history, explored in depth the whole subject of sovereignty within the United States, and, as a consequence, the very nature of our Federal Union.

As we shall discover, it was the intention of the Founding Fathers of the United States that sovereignty should remain vested in the peoples of the several States of the Federal Union. Yet, as a consequence of the War Between the States, sovereignty was transferred to the Government of the United States, which has ever since accumulated power in an attempt to regulate everything and control everybody. We shall therefore conclude our inquiry by considering the dire consequences of this trend upon the liberties and rights of the American people. As we shall discover, the grand battle of the ages to determine who shall be the *Master* continues unabated, even into the Twenty-First Century.

Chapter Two

The Rise of the Age of Reason

The student of constitutional government in the United States hardly needs to be reminded that terminology is frequently coined or originated to describe something which may have existed long before the word itself is first introduced to identify it. This is an observation that applies to all spheres of human existence, not merely to political science. The term "cells," for instance, illustrates this concept. The cells comprising the human body, needless to say, have existed since God created the first man, and it would be absurd to even suggest that the cells of the human body did not exist until mankind invented a name for them upon discovering the cellular nature of tissue through the microscope. In similar fashion, it must be understood that sovereignty existed long before it was formally defined and named. Indeed, such sovereignty may well have been referred to by another name by ancient commentators, or it may have been a concept too intangible for precise language. Yet, the *supreme political power* has necessarily existed since the origin of civil society, whether named or not.

The reason why we here stress this simple truth is owing to the fact that the *term* "sovereignty" was invented during a period when governments had generally succeeded in stealing the supreme authority from the people. In fact, the term was coined by the proponents of government supremacy in an effort to justify the claim that kings possessed an unlimited right or power to reign over their subjects. Owing to such origins of the term itself, some political writers, such as John Taylor of Caroline, were reluctant to use the term as applicable to anything other than the absurd Divine Rights of Kings theory of government.

When properly defined and understood, however, sovereignty is an essential concept to comprehend, for it signifies the supreme authority within a body politic. Such a supreme power must, of necessity, exist within every political community, whether it resides in the people or in their government. There is nothing improper in using the term, provided it is properly defined and properly assigned to those who of *natural right* should possess it.

According to Leslie Lipson, in *The Great Issues of Politics*, the term sovereignty was first employed in the Sixteenth Century. By that time, however, leading political commentators were contending that such a supreme power was invested in the government. The Frenchman, Jean Bodin, for example, who published his *Six Books Concerning the Republic* in 1576, declared: "Sovereignty is a power over citizens and subjects that is supreme and above the law."[1]

That the word "sovereignty" and the word "subjects" could be used in the same sentence illustrates that, by 1576, the natural law concept of government had been perverted. Advocates of sovereignty during this period correctly observed that the very concept of a "law" implies a "law-giver" who of necessity must be superior to the laws he creates. From such authority flow the laws of society, and without such authority the laws could have no binding validity. It was also clearly understood at the time that he who makes a law without authority, makes no law at all. Yet, it was solemnly proclaimed that the supreme authority that stood over the law was not the people, but their king. Such a contention, it scarcely needs to be mentioned, directly condoned a government of unlimited powers.

Regarding this misuse of the concept of sovereignty, Professor Leslie Lipson has noted:

> In rejecting the view that the functions of the state should be exercised within a limited sphere, [the false concept of] sovereignty asserted the limitless range of governmental activity. When sovereignty was pronounced to be one and indivisible [and invested in government], this meant that the state was to assume (or resume what it enjoyed in Graeco-Roman days) the general direction and supervision of society. [2]

Commenting on the triumph of consolidating or centralizing doctrines following the Middle Ages, Professor Lipson has observed how such a trend subverted the concept of distributed or local government:

> When the changeover occurred from the medieval to the nation-state, and from a feudal to a mercantilist economy, the attempt was made in theory and in practice to construct government upon the opposite principles. In place of localism, the accent was put upon *centralization*....To achieve this, it was, of course, necessary for the king to triumph over the aristocracy....But royal supremacy over the nobles brought an additional consequence besides centralization. The power that redounded to the king at the center was there concentrated in his office. Monarchy became the magnet, attracting local loyalties to the capital and the court, and overriding the separatist tendencies of competing institutions. With centralization, therefore, came integration. From both of these the king was the gainer. *In theoretical terms these facts were*

---

[1] Leslie Lipson, *The Great Issues of Politics*, Second Edition, Prentice-Hall, Inc., Englewood Cliffs, 1960, quoted on pp. 176-177.

[2] *Ibid.*, p. 177.

> *synthesized in the new doctrine of "sovereignty."* The *consolidation of power*, which this term signified, meant the recognition of one supreme will, paramount over other central agencies and local particularisms. The identification of the symbol of sovereignty with the office of monarchy was easily brought about. The king was "the sovereign" personified. What could be more simple?
>
> Thus was inaugurated in Europe a period in which monarchy attained its zenith, accumulating so much as to merit the description "absolute." Never was this absolutism more fittingly epitomized than by Louis XIV of France, the Sun-King. In his remark: "L'Etat, c'est moi," a comment whose boast of personal pre-eminence exceeds even the claim of Adolf Hitler, "For twenty-four hours I was the supreme court of Germany," or the statement, "I am the law," attributed to a sometime mayor of Jersey City. [emphasis added] [3]

The concept of sovereignty had thus been completely subverted by the end of the Middle Ages. Accompanying the pronouncement of a sovereign government was the consolidation of political power into one centralized set of hands. Indeed, such is always the inevitable consequence of proclaiming a sovereign government, for a *sovereign government* and a *government of unlimited powers* are one and the same.

As a consequence of this subversion of political supremacy, the subject peoples suffering under these governments lost their natural rights. The people were allowed to possess only such "rights" as the king saw fit to grant, and he alone defined what those rights should be. And any king that granted rights and privileges could, at his pleasure, reclaim or withdraw what he had granted to his subjects.

Those who championed the Divine Rights of Kings in their day based their assertions upon perversions of Holy Writ, twisting and torturing the words of God to fit their needs. Some of the best arguments ever made for a sovereign government may be found in the writings of Sir Robert Filmer and Thomas Hobbes in England. For nearly half a century, their arguments were the leading lights of the time in Great Britain, and it was not until a parliamentary struggle near the end of the Seventeenth Century, known as the Glorious Revolution, that the absurdity of the Divine Rights of Kings was theoretically defeated by a brilliant philosopher named John Locke.

Thomas Hobbes and the Leviathan State

Assertions for the sovereignty and supremacy of government produced a

---

[3] *Ibid.*, pp. 293-294.

book written by Thomas Hobbes that has ever since stood as the "bible" and main inspiration for all who adore totalitarian government. Within that book, styled *Leviathan*, and published in 1651, Mr. Hobbes made an eloquent and ardent defense of a supreme government with unlimited power. Symbolizing the Leviathan State was an artificial man wearing a crown, whose body was composed of countless tiny real men, a fitting symbol to represent the theoretical annihilation of individuality under a sovereign government. It is of particular interest to note that Mr. Hobbes considered sovereignty to be the *soul* of his tyrannical monster.

The *Leviathan State* of Thomas Hobbes contained all of the elements associated with a sovereign government, including consolidation of power and collectivization. Accordingly, the *Leviathan* is still considered "must" reading by modern-day collectivists. In his introduction to a modern edition of the *Leviathan*, for instance, Professor Francis B. Randall noted that "Hobbes is much approved of in Communist circles." [4]

As Professor Randall has noted:

> *Leviathan* contains the most powerful argument ever made in any culture, at any time, on behalf of really strong government. And the argument about the merits of strong government has been one of the absolutely crucial debates in which men have been engaged for nearly 2,500 years, never more so than at the present moment, when discussions about "freedom," "socialism," "democracy," and "totalitarianism" take place day and night around the entire world. [5]

Along the same lines of Thomas Hobbes' *Leviathan*, Sir Robert Filmer penned his famous *Patriarcha, or the Natural Power of Kings*, which was published posthumously in 1680. Although both men wrote in defense of sovereign government, the emphasis of each book was different from the other. Mr. Hobbes was more far-reaching and general in his conceptualization of absolutism, asserting that totalitarian government is the only alternative to the chaos and lawlessness of anarchy. Sir Robert Filmer, on the other hand, focused his efforts on attempting to justify a sovereign government by espousing the *Divine Rights of Kings*, claiming that kings are or should be considered the direct heirs of Adam and are thereby vested with a supposed natural right to rule mankind. To refute the allegations made by both of these advocates of absolutism became the task of John Locke, whose *Two Treatises on Government* still stands as one of the most penetrating arguments ever written on behalf of the sovereignty of the people and the natural rights of man.

---

[4] Thomas Hobbes, *Leviathan*, Washington Square Press, Inc., New York, 1964, p. xiii.

[5] *Ibid.*, p. ix.

The Father of the Age of Reason

John Locke's great masterpiece, *Two Treatises of Government*, was divided into two volumes of dissertations, each dealing with the separate arguments of England's two most distinguished advocates of government supremacy over the people. The *First Treatise of Government* was directed toward the fallacious theories espoused by Sir Robert Filmer. The *Second Treatise of Government*, on the other hand, was written primarily to refute the more generalized theories of Thomas Hobbes.

Although Mr. Locke aimed his critique of the Divine Rights Theory of Government directly at Sir Robert, specifically naming him as the opponent, his refutation of Thomas Hobbes and the Leviathan State was more indirect. Thus, he never mentioned Mr. Hobbes by name, but chose instead to present the true theory of civil society to replace the spurious notions that result in a Leviathan State. With the success of the Glorious Revolution and the destruction of the Hobbesian Theory of Government, the *Two Treatises of Government* was widely acclaimed and its author, John Locke, became acknowledged as the Father of the Age of Reason.

Before considering the absurdities of the theory of a Divine Rights of Kings, we are again reminded that what might seem plainly foolish and palpably ridiculous to some is capable of fooling and deceiving others, and that while some condemn others for playing the role of fools, they are themselves deceived by nonsense in another form. In modern America, for example, we note that very few Americans would vote for a candidate calling himself a *Socialist*, but millions would vote for a Socialist calling himself a Democrat or a Republican.

While it might appear foolish for a people to ever seriously believe or contend that a government possesses sovereignty due to the supposed Divine Rights of Kings, would it be any less foolish for another people at another time in history to allow their government to steal their sovereignty under the pretext of vesting that sovereignty in a Nation that does not exist? Yet, as we shall discover before the end of our treatise, that is precisely the theory advanced to supposedly justify the theft of sovereignty from the American people!

In the Preface of his two treatises, John Locke asserted:

> Reader,
>
> Thou hast here the Beginning and End of a Discourse concerning Government....Teachers, [who] have so dangerously misled others, should be openly shewed of what Authority this their Patriarch [Sir Robert Filmer] is, whom they have so blindly followed, that so they may either retract what upon so ill Grounds they have vented, and cannot be maintained, or else justifie those Principles which they have Preached up for Gospel; though they had no better an Author than an English Courtier....I wish, where they have

> done the Truth and the Public wrong, they would be as ready to Redress it and allow its just Weight to this Reflection, viz. That, *there cannot be done a greater mischief to prince and people than the propagating wrong notions concerning government*....If any one, concerned really for Truth, undertake the Confutation of my Hypothesis, I promise him either to recant my mistake, upon fair Conviction; or to answer his Difficulties. But he must remember two Things;
>
> First, That Cavilling here and there, at some Expression, or little incident of my Discourse, is not an answer to my Book.
>
> Secondly, That I shall not take railing for Arguments, nor think either of these worth my notice: Though I shall always look on my self as bound to give satisfaction to any one who shall appear to be conscientiously scrupulous in the point, and shall shew any just Grounds for his Scruples. [emphasis added] [6]

Particular attention should be directed to Mr. Locke's correct assertion that "there cannot be done a greater mischief to prince and people than the propagating wrong notions concerning government." As in his time, modern teachers should heed this maxim, for all too often they preach falsehoods as if they were Gospel, never taking the time to verify the principles they teach. Their students also have a tendency to propagate those falsehoods to the next generation, until, over a period of time, the pristine principles of a system of government are totally obliterated from view behind a cloud of hazy confusion, false theories, and even dangerous misconceptions. What greater mischief, John Locke inquired, could possibly exceed the propagation of falsehoods concerning government by teachers?

The First Treatise of Government

The topic of John Locke's *First Treatise of Government*, as we have previously stated, was a refutation of the theory of the Divine Rights of Kings as espoused by Sir Robert Filmer. So important did Mr. Locke consider the concept of sovereignty in this task that, of the eleven chapters in the *First Treatise of Government*, six of them – more than fifty percent – contained the word "sovereignty" or "sovereign" in their very titles. Chapter Three, for instance, is titled, "Of Adam's Title to Sovereignty, by Creation." Chapter Four is titled, "Of Adam's Title to Sovereignty, By Donation." Chapter Five is titled, "Of Adam's Title to Sovereignty, by the Subjection of Eve." Chapter Six is entitled, "Of Adam's Title to Sovereignty, by Fatherhood." Chapter Seven is titled, "Of

---

[6] John Locke, *Two Treatises of Government*, A Mentor Book from New American Library, New York, Revised Edition, 1960, pp. 171-173.

Fatherhood and Property, Consider'd Together as Fountains of Sovereignty." And Chapter Eight is titled, "Of the Conveyance of Adam's Sovereign Monarchial Power."

Even within those chapters that did not contain the word "sovereignty" in their titles, the subject of sovereignty was central to the refutation of the theory of the Divine Rights of Kings. The reader of the *First Treatise of Government* cannot fail to grasp the understanding that the chief difference between freedom and slavery centers around the question of who is sovereign. Indeed, John Locke set the tone of his work with an opening statement that began, "Slavery is so vile and miserable an Estate of Man." [7]

Summarizing the concepts that he wished to refute, Mr. Locke wrote:

> If any one think I take too much liberty in speaking so freely of a Man, who is a great Champion of absolute Power, and the Idol of those who Worship it; I beseech him to make this small allowance for once, to one, who, even after the reading of Sir Robert's book, cannot but think himself, as the Laws allow him, a Freeman: And I know no fault it is to do so, unless any one better skill'd in the Fate of it, than I, should have it revealed to him, that this Treatise, which has lain dormant so long, was when it appeared in the World, to carry by strength of its Arguments, all Liberty out of it; and that from thenceforth our Author's short Model was to be the Pattern in the Mount, and the perfect Standard of Politics for the future. His System lies in a little compass, 'tis no more but this,
>
> *That all Government is absolute Monarchy.*
>
> And the Ground he builds on, is this,
>
> *That no Man is Born free.*
>
> In this last age a generation of men has sprung up among us, who would flatter princes with an Opinion, that they have a Divine Right to absolute Power, let the Laws by which they are constituted, and are to govern, and the Conditions under which they enter upon their Authority, be what they will, and their Engagements to observe them never so well ratified by solemn Oaths and Promises. To make way for this doctrine they have denied Mankind a Right to natural Freedom, whereby they have not only, as much as in them lies, exposed all Subjects to the utmost Misery of Tyranny and Oppression, but have also unsettled the Titles, and shaken the Thrones of Princes: (For they too, by these Mens systeme, except only one, are all born Slaves, and by Divine Right, are Subjects to Adam's right Heir); As if they had design'd to make War upon all Government, and subvert the very Foundations of Human Society, to serve their present turn.
>
> However we must believe them upon their own bare Words, when they tell us, we are all born Slaves, and we must continue so; there is no remedy for it: Life and Thraldom we enter'd into together, and can never be quit of the one, till we part with the other. Scripture or Reason I am sure doe not any where say so notwithstanding the noise of divine right, as if Divine Au-

---

[7] *Ibid.*, p. 175.

> thority hath subjected us to the unlimited Will of another....
>
> By whom this Doctrine came at first to be broach'd, and brought in fashion amongst us, and what sad Effects it gave rise to, I leave to *Historians* to relate, or to the Memory of those who were Contemporaries with Sibthorp and Manwering to recollect. My business at present is only to consider what Sir R.F. who is allowed to have carried this Argument farthest, and is supposed to have brought it to perfection, has said in it; for from him every one...has learned...this short System of Politics, *viz. Men are not born free,* and *therefore could never have the liberty to choose either Governors, or Forms of Government. Princes have their Power Absolute, and by Divine Right, for Slaves could never have a Right to Compact or Consent. Adam was an absolute Monarch, and so are all Princes ever since.* [8]

Here, then, is the consolidating and collectivist argument against which John Locke directed his intellect to explode within the *First Treatise of Government*. By rejecting the Divine Rights of Kings concept of government, it should be noted, Mr. Locke did not reject either God or the Bible. To have done so would have been out of character for the Father of the Age of Reason. A devout Christian, Mr. Locke was a firm believer in the inerrancy of the Scriptures and even wrote a treatise espousing *The Reasonableness of Christianity*. Therefore, it was not against Holy Writ that John Locke wrote, but against the perversions and distortions of the Bible used by Sir Robert Filmer to supposedly justify the Divine Rights of Kings.

Exploding the Divine Rights of Kings

According to the Divine Rights of Kings Theory of Government, sovereignty is derived from God, which is the only contention put forth by that theory with which John Locke concurred. Such sovereignty, opined Sir Robert Filmer, was vested in Adam by the Creator of the Universe, and such sovereignty was transferred to Adam's oldest son upon his death. This mode of bequeathing sovereignty from one generation to the next supposedly continued uninterrupted throughout history, and within each generation there was supposedly only one human being who could rightfully claim to be the sovereign ruler of the whole world. As chance would have it, England was the fortunate nation to possess the truly royal family, the only one in the world directly descended from Adam!

This line of reasoning, needless to say, presented many problems, as John Locke clearly illustrated in his *First Treatise of Government*. To begin with, Mr. Locke pointed out that, even if we agree that Adam was the world's first

---

[8] *Ibid.*, pp. 176-178.

sovereign monarch, it is impossible to determine who is truly Adam's sole heir in the modern world. In addition, he denied Sir Robert's contention that God's chosen line of succession was necessarily through the oldest son of each succeeding generation.

The biblical illustration of Esau and Jacob is but one example to refute Sir Robert's contention. Esau selling his birthright to his brother did not conform to the Divine Rights of Kings theory. Nor did the case of Joseph and his eleven brothers bowing before him in Egypt. Jacob's dual blessing of Manasseh and Ephraim, in which the younger son received the principal blessing, also failed to conform to the Divine Rights theory. Of the twelve sons of Jacob, it was Judah – who was not the eldest – who gave rise to the line of kings in Israel, from which Jesus Christ was born. These are just a few illustrations that mitigated against the theory of sovereignty espoused by Sir Robert Filmer.

According to the *Lockean Theory of Government*, all mankind must be the true heirs of Adam in common. Yet, the greatest argument against Sir Robert's line of reasoning was the simple observation that the Scriptural lineage of dominion noted by him was merely *familial*, not universal. When Jacob purchased the birthright from his brother and deceitfully obtained his father's blessing, for instance, this did not entitle him to be the universal monarch of the world. The blessing merely bequeathed upon him dominion within his own family.

If God had intended for one man in each generation to possess sovereignty, then His will would surely have been for all mankind to live within a single society or body politic under a single ruler. Yet, Scripture reveals God's will to have been otherwise. God Himself scattered the peoples of the earth into separate Nations speaking different tongues at the Tower of Babel.

In Genesis 9:6, God's will is expressed as follows: "Whoso sheddeth man's blood, by man shall his blood be shed; for in the image of God made he man." [9] This is the most positive authorization for sovereignty that could be expressed, and it is clear that it extends sovereignty to all men equally. All men are made equally in the "image of God," and in God's eyes all men are therefore created equal. Thus, it is illogical and unreasonable to argue that God would vest sovereignty in only one man to rule over everyone else by natural right and without limitation of power. The correct interpretation of Holy Writ is that God vested sovereignty in all men equally, and that the people of each society were then empowered to institute government for themselves and to delegate certain limited powers to that government.

By proper interpretation of the Word of God, the concept of a sovereign government is utterly demolished. Men are not by nature born slaves, and rul-

---

[9] C.I. Scofield (ed.), *The New Scofield Reference Bible*, Oxford University Press, New York, 1967, pp. 13-14.

ers do not possess sovereignty by natural right. Rather, men are born free by nature, and the people in every society possess sovereignty by *natural right*. By Natural Law, a government may rightfully possess and exercise only those powers that have been *delegated* to it by the people.

The burden and the honor of asserting these basic truths fell to John Locke, and because of his great contributions to our understanding of Natural Law, the Age of Reason was born. The consequences of the ascendancy of the Lockean Theory of Government to predominance was the rise of a thriving middle class, the re-emergence of freedom in the world, and the recognition of the true concept of sovereignty as the cornerstone of human liberty.

The Second Treatise of Government

While John Locke devoted his *First Treatise of Government* to refuting the perverted concept of sovereignty based on the Divine Rights of Kings, in his *Second Treatise of Government* he set forth the true principles of sovereignty based on Natural Law and the compact or contract nature of civil society. Whereas the former treatise had been essentially *negative* in tone, to refute the notions put forth by Sir Robert Filmer, the latter treatise was essentially *positive* in nature, by offering mankind an alternative to the Leviathan State espoused by Thomas Hobbes.

According to the Hobbesian concept of the Leviathan State, mankind is so wicked, anarchic, and debased, that it could never constitute a government of *limited powers* by agreement or compact. Furthermore, because men are so prone to chaos and violence, they must be kept in a State of Slavery by their government. John Locke, however, rejected this entire Hobbesian philosophy by asserting that mankind, although prone to anarchy, is basically rational and capable of creating civil society and instituting government by *consent* and *agreement*.

Commenting on the *Second Treatise of Government*, Professor Thomas P. Peardon has observed:

> The political philosophy of the *Second Treatise*, like all political philosophies, rests upon an interpretation of human nature. Locke viewed man as a pretty decent fellow, far removed from the quarrelsome, competitive, selfish creature found in Hobbes. He has more inclination to society and is more governed by reason, "the common rule and measure God has given to mankind." The rationality ascribed to man by Locke is a pervasive characteristic going beyond the cunning calculation of interests upon which Hobbes depended to induce individuals in the state of nature to inaugurate society by a compact after which they must be held in society largely by force. It could be relied upon to produce a good deal of order even without

> be relied upon to produce a good deal of order even without the sanctions of government and to help maintain government once it was set up. This was especially so since Locke saw that man prefers stability to change. For "people are not so easily got out of their old forms as some are apt to suggest." [10]

The astute reader undoubtedly has noticed the similarity between this concept espoused by John Locke and the nature of man alluded to in our Declaration of Independence. "Prudence, indeed, will dictate that Governments long established should not be changed for light and transient causes;" Thomas Jefferson noted in that document, "and accordingly all experience hath shown, that mankind are more disposed to suffer, while evils are sufferable, than to right themselves by abolishing the forms to which they are accustomed." [11]

As Professor Peardon noted:

> From this interpretation of human nature, it followed rationally that the state of nature (that is, the condition in which men were before political government came into existence or would be if government did not exist) was no condition of war and anarchy as Hobbes had declared. On the contrary, "men living together according to reason, without a common superior on earth with authority to judge between them, is properly the state of nature." The state of nature thus understood is prepolitical since it lacks "a common superior on earth with authority to judge." But it can hardly be called presocial. In it men live together under the guidance of the Law of Nature by which their rights and responsibilities are determined.
>
> The conception of the Law of Nature is fundamental in Locke and marked one of the numerous respects in which he may be said to link emerging British constitutionalism to traditional ways of thought. For him it was really an objective rule and measure emanating from God and ascertainable by human reason. It provided a test or criterion by which political institutions and behavior could be limited and judged. It was prior to and more fundamental than the positive laws enacted by the state. And it bound men to obedience to just government once inaugurated by consent. "For truth and keeping of faith belongs to men as men, and not as members of society." Here was Locke's main solution to the problem of why men ought to obey.
>
> In one very important respect, however, Locke certainly contributed to a fundamental reformation of the Law of Nature. He gave it a sharp bias toward individualism. The precepts of the Law of Nature as stated by him are concerned mostly with individual rights rather than with individual responsibilities to society. Under the Stuarts the scales of government had been weighted heavily on the side of authority. The balance was to be more than redressed in the era whose birth was signalized by the Revolution of 1688 [*i.e.*, the Glorious Revolution]. And so the chief lesson John Locke learned from the Law of Nature was that even before government existed men were

---

[10] John Locke, *The Second Treatise of Government*, The Bobbs-Merrill Company, Inc., New York, 1952, p. xii.

[11] *Our Heritage From Our Great Documents*, West Texas Schools American Heritage Project, Abilene, p. 27.

> free, independent, and equal in the enjoyment of inalienable rights, chief among them being life, liberty and property.
>
> Among these rights, property receives the most attention in the *Second Treatise*. Its protection is represented as being the primary function of government....Locke's theory...loomed large in the rise of middle-class notions of the functions of government. For Locke was modifying the dominant trend of previous Natural Law thought most strikingly when he made property a natural right preceding civil society and not created by it. By merely applying his labor to the gifts of nature man creates property. He cannot be deprived of it by government which it precedes.
>
> ...Locke was aware that some might conclude that the blessings of the state of nature were preferable to the constraints of government. He tries to destroy this position by dwelling upon the "inconveniences" (which might be summed up as a lack of security and certainty in the enjoyment of property and rights) under which man in the state of nature must live and for the elimination of which he should be willing to set up civil society.
>
> The anarchists would argue that the cure was worse than the disease. Extreme libertarians can always derive support from Locke. But he himself believed that if government is based on consent men can still preserve that freedom, independence, and equality with which they are endowed by nature. To secure this end, of course, he resorted to the notion of the social compact. It is impossible to be sure if he believed such an original contract had actually occurred in history or was merely using the concept as an expository or controversial device. Locke was not very historically minded and may have believed that he was describing what had really taken place in the remote past when political society was born. He cites some examples drawn from history and from accounts of America in support of the historicity of the state of nature and the social contract. But the point is not really important. Locke based his government on consent because that seemed reasonable to him.... [12]

The Social Contract

When God delegated sovereignty to mankind, the human race lived in what John Locked termed the *State of Nature*, a state in which there was no government, statutory laws, or Nations. This delegation, it must be emphasized, was an authorization that vested sovereignty in all people as individuals, and not directly in human government. *Human government is the creation of man, not of God.* Thus, while God acted to bestow sovereignty upon the human race, it remained for mankind to establish its own civil societies and institute its own forms of government.

While living within this State of Nature, every man had the natural right

[12] *Ibid.*, pp. xii-xv.

to exercise all the powers we now commonly associate with organized government. Each man could therefore administer justice in this state and, if need be, execute a criminal. Although historical illustrations of mankind living in a State of Nature are naturally quite rare, we are fortunate to have the Bible as a guide. In reference to the early conditions among the Israelites, Judges 17:6 says that, "In those days *there was* no king in Israel, *but* every man did *that which was* right in his own eyes." [13] Another reference to this natural state in which the Israelites once lived is found in Judges 21:25: "In those days *there was* no king in Israel; every man did *that which was* right in his own eyes." [14]

Although such a state might seem idyllic when considered as an abstract concept, it was, as John Locke noted, a State of Insecurity, wherein no man's rights were truly protected from the invasions of criminals. It was to provide greater protection for their lives, liberties, and properties that men resolved to leave the State of Nature, enter into civil societies, and institute governments.

The importance that John Locke attached to this concept is evident by the fact that he devoted nearly half of the *Second Treatise of Government* to explaining the State of Nature and the original creation of civil society. And the reason for his emphasis on those topics is not difficult to understand. By focusing so much attention on the creation of civil society and the natural rights that existed *before* the establishment of human government, Mr. Locke wished to leave no doubt as to the true *purpose* of civil society and government – to the true *reason* why mankind entered into civil society and created government.

John Locke began what might be considered the most important chapter of the *Second Treatise of Government*, entitled "Of the Ends of Political Society and Government," with these words:

> If Man in the State of Nature be so free, as has been said; If he be absolute Lord of his own Person and Possessions, equal to the greatest, and subject to no Body, why will he part with his Freedom? Why will be give up this Empire, and subject himself to the Dominion and Controul of any other Power? To which 'tis obvious to Answer, that though in the state of Nature he hath such a right, yet the Enjoyment of it is very uncertain, and constantly exposed to the Invasion of others. For all being Kings as much as he, every Man his Equal, and the greater part no strict Observers of Equity and Justice, the enjoyment of the property he has in this state is very unsafe, very unsecure. This makes him willing to quit a Condition, which however free, is full of fears and continual dangers: And 'tis not without reason, that he seeks out, and is willing to joyn in Society with others who are already united, or have a mind to unite for the mutual *Preservation* of their Lives, Liberties and Estates, which I call by the general name, *Property*.

---

[13] C.I. Scofield (ed.), *The New Scofield Reference Bible*, Oxford University Press, New York, 1967, p. 310.
[14] *Ibid.*, p. 316.

> The great and *chief end* therefore, of Mens uniting into Commonwealths, and putting themselves under Government, *is the Preservation of their Property.* [15]

Vested with political authority, mankind was free to either continue within the State of Nature or to pool political authority within *civil societies* and create *body politics* or Nations. There are two manners in which such societies could have been formed – either by consent or by force. If by force, then the very creation of such a political society was in itself a crime. Only by the consent of all could such a civil society be legitimately created.

Within the *Second Treatise of Government*, John Locke presents the concept of a *social contract* as the rightful means of creating a civil society:

> Men being, as has been said, by Nature, all free, equal and independent, no one can be put out of this Estate, and subjected to the Political Power of another, without his own *Consent.* The only way whereby any one devests himself of his Natural Liberty, and *puts on the bonds of Civil Society* is by agreeing with other Men to joyn and unite into a Community, for their comfortable, safe, and peaceable living one amongst another, in a secure Enjoyment of their Properties, and a greater Security against any that are not of it. This any number of Men may do, because it injures not the Freedom of the rest; they are left as they were in the Liberty of the State of Nature. When any number of Men have so *consented to make one Community* or Government, they are thereby presently incorporated, and make *one Body Politick*, wherein the *Majority* have a Right to act and conclude the rest. [16]

Although Mr. Locke was a philosopher, not an historian, there are, in fact, actual historical examples that illustrate his concept of a social contract. Perhaps the most significance example is the creation of a civil society by the Pilgrims upon their arrival in the New World in 1620. Those settlers were wise enough to realize that their new colony would be beyond the reach of the laws of any European country and that they had, upon arriving in the New World, entered into a State of Nature. In order to better safeguard their rights and promote their welfare, they resolved to formally draft and sign an agreement to establish a civil society amongst themselves.

Within this Mayflower Compact, which was signed aboard the *Mayflower* by every adult male on November 21, 1620, the Pilgrims agreed to "solemnly and mutually in the presence of God, and one of another, covenant and combine ourselves together into a civil body politic, for our better ordering and preservation." [17] The civil society thus created by mutual consent would be

---

[15] John Locke, *Two Treatises of Government, Op. cit.*, p. 395.
[16] *Ibid.*, pp. 374-375.
[17] *Our Heritage From Our Great Documents, Op. cit.*, p. 11.

empowered "to enact, constitute and frame such just and equal laws, ordinances, acts, constitutions and offices, from time to time, as shall be thought most meet and convenient for the general good of the Colony," and the Pilgrims formally promised "all due submission and obedience." [18]

Although John Locke did cite specific historical examples in support of the concept of a social contract as the valid and proper foundation of civil society, he was undoubtedly aware that not all Nations historically rested upon such foundation. Indeed, the history of mankind is replete with illustrations of Nations being conquered by invading armies and of populations being forced to submit to governments without their consent.

But such historical misdeeds to not negate the Lockean Theory of Government, for Mr. Locke, in propounding his thesis, was not giving a general *history* lesson of the human race, but a *moral* lesson of *right and wrong*. John Locke was simply stating that there is one and only one legitimate foundation for civil society, and that is the *consent* and *agreement* of the members who are forming that body politic. Since all men are created equal and are equally vested with sovereignty in the natural State of Nature, reason dictates that men could form a civil society among themselves only by the unanimous consent of every member of that society. This is the theory that lies at the foundation of the concept of *government- by-the-consent-of-the-governed*. We might add that, without this foundation, it would not be possible for liberty to coexist with civil society, for freedom cannot exist where men are forced to enter into a political society against their will.

Regarding John Locke's concept of the social contract, Professor Thomas P. Peardon has noted:

> [H]e used it so as to preserve natural freedom as much as possible. Men surrender *only* the right of enforcing the Law of Nature. *All other rights they retain as fully as before.* Moreover, since men are by nature free, independent, and equal, the contract must be *unanimous*. Those who wish to remain in the state of nature are permitted to do so. Thus, Locke hoped, government would be both limited in its powers and based firmly on consent. [emphasis added] [19]

America's Founding Fathers certainly understood and accepted this Lockean concept, as is illustrated by a letter written to Thomas Jefferson by James Madison on February 4, 1790:

> On what principle is it that the voice of the majority binds the minority? It does not result, I conceive, from a Law of Nature, but from com-

[18] *Ibid.*, p. 11.
[19] John Locke, *Op. cit.*, p. xv.

> pact founded on utility? A greater proportion might be required by the fundamental Constitution of Society, if under any particular circumstances it were judged eligible. Prior, therefore, to the establishment of this principle, *unanimity* was necessary; and rigid theory accordingly presupposes the assent of every individual to the rule which subjects the minority to the will of the majority. [20]

The United States of America is quite fortunate and perhaps unique in the annals of history, in that American civilization was actually *founded* upon the wholesome principles espoused by John Locke in the *Second Treatise of Government.* As we shall soon discover when we examine more thoroughly what may be termed the *American Theory of Government,* such concepts as consent and agreement were fundamental in laying the foundations of the American political system.

Other Nations were not so fortunate to have their foundations established on such pristine principles. And here we might inquire: Is there no hope for such Nations to ever enjoy the blessings of natural liberty? To answer this question, we must observe the fundamental maxim that the misdeeds of the past cannot perpetually enslave future generations. The present generation of any Nation, whether founded on proper principles or not, may resume their liberties by resolving to henceforth conduct their affairs based upon the natural rights of man.

The Concept of Tacit Consent

It is of great importance to note that, in forming a civil society, the generally recognized intention of those creating it is that the society should endure permanently, so that succeeding generations of that society may enjoy its blessings. In such a case, it is not necessary for every individual in succeeding generations to formally renew the social contract. By virtue of the fact that a man is born into an existing society and is reared under the protections offered by that society, he automatically becomes a member of that society and owes allegiance to that society's sovereign, which, in a society based on proper principles, is the whole people of that Nation.

A man thus born into an existing society has only two legitimate alternatives available to him. First, he may assume a place within that society and continue to enjoy its blessings, thereby giving his *tactic consent* to its existence. Secondly, he may leave that Nation and relocate to another State more suitable to

---

[20] James Madison, *The Complete Madison: His Basic Writings,* Harper & Brothers, Publishers, New York, 1971, p. 31.

his liking.

It should be noted, however, that some – not all, but *some* – modern-day libertarians find it difficult to accept the concept of tacit consent. Typical of such views are those expressed by Professor Michael S. Rozeff of the University of Buffalo, who expressed his rejection of the concept of tacit consent in an article published by LewRockwell.com on September 20, 2005. Within this essay, Professor Rozeff declared:

> Do you and I willingly give up our freedom and property for the benefits of living in these United States? Do we tacitly consent to oppression by not moving to another country? Do we tacitly consent to the authority of our governments by not rebelling, by not throwing the tea into Boston harbor?
>
> John Locke and many today say "yes": we tacitly accept the State by paying our taxes, by receiving its benefits (such as property protection!), and by not emigrating. They say we acquiesce in an implicit contract in which we give up freedom or accept compulsion in exchange for other things that we value.
>
> This view is dead wrong. Why is it wrong? We are born into a system, we are chained from the start. The deck is stacked against us. The State has powers that it accumulated many decades ago, before you and I were born, and has accumulated since. We can change our position only at great cost. If we calculate whether to consent or not, we seemingly consent because we expect that to fight will cost us dearly without our securing a gain. We are not making a social contract freely entered into. There are guns to all our heads, one of which is PAY YOUR TAXES. Protest that and you go to jail. Call this consent?....
>
> Tacit consent is myth. What we really have is tacit submission....[21]

To answer Professor Rozeff, we must note that a civil society, once established, is a sovereign body politic and is thereby vested with a right to defend its territory and jurisdiction from any citizen – who, *as an individual member of society*, is not sovereign – that might prefer to live in a State of Nature *within the territory and jurisdiction of the established, sovereign State*. To allow such a right to an individual citizen would be to violate the rights of every other citizen within that body politic, for it is clear that the remaining members of that sovereign State could not remain secure in their rights if any person of the community could suddenly establish a State of Nature within its territory at will and thereby withdraw his loyalty to the State.

It is also evident from Professor Rozeff's essay that some confusion exists as to exactly what is being consented to through the concept of tactic consent.

---

[21] Michael S. Rozeff, "Tacit Submission," http://www.lewrockwell.com/rozeff/rozeff26.html, September 20, 2005.

Theoretically, the *state* and the *government* of that State are not identical entities. The State is the whole body of the people of a sovereign nation. *The State is the sovereign people, the supreme authority within the society, and the entity to whom loyalty and allegiance are due.* The government, on the other hand, is merely an agent of that State, and, when properly constituted, has only limited powers and may be modified by the majority of the people or even abolished and replaced as required.

Thus, whenever an individual is born into a society in which the government is improperly constituted or has escaped from the confining chains of its constitution, the only rightful choices available to an individual citizen are to relocate to another country or to *tacitly consent to the existing civilization* and acknowledge his citizenship in that existing State, while resolving to work for political change within his country. While individuals in a State of Nature have a natural right to join or refuse to join with others to establish a civil society, no *citizen of an existing society* has a natural right to undermine or destroy a sovereign State. In this regard, the natural right of sovereignty extends only to the building of a civilization, not to its destruction.

To illustrate the point being made, let us consider two statements. "I consent to my citizenship in this country, and acknowledge that I owe loyalty and allegiance to my fellow citizens, who constitute the sovereign power in my country." "I consent to my citizenship in this country, and acknowledge that I owe loyalty and allegiance to its government." These two statements are profoundly different. In fact, these two statements express sentiments diametrically opposed to one another. In a political system that is properly constituted, sovereignty is acknowledged as being vested in the people of the State, and loyalty is owed to the Nation – which is the whole people. The government within such a system should be considered as the mere humble servant of this Nation of people.

Regarding the concept of *majority rule*, it has already been noted that unanimity should be a requirement for the *creation* of civil society. But once formed, some form of simple majority rule should be sufficient to conduct the civil affairs of that society. Of course, as is the case in every instance of majority rule, sovereignty authorizes the majority of the people, in the manner described previously, to act for the whole people and to bind the minority *only in those cases wherein the majority has a natural right to rule.* Although the powers associated with sovereignty may be unlimited, *those who exercise sovereignty are bound by Natural Law to restrict the use of this authority to those ends established by God.* And those ends, clearly, are to enforce an observance of the Laws of Nature and to secure every individual in the enjoyment of his personal rights.

To state this matter in different words, no sovereign Nation has any right to use the political authority delegated by God to enslave others or to plunder the people. Sovereignty has been delegated to mankind by the Creator for the purpose of enforcing an observance of Natural Law and of protecting the inalienable rights of the citizens of an established State. The use of that political power for any other purpose is a violation of Natural Law and contrary to the will of God, and may aptly be considered unjust and criminal.

The government created by a sovereign people, needless to say, is even more limited in the exercise of political powers. The sovereign people of a State are limited by Natural Law, whereas their government is limited by Constitutional Law. When creating a government, the people delegate to it such powers as they deem proper and automatically retain or reserve all powers not specifically delegated. Even if this were not specifically or formally stated when creating a government, it would logically apply for a very obvious reason. The people of a Nation or State, who are vested with sovereignty, posses political powers naturally. Their government, on the other hand, possesses no inherent or natural powers, unless it has stolen sovereignty from the people. Such a government may rightfully possess only the powers that are specifically *delegated* to it by compact and consent. It is this concept, perhaps, that constitutes the greatest contribution of the *Second Treatise of Government* to our understanding of sovereignty and Natural Law.

The Powers of Government

Within the *Second Treatise of Government*, John Locke took pains to differentiate between civil society and government, noting that the creation of each constituted separate political actions. Vested with sovereignty, the people within a body politic may rightfully institute government for themselves and delegate certain powers to that government. In fact, *the ability to create a government and to define its powers is the hallmark of sovereignty*. And in so creating a government, those who possess sovereignty do not forfeit their supremacy to that government. Sovereignty – the supreme political authority – continues to be vested in the people of that society.

So important is this concept that we would be well advised to dwell further upon the points herein presented. It is a common mistake to look upon the powers exercised by a government and to falsely conclude that those are sovereign powers and to perhaps conclude that the government that exercises those powers must be sovereign, or at least partially sovereign. This mistake stems from an erroneous definition of sovereignty.

The ordinary powers of government do not constitute the supreme authority within a Nation. To be certain, such powers as that of declaring war and of taxation are very important powers. Yet, such powers do not, in themselves, constitute sovereignty. *Sovereignty is the supreme political authority within a State.* It is the power that can create a government, delegate powers to that government, define its ends, and even remove powers from that government. Indeed, as the author of the *Second Treatise of Government* points out in the chapter entitled, "Of the Dissolution of Government," the sovereign people within civil society have the right to abolish their existing government and to replace it with a new government. *That level of authority is sovereign power!*

Improper notions of sovereignty and the powers of government invariably result in theories that transfer sovereignty from its rightful owner to the government. And as we have observed previously, the concept of sovereignty lies at the heart of the question: Who is the master and who is the servant? A sovereign government is, by its very nature, a totalitarian tyranny, and the hapless people who must live under such a despotic government are truly slaves.

Two such falsehoods concerning sovereignty that have arisen in modern times are the concepts of "delegated sovereignty" and "divided sovereignty." Even those whose principles are otherwise sound have made the mistake of asserting these fallacies, not realizing that the logical conclusion of those concepts is a government of unlimited powers.

John T. Flynn, a well-respected and distinguished advocate of liberty, provided an illustration of this fallacy in his book, *The Decline of the American Republic*, in which he mistakenly equated the delegated powers exercised by government with sovereignty. The result of this mistake was unmistakably a sovereign, supreme government. "The Federal Government," he wrote, "*while sovereign*, does not have all of its own *sovereignty authority* entrusted to one set of hands." [emphasis added] [22]

Another well-respected conservative commentator to make this mistake was E.W.R. Ewing, who wrote an article entitled, "The Secession of 1861 Founded Upon Legal Right." Within this article, Mr. Ewing stated that, "The United States Government does not enjoy spontaneous or original or inherent sovereignty; all of its sovereign powers are delegated."[23]

Mr. Ewing then quoted a legal authority and the United States Supreme Court in support of the contention of a supreme or sovereign government:

> As summarized by a leading law authority, deduced from universally admitted decisions, here is full government in America:
>
> "The powers of sovereignty in the United States are divided between the government of the Union and those of the States. *They are each sovereign* with respect to the objects committed to it, and neither sovereign with respect to the objects committed to the other."...

[22] John T. Flynn, *The Decline of the American Republic*, The Devin-Adair Company, New York, 1955, p. 30.
[23] E.W.R. Ewing, "The Secession of 1861 Founded Upon Legal Right," *The Gray Book*, Gray Book Committee S.C.V., Published in behalf of The Sons of Confederate Veterans, Hattiesburg, p. 43.

> In 1904 the Supreme Court of the United States stated the same fact in these words:
>
> "In this Republic there is a dual system of government, national and State, and each within its own domain is *supreme*." [emphasis added] [24]

Within these passages, the Government of the United States is frankly proclaimed to be sovereign. The only limitation upon the sovereignty supposedly invested in the Federal Government is the sovereignty supposedly invested in the State governments. After this, it would appear, there is simply no more sovereignty that could remain in the hands of the people, who alone have a natural right to political supremacy. The fact that these erroneous concepts could be asserted by authorities no less prestigious and eminent than the Supreme Court of the United States and leading legal experts illustrates how important it is for the general public to properly understand the true nature of sovereignty.

Such a concept is highly reminiscent of the olden days of monarchy when kings proclaimed themselves to be sovereign by Divine Right, demanding that the people be their loyal subjects and bow low before them. Yet, as we have already ascertained, the rise of the Age of Reason exploded the myth of a sovereign government as a legitimate notion. Such careless usage of false concepts as those noted above cannot serve as sound principles to resurrect that which was cast into the trash bin centuries ago.

The Nature of Supremacy

Within his essay, E.W.R. Ewing stressed "the distinction: the sovereignty of the United States is *delegated*; that of each State is *inherent*." [25] Furthermore, he stated, "There can be no such thing as *limited* sovereignty. There is division of sovereign powers....But sovereignty is a self-explanatory word...." [26]

The key to understanding the fallacy of this notion of "delegated sovereignty" and "divided sovereignty" was provided by this author himself, in the assertion that, "There can be no such thing as *limited* sovereignty." If sovereignty is the *supreme* political power of a society, then it is apparent that it cannot possibly be *limited, divided*, or *delegated*. The very definition of "delegated" denies that sovereignty can be delegated to any government, for the concept of *delegation* implies that a government holds its powers only as a *trust*. If the government possessed sovereignty, then it would possess, not *delegated powers*, but

---

[24] *Ibid.*, p. 44.
[25] *Ibid.*, p. 45.
[26] *Ibid.*, p. 48.

inherent or natural powers. In fact, if a government possessed sovereignty, then it could assign to itself any political power that it wished to exercise, thereby eliminating the necessity of having powers delegated to it by some other authority. The very expression, "delegated sovereignty," is therefore a self-contained contradiction.

Those who mistakenly contend for "delegated sovereignty" and "divided sovereignty," as we have previously noted, are confusing the ordinary powers of government with sovereignty, which is the supreme political power, or the *source* of all legitimate governmental powers. Simply because a government may exercise such important powers as declaring war, regulating commerce, and conducting foreign affairs, does not automatically render that government sovereign. Those are not sovereign powers! If the government holds its powers as a trust, is limited by a constitution, and is responsible to those who created it, then it is plain to discern that those who created it must retain sovereignty and may alter or abolish their created servant at will.

At this point in our inquiry into the nature of sovereignty, it should be obvious that the notion of "limited sovereignty" is also a self-contained contradiction. Sovereignty is the *supreme political power* within a civil society. Does the concept of "limited supremacy" have meaning? While it is quite possible to divide and thereby limit the sphere of powers delegated to a government, the supreme power that can create a government cannot be limited, divided, or shared. Either the people are the masters within a civil society, or they are not. No man, it has been said, can serve two masters; there can be only one master in a kingdom, a Nation, a society, or a Republic. The very idea of two masters within the same kingdom would set the stage for conflict, turmoil, and civil war. One or the other must and will ultimately triumph over the other.

Supremacy is an exclusive concept. As with other such exclusive concepts – such as the ideas inherent in the words *tallest, shortest, biggest,* and *best* – the very concept of sovereignty renders it a solitary attribute or possession. Several illustrations are here offered for consideration, for the point to be made is one of great significance in adequately understanding the true nature of sovereignty.

Within every library may be found a book that is taller than any other book. That one book may thus be described as the *tallest* book in that library. In making such an assertion, it is inherently implied that it alone shares this attribute, and that no other book in that library is as tall as it is. The same may be said of the shortest book, or the heaviest book, or the best book in that library. In each case, there can be only one book that has the stated attribute. The idea of limited, divided, or shared characteristics is rejected by the very meaning of those words. There cannot be two tallest books in the same library. Nor can there be two shortest books, two heaviest books, or two best books in the same library.

The same rule applies to the concept of sovereignty. As we have already noted, sovereignty is defined as the *supreme political power* within civil society, and supremacy implies that there can be only one master within a body politic. There simply cannot be more than one supreme or highest authority within a political kingdom.

If there could remain any doubt on this concept, then let us offer one further illustration. By way of example, let us consider the situation of two Nations, which we shall designate as Nation A and Nation B, who desire to establish an association or union between themselves. Prior to the formation of this association, each Nation is undeniably sovereign and independent. Thus, in forming a union between them, there are only two logical alternatives in regard to sovereignty.

The first option, of course, is for both Nations to agree to merge into a single State or body politic, which we may style Nation C, in which the two separate societies become one society or Nation. In such a case, Nation C would be sovereign, and neither Nation A nor Nation B would be sovereign. In fact, neither Nation A nor Nation B would continue to exist as States or Nations. Within this union, there would exist no conflict of supremacy.

The second option available to Nation A and Nation B upon the formation of their union would be for each to retain its separate sovereignty. In such a case, Nation A and Nation B would continue to be separate sovereign States. But the union formed between them, even if properly styled with a name, such as the United Nations or the United States, would not be sovereign, for it, in itself, would not be a real Nation, but merely a political association. Once again, there would exist no conflict of supremacy within this union. The citizens of Nation A would owe allegiance to only one sovereign – Nation A. And the citizens of Nation B would owe allegiance to only one sovereign – Nation B.

If we wish to set aside logic and reason, there is a third option. Nation A and Nation B could create through their union a new, sovereign Nation C, while attempting to continue to exist as separately sovereign Nations themselves. In such a case, there would exist a conflict of logic as to who was sovereign. Within Nation A, for example, there would exist two supposedly sovereign authorities, each claiming supremacy over the other. The same would be true within Nation B, for Nation C would attempt to share political supremacy with it. The internal contradictions of such a system of conflicting supremacy would prove to be its very destruction.

Just as a man can hire a security guard to protect his property, without ceasing to own his possessions, so may a sovereign people create a government without ceasing to possess their natural political supremacy. Ordinary political powers may be delegated to government, divided among several governments, and limited by written constitutions, but sovereignty cannot be removed from the people except by theft or usurpation, accompanied by false theories of government designed to justify such grand larceny.

Government is, always has been, and always will be, the most effective, highly organized *instrument of power* ever devised by mankind. A government has access to the pockets of the people through taxation and has at its command martial forces sufficient to enforce its will. As an instrument of power, a government is no better and no worse than those who administer it. As such, within every society, there will inevitably arise those who seek to use this instrument of power to plunder the nation and enslave the people. When that happens, the dangerous servant we call government is subverted into a frightening and fearful master.

Chapter Three

Sovereignty in the United States

The peoples who migrated to the New World and settled along what is now the Eastern seaboard of the United States found what may be regarded as the last great geographical area on earth that was still in the State of Nature. Except for a relatively few native Indians, North America was a vast and unsettled wilderness governed only by the Laws of Nature. Some European colonists, upon arriving in the New World, followed the pattern established by the Pilgrims in the Mayflower Compact, wherein civil society was established by formally expressed consent. Other societies were formed more informally and by tacit consent.

Eventually, that portion of North America that had been civilized became, either through agreement, purchase, or conquest, colonies of Great Britain. Those colonies destined to become the original thirteen States of the American Union were Georgia, South Carolina, North Carolina, Virginia, Maryland, New Jersey, New York, Pennsylvania, Connecticut, Rhode Island, Massachusetts, Delaware, and New Hampshire. While in their colonial status, needless to say, none of these colonies possessed political sovereignty, but they did share the common sovereignty of the mother country by virtue of the fact that the colonists held the rights of Englishmen.

Following a period of escalating conflict with the mother country, the thirteen American colonies, acting in concert, but each acting for itself, declared themselves sovereign and independent of Great Britain. The great principles of the American Revolution were formally expressed within the Declaration of Independence, which was issued to a candid world on July 4, 1776. Those principles espoused within that Declaration formed the foundation for the American system of government and clearly indicated the true extent of the influence of the Lockean Theory of Government on the minds of the American people.

Commenting on the profound influence of John Locke among the American patriots, C. Edward Merrian noted:

> Locke, in particular, was the authority to whom the Patriots paid greatest deference. He was the most famous of Seventeenth Century democratic theorists, and his ideas had their due weight with the colonists. Almost

> every writer seems to have been influenced by him, many quoted his words, and the argument of others shows the unmistakable imprint of his philosophy. The first great speech of Otis was wholly based upon Locke's ideas; Samuel Adams, on the "Rights of the Colonists as Men and as British Subjects", followed the same model. Many of the phrases of the Declaration of Independence may be found in Locke's Treatise; there is hardly any important writer of this time who does not openly refer to Locke, or tacitly follow the lead he had taken. The argument in regard to the limitations upon Parliament was taken from Locke's reflections on the "supreme legislature" and the necessary restrictions upon its authority. No one stated more strongly than did he the basis for the doctrine that "taxation without representation is tyranny". No better epitome of the Revolutionary theory could be found than in John Locke on civil government. [1]

The influence of John Locke on the mind of Thomas Jefferson, the author of the Declaration of Independence, may be ascertained by noting that in the parlor of his home at Monticello hung portraits of three men. Mr. Jefferson would often tell his visitors that he considered those men to be the three greatest individuals who had ever lived. It is of special consequence to our understanding of the influence of Natural Law thought on the minds of America's Founding Fathers to note that one of the paintings was a portrait of John Locke, the Father of the Age of Reason.

Although the strong influence of John Locke on Mr. Jefferson's natural rights philosophy was unmistakable within the Declaration of Independence, its author insisted that he was merely expressing "the American mind" within that remarkable document. In a letter to a friend in 1825, for instance, Thomas Jefferson explained that the principles contained with the Declaration constituted the common understanding of the Laws of Nature shared by all Americans:

> [The essential thing was] not to find out new principles, or new arguments, never before thought of, not merely to say things which had never been said before; but to place before mankind the common sense of the subject, in terms so plain and firm as to command their assent....Neither aiming at originality of principles or sentiments, nor yet copied from any particular and previous writing, it was intended to be an expression of the American mind....All its authority rests then on the harmonizing sentiments of the day, whether expressed in conversation, in letters, printed essays, or the elementary books of public right, as Aristotle, Cicero, Locke, Sidney, etc. [2]

---

[1] Verna M. Hall, *Christian History of the Constitution of the United States of America*, Volume 1, The American Christian Constitution Press, San Francisco, 1960, quoted on p. 51.

[2] Carl Becker, *The Declaration of Independence: A Study in the History of Political Ideas*, Vintage Books, New York, 1970, quoted on pp. 25-26.

The Declaration of Independence

The Declaration of Independence may be divided by content into three distinct sections. The first section, which is perhaps the most famous and often quoted, summarizes the Lockean Theory of Government and reaffirms the right of the colonies to self-government. The second section, which is of interest primary as an historic list of colonial grievances, provides the specific reasons why the colonies decided to withdraw or secede from the British Empire. Finally, the third section contains the actual declaration by the colonies – which would henceforth be States – of their sovereignty and independence from Great Britain.

John Locke's influence on what Thomas Jefferson referred to as "the American mind" can be ascertained from a plain reading of the first section of the Declaration of Independence:

> When, in the course of human events, it becomes necessary for one people to dissolve the political bands which have connected them with another, and to assume, among the powers of the earth, the separate and equal station to which the Laws of Nature, and of nature's God entitle them, a decent respect to the opinions of mankind requires that they should declare the causes which impel them to the separation.
>
> We hold these truths to be self-evident, that all men are created equal; that they are endowed by their Creator with certain unalienable rights; that among these, are life, liberty, and the pursuit of happiness. That, to secure these rights, governments are instituted among men, deriving their just powers from the consent of the governed; that, whenever any form of government becomes destructive of these ends, it is the right of the people to alter or to abolish it, and to institute a new government, laying its foundation on such principles, and organizing its powers in such form, as to them shall seem most likely to effect their safety and happiness. Prudence, indeed, will dictate that governments long established, should not be changed for light and transient causes; and, accordingly, all experience hath shown, that mankind are more disposed to suffer, while evils are sufferable, than to right themselves by abolishing the forms to which they are accustomed. But, when a long train of abuses and usurpations, pursuing invariably the same object, evinces a design to reduce them under absolute despotism, it is their right, it is their duty, to throw off such government, and to provide new guards for their future security. [3]

Within these passages of the Declaration of Independence, we see a masterful summary of the Lockean Theory of Government, as expressed in the majestic style of Thomas Jefferson. So general are the principles presented within

[3] Alexander H. Stephens, *A Constitutional View of the Late War Between the States; Its Causes, Character, Conduct and Results*, Volume 1, Kraus Reprint Co., New York, 1970 (orig. pub. 1868), quoted on pp. 545-546.

this section of the Declaration, that they apply not merely to the thirteen American colonies, but to all Nations and all peoples, anywhere and at any time in history. The expression used in the first sentence of "one people," in fact, does not refer to any specific society, but to *any* people. By substituting the word "any" for "one" within that phrase, the full import of the phrase becomes even more obvious: "When, in the course of human events, it becomes necessary for *any* people to dissolve...."

That passage within the Declaration of Independence that begins with the words, "We hold these truths to be self-evident," is undeniably the most cherished and most often quoted passage within that revered document. Within this passage, Mr. Jefferson stated that "all men are created equal," meaning that no one has a Divine Right to lord over humanity. The author of the Declaration also stated that God exists, a belief that provides an essential foundation for the entire Lockean Theory of Government. Without God, there can be no inalienable rights, no sovereignty vested in the people, and no Natural Law. But the Declaration boldly proclaims that there is a God and that God created all men equally and endowed them with certain inalienable rights. The purpose of government, asserted Mr. Jefferson, is merely to safeguard the individual rights of the people.

Thomas Jefferson concluded this section of the Declaration of Independence by noting that people tend to be conservative by nature and do not – and should not – replace governments for trivial reasons. Yet, whenever government fails to safeguard the rights of the people, or becomes itself a threat to their rights, the people – who are collectively the master within political society – not only have a right, *but are duty bound*, to replace that government with a new one, "laying its foundation on such principles."

Never before had any Nation been founded on such principles. Other countries, such as Great Britain, had attempted to adapt such concepts to their existing political systems, with varying degrees of success. But until July 4, 1776, no Nation had ever established its *foundation* on the Lockean Theory of Government. On that date, thirteen newly sovereign American States were ushered into the world boldly declaring the Lockean principles of Natural Law and natural rights as their foundations.

Immediately after declaring their independence from Great Britain, the thirteen sovereign States proceeded to reconstitute themselves on the principles of the Lockean Theory of Government, beginning with a recognition of the sovereignty of the people and the principle that all legitimate political power emanates from that fount of authority. Accordingly, they unanimously rejected *Monarchy* as a form of government, since it was deemed incompatible with popular sovereignty. In similar fashion, they rejected *Democracy* as a form of government, since it was based on unlimited majority rule, which was deemed as one path toward a sovereign government. By selecting the *republican form* of government, they acknowledged the right of the majority to rule, but only within the limitations constitutionally established. Finally, these thirteen sovereign States formed a *Federal Union* between themselves to further safeguard their rights from aggressive foreign powers. Because the newly sovereign American States created a Federal Republic, they added a new dimension to the Lockean concept called *federalism*, thereby creating a uniquely American Theory of Government.

The American Mind

Although there would be many other Nations that would pay lip service to the concept of the sovereignty of the people, only in the United States of America was that concept translated into a reality. As the young Republic grew in territory, population, and prestige, the entire world looked upon the American States with envy and wonder. When a young Frenchman named Alexis de Tocqueville toured the United States in 1831, he was so moved by the civilization, culture, and political system of the United States that he wrote two volumes on his impressions, entitled *Democracy in America*, which were originally published in 1835 and 1840.

Among the unique qualities of American civilization that made a lasting impression on this twenty-five year old Frenchman was the concept of the sovereignty of the people. In fact, he devoted an entire section of the first volume of his book to his observations on "The Principle of the Sovereignty of the People of America."

Commenting on this principle, Alexis de Tocqueville wrote in *Democracy in America*:

> Whenever the political laws of the United States are to be discussed, it is with the doctrine of the sovereignty of the people that we must begin.
>
> The principle of the sovereignty of the people, which is always to be found, more or less, at the bottom of almost all human institutions, generally remains there concealed from view. It is obeyed without being recognized, or if for a moment it is brought to light, it is hastily cast back into the gloom of the sanctuary.
>
> "The will of the nation" is one of those phrases that have been most largely abused by the wily and the despotic of every age. Some have seen the expression of it in the purchased suffrages of a few of the satellites of power; others, in the votes of a timid or an interested minority; and some have even discovered it in the silence of a people, on the supposition that the fact of submission established the right to command.
>
> In America the principle of the sovereignty of the people is neither

> barren nor concealed, as it is with some other nations; it is recognized by the customs and proclaimed by the laws; it spreads freely, and arrives without impediment at its most remote consequences. If there is a country in the world where the doctrine of the sovereignty of the people can be fairly appreciated, where it can be studied in its application to the affairs of society, and where its dangers and advantages may be judged, that country is assuredly America.
>
> ...The people reign in the American political world as the Deity does in the universe. They are the cause and the aim of all things; everything comes from them, and everything is absorbed in them. [4]

This Frenchmen elsewhere in his book paid a great tribute to our young Republic:

> At the present day the principle of the sovereignty of the people has acquired in the United States all the practical development that the imagination can conceive. It is unencumbered by those fictions that are thrown over it in other countries, and it appears in every possible form, according to the exigency of the occasion. [5]

According to Alexis de Tocqueville, the principle of the sovereignty of the people in the United States extended its influence to the people's habits, religion, and family life, and even had a profound impact on their notions of popular government:

> In the United States the sovereignty of the people is not an isolated doctrine, bearing no relation to the prevailing habits and ideas of the people; it may, on the contrary, be regarded as the last link of a chain of opinions which binds the whole Anglo-American world. That Providence has given to every human being the degree of reason necessary to direct himself in the affairs that interest him exclusively is the grand maxim upon which civil and political society rests in the United States. The father of a family applies it to his children, the master to his servants, the township to its officers, the county to its townships, the State to the counties, the Union to the States; and when extended to the nation, it becomes the doctrine of the sovereignty of the people. [6]

As is evident from these passages from *Democracy in America,* it was rapidly becoming apparent to the entire world, as early as 1831, that the United States was destined for greatness beyond that of ordinary Nations. Nor was it any secret why American civilization would rise to unprecedented heights in

---

[4] Alexis de Tocqueville, *Democracy in America*, Volume 1, Vintage Books, New York, 1945, pp. 57 and 60.

[5] *Ibid.*, Volume 1, p. 59.

[6] *Ibid.*, Volume 1, pp. 435-436.

terms of prosperity, strength, and glory. America was destined to greatness because the American political system had been founded upon the proper principles of Natural Law, natural rights, and the sovereignty of the people.

Blackstone's Commentaries

Although John Locke was an English philosopher and the Glorious Revolution directly associated with his principles was aimed at reforming Great Britain, the Lockean Theory of Government had a significantly more profound influence on the thinking of Americans than it did on the thinking of the British, whose long history of monarchical government hindered the acceptance of the sovereignty of the people in the British Isles. For that reason, it became necessary for leaders in our young Republic to exercise care and caution when adopting books penned by British authors as teaching guides in American schools and universities. Perhaps the most famous case was the adoption of Sir William Blackstone's authoritative work, entitled *Commentaries on the Laws of England*, which was originally published in 1765-1769, as the standard for qualifying lawyers in the United States.

This great work was highly regarded, even in the United States, for Blackstone's *Commentaries* established the theoretical basis for a justice system founded upon fairness and the rule of law. Yet, there was one difficulty in adopting it for use in the American Republic. Its author did not understand that sovereignty was, as a natural right, vested in the people within civil society. Instead of advocating the sovereignty of the people, Sir William Blackstone stated that sovereignty can only be vested in government.

As this distinguished British author erroneously stated:

> How the several forms of government we now see in the world at first actually began, is a matter of great uncertainty, and has occasioned infinite disputes. It is not my business or intention to enter into any of them. However they began, or by what right they subsist, there is and must be in all of them a supreme, irresistible, absolute, uncontrolled authority, in which the JURA SUMMI IMPERII, or the rights of sovereignty, reside. And this authority is placed in those hands, wherein...the qualities requisite for supremacy, wisdom, goodness, and power, are the most likely to be found.
>
> The political writers of antiquity will not allow more than three regular forms of government; the first, when the sovereign power is lodged in an aggregate assembly consisting of all the free members of a community, which is called a democracy; the second, when it is lodged in a council, composed of select members, and then it is stiled an aristocracy; the last, when it is intrusted in the hands of a single person, and then it takes the name monarchy. All other species of government, they say, are either corruptions of, or re-

> ducible to, these three.
>
> By the sovereign power, as was before observed, is meant the making of laws; for wherever that power resides, all others must conform to, and be directed by it, whatever appearance the outward form and administration of the government may put on. For it is at any time in the option of the legislature to alter that form and administration by a new edict or rule, and to put the laws into whatever hands it pleases; by constituting one, or a few, or many executive magistrates: and all the other powers of the state must obey the legislative power in the discharge of their several functions, or else the constitution is at an end. [7]

Such a conception of sovereignty is surprising, considering that it was written more than seventy years after John Locke's *Second Treatise of Government* should have forever crushed the idea of a sovereign government as a legitimate concept. Yet, the work contained many concepts on law that were of great value to our young Republic. The question confronting the United States was how to obtain the great mass of good within Blackstone's *Commentaries* while maintaining the principle of the sovereignty of the people.

The solution to this dilemma was found by including special notes correcting Sir William's mistaken notions on sovereignty when publishing Blackstone's *Commentaries* in the United States. Thus, in 1803, a special American edition of Blackstone's *Commentaries*, compiled by St. George Tucker, was published under the title of *Blackstone's Commentaries: With Notes of Reference to the Constitution and Laws, of the Federal Government of the United States, and of the Commonwealth of Virginia.*

In reference to Sir William Blackstone's assertion that, "Sovereignty and Legislature are indeed convertible terms; one cannot subsist without the other," St. George Tucker offered this clarification:

> The generality of expression in this passage might lead those who have not considered with attention the new lights which the American Revolution has spread over the science of politics, to conclude with the learned commentator, that, "By the sovereign power, is meant the making of laws; and wherever that power resides, all others must conform to and be directed by it, whatever appearance the outward form and administration of justice may put on. It being at any time in the option of the legislature to alter that form and administration by a new edict or rule, and to put the execution of the laws into whatever hands it pleases: and all the other powers of the state must obey the legislative power in the execution of their several functions...or else the constitution is at an end."...
>
> ...But the American Revolution has formed a new epoch in the history of civil institutions, by reducing to practice, what, before, had been supposed to exist only in the visionary speculations of theoretical writers....The

---

[7] Stephen L. Corrigan, http://members.nuvox.net/~on.stephenc/repf.html, quoted in website.

> world, for the first time since the annals of its inhabitants began, saw an original written compact formed by the free and deliberate voices of individuals disposed to unite in the same social bonds; thus exhibiting a political phenomenon unknown to former ages. This memorable precedent was soon followed by the far greater number of the States in the Union, and led the way to that instrument, by which the Union of the Confederated States has since been completed, and in which, as we shall hereafter endeavour to shew, the sovereignty of the people, and the responsibility of their servants are principles fundamentally, and unequivocally, established; in which the powers of the several branches of government are defined, and the excess of them, as well in the *legislature*, as in the *other* branches, finds limits, which cannot be transgressed without offending against that greater power from whom all authority, among us, is derived; to wit, the PEOPLE.
>
> To illustrate this by an example. By the Constitution of the United States, the solemn and original compact here referred to, being the act of the people, and by them declared to be the supreme law of the land, the legislative powers thereby granted, are vested in a Congress, to consist of a Senate and House of Representatives. As these powers, on the one hand, are extended to certain objects, as to lay and collect taxes, duties, &c. so on the other they are clearly limited and restrained; as that no tax or duty shall be laid on articles exported from any State...nor any preference given by any regulation of commerce or revenue to the ports of one State over those of another, &c. These, and several others, are objects to which the power of the legislature does not extend; and should Congress be so unwise as to pass an act contrary to these restrictions, the other powers of the state are not bound to obey the legislative power in the execution of their several functions, as our author expresses it: but the very reverse is their duty, being sworn to support the Constitution, which unless they do in *opposition* to such encroachments, the Constitution would indeed be at an end.
>
> Here then we must resort to a distinction which the institution and nature of our government has introduced into the Western hemisphere; which, however, can only obtain in governments where power is not usurped but delegated, and where authority is a trust and not a right...nor can it ever be truly ascertained where there is not a written constitution to resort to. A distinction, nevertheless, which certainly does exist between the indefinite and unlimited power of the people, in whom the sovereignty of these States, ultimately, substantially, and unquestionably resides, and the definite powers of the Congress and State legislatures, which are severally limited to certain and determinate objects, being no more than emanations from the former, where, and *where only*, that legislative essence which constitutes sovereignty can be found. [8]

As this learned writer noted, it is necessary to acknowledge the sovereignty of the people as the foundation of the American system of government,

---

[8] St. George Tucker, *Blackstone's Commentaries: With Notes of Reference to the Constitution and Laws, of the Federal Government of the United States, and of the Commonwealth of Virginia*, Volume 1, http://www.constitution.org/tb/t1a.htm, (orig. pub. 1803).

for such an acknowledgement is the principle on which the concept of constitutionally limited government is derived. The people, not any government, asserted St. George Tucker, constitute the sovereign power in the American political system. The government, within our political system, possesses only those powers that are delegated to it by the sovereign, and which it holds as a trust. The government has no right to assume any power, either by undisguised usurpation or by pretending to possess implied or inherent powers. Unless these basic principles are acknowledged, despotism would be inevitable in the United States and "the Constitution would indeed be at an end."

In another note, St. George Tucker added to his previous observations on the importance of acknowledging the sovereignty of the people:

> A Nation or State is a body politic, or a society of men united together to promote their mutual safety, and advantage, by means of their union.
>
> From the very design, that induces them to form a society that has its common interests, and ought to act in concert, it is necessary that there should be established a public authority, to order and direct what ought to be done, by each, in relation to the end of the association.
>
> This political authority, is by some writers denominated the sovereignty; but, for reasons which will be hereafter explained, I prefer calling it the government, or administrative authority of the state, to which each citizen, subjects himself by the very act of association, for the purpose of establishing a civil society.
>
> All men being by nature equal, in respect to their rights, no man nor set of men, can have any natural, or inherent right, to rule over the rest.
>
> This right cannot be acquired by conquest, for the few, are, in a state of nature, unable to subdue the many.
>
> Were it ever possible that the few could triumph over the many, the power thus acquired, can not be transmissible by inheritance, since it may fall into hands incapable of maintaining it.
>
> The right of governing can, therefore, be acquired only by consent, originally; and this consent must be that of at least a majority of the people.
>
> Since no person possesses any inherent right to govern, or rule over, the rest; and since the few cannot possess, naturally power enough to subdue the many; the majority of the people, and, much more the whole body, possess all the powers, which any society, State, or Nation, possesses in relation to its own immediate concerns.
>
> This power which every independent State or Nation, (however constituted, or by whatever name distinguished, whether it be called an empire, kingdom, or republic and whether the government be in its form a monarchy, aristocracy, or democracy, or a mixture or corruption of all them,) possesses in relation to its own immediate concerns, is unlimited, and unlimitable, so long as the Nation or State retains its independence; there being no power upon earth, whilst that remains, which can control, or direct the operations, or will, of the State in those respects.

> This unlimitable power, is that supreme, irresistable, absolute, uncontrollable authority, which by political writers in general, is denominated the SOVEREIGNTY; and which is by most of them, supposed to be vested in the government, or administrative authority, of the State: but, which, we contend, resides only in the people; is inherent in them; and unalienable from them.
>
> Except in very small States, where the government is administered by the people themselves, in person, the exercise of the sovereign power is confined to the establishment of the constitution of the State, or the amendment of its defects, or to the correction of the abuses of the government.
>
> The constitution of a State is, properly, that instrument by which the government, or administrative authority of the State, is created: its powers defined, their extent limited; the duties of the public functionaries prescribed; and the principles, according to which the government is to be administered, delineated....
>
> Legitimate government can therefore be derived only from the voluntary grant of the people, and exercised for their benefit.
>
> The sovereignty, though always potentially existing in the people of every independent Nation, or State, is in most of them, usurped by, and confounded with, the government. Hence in England it is said to be vested in the parliament: in France, before the revolution, and still, in Spain, Russia, Turkey and other absolute monarchies, in the crown, or monarch; in Venice, until the late conquest of that State, in the doge, and senate, &c.
>
> As the sovereign power hath no limits to its authority, so hath the government of a State no rights, but such as are purely derivative, and limited; the union of the SOVEREIGNTY of a State with the GOVERNMENT, constitutes a state of USURPATION and absolute TYRANNY, over the PEOPLE.
>
> In the United States of America the people have retained the sovereignty in their own hands: they have in each State distributed the government, or administrative authority of the State, into two distinct branches, internal, and external; the former of these, they have confided, with some few exceptions, to the State government; the latter to the Federal Government.
>
> Since the union of the sovereignty with the government, constitutes a state of absolute power, or tyranny, over the people, every attempt to effect such an union is treason against the sovereignty, in the actors; and every extension of the administrative authority beyond its just constitutional limits, is absolutely an act of usurpation in the government, of that sovereignty, which the people have reserved to themselves. [9]

Within these passages, it can be observed that the concept of the sovereignty of the people was deeply rooted in the minds of the American people from the very birth of our Republic, making the United States of America

---

[9] St. George Tucker, *Blackstone's Commentaries: With Notes of Reference to the Constitution and Laws, of the Federal Government of the United States, and of the Commonwealth of Virginia*, Volume 1, http://www.constitution.org/tb/t1b.htm, (orig. pub. 1803).

unique in the annals of the history of the human race. So great was the importance of this great principle of popular sovereignty that it was necessary to append notes of correction regarding sovereignty to Blackstone's *Commentaries*. And so great was this principle in the American mind that, as St. George Tucker stated in unmistakable language, a sovereign government should be regarded as *the definition of tyranny*, and any attempt to transfer sovereignty from the people to the government should be regarded as *treason*.

The Republican Form of Government

The Declaration of Independence established the principle of the sovereignty of the people as the foundation for the American Theory of Government. Within that Declaration, the will of the people is proclaimed to be superior to that of the government, and government is properly relegated to the role of servant of the people. After the thirteen American States had secured their independence from the British Empire, the concept of the sovereignty of the people played a significant role in determining the type of government established in the United States.

Inherent in the principle of the sovereignty of the people is the notion of *popular government* – a government that represents the interests of the people, is controlled and limited by them, and is accountable to them. It was only natural, therefore, following the War of Independence, that the Founding Fathers should reject any and all proposals for the creation of a monarchy, an aristocracy, or any other type of unrepresentative government. Nothing less than a republican form of government would suffice for each of the States, and nothing less than a Federal Republic would suffice for the Union of those States.

James Madison, who has earned the endearing title of "Father of the Constitution," explained the basis of our form of government in the February 20, 1792 issue of the *National Gazette*, wherein he declared:

> No government is perhaps reducible to a sole principle of operation....It is useful, nevertheless, to analyse the several kinds of government, and to characterize them by the spirit which predominates in each....
>
> May not governments be properly divided, according to their predominant spirit and principles into three species of which the following are examples?
>
> First. A government operating by a permanent military force which at once maintains the government, and is maintained by it; which is at once the cause of burdens on the people, and of submission in the people to their burdens. Such have been the governments under which human nature has groaned through every age....

> Secondly. A government operating by corrupt influence; substituting the motive of private interest in place of public duty; converting its pecuniary dispensations into bounties to favorites, or bribes to opponents; accommodating its measures to the avidity of a part of the nation instead of the benefit of the whole; in a word, enlisting an army of interested partizans, whose tongues, whose pens, whose intrigues, and whose active combinations, by supplying the terror of the sword, may support a real domination of the few, under an apparent liberty of the many. Such a government, wherever to be found, is an imposter....
>
> Thirdly. A government deriving its energy from the will of the society, and operating by the reason of its measures, on the understanding and interest of the society. Such is the government for which philosophy has been searching, and humanity been fighting, from the most remote ages. Such are republican governments which it is the glory of America to have invented, and her unrivalled happiness to possess. [10]

As the astute reader has undoubtedly concluded, after reading these words of the Father of the Constitution, the form of government established by our Founding Fathers is not really the same type of government we have in actual operation today. Our Founding Fathers clearly established the third type of government described by James Madison. Equally clear, our modern Welfare State has completed the transformation of our governmental system into the second type described by Mr. Madison, a political system that pretends to be the servant of society, but is in fact the servant of special interest groups.

The concept of the sovereignty of the people was the principle that guided our Founding Fathers toward the creation of representative, constitutionally limited government for the United States. Every State then existing voluntarily reconstituted itself under the republican form of government, and a special provision was inserted into the Federal Constitution to guarantee that form of government to every State in the Union.

While a few delegates to the Philadelphia Convention of 1787 did express fondness for aristocratic and monarchical forms of government, the overwhelming majority of that Federal Convention was firmly attached to the principle of the sovereignty of the people, which was regarded as compatible only with the republican form of government. This principle also inspired the Founding Fathers to view the powers of the Federal Government, like those of the State governments, as limited to only those delegated to it. They emphatically rejected all notions that any government could possess or exercise powers by natural or inherent right. Thus, within the Constitution of 1787, the first three words are, "We the people," words that clearly reveal the rightful source of all political power within our political system.

---

[10] James Madison, *The Complete Madison: His Basic Writings*, Harper & Brothers, Publishers, New York, 1971, pp. 35-36.

Following the adoption of our current Federal Constitution, two political parties appeared in the infant Republic. One – lead by Thomas Jefferson – was devoted to preserving the sovereignty of the people, and the other – lead by Alexander Hamilton – was devoted to transforming the Federal Government into a sovereign general government. John Taylor of Caroline was destined to become the principal philosopher of the Jeffersonians, and within his books and pamphlets, he frequently referred to the notion of the sovereignty of the people as the true and proper foundation of the American Theory of Government.

The Philosophy of John Taylor of Caroline

John Taylor of Caroline, who had held the rank of Colonel in the Continental Army during the Revolutionary War, based the argument for States' Rights and strictly limited constitutional government on the natural sovereignty of the people, which he recognized as being equivalent with the sovereignty of the States. The expression "of Caroline" following his name is a reference to his *county* of origin within the State of Virginia, and his use of that style of personal reference was in not unusual in his day, as evidenced by its usage by others, such as Thomas Jefferson of Albemarle and John Randolph of Roanoke. Among the books authored by John Taylor of Caroline were *Arator*, *Tyranny Unmasked*, *Construction Construed and Constitutions Vindicated*, *New Views of the Constitution of the United States*, and *An Inquiry into the Principles and Policy of the Government of the United States*.

Professor C. William Hill, Jr., in his book, *The Political Theory of John Taylor of Caroline*, noted that Mr. Taylor "agreed with Locke's doctrine of popular sovereignty" and occasionally mentioned Mr. Locke in his works. [11] And Professor Henry H. Simms, in his book, *Life of John Taylor*, noted that Mr. Taylor "became the central figure in the Virginia State Rights School." [12] Perhaps the greatest admirer of Mr. Taylor's brilliant philosophical works was none other than Thomas Jefferson himself.

In his book, *The Social Philosophy of John Taylor of Caroline*, Eugene Tenbroeck Mudge compiled these written statements made by Mr. Jefferson:

> Col. Taylor and myself have rarely, if ever, differed in any political principle of importance. Every act of his life, and every word he ever wrote,

[11] C. William Hill, Jr., *The Political Theory of John Taylor of Caroline*, Fairleigh Dickinson University Press, Rutherford, 1977, p. 41.

[12] Henry H. Simms, *Life of John Taylor: The Story of a Brilliant Leader in the Early Virginia State Rights School*, The William Byrd Press, Inc., Richmond, 1932, p. 177.

> satisfies me of this....[*Construction Construed and Constitutions Vindicated*] is the most effective retraction of our government to its original principles which has ever yet been sent by heaven to our aid. Every State in the Union should give a copy to every member they elect....On all important questions, it contains the true political faith....[But the damage has been done], I fear [*New Views of the Constitution of the United States*] is the voice of one crying in the wilderness. [13]

Thomas Jefferson did not merely approve of the works written by his fellow Virginian; he was also influenced by the philosophy of John Taylor of Caroline. Regarding *Construction Construed and Constitutions Vindicated*, for example, the Sage of Monticello noted that, "I acknowledge it has corrected some erring opinion into which I had slidden without sufficient examination." [14]

Commenting the views of John Taylor of Caroline toward the concept of the sovereignty of the people, Eugene Tenbroeck Mudge noted:

> What, then, is Taylor's conception of the system of government of the United States? Every chapter of every book contains frequent statements of the principle of popular sovereignty which he held to be a basic element of our theory of government....[Especially in his later books,] the argument is based on a theory of natural sovereignty or natural self-government and the implications therefrom for the doctrine of States' Rights, for a limitation of the power of the Supreme Court, for a reorganization of the banking system, for a nullification of the protective tariff, and in general for the removal of the repressions which impede the growth of agriculture....[T]he *Inquiry* contains numerous references to the right of self-government and to the sovereignty of state nations or of the people of the States....The later works, although no less repetitious and unorganized, do nevertheless present a complete theory of sovereignty based on the ideas which were little more than mentioned in the *Inquiry*....In the earlier writing Natural Law and popular sovereignty are treated as items of the good moral principles of government....The net result is an absolute moralistic dualism of good and bad principles, in which the good principles are identified with enlightened self-interest, or Natural Law, and the bad principles with fraud and force, artificiality, special privilege, sovereign government, or the English form of government. [15]

Such notions of sovereignty as expressed by John Taylor of Caroline and other Jeffersonians in the early days of the Republic were in complete accord

---

[13] Eugene Tenbroeck Mudge, *The Social Philosophy of John Taylor of Caroline: A Study in Jeffersonian Democracy*, AMS Press, New York, 1968 (orig. pub. 1939), quoted on p. 3.

[14] Russell Kirk, *John Randolph of Roanoke: A Study in American Politics*, Henry Regnery Company, Chicago, 1964, quoted on p. 81.

[15] Eugene Tenbroeck Mudge, *Op. cit.*, pp. 34-35.

with the concept of sovereignty generally understood and acknowledged by all Americans at the time the Constitution of 1787 was ratified by the States. In the *Federalist Papers*, for example, we find numerous and favorable references to the sovereignty of the people. Let us turn, now, and briefly look at the contributions made by the *Federalist Papers* to our general understanding of sovereignty in the United States.

The Federalist Papers

James Madison, one of the Republic's early Jeffersonians, had this to say in the *Federalist*, No. 46:

> The Federal and State governments are in fact but different agents and trustees of the people, constituted with different powers and designed for different purposes.... *The ultimate authority*, wherever the derivative may be found, *resides in the people alone*, and that it will not depend merely on the comparative ambition or address of the different governments whether either, or which of them, will be able to enlarge its sphere of jurisdiction at the expense of the other. [emphasis added] [16]

In the *Federalist*, No. 39, the Father of the Constitution wrote:

> If we resort for a criterion to the different principles on which different forms of government are established, we may define a Republic to be, or at least may bestow that name on, a government which derives all its powers directly or indirectly from the great body of the people.... [17]

Unlike most of his contemporaries, Alexander Hamilton, both before and after the adoption of our present Federal Constitution, strongly disliked the concept of popular government and the principle of the sovereignty of the people. In a five-hour oration before his fellow delegates at the Philadelphia Convention of 1787, he had urged them to abolish altogether these concepts in the American Theory of Government. Although that Convention rejected his proposal, Mr. Hamilton patriotically championed the cause of the new Constitution during the Ratification Period. And while he candidly admitted that no man's views were more remote from the Federal Constitution than his were known to be, he collaborated with James Madison and John Jay to pen the *Federalist Papers* in support of adopting the Constitution of 1787.

---

[16] Alexander Hamilton, James Madison, and John Jay, *The Federalist Papers*, A Mentor Book from New American Library, New York, 1961, p. 294.
[17] *Ibid.*, p. 241.

After the adoption of our current Federal Constitution, Mr. Hamilton assumed the leadership of the Federalist Party, a faction determined to subvert the new Constitution and to create a sovereign general government. Yet, within the *Federalist Papers*, written in an effort to persuade the State of New York to ratify the federal compact, Alexander Hamilton tried to set aside his personal convictions and to present the true principles on which our Constitution rests.

In the *Federalist*, No. 84, for instance, Mr. Hamilton made these comments in reference to a proposed Bill of Rights:

> Here, in strictness, the people surrender nothing; and as they retain everything they have no need of particular reservations. "We, the people of the United States, to secure the blessings of liberty to ourselves and our posterity, do *ordain* and *establish* this Constitution for the United States of America." Here is a better recognition of popular rights than volumes of those aphorisms which make the principal figure in several of our State bills of rights and which would sound much better in a treatise on ethics than in a constitution of government. [18]

At the conclusion of the *Federalist*, No. 22, Alexander Hamilton succinctly summarized the concept of the sovereignty of the people in the United States with these words:

> The fabric of American empire ought to rest on the solid basis of the consent of the people. The streams of national power ought to flow immediately from that pure, original fountain of all legitimate authority. [19]

It should be clear that the concept of the sovereignty of the people, as established in the Lockean Theory of Government and reaffirmed by the Declaration of Independence, forms the basis of the American Theory of Government. That concept was clearly incorporated into our constitutional system of government and is responsible for determining that our forms of government – both State and Federal – would be republican in nature.

Yet, it remains to be determined, Which people are sovereign in the United States? To be certain, within the United States of America, it is the people, and not any government, which is sovereign. But the question remains of exactly which people in the United States are vested with sovereignty. Does the American Theory of Government hold that sovereignty is vested in all the people of the United States, considered as a single sovereign Nation? Or does that theory hold that sovereignty is vested in the people of each State, separately?

---

[18] *Ibid.*, p. 513.
[19] *Ibid.*, p. 152.

These questions are not immaterial and, in fact, constitute one of the most crucial issues ever debated in the United States of America. Therefore, we should turn our attention to answering those critical questions and to ascertaining the true nature of our federal system of government, as established by our Founding Fathers.

Chapter Four

The American Theory of Government

The Lockean Theory of Government was reaffirmed and enshrined within the Declaration of Independence, which was issued to a candid world on July 4, 1776. Within that cherished document, the concept of the sovereignty of the people was boldly proclaimed as the only just foundation of civil society. Government exists to serve the interests of society and to safeguard the rights of man, proclaimed the Declaration, and whenever government fails to effect that great end, or becomes itself a threat to society, it is the right – and the duty – of the people to alter or abolish it. Furthermore, stated the Declaration of Independence, it was the intent of the people of the colonies to become independent States and to establish new governments based on those great principles.

As we have already observed, the great principle of the Lockean Theory of Government and of the American Declaration of Independence – the sovereignty of the people – did indeed become the foundation of the American system of government, cherished by most and acknowledged by all of the Founding Fathers of the United States. But the question that remains to be answered is, Who exactly is sovereign in the United States? Clearly, no government can rightfully be sovereign within our political system, for the American Theory of Government is based on the concept of the sovereignty of the people. Yet, which people in the United States are sovereign? Are the peoples of each State sovereign? Or are the American people, considered as a single consolidated Nation, vested with sovereignty? It is the application of the Lockean Theory of Government to our federal system of government that creates a uniquely American Theory of Government.

One key to answering our question of who is sovereign lies in understanding who declared independence in the Declaration of Independence. Within that Declaration, did a consolidated American Nation declare its independence of Great Britain? Or did thirteen colonies declare their independence as sovereign States? For what purpose was the War of Independence waged? And who was recognized as sovereign within the Treaty of Paris of 1783, which formally concluded the Revolutionary War? The answers to these questions will go far toward answering the paramount question of who is sovereign in the United States of America.

Of course, as history plainly reveals, a proposal was made by New Hampshire within the Second Continental Congress that the thirteen colonies should declare themselves to be a single, independent State or Nation within the Declaration of Independence. The idea that the American Revolution should be conducted to convert the thirteen separate colonies into a single Nation, however, was rejected by the other colonies. Instead of adopting New Hampshire's suggestion, it was finally resolved by the colonies to declare themselves individually independent, ensuring thereby that each colony would become a separate sovereign State.

Accordingly, within the final section of the Declaration of Independence, Thomas Jefferson asserted:

> We, therefore, the representatives of the United States of America, in General Congress, Assembled, appealing to the Supreme Judge of the world for the rectitude of our intentions do in the Name, and by Authority of the good People of these Colonies, solemnly publish and declare, that these United Colonies are, and of Right ought to be *free and independent States*; that they are Absolved from all Allegiance to the British Crown, and that all political connection between them and the *State of Great Britain*, is and ought to totally dissolved; and that as *free and independent States*, they have full Power to levy War, conclude Peace, contract Alliances, establish Commerce, and all other Acts and Things which *Independent States* may of right do. [emphasis added] [1]

The American Concept of Statehood

To ascertain exactly who was declared sovereign by the Declaration of Independence it is necessary to determine what was meant by that crucial term *State*. As the reader has undoubtedly observed, that term – in its singular and plural forms – appeared within the final section of the Declaration of Independence four times, three times in reference to fourteen specific States and once in reference to independent States in general. Thirteen of those specific States, needless to say, were the British colonies who were asserting their independence through that instrument. Yet, the Declaration also employed the term to refer to Great Britain, within the phrase, "the State of Great Britain." Using the Declaration of Independence as our guide, therefore, it may be deduced that the American concept of a "State" is a sovereign body politic or an independent, sovereign Nation. And this is precisely what each of the thirteen American States was declaring itself to be within that document.

---

[1] Alexander H. Stephens, *A Constitutional View of the Late War Between the States; Its Causes, Character, Conduct and Results*, Volume 1, Kraus Reprint Co., New York, 1970 (orig. pub. 1868), quoted on p. 548.

The *cause* for which the American Revolution was waged, it becomes apparent, was to secure for each British colony the status of sovereign Statehood, or a position in the natural world equal to that held by Great Britain and all other independent Nations. According to the Declaration of Independence, Great Britain was a "State," North Carolina was a "State," Virginia was a "State," Maryland was a "State," Pennsylvania was a "State," Connecticut was a "State," Rhode Island was a "State," Massachusetts was a "State," Delaware was a "State," New York was a "State," New Jersey was a "State," and New Hampshire was a "State." All the powers of government naturally inherent in sovereignty, including "full Power to levy War, conclude Peace, contract Alliances, establish Commerce, and all other Acts and Things which Independent States may of right do," were conveyed by the Declaration of Independence, not upon the United States as a single Nation, but upon each and every one of the thirteen States *separately*.

This separate State sovereignty was acknowledged and recognized within the Treaty of Paris of 1783, which formally terminated the War of Independence, in which his "Britannic Majesty" solemnly acknowledged:

> ...the said United States, viz. New-Hampshire, Massachusetts-Bay, Rhode-Island and Providence Plantations, Connecticut, New-York, New-Jersey, Pennsylvania, Delaware, Maryland, Virginia, North-Carolina, South-Carolina, and Georgia, to be free, *sovereign*, and independent States; as such he treats with them, and relinquishes all claim to their government and territorial rights. [2]

Thus, the *cause* for which the American States waged their War of Independence, and which was expressed and asserted in the Declaration of Independence, was formally recognized and acknowledged in the treaty that officially terminated the hostilities between those American States and the State of Great Britain. Of course, it hardly needs to be pointed out that, had the term "sovereign" been entirely omitted from the Treaty of Paris of 1783, sovereignty would have been implied in the *inherent meaning* of the term "State." But it was not left out of the treaty, and its inclusion leaves no doubt whatsoever that the thirteen former British colonies were internationally recognized as "free, sovereign, and independent States."

With equal propriety, our sovereign States could have assumed, instead of the title of State, another title that would have equally affirmed their sovereignty, such as the term "Nation" or "Country." According to the third edition of *Roget's International Thesaurus*, the concept inherent in the term "State"

---

[2] John Taylor, *New Views of the Constitution of the United States*, Da Capo Press, New York, 1971, quoted on p. 177.

qualifies it to be associated with the terms *country*, *nation*, *nationality*, *polity*, *body politic*, *republic*, *commonwealth*, *kingdom*, *empire*, and *domain*. By definition, a "State" is a corporate or civil society with one people in the political sense. It is a self-governing Nation and a sovereign polity.

The very fact that the term "State" conveys sovereignty has caused much grief to the Consolidating School of Thought, which is bent upon achieving a "national sovereignty" over the States of our Union. While forced to admit that the term "State" does indeed convey sovereignty in its usual application, this consolidating school has advanced the fallacious notion that the States of our Federal Union are not really States.

Typical of this strange mode of reasoning is the argument presented by Philip Dorf, Abraham Leavitt, and Curtis L. Pfaff in their book, *Visualized American Government*, which was published in 1971. According to these authors:

> A *state* is an organized political society which possesses sovereign powers over all inhabitants of a clearly defined area....We can locate them on the map and trace their respective boundaries. We know that if we enter the territory of any one of these states we are subject to its jurisdiction. But the Organization of American States is not a state; neither is the United Nations, nor the International Labor Organization. None of these possesses sovereign power over lands and people. [3]

After stating these truths, these authors then assert:

> The use of the term "State" for the fifty members of our Federal Union sometimes is confusing. This is a special use of the term, since our States possess only *limited* sovereignty under the Federal Constitution. [4]

Perhaps, according to this view, our States should have styled themselves "Limited States" or "Partial States," and our federation should have been styled the "Unified State of America" or the "United Partial States of America." But word games we leave to the Consolidating School of Thought, whose ends can only be achieved by subverting the Constitution and undermining the true meaning of words.

The assertion that our Founding Fathers were negligent or careless in their terminology defies both common sense and the historical development of the United States of America. When Thomas Jefferson, within the Declaration of Independence, used the term "State" to describe each former colony and to

---

[3] Philip Dorf, Abraham Leavitt, and Curtis L. Pfaff, *Visualized American Government*, Oxford Book Company, New York, 1971, p. 2.

[4] *Ibid.*, p. 2.

describe Great Britain, he could not have had in mind two different meanings for the same term – a normal meaning of the term when applied to Great Britain, and a special one when applied to our own States. Common sense alone rejects such an assertion, for Mr. Jefferson, within the Declaration, was proclaiming that our States are in fact the equivalent of the State of Great Britain in regard to sovereignty. If any doubt could still remain on this subject, then we may refer again to the Treaty of Paris of 1783, wherein each State was mentioned by name and recognized as sovereign and independent.

John Taylor of Caroline, the brilliant philosopher of the American Theory of Government, clearly realized the significance and implications inherent in the word "State." In his book, *New Views of the Constitution of the United States*, which was originally published in 1823, Mr. Taylor made the following observations:

> The meaning of the word "State" accords with that of the words associated with it. Used in reference to individuals, it comprises a great variety of circumstances, but in reference to the publick, it means a political community. Johnson thus expounds it, and adds, that it implies a republick, or a government not monarchial. What other word was more proper to describe the communities recognized by the Declaration of Independence, the Union of 1777, and the Union of 1787? Can the same word have been intended to convey an idea in the last, inconsistent with the idea it conveys in the two first instruments? Neither monarchy nor aristocracy would have fitted the case, and the word republick itself would have been exposed to uncertainties, with which the word State is not chargeable; because it has been applied to governments discordant with those which were established by our revolution. As no word more explicitly comprises the idea of a sovereign independent community; as it is used in conjunction with a declared sovereignty and independence; as it is retained by the Union of 1787, and in all the operations of our governments; and as sovereign powers only could be reserved by States; there seems to be no sound argument by which it can be deprived of its intrinsick meaning, contrary to these positive constructions. [5]

The term under consideration was certainly understood by James J. Kilpatrick, who made the following observations in his brilliant book, *The Sovereign States*, which was published in 1957:

> To review the process by which the colonies became States is not necessarily to answer the basic question, What is a *State*? It is a troublesome word. The standard definition is that a State is "a political body, or body politic; any body of people occupying a definite territory and politically organized under one government, especially one that is not subject to external control." Chief Justice Chase, in *Texas vs. White*, put it this way: "A State, in

[5] John Taylor, *Op. cit.*, pp. 6-7.

the ordinary sense of the Constitution, is a political community of free citizens, occupying a territory of defined boundaries, and organized under a government sanctioned and limited by a written Constitution, and established by the consent of the governed." In the Cherokee case, John Marshall described a State as "a distinct political society, separated from others, capable of managing its own affairs and governing itself."

Thus, variously, a State is defined as a body, a community, and a distinct society. Plainly, mere boundary lines are not enough; a tract of waste and uninhabited land cannot constitute a State. Nor are people, as such, sufficient to constitute a State....

...[T]he State is seen as a continuing political being, controlled by its citizens and yet controlling them. The State can be bound in ways that its own people cannot be bound; it can exercise powers that no citizen or group of citizens may exercise for themselves [except in the State of Nature]. The State may buy, sell, hold, grant, convey, it may tax and spend, it may sue, and if it consent, be sued; it exists to create law and to execute law, to punish crime, administer justice, regulate commerce, enter into compacts with other States. Yet there is no State until a community of human beings create a State; and no State may exist without the will and power of human beings to preserve it.

It is this combination of will and power which lies at the essence of the State in being. *This is sovereignty.* In the crisp phrase of John Taylor of Caroline, sovereignty is "the will to enact, the power to execute." Long books have been written on the nature of sovereignty, but they boil down to those necessities: The will to make, the power to unmake.

It was this power, this will, that the people-as-States claimed for themselves in 1776. Henceforth, they said, we are sovereign: The State government is not sovereign, nor is any citizen by himself sovereign [except in the State of Nature]. By the "sovereign State" we mean citizens, the State; we collectively, within our established boundaries; this community of people; we alone who are possessed of the power to create or to abandon.

God knows it was a great, a priceless, power these people-as-States claimed for themselves. True, not everyone saw it that way. Mr. Justice Story, for one, never grasped the concept of States. Nor did [Andrew] Jackson. Albert J. Beveridge, in his biography of [Chief Justice John] Marshall, refers sneeringly to the States as "these pompous sovereignties," but in a way, Beveridge's is perhaps a high acknowledgement of the simple truth: These infant States *were* sovereignties, and the people within them were proudly jealous of the fact. The saw themselves, in Blackstone's phrase, "a supreme, irresistible, absolute, uncontrolled authority." This, among other things, was the aim they had fought for. It cannot be imagined that they ever would have relinquished this high power of sovereignty except in the most explicit terms. [emphasis added] [6]

If further proof were needed that the States of our Federal Union truly

[6] James Jackson Kilpatrick, *The Sovereign States*, Henry Regnery Company, Chicago, 1957, pp. 8-10.

are States, then we may offer the adoption of English common law by each of the original States as clear evidence. The *common law*, of course, is that fundamental law of civil society that is basic and fundamental in nature, as distinguished from *statutory law*, or law formally enacted by a legislative body. Each State of the American Union has its own common law, whereas the United States, considered as a whole, has no common law.

Regarding the common law within our federal system, John Willey Willis has noted in his contribution to the *Catholic Encyclopedia* that not all States within our Union have the same common law. While the States, in general, have adopted the English common law, the State of Louisiana stands out as an exception, inasmuch as its common law is based on the civil law of Rome. As Mr. Willis wrote:

> When the thirteen American colonies achieved their independence, the English common law, as it existed with its legal and equitable features in the year 1607, was universally held by the courts to be the common law of each of the thirteen States which constituted the new confederated Republic known as the United States of America. As the United States have increased in number, either by the admission of new States to the Union carved out of the original undivided territory, or by the extension of territorial area through purchase or contest, the common law as it existed at the close of the War of the American Revolution has been held to be the common law of such new States with the exception that, in the State of Louisiana, the civil law of Rome, which ruled within that vast area originally called Louisiana, has been maintained, subject only to subsequent legislative modifications. [7]

The Views of John Taylor of Caroline

In the view of John Taylor of Caroline – America's greatest philosopher – the organic structure of the United States of America rests upon the foundation of the sovereignty of the States, for the States and the American people, within our political system, are equivalent. Writing of Mr. Taylor's views, Eugene Tenbroeck Mudge made the following observations:

> Sovereignty is defined as "a will to enact, and a power to execute." Its *locus* is self-evident. "The existence of societies supposes a sovereignty in each society, and this sovereignty can only be found in the people of each State as associated." Sovereignty follows from "the natural right of mankind to establish societies for themselves." It is, not individual, but social. "There is no sovereignty among men, except that species which resides in the people or

[7] John Willey Willis, *Catholic Encyclopedia*, Volume IX, http://www.newadvent.org/cathen/09068a.htm, Online Edition, 1999 (orig. pub. 1910).

society," and its power is supreme. "Sovereignty is the highest degree of political power, and the establishment of a government, the highest proof which can be given of its existence." Sovereignty is always present in some form. It is indestructible....

These ideas should not be taken to imply that Taylor was an extreme democrat as was Thomas Paine. On the contrary, he feared too much the inevitable consequences of undivided, irresponsible political power in whatever form to express an unbounded esteem for the people. Though the people are sovereign and capable of self-government, every phase of their government must be restrained by a rigid code of political law. Even majorities, unless restrained, are capable of tyranny. Taylor's treatment of the issue of sovereignty seems to be directed more to minimize the power of the Federal Government and its factional allies than to strengthen the power and prestige of the people, for it is on the basis of the sovereignty of the peoples of the States that he urges a sweeping curtailment of the powers of the executive and judicial branches of the government of the Union.

Sovereignty, Taylor believes, is a dangerous concept and likely to be double-edged. Actually it should not be used to describe things temporal, for it is essentially an attribute of God....Taylor's antipathy to the concept follows from his theory that the course of political history may be explained in terms of the degree of usurpation of private property by governments which claim a sovereign power over persons and property.

Nevertheless the term is not discarded, for Taylor proceeds to argue that sovereignty follows from the natural right of mankind to establish societies for itself....

Sovereignty, then, is an attribute of the natural right of self-government, applies exclusively to a people, and is the soundest basis for social liberty. The people are the only safe repository for sovereign power, because they are not inclined to oppress a minority. This is on the assumption that they must generally perceive that any booty which would result from exploitation of a minority could not be satisfactorily distributed among the vast numbers of the majority. This form of oppression is as unlikely as for one hundred men together to own one slave. On the other hand, a minority can always live off a majority and is therefore a potential source of oppression. From this it follows significantly that although sovereign nations are prone to error they are incapable of adding fraud to error, while both fraud and error are essential parts of the mechanisms of sovereign governments....

Sovereignty is indivisible. "Our principle [is] that complete sovereignty resides only in the people of each State." And if the people are sovereign, the government is not. "Our maxim is that a government is, not a sovereign, but a trustee of the sovereignty of the people, invested only with limited powers and composed of co-ordinate departments established to discharge specified duties." No sovereignty can be deduced from delegated power. Since all the rights of government are "conventional," not "natural," government cannot claim any of the rights or prerogatives of sovereignty....

On the basis of the sovereignty of the people Taylor develops an interesting corollary. The Bill of Rights, which the Republicans were instrumental in obtaining, is theoretically superfluous, because it follows inevitably

> from the right of self-government that all powers not delegated remain in the people; and it is dangerous, because the mere existence of such a document implies, as in England, not that government derives rights from the people, but that the people derive their rights from government. At any rate, the Bill of Rights for each State rather than that of the general government is the real guarantor of popular rights.
>
> At one point Taylor makes a statement that requires more explanation than he offers. Writing on the theme of the nature of the Union, he says, "the people have two rights of self government, one for federal or general purposes, the other for State or local purposes." This means, presumably, that by virtue of their inherent sovereignty an associated people may set up as many governments as it chooses and that in the United States each people has been content to establish two – one for the local internal affairs of the individuals of each State and one for the common external affairs of all the States.
>
> Further light is thrown on the question of sovereignty by a discussion of the term in *The Federalist,* "sovereignty of spheres," or the supremacy in their respective spheres of the two divisions of government, State and Federal....However, the principle of spherical sovereignty is as meaningless as the music of the spheres. The constitutional enjoyment of ex post facto laws and of laws impairing the obligation of contracts is an indication that governments in our system are not sovereign. The idea of a sovereignty of spheres of government is incongruous with the idea of a government of specific delegated powers. Sphere implies limitation, whereas sovereignty implies lack of any limitation....[I]f the principle of the sovereignty of spheres is accepted, the real danger is that in the course of time the just claim of the people to complete sovereignty may be lost sight of and popular sovereignty may be defeated forever by the principle of the sovereignty of governments. [8]

The Articles of Confederation

Through the Declaration of Independence, each of the thirteen British colonies along the Atlantic seaboard in North America became, on July 4, 1776, severally sovereign and independent States. As such, each State exercised its sovereignty by creating a new State government and State Constitution for itself. Yet, realizing their own individual weakness against the aggressions of hostile foreign powers, these thirteen American sovereign States resolved to band together for mutual protection. In fact, at the same time they resolved to declare their independence of the Government of Great Britain, the States decided to draft a plan of political Union styled the Articles of Confederation.

Within the Declaration of Independence, an entity is mentioned that

---

[8] Eugene Tenbroeck Mudge, *The Social Philosophy of John Taylor of Caroline: A Study in Jeffersonian Democracy,* AMS Press, New York, 1968, pp. 35-42.

was termed the "United States of America." This entity, as it existed at the time, was merely a loose *military alliance* among the sovereign States. This United States of America was clearly not a sovereign body politic or civil society or Nation, for the Declaration recognized only the thirteen American States and the State of Great Britain. And within the Treaty of Paris of 1783, it was the thirteen American States – not a single American Nation styled the United States of America – that was acknowledged as being free, independent, and sovereign.

By 1781, all thirteen American States had formally ratified the Articles of Confederation. This first Federal Constitution for the United States of America created a *Federal Government* and a *Federal Union* between the sovereign States. In the terminology of political science, the form and system of the new Union constituted a *Federal Republic*. The objective of those Articles was to establish a league or federation of sovereign States, in which each State government retained political control over the domestic affairs of the State, while what John Locke termed *federative powers* – powers relating to foreign affairs – were delegated to the Federal Government.

The Declaration of Independence had asserted that, among the powers possessed by sovereign States was the power of forming alliances. In creating the Federal Union under the Articles of Confederation, the States once again proved themselves to be sovereign. By establishing this political Union, the States created a new government, delegated powers to that government, formed a political alliance or Union between themselves, and voluntarily agreed to accept certain restraints on the exercise of their respective sovereign powers.

Lest there should be any doubt as to where the seat of sovereignty was situated within this Federal Union, the Articles were not silent on the subject. Article II asserted in plain terms that, "Each State retains its sovereignty, freedom, and independence, and every power, jurisdiction, and right, which is not by this Confederation expressly delegated to the United States in Congress assembled." [9]

Article II not only stated the obvious fact that the States retained their sovereignty within the Federal Republic, but it also revealed who was the recipient of all powers delegated to the United States. The phrase, "the United States in Congress assembled," clearly indicated that everything yielded by the States to the United States was invested in the Federal Government. Thus, had any sovereignty been yielded to the "United States," it would have ended up – not in the possession of some consolidated Nation of the whole American people – but *in the hands of the Federal Government*. This is an important concept to recognize and fully comprehend.

---

[9] Alexander H. Stephens, Volume 1, *Op. cit.*, quoted on p. 549.

It is readily apparent that, in forming the Federal Union under the Articles of Confederation, no new State or Nation or Body Politic was created. The American people remained, as before the creation of the Union, politically organized in thirteen sovereign States. The only two entities created by the Federal Union were an alliance for limited purposes between those States and a Federal Government. An alliance is not a civil society. Instead of adopting the name "United States of America," other names for such a political Union could have been the "Alliance of the Thirteen American States," the "American States Allied," or even the "United Front of the Sovereign American States."

Article III of the original Articles of Union also dealt with the question of sovereignty by asserting that, "The said States hereby severally enter into a firm league of friendship with each other, for...." [10] What followed those words were obviously the *reasons* why the sovereign States had created the Federal Union. Among the reasons listed in this article for which the States had united was to provide mutual defense against "attacks made upon them, or any of them, on account of religion, sovereignty, trade, or any other pretence whatever." [11] Thus, the very purpose for which the United States of America was created was *to preserve and defend the sovereignty of the States!*

The Constitution of 1787

When the sovereign American States found the Articles of Confederation inadequate to meet the exigencies of their Federal Union, they resolved to replace that compact with another one. Delegates from twelve of the States met in Philadelphia in the summer of 1787 and drafted a new Federal Constitution, which was subsequently ratified by all thirteen States, each State bound only by its own assent to the new plan of government. This new Constitution, which went into effect in 1789, established a new Federal Union with a Federal Government possessing invigorated delegated powers. The style of the original Union – the "United States of America" – was retained and applied to the invigorated Union, clearly indicating that the organic structure of the United States had not been altered.

The only difference in authority between the Articles of Confederation and the Constitution of 1787 is that the former was ratified by the State governments, while the latter was ratified by the peoples of the States, whose sovereign will was expressed through State Ratifying Conventions. Both compacts, however, were ratified by the States. The new Federal Constitution, in fact,

---

[10] *Ibid.*, Volume 1, quoted on p. 549.
[11] *Ibid.*, Volume 1, quoted on p. 549.

recognized the States and the American people as being equivalent. While the Preamble speaks of "We the people of the United States" as establishing and ordaining the compact, Article VII speaks of the Constitutional Union as being one "between the States" who ratified it. [12] If the States and the people are not equivalent, then the Federal Constitution is inconsistent with itself.

The fact that the States voluntarily placed limitations upon themselves within the Constitution of 1787 does not imply that they thereby ceased to be sovereign in adopting it. Those same States had voluntarily placed limitations on themselves within the Articles of Confederation as well; yet, as we have observed, they did not thereby lose their sovereignty. Nor does the Supremacy Clause – which asserts that the Constitution, all laws made in pursuance of it, and all treaties made under its authority, shall be the *supreme law* of the land – detract from the principle of State sovereignty. The power that *decrees* that any law should be deemed supreme is obviously the supreme political power. The Constitution, legitimate federal laws, and treaties can be considered the supreme law of the land, not because the Federal Government or any consolidated Nation of people so decrees that such shall be the case, but only because the sovereign States, within their compact of government, have so decreed.

It is true, of course, that the Constitution of the United States creates a judicial entity styled the *Supreme* Court. However, the supremacy referred to in the name of the highest federal judicial tribunal is not *political* supremacy, but *judicial* supremacy. In fact, the highest federal court is so named only to distinguish it from other federal courts that the Congress might create. Thus, the name *Supreme Court* is intended only to establish its superiority over the lower or *inferior* federal courts. And it must be noted that *each one of the sovereign States has its own Supreme Court as well.* Although the Supreme Court of the United States – in the hands of activist judges – might act as though it were supreme over everything, including the Federal Constitution, the States, and even God Himself, it is, in fact, merely superior to the inferior federal courts.

Admittedly, the Federal Constitution delegates important powers to the Government of the United States. Yet, if the delegation of important powers necessitates a transfer of sovereignty, then the whole foundation of civil society would collapse. An owner of a bank, for instance, may hire a security guard to protect his property. To be sure, the guard has been delegated important powers – so important that he carries a gun. Yet, would anyone dare to assert that the guard is the master of the bank, and not merely the servant of his employer? And what else is government, but a security guard for the rights of man?

Do sovereign people, upon instituting civil society and creating government, surrender their supremacy or sovereignty to that government? Or do

[12] *Ibid.*, Volume 1, quoted on pp. 557 and 566.

they merely delegate certain powers to it to hold as a trust and to serve their needs? Then, in creating the Federal Government, did the sovereign States surrender their supremacy or sovereignty to that government? Or did they merely delegate certain powers to the Federal Government and entrust it to act only on their behalf and in their interests? The answers to these questions form the ground on which the American Theory of Government is constructed.

The United States of America

The States who created the "United States of America" – first as loose military alliance, then as a Confederation under the Articles of Confederation, and finally as a Confederation under our present Federal Constitution – did not cease to exist. Nor was any new Nation – a so-called *State of America* – born during this process. In creating their political Union, the sovereign States merely divided the powers of government among their State governments and a common Federal Government.

Perhaps it may help to better comprehend this concept by utilizing the analogy of a train of wagons heading West during the pioneer days of American history. When confronted with hostile Indians, those wagons would often perform a routine defensive measure known as "circling the wagons." It would certainly be absurd to claim that, in performing this maneuver, the separate wagons ceased to exist, or that a new consolidated wagon was created by the encircling process. In reality, the number of wagons would remain unchanged, and the defensive circle would not be a wagon at all.

If this concept can be easily understood when applied to the wagon trains of the Old West, then it should be just as easy to comprehend when applied to sovereign States who form a political alliance for mutual defense. The States who formed the American Federal Union did not vaporize into thin air, and no new State was created by the political alliance. Thirteen States existed before the adoption of the Constitution of 1787, and those same thirteen States existed after its adoption. The Union is not a sovereign State – it is merely a *political alliance* between sovereign States.

Because the States remain sovereign within our system of government, it is truly *federal* in nature, as opposed to a *national* system of government. Within other countries, local districts or provinces are sometimes created to serve as branches of a National Government for its administrative convenience. In those countries, the local districts or provinces are not sovereign, and the system of government remains national, not federal, in character and substance. In the United States of America, however, our political system rests on precisely opposite principles. The American States first became sovereign, and then they created a Federal Government to conduct their foreign affairs, while retaining their sovereignty.

In adopting the Federal Constitution of 1787, as we have already ascertained, no new American Nation was created. The title of the old Confederation – "the United States of America" – and the title of the members of the Federal Union – "the States" – were retained in our present federal compact. If such a drastic change as the transfer of sovereignty from the old States to an entirely new State of America had been intended, the Federal Constitution would assuredly have mentioned it. Yet, the only States recognized by our present Constitution are those that existed prior to its adoption and those that have, from time to time, been admitted into the Union on the same footing, in regard to their sovereignty, as the original thirteen States.

Within his monumental book, *The Rise and Fall of the Confederate Government*, which was originally published in 1881, Jefferson Davis – the first and only President of the Confederate States of America – noted:

> To whom, in fine, *could* the States have surrendered their sovereignty? Not to the mass of the people inhabiting the territory possessed by all the States, for there was no such community in existence, and they took no measures for the organization of such a community. If they had intended to do so, the very style, "United States," would have been a palpable misnomer, nor would treason have been defined as levying war against *them*. Could it have been transferred to the Government of the Union? Clearly not, in accordance with the ideas and principles of those who made the Declaration of Independence, adopted the Articles of Confederation, and established the Constitution of the United States; for in each and all of these the cornerstone is the inherent and inalienable sovereignty of the people. To have transferred sovereignty from the people to a government would have been to have fought the battles of the Revolution in vain – not for the freedom and independence of the States, but for a mere change of masters. Such a thought or purpose could not have been in the heads or hearts of those who molded the Union, and could have found lodgment only when the ebbing tide of patriotism and fraternity had swept away the landmarks which they erected who sought by the compact of Union to secure and perpetuate the liberties then possessed. The men who had won at great cost the independence of their respective States were deeply impressed with the value of union, but they could never have consented, like "the base Judean," to fling away the priceless pearl of State sovereignty for any possible alliance. [13]

Perhaps it was John Randolph of Roanoke who best expressed the sentiments shared by the generation of our Founding Fathers, when he said that, "Asking one of the States to surrender part of her sovereignty is like asking a

---

[13] Jefferson Davis, *The Rise and Fall of the Confederate Government*, Volume 1, Thomas Yoseloff, New York, 1958 (orig. pub. 1881), p. 156.

lady to surrender part of her chastity." [14]

Let us, for the sake of argument, assume all the possibilities conceivable with regard to sovereignty in the United States. Conceivably, there are only three possibilities compatible with the basic premise that only people, and not government, should possess political supremacy. The first possibility is that each of our States – meaning the *people* of each State – is sovereign. The second possibility is that our States are partially sovereign, while an entity we may refer to as the State of America holds the remainder of that supposedly divided sovereignty. Finally, the third alternative is that the United States – a consolidated State of America – possesses all sovereignty.

Now let us ask a few pertinent questions that will help to reveal which of these three possibilities is the most reasonable and consistent with our present Federal Constitution. The Federal Union exists between whom? According to Article VII of the federal compact, the Union exists "between the States" who ratified the Constitution. The State of America is not even a member of the Union. If it exists, it can exist only as a foreign Nation with an alien population.

Which people elect, indirectly through the Electoral system, the President and Vice-President of the United States? The peoples of each of our fifty States may vote in federal elections; but they vote as States, with each State having Electoral Votes equal to its number of Senators added to its number of U.S. Representatives. The so-called State of America cannot vote for any federal officer and has absolutely no Electoral Votes at all. As a consolidated Nation, the American people cannot vote in any federal election. But they can vote as States.

Which people are represented in the Federal Legislature? Once again, the American people, as a consolidated State of America, are totally unrepresented in either chamber of Congress. The State of America has not one member of the House of Representatives, and has no Senator in the Senate. On the other hand, the people of each State, as a State, have at least one Representative in the lower chamber of Congress and two Senators in the Senate.

In the event of a tie in a Presidential election, the House of Representatives shall chose the President, with the representation from each State having one vote. How many votes would the State of America have in such a proceeding? Of course, it would not have any vote because the Constitution of the United States does not recognize the existence of the State of America.

Which people established and ordained the Federal Constitution? In adopting the federal compact, each State ratified it on its own behalf. Did the

---

[14] Russell Kirk, *John Randolph of Roanoke: A Study in American Politics*, Henry Regnery Company, Chicago, 1964, quoted on p. 67.

State of America have the opportunity to consent to the compact? The Constitution provides a means whereby the States may modify the compact by the amendment process. Either the States or Congress may propose an amendment. Can the State of America propose an amendment? The Constitution stipulates that the assent of three-fourths of the States shall be required to adopt a proposed amendment. The State of America is not even allowed to cast a vote for a proposed amendment, because it does not constitutionally exist.

Finally, let us ask the very pertinent question, To whom are all powers not delegated reserved? The Tenth Amendment to the Federal Constitution answers this question in these words: "The powers not delegated to the United States by the Constitution, nor prohibited by it to the States, are reserved to the States respectively, or to the people." [15]

Only those who created the Government of the United States and delegated powers to it could possibly *reserve* the powers not delegated, inasmuch as the reserved powers remain precisely where they were prior to the creation of our present Federal Union. Since the State of America did not create the Union, did not create the Federal Government, and did not possess any powers to delegate to it, the State of America obviously cannot have any reserved powers and rights. If such a State of America exists, it can exist only as a Nation of Slaves!

As Jefferson Davis of Mississippi noted in his book:

> It was without any change of title – still as "United States" – without any sacrifice of individuality – without any compromise of sovereignty – that the same parties entered into a new and amended compact with one another under the present Constitution. Larger and more varied powers were conferred upon the common government for the purpose of insuring "a more perfect Union" – not for that of destroying or impairing the integrity of the contracting members.
>
> The point which now specially concerns the argument is the historical fact that, in all these changes of circumstances and of government, there has never been one single instance of action by the "people of the United States in the aggregate," or as one body. Before the era of independence, whatever was done by the people of the colonies was done by the people of each colony separately and independently of each other, although in Union by their delegates for certain specified purposes. Since the assertion of their independence, the people of the United States have never acted otherwise than as the people of each State, severally and separately. The Articles of Confederation were established and ratified by the several States, either through conventions of their people or through the State legislatures. The Constitution which superseded those articles was framed...by delegates chosen and empowered by the several States, and was ratified by conventions of

[15] Alexander H. Stephens, Volume 1, *Op. cit.*, quoted on p. 569.

> the people of the same States – all acting in entire independence of one another. This ratification alone gave it force and validity. Without the approval and ratification of the people of the States, it would have been, as Mr. Madison expressed it, "of no more consequence than the paper on which it was written." It was never submitted to "the people of the United States in the aggregate," or *as a people.* Indeed, no such political community as the people of the United States in the aggregate exists at this day or ever did exist. Senators in Congress confessedly represent the States as equal units. The House of Representatives is not a body of representatives of "the people of the United States," as often erroneously asserted; but the Constitution, in the second section of its first article, expressly declares that it "shall be composed of members chosen by *the people of the several States.*"
>
> Nor is it true that the President and Vice-President are elected, as it is sometimes vaguely stated, by the vote of the "whole people" of the Union. Their election is even more unlike what such a vote would be than that of representatives who in numbers at least represent the strength of their respective States. In the election of President and Vice-President the Constitution (Article II) prescribes that "*each State* shall appoint, in such manner as the Legislature thereof may direct, a number of electors" for the purpose of choosing a President and Vice-President. The number of these electors is based partly upon their equal sovereignty, partly upon the unequal population of the respective States.
>
> It is, then, absolutely true that there has never been any such thing as a vote of "the people of the United States in the aggregate"; no such people is recognized by the Constitution; and no such political community has ever existed. It is equally true that no officer or department of the general government formed by the Constitution derives authority from a majority of the whole people of the United States, or has ever been chosen by such majority. As little as any other is the United States Government a government of a majority of the mass. [16]

It should be evident at this point that, at the present time, the United States of America constitutionally consists of fifty sovereign States. There is no consolidated Nation of Americans styled the State of America or any other name. The United States is neither wholly nor partially sovereign. Only the States of the Federal Union rightfully possess sovereignty.

According to the American Theory of Government, the States are the *masters* within our political system. The State governments and the Federal Government are their *servants.* All of our constitutions – State and Federal – represent the sovereign will of the peoples of the several States. No other people exist in the United States other than the peoples of the States and Territories of the United States.

---

[16] Jefferson Davis, *Op. cit.*, Volume 1, pp. 119-120.

A Federal Republic

Whenever two or more sovereign States form a Union while retaining their separate sovereignty, they create a political association known as a *Federal Republic*. This was a concept advanced in the most internationally distinguished book on Natural Law in existence during the early days of our Republic, the *Law of Nations*, which was penned by Emmerich de Vattel. As we have previously noted, this book, which was first published in 1758, had a profound influence on the thinking of most of the civilized world. Among Americans, its impact was as significant as the great works of John Locke. In fact, so esteemed was this book that, when an official standing portrait of Jefferson Davis was made in 1861, he was portrayed holding his left hand on Vattel's *Law of Nations*.

In one chapter of his book, "Nations or Sovereign States," Mr. Vattel declared that, "Every Nation which governs itself, under whatever form, and which does not depend on any other Nation, is a *sovereign State*." [17] Elsewhere, he likened sovereign political communities to sovereign individuals exercising their freedom of personal rights: "The Law of Nations is the law of sovereigns; free and independent States are moral persons...." [18]

Within this same chapter, Mr. Vattel noted:

> Several sovereign and independent States may unite themselves together by a perpetual confederacy, without each in particular ceasing to be *a perfect State*. They will form together a Federal Republic: the deliberations in common will offer no violence to *the sovereignty of each member*, though they may, in certain respects, put some restraint on the exercise of it, in virtue of voluntary engagements. A person does not cease to be free and independent, when he is obliged to fulfill the engagements into which he has very willingly entered. [19]

In the *Federalist*, No. 40, James Madison explained that the basic principles of the Constitution of 1787 are no different than the fundamental principles of the Articles of Confederation:

> I ask, What are these principles? Do they require that in the establishment of the Constitution the States should be regarded as distinct and independent sovereigns? They are so regarded by the Constitution pro-

---

[17] Emmerich de Vattel, *The Law of Nations or the Principles of Natural Law Applied to the Conduct and to the Affairs of Nations and of Sovereigns*, Translation of the Edition of 1758, Carnegie Institution of Washington, Washington, 1916, p. 11.

[18] *Ibid.*, p. 12.

[19] Jefferson Davis, *The Rise and Fall of the Confederate Government*, Volume 1, Thomas Yoseloff, New York, 1958 (orig. pub. 1881), quoted on p. 145.

> posed....Do these principles, in fine, require that the powers of the general government should be limited, and that, beyond this limit, the States should be left in possession of their sovereignty and independence? We have seen that in the new government, as in the old, the general powers are limited; and that the States, in all unenumerated cases, are left in the enjoyment of their sovereign and independent jurisdiction.
>
> The truth is that the great principles of the Constitution proposed by the Convention may be considered less as absolutely new than as the expansion of principles which are found in the Articles of Confederation. [20]

In the *Federalist*, No. 39, the Father of the Constitution asserted that State sovereignty and our federal system of government were mutually supportive of one another:

> That it [the adoption of the Constitution] will be a federal and not a national act... – the act of the people, as forming so many independent States, not as forming one aggregate Nation – is obvious from this single consideration: that it is to result neither from the decision of a *majority* of the people of the Union, nor from that of a *majority* of the States. It must result from the *unanimous* assent of the several States that are parties to it, differing no otherwise from their ordinary assent than in its being expressed, not by the legislative authority, but by that of the people themselves. Were the people regarded in this transaction as forming one Nation, the will of the majority of the whole people of the United States would bind the minority, in the same manner as the majority in each State must bind the minority; and the will of the majority must be determined either by a comparison of the individual votes, or by considering the will of the majority of the States as evidence of the will of a majority of the people of the United States. Neither of these rules has been adopted. Each State, in ratifying the Constitution, is considered as a sovereign body independent of all others, and only to be bound by its own voluntary act. In this relation, then, the new Constitution will, if established, be a *federal* and not a *national* Constitution. [21]

Even Alexander Hamilton, in the *Federalist*, No. 81, acknowledged that the States were sovereign:

> It is inherent in the nature of sovereignty not to be amenable to the suit of an individual *without its consent*. This is the general sense and the general practice of mankind; and the exemption, as one of the attributes of sovereignty, is now enjoyed by the government of every State in the Union. [22]

---

[20] Alexander Hamilton, James Madison, and John Jay, *The Federalist Papers*, A Mentor Book from New American Library, New York, 1961, pp. 249-251.
[21] *Ibid.*, pp. 243-244.
[22] *Ibid.*, p. 487.

In the *Federalist*, No. 82, Mr. Hamilton stated:

> The erection of a new government, whatever care or wisdom may distinguish the work, cannot fail to originate questions of intricacy and nicety; and these may, in a particular manner, be expected to flow from the establishment of a Constitution founded upon the total or partial incorporation of a number of distinct sovereignties. [23]

Even Philip Dorf, Abraham Leavitt, and Curtis L. Pfaff, in their book, *Visualized American Government*, although claiming that the term "State" has a special meaning when applied to the members of the American federation, have admitted the following undeniable truth:

> The fifty States which comprise the Federal Union vary greatly in area and in population. They range from little Rhode Island whose area is only 1,248 square miles, to vast Alaska, which, with its 586,400 square miles, is considerably larger than any European country except Russia; from sparsely settled Alaska, [which has fewer than one million inhabitants]...to California [which has tens of millions of inhabitants]....Nevertheless, despite variations in size, all the States are considered to stand on a level of *mutual equality as regards their sovereignty, power, and relations with one another*. [emphasis added] [24]

According to the American Theory of Government, only people may rightfully possess sovereignty. Government, within our system, may possess and exercise only those powers that are constitutionally delegated to it. The government is entrusted to hold that power and has no rights, only duties and obligations to the people it was created to serve. For this reason, we must once again emphasize that, when speaking of States' Rights and the sovereignty of the States within our Federal Union, we are speaking of the natural rights of the peoples of the several States, and not of any government.

Considered in its most basic composition, a State consists of only three elements – territory, government, and people. Whenever speaking of a State, therefore, it must be deduced by reason and logic which of these three elements is being referenced. We could, for example, say that Mississippi is a very scenic State. Clearly, we are here referring to her geographic or physical qualities, such as her hills and valleys, rivers and streams, and forests and pastures. We could also say that the State of Mississippi enacted new highway legislation last year. Common sense dictates that we are here referring to the government of that State. On the other hand, we could assert that Mississippi is a sovereign State.

---

[23] *Ibid.*, p. 491.
[24] Philip Dorf, Abraham Leavitt, and Curtis L. Pfaff, *Op. cit.*, p. 155.

We are here obviously referring to the people of that State, for, according to the American Theory of Government, only people may rightfully possess sovereignty.

In their book, *The South Was Right!*, James Ronald Kennedy and Walter Donald Kennedy offered this concise explanation of the concept of sovereignty:

> The State government is not sovereign, nor is any citizen individually. By the term "sovereign State" we refer to the citizens of the State collectively. John C. Calhoun described the State as the "sovereign community." The State, as the agent of the people, exercises sovereign authority by the consent of those who created it (i.e., the people of the State). A State, as the agent of the sovereign community, may delegate a portion of its powers to another government, but it can not delegate a portion of sovereignty. Sovereignty, like chastity, is not transferable or divisible. [25]

Jefferson Davis of Mississippi made the following observations in his book, *The Rise and Fall of the Confederate Government*:

> No doubt, the States – the people of the States – if they had been so disposed, might have merged themselves into one great consolidated State, retaining their geographical boundaries merely as matters of convenience. But such a merger must have been distinctly and formally stated, not left to deduction or implication.
>
> Men do not alienate even an estate, without positive and express terms and stipulations. But in this case not only was there no express transfer – no formal surrender – of the preexisting sovereignty, but it was expressly provided that nothing should be *understood* as even *delegated* – that everything was reserved, unless granted in express terms. The monstrous conception of the creation of a new people, invested with the whole or a great part of the sovereignty which had previously belonged to the people of each State, has not a syllable to sustain it in the Constitution, but is built up entirely upon the palpable misconstruction of a single expression in the Preamble.
>
> In denying that there is any such collective unit as the people of the United States in the aggregate, of course I am not to be understood as denying that there is such a political organization as the United States, or that there exists, with large and distinct powers, a *Government* of the United States; but it is claimed that the Union, as its name implies, is constituted of States. As a British author, referring to the old Teutonic system, has expressed the same idea, the States are the integers, the United States the multiple which results from them. The Government of the United States derives its existence from the same source, and exercises its functions by the will of the same sovereignty that creates and confers authority upon the State governments. The people of each State are, in either case, the source. The only

---

[25] James Ronald Kennedy and Walter Donald Kennedy, *The South Was Right!*, Pelican Publishing Company, Gretna, 1994, p. 223.

> difference is that, in the creation of the State governments, each sovereign acted alone; in that of the Federal Government, they acted in cooperation with the others. Neither the whole nor any part of their sovereignty has been surrendered to either Government. [26]

As Thomas Jefferson once observed, the objective of our federal system of government is to make us one in our foreign affairs, while leaving each State independent in its internal or domestic affairs. The purpose of the Government of the United States is to conduct the common foreign affairs of the several States, presenting to the world a common front. From the vantage point of foreign nations, the United States should appear as one great and powerful Nation. The powers delegated to the Federal Government by the Constitution, as we would expect, are the powers requisite to conduct foreign affairs of the United States, such as appointing ambassadors, declaring war, maintaining the armed forces of the United States, and, of course, levying taxes to fund these legitimate activities.

The powers reserved to the several States by the Federal Constitution include those required to conduct the internal or domestic affairs of the States. This fact, coupled with the fact that sovereignty is vested in each State, makes each State government the *primary government* within our political system. In fact, if there is any level of government within our political system that may be fairly termed a *National Government*, it would be each State government, for the States, by definition, are sovereign Nations. It was the State governments, not the Federal Government, which our Founding Fathers intended to be responsible for the security and preservation of the lives, liberties, and properties of the American people.

Within his book, Jefferson Davis stressed eight key propositions on which the American Theory of Government is built:

> 1. That the States of which the American Union was formed, from the moment when they emerged from their colonial or provincial condition, became severally sovereign, free, and independent States – not one State, or Nation.
>
> 2. That the Union formed under the Articles of Confederation was a compact between the States, in which these attributes of "sovereignty, freedom, and independence," were expressly asserted and guaranteed.
>
> 3. That, in forming the "more perfect Union" of the Constitution, afterward adopted, the same contracting parties formed an *amended compact*, without any surrender of these attributes of sovereignty, freedom, and independence, either expressed or implied: on the contrary, that, by the Tenth Amendment to the Constitution, limiting the power of the government to its express grants, they distinctly guarded against the presumption of a surrender

[26] Jefferson Davis, *Op. cit.*, Volume 1, pp. 155-156.

of anything by implication.

4. That Political Sovereignty resides, neither in individual citizens, nor in unorganized masses, nor in fractional subdivisions of a community, but in the people of an organized political body.

5. That no "republican form of government," in the sense in which that expression is used in the Constitution, and was generally understood by the founders of the Union – whether it be the government of a State or of a confederation of States – is possessed of any sovereignty whatever, but merely exercises certain powers delegated by the sovereign authority of the people, and subject to recall and reassumption by the same authority that conferred them.

6. That the "people" who organized the first Confederation, the people who dissolved it, the people who ordained and established the Constitution which succeeded it, the only people, in fine, known or referred to in the phraseology of that period – whether the term was used collectively or distributively – were the people of the respective States, each acting separately and with absolute independence of the others.

7. That, in forming and adopting the Constitution, the States, or the people of the States – terms which, when used with reference to acts performed in a sovereign capacity, are precisely equivalent to each other – formed a new *government*, but no new *people*; and that, consequently, no new sovereignty was created – for sovereignty in an American Republic can belong only to a people, never to a government – and that the Federal Government is entitled to exercise only the powers delegated to it by the people of the respective States.

8. That the term "people," in the Preamble of the Constitution and in the Tenth Amendment, is used distributively; that the only "people of the United States" known to the Constitution are the people of each State in the Union; that no such political community or corporate unit as one people of the United States then existed, has ever been organized, or yet exists; and that no political action by the people of the United States in the aggregate has ever taken place, or ever can take place, under the Constitution. [27]

To be certain, the people of the United States actually do exist. With equal validity, it may be said that all the people in the world actually exist. But all the people in the world do not exist as one State of Nation, for they exist *politically* as many Nations. In similar fashion, the people of the United States do exist, but they are politically organized as States of the Federal Union. In that capacity, and only in that capacity, are they vested with sovereignty.

Proper Terminology

Now that we have a proper understanding of the American Theory of

[27] *Ibid.*, Volume 1, pp. 157-158.

Government, it should be obvious that there is a proper set of terminology that may be applied to our political system, as well as an improper set of terminology. Words and terms have definitions and imply ideas. The proper set of terminology will convey a true and proper understanding of our system of government, while improper terminology serves no other purpose than to befuddle, confuse, and mystify.

The *science of government*, like biology or chemistry or astronomy, truly is a science. As such, it utilizes terms that have specific meanings and words that convey specific concepts. What would we think of a professor of medicine, for example, who employed such terms as "funny bone" and "belly" and "shin bone" when referring to the ulnar nerve, the abdomen, and the tibia? What would we think of a chemistry textbook that used the terms "element," "compound," and "atom" as though they were interchangeable and equivalent terms? What should we think of an astronomy professor who asserted that "planets" and "stars" are equivalent?

In similar fashion, what should we think of a political science textbook or professor who asserted the equivalency of such concepts as a Federal Government and a National Government, a Federal Constitution and a National Constitution, and a Republic and a Democracy; or that asserted limited, divided, or delegated sovereignty; or that even denied altogether the sovereignty of the States in our system of government?

It should be apparent that there are only certain terms that may be *properly* applied to the American system of government. The following are among the words and terminology that may be considered proper and in accord with the American Theory of Government: *Government of the United States, Federal Government, Federal Constitution, Federal Union, Federal Republic, federal system, republican form of government, delegated powers of government, State sovereignty, States' Rights, sovereign States*, and the *sovereignty of the people*. The word "Confederate" can be used in the place of "Federal," inasmuch as the two terms are synonymous and mean *of a league*. Thus, the Federal Government is literally the *Government of a league of States* styled the United States of America.

In similar fashion, and for obvious reasons, some words and terms are not only inappropriate when applied to our political system, but actually are subversive of the American Theory of Government. Among these improper terms are the following: *National Government, National Constitution, National Union, National Republic, National Democracy, national system, democracy, natural powers of government, inherent powers of government, sovereign powers of government, implied powers of government, supreme National Government, supreme government, sovereign government, national sovereignty, country*, and *Nation*.

Special attention should be directed to the last two improper terms listed above – "country" and "Nation." Constitutionally speaking, there is no Nation – with a capital "N" – known as the United States of America. Strictly speaking, the only true countries or Nations within our political system are the sovereign States. The United States is merely a league of Nations or a federation of States. It is not a single State, Nation, or Country.

Often we hear or read loose expressions that refer to the United States as a country or nation – with a little "c" or a little "n" – in which the intent is not to deny the sovereignty of the States. We might hear someone say, for example, "America is the greatest nation in the world!" While such sentiments might be considered appropriate, or even patriotic, statements such as this should never be confused with a treatise on the Constitution. In the example here cited, for instance, we understand that the speaker is referring to the United States of America – not literally to the entire Western Hemisphere, which is known as America. We also understand that the term "nation" is not used in the strict sense of political science, but is meant as a reference to our federation of sovereign States.

Proper and precise terminology should always be preferred over vague, and even improper, terminology when referring the American political system. Yet, whenever loose expressions are encountered, they must be interpreted in the spirit in which they were uttered or written. Careless use of terminology is an insufficient argument to support the subversion of fifty sovereign States!

A Lesson in Confusion

The true organic structure of the United States of America, as defined by the American Theory of Government, is not a complex or mysterious concept to comprehend. Yet, there are many – including professors at some of our great universities – who profess total bewilderment as to how thirteen sovereign States could ever form a Federal Union without losing their sovereignty to the Federal Government or to some consolidated State of America. Such confusion is greatly augmented by the improper mixture of appropriate and inappropriate terminology to describe our system of government.

An excellent illustration of this mystifying process can be found in *The Framing of the Federal Constitution*, written by Richard B. Morris and published in 1986 as Handbook 103 by the U.S. Department of the Interior. In the Preface of this book, the following summary of the work of our Founding Fathers is provided

> The American system of government springs from the work of 55 delegates meeting in Convention in Philadelphia during the summer of

> 1787. The document they wrote and presented to their countrymen for approval was the Federal Constitution. This work gave the nation a National Government based on the principle of popular sovereignty and the paradoxical idea of a "sovereign Union of sovereign States." That a people could, by purposeful deliberation, make themselves into a Nation was an event heretofore without parallel. [28]

As to how a *Federal Constitution* could bring into existence a *National Government* is truly a mystery. It is as mysterious as the "paradoxical idea" of a *sovereign Union* co-existing with *sovereign States*. By this account, our system of government is founded upon "popular sovereignty," a "sovereign Union," and "sovereign States." But the mystery presented in the Preface only deepens in the book's Introduction:

> In the summer of 1787, some 55 delegates met in Convention in the State House in Philadelphia and devised a new National Government, then loosely allied in a "league of friendship" under the Articles of Confederation....In mid-September they gave to their countrymen the final document, four pages of parchment setting forth a plan of Union....
>
> The document was the Federal Constitution. It provided for a sovereign government with clearly defined powers and responsibilities. In spare, eloquent language, the delegates...steered between the equal dangers of tyranny and ineffectualness with...strict limitations on powers granted...and the vesting of sovereignty in the people themselves and not in offices and institutions. [29]

It would be difficult to make a simple concept more complicated, confusing, and mysterious than this. Devising *a new National Government* somehow resulted in a *Federal Constitution*. That *Federal Constitution* somehow provides for a *sovereign government*, yet *vests sovereignty in the people themselves* and not in offices and institutions. It was the action of the delegates at the Constitutional Convention of 1787, and not the Declaration of Independence of 1776, that vested sovereignty in the people. Sovereignty is thus vested in the people, in the Union, in the States, and in the Federal Government – evidently, sovereignty is vested everywhere except in the humble State governments! The *sovereign Federal Government*, which, by definition, is a government of unlimited powers, somehow possesses *clearly defined powers and responsibilities*. And that *sovereign government* with unlimited powers somehow has placed over it *strict limitations on powers granted.*

This is precisely the type of befuddlement, inconsistency, confusion,

---

[28] Richard B. Morris, *The Framing of the Federal Constitution*, Handbook 103, U.S. Department of the Interior, Washington, D.C., 1986, p. 2.
[29] *Ibid.*, p. 6.

mystery, and tortured logic that results from any and all attempts to deny the true sovereignty of the States within the Federal Union. Invariably, all such attempts to deny the sovereignty of the States lead, directly or indirectly, to a sovereign Federal Government. Only the true concept of sovereignty, on which the American Theory of Government is founded, is capable of preserving unimpaired the sovereignty of the people, thereby ensuring that they, and not any government, constitute the *master* within the American political system.

Chapter Five

Review and Summary

Thus far in our examination of the principles related to the concept of sovereignty, we have ascertained the nature of sovereignty, the origin of sovereignty, the various types of sovereignty, the relationship between sovereignty and the social contract, the seat of sovereignty in the United States of America, and the relationship between sovereignty and the American Theory of Government. It has been shown that sovereignty in the United States, according to the American Theory of Government, is vested in the people and not in any government. It has also been shown that, by the terms of that theory, sovereignty is vested in the peoples of each State of the Federal Union.

As simple as these concepts might be, the Consolidating School of Thought has clouded the true nature of sovereignty in the hope that, out of such confusion and mystery, a consolidated, highly centralized, all-powerful, sovereign Federal Government may emerge. The various schemes and devices employed by the consolidators to rear a sovereign government on the ruins of State sovereignty shall be our next topic for consideration. Before proceeding, however, we should summarize the basic principles regarding political sovereignty that have already been established on historical fact and sound reasoning. From our examination of sovereignty thus far presented, the following truths have been firmly ascertained.

1. Sovereignty may be generally defined as a supreme power or authority that is granted to mankind by the Creator. The same God that made all men in His image and endowed all men equally with the inalienable rights of life, liberty, and property, also endowed all men with Personal Sovereignty over themselves. In addition, when God instituted Holy Matrimony, He endowed all husbands with Patriarchal Sovereignty to be the heads of their own households, and He endowed all parents with Parental Sovereignty over their own children. Finally, when God allowed mankind the authority to enforce the laws of nature and to punish criminals, He endowed all men with Political Sovereignty. There are thus four basic types of sovereignty, of which our primary focus is on Political Sovereignty, the type of sovereignty that involves the formation of civil society, government, and constitutions. Since our focus is on Political Sovereignty, we have referred to it simply as sovereignty in the course of our inquiry.

2. Before the advent of human government, mankind lived in what has been called a State of Nature, in which each man was vested with sovereignty. Accordingly, every man within this state had the right to enforce an observance of the Laws of Nature. Although some societies and governments may have historically been formed in violation of the natural rights of man, the proper and rightful formation of civil society and government can be ascertained by proper reasoning. Upon forming civil society by rightful methods, each man comprising the community should voluntarily consent to surrender his sovereignty to the society as a whole to form, together with the other citizens, a sovereign State. This consent and understanding constitutes a social contract. Later generations, born into an existing civil society, give their tacit consent to the social contract by continuing to live within the society and enjoying its protection and benefits. Although the initial formation of a civil society should be based upon the unanimous consent of all those who are to be its citizens, once a society is formed, the majority may rightfully conduct the affairs of the State.

3. Although Political Sovereignty was rendered a collective function and possession of the State upon the formation of civil society, the other three types of sovereignty – Personal, Patriarchal, and Parental – remained individual possessions and functions as they were in the State of Nature. Every man, even within a body politic, remains master over his own life, over his own family, and over his own property. Indeed, the very reason or purpose for which civil society was formed was to provide greater protection and security for individual human rights. Thus, while mankind does need governments to better protect itself from criminals, there can never be any justification for a dictatorship or a Big Brother type of government to dictate how the people should live their lives.

4. A civil society or State, which is sovereign, may create a constitution and thereby institute government, delegating to that government only such powers as are deemed proper and necessary to protect the society from criminals and the aggressions of hostile foreign powers. In creating the government, the State or civil society does not surrender any portion of its sovereignty, but remains the supreme political authority. The government that the State creates has only limited, delegated powers that it holds as a trust, and it is a servant of the people of the State, who, in their sovereign capacity, are the masters within the political system. The government is distinct from the State, for the latter is sovereign while the former is not.

5. Government is organized power, with access to the pockets of the people and the ability to enforce its will with martial power. Although human government, in its proper application, is a great blessing for mankind, it is, in actual practice, like fire, a dangerous servant and a fearful master. Throughout every age, there have been those who sought to undermine the true purpose of

human government and to subvert it into an instrument of oppression and tyranny. When criminals gain control of a government, they invariably attempt to rob the people of their natural sovereignty by insisting that the government may decide for itself how much power it may exercise. And such criminals invariably promote collectivism as a means of plundering the hapless people under its jurisdiction.

6. The significance of sovereignty in determining the fate and welfare of a society can never be overemphasized. As sovereignty determines who is the master and who is the servant within any political system, it is clear that whoever possesses it will determine the destiny of the civilization. If the people remain sovereign, they are the masters, and their government is their servant. But if the government steals that sovereignty, it becomes the master, and the people are reduced to slavery.

7. Prior to the Age of Reason, human government had been subverted to the extent that grandiose theories were advanced in attempts to supposedly justify the enslavement of the human race. Among these perverted concepts were the Divine Rights of Kings theory and the plea for a Leviathan State. John Locke, in spearheading the Age of Reason, exploded these fallacious concepts and reaffirmed the sovereignty of the people and the social contract foundation of civil society. According to the Lockean Theory of Government, men left the State of Nature, formed civil society, and put themselves under government for the purpose of providing greater security for their individual human rights. Furthermore, stated this theory, civil society and government are created by consent and agreement, and the government, therefore, may possess only delegated powers, or those powers specifically assigned to it by the people. The people rightfully retain sovereignty, or political supremacy, as well as all powers not specifically delegated to their government. While the people within society possess natural rights, the government possesses no rights at all, but only duties to perform and obligations to the governed. The Lockean Theory of Government established the foundations of the concepts of government-by-the-consent-of-the-governed and constitutionally limited government.

8. The Lockean Theory of Government deeply influenced the thinking of the American people to such an extent that, when writing the Declaration of Independence, Thomas Jefferson gave a summary of that political theory, calling it an expression of the American mind. Within that Declaration, the thirteen colonies declared their independence from Great Britain and proclaimed themselves to be free and sovereign States equal to the State of Great Britain in regard to sovereignty and empowered to do all acts which sovereign States may rightfully do. The word "State," as first used within the Declaration, later in the Articles of Confederation, and still later in the Constitution of 1787, implies a sovereign body politic. The American Revolution was fought to secure

that asserted sovereignty of the American States. And within the Treaty of Paris of 1783, the States secured international recognition of their separate and individual sovereign status.

9. As sovereign bodies, the thirteen American States were free to form alliances and associations with other sovereign States. Accordingly, they formed a Federal Union with each other, known as the United States of America, under a Federal Constitution styled the Articles of Confederation. Those Articles specifically acknowledged the obvious fact that the States of the Union were sovereign. Furthermore, those Articles expressed the purpose of the United States to be the preservation and defense of the sovereignties of the several States. When the States adopted a new Federal Constitution in 1789, it was based on the same principles as the Articles of Confederation. Under each of the two federal compacts, the Federal Union existed between the States, and each Union bore the same name, the United States of America.

10. The application of the Lockean Theory of Government to the American federal system resulted in the creation of a uniquely American Theory of Government. According to this theory, only the people possess sovereignty or political supremacy. All levels of government are servants of the people and may rightfully exercise only delegated powers. The State governments constitute the primary level of government and are entrusted with powers to provide for the domestic needs of the people and to safeguard their human rights. The Federal Government, on the other hand, is vested with powers to conduct foreign and interstate affairs. Sovereignty is vested in the people of each State, who, in their sovereign capacity, are the equivalent of the State. There is no such thing as delegated sovereignty, divided sovereignty, or limited sovereignty within our political system. The American Theory of Government dictates that only the States are sovereign. Any and all attempts to deny this truth invariably result in vesting sovereignty in the Government of the United States.

11. Finally, in the creation of the Federal Union styled the United States of America, no consolidated State or Nation of people was created. In adopting our present Federal Constitution, the people remained politically organized as sovereign States. The State of America – as a consolidated Nation – does not constitutionally exist. The people of the United States, of course, do indeed exist, but they exist politically only as sovereign States. They vote in federal elections only as States. They are represented in the Federal Government only as States. They created the Federal Union only as States. They reserve all powers not delegated to the Federal Government only as States. They are recognized by the supreme law of the land only as individual citizens or as sovereign States, and they may alter or amend the Federal Constitution only as States. In terms of sovereignty, supremacy, dominion, and mastery, the people are the States,

and the States are the people. The political rights of the people and the rights of the States are synonymous and equivalent concepts. State sovereignty and States' Rights, therefore, are concepts equal in meaning to the sovereignty of the people and the political rights of the American people.

The history of the formation of the Federal Union and the creation of the Federal Republic leave no doubt whatsoever that, within our federal system, each State is sovereign. An attempt was made, it is true, within the Constitutional Convention of 1787, to reduce these sovereignties to mere departments of a consolidated, supreme National Government. That project, however, was defeated within the Philadelphia Convention, and the result of the Convention was a Federal Constitution, not a national one.

Following its defeat within the Philadelphia Convention, the consolidating school remained unrelenting and continued to pursue its objective of consolidating sovereignty in the United States, and ultimately of transforming the Government of the United States into a supreme National Government. The schemes, designs, artifices, and perverted theories expounded by the consolidating school require our careful attention. For that reason, to examine these schemes and distorted concepts shall be our next topic for consideration.

Chapter Six

The Rise of the Consolidating School

The consolidating school has been in existence in the United States from the very beginning. The discord it has sown among brethren of the same political Union is amply recorded on the pages of history. And with grief and shame it must be admitted that the consolidating school has managed to maneuver itself into a position of authority and control in the United States, both in and out of government. It has laid its hands upon the reins of government and has usurped power right and left. Perhaps worse than that, the consolidators have seized control of the education process in the United States, and today controls the teaching of students in our government-run indoctrination centers called public schools, from the kindergarten level to the post-graduate level. It also has a near monopoly on the writing, publication, and distribution of books on the subjects of economics, history, and political science. Adding to its noxious control over the American mind, it exerts tremendous influence on and control of the news media, from radio and television, to newspapers and magazines. Assuredly, as John Locke once stated, there is nothing more dangerous to the natural rights of man than the propagation of false theories concerning government.

Of course, it would be virtually impossible for even the most zealous consolidator to pretend that the States of our Union do not exist, or that the State governments do not or should not exercise any powers. The existence of the States is a fact that even the consolidating school must acknowledge. Yet, by sleight of hand, the art of misconstruction, the use of improper terminology, and even an appeal to the results of the use of brute force, the Consolidating School of Thought has managed to advance theories and explanations of government that render the States little more than administrative districts of a supreme, consolidated, national sovereignty.

We have already cited several examples of the confused and confusing explanations of our federal system of government that are offered by modern-day expounders of the Constitution. One explanation, as we have noted previously, attempts to deny the sovereignty of the States by denying that the States within the Federal Union are really States. Perhaps the most extreme example of utter confusion we have already examined is the one offered by Professor

Richard B. Morris in his 1986 book, *The Framing of the Federal Constitution*, in which the claim is made that sovereignty in our political system is supposedly vested simultaneously in the American people, the States, the Federal Union, and the Government of the United States. It was further asserted that our *Federal* Constitution somehow established a Nation and a *National* Government.

Such examples illustrate the more extreme excesses of absurdity to which the use of improper terminology and erroneous theories of government have given rise. There are, of course, more responsible modern-day history and political science textbooks that have been published, which present a more truthful explanation of the constitutional history of the United States. Such textbooks candidly acknowledge that the modern American system of government is not the same as the system established by the Founding Fathers. Invariably, the reason or excuse given for this subversion of our constitutional system is always the same.

A typical example of what modern students are taught regarding our system of government and the concept of sovereignty may be found in the Eleventh Edition of the political science textbook, *Government by the People*, which was published in 1981. Its three authors were James MacGregor Burns of Williams College, J.W. Peltason of the American Council on Education, and Thomas E. Cronin of Colorado College. Within the chapter entitled, "American Federalism: Constitutional Dynamics," these authors offer an assessment and explanation of the American federal system of government.

These writers begin their explanation of the American system of government by acknowledging that it was originally constituted as a federal system simply because the Founding Fathers had no other practical alternative:

> We have a federal form of government in part because in 1787 there was really no other choice. After confederation had been found unsuccessful, the only choice open to those who wanted a more closely knit Union was federation. A unitary system was out because most of the people were too deeply attached to the State governments to permit the States to be subordinated to central rule. Consolidation of the States into a single unitary government was impossible short of military conquest by the more populous States. [1]

The American people during the Constitutional Period were so firmly attached to the principles of federalism and States' Rights that they would have rejected a National Government had one been presented for their consideration. Indeed, nothing short of military conquest could have induced them to accept a consolidation of their governmental system. That any modern-day

[1] James MacGregor Burns, J.W. Peltason, and Thomas E. Cronin, *Government by the People*, Eleventh Edition, Prentice-Hall, Inc., Englewood Cliffs, 1981, p. 48.

textbook could acknowledge these truths is quite remarkable, and the acknowledgement of such truths by these authors makes their subsequent contentions even more remarkable.

As the authors of this textbook explain, "Federalism embodies the American suspicion of concentrated power, for Americans tend to equate freedom and federalism." Furthermore, they state that "federalism does lessen 'the risk of a monopoly of political power,'" and that, within the federal system, "national majorities could be checked by local majorities." "Federalism," the authors note, "by providing numerous areas for decision-making, involves many people and helps to keep government closer to the people." [2]

Yet, in spite of the fact that our system of government was established on the principles of federalism and State sovereignty, and that such principles are requisite to prevent a monopoly of power in Washington, D.C., these authors note that our political system has been transformed into precisely that type of system that was widely abhorred by the American people when the Constitution was adopted:

> There may be a few subjects – for example, regulation of marriage, divorce, and minimum wages for State employees – about which the Supreme Court might raise objections to national legislation because of the principles of federalism, but it is now fairly accurate to say that Congress has power to do whatever it believes is necessary and proper to promote the general welfare. [3]

Any government that may exercise power to do whatever it professes to be necessary and proper to promote whatever it professes to be the general welfare is, by definition, a *government of unlimited powers* – a supreme, sovereign government! Incredibly, this is how the modern-day Government of the United States is described, even by those who acknowledge that such a government was never intended by those who framed and adopted our Federal Constitution. "Federalism, in short," these authors say, "no longer imposes serious constitutional restraints on the powers of Congress, the President, or the Federal Courts." [4]

How did this come about? How did the American people lose their federal system, with its constitutionally limited government, that served to protect them from a monopoly of power? The authors of *Government by the People* explain that, from the very birth of our Republic, there existed two opposing schools, a *States' Rights school* devoted to preserving our constitutional system of government and a *consolidating school* whose aim was the subversion of that sys-

---

[2] *Ibid.*, pp. 50-51.
[3] *Ibid.*, pp. 57-58.
[4] *Ibid.*, p. 58.

tem and the erection upon its ruins of a highly centralized and sovereign National Government.

As these authors write:

> The nationalist position, supported by Chief Justice John Marshall, Abraham Lincoln, Theodore Roosevelt, Franklin Roosevelt, and throughout most of our history by the Supreme Court, rejects the whole concept of the Constitution as an interstate compact. Rather, the Constitution is a *supreme law* established by the people. The National Government is an agent of the *people*, not of the States, for it was the people who drew up the Constitution and created the National Government....They intended that the central government's powers should be liberally defined and that it not be denied authority unless the Constitution so clearly states. [5]

"The nationalist interpretation of government," these authors claim, "finally triumphed at Appomattox Courthouse after the Civil War." [6] Thus, even though the American people at the time of the adoption of our present Federal Constitution would never have accepted a consolidated National Government, modern Americans today are living under such a government because those who hated our constitutional system waged the War Between the States and conquered the sovereign States. And our true constitutional system remains hidden from view today because we are ruled by politicians who continue to prefer a monopoly of power to our legitimate federal system of government. This conspiracy to subvert the Constitution of the United States, though openly acknowledged, is neither condemned nor praised by these authors, but is merely stated as a fact, as though the mere fact of a victory in a war is sufficient to justify the consolidating school's "interpretation of government."

That this conclusion is typical of what is presented today within our education system is attested to by an examination of numerous other textbooks of history and political science. If further illustrations were required, then we may offer the sixth edition of *Introduction to American Government*. Its two authors were a Professor of Political Science at the University of California, P. Orman Ray, and a Professor of Political Science at the University of Wisconsin, Frederic A. Ogg. This book, which was first published in 1922, with the sixth edition appearing in 1938, is representative of textbooks published after the War Between the States in glorifying the triumph of a supreme National Government over the once-sovereign States of our Federal Union.

As Professors Ogg and Ray wrote:

> Having struggled with the problem of the future position of the

---

[5] *Ibid.*, pp. 58-59.
[6] *Ibid.*, p. 60.

> States as with no other issue entering into their discussions, the Constitution's makers may be supposed to have done their best to define the relations of nation and States clearly and comprehensively....
>
> ...Throughout the first half of our national history, the fundamental matter in dispute was not merely the tenuous line of separation between national and State powers, but the very nature of the Union itself. Was the United States, under the Constitution, a true and indivisible nation; or was it only a league of sovereign States as before 1789? The question may sound hollow to our ears, but it once stirred the profoundest thought and emotion of American political leaders. That the States were not mere administrative subdivisions, nor yet only subordinate areas with a limited autonomy conferred by the central government, was conceded by all. They were, as everybody knew, distinct, original, indestructible political entities, with extensive inherent powers. But did this mean that they were "sovereign"? Or were their people so merged in a common, superior, national organization that the States also, as political units, had become inextricably embedded in it? [7]

The authors of *Introduction to American Government* offered this happy explanation of how the consolidating school achieved its victory over the States' Rights school by the superiority of military strength:

> Happily, the logic of events has gone far toward clearing up all reasonable doubt on this score. As every student of our history knows, the trend since 1789 has been decidedly in the direction of a strong National Government based on an indissoluble Union of States. In a remarkable series of decisions in cases turning on constitutional questions, the Supreme Court, notable during John Marshall's long service as Chief Justice (1801-35), consistently – and with powerful effect – gave its support to the nationalist view. The denial and total extinction of the alleged right of a State to nullify acts of Congress, notwithstanding momentary successes of nullificationists in South Carolina and Georgia, worked to the same end. And – passing over a great number of other contributing factors – the failure of secession in 1860-1865, followed by general (even though in some quarters reluctant) acquiescence in the conclusion that a State cannot secede, *clinched the victory of nationalism and stamped the Union with the quality of permanence which it unmistakably possesses in our own day.* [emphasis added] [8]

Might Makes Right

According to the modern apologists for the consolidating school's subversion of our Constitution, the question of the sovereignty of the States needs

---

[7] Frederic A, Ogg and P. Orman Ray, *Introduction to American Government*, Sixth Edition, D. Appleton-Century Company Incorporated, New York, 1938, pp. 72-73.
[8] *Ibid.*, p. 73.

no longer to be even considered today, for the question was intensely debated prior to the War Between the States, and the victory of the consolidators in that war, through force of arms, provided the final answer. The States are not sovereign, according to this novel and despicable theory, because the Government of the United States conquered them! And this supposedly settles the matter conclusively, as we are quite "happily" informed.

We are immediately reminded of the words of Mao Tse-tung, the bloody Communist butcher of the Chinese people, who asserted in "Problems of War and Strategy" on November 6, 1938, that, "Every Communist must grasp the truth, 'Political power grows out of the barrel of a gun.'" [9] Those who argue that the question of State sovereignty was answered by the outcome of the War Between the States share Mao's philosophy, which is nothing more than the law of brute force – the law of the savage and the law of the bully – the cornerstone of all sovereign governments. In effect, such apologists for Big Government are claiming that an appeal to force, rather than an appeal to reason, is the proper course of civilized societies. They are stating the immoral concept that *might makes right.*

According to the Consolidating School of Thought, the States of the Federal Union are not sovereign, but are prisoners of the Federal Government and cannot escape from the Union they originally created. The Government of the United States is one of constitutionally limited powers, this consolidating theory acknowledges, although the Constitution is whatever the Federal Government says it is. Congress has the unlimited power to pass any law that it deems necessary and proper to promote whatever it claims is the general welfare. The President of the United States may rule by executive order, may usurp whatever powers he pleases, and may declare himself to be the King of the World. And the Constitution of the United States is whatever the Supreme Court of the United States says it is. Reverence paid to the awesome powers of the Federal Government is even portrayed as patriotic. But any State that attempts to challenge the Federal Government's right to assume any powers it pleases will find itself staring down the barrel of a gun.

As Supreme Court Justice Salmon P. Chase succinctly phrased the matter, "State sovereignty died at Appomattox." [10] Since might makes right in this war-begotten theory of government, all the historical facts proving that the States are sovereign – together with the wise words of wisdom of men such as Thomas Jefferson, John Taylor of Caroline, James Madison, and John C. Calhoun – are discarded in the ash heap. Resurrected are the corrupt and erroneous philosophies of Alexander Hamilton, John Marshall, Daniel Webster, Jo-

---

[9] Mao Tse-tung, *Quotations From Chairman Mao Tsetung*, Foreign Language Press, Peking, 1972, p. 61.

[10] James Ronald Kennedy and Walter Donald Kennedy, *The South Was Right!*, Pelican Publishing Company, Gretna, 1994, quoted on p. 219.

seph Story, and Abraham Lincoln.

Because the Government of the United States conquered the sovereign States in the War Between the States, Professors Ogg and Ray made this assertion in their textbook: "The verdict of history is that the ultimate, *i.e.*, sovereign authority in this country is, not each State for itself, not yet the Government of the United States, but the people of the country considered as a whole." [11]

Thus, under the pretense of vesting sovereignty in a mythological Nation of Americans, the consolidators have succeeded in stealing sovereignty from the genuine peoples of the several States and vesting it in the Government of the United States. And this, we are happily informed, is the "verdict of history," a verdict that must take precedence over historical facts, truth, justice, logic, reason, and common sense, to say nothing of the liberties of the American people. Yet, must the American people accept this so-called verdict of history? Are the people of the United States to be forever condemned to accept this verdict? Can the criminal misdeeds of the consolidating school justify the permanent subjugation of the States, the subversion of the Constitution, and the subjection of the American people to a monopoly of power in their Federal Government?

If we accept the misdeeds of the consolidating school as the final verdict of history, then we are overthrowing all traditional concepts of morality, ethics, decency, and civilization, all of which assert that reason, and not force, should settle disputes among men. To accept the immoral principle that might makes right is to accept and condone all the misdeeds of the human race that have been sustained by brute force, from the communist enslavement of Red China to the extermination of the Jews by Adolph Hitler. Since the Communists and the Nazis who perpetrated those heinous crimes did so with superior force, we must concede that their arguments and their deeds were correct. Is the reader willing to make such a concession?

Even if the so-called verdict of history is supposedly on the side of the consolidating school in America, the *truth* is on the side of the advocates of the sovereignty of the States. And which should we prefer – the verdict of history, or the verdict of truth? For all honest men, the answer is self-evident.

Before turning our attention to an examination of the early machinations of the consolidators in the United States, we should devote some attention to one other point raised by Professor Ogg and Professor Ray in their textbook. In happily concluding that State sovereignty does not exist within our modern political system, these two authors were careful to avoid directly vesting that sovereignty in the Government of the United States.

---

[11] Frederic A, Ogg and P. Orman Ray, *Op. cit.*, p. 73.

The concept of the sovereignty of the people is too deeply ingrained in the American mind to directly and boldly proclaim that such supremacy is invested in a sovereign National Government. Such an assertion, although sometimes made by the consolidating school, would not be readily accepted by the general public, for even modern Americans are still somewhat aware of the concept that government should be the servant of the people. Thus, the *indirect method* of vesting sovereignty in the Federal Government is the more preferred approach of the Consolidating School of Thought. This feat is accomplished by claiming that sovereignty is vested in a consolidated State of America that does not exist. Since the State of America is a figment of the imagination, the sovereignty supposedly vested in it ends up in the hands of the Government of the United States. And that government may then lay claim to a field of unlimited powers while paying lip service to the sovereignty of the people.

Here we should pause to reflect on what may be the greatest irony of our time. In bygone ages, efforts to supposedly justify the supremacy of government gave the world the distorted concepts of the Divine Rights of Kings and the supposed necessity of a Leviathan State to rule over anarchic mankind. To the modern mind, the theories used to justify these absurdities ring hollow, and modern man may well wonder how anyone could ever have been so foolish as to believe those nonsensical notions. Yet, as we have seen, modern Americans are expected to swallow notions of government that are even more absurd and ridiculous. How could any reasonable person reject the Divine Rights of Kings as foolishness, yet allow the Federal Government to steal sovereignty from the States under the pretext of vesting that sovereignty in a consolidated Nation of people that does not exist?

The Constitutional Convention of 1787

More than two hundred years have passed since the founding of the American Republic. During that course of time, it has become a tradition for modern Americans to attribute to the generation of our Founding Fathers attributes beyond what mere mortals possess, and modern Americans tend to regard the generation of our Founders as one in which all the people were of one mind and one heart in the cause of independence and liberty. The truth, however, is that that generation, like any other generation of people who have ever lived, was not really of one heart and mind. When Thomas Jefferson wrote that the Declaration of Independence, for example, was an *expression of the American mind*, he meant only that it was an expression of the sentiments of the *majority* of the American people.

Historians generally agree that, at the time of the American Revolution, approximately one-third of the American colonists were Tories who favored the success of British imperial forces over the American patriots. The fact that the thirteen colonies had formally declared their independence of Great Britain and had become sovereign States meant that those Tories were, in actuality, traitors to their own peoples. Some of the Tories even committed acts of treason by aiding the British during the War of Independence and betraying the American forces.

If such divisions among the American people could exist during the Revolutionary War, it should come as no surprise that divisions in sentiments and principles existed afterwards. Such divisions certainly existed during what historians have called the "Critical Period" under the Articles of Confederation and were even evident within the Philadelphia Convention of 1787. That such divisions remained after the adoption of our present Federal Constitution cannot be denied and explains the formation of political parties during the earliest days of the Republic.

So well defined had these divisions of sentiments and principles become by 1787, that, within the Constitutional Convention it was possible to clearly identify three separate factions. Although these parties were not formally named at the time, their existence was apparent to all honest observers. One delegate from Maryland, Luther Martin, was able to recognize and differentiate these factions and to describe them in detail:

> One party, whose object and wish it was to abolish and annihilate all State governments, and to bring forward one general government over this extensive continent of a monarchial nature, under certain restrictions and limitations. Those who openly avowed this sentiment were, it is true, but few; yet it is equally true that there was a considerable number, who did not openly avow it, who were, by myself and many others of the Convention, considered as being in reality favorers of that sentiment....
>
> The second party was not for the abolition of the State governments nor for the introduction of a monarchial government under any form; but they wished to establish such a system as could give their own States undue power and influence in the government over the other States.
>
> The third party was what I considered truly federal and republican. This party was nearly equal in number with the other two, and was composed of the delegates from Connecticut, New York [excluding Alexander Hamilton], New Jersey, Delaware, and in part from Maryland; also of some individuals from other representations. This party were for proceeding upon terms of federal equality; they were for taking our present federal system [under the Articles of Confederation] as the basis of their proceedings, and, as far as experience had shown that other powers were necessary to the Federal Government, to give those powers. They considered this the object for which

they were sent by their States, and what their States expected from them. [12]

If proper names could be ascribed to these factions within the Federal Convention of 1787 based upon their principles and sentiments, then the first party described by Luther Martin could be labeled the *National Monarchists*, a party whose most vocal members were Alexander Hamilton and Gouverneur Morris. Although this party was the weakest and least influential one within that Convention, it preferred the replacement of the existing federal system with a national system, to be governed by a sovereign National Government of a monarchical nature.

The second party described by Mr. Martin could be labeled the *National Republicans*, a faction whose most prominent members included James Madison and James Wilson. Although this party was stronger than the National Monarchists within the Convention, they did not possess sufficient strength to command a majority of opinion. This faction favored a republican form of government, although they were very determined to replace the existing federal system of government with a national system to be governed by a supreme National Government that would force the State governments into obedience.

The third party described by Luther Martin may be labeled the *Federal Republicans*, whose most prominent members included Luther Martin and Roger Sherman. This party was committed to the republican form of government, the concept of federalism, and the creation of a new Union founded upon the sovereignty of the States. Approximately half of the delegates to the Grand Convention supported these views, and their views undeniably reflected the sentiments of the overwhelming majority of the American people.

Commenting further on these parties within the Philadelphia Convention, Luther Martin noted that the National Monarchists and the National Republicans, in an effort to overwhelm the Federal Republicans with the Federal Convention, formed a coalition or alliance. "The first party, *conscious that the people of America would reject their system*, if proposed," he stated, "joined the second, well knowing that by departing from a federal system, they paved the way for their favourite object, the destruction of the State governments, and the introduction of monarchy."[13]

It is of interest to note that, during the long, hot summer of 1787, each of these three parties introduced its own proposed plan of government to the Federal Convention. The National Republicans, evidently believing that surprise and boldness were the keys to victory, made their move almost immedi-

---

[12] Jefferson Davis, *The Rise and Fall of the Confederate Government*, Volume 1, Thomas Yoseloff, Cranbury, 1958 (orig. pub. 1881), quoted on p. 95.
[13] John Taylor, *New Views of the Constitution of the United States*, Da Capo Press, New York, 1971 (orig. pub. 1823), quoted on p. 42.

ately after the Convention got underway, as soon as the proceedings had been shrouded in a cloak of secrecy. Their proposal has often been referred to as the *Virginia Plan*, a plan that audaciously called for the creation of a strong, energetic, supreme National Government. This scheme of government bristled with the words "supreme" and "National Government," making it clear that what was envisioned was the conquest of the sovereign States. At one point during the proceedings, the plan repeated the term "national" no less than twenty-six times! Not surprisingly, this proposed National Government would be empowered to force submission from the States by having a veto power over State legislation.

The Virginia Plan was thrust upon the Convention before all the delegates had even arrived in Philadelphia. As a consequence, by the time some of the delegates arrived to take part in the Convention's proceedings, they discovered that the Convention had already resolved to replace the federal system of government with a national system. Yet, with the arrival of more delegates to the Convention, opposition to the proposed Virginia Plan grew stronger. Before long, the Federal Republicans resolved to propose their own plan of government to the Convention, one that was wholly federal in nature. This new proposal has often been referred to as the *New Jersey Plan*. Although the Convention promptly rejected this federal plan, its introduction marked the beginning of the end for the Virginia Plan. As the Convention proceeded, the Federal Republicans succeeded in transforming the Virginia Plan into a genuinely federal system.

Perhaps the signal event that marked the turning point in the Federal Convention was the proposal by the Federal Republicans that the term "National Government" be removed from the evolving compact of government and replaced by terminology proper for a federal system of government. With the adoption of this proposal, the words *National Government* were deliberately stricken out of the evolving Constitution and replaced by the words *Government of the United States*. The Federal Republicans also succeeded in removing the concept of governmental supremacy from the evolving plan of government. In the end, it would be the Constitution and laws and treaties made in pursuance of it – and not the Federal Government itself – that would be declared supreme by the new plan of Union.

Alarmed by the growing successes of the Federal Republicans, the National Monarchists made their move in the Convention by introducing a third plan of government. Although their plan was never seriously considered, and therefore has never been formally named by historians, it was proposed by Alexander Hamilton, who advocated its adoption in a five-hour oration, the longest speech given in the Philadelphia Convention. It is important that we understand this proposed plan of government, for it represented the crystallization of thought that would quickly give rise to the Consolidating School of Thought in the United States.

Alexander Hamilton's Plan of Government

Alexander Hamilton's proposed plan called for the subjugation of the States. He candidly confessed that he would prefer to abolish the States completely, but was willing to tolerate their existence if they could be controlled completely by a centralized government. He therefore advocated that the State Governors should be appointed by a National Government and that this national representative could veto any State laws deemed to be in conflict with the supremacy of the centralized government. His proposed supreme National Government was candidly intended to represent an aristocracy of wealth, a type of government often referred to as a *plutocracy*. This National Government would be sovereign and thus empowered to pass any law it deemed proper without restriction. The President of the United States, under this plan, would be a totalitarian dictator, exercising more powers than any king of old could ever claim under the Divine Rights of Kings theory. Mr. Hamilton's plan was, in essence, the application of the concept of a Leviathan State to the United States of America, a plan for a socialistic totalitarian government.

Regarding the plan proposed to the Constitutional Convention by Mr. Hamilton, the distinguished historian, Claude G. Bowers, has noted the following in his book, *Jefferson and Hamilton*:

> The plan was a direct contradiction of that which was adopted. There is nothing conjectural about the fact – the records are indisputable. We have the plan, the brilliant five-hour oration in its behalf, the brief from which he spoke. These have come down to us, not from his enemies, but from his partial biographers, his son the editor of his "Works," and the report of Madison on the authenticity of which he himself passed. This plan provided for the election of a President for life; for Senators for life or during good behavior, and by electors with a property qualification; and for the crushing of the sovereignty of the States through the appointment by the President of Governors with a life tenure and the power to veto any act of the State legislatures, though passed unanimously. Not only was the President enabled under this plan to negative any law enacted, but he had the discretionary power to enforce or ignore any law existing. Though his President, serving for life, was not called a king, he was to be armed with more arbitrary power than was possessed by the King of England. His English eulogist does not overstate when he says that "what he had in mind was the British Constitution as George III had tried hard to make it," and failed because the English people would not tolerate it. This interpretation of Hamilton's purpose is reenforced

by another of his most brilliant disciples who asserts that "Hamilton's governor [President] would have been not dissimilar to Louis XIV and could have said with him, 'L'etat c'est moi.'...Thinly veiled, his plan contemplated an elective king with greater powers than those of George III, an imitation House of Lords, and a popular House of Commons with a limited tenure." Even so this plan confessedly fell far short of his conception of an ideal government. In the brief for his speech we are left in no doubt as to his partiality for a monarchy, in which the aristocracy should have a special power. "The monarch...ought to be hereditary, and to have so much power that it would not be his interest to risk much to acquire more." As for the aristocracy, "they should be so circumstanced that they can have no interest in a change." We should be "rescued from the democracy." As to the republican form of government – "Republics are liable to corruption and intrigue," and, since "a republican government does not admit of a vigorous execution, it is therefore bad."

Later, in one of his few discussions, he said that "those who mean to form a solid republican government ought to proceed to the confines of another government." His republic, and in his great speech he had conceded that no other form would be accepted by the people, "was to be an aristocratic as distinguished from a democratic republic, and the power of the separate States was to be effectually crippled." In one of his brief Convention talks he said of the States that "as States he thought they should be abolished." Even after the Constitution had been adopted, he believed that one of the objects of administration should be "to acquire for the Federal Government more consistency than the Constitution seems to promise for so great a country," to the end that it "may triumph altogether over the State governments and reduce them to an utter subordination, dividing the large States into simpler districts." Such were the ideas urged by Hamilton in the forceful five-hour speech which Gouverneur Morris thought the most brilliant intellectual exhibition he had ever witnessed. After this exhaustive exposition, he took but little part. Toward the close he explained his comparative silence: "He had been restrained from entering into the discussions by his dislike of the scheme of government in general." This distaste did not diminish as the Convention closed its labors, and he accepted the Constitution in the end "as better than nothing." His motive for joining in recommending it to the people is conclusively shown in his last Convention utterance: "No man's ideas are more remote from the plan than my own are known to be; but is it possible to deliberate between anarchy and convulsion on one side, and the chance of good to be expected from the plan on the other?" [14]

The Denial That State Sovereignty Ever Existed

It has often been noted that the Philadelphia Convention of 1787 failed

---

[14] Claude G. Bowers, *Jefferson and Hamilton: The Struggle for Democracy in America*, Houghton Mifflin Company, Boston, 1925, pp. 30-32.

to include within the Constitution a positive statement that the States, within the Union to be established by it, would retain their sovereignty. Had that Convention inserted such a direct, positive statement within our present Federal Constitution, would it have made any difference? Would such a statement have prevented those who later denied the sovereignty of the States from making such claims?

In considering these questions, an exchange of dialogue that occurred within the Constitutional Convention between Elbridge Gerry of Massachusetts and Luther Martin of Maryland is instructive. In June, Mr. Gerry declared to the Convention that, "we *never were* independent States, *were not such now, and never could be,* even on the principles of the Constitution," referring, of course, to the Articles of Confederation. "The States," he insisted, "and the advocates for them, were intoxicated with the idea of their *sovereignty.*" [15]

Fortunately, there were enough delegates attending that Federal Convention who were sufficiently "intoxicated" with the notion of State sovereignty to ensure that the Convention's final product was a Constitution founded on the sovereignty of the peoples of the several States. As for the difficulty encountered by some of the delegates to understand that the States, under the Articles of Confederation, were truly sovereign, Luther Martin told the Convention that "the language of the States being *sovereign and independent,* was once familiar and understood; though it seemed now so strange and obscure." According to the records of the Convention, "He read those passages in the Articles of Confederation which described them in that language." [16]

Those passages which Mr. Martin, an eminent lawyer from Maryland, read to the Grand Convention were undoubtedly the second and third articles of the then-existing supreme law of the land. One of them specifically asserted that the States were sovereign. The other one stated that the purpose of the Federal Union – the very reason why the United States of America was created – was to preserve, protect, and defend the sovereignty of the States. Despite these plain assertions within the Articles of Confederation, however, there were obviously some prominent individuals at the time who could not, or pretended that they could not, grasp the fact that the States were sovereign under the Articles.

Therefore, if anyone today thinks that the question of State sovereignty could have been made even more clear and obvious by the insertion in the Federal Constitution of 1787 of a positive statement expressly asserting the sovereignty of the States, then this dialogue between Mr. Gerry and Mr. Martin should conclusively settle the matter. Even at a time when the supreme law of

---

[15] Jonathan Elliot (ed.), *Elliot's Debates,* Volume 5, Published under the Sanction of Congress, Washington, D.C., 1845, p. 259.

[16] *Ibid.*, Volume 5, p. 259.

the land expressly asserted State sovereignty in plain words, there were those who dared to assert that the States were not really sovereign. It should be evident, then, that even if similar positive assertions of State sovereignty had been inserted into our present Federal Constitution, those who deny the sovereignty of the States would continue to do so.

From the very beginning, it is clear that, whether or not State sovereignty was positively asserted in the federal compact, the consolidating school was determined to either deny its existence or to snuff it out and transfer such sovereignty to a supreme National Government. *The drafting of our present Federal Constitution represented a highly significant defeat for the consolidating school.* The plan of government that emerged from the Philadelphia Convention of 1787 was strictly federal in nature, providing for a Federal Union that would exist *between sovereign States.*

The Inconsistencies of the Federalist Papers

After the Federal Constitution of 1787 had been written and approved by the Philadelphia Convention, the proposed new plan of government was submitted to the sovereign States for their ratification. The new federal compact, as stipulated in its Seventh Article, would be considered duly adopted only if ratified by at least nine States. But in ratifying the compact, each State could be bound only by its own accession. If any State refused to ratify the new Federal Constitution, it would not be a member of the new Federal Union. Rhode Island, in fact, hesitated so long in ratifying the new Constitution, that, when it finally entered the new Union, the newly formed Federal Government was already in operation and entertaining legislation that regarded Rhode Island as a foreign Nation.

One State after another eventually did ratify the new compact, but in some States the opposition was strong. To allay fears that the new Federal Constitution would subvert the sovereignty of the States, the proponents of ratification styled themselves *Federalists* and branded their opponents as *Antifederalists.* In one State Ratifying Convention after another, the Federalists repeatedly assured the people that the new Constitution was truly federal and republican in nature, and that, in adopting the new plan of Union, the States would retain their sovereignty.

Some State Ratifying Conventions insisted on examining every questionable clause in the proposed Constitution to ensure that a plot to sneak a supreme National Government through the back door was not being attempted. In every case, the Federalists solemnly assured all doubters that such fears were groundless. To further appease the Antifederalists, the Federalists agreed that, after the new plan was adopted, a Bill of Rights would be added to the Federal Constitution to provide additional safeguards for the rights of man and the sovereignty of the States.

With such assurances, the Constitution was finally ratified by the minimum nine States required to ensure its success. But hope was held that the other four States would also join the new Federal Union. After Virginia's great debate on the proposed compact and its final acceptance of the new compact, all eyes turned to New York, where the Antifederalists were particularly well represented in that State's Ratifying Convention. The Federalist faction within the New York State Ratifying Convention was led by Alexander Hamilton, and it is clear from Mr. Hamilton's speeches to the Convention that he understood fully that the Constitution of 1787 truly was federal and republican in nature.

To assist in the goal of persuading the Empire State to ratify the new Constitution, Alexander Hamilton collaborated with John Jay and James Madison in writing a series of essays extolling the new plan of government under the common pseudonym of "Publius." Historians have since identified, with only minimal doubt, which of the three men actually wrote each essay, and the essays themselves have been collected and published under the title of *The Federalist Papers*.

Although the *Federalist Papers* do contain a great deal of truth and have been widely acclaimed by statesmen and historians alike, those essays should not be regarded as perfect in every detail, for they contain a number of inconsistencies and misapplications of political terminology. All three of the authors, of course, were ardent nationalists at the time they penned the essays, personally preferring a strong, supreme National Government for the United States. And Mr. Hamilton was a monarchist who personally despised the republican form of government. It should come as no surprise, therefore, that, try as they may to present an honest assessment of the principles of the new Federal Constitution, their own personal biases should surface from time to time within the essays.

Within the *Federalist Papers*, John Jay did not really touch upon the question of sovereignty, for he authored only a few of the essays. Mr. Madison and Mr. Hamilton, however, considered that subject in numerous essays. Of these two men, the Father of the Constitution displayed greater consistency in both terminology and explanation. Although careless at times, James Madison clearly described the system of government under the new compact to be federal, not national. Alexander Hamilton, unfortunately, was rather careless and inconsistent in his contributions to the essays. Since he was destined to assume the inglorious role of *Father of the Consolidating School* in the United States, his views, as expressed in those essays, become especially interesting.

In the *Federalist*, No. 81, Alexander Hamilton wrote:

> It is inherent in the nature of sovereignty not to be amenable to the suit of an individual ***without its consent***. This is the general sense and the general practice of mankind; and the exemption, as one of the attributes of sovereignty, is now enjoyed by the government of every State in the Union. [17]

In the *Federalist*, No. 82, Mr. Hamilton termed the States "distinct sovereignties." [18] Within the *Federalist*, No. 33, he declared that, "The necessity of a concurrent jurisdiction in certain cases results from the division of the sovereign power." [19]

In the *Federalist*, No. 32, Alexander Hamilton asserted:

> But as the plan of the Convention aims only at a partial Union or consolidation, the State governments would clearly retain all the rights of sovereignty which they before had, and which were not, by that act, *exclusively* delegated to the United States. This exclusive delegation, or rather this alienation, of State sovereignty would only exist in three cases: where the Constitution in express terms granted an exclusive authority to the Union; where it granted in one instance an authority to the Union, and in another prohibited the States from exercising the like authority; and where it granted an authority to the Union to which a similar authority in the States would be absolutely and totally *contradictory* and *repugnant*. [20]

In the *Federalist*, No. 32, the Father of the Consolidating School made these comments:

> I repeat here what I have observed in substance in another place, that all observations founded upon the danger of usurpation ought to be referred to the composition and structure of the government, not to the nature or extent of its powers. The State governments by their original Constitutions are invested with complete sovereignty. [21]

And, as one final selection, in the *Federalist*, No. 9, Alexander Hamilton stated the following:

> The definition of a *Confederate Republic* seems simply to be, an "assemblage of societies" or an association of two or more states into one state. The extent, modification and objects of the Federal authority are mere matters of direction. So long as the separate organisation of the members be not abolished, *so long as it exists by a constitutional necessity for local purposes*,

[17] Alexander Hamilton, James Madison, and John Jay, *The Federalist Papers*, A Mentor Book from New American Library, New York, 1961, p. 487.
[18] *Ibid.*, p. 491.
[19] *Ibid.*, p. 201.
[20] *Ibid.*, p. 198.
[21] *Ibid.*, p. 196.

> *though it should be in perfect subordination to the general authority of the Union*, it would still be, in fact and in theory, an association of States, or a confederacy. The proposed Constitution, so far from implying an abolition of the State governments, makes them constituent parts of the national sovereignty by allowing them a direct representation in the Senate, and leaves in their possession certain exclusive and very important portions of sovereign power. This fully corresponds, in every rational import of the terms, with the idea of a Federal Government. [22]

Within these six selections from Mr. Hamilton's contributions to the *Federalist Papers*, we find gross inconsistencies with respect to the question of sovereignty and the new Federal Constitution, as well as a highly significant false definition of what constitutes a "Confederate Republic." Within the *Federalist*, No. 81, as we have demonstrated, Mr. Hamilton acknowledged that the States are sovereign. In the *Federalist*, No. 82, he again assigned sovereignty to the States of the Union. In the *Federalist*, No. 33, however, he advocated a so-called divided sovereignty under the new Constitution between the States and a "nation." In the *Federalist*, No. 32, Alexander Hamilton stated that the States would possess sovereignty under the new compact, and that this would not be a partial sovereignty or sovereignty shared with a "nation," but a "complete sovereignty." Strangely, however, he did not acknowledge the sovereignty of the people, but claimed that such "complete sovereignty" was vested in the government of each State. And, finally, within the Federalist, No. 9, he advocated both a divided sovereignty and a "national sovereignty."

As is evident, Alexander Hamilton's various explanations of sovereignty within the *Federalist Papers* constituted an exercise in confusion and befuddlement. Whether Mr. Hamilton was confused as to the true nature of sovereignty under the proposed compact, or whether he hoped to confound his readers, is a matter for speculation. Whatever explanation seems more plausible, it is clear that he claimed that sovereignty was vested in the States, that sovereignty was vested in the State governments, that sovereignty was vested in the Federal Government, and that sovereignty was vested in a consolidated American Nation. While acknowledging that the States enjoyed complete sovereignty, Mr. Hamilton claimed that sovereignty was divided between the States and a consolidated Nation.

Alexander Hamilton's definition of a Confederate Republic within the *Federalist*, No. 9, is especially intriguing. At first glance, it appears that Mr. Hamilton was paying homage to the States' Rights School of Thought by plainly acknowledging that, under the Constitution of 1787, the States would be sovereign and would together constitute a Federal Republic or, what is an

[22] *Ibid.*, p. 76.

equivalent expression, a Confederate Republic.

Upon closer examination, however, several disturbing concepts within that essay come to light. It should be noted, for example, that Mr. Hamilton, while referring to the system of government as a "confederacy," advocated a "national sovereignty." Although the States, it would appear from his explanation, might possess a so-called partial sovereignty, such sovereignty was supposedly vested, not in the people of each State, but in their State *government*, a concept that is highly un-American in principle. Finally, it should be noted that, within this essay, Mr. Hamilton defined a Confederate Republic as an association of two or more States that results in the creation of a new consolidated State.

Alexander Hamilton's definition of a Federal Republic differed significantly from the commonly accepted definition given by such noted luminaries as Emmerich de Vattel in his celebrated *Law of Nations*. The true definition of a Federal Republic, of course, is a political alliance between sovereign States. The alliance, needless to say, is neither a State in itself nor is it sovereign. The only States within a Federal Republic are the members of the Federal Union, who alone possess sovereignty.

After the adoption of the Constitution of 1787, it was a common practice of the consolidators to attempt to subvert the American Theory of Government by insisting that the adoption of the federal compact somehow created a consolidated Nation or State of America, and that this consolidated State should at least "share" sovereignty with the real States in the Union, if not possess all sovereignty. Of course, no such consolidated State of America existed then, or now exists, and the true objective was, and is, to steal sovereignty from the States and transfer it to the Government of the United States, under the pretense of vesting such sovereignty in a consolidated Nation of Americans.

Regarding Alexander Hamilton's conduct during the Ratification Period, historian Richard B. Morris noted:

> *The Federalist* papers reflect a certain divergence of opinion between Hamilton and Madison on the role of the States in the new Federal Government. Hamilton saw the proposed Constitution as designed to establish a "consolidated system," one in which the States would be subordinated to the authority of the Union. In *Federalist* No. 22 he asserts: "The fabric of American empire ought to rest on the solid basis of the consent of the people." Madison, on the other hand, felt that the people's assent to the Constitution was to be given not as individuals but through their respective States, and that the act establishing the Constitution would be "federal" rather than "national." Hamilton believed that the powerful States and State machines menaced popular liberty and that the Federal Government was the bulwark of the people's rights. However, *he could not afford to be too blunt in expressing his views during the contest over ratification*, and he constantly sought to reassure

> the States' Rights politicians that State sovereignty would not be jeopardized and that the first loyalty of the citizens would be to their own States. [emphasis added] [23]

The Formation of Political Parties

As soon as the new Federal Constitution had been ratified by the requisite number of States, steps were taken to create the new Federal Government even before the few reluctant States had resolved to join the new Union. George Washington of Virginia was unanimously elected as the first President of the United States, and the First Congress convened at the temporary site of the new government in New York City. For his Cabinet, President Washington appointed four men, including Alexander Hamilton as the first Secretary of the Treasury and Thomas Jefferson as the first Secretary of State.

In a letter written to William Short on January 8, 1825, Thomas Jefferson explained the conditions he had found upon arriving in New York City to assume his new duties as Secretary of State in the Washington Administration. He also explained how the zeal for monarchy evolved over ensuing years into a conspiracy to consolidate all powers in the Federal Government.

As Mr. Jefferson wrote:

> When I arrived at New York in 1790, to take a part in the administration,...I found a state of things, in the general society of the place, which I could not have supposed possible. Being a stranger there, I was feasted from table to table, at large set dinners, the parties generally from twenty to thirty....I was astonished to find the general prevalence of monarchical sentiments, insomuch that in maintaining those of Republicanism, I had always the whole company on my hands, never scarcely finding among them a single co-advocate in that argument, unless some old member of Congress happened to be present. The farthest that any one would go in support of the Republican features of our new government, would be to say, "the present constitution is well as a beginning, and may be allowed a fair trial, but it is, in fact, only a stepping stone to something better." Among their writers, Denny, the editor of the Portfolio, who was a kind of oracle with them, and styled the Addison of America, openly avowed his preference of monarchy over all other forms of government, prided himself on the avowal, and maintained it by argument freely and without reserve, in his publications. I do not, myself, know that the Essex junto of Boston were monarchists, but I have always heard it so said, and never doubted.
>
> ...Monarchy, to be sure, is now defeated, and they wish it should be forgotten that it was ever advocated. They see that it is desperate, and treat its

[23] Richard B. Morris (ed.), *The Basic Ideas of Alexander Hamilton*, Washington Square Press, Inc., New York, 1956, p. 223.

> imputation to them as a calumny, and I verily believe that none of them have it now in direct aim. Yet the spirit is not done away. The same party takes now what they deem the next best ground, the consolidation of the government; the giving to the Federal member of the government, by unlimited constructions of the Constitution, a control over all the functions of the States, and the concentration of all power ultimately at Washington. [24]

The new Federal Government had scarcely commenced its operations when Alexander Hamilton, from his strategic position as Secretary of the Treasury, made his move to inaugurate a campaign intended to subvert the Federal Constitution, undermine State sovereignty, and convert the Republic into a plutocracy in which the affairs of the government would be conducted for the primary benefit of an *aristocracy of wealth*. It was Mr. Hamilton's stated view that there were only two ways in which an unconstitutional, supreme National Government could be erected on the ruins of the sovereign States. One method was to utilize *force* – to usurp the reserved powers of the States and to coerce obedience by military might. The other method was to appeal to the *interests* of those who would be willing to support the ambitions of consolidating politicians in exchange for pecuniary advantages dispensed by the Federal Government. Although the first method was not entirely ruled out, the Father of the Consolidating School resolved to rely primarily on the second method.

Mr. Hamilton, who boasted that *a national debt is a national blessing*, promptly proposed a number of measures that would tax all Americans for the specific benefit of the commercial and industrial interests, which happened to be primarily situated in the Northern quarter of the Union. These measures advocated by the Secretary of the Treasury were modeled after the corrupt practices of the British Government, and in copying the bad practices of that government, Mr. Hamilton verified the veracity of an observation made by the Adam Smith in *The Wealth of Nations*, that, "There is no art which one government sooner learns of another, than that of draining money from the pockets of the people." [25]

In his book, *Inquiry into the Origin and Course of Political Parties in the United States*, which was published posthumously in 1867, ex-President Martin Van Buren summarized the fiscal and economic policies of the Hamilton System as follows:

> The measures which Hamilton deemed indispensable to the success of the new government, in addition to those authorized by the Constitution,

---

[24] Richard S. Poppen (ed.), *Thomas Jefferson: The Declaration of Independence and Letters, Addresses, Excepts and Aphorisms*, St. Louis, 1904, pp. 146-147.

[25] Adam Smith, *An Inquiry into the Nature and Causes of the Wealth of Nations*, The Modern Library, New York, 1965 (orig. pub. 1776), p. 813.

> consisted of
>
> *First.* A funding system upon the English plan, with authority to assume the separate debts of the States;
>
> *Second.* A National Bank; and,
>
> *Third.* An unrestricted exercise by Congress of the power to raise money, and the employment of the national revenue in patronizing individual, class, and corporate interests, according to the plan detailed in his report, nominally on manufactures, but embracing an infinite variety of other concerns. [26]

Commenting on the effects of the Hamiltonian System, Mr. Van Buren wrote:

> The advantages Hamilton anticipated from these measures consisted of the effect which the fact of their establishment would have upon every question of constitutional power, the popularity and political influence which the administration would acquire in and through their organization, and greater than all, of their inevitable influence upon the future character of the institutions of the country....If he had succeeded in these points and secured his advances, he would have been fully warranted in regarding the enumeration of the powers of Congress contained in the Constitution as a sham, and the brief clause he proposed in the Convention, giving to the national legislature power to pass all laws which it should judge necessary to the common defense and general welfare of the Union, as inserted in its place. [27]

Even in foreign affairs, Alexander Hamilton attempted to exert a strong influence in favor of the chief enemy of the United States at that time, Great Britain. In their textbook, *The United States: The History of a Republic*, historians Richard Hofstadter, William Miller, and Daniel Aaron noted that Mr. Hamilton, during his service in the Washington Administration, was, in fact, working as a British secret agent:

> For years, while serving as Washington's closest adviser, Hamilton had also served as a secret consultant – "No. 7" in the British cipher – with British secret agents in the United States....As early as October, 1789, Hamilton told Major George Beckwith, his secret contact reporting on American affairs: "I have always preferred a connexion with you, to that of any other country, *we think in English*, and have a similarity of prejudices and predilections." Thereafter, Hamilton let nothing pass to Britain's disadvantage. [28]

---

[26] Martin Van Buren, *Inquiry into the Origin and Course of Political Parties in the United States*, Augustus M. Kelley, Publishers, New York, 1967 (orig. pub. 1867), p. 140.
[27] *Ibid.*, pp. 141-142.
[28] Richard Hofstadter, William Miller, and Daniel Aaron, *The United States: The History of a Republic*, Prentice-Hall, Inc., Englewood Cliffs, 1967, pp. 193-194.

The British Government watched with keen interest the development and adoption of the Hamilton System by the young American Republic. In London, there was no doubt as to the true consequences of Mr. Hamilton's measures. "Let the Americans," said William Pitt the elder, "adopt their funding system, and go into their banking institutions, and their boasted independence will be a mere phantom." [29]

No one knew better than Alexander Hamilton that the measures he proposed were palpably unconstitutional. The proposal for the First Bank of the United States, in fact, was made by the Secretary of the Treasury in spite of the knowledge that the Philadelphia Convention of 1787 had considered giving to the Federal Government the power to incorporate, but had rejected the proposal precisely because such a power might be used to incorporate a National Bank.

As Mr. Hamilton's schemes became known throughout the Union, those who stood to gain from his proposed fiscal and economic system became his zealous advocates and supporters, while those who were devoted to honest government and the sovereignty of the States began to unite in order to form an opposition faction. Within the Congress, there arose statesmen, including James Madison, who openly voiced opposition to the Hamiltonian system, using the word "unconstitutional" to describe its policies and acts. Yet, it was within President Washington's Cabinet where Mr. Hamilton encountered the man who was destined to become his primary adversary. On virtually every subject that arose for discussion at Cabinet meetings, the Secretary of the Treasury found that the Secretary of State was determined to oppose him. "In these discussions," Thomas Jefferson wrote years later, "Hamilton and myself were daily pitted in the Cabinet like two cocks." [30]

The two factions quickly matured into formal political parties. Those who championed the Hamiltonian System called their faction the *Federalist Party,* and their undisputed leader was Alexander Hamilton of New York. The name selected by the consolidating school was ironic, in that the principles they advocated were precisely the opposite of what their party name implied. In adopting this title for their party, the Federalists undoubtedly hoped to establish in the public mind a link between themselves and those who had advocated adoption of the Constitution during the Ratification Period.

The opposition party, which styled itself the *Democratic-Republican Party* – also referred to as the *Federal Republican Party* or the *Republican Party,* for short – rallied around the leadership of Thomas Jefferson of Virginia. Al-

---

[29] William M. Gouge, *The Curse of Paper-Money and Banking,* Greenwood Press, Publishers, New York, 1968 (orig. pub. 1833), quoted on p. 1.
[30] Andrew M. Allison, *The Real Thomas Jefferson,* Second Edition, National Center for Constitutional Studies, Washington, D.C., 1983, quoted on p. 162.

though the Washington Administration has been described by some historians as Federalist, the truth is that George Washington personally remained aloof from both parties. President Washington, it is true, generally did approve of and support Mr. Hamilton's measures, but his support was based on a misplaced confidence in the Secretary of the Treasury. As Mr. Jefferson noted, the President did not understand the true nature, implications, and far-reaching consequences of Mr. Hamilton's fiscal, economic, and political maneuvers.

In regard to where the two political parties stood on the question of the sovereignty of the people of the States, J. Clarence Stonebraker noted in his book, *The Unwritten South*:

> These two parties were termed, the one the Jeffersonian, and the other the Hamiltonian. The one holding that the people should be masters of the government; the other that the government should be the masters of the people. The one being in favor of a government of the people with powers cautiously limited and clearly defined in the Constitution, the other in favor of what they called "a strong government," with similar powers to a monarchy, without its name. [31]

It was obvious from the very beginning of the Republic that these two political parties represented divergent interests that would endure for as long as the United States existed. Although specific political parties would come and go over the course of American history, these two opposing and competing *schools of thought and action* would continue to divide the American people. The *Jeffersonians* of all succeeding generations – who would advocate federalism and constitutionally limited government – were the political heirs of Thomas Jefferson and belonged to what we may term the *States' Rights School of Thought.* The *Hamiltonians* of all succeeding generations – who would advocate a supreme, sovereign National Government – were the political heirs of Alexander Hamilton and belonged to what we may term the *Consolidating School of Thought.*

The word "consolidation," as used here, means a *consolidation of the government* by the usurpation of the reserved rights and powers of the sovereign States. Although the word was widely employed and commonly understood in Nineteenth Century America, today this concept is more often referred to by the expression, *centralization of power.* Inasmuch as we are primarily interested in presenting the conspiracy to centralize powers during the ante-bellum period of our history, we will use the terminology more popular during that period – consolidation.

The high tide of the Federalist Party came with the 1796 election of John Adams to succeed George Washington as President of the United States.

---

[31] J. Clarence Stonebraker, *The Unwritten South*, Eighth Edition, 1908, p. 15.

While this election was clearly a victory for the Federalists, the fact that Thomas Jefferson was elected to the office of Vice-President of the United States gave hope to the Democratic-Republicans that the reign of the Federalists would be short-lived.

Fearful of the growing popularity of the opposition party, the Federalists resolved to curtail freedom of speech and make criticism of President Adams a crime by passing the infamous Alien and Sedition Acts. The passage of those acts presented the young Republic with its first major political crisis in which the freedom of the American people was a stake. Determined to save the liberties of the people, James Madison and John Taylor of Caroline collaborated to induce the State of Virginia to enact the Virginia Resolutions of 1798. And Thomas Jefferson penned similar resolutions that were adopted by the State of Kentucky. These historically famous *Kentucky and Virginia Resolutions of 1798* boldly asserted that the States of the Federal Union were sovereign and that, in cases of a dangerous and unconstitutional federal action, a sovereign State could interpose its authority and nullify the federal act to arrest the progress of evil.

Although the Federalists condemned this action by two sovereign States, insisting that the principles they espoused were rank heresy, the Kentucky and Virginia Resolutions of 1798 were popular with the American people and succeeded in rallying public sentiment against the consolidating school. In the 1800 Presidential election, Thomas Jefferson succeeded in securing enough votes to throw the election into the House of Representatives. A bitter contest erupted within the House over the question of who should become the third President of the United States, Mr. Jefferson or Aaron Burr. As ironic as it might seem, Alexander Hamilton's personal dislike of Mr. Burr exceeded his political approbation of Mr. Jefferson, which induced him to throw his support to Thomas Jefferson. By this means, the Hermit of Monticello was elected as the third U.S. President in what many Democratic-Republicans hailed as the great *Revolution of 1800.*

The Federalist Party seemed to sense that its demise was inevitable. One of the last acts in public office by President Adams was to make his infamous *midnight appointments* in a desperate effort to place as many Federalists in appointed positions as possible before Mr. Jefferson was inaugurated into office.

The election of Thomas Jefferson to the Presidency was indeed the beginning of the end for the Federalist Party. A few years afterwards, that party received another blow when Alexander Hamilton was killed in a duel with Aaron Burr. Many Federalists lamented that, with Mr. Hamilton's death, the brains had been blown out of the party. Although the Federalist Party remained in existence for more than a decade after Mr. Hamilton's untimely death, it faced a number of defeats in one election after another, as it headed slowly into oblivion.

Even though the Republic was still in its infancy at the time of Mr. Hamilton's death, it had become obvious to a number of Federalists that the States' Rights School of Thought was too strong and too popular with the American people to be defeated in the ordinary course of political action and debate. Alexander Hamilton himself realized that nothing short of a civil war, or a War Between the States, would be sufficient to force consolidation on the resisting people of the United States. We know that Mr. Hamilton entertained such thoughts, not because of any accusation from his political enemies, but by the acknowledgement of one his most admiring political associates, Gouverneur Morris of Pennsylvania.

In a letter written to Governor Aaron Odgen in December of 1804, Mr. Morris stated:

> Our poor friend Hamilton bestrode his hobby [to subvert the Constitution and establish a consolidated government] to the great annoyance of his friends and not without injury to himself. More a theoretic than a practical man, he was not sufficiently convinced that a system may be good in itself and bad in relation to particular circumstances. He well knew that his favorite form was inadmissible unless as the result of civil war; and I suppose that his belief in what he called an approaching crisis arose from a conviction that the kind of government most suitable, in his opinion, to this extensive country, could be established in no other way. [32]

A Balance of Power

Thomas Jefferson was easily re-elected to a second term as President of the United States, after which he voluntarily refused to run again for political office. But the popularity of the Democratic-Republicans was at high tide, setting the stage for what historians have termed the *Virginia Dynasty*. When Mr. Jefferson declined to serve a third term in office, the Democratic-Republican Party nominated James Madison for the Presidency. Following Mr. Madison's two-terms in office, the party nominated James Monroe for that office. He also served two terms in the Presidency.

The repeated success of the Democratic-Republican Party proved that most Americans in the early days of the Republic overwhelmingly rejected the thoughts and deeds of the consolidating school and enthusiastically supported the States' Rights School of Thought. For nearly a quarter of a century, the Jeffersonian advocates of States' Rights held the dominant hand in the affairs of

---

[32] Martin Van Buren, *Op. cit.*, quoted on pp. 80-81.

the Republic, as the remarkable longevity of the Virginia Dynasty attests.

So disillusioned were the Federalists that, when war with England broke out in 1812, many of them openly and enthusiastically sided with the enemy. At their Hartford Convention of 1814, a number of Federalists actually favored the secession of the New England States from the Federal Union, some undoubtedly having in mind a reunification with the old mother country, Great Britain. But before the Federalists could carry out such schemes, they were greatly embarrassed by the stunning victory of General Andrew Jackson in the Battle of New Orleans and the end of the war with an American victory.

Shortly after the War of 1812 ended, Matthew Carey's book, *The Olive Branch*, was published. Within this remarkable work, its author revealed the true extent of the nefarious and shameful acts of the New England Federalists during the war and offered an olive branch on behalf of New England to the other quarters of the Federal Union, in the hopes of securing peace and harmony in the Federal Republic. As Mr. Carey explained, the New England Federalists went far beyond merely contemplating secession from the Union. They also engaged in treasonous activities, such as endeavoring to financially cripple the Federal Government and welcoming with open arms the invading British troops during the War of 1812.

The Federalist Party, having been permanently defeated and soundly discredited as a consequence of its treasonous actions, was truly doomed to fade away into oblivion. But before this political party breathed its last dying gasps, the consolidating school was determined to use this party to make one final insult upon the Federal Republic. Observing that the stronghold of the Jeffersonians lay in the Southern quarter of the Union, and that the spirit of Manifest Destiny would result in a number of new States being added to the Union over the course of the next few decades, the consolidators resolved to pursue a strategy to introduce a new, emotional issue in the federal forum that would drive a wedge between North and South. Their goal was to isolate the Southern States to such an extent that, over a period of time, the Southern States would find themselves confronted by an overwhelming, hostile numerical majority arrayed against them.

The proposed admissions of Missouri and Maine into the Federal Union in 1820 provided the opportunity for the consolidating school to make its move. Suddenly, the Hamiltonians feigned shock and moral indignation to discover that chattel slavery existed in the Southern States. Such an horrific evil, they argued, should not be allowed to spread to new States that would enter the Union, but should be quarantined in those Southern States where it already existed. From the ensuing political turmoil that this maneuver engendered emerged the *Missouri Compromise of 1820*, which drew a line across the continent and divided the United States into two sub-confederacies, ironically styled the "Free States" and the "Slave States." By the terms of the Missouri Compromise of 1820, for each new "Slave State" admitted into the Union, a "Free State" would also be admitted, thereby ensuring that the number of "Free States" would always equal the number of "Slave States."

At the time this alarming "compromise" was promulgated, it was widely understood that the motivations of the consolidating school were anything but humanitarian in nature. It was not a genuine concern for the welfare of the slaves in the Southern States that stirred the hearts of the consolidating politicians, but a zeal to acquire a so-called *balance of power* that could ultimately be tipped in favor of the consolidating school. To achieve that objective, they were willing to destroy the fraternal Union of States and divide the American people on a false issue grounded in emotions and passions.

It was immediately obvious to all honest observers that the introduction of slavery as an issue for debate in the federal arena would cultivate emotional hatred toward the Southern States and inflame the feelings of peoples in other parts of the Union. This stratagem was merely a clever adoption of the old divide-and-conquer strategy, employed by the consolidating school to obtain what they could not acquire by honest means.

No one was more alarmed by this turn of events than Thomas Jefferson, who claimed that it filled him with terror, like a fire bell in the night. In a letter to William Pinkney on September 30, 1820, the Sage of Monticello wrote:

> The Missouri question is a mere party trick. The leaders of Federalism, defeated in their schemes of obtaining power by rallying partisans to the principle of monarchism, a principle pf personal not of local division, have changed their tack, and thrown out another barrel to the whale. They are taking advantage of the virtuous feelings of the people to effect a division of parties by a geographical line; they expect that this will insure them, on local principles, the majority they could never obtain on principles of Federalism; but they are still putting their shoulder to the wrong wheel; they are wasting Jeremiads on the miseries of slavery, as if we were advocates for it. Sincerity in their declamations should direct their efforts to the true point of difficulty, and unite their councils with ours in devising some reasonable and practicable plan of getting rid of it. Some of these leaders, if they could attain the power, their ambition would rather use it to keep the Union together, but others have ever had in view its separation....But this scheme of party I leave to those who are to live under its consequences. We who have gone before have performed an honest duty, by putting in the power of our successors a state of happiness which no nation ever before had within their choice. If that choice is to throw it away, the dead will have neither the power nor the right to control them. [33]

[33] Richard S. Poppen (ed.), *Op. cit.*, pp. 129-130.

John Taylor of Caroline was also deeply concerned by this new twist in the strategy of the consolidating school. By splitting the Union into two sub-confederacies and by insisting on the maintenance of a balance of power between those sub-confederacies, Mr. Taylor argued, the stage had been set for a civil war between the rival sub-confederacies, for a civil war is always the end result of a power struggle. Thus, by 1820, the Hamiltonians had laid the groundwork for the War Between the States, a war which Alexander Hamilton himself believed to be necessary to force a consolidated, supreme, sovereign National Government on the American people.

By 1824, the Federalist Party had faded into oblivion. But the consolidating school certainly had not ceased to exist. In another surprising stratagem, the consolidators, upon abandoning their old party, promptly infiltrated the Democratic-Republican Party, and the former Federalists solemnly announced their conversion to Jeffersonian principles. In the Presidential election of 1824, there were no less than four candidates for the Presidency – John Quincy Adams, Andrew Jackson, Henry Clay, and William Crawford – each one claiming to be the true candidate of the Party of Jefferson, but all save Mr. Crawford dubbed pseudo-Republicans by Mr. Jefferson himself. The result of this political turmoil was the election of the consolidator, John Quincy Adams, to the Presidency and the destruction of the Democratic-Republican Party.

During the Administration of President John Quincy Adams, the Jeffersonians reorganized into the *Democratic Party*, while the Hamiltonians formed the *National Republican Party*. In the election of 1828, Andrew Jackson of the Democratic Party was elected to the Presidency. But when President Jackson threatened to use military action to coerce the State of South Carolina during the nullification crisis, the Jeffersonians temporarily abandoned the Democratic Party to reorganize as the short-lived *Anti-Jackson Democratic Party*. And by the end of President Jackson's second term in office, the Hamiltonians had once again reorganized in the new *Whig Party*. The political chaos and confusion that abounded during this period is evident from the fact that John C. Calhoun of South Carolina was the Vice-President of the United States during the Administrations of both President Adams and President Jackson.

Toward the end of his life, Thomas Jefferson clearly foresaw the dangers to the United States that lay in the future and repeatedly warned his countrymen of the threat posed by the consolidating school. Typical of such warnings are these words expressed by Mr. Jefferson:

> I see with the deepest affliction the rapid strides with which the federal branch of our government is advancing towards the usurpation of all the rights reserved to the States, and the consolidation in itself of all powers, domestic and foreign; and that, too, by constructions which, if legitimate, leave

no limits to their power. [34]

A government of unlimited power – *a sovereign government* – that was the danger which Thomas Jefferson foresaw and sought to warn his countrymen to avoid. With his death on July 4, 1826, the last survivors of the generation of our Founding Fathers were quickly passing from the scene. That generation had successfully waged the War of Independence and established a Federal Union between the sovereign States. That generation had also witnessed a terrific struggle between the forces of consolidation and those determined to preserve constitutionally limited government, a struggle lead by the two titans of that period, Alexander Hamilton and Thomas Jefferson.

So great was the influence of these two political leaders in the American mind that it was not uncommon for children born during the early years of the Republic to be named in honor of one or the other. When the Southern States seceded from the Union and created the Confederate States of America in 1861, they chose Jefferson Davis, who had been named in honor of Thomas Jefferson, as their President. Ironically, the man selected to become the Vice-President of the Confederate States of America was Alexander Hamilton Stephens of Georgia, who had been named in honor of the Father of the Consolidating School.

The Marriage of Plutocracy and Socialism

Despite the early victories of the States' Rights school over the consolidating school during the days of Mr. Jefferson and Mr. Hamilton, the consolidating school was determined to ultimately win the great struggle for power and control over the Government of the United States. But to accomplish that objective, they realized that a change in strategy was required, particularly in how the American people perceived the two opposing schools of thought and action.

Initially, the consolidators had made no attempt to conceal their disdain and contempt for the American people, and they openly proclaimed their preference for an elitist or aristocratic rule founded on wealth and privilege, a system which political scientists often refer to as *plutocracy*. Within the Constitutional Convention, for example, Alexander Hamilton openly professed his dislike for the citizenry and urged the delegates to adopt a plan of government that would cater to the interests of the rich. And when the Convention was considering the composition of the United States Senate, Gouverneur Morris

---

[34] Samuel B. Pettengill, *Jefferson: The Forgotten Man*, America's Future, New York, 1938, quoted on p. 83.

suggested that the upper House of Congress be reserved as the domain for the wealthy elite in society, saying that he hoped the Senate, thus constituted, would show America and the world *the weight of aristocracy*. The Convention, needless to say, rejected that proposal and instead created a Senate that would serve as a living monument to the sovereign equality of the States.

The succeeding generation of consolidators recognized the error of being too candid in support of plutocracy and resolved to mix demagoguery and flattery of the people with their drive to transfer sovereignty from the people to the Government of the United States. In addition, the new generation of Hamiltonians resolved to greatly expand the system of plunder and redistribution of wealth by advocating internal improvements and protective tariffs.

In advocating the federal funding of *Internal Improvements*, the consolidating school sought to use public monies to bankroll the domestic economic development of favored States through the construction of roads, canals, schools, and other infrastructure. The States benefiting from such federal funding, needless to say, would naturally tend to patronize those politicians who were bestowing them with "free" money from the public treasury. And those business enterprises that profited from such construction projects would obviously become the zealous supporters of their financial benefactors. Of course, there was, is not, and never will be, any such thing as "free" money bestowed by the Federal Government. Whatever monies it doles out must first be taken from the American people through taxation. The system of internal improvements advocated by the consolidating school, therefore, constituted a system of plunder, redistribution of wealth, and corruption. As such, it was decidedly socialistic in nature, representing the marriage between socialism and plutocracy.

Protective tariffs were promoted by the consolidating school for the same purpose and objective. The consolidators openly proclaimed that the tariffs they advocated were intended, not to fund the legitimate activities of the Federal Government, but to provide special privileges for favored commercial and industrial interests who would benefit from the stifling of foreign competition afforded by high tariffs on imported goods. The objective of protective tariffs was to replace the constitutional *free enterprise* economic system with an unconstitutional socialistic system founded on government intervention in and regulation of the marketplace.

No knew better than the consolidating politicians that the system they advocated was subversive of the Federal Constitution. Although that Constitution did delegate the power to tax – including the power to levy tariffs – the power to tax was restricted in its purpose. Congress had been delegated the power to tax only to fund the enumerated powers and legitimate ends defined by the Constitution. Congress had, for example, the power to raise and maintain an army. To fund that army, Congress could rightfully levy taxes, including tariffs. But no power had been delegated to Congress to promote or encourage favored industries and commercial activities, for that would be a clear violation of its obligation to provide for the *general welfare* of the United States. Thus, tariffs levied for the purpose of taxing all Americans for the benefit of favored interest groups were palpably unconstitutional.

As a consequence of these policies based on plunder and avarice, new words soon entered into the political vocabulary of the ante-bellum period of the Republic, including *pork barrel* and *logrolling*. And the corrupting effects of these pernicious public policies had a devastating influence on the character of both the American people and the politicians who were elected to office. Under the influence of these policies, politicians would not be elected based on their patriotism or their record of noble public service, but on their ability to secure largesse from the public treasury, and a politician might be required to explain to his constituents why he had not managed to acquire even greater federal subsidies for his district.

The effects of such a system on the character of the voting public was even more alarming. Such a system was deliberately designed to encourage the American people to look to the Government of the United States for subsidies and handouts, and far too many Americans quickly demonstrated a willingness to sell their votes to the highest bidder in each election. Had an unprincipled politician attempted to purchase votes with his own money, he would have been denounced as thoroughly corrupt and his actions would have been deemed criminal. Yet, if that same politician offered to buy votes with monies from the federal treasury, he would all too often be hailed as a great statesman and be sent to Washington to serve in a public office.

The fact that the favored interest groups benefiting from this system of plunder and patronage lay primarily in the Northern States added a geographic or *sectional dimension* to the corrupt system. Southerners watched in dismay and alarm as a golden stream of treasure flowed steadily from their States into the coffers of favored monied interests in the Northern States, due solely to the deliberate and unfair interference in economic affairs by the Federal Government. Adding to the concerns of the Southern members of the Union, the consolidators were determined to wage tactical, sectional warfare over the issue of chattel slavery, while abolitionists, growing bolder and more radical with each passing year, loudly denounced Southerners as evil and vehemently cursed the Federal Constitution because it recognized the property rights of the slaveholders of the Southern States.

Unlike their Federalist predecessors, the National Republicans, later renamed the Whigs, proved to be clever politicians and ruthless demagogues. Their greatest contribution to the consolidating conspiracy was to marry plutocracy and socialism by combining the Hamiltonian System with demagogic appeals to unlimited numerical majority rule and by appealing to the greed and avarice of the general public. The Whigs boldly asserted, for example, that their protective tariffs translated into more jobs and higher wages for working Americans, but conveniently failed to add that those same protective tariffs also meant artificially inflated prices for goods and services consumed by the American people.

Although the consolidators of the Whig Party feigned loyalty to "the people," their primary loyalty was always to what John Taylor of Caroline called the *monied aristocracy*. This economic power, situated chiefly in the New England States, has been in existence since the earliest years of the Republic and has been referred to by various names over the years, but its power and control over the affairs of government have been remarkably consistent and extensive. Martin Van Buren referred to it as the *money power*, the Pujo Committee at the beginning of the Twentieth Century called it the *money trust*, and a Dwight D. Eisenhower used the expression *military-industrial complex* to describe it. In more recent years, this concentrated economic and political power has been referred to as the *Establishment*, or more precisely the *Left-Wing Establishment*. Various terms have been used over the years to refer to those who belong to or represent this economic-political power, ranging from *international bankers* to the *Insiders*. By whatever terminology we use to describe this power and its members and supporters, this has been the power ultimately behind the consolidating conspiracy in the United States of America.

When this marriage of plutocracy and socialism was first presented to the public, it was promoted under the ironic label of the *American System*. The acknowledged *Father of the American System* was Henry Clay, the Kentucky politician of ante-bellum fame whom Andrew Jackson once referred to as the *Judas of the West* for his betrayal of genuine Western interests in favor of the interests of the monied aristocracy. Daniel Webster of Massachusetts soon added his prestige to the American System by enthusiastically promoting this criminal system of plutocracy and socialism.

In his book, *The Real Lincoln*, which was published in 2002, Professor Thomas J. DiLorenzo offered insights into the sinister nature of the American System and the characters of its principal advocates during the ante-bellum years of the Republic. Regarding Henry Clay, the system's founding father, for instance, Professor DiLorenzo stated that he "was the political heir to Alexander Hamilton and so championed centralized governmental power driven by political patronage" for the benefit of the monied aristocracy. [35]

The corrupting influence of Henry Clay's misnamed American System,

---

[35] Thomas J. DiLorenzo, *The Real Lincoln: A New Look at Abraham Lincoln, His Agenda, and an Unnecessary War*, Forum, 2002, p. 62.

Professor DiLorenzo noted, could be seen in the Kentuckian's activities from 1822 to 1824. With $40,000 in personal debt, this politician left Congress for two years in 1822 to serve the Second Bank of the United States as a general counsel. As compensation for his services to the bank, both as general counsel and as a United States Senator, Henry Clay received in just two years what amounted to one million dollars in current dollars.

As Professor DiLorenzo pointed out, Senator Daniel Webster was even more personally corrupt than Senator Clay:

> Another Whig, Daniel Webster, never even bothered to resign from Congress before collecting "compensation" from the bank. He simply demanded a "retainer" from the bank as a payoff for being one of the bank's chief spokespersons, along with Clay, in Congress. He once wrote to Nicholas Biddle, the bank's president, "I believe my retainer has not been renewed or *refreshed* as usual. If it be wished that my relation to the Bank should be continued, it may be well to send me the usual retainer." [36]

Regarding the criminal American System promoted by Daniel Webster and Henry Clay, Professor DiLorenzo stated:

> Economists have a...word for the combination of policies known as the American System – namely, *mercantilism*. As defined by economist Murray Rothbard, mercantilism, "which reached its height in the Europe of the seventeenth and eighteenth centuries," was "a system of statism which employed economic fallacy to build up a structure of imperial state power, as well as special subsidy and monopolistic privilege to individuals or groups favored by the state." More specifically, protectionism (legal protection from international competition through trade tariffs and quotas) was a means by which a government could dispense favors to well-connected (and well-financed) special interest groups, which in turn provided financial and other support for the politicians dispensing the favors. It benefits both those industries that are protected from competition and the politicians, but harms everyone else. Consumers pay higher prices because of the reduced competition, and they also have fewer choices. Potential competitors are kept out of the market, which means a loss of jobs. Protectionism always reduces the wealth of nations – which is why Adam Smith gave his magnum opus that very name.
>
> The special interest groups that benefit from protectionism have always employed small armies of intellectuals and publicists whose job is primarily to confuse the public about their true intentions. They have always attempted to convince the public that economic policies that in reality only benefit a small special interest group are good for "the nation."...
>
> The same can be said for another element of mercantilism – tax-funded subsidies to politically well connected businesses and industries.

[36] *Ibid.*, p. 65.

> These subsidies generally benefit only those businesses that are lucky enough to get them, at the expense of the taxpayers generally. Much of the public has finally caught on to this fact; today, the progressive-sounding phrase, "internal improvement subsidies" is usually denigrated (and rightly so) as "corporate welfare" or "welfare for the well-to-do."
>
> Nationalized banking was always part and parcel of the mercantilist agenda as well, for mercantilists have always advocated having the government simply print paper money in order to finance their special-interest subsidies....
>
> Obviously, mercantilism has the potential for generating a great deal of political corruption, as is always the case with any system in which governments are empowered to dispense taxpayers' revenues to special-interest groups, rather than being restricted to spending money only on things that benefit the public as a whole. But it is exactly this potential for corruption, and the ability to literally buy votes and political support with taxpayers' funds, that attracts power-hungry politicians to mercantilism. It may be bad for the economy, but it has great potential for advancing one's political career. The Whigs always understood this perfectly clearly, which is why they made mercantilism, euphemistically referred to as "the American System," their top policy goal....
>
> All of these policies tend to generate a centralization of governmental power as well, which is why they were the focus of American political debate from the time of the founding until the 1860s. At that point the debate was ended; the consolidators, led by Lincoln and the Republican Party, had won the debate, literally, by force of arms. [37]

Until such time as the consolidators were able to "win" the great contest between consolidation and States' Rights by resorting to brute force, and thus establish for their side the so-called verdict of history, they were confronted with the difficult task of attempting to justify their criminal system of fraud and plunder by argument and persuasion. The States' Rights school did not merely assail the consolidating system because it was based on grand theft. They also accused it – and correctly so – of being *unconstitutional* and *subversive* of our system of government.

The States' Rights school understood all too well that the Federal Government could and would *control* whatever it subsidized. If that government subsidized agriculture, for instance, it would soon control agriculture. And, as Thomas Jefferson wisely observed, if we were ever directed from Washington when to sow and when to eat, we would soon want bread. If the American System of the Whig Party became entrenched in our political system, the States' Rights school realized, all power would ultimately be centralized in Washington, and the Federal Government would control everyone and regulate everything on behalf of the monied aristocracy. The inevitable result of the consoli-

---

[37] *Ibid.*, pp. 56-59.

dating conspiracy would be the replacement of the constitutional Republic with a draconian Leviathan State.

The Orator of Consolidation

Confronted with the stern opposition of the States' Rights school, the consolidating school was forced to defend its unconstitutional system by insisting that its socialistic American System was as all-American as Mom and Apple Pie. If the name selected for this un-American system was insufficient to deceive the unwary, then the Consolidating School of Thought would resort to presenting distorted accounts of the historical development of the United States to deny that the States really are sovereign and to advance theories that would supposedly justify a sovereign National Government sufficiently empowered to redistribute wealth.

Developing the Consolidating School of Thought, however, was not an easy task, since all the available facts proved that the States' Rights School of Thought was intellectually honest and correct. It was not until the middle of the ante-bellum period of our Republic that a gifted orator could be found to advance the cause of the consolidating school by enshrining it in the rhetoric of the demagogue. Although Daniel Webster was thoroughly corrupt as a politician and possessed manners that often offended even his admirers, he truly was a gifted orator, possessing a booming voice that resonated in the Senate chamber during his famous debate with Robert Y. Hayne in 1830 and his equally famous debate with John C. Calhoun in 1833. For his rhetorical contributions to the cause of the consolidating conspiracy, Daniel Webster may be considered America's greatest *Orator of Consolidation*.

Even after Mr. Webster's death, the consolidating school has gone to great lengths to honor one its own. Although Daniel Webster never attained the level of deification that Abraham Lincoln achieved in consolidationalist folklore, he has often been reverently referred to as America's greatest expounder of the Constitution, as a man who put patriotism above sectional feelings, and as America's greatest orator. Throughout the Northern States, schoolchildren were taught to quote Senator Webster's words about the Union and liberty being one and the same forevermore, in spite of the fact that such sentiments contradicted the principles of the Declaration of Independence, which asserted that it was not only the right of the people – *but their solemn duty* – to alter or abolish their government should it become oppressive, and in spite of the fact that it contradicted Thomas Jefferson's wise maxim that eternal vigilance – and not a blind, childlike trust in government – was the true price of liberty. One of the myths that arose in regard to the Massachusetts politician contends that Mr. Webster's debating skills were so great that he could even win a debate with the Devil himself.

Yet, as Senator Webster himself once observed, there is nothing as strange or as fascinating as the truth, and the truth is that Daniel Webster, the man, and Daniel Webster, the legend, were two very different people. He was, from the very start of his political career, a sectional man, interested only in the welfare of the shipping, commercial, and industrial interests of the New England States. The public record reveals that he was not devoted to high and lofty principles, but to sectional aggrandizement, and that he was very inconsistent in his constitutional principles.

Born in the State of New Hampshire, Mr. Webster studied law and graduated from Dartmouth College in 1801. Following a legal apprenticeship, he opened a law practice in Portsmouth, New Hampshire, in 1807. A firm advocate of the Hamiltonian System, Mr. Webster joined the Federalist Party and stayed in that party until the bitter end. In 1812, he was elected to the U.S. House of Representatives to represent the Granite State in the lower house of Congress, where his voice was consistently raised in opposition to the defensive measures of the United States in the War of 1812. After two more terms, Daniel Webster left Congress in 1816 and relocated to Boston, Massachusetts.

In 1823, Mr. Webster was again elected to Congress, this time representing the State of Massachusetts, and in 1827 he was elected by his State to the Senate of the United States, where he promptly formed a working relationship with Henry Clay to advance the cause of Mr. Clay's American System. In 1836, Senator Webster ran for the Presidency as one of three Whig Party candidates vying for that high office, but he carried only his own State. For the remainder of his life, the Massachusetts Senator vainly aspired to the Presidency. But the closest he could come to such a high position was to serve as the Secretary of State in the Administration of President Millard Fillmore.

At the time Daniel Webster's political career was launched, Thomas Jefferson was the President of the United States. Great Britain, still hostile toward the young Republic, was increasingly violating American rights on the high seas. In response, Mr. Jefferson urged the adoption of the Embargo, in an effort to avoid war with what was then the most powerful Nation on earth. The mercantile interests, largely concentrated in New England, bitterly resented the Embargo, even though it was chiefly to protect their commercial and shipping interests that the Federal Government had acted. Suffering from an economic recession caused by the Embargo, the New England Federalists directed their hatred toward President Jefferson, and their case was expressed in the form of a pamphlet written anonymously by Daniel Webster.

"The Government of the United States is a delegated, *limited* government," Mr. Webster wrote, insisting that the Embargo was unconstitutional.

He asserted that the Federal Constitution, in delegating the power to regulate commerce to the Federal Government, did not empower that government to destroy commerce or harm the interests of any section of the Union. "This, it would seem, is not regulating commerce by an Embargo. It is, in effect, carrying on war, at the expense of one class of the community." [38]

War with Great Britain finally broke out in 1812, and the New England Federalists, including Daniel Webster, strongly sympathized with the enemy. When the Federalists of Rockingham County, Massachusetts, met in Convention, Daniel Webster presented to the assembly a letter address to President James Madison. This *Rockingham Memorial*, which was endorsed by the convention, ominously announced that the war efforts of the Government of the United States, if continued, might induce the New England to secede from the Union. And should that occur, the letter asserted, the blame for the dissolution of the Union would lie with the Federal Government and the supporters of the war effort in the Southern States. The secession of the Northern States, Mr. Webster wrote, could occur when "one portion of the country" undertook "to control, to regulate, and to sacrifice the interest of another," and when a "small and heated majority" disregarded the rights of a "large and heated minority." [39]

Regarding this Rockingham Memorial, historian Richard N. Current noted in his book, *Daniel Webster and the Rise of National Conservatism*, that, "On this platform Webster was nominated for Congress. He was easily elected." [40] Mr. Webster, it should be stressed, was elected to a federal office as an avowed supporter of States' Rights and State sovereignty, as a man who advocated the right of a State to secede from the Federal Union, as a champion of a strict construction of the Constitution, and as an advocate of the concept that the Federal Government should not regulate the affairs of the United States to the detriment of any quarter of the Union. He was not, of course, dedicated to those principles for their own sake, but only because such principles best served, at the time, the interests of the New England mercantile class that supported him. As their interests and views changed over time, so would his.

Concerning Daniel Webster's alleged patriotism and unfaltering love of country above all else, Richard N. Current has offered this interesting chapter in Mr. Webster's political career:

> In Hartford a group of New England Federalists met to demand constitutional reforms, seemingly at the price of their section's remaining in the Union. Webster himself...*kept up his obstructionist activities in the House at Washington, while the government grew increasingly desperate.*
>
> In its extremity the Administration decided to draft men into the

---

[38] Richard N. Current, *Daniel Webster and the Rise of National Conservatism*, Little, Brown and Company, Boston, 1955, quoted on p. 12.
[39] *Ibid.*, quoted on p. 14.
[40] *Ibid.*, p. 14.

regular army from the militia, which in some of the New England States the governors ordered not to fight. *The conscription bill was lost when Webster rose in the House (December 9, 1814) to launch his rumbling oratory. The draft, he argued, was unconstitutional.* True, Congress had power to raise armies but not by any means, however violent, that it might choose. Congress also had the power to borrow money but not, thereby, the right to impose a forced loan. Though not limited by specific clauses of the Constitution, those powers were restrained by the general spirit of the whole document, and a "free constitution" must be construed only according to "free principles." The draft – "this horrible lottery" – was worse than unconstitutional. It was criminal: "...'tis murder."

No such law could ever be carried out, Webster warned. "The operation of measures thus unconstitutional and illegal ought to be prevented by a resort to other measures which are both constitutional and legal. It will be the solemn duty of the State governments to protect their own authority over their own militia and to *interpose* between their citizens and arbitrary power." *This kind of interposition between the Federal Government and their own people was one of the "highest obligations" of the States, Webster averred, and then to prove his point he quoted from the New Hampshire bill of rights.* His people would fight – but only for their freedom. "If Administration has found that it can not form an army without conscription, it will find, if it venture on these experiments, that it can not enforce conscription without an army."

Webster referred to "the state of things in New England," meaning in particular the assembling of the Federalists at Hartford, and denied that they were in any sense disunionists. "Those who cry out that the Union is in danger," he maintained, "are themselves the authors of that danger. They put its existence to hazard by measures of violence, which it is not capable of enduring." That was to say, the [Democratic-] Republicans of the South and West themselves had brought the country to its dire pass, against the counsels of true unionists. "They alone, Sir, are friends to the Union of the States who endeavor to maintain the principles of civil liberty in the country, and to preserve the spirit in which the Union was framed."

After this speech Webster grimly rejoiced in private that the government could not collect taxes, borrow money, or recruit soldiers. "What can it do?" he asked. "The Govt. *cannot last*, under this war & in the hands of these men, another twelve month. Not that the opposition will break it down, but it will break itself down. It will go out."

He soon was disappointed. Just two days after he had written down his "sober opinion," Henry Clay and the other peacemakers in Ghent signed a treaty which, when ratified, would end the war. News of the signing, on the day before Christmas, did not reach Washington until after dispatches telling of Andrew Jackson's smashing victory, January 8, 1815, over the invading British at New Orleans. These tidings of victory and peace embarrassed and refuted the delegation arriving from Hartford with the Federalist hint that the [Democratic-] Republicans must reform or perish, along perhaps with the Union itself. *The American people got the impression that their country had won the war, and in their eyes the Federalist Party was discredited as almost trea-*

sonable. [emphasis added] [41]

As has been demonstrated, not only did Daniel Webster advocate State Interposition and Nullification during his early years in public office, but he did so at a time when such intervention to prevent the execution of federal laws might well have resulted in the defeat of the United States in a war against an invading power. As for the patriotism of Mr. Webster, Professor Current noted that, "He seemed to view defeat on the battlefield as a misfortune of the party in power, not of the country, and certainly not of the Federalists or himself." [42]

Within his biography of the Orator of Consolidation, Richard N. Current illustrated that Daniel Webster, during his early years in office, clearly understood that our political system rested on the principle of constitutionally limited government:

> During his first decade in politics, 1807-1816, Webster had acted as if his vision seldom extended beyond the boundaries of his native New Hampshire. He made his debut in public life as a strict constructionist and an anti-nationalist. He insisted that Congress, under the Constitution, could exercise only "delegated, *limited*" powers. Advocating State Rights, he carried his argument to the point of recommending a kind of nullification when he maintained that his State had a "solemn duty" to "interpose" between its citizens and the Federal Government. He even hinted at secession as a justifiable recourse when a majority in the nation oppressed or tyrannized a minority within the State. And he voiced the theories of *laissez faire*, criticizing tariff protection as probably unconstitutional and certainly inexpedient.
>
> These things he did as the agent of a fairly compact and homogenous mercantile community. The interests he represented were to change, and so were some of his ideas. He was to spend the better part of his long career in defending principles he had attacked and condemning others he had approved during his apprentice years. [emphasis added] [43]

As Professor Current indicated, Daniel Webster's conversion to nationalism and the principles of consolidation began when he came under the influence of the monied aristocracy:

> The founder of the Boston Manufacturing Company, Francis C. Lowell, member of an old merchant family and inventor of the power loom, introduced Webster to a philosophy of moderate and selective protectionism. Lowell spent the winter of 1815-1816 in Washington. "I was much with him," Webster afterwards recalled. "I found him full of exact, practical knowledge, on many subjects." The knowledgeable manufacturer remained

---

[41] *Ibid.*, pp. 16-18.
[42] *Ibid.*, p. 16.
[43] *Ibid.*, pp. 22-23.

on hand to advise the Congressman during the debates on the tariff of 1816.[44]

Undeniably talented and gifted with a flare for oratory, Daniel Webster's subservience to the bidding of the monied aristocracy proved quite profitable. As Richard N. Current pointed out, "During the 1820's he was probably the most highly paid lawyer in the United States." [45] His willingness to sacrifice principles to promote the interests of the rich and powerful in his own section also proved beneficial to his political career, and Mr. Webster "talked like a thoroughgoing Hamiltonian." [46]

"Having begun so strongly, on the high plane of principle," noted Professor Current, "Webster weakened his case when he descended to details and began to make exceptions." Continuing, Mr. Current adds that, "He was no longer standing on principle: he was poised to represent, as precisely as he could, the balance of contending interests at home. When that balance should swing to the protectionist side, so would he." [47]

Adding to Mr. Webster's lack of credibility as an expounder of constitutional principles was his desire for rich living, often beyond his means. Accordingly, he developed the habit of accepting easy loans and outright gifts from rich benefactors, who in turn were rewarded for their generosity by his votes cast in Congress and by his public support for causes favored by the special interest groups. "He came more and more to crave money, as an addict craves the drug," Richard N. Current wrote, "and he was to satisfy that craving in ways that eventually hurt his reputation." [48]

During the Presidential election of 1828, which pitted Andrew Jackson against John Quincy Adams, a Boston newspaper named the *Jackson Republican* accused some prominent former Federalists, in particular Daniel Webster, of engaging in treasonous conduct during the War of 1812. After the election, Mr. Webster filed suit against the newspaper for libel. During the ensuing trial, the counsel for the defense argued that, in implicating Mr. Webster in secessionist schemes, the newspaper had not really imputed to him any treasonable designs. "The several States are independent and not dependent," the defense attorney asserted. "Every State has a right to secede from the Union without committing treason." [49] As authority for such a defense, the newspaper's counsel introduced two documents penned years earlier by Mr. Webster himself. One was his 1808 pamphlet on the Embargo and the other was his 1812 Rock-

---

[44] *Ibid.*, p. 22.
[45] *Ibid.*, p. 26.
[46] *Ibid.*, p. 34.
[47] *Ibid.*, p. 40.
[48] *Ibid.*, p. 50.
[49] *Ibid.*, quoted on p. 58.

ingham Memorial. Faced with such evidence, the jury could not agree among themselves whether or not the editor had defamed Daniel Webster.

It was during his years as a United States Senator from Massachusetts that Mr. Webster provided his greatest service for the cause of consolidation. As the great Orator of Consolidation, Senator Webster was thoroughly committed to that expanded Hamiltonian System known as the American System. In his biography of Senator Webster, Richard N. Current summarized the nationalistic and socialistic views of the Massachusetts politician:

> The great harmonizer of all interests, as Webster now saw it, was a wise and active Federal Government stimulating and regulating economic activity by means of a national banking system, a protective tariff, and expenditures for internal improvements.
>
> Most important was the banking system....
>
> The...philosophy of Webster thus had no place for *laissez faire*. When Silas Wright proposed that the government tend to its own business and let the people attend to theirs, Webster expressed his horror at this "ominous" and "ill-boding" doctrine which constituted "the whole principle and policy of the administration, at the present critical moment." And when Calhoun objected that credit was private property, and that the government had no right to interfere with it, Webster replied: "Government does interfere and place restrictions in a thousand ways upon every kind of individual property; and it is done, and is necessarily done, by every government, for the good of the whole community." [50]

Perhaps the arrogance of Daniel Webster centered not so much in what he advocated on behalf of the plutocrats that he represented, as in his insistence that what was good for New England was good for America. "Throughout his career as a nationalist," Professor Current observed, "Webster maintained that the interests of New England and of the nation as a whole were identical, that the manufacturing interest was a general interest." [51] And this contention was made in spite of the loud and repeated protests of the other sections of the Union, and especially of the Southern quarter of the Union. "He deserves such credit or blame," Professor Current noted, "as attaches to being the first to introduce the epithet *un-American* into political debate." [52] It was, perhaps, Daniel Webster's greatest contribution to the consolidating school to widely spread the foolish notion that a socialistic Big Government, unencumbered by constitutional restrictions, and possessed of sovereignty that rightfully belongs to the States, is the true American System of Government.

---

[50] *Ibid.*, pp. 104-106.
[51] *Ibid.*, p. 192.
[52] *Ibid.*, p. 146.

From Whigs to Radical Republicans

Daniel Webster reached the pinnacle of his glory as the Orator of Consolidation during the Webster-Hayne Debate of 1830 and the Webster-Calhoun Debate of 1833. Although Senator Webster was a true master of expressing general sentiments designed to stir the emotions, his arguments invariably weakened when he descended into an examination of the details of our constitutional system of government. In an effort to overcome these difficulties in details, the consolidating school looked with hope to Justice Joseph Story, the eminent author of the three-volume *Commentaries on the Constitution*. But in this, they were also disappointed. Try as they may, the consolidating school was not able to present a genuine theory or philosophy to defend, or even to justify, their illegal system of fraud, plunder, and corruption. In time, they would discover that, when the truth is on the other side of a great issue, nothing works better than an application of brute force to resolve a dispute.

Opposing the Whigs was the Democratic Party, which was the political heir of the original Party of Jefferson and whose leading light was the distinguished John C. Calhoun of South Carolina. Although the rapid growth in population of the Northern States quickly gave the consolidators greater resources with which to work, for a number of years the States' Rights school succeeded in maintaining the precarious balance of power in the Union by superior statesmanship and by appealing to the more conservative elements in the Northern and Western quarters of the Union for political support.

The consolidating school succeeded in creating a crisis in 1832 that nearly caused the Federal Union to split asunder. By their continuous increases in the oppressive protective tariff system, the burden of taxation on the Southern States compelled South Carolina, which by then had assumed from Virginia the leadership in the States' Rights school, to interpose its sovereign authority and nullify the unconstitutional act of Congress. When President Andrew Jackson threatened to use military force to coerce the submission of the Southern State, it appeared to many that a War Between the States was imminent. Although such a war was postponed and the crisis abated by a reduction in the protective tariffs, the Whigs continued relentlessly their advocacy of their American System.

Following the Mexican-American War, in which the United States gained additional Western territories that would be subsequently admitted into the Union as new States, the old struggle for a balance of power again reared its ugly head. By the terms of the misnamed Compromise of 1850, the old balance of power was cast aside and the Northern States openly demonstrated that, by virtue of the numerical superiority of their populations, they would thereafter be the dominant power in the Federal Union. As a consequence, the Southern

States could expect to decline in status within the Union with each passing year, destined to assume a subservient role.

In 1850, John C. Calhoun died. A few years later, Senator Daniel Webster and Henry Clay passed away. With the passing of these political giants, the age of compromise also passed away, as the great contest between the States' Rights school and the consolidating school quickly grew more ugly and ruthless. In 1854, the Whig Party merged with the newly formed Free Soil Party to establish the *Republican Party.* From its inception, the Republican Party was dedicated to three main objectives: 1. To so thoroughly dedicate the United States to the plutocratic-socialistic, consolidating American System that it could never be revoked; 2. To crush the Southern States and force them into obedience; and 3. To replace the Federal Government with a supreme, sovereign National Government.

Perhaps it was a little-known, obscure Illinois demagogue named Abraham Lincoln who best summarized the political strategy of the Republican Party in his debate with Stephen A. Douglas for a seat in the United States Senate. As Mr. Lincoln stated, the Union should no longer exist half free and half slave. The balance of power between the sections, in other words, had been decisively tilted in favor of the Northern States, which by then had attained a substantial majority in population over the Southern States. Compromise and concession would no longer be acceptable to the consolidating school, and the full meaning of Mr. Lincoln's words was not lost on the people of the South. The Southern States had been targeted for subjugation.

Adding to this cause for alarm in the Southern States, Northern abolitionists had succeeded in creating among the Northern people in general an increasingly aggressive and hostile attitude toward the people of the Southern States. Initially, Americans in general – North, South, East, and West – were disgusted by the antics of the crazed abolitionists. When Wendell Phillips, for example, declared before a crowd, "My CURSE be on the Constitution of these United States," the general reaction of the public was one of shocked disbelief. [53] And when William Lloyd Garrison delivered a harangue on slavery in Boston in the early 1830's, the good people of that city angrily attempted to tar and feather him. Yet, when John Brown led his murderous attack on Harper's Ferry three decades later in a quest to terrorize the population there and to inaugurate a slave revolt, the people of Boston celebrated his actions and regarded him as some kind of saint.

Two years before John Brown's terrorist attack on the State of Virginia, Hinton Helper's book, *The Impending Crisis*, was published. Within this book,

---

[53] Henry Mayer, *All on Fire: William Lloyd Garrison and the Abolition of Slavery*, St. Martin's Press, New York, 1998, quoted on p. 319.

Mr. Helper gleefully announced that the destruction of the civilization in the Southern States was imminent. He taunted the people of the South with the claim that they were helpless to prevent their own doom and even dared them to attempt to save themselves. The book was officially endorsed by the Republican Party, which funded its widespread distribution throughout the United States.

When the Republican Party nominated Abraham Lincoln for the Presidency in 1860, the people of the Southern States desperately turned to the Democratic Party as their only hope to remain secure within the Union. But they were to be sorely disappointed when the Democratic Party split into Northern and Southern factions, with each faction nominating separate candidates for office.

The result of the political split in the State's Rights school gave to the consolidating school a highly significant victory, and Abraham Lincoln was elected President of the United States. Although Mr. Lincoln had received less than forty percent of the populate vote, he had nonetheless received a majority of the electoral votes as defined by our federal system of electing a President. And in this regard, it is more than of passing interest to note that, had the United States been a consolidated Nation, as claimed by the consolidating school, Mr. Lincoln would not have been victorious in the election, for he failed to receive the support of a numerical majority of the votes cast in the election. But because Mr. Lincoln received the majority of the electoral votes in what amounted to a purely sectional victory over the Southern States, he became the first Republican elected to the White House.

Fearing for their lives, the Southern people resolved that the time had come to escape impending subjugation at the hands of the Republican Party. The States of the Deep South seceded from the Union before Mr. Lincoln was sworn into office. After Abraham Lincoln assumed the duties of the Presidency and indicated a desire to wage war upon the seceded States, the border States promptly seceded and joined the other Southern States in forming their own Federal Republic, styled the Confederate States of America.

The Conquest of the States

Before his death, Alexander Hamilton had predicted that a supreme, sovereign National Government could not be attained in the United States by peaceful means, that such a government could be established only by forcing it upon the American people with military coercion. A civil war, or War Between the States, he foresaw, would be necessary to ensure the victory of the consolidating school. History has unfortunately proven Mr. Hamilton's prediction to be correct.

For four long and grueling years, the armies of two great Federal Republics collided on the field of battle, as the Government of the United States waged a war of conquest against the seceded Southern States. The consolidating school was determined that the Southern States should not be allowed to escape from the role of subjugation intended for them. Yielding at last to the martial power of the Northern States, the Southern States were finally forced to surrender, thereby ending the War Between the States. Few Americans at the time fully grasped the true significance of this consolidating victory over the Southern States. Even fewer today fully comprehend the profound effect the Yankee victory had on our system and form of government.

Jefferson Davis certainly had no difficulty comprehending the subversive and destructive results of the conquest of the States by the Government of the United States. In his book, *A Short History of the Confederate States of America*, which was published in 1890, the leader of the Lost Cause offered this candid assessment:

> With the capture of the capital, the dispersion of the civil authorities, the surrender of the armies in the field, and the arrest of the President, the Confederate States of America disappeared as an independent power, and the States of which it was composed, yielding to the force of overwhelming numbers, were forced to rejoin the Union from which, four years before, they had one by one withdrawn. Their history henceforth became a part of the history of the United States.
>
> With the cessation of all hostilities against the power of the Government of the United States nothing remained to be done but for the sovereigns, the people of each State, to assert their authority and to restore order. If the principle of the sovereignty of the people – the corner-stone of our political institutions – had survived and was still in force, it was necessary only that the people of each State should reconsider and revoke their ordinances of secession, and again recognize the Constitution of the United States as the supreme law of the land. This simple process would have placed the Union on its original basis, and have restored what had ceased to exist – the Union by consent. Unfortunately, such was not the intention of the conqueror. The union of free wills and brotherly hearts, under a compact ordained by the people, was not his object. Henceforth there was to be established a Union by force. Sovereignty was to pass from the people to the Government of the United States, and to be upheld by those who had furnished the money and the soldiers for the war. [54]

This criminal conquest of the States and the forced transfer of sovereignty from the people to the Government of the United States paved the way

[54] Jefferson Davis, *A Short History of the Confederate States of America*, Sprinkle Publications, Harrisonburg, 2002 (orig. pub. 1890), p. 503.

for an incessant process of centralization of power, a process which, by the Twentieth Century, had resulted in the unmistakable appearance of a Big Brother Government in Washington, D.C.

Commenting on this remarkable transformation within our political system, William Bennett Bizzell wrote the following in his book, *Judicial Interpretation of Political Theory*, which was published in 1914:

> The history of the transformation of the terms "Federal Government" or "Confederacy" (as the general government was usually referred to up to the time of the Civil War *by both North and South*) into the "Nation" is of interest and consequence in the development of our political ideas. Lincoln, in his debate with Douglas in 1858, used the term "Confederacy," in speaking of the Union, but when Confederacy was applied to the seceding States in the South, the term was generally abandoned by the North, and *with its abandonment the old idea of the word was surrendered also*. Lincoln, in his Gettysburg Address, speaks of "a new Nation conceived in liberty and dedicated to the proposition that all men are created equal." From this time on it was often asserted that we had become *a Nation with a big N*. This is interesting when we *contrast* this sentiment with that of the Constitutional Convention; for in the first draft of the Constitution the word "national" was *struck out twenty-six times* and the words "Government of the United States" substituted. But the new word had taken a deep hold upon the people, and its frequent use by public speakers and the current literature of the period gave it *permanence in our political vocabulary. With the appropriation of this term came the tendency of the party in power to extend the powers of our governmental agencies, especially that of the executive power*....It was but a step for the Republican Party to go from the Reconstruction Acts to *a policy of increased centralization*.... [emphasis added] [55]

To those who adore the awesome power of the Government of the States in modern-day America and who worship at the altar of Big Brother, the conquest of the sovereign States of our Federal Union will always be regarded as a blessed event in the historical evolution of our Federal Union. And they will happily inform their countrymen that the subjugation of the States and the transfer of sovereignty from the people to the Federal Government is the *verdict of history* from which no appeal can be made.

But to those who value truth, justice, and the natural rights of man, might does not make right, and the criminal conquest of the once-sovereign States of our Federal Union constituted a tragedy of monumental proportions that can and should be corrected. And if sufficient numbers of Americans are willing to rise up and demand the restoration of the sovereignty of the people

---

[55] William Bennett Bizzell, *Judicial Interpretation of Political Theory: A Study in the Relation of the Courts to the American Party System*, G.P. Putnam's Sons, New York, 1914, pp. 67-68.

of the States, constitutionally limited government can be restored to the United States, and the Government of the United States can once again be forced to assume its legitimate role as the servant – and not the master – of the American people.

Chapter Seven

Two Schools of Thought

As we have observed, the consolidating school has wrought great turmoil and misery in the United States of America. That school has waged a war of conquest against the States and robbed the people of their supremacy within our political system. But as might does not make a right, such a theft can only be regarded as a crime that should not be allowed to stand by a people determined to regain their freedom and to reassert their mastery over the Government of the United States.

If the American people ever hope to regain what is rightfully theirs, then it is imperative that the general public has a proper understanding of the true principles of our constitutional system of government. We have already observed the great conflict between the consolidating school and the States' Rights school in terms of political parties and struggles to determine which one would emerge triumphant. Now we should direct our attention to the *theories* and *principles* espoused by each school, for, in many respects, the false theories espoused by the consolidators are just as dangerous as their actions have proven to be.

The question of sovereignty, as has been demonstrated, lies at the heart of the struggle between consolidation and States' Rights in the United States of America. Both theoretically and historically, the question of sovereignty has a direct bearing on the whole nature of our political system and constitutes the foundation of the true American Theory of Government. Despite the confusion over this question which has been created by the consolidating school, sovereignty in the United States is not a difficult concept to understand.

To recap the basic principles of the American Theory of Government, the American Revolution had but one objective – to secure the separate sovereignties of the thirteen original States. To assert this objective, the Continental Congress, representing those States, issued to a candid world the unanimous and unilateral Declaration of Independence on July 4, 1776. That great document asserted that each of the former colonies was declaring its freedom and independence. The term "States" was employed in its plural sense within the Declaration, for the colonies had rejected the suggestion that they should become a single State or Nation.

Following the successful outcome of the War for Independence, the newly independent American States signed a formal treaty of peace with Great Britain that terminated the hostilities. Within that Treaty of Paris of 1783, Britain acknowledged that each of her former American colonies had become a sovereign State, listing each State by name. Two years earlier, those thirteen sovereignties had formally established a political Union, styled the United States of America, under the Articles of Confederation, in which the sovereignty of the States was specifically recognized. Those Articles also expressly asserted that the purpose of the United States of America was to protect and defend the sovereignty of the States.

To render the Federal Government more adequate to the exigencies of the Union, a Constitutional Convention was held in Philadelphia in the summer of 1787, the result of which was our present Federal Constitution. The new federal compact, unlike the old Articles, contained no clause or phrase that expressly referred to the subject of sovereignty. That, in itself, is highly significant, inasmuch as the Constitution of 1787 is founded on the concept that the States, in forming their new Union, yielded nothing that was not expressly delegated. The silence of our present Constitution on this matter can only be interpreted to mean that the seat of sovereignty, as it existed previously, had not been altered by its adoption.

Further proof that the Constitution of 1787 rests upon the sovereignty of the States may be deduced from the federal mode in which it was drafted and adopted. The Convention that drafted it was a *Federal* Convention, representing the States, not the American people as one aggregate body politic, and the delegates to that Philadelphia Convention voted as States, with each State having one vote. After the Constitution had been drafted, it was submitted to the American people for their approval, a process that directly acknowledged the sovereignty of the people. Yet, it was not submitted to the American people as one sovereign State or Nation. Instead, it was submitted to the people as sovereign States. In ratifying the new compact, each State was to be bound only by its own voluntary accession to the new plan of government. As stipulated in Amendment VII of the Federal Constitution, its ratification by a minimum of nine States was required to establish the new Union between the ratifying States, and in this voting process, each State had one vote.

The purpose of the new compact was not to establish a political system for the States different from the system which had existed under the Articles. Its stated objective was to institute *a more perfect Union* – a more perfect Federal Union. Terms such as *Federal Union*, *Federal Constitution*, *Federal Government*, and *Federal Republic* were all used to describe our public institutions under the Articles of Confederation; and they continue to describe our political institutions under the Constitution of 1787 as well. The latter was expressly created for a league of States known as the *United States of America*, the very same title given to the federation of sovereign States that had existed under the Articles. The Articles of Confederation had established a Federal Union *between the States*, and, according to the express words of the Constitution of 1787, it, too, established a Federal Union *between the States*.

The States' Rights School of Thought

No political theorist of the States' Rights School of Thought has contributed more toward a proper understanding of the principles on which the Federal Constitution is founded than John Taylor of Caroline. The chapter entitled "Sovereignty" within his 1823 book, *New Views of the Constitution of the United States*, was especially significant in establishing the intellectual basis of the concept of States' Rights.

Within that chapter, Mr. Taylor made the following observations:

> The reader has perceived that the question concerning State powers, is condensed in the word sovereignty, and therefore any new ideas upon the subject, if to be found, would not be unedifying. A will to enact, and a power to execute, constitute its essence. Take away either, and it expires. The State governments and the Federal Government, are the monuments by which State sovereignty, attended with these attributes, is demonstrated. But as the consolidating school will not see it, I will endeavour further to establish its existence, in order to prevent these beautiful examples of political science from falling into ruin.
>
> The Constitution, like the Declaration of Independence, was framed by deputies from the "States of New-Hampshire," &c. and at the threshold of the transaction, we discern a positive admission of the existence of separate States invested with separate sovereignties. This admission expounds the phrase "We, the people of the United States," which co-operates with the separate powers given to their deputies in the Convention, and is distinctly repeated by the words "do ordain and establish this Constitution for *the United States of America*." Had the sovereignty of each State been wholly abandoned, and the people of all been considered as constituting one nation, the idea would have been expressed in different language. Suppose that Fredonia had been assumed as an appellation comprising the territories of all the States, and that a consolidated Nation had been contemplated by the Convention, would it have framed, ordained, and established, a Constitution by States for States, or by Fredonians for Fredonia. The appellation adopted by the Declaration of Independence was, "The United States of America." The first Confederation declares, that the style of this Confederacy shall be, "The United States of America." And the Union of 1787, ordains and establishes the Constitution for "The United States of America." The three instruments, by adhering to the same style, co-extensively affirmed the separate sovereign-

ties of these States. It was a style proper to describe a Confederacy of independent States, and improper for describing a consolidated Nation. If neither the Declaration of Independence nor the Confederation of 1777, created an American Nation, or a concentrated sovereignty, by this style, the conclusion is inevitable, that the Constitution was not intended to produce such consequences by the same style. The word America is used to designate the quarter of the globe in which the recited States were established, and not to designate a Nation of Americans. A league or union of the kingdoms of Europe for limited objects, distinctly reciting the name of each kingdom, would not have created a consolidated Nation of Europeans....If the word State does not intrinsically imply sovereign power, there was no word which we could use better calculated for that purpose....

This construction bestows the same meaning upon the same words in our three constituent or elemental instruments, and exhibits the reason why the whole language of the Constitution is affianced to the idea of a league between sovereign States, and hostile to that of a consolidated Nation. There are many States in America, but no State of America, nor any people of an American state. A Constitution for America or Americans, would therefore have been similar to a Constitution for Utopia or Utopians.

Hence the Constitution is declared to be made for the "United States of America," that is, for certain States enumerated by their names, established upon that portion of the earth's surface, called America. Though no people or Nation of America existed, considering these words as defining a political association, States did exist in America, each constituted by a people. By these political individual entities, called States, the Constitution was framed; by these individual entities it was ratified; and by these entities it can only be altered. It was made by them and for them, and not by or for a Nation of Americans....If each State, or the people of each State, did not possess a separate sovereignty, they had no right to convey or retain powers. If they had a right both to convey and to retain powers, it could be in virtue of State sovereignty. Admitting the utmost which can be asked, and more than ought to be conceded, by supposing that these sovereignties, in conveying limited powers to the Federal Government, conveyed also a portion of sovereignty, it must also be allowed, that by retaining powers, they retained also a portion of sovereignty. If sovereignty was attached to the ceded powers, it was also attached to the powers not ceded, because all or none of the powers of the States must have proceeded from this principle. In this observation, no use is made of the power reserved to the States to amend the federal form of government, by which a positive sovereignty is retained to the States over that government, subversive of the doctrine, that the Constitution bestows a sovereignty upon it over the States. But a delegation of limited powers, being an act of sovereignty, could not be a renunciation of the sovereignty attached to the powers not delegated. A power to resume the limited delegation, was the strongest expression of sovereignty, and rejects the idea, that the delegated authority may positively or constructively subject the sovereign power to its own will; that no sovereignty may destroy an actual sovereignty. By this power of amendment, the States may re-establish the Confederation of 1777, and thus unquestionably revive their separate sovereignties said to be extinct;

because they are positively asserted by that Confederation. If it is not absurd, it is yet a new idea, that a dead sovereignty contains inherent power to revive itself whenever it pleases.

The mode of making amendments to the Constitution, expresses its true construction, and rejects the doctrine, that an American people created a Federal Government. Their ratification is to be the act of States....

An adherence to our original principle of State sovereignty is demonstrated both by the Confederation and Constitution. Unanimity was necessary to put the first, and a concurrence of nine States to put the second, into operation. The operation of the first, when ratified, was to extend to all the States, and the operation of the second, "to the States ratifying only." Both consequences are deduced from State sovereignty, by which one State could defeat a Union predicated upon unanimity, and four States might have refused to unite with nine. The latter circumstance displays the peculiar propriety of ordaining and establishing the Constitution "for the United States of America." The refusing States, though States of America, did not constitute a portion of an American Nation; and their right of refusal resulted from their acknowledged sovereignty and independence. "The United States of America" would have consisted of nine States only, had four refused to accede to the Union; and therefore thirteen States could not have been contemplated by the Constitution, as having been consolidated into one people. Hence it adheres to the idea of a league, by a style able to describe "the United States of America," had they consisted but of nine, and avoids a style applicable only to one Nation or people consisting of thirteen States. By acknowledging the sovereignty of the refusing, it admits the sovereignty of the concurring States. Assent or dissent, was equally an evidence of it. The limitation of federal powers by assent, establishes the principle from which the assent flowed. There could be no sound assent, nor any sound limitation, unless one was given, and the other imposed, by a competent authority; and no authority is competent to the establishment of a government, except it is sovereign. The same authority could only possess the right of rejecting the Constitution. Had it been the act of an American Nation or people, a State would have possessed no such right. The judicial sages have allowed the federal to be a limited government, but how can it be limited if the State sovereignties by which it was limited, do not exist, and if the State powers reserved, which define the limitation, are subject to its control?

Having proved that State sovereignties were established by the Declaration of Independence; that their existence was asserted by the Confederation of 1777; that they are recognized by the Constitution of 1787, in the modes of its formation, ratification, and amendment; that this Constitution employs the same words to describe the United States, used by the two preceding instruments; that the word State implies a sovereign community; that each State contained an associated people; that an American people never existed; that the Constitution was ordained and established, for such States situated in America, as might accede to a Union; that its limited powers was a partial and voluntary endowment of State sovereignties, to be exercised by a Congress of the States which should unite; that the word Congress implies a deputation from sovereignties, and was so expounded by the Confederation;

> and that a reservation of sovereign powers cannot be executed without sovereignty; the reader will consider, whether all these principles, essential for the preservation both of the Federal and State governments, were intended to be destroyed by the details of the Constitution. The attempt to lose twenty-four [or fifty, by today's reckoning,] States, in order to find a consolidated Nation, or a judicial sovereignty, reserves the mode of reasoning hitherto admitted to be correct, by deducing principles from effects, and not effects from principles. But in construing the Constitution, we shall never come at truth, if we suffer its details, intended to be subservient to established political principles, to deny their allegiance, and rebel against their sovereigns. A will to act, and a power to execute, constitutes sovereignty. The State governments, say the Federalist [Papers], are no more dependent on the Federal Government, in the exercise of their reserved powers, than the Federal Government is on them, in the exercise of its delegated powers.
>
> The treaty between his Britannick majesty and the *United States of America*, acknowledges "the said United States, viz. New-Hampshire, Massachusetts-Bay, Rhode-Island and Providence Plantations, Connecticut, New-York, New-Jersey, Pennsylvania, Delaware, Maryland, Virginia, North-Carolina, South-Carolina, and Georgia, to be free, *sovereign*, and independent States; as such he treats with them, and relinquishes all claim to their government and territorial rights." This king acknowledges, individually, the sovereignty of the States; he relinquishes to them, individually, his territorial rights; three eminent envoys demanded this acknowledgement and relinquishment, as appertaining, individually, to the States; a Congress of the United States ratified the act and the doctrine; the treaty was then unanimously hailed, and is still generally considered, as a consummation of right, justice, and liberty; but now it is said that the States are corporations, subordinate bodies politick, and not sovereign. By the admirers of royal sovereignty, the treaty ought to be considered as valid; by those who confide in authority, it ought to be considered as authentick; by such as respect our revolutionary patriots, it ought to be venerated; and by honest expositors of the Constitution, it will be allowed to afford conclusive proof, that the phrase "United States of America," used both in the treaty and the Constitution, implied the existence, and not the abrogation, of State sovereignty. Consolidators, suprematists, and conquerors, however, will all equally disregard any instrument, however solemn and explicit, by which ambition and avarice will be restrained, and the happiness of mankind improved. [1]

As is readily apparent from these passages, John Taylor of Caroline was undeniably the greatest American political philosopher who ever lived. His understanding of the American Theory of Government was unsurpassed, and his ability to expound the true principles of our political system was unmatched by any other theorist. Further evidence that Mr. Taylor clearly understood and appreciated the great principles upon which our system of government was

---

[1] John Taylor, *New Views of the Constitution of the United States*, Da Capo Press, New York, 1971 (orig. pub. 1823), pp. 171-177.

founded may be found in his book, *Construction Construed and Constitutions Vindicated*:

> I cannot conceive that the Constitution could have contained any thing more hostile to the doctrine "that the sovereignty or supremacy over the government of the Union, rested in the people of the United States, not in their political, but natural capacity." It clearly discloses an opinion, that there were no such people, politically speaking; nor can I discern a vestige of the people inhabiting the territories of the United States, having ever formed themselves, or attempted to form themselves, into any political society or civil government. By this new doctrine, however, *the checks provided to controul the powers of the government of the Union are ingeniously evaded*. It asserts, that the government of the Union is responsible to the sovereignty of the people presiding throughout the Union, and not to the sovereignty of the people residing in each State. Now as an effective sovereignty of the people can only result from their having constituted into a civil society, and the first people having never done so, an acknowledgement of a sovereignty which does not exist, only annuls that which does; and escapes altogether from any species of loyalty to this superior authority. It brings us back to the old ground of a tacit compact between governments and subjects. The people of each State invested their governments with limited powers. They have also established a government of the Union with powers infinitely more limited, than those originally bestowed on the State governments. But if a tacit social compact between this last government, and the people individually of all the States, should be admitted, *all these specifications would be abolished*; because, as it is unwritten, the government of the Union might construe it as was most convenient to itself, as all governments have done, which have condescended to acknowledge implied obligations only....
>
> ...[The Ninth Amendment] prohibits a *construction* by which the rights retained by the people shall *be denied or disparaged*; and the...[Tenth Amendment] "reserves *to the States respectively or to the people* the powers not delegated to *the United States*, nor prohibited *to the States*." The recision of these expressions is happily contrived to defeat a construction, by which the origin of the Union, or the sovereignty of the States, could be rendered at all doubtful....
>
> ...Not a single one of the United States would have consented to have dissolved its peoples, to have reunited them into one great people, to have received State governments or unrestricted legislation from this great people, so ignorant of local circumstances, and so different in local habits. This reasoning would I think have been sufficient to ascertain the people by whom the Constitution was made, had it contained no internal evidence of the sense in which it uses that term....
>
> The powers reserved are those "not delegated by the Constitution." They could only be *reserved* by those who possessed them. They were not powers possessed by a consolidated people of all the States, but by a distinct people of each State; and as those who reserved were those who delegated, it follows, either that the reservation was to a consolidated people of all the

> States, or that the delegation of powers flowed from the people of the separate States. Perhaps the interpolation of a grantor and reserver of powers into the Constitution, who had nothing either to grant or to reserve, may have arisen from an erroneous construction of the word "or." If the remark just made is correct, consistency decides its true meaning. "Are reserved to the States respectively *or* to the people." This word is used either to couple synonyms, or to denote opposition. The words "State and people" had the same, and also a different meaning: The same, as an associated people constituted a State; and a different meaning, from the right of self-government attached to mankind. But another construction seems to me to be the true one. "Or" is used merely to conjoin two words considered as completely synonymous; and the latter is introduced as an expletive of the former, lest it should be interpreted to mean "governments." The word "States" had been so often used in the Constitution, with which it had been charged previously to its adoption; by defining "States and people" as words synonymously used, effectually to defeat the pretence, that the term "people" meant the people of all the States, instead of the people, "respectively" of each State. A construction which supposes that all the inhabitants of all the States, and not the people of each State, were meant, would produce consequences which never could have been contemplated. The reservation would have been in favour of two incongruous objects, and therefore both could not reap its benefits. Being in the disjunctive, it might have been fulfilled by acknowledging the right of either, although the other should get nothing. By selecting the inhabitants of all the States in one mass, as the assignee of the reserved powers, the government of the Union might extend their own powers; since there could be no loss, in conceding powers to those who could neither receive, exercise, nor preserve them. [emphasis added] [2]

Elsewhere in the same book, Mr. Taylor made the following comments in regard to the nature of the Federal Union:

> The plural "States" rejects the idea, that the people of all the States considered themselves as one state. The word "united" is an averment of pre-existing social compacts, called States; and these consisted of the people of each separate State. It admits the existence of political societies able to contract with each other, and who had previously contracted. And the words "more perfect Union" far from implying that the old parties to the old Union were superseded by new parties, evidently mean, that these same old parties were about to amend their old Union....
>
> The term "union" has never been applied to describe a government, established by the consent of individuals; nor do any of our State Constitutions use it in that sense. They speak indeed of individuals "uniting" to form a government, not to form a union; and I do not recollect that a single compact between individuals for the establishment of a government, has ever

[2] John Taylor, *Construction Construed and Constitutions Vindicated*, Da Capo Press, New York, 1970 (orig. pub. 1820), pp. 45-48.

> been called a union; though a multitude of cases exist, in which that name has been given to agreements between independent States. If therefore this term comprised the whole evidence, to prove that our Union was the act of distinct bodies politick, composed of the people within different geographical boundaries, and not a number of people, encircled by one line, without any such discrimination, it would be sufficient. [3]

It is worthy of note that, despite the fact that Mr. Taylor's great works were first published nearly two centuries ago, no one has ever seriously attempted to answer him. As an expounder of the Constitution of the United States, John Taylor of Caroline still stands as the undisputed master. If the so-called verdict of history is on the side of the consolidating school, then the verdict of truth and justice is on the side of the advocates of States' Rights and the sovereignty of the people.

The Views of John C. Calhoun

Following the deaths of John Taylor of Caroline in 1824 and Thomas Jefferson in 1826, the intellectual leadership of the States' Rights School of Thought passed to John Caldwell Calhoun of South Carolina. One of the greatest contributions to the States' Rights School of Thought made by this distinguished political theorist of the Old South was his brilliant response to Senator Daniel Webster in the famous Webster-Calhoun Debate of 1833, a debate which we shall examine in more detail later. The Southern statesman's contribution to the cause of expounding the true principles of constitutional government, however, were by no means confined to that great debate.

In April of 1845, Mr. Calhoun informed a friend that he had commenced "an enquiry into the elements of political science, preliminary to a treatise on the Constitution of the U. States; but I know not whether I shall ever have time to finish it." [4] John C. Calhoun, who died in 1850, lived long enough to complete the preliminary inquiry, *A Disquisition on Government*, and the treatise, *A Discourse on the Constitution and Government of the United States*, although he did not live to see either work in print.

Assessing John C. Calhoun's conceptions of sovereignty in the United States, historian Richard N. Current, in his biography of the Senator from South Carolina, has written:

> To Calhoun, it seemed...ridiculous to suppose that sovereignty ever

---

[3] *Ibid.*, pp. 42-43.

[4] John C. Calhoun, *A Disquisition on Government and Selections from the Discourse*, The Bobbs-Merrill Company, Inc., Indianapolis, 1953, quoted on p. vii.

had belonged or could belong to the people of the United States as a whole. It belonged to the *people*, yes, but to the peoples of the separate *States*. The American people had never been a political entity. "During their colonial condition they formed distinct communities – each with its separate character and government, and in no way connected with each other, except as dependent members of a common empire." The first effect of the Revolution was to leave the colonies as independent States – independent from one another as well as from the former British government. "Its next effect was to transfer the sovereignty which had heretofore resided in the British Crown, not to the *governments* of, but to the *people* composing the *several* States."

To some it might appear that, in the process of transfer from the British Crown to the American States, sovereignty must have been divided and, indeed, divided twice – first, as between Britain and America, and second, as among the thirteen States. But it did not seem so to Calhoun.

After the Declaration of Independence and the extinction of British authority in the colonies, he explained further, nothing remained of the colonial governments except the "popular and representative" branches. "But a representative government, even when entire, cannot possibly be the seat of sovereignty – the supreme and ultimate power of a State. The very term *representative* implies a superior in the individual or body represented." That superior, in the case of the new States, was the body of voters in each of them. "The mere will of the sovereign communities – aided by the remaining fragments, the popular branches of their several colonial governments – speedily ordained and established governments, each for itself." That is, each State adopted a Constitution.

> Thus commenced the division between the constitution-making and the law-making powers – between the power which ordains and establishes the fundamental laws – which creates, organizes, and invests government with its authority, and subjects it to restrictions – and the power that passes acts to carry into execution the powers thus delegated to the government. The one, emanating from the people as forming a *sovereign community*, creates the government; the other, as a representative appointed to execute its powers, enacts laws to regulate and control the conduct of the people regarded as *individuals*. This division between the two powers – thus necessarily incident to the separation from the parent country – constitutes an element in our political system as essential to its formation as the great and primary territorial division of independent and sovereign States....

...Calhoun argued that the people of each State, acting in their sovereign capacity and in a special way, had set up a Constitution and, through it, had delegated certain powers to the State government. The same people, acting again in their sovereign capacity, later established a second Constitution and, through this one, delegated certain other powers to the Government of the United States. Thereafter the people of each State possessed two governments, and these two, within their respective spheres, were equal and coordinate. Neither was above the other, but the sovereign people of each

State were above both. As Calhoun expressed the essential idea:

> Ours is a system of governments, compounded of the separate governments of the several States composing the Union and of one common government of all its members, which was created by their agency. Each was framed by written Constitutions; those of the several States by the people of each State, acting separately and in their sovereign character; and that of the United States by the same, acting in the same character – but jointly instead of separately.

The sovereign communities, according to Calhoun, delegated only governmental powers and not one bit of their respective sovereignties....

> ...[T]he people of the several States, in their sovereign capacity, agree to unite themselves together in the closest possible connection that could be formed without merging their respective sovereignties into one common sovereignty – to establish one common government for certain specific objects which, regarding the mutual interest and security of each and all, they supposed could be more certainly, safely, and effectually promoted by it than by their several separate governments.

True, Calhoun conceded, the Preamble of the Constitution reads that "We the people of the United States" ordain and establish the new government. But this phrase proves nothing, he said. The term "United States" had been used earlier to designate the thirteen States in Congress assembled, even though the Articles of Confederation specifically recognized the sovereignty of the separate States. Here was a mere problem of semantics, Calhoun thought (though, of course, he did not use that word; it had not yet been invented). The phrase "the people of the United States" could be ambiguous, for it was sometimes used in a territorial or geographical sense. "In this sense, the people of the United States may mean *all* the people living within these limits, without reference to the States or Territories in which they may reside, or of which they may be citizens," Calhoun admitted. But he said the phrase, in its political sense, refers to "*the States united*, which inversion alone, without further explanation, removes the ambiguity." There was, strictly speaking, no United States. There were only the States United.

The Constitution, Calhoun repeated over and over, was a "compact" between the States (that is, between the sovereign communities). By this compact they set up a Federal Government for common ends. In lawyer's language, the States were the principals, and the Federal Government was the agent whom they had authorized to act for them. The principals gave specific instructions to the agent in the compact that the principals had made among themselves. That is, they specified the powers and purposes of the Federal Government in the Constitution. Naturally, according to Calhoun's reasoning, the States themselves must interpret the Constitution and decide when or whether the Federal Government was exceeding its powers – just as, in law, the principal determines whether his agent is carrying out the instructions given to him. Calhoun wrote:

> Against these conclusive arguments, as they seem to

> me, it is objected that, if one of the parties has the right to judge of infractions of the Constitution, so has the other; and that, consequently, in cases of contested powers between a State and the general government, each would have a right to maintain its opinion, as is the case when sovereign powers differ in the construction of treaties or compacts; and that, of course, it would come to be a mere question of force. The error is in the assumption that the general government is a party to the constitutional compact. The States, as has been shown, formed the compact, acting as sovereign and independent communities. The general government is but its creature; and though in reality a government, with all the rights and authority which belong to any other government, within the orbit of its powers, it is nonetheless a government emanating from a compact between sovereigns, and partaking, in its nature and object, of the character of a joint commission, appointed to superintend and administer the interests in which all are jointly concerned; but having, beyond its proper sphere, no more power than if it did not exist.
>
> If, in Calhoun's logic, it was erroneous to suppose that the Federal Government had an equal right to judge, it was of course still more erroneous to suppose that the Federal Government had an exclusive right to judge. The Supreme Court of the United States was only a branch of the Federal Government. So the Supreme Court could no more decide constitutional issues involving State powers than an agent or commissioner could decide the intent of the principal who commissioned and instructed him. [5]

Professor Current's presentation and analysis of the theoretical views of John C. Calhoun are essentially correct and accurate, except in one detail. As the matter involves a principle of great importance, we cannot pass it over without comment. "To some it might appear that, in the process of transfer from the British Crown to the American States, sovereignty must have been divided and, indeed, divided twice – first, as between Britain and America, and second, as among the thirteen States," Professor Current stated. "But it did not seem so to Calhoun." The concept of a "divided" sovereignty, as presented by Professor Current, requires closer attention.

While in a colonial status, a territory forms a part of the whole society of a greater Nation and thereby shares the *common sovereignty* of that entire Nation. Upon becoming independent of the mother country, however, the former colony would become a separate State or Nation. The mother country, of course, would remain sovereign *within its own jurisdiction*. Since there would not exist any overlap of supreme authority, there could be no divided sovereignty. Each independent Nation would be separately sovereign, free, and in-

---

[5] Richard N. Current, *John C. Calhoun*, Washington Square Press, Inc., New York, 1963, pp. 62-68.

dependent.

The notion of a "divided" sovereignty is a false concept advanced by the consolidating school in the United States as one of several ways of undermining the political supremacy of the States in our system of government. What the Consolidating School of Thought advocates, in utilizing this notion of a divided sovereignty, is that each State in the Union *shares* sovereignty with a fictitious Nation of Americans. The idea that the States of the Federal Union are, or could possibly be, half-sovereign is a totally absurd conception. And as Professor Current noted, Senator Calhoun wisely rejected such a foolish notion.

Richard N. Current succinctly summarized the political philosophy of John C. Calhoun – and the true foundation of the American Theory of Government – as follows:

> *Sovereignty*, the ultimate and supreme power within a body politic, is not to be confused with governmental powers. The one is the source for the others. Governmental powers, which are derived from sovereignty, may be delegated and divided; sovereignty itself cannot be. In the United States, sovereignty resides in the people of each of the separate States. [6]

Admittedly, there are many Americans who are simply fascinated and awestruck to contemplate the powers of the Government of the United States, totally failing to realize that there rightfully exists a power superior to all those exercised by the Federal Government. And while it may be true that, ever since its military conquest of the States in the War Between the States, the Federal Government has continuously usurped powers, it is equally true that it was not the intent of the Founding Fathers that the powers of the Government of the United States should be as great as those of the State governments. According to James Madison, in the *Federalist Papers*, the Federal Government's powers are supposed to be few and well defined, while those of the State governments should be more extensive in comparison.

Yet, the Consolidating School of Thought exhibits an unnatural reverence for the powers exercised by the Federal Government, and the result of such an unhealthy fascination is the glorification of power for its own sake. Such a worshipful view of the powers of government easily leads to the false assumption that governmental powers and sovereignty are equivalent.

As Professor Richard N. Current noted:

> "In America," to quote [John] Marshall, "the powers of sovereignty are divided between the government of the Union and those of the States. They are each sovereign, with respect to the objects committed to them."

---

[6] *Ibid.*, p. 104.

> Like most of his American contemporaries, Marshall did not distinguish clearly between *sovereignty* and *governmental powers*. But Calhoun did.[7]

When the various concepts of sovereignty – from State sovereignty, to divided sovereignty, to a consolidated sovereign Nation – are carefully analyzed and assessed, the invariable conclusion is that only the States' Rights School of Thought has ever advocated a theory of sovereignty in which the people, and only the people, possess that supreme authority. The sundry falsehoods advanced by the Consolidating School of Thought lead, directly or indirectly, to a sovereign and supreme National Government.

As John C. Calhoun noted:

> There is no difficulty in understanding how powers, appertaining to sovereignty, may be divided; and the *exercise* of one portion delegated to one set of agents, and another portion to another; or how sovereignty may be vested in one man, or in a few, or in many. But how sovereignty itself, the supreme power, can be divided – how the people of the several States can be partly sovereign and partly *not* sovereign, partly supreme and partly *not* supreme – it is impossible to conceive. *Sovereignty is an entire thing; to divide is to destroy it.* [emphasis added][8]

Because the States are sovereign, they – and they alone – rightfully possess the authority to be the judges as to the extent of powers which the Federal Government may lawfully exercise. This, of course, is the highest attribute of sovereignty – the power to create a government, delegate powers to it, and establish the limits to its powers. Should the Federal Government succeed in usurping from the States the power to be the final arbiter in questions of contested power, it would become the sovereign lord and master within the political system.

Professor Current summarized the views of John C. Calhoun on this matter as follows:

> By what procedure...could the States, together, interpret the Constitution?
>
> Calhoun found the answer in the amending process. The States could *interpret* the Constitution in the same way that they could *amend* it – and in essentially the same way they had used to *ratify* it in the first place....
>
> The question remained: how would the amending process be put into operation when needed? Calhoun answered that it was the duty of the Federal Government, before undertaking to exercise any power not clearly delegated to it in the Constitution, to seek an amendment specifically dele-

---

[7] *Ibid.*, p. 62.

[8] *Ibid.*, quoted on p. 62.

gating that power. The burden of proof rested with the Federal Government, since it, after all, was only an agent of the States. [9]

Jefferson Davis and Alexander H. Stephens

Following the death of John C. Calhoun in 1850, the philosophical leadership of the States' Rights School of Thought fell to Jefferson Davis of Mississippi, a prominent statesman in the Democratic Party who represented his State in the United States Senate, served with distinction in the Mexican-American War, and held a the position of Secretary of War in the Cabinet of President Franklin Pierce. When the Southern States seceded from the Union and formed the Confederate States of America, Mr. Davis was selected to serve as the President of the Southern Confederacy, and upon his capture at the conclusion of the War Between the States, he was imprisoned by the conquerors of the American States. Although he was accused of treason, he was never tried in a court of law, but was eventually released when his continued confinement without trial became a political embarrassment to the Republican Party. The Leader of the Lost Cause spent the last years of his life at Beauvoir, his home at Biloxi, Mississippi, where he penned his masterpiece, *The Rise and Fall of the Confederate Government*, which was published in 1881. In 1890, a year after his death, his other book, *A Short History of the Confederate States of America*, was published.

A contemporary of Jefferson Davis who contributed to the States' Rights School of Thought was Alexander H. Stephens of Georgia. Prior to the War Between the States, Mr. Stephens had been a member of the Whig Party and an opponent of secession. But upon the formation of the Confederate States of America, he was elected to the office of Vice-President of the Southern Confederacy. After the Government of the United States had succeeded in enslaving the Southern States and establishing the tyranny of Radical Reconstruction, Mr. Stephens, in retirement at his home at Liberty Hall, wrote his brilliant work, *A Constitutional View of the Late War Between the States*, which was published in 1868. On the title page of this book is an aphorism that aptly summarizes the sentiments of the States' Rights School of Thought and clearly distinguishes that school from the unprincipled consolidators: "Times change and men often change with them, but principles never!" [10]

Within his book, *The Rise and Fall of the Confederate Government*, Jefferson Davis wrote:

---

[9] *Ibid.*, pp. 68-69.

[10] Alexander H. Stephens, *A Constitutional View of the Late War Between the States; Its Causes, Character, Conduct and Results*, Volume 1, Kraus Reprint Co., New York, 1970 (orig. pub. 1868), title page.

> We have seen that the united colonies, when they declared their independence, formed a league or alliance with one another as "United States." This title ante-dated the adoption of the Articles of Confederation. It was assumed immediately after the Declaration of Independence, and was continued under the Articles of Confederation; the first of which declared that "the style of this Confederacy shall be 'The United States of America'"; and this style was retained – without question – in the formation of the present Constitution. The name was not adopted as antithetical to, or distinctive from, "confederate," as some seem to have imagined. If it has any significance now, it must have had the same under the Articles of Confederation, or even before they were adopted.
>
> It has been fully shown that the States which thus became and continued to be "united," whatever form their union assumed, acted and continued to act as distinct and sovereign political communities. The monstrous fiction that they acted as *one people "in their aggregate capacity"* has not an atom of fact to serve as a basis.
>
> To go back to the very beginning, the British colonies never constituted one people. Judge [Joseph] Story, in his "Commentaries" on the Constitution, seems to imply the contrary, though he shrinks from a direct assertion of it, and clouds the subject by a confusion of terms. He says: "Now, it is apparent that none of the colonies before the Revolution were, in the most large and general sense, independent and sovereign communities. They were all originally settled under and subjected to the British Crown." And then he proceeds to show that they were, in their colonial condition, not *sovereign* – a proposition which nobody disputed. As colonies, they had no claim, and made no pretension, to sovereignty. They were subject to the British Crown, unless, like the Plymouth Colony, "a law unto themselves," but they were *independent of each other* – the only point which has any bearing upon their subsequent relations. There was no other bond between them than that of their common allegiance to the Government of the mother-country. As an illustration of this may be cited the historical fact that, when John Stark, of Bennington memory, was before the Revolution engaged in a hunting expedition in the Indian country, he was captured by the savages and brought to Albany, in the colony of New York for a ransom; but, inasmuch as he belonged to New Hampshire, the government of New York took no action for his release. There was not even enough community of feeling to induce individual citizens to provide money for the purpose. [11]

This is but one sample from the potent book penned by Jefferson Davis, and we shall certainly hear more from him as we proceed in our examination of the clash of ideologies between the advocates of States' Rights and those of consolidation. It is of significance to note that this book, like the one penned by Alexander H. Stephens, has never been answered. The response of the Consolidating School of Thought to each book has been a remarkable silence. Being

---

[11] Jefferson Davis, *The Rise and Fall of the Confederate Government*, Volume 1, Thomas Yoseloff, New York, 1958 (orig. pub. 1881), pp. 114-115.

unable to answer the States' Rights School of Thought, they prefer to ignore the great philosophical, theoretical, and historically accurate works that sustain the true American Theory of Government. And they undoubtedly hope that everyone else will ignore those works as well.

The Consolidating Doctrines of Judge Story

When one takes the time to actually analyze and compare the two competing political philosophies – the States' Rights School of Thought and the Consolidating School of Thought – one is struck by the utter absurdity of the latter, which is grounded on distortions of historical facts, misinterpretations the plain language of the Constitution, and concepts unsupported by logic and common sense. The reason for this, of course, is that the Consolidating School of Thought is a pseudo-philosophy originated in corruption and designed to cloak avarice and usurpations of power in the garments of legitimacy and respectability. As the consolidating school came to understand all too well, it was far easier to crush the States' Rights school with brute force than it was to win a debate with its advocates.

Faced with repeated defeats in the great debate over constitutional principles, the consolidators turned hopefully to Justice Joseph Story to provide them with the ideological arguments that would supposedly justify their contention for a consolidated Nation of Americans vested with a national sovereignty. Considered by the consolidating school to be "the foremost of American legal writers," Joseph Story graduated from Harvard in 1798 and was admitted to the bar in 1801. During a six-year period starting in 1805, Mr. Story was politically active, serving in the State legislature and in Congress, and serving as Speaker of the Massachusetts House of Representatives. In 1811, President James Madison appointed him to the Supreme Court of the United States, believing that Mr. Story was sincerely devoted to the principle of constitutionally limited government. After his appointment to that position at age 32, however, Mr. Story surprised everyone by becoming a disciple of Chief Justice John Marshall, an ardent nationalist and consolidator. Not only did Justice Story become a militant abolitionist and hater of the Southern quarter of the Federal Union, but he thoroughly adopted the Hamiltonian mentality as to the nature of the Federal Republic.

In 1829, while continuing to serve on the United States Supreme Court, Joseph Story became the first Dane Professor of Law at Harvard University. His position at Harvard afforded him the opportunity to write and publish a number of commentaries, including his highly significant *Commentaries on the Constitution of the United States; With a Preliminary Review of the Constitutional*

History of the Colonies and States, Before the Adoption of the Constitution, a three-volume tome that was first published in 1833. Shortly afterwards, a condensed, one-volume version was published for use as a textbook for high school and college students.

Regarding Judge Story's great contributions to the Consolidating School of Thought, Jon Roland has written:

> Many Americans who are alarmed about the exercise of powers by government, especially the central government, that go beyond those delegated by the Constitution, think that most of these usurpations began with the New Deal, but an examination of the constitutional history of the United States reveals that efforts to exercise unconstitutional powers date back to the beginning of the Republic.
>
> Perhaps the two most revealing issues that divided early Americans centered on the Alien and Sedition Act of 1798 and proposals to establish a National Bank. The former provoked a vigorous response, represented by the Kentucky Resolutions of 1798 and 1799 and the Virginia Resolution of 1798, led by Thomas Jefferson and James Madison, the leaders of those favoring a strict construction of the delegation of powers to the central government.
>
> When Joseph Story was appointed to the Supreme Court at the instigation of Jefferson and Madison, his views on constitutional interpretation were similar to theirs, but the fourth Chief Justice of the Supreme Court, John Marshall, favored a broader interpretation of delegated powers, and under Marshall's influence Story's views changed. He began to find implied powers in the words of the Framers, mainly in the Commerce Clause, discussed in his *Commentaries* in Book III Chapter XV, and the Necessary and Proper Clause, discussed in Book III, Chapter XXIV.
>
> ...[B]y opening the door to expansion of powers by re-interpreting the language of the Constitution rather than by amending it, and writing a work, these *Commentaries*, which dominated constitutional interpretation for the next 100 years, he certainly laid the basis for these usurpations [perpetrated by the Federal Government in later years], which would be further advanced by Justice Oliver Wendell Holmes before the Supreme Court became packed with justices appointed by President Franklin D. Roosevelt and his successors. [12]

Within his *Commentaries on the Constitution*, Judge Story declared:

> [T]he Colonies did not severally act for themselves, and proclaim their own independence....[T]he Declaration of Independence of all the Colonies was the united act of all. It was "a Declaration by the Representatives of the United States of America, in Congress assembled;" "by the Delegates, appointed by the Good People of the Colonies," as in a prior Declara-

---

[12] Jon Roland, "Introduction", http://www.constitution.org/js/js_002.htm.

> tion of Rights they were called. It was not an act done by the State governments, then organized; nor by persons chosen by them. It was, emphatically, the act of the *whole People* of the United Colonies, by the instrumentality of their Representatives, chosen for that, among other purposes....It was an act of original, inherent Sovereignty, by the People themselves....It was, therefore, the achievement of the whole for the benefit of the whole. The People of the United Colonies made the United Colonies free and independent States, and absolved them from all allegiance to the British Crown....
>
> In the debates in the South Carolina Legislature, in January, 1788, respecting the propriety of calling a Convention of the People, to ratify or reject the Constitution, a distinguished Statesman used the following language: "This admirable manifesto [*i.e.*, the Declaration of Independence] sufficiently refutes the doctrine of the individual Sovereignty and Independence of the several States. In that Declaration, the several States are not even enumerated; but, after reciting, in nervous language, and with convincing arguments, our right to Independence, and the tyranny which compelled us to assert it, the Declaration is made in the following words: 'We, therefore, the Representatives of the United States, etc., do, in the name, etc., of the Good People of these Colonies, solemnly publish, etc., that these United Colonies are, and of right ought to be, free and independent States.'" The separate Independence and individual Sovereignty of the several States were never thought of by the enlightened band of patriots who framed this Declaration. The several States are not even mentioned by name in any part, as if it was intended to impress the maxim on America, that our freedom and independence arose from our Union, and that without it, we could never be free or independent. Let, us, then, consider all attempts to weaken this Union by maintaining that each State is separately and individually independent, as a species of political heresy, which can never benefit us, but may bring on us the most serious distresses.
>
> In the next place, we have seen that the power to do this act was not derived from the State governments; nor was it done generally with their cooperation. The question, then, naturally presents itself, if it is to be considered as a National act, in what manner did the Colonies become a Nation, and in what manner did Congress become possessed of this National power? The true answer must be that, as soon as Congress assumed powers, and passed measures, which were, in their nature, National, to that extent, the People, from whose acquiescence and consent they took effect, must be considered as agreeing to form a Nation. [13]

It is from such bizarre and distorted perversions of American history as this that the Consolidating School of Thought seeks to justify the creation of a supreme National Government with unlimited powers on the ruins of a Federal Government with strictly limited powers. From audacious distortion of historical facts, Judge Story managed to deduce a consolidated, sovereign American Nation directly from the Declaration of Independence!

---

[13] Alexander H. Stephens, *Op. cit.*, Volume 1, quoted on pp. 61-64.

Strange, indeed, is the contention that the Declaration of Independence established a single, consolidated State of America, when the Treaty of Paris of 1783, which formally ended the War of Independence, expressly declared that the thirteen American States were severally sovereign and independent. Even more strange, if what Judge Story wrote is true, is how that unitary sovereign State of America could adopt the Articles of Confederation, in which the separate States were expressly declared to be sovereign. In the Consolidating School of Thought, facts which do not support their strange theories are conveniently overlooked as being irrelevant.

Let us suppose for a moment, for sake of argument, that Joseph Story's interpretation of the Declaration of Independence is correct. If the purpose of the War of Independence was to secure the sovereignty and independence of a consolidated American Nation, then why did the American patriots accept the Treaty of Paris of 1783, in which their separate States were acknowledged as free, sovereign, and independent? And why would those same American patriots establish a Federal Union under the Articles of Confederation, in which the sovereignty of the separate States was not only expressly declared, but in which the security of that State sovereignty was identified as the purpose of the Union? These are questions which Joseph Story, and all others who advocate his line of reasoning, have never been able to provide an answer that is consistent with their conception of a single sovereign Nation.

The fact that the thirteen original American States fought together in the American Revolution is not as important or significant as the fact that they were waging war to secure their separate and distinct sovereignties. They acted in concert only as a military tactic, for the sake of convenience, and they even enlisted the assistance of such foreign powers as France.

Attention should be given to Judge Story's insistence that the role of the State governments in securing American independence from Great Britain was insignificant to non-existent. That contention is a blatant lie. Within the Second Continental Congress, the representatives of the colonies waited to receive instructions and authorizations from their respective colonial governments before voting on the question of independence. And in voting for a Declaration of Independence, the delegates to the Second Continental Congress voted as States, with each State having one vote.

It was the State governments who provided soldiers for the Continental Army in the War of Independence and who provided the funds necessary to sustain the war effort. When the British marched on Lexington and Concord, it was the Massachusetts State militia that met them on the field of battle and fired the famous shot heard around the world. Yet, Joseph Story would have us believe that the State governments played little or no role in the American Revolution, and that the process of securing independence from Great Britain was the act of the people of America as one body politic on behalf of a consolidated Nation of Americans.

Had the Founding Fathers intended to merge the thirteen colonies into one Nation, they would have declared, within the Declaration of Independence, that the colonies had become a free and independent *State.* By declaring, instead, that the colonies had become "free and independent *States,*" their intention was clearly to declare and assert the *separate* sovereignties of each former colony.

As one final observation, we note Judge Story's assertion that, "as soon as Congress *assumed* powers, and passed measures, which were, in their nature, National, to that extent, the People, from whose acquiescence and consent they took effect, must be considered as agreeing to form a Nation." The true American Theory of Government is that government possesses and may lawfully exercise only those powers that are expressly delegated to it by a constitution of government. The concept of *assumed powers* is alien to our constitutional system of limited government, for if any government could rightfully *assume* powers, it would be impossible to limit its powers. Such a government would itself be the sovereign power of the Nation it ruled.

Perhaps what Judge Story had in mind, when writing this passage, was that, whenever the Federal Government assumes power by usurpation, and the American people allow this to happen without sufficient challenge, our political system is subverted and the Government of the United States thereby begins the process of evolving into a totalitarian, supreme, sovereign National Government in utter violation of the supreme law of the land. If this is what Joseph Story meant, then we could not agree more with him.

These passages from Judge Story's *Commentaries on the Constitution,* which we have cited above, constitute but one example showing the distortions and misinterpretations of historical events that were propagated to build up the Consolidating School of Thought. Over the years, a number of distinguished advocates of the States' Rights School of Thought have thoroughly analyzed and debunked Judge Story's fallacious conceptions, including Jefferson Davis, Alexander H. Stephens, and, in more modern times, James Ronald Kennedy and Walter Donald Kennedy. Perhaps the most thorough and penetrating analysis of Judge Story's misconceptions was the one presented by Mr. Stephens in his great work, *A Constitutional View of the Late War Between the States.*

Refuting Judge Story's Misconceptions

Regarding Judge Story's perverted consolidating doctrines, Alexander H.

Stephens offered these comments:

> Now what I have to say in reply to Judge Story's argument, is, that it would be conclusive of the question if it were sustained by the facts; but being so directly in opposition to the great unquestionable facts of our history – facts which Mr. [John L.] Motley [a consolidator who denounced the sovereignty of the States on behalf of the Radical Republicans after the War Between the States] could not venture to gainsay – facts as well established as that America was discovered by Columbus, or that the colonies were subject to the British Government at the time of their Declaration of Independence – it is utterly untenable....
>
> ...I do not question the fact that the Colonies, under their Charter Governments, were not Sovereign, or that they never pretended to be Sovereign, or that they did not claim a local allegiance. What has that to do with the question? Nor do I dissent from the statement that the Declaration of Independence was not made by these Charter Governments, nor that they were not competent or authorized to adopt it. No truth is better established than that – but what has this to do with the question? That the Declaration of Independence was entirely revolutionary in its character is also true. All admit it. The Declaration was made with a view to overthrow these very Governments, as they were then administered, and the authority of the British Crown, under whose auspices they had been established, or by which they were then attempted to be controlled. What need had Judge Story to state this fact in the line of his argument?...It was an act of "original inherent Sovereignty by the people themselves, resulting from their right to change the form of government, and to institute a new government, whenever necessary for their safety and happiness." This I fully agree to. But this was done by the Paramount authority of the people of each Colony respectively for themselves. The Declaration itself was made by the people of each Colony, for each Colony, through representatives acting by the Paramount authority of each Colony, separately and respectively. The Declaration of Independence was, in this way, a joint act of all the Colonies, for the benefit of each separately, as well as for the whole. The Congress that made it was a Congress of States. The deputies or delegates from no State assumed to vote for it until specially instructed and empowered so to do. Massachusetts had instructed and empowered her delegation so to act as early as January before; South Carolina in March; Georgia in April; North Carolina in April; Rhode Island in May; Virginia in May; New Hampshire in June; Connecticut in June; New Jersey in June; Maryland in June; Pennsylvania and New York were the last. The powers and instructions from these States did not arrive until after the 1st day of July, which caused a postponement of final action of the Congress on the Declaration until the 4th day of that month, when, full powers being received from all the States, it was then, after being voted upon by States and carried by States, unanimously proclaimed by all the States, so in Congress assembled. The Declaration of Independence was, be it remembered, voted upon and carried by States, and proclaimed by and in the name of States.

This is the history of the matter. But the statement adopted by Judge Story, of the reported remarks of Mr. Pinckney of South Carolina, is even more extraordinary still.

The statement is, "that the separate independence and individual Sovereignty of the several States were never thought of by the enlightened band of patriots who framed this Declaration."

That these men did look forward hopefully for a continued Union of States, under a Compact to be formed securing the Independence and Sovereignty of each, I do not doubt; but that they did not then consider each as an Independent Sovereign power, is wholly at variance with all the attending facts. The very Declaration itself shows this conclusively without going farther into a detail of these facts. The very title shows how it was made. Here it is: "In Congress, July 4, 1776, the unanimous Declaration of the thirteen United States of America." It was the Declaration of States in Congress assembled, by their deputies, empowered by the Paramount authority of each, to make it. The Declaration was not that they were to be *one State*, as New Hampshire had instructed her representatives to make it, but, in their own language, "thirteen free, Sovereign and Independent States." This was in strict accordance with the instructions of their constituents. The people of the several Colonies would not consent for a Declaration to be made in any other way. This appears from the instructions of all the Colonies or States except New Hampshire. In their several instructions and powers for the Declaration of Independence, were instructions and powers for forming a Confederation of Independent States. So universal was this sentiment, that Richard Henry Lee's first motion for the Declaration of Independence, early in June, was not only for Independence, but farther – for "a plan of Confederation, to be prepared and transmitted to the respective Colonies for their consideration and approbation."

The plan for a Confederation of separate Independent Sovereign States, was moved in the very resolution which proposed the Declaration of their Independence. And subsequently, on the 24th of June, 1776, the Congress declared, by resolution, that "all persons abiding within any of the United Colonies and deriving protection from the laws of the same, owed allegiance to the said laws, and were members of such Colony; and that all persons passing through, or making a temporary stay in any one of the Colonies being entitled to the protection of the laws, during the same, *allegiance thereto....*"

Judge Story says that this Declaration has always been treated as an act of Paramount and Sovereign authority, complete and perfect *per se*, and *ipso facto*, working an entire dissolution of all political connection with and allegiance to Great Britain. This is certainly true to the letter. He very cautiously, however, abstains from stating, by whose Paramount and Sovereign authority it was done, and to what Paramount authority allegiance under it was due, and declared to be due, by the States themselves in Congress assembled. We have seen that it was done by the authority of each State severally and respectively, and that the allegiance of the citizens of each was declared to be due to each severally and respectively.

Strange, indeed, is it, that Judge Story should assert, as he does, "that we have seen that the power to do this act was not derived from the State governments, nor was it done generally with their co-operation." This language is exceedingly ambiguous. If he meant that it had been seen that the act was not done by the authority, nor with the co-operation of the Royal Charter Governments, no fact is more readily admitted; and none could be stated, less relevant, or less pertinent; but, if he meant to say that it was not done entirely by the authority of the new Revolutionary Governments, erected in each State by virtue of the asserted Sovereignty of the People thereof, respectively, then, his statement is utterly unsustained by the record itself, as well as in direct conflict with the whole history of the times. The Delegates themselves say, in the paper signed by them, that it was done in the name, and by the authority, of the People of the Colonies. That is, the Sovereign authority of the People of each Colony, respectively. For not one of them had any authority to speak for the People of any Colony, except the one he was delegated to represent; nor did any one assume or presume to speak for his own Colony, until empowered to do so. The object of Judge Story seems to have been to produce the impression, without positively stating the fact so in truth to be, that the Declaration of Independence was a National act...."The question," says he, "then naturally presents itself, *if it is to be* considered a National act [he does not affirm that it was, but says *if it is to be considered so*], in what manner did the Colonies become a Nation, and in what manner did Congress become possessed of this National power? The true answer [*that is, if it is to be considered so,* he goes on to say] must be that, as soon as Congress *assumed* powers and passed measured which were National, to that extent, the people, from whose acquiescence and consent they took effect, must be considered as agreeing to form a Nation!"

Such an argument and such a conclusion, founded upon such an IF, you must allow me to say, require all Judge Story's reputation, to entitle them to even a moment's notice, or to elevate them to the dignity of serious consideration.

...It was exceedingly important...for the establishment of this theory of a unity of the people now as one Nation, to get a conclusion somehow, that the States were never separately Sovereign. But nothing is easier to be done, than to show that his conclusion, so drawn, from premises of the imagination entirely, has not a solitary fact to stand upon.

Our history at this period rests not upon legends and fables. That Congress itself did not regard their act as the result of assumed, or unauthorized powers, their acts at the time abundantly show. That they did not consider the Declaration of Independence as a National act, or put any such construction upon it, as Judge Story has done, appears clearly from what they were then doing. At the very time the Declaration of Independence was made, a Committee, consisting of one delegate from each State, was organized to prepare articles of Confederation between the States, as separate, distinct Sovereign political Communities. That Committee, which was appointed on the 11th of June, even before the Declaration of Independence was agreed to, and in anticipation of it, reported the Articles of Confederation, before referred to, which, Mr. Curtis says, was the first written Constitution of the United States....These Articles were reported on the 12th day of

July, eight days after the Declaration. Moreover, this argument and conclusion of Judge Story are utterly inconsistent with the facts acknowledged and set forth in the treaty of Peace with Great Britain, in 1783....

The fifth article of the treaty clearly shows how the States, the other party to it, understood it. This is in these words:

"It is agreed that the Congress shall earnestly recommend it to the legislatures of the respective States, to provide for the restitution of all estates, rights and properties, which have been confiscated, belonging to real British subjects, and also of the estates, rights and properties of persons resident in Districts in possession of his Majesty's arms, and who have not borne arms against the United States. And that persons of any other description shall have free liberty to go to any part or parts of any of the thirteen United States, and therein to remain twelve months, unmolested in their endeavors to obtain the restitution of such of their estates, rights and properties, as may have been confiscated; and that Congress shall also earnestly recommend to the several States a reconsideration and revision of all acts or laws regarding the premises, so as to render the said laws or acts perfectly consistent, not only with justice and equity, but with that spirit of conciliation, which on the return of the blessings of peace should universally prevail. And that Congress shall also earnestly recommend to the several States, that the estates, rights and properties of such last mentioned persons, shall be restored to them, they refunding to any persons who may be now in possession, the *bona fide* price (where any has been given) which such persons may have paid on purchasing any of the said lands, rights or properties, since the confiscation. And it is agreed, that all persons who have any interest in confiscated lands, either by debts, marriage settlements, or otherwise, shall meet with no lawful impediment in the prosecution of their just rights."

So far from the Federal Government assuming a national character at that time, it would not presume to bind the States or enter into an obligation upon matters that related to their own separate Sovereign Jurisdiction. That Government only engaged to use its influence in recommending to the Sovereign States respectively certain stipulations. This statement of Judge Story is the more remarkable, because it is in direct conflict with numerous decisions of the Supreme Court of the United States.

This Court, in the case of *McIlvaine* vs. *Coxe, 2d Peter's Condensed Reports*, page 86, in 1805, held that, "on the 4th of October, 1776, the State of New Jersey was completely a Sovereign, Independent State, and had a right to compel the inhabitants of the State to become citizens thereof."...

One of the points in this case was citizenship, and to what power allegiance was due; or in other words, where Sovereignty or Paramount authority under our system then resided – that is, under the Confederation. These, as we settled in the beginning, belong to Sovereignty and follow it. In this case the Supreme Court of the United States decided that both citizenship and allegiance, in 1776, after the Declaration of Independence, belonged to the States severally and respectively....

In another case decided by the same court, in February, 1796, nine years before *Ware*, etc., vs. *Hylton*, etc., 3 *Dallas*, 199, Chase, Justice, in delivering his opinion, says:

..."I consider this [Declaration of Independence] as a Declaration, not that the United Colonies JOINTLY, in a *collective* capacity, were Independent States, etc., but that each of them was a Sovereign and Independent State; that is, that each of them had a right to govern itself by its own authority and its own laws, without any control from any other power upon earth!"

Is authority clearer, stronger, or higher, needed to show the utter groundlessness of Judge Story's argument? If so let us turn to what Chief Justice [John] Marshall said, in delivering the decision of the Supreme Court of the United States, in the great case of *Gibbons* vs. *Ogden*, in 1824. Here it is:

"As preliminary to the very able discussion of the Constitution which we have heard from the bar, and as having some influence on its construction, reference has been made to the political situation of these States anterior to its formation. It has been said that they were Sovereign, were completely Independent, and were connected with each other only by a league. This is true!"

Judge Marshall here distinctly affirms, judicially affirms, from the Bench of the Supreme Court of the United States, that the States were separate and distinct Sovereignties when the Articles of Confederation were entered into, and that these articles were but a league between Sovereign Powers.

...Judge Story's account of the matter, and his whole argument built upon it, has not a single fact to rest upon.... [14]

The Duplicity of the Consolidating School

In his book, *The Rise and Fall of the Confederate Government*, Jefferson Davis made these observations:

That the States were severally sovereign and independent when they were united under the Articles of Confederation, is distinctly asserted in those articles, and is admitted even by the extreme partisans of consolidation. Of right, they are still sovereign, unless they have surrendered or been divested of their sovereignty; and those who deny the proposition have been vainly called upon to point out the process by which they have divested themselves, or have been divested of it, otherwise than by usurpation.

Since Webster spoke and Story wrote upon the subject, however, the sovereignty of the States has been vehemently denied, or explained away as only a partial, imperfect, mutilated sovereignty. Paradoxical theories of "divided sovereignty" and "delegated sovereignty" have arisen, to create that "confusion of ideas," of which Judge Story speaks. Confounding the sovereign authority of the *people* with the delegated powers conferred by them upon their *governments*, we hear of a Government of the United States "sovereign within its sphere," and of State governments "sovereign in *their*

[14] *Ibid.*, Volume 1, pp. 66-78 and 80-81.

> sphere"; of the surrender by the States of *part* of their sovereignty to the United States, and the like. Now, if there be any one great principle pervading the Federal Constitution, the State Constitutions, the writings of the fathers, the whole American system, as clearly as the sunlight pervades the solar system, it is that *no* government is sovereign – that all governments derive their powers from the people, and exercise them in subjection to the will of the people – not a will expressed in any irregular, lawless, tumultuary manner, but the will of the organized political community, expressed through authorized and legitimate channels. The founders of the American Republic never conferred, nor intended to confer, sovereignty upon either their State or Federal Governments.
>
> If, then, the people of the States, in forming a Federal Union, surrendered – or, to use Burlamaqui's term, transferred – or if they meant to surrender or transfer – *part* of their sovereignty, to whom was the transfer made? Not to "the people of the United States in the aggregate"; for there was no such people in existence, and they did not create or constitute such a people by merger of themselves. Not to the Federal Government; for they disclaimed, as a fundamental principle, the sovereignty of any government. There was no such surrender, no such transfer, in whole or in part, expressed or implied. They retained, and intended to retain, their sovereignty in its integrity – undivided and indivisible. [15]

One objective of the Consolidating School of Thought has ever been to obscure the meanings of key words and terms to define our political system. The word "federal," for instance, has a true meaning that is synonymous with the word "confederate." But the Consolidating School of Thought has long sought to redefine the word "federal" so that it is synonymous with the word "national."

Joseph Story not only attempted to mystify the concept of sovereignty in the United States, but even assured his readers that the mystery and confusion were inherent in the term. "The term 'sovereign' or 'sovereignty,'" wrote the crafty Justice and law professor, "is used in different senses, which often leads to a confusion of ideas, and sometimes to very mischievous and unfounded conclusions." [16] "But, indeed," proclaimed John Lothrop Motley, himself a rabidly fanatical consolidator of Radical Republican fame, "the words 'sovereign' and 'sovereignty' are purely inapplicable to the American system." [17]

Mr. Motley, illustrating typical Radical Republican thinking, proceeded to say:

> In the Declaration of Independence the provinces declare themselves "free and independent States," but the men of those days knew that the word

[15] Jefferson Davis, *Op. cit.*, Volume 1, pp. 142-143.
[16] *Ibid.*, Volume 1, quoted on p. 141.
[17] *Ibid.*, Volume 1, quoted on p. 143.

> "sovereign" was a term of feudal origin. When their connection with a time-honored feudal monarchy was abruptly severed, the word "sovereign" had no meaning for us. [18]

It is grotesque distortions and perversions of plain truths such as this, our modern-day historians and political scientists insist, that supposedly triumphed over State sovereignty as a consequence of the so-called verdict of history in the War Between the States. If such a twisted theory as this can prevail over that of States' Rights, then it can only be owing to the force of arms, and most assuredly not to the force of logic and reason.

Although such views as those of Mr. Motley scarcely deserve a response, much less serious consideration, all attacks upon the true American Theory of Government require a response, no matter how foolish and unsubstantiated they are. The Treaty of Paris of 1783, as we have previously observed, contained the term sovereignty and plainly indicated that the term applied to the thirteen original States of our Federal Union. The Articles of Confederation also contained the term in question and unequivocally acknowledged that the word applied to the sovereign States of the American Union. These were the works of the "men of those days" – of our Founding Fathers. Unlike Mr. Motley, the Founders of our Republic certainly considered sovereignty a crucial concept.

The State of Massachusetts, which is historically renowned for producing eminent consolidators – including Mr. Motley and others like him – was originally lead by distinguished patriots who cherished and espoused the concept of State sovereignty. Shortly after the Declaration of Independence was issued by the Second Continental Congress, those early leaders of the Bay State drafted a Constitution for Massachusetts that declared, in part:

> The people inhabiting the territory formerly called the Province of Massachusetts Bay do hereby solemnly and mutually agree with each other to form themselves into a free, *sovereign*, and Independent body politic, or State, by the name of The Commonwealth of Massachusetts.[19]

James Madison certainly thought that the terms "sovereign" and "sovereignty" were applicable to the American political system, for he repeatedly used the words to describe the status of the States within the Virginia State Ratifying Convention as well as within his contributions to the *Federalist Papers*. Even Alexander Hamilton, the Father of the Consolidating School in the United States, repeatedly used the terms in his contributions to those essays. In the

---

[18] *Ibid.*, Volume 1, quoted on p. 143.
[19] *Ibid.*, Volume 1, quoted on p. 143.

Federalist, No. 81, for example, Mr. Hamilton said that the attribute of a State not to be sued without its consent constitutes "one of the attributes of sovereignty" now possessed by "every State in the Union." [20]

Regarding the significance placed upon the concept of sovereignty by the "men of those days," Jefferson Davis wrote:

> Benjamin Franklin advocated equality of suffrage in the Senate as a means of securing "the *sovereignties* of the individual States." James Wilson, of Pennsylvania, said sovereignty "is in the people before they make a Constitution, and remains in them," and described the people as being "thirteen independent sovereignties." Gouverneur Morris, who was, as well as Wilson, one of the warmest advocates in the [Constitutional] Convention of a strong central government, spoke of the Constitution as "a *compact*," and of the parties to it as "each enjoying *sovereign* power." Roger Sherman, of Connecticut, declared that the Government "was instituted by a number of *sovereign States*." Oliver Ellsworth, of the same State, spoke of the States as "sovereign bodies." These were all eminent members of the Convention which formed the Constitution.
>
> There was scarcely a statesman of that period who did not leave on record expressions of the same sort. But why multiply citations? It is very evident that the "men of those days" entertained very different views of sovereignty from those set forth by the "new lights" of our day. Far from considering it a term of feudal origin, "purely inapplicable to the American system," they seem to have regarded it as a very vital principle in that system, and of necessity belonging to the several States – and I do not find a single instance in which they applied it to any political organization, except the States. [21]

The word "federal" literally means *of a league*. The term *Federal Government* literally means *Government of a League of States*, while the term *Federal Constitution* literally means *Constitution of the League of States*. And the term *Federal Union*, therefore, inherently implies that our system consists of a league of sovereign States that have banded together to provide greater security against hostile foreign powers. There is nothing mystical or obscure about the nature of sovereignty in the United States of America.

Confusion arises, however, when cleverly deceptive theories are advanced with the objective of distorting the facts and substituting mythology for truth. A denial of the fact that the people who ordained and established the Federal Constitution were divided into separate and distinct sovereignties, for example, could serve no other purpose than that of consolidation. And any attempt to confuse the real people of the several States with a mythical Nation of Americans can serve no other purpose than that of transferring sovereignty from the

[20] Alexander Hamilton, James Madison, and John Jay, *The Federalist Papers*, A Mentor Book from New American Library, New York, 1961, p. 487.

[21] Jefferson Davis, *Op. cit.*, Volume 1, pp. 144-145.

real people to their government, while pretending to vest it in a mythical people.

As Russell Hoover Quynn has pointed out, "'The people'...are the States. The people do not speak, never have, never can, speak in their sovereign capacity, without a subversion of our whole system, otherwise than as *people of the States.*" [22] Jefferson Davis also noted this key concept, stating that, "It is merest self-stultification to admit the sovereignty of the people and deny it to the *States* in which alone they have community existence." [23]

The Outlandish Assertions of Edward Everett

One of the commentators on political theory from the consolidating school whose doctrines were especially outlandish was Edward Everett of Massachusetts fame. Possessing strong ambitions to advance his political career, Mr. Everett became an ardent advocate of the extreme wing of the Consolidating School of Thought.

Regarding the twisted political doctrines advanced by the cunning New England politician, Jefferson Davis of Mississippi observed:

> Mr. Edward Everett, in his Fourth-of-July address, delivered in New York in 1861, following the lead of Judge Story, and with even less caution, boldly declares that, "before their independence of England was asserted, they (the colonies) constituted *a provincial people.*" To sustain this position – utterly contrary to all history as it is – he is unable to adduce any valid American authority, but relies almost exclusively upon loose expressions employed in debate in the British Parliament about the period of the American Revolution – such as "that people," "that loyal and respectable people," "this enlightened and spirited people," etc., etc. The speakers who made use of this colloquial phraseology concerning the inhabitants of a distant continent, in the freedom of extemporaneous debate, were not framing their ideas with the exactitude of a didactic treatise, and could little have foreseen the extraordinary use to be made of their expressions nearly a century afterward, in sustaining a theory contradictory to history as well as to common sense. It is as if the familiar expressions often employed in our time, such as "the people of Africa," or "the people of South America," should be cited, by some ingenious theorist of a future generation, as evidence that the subjects of the Khedive and those of the King of Dahomey were but "one people," or that the Peruvians and the Patagonians belonged to the same political community.
>
> Mr. Everett, it is true, quotes two expressions of the Continental Congress to sustain his remarkable proposition that the colonies were "a

---

[22] Russell Hoover Quynn, *The Constitutions of Abraham Lincoln and Jefferson Davis*, Exposition Press, New York, 1959, p. 22.

[23] *Ibid.*, quoted on p. 22.

people." One of these is found in a letter addressed by the Congress to General Gage in October, 1774, remonstrating against the erection of fortifications in Boston, in which they say, "We entreat your Excellency to consider what a tendency this conduct must have to irritate and force *a free people*, hitherto well disposed to peaceable measures, into hostilities." From this expression Mr. Everett argues that the Congress consider themselves the representatives of "a people." But, by reference to the proceedings of the Congress, he might readily have ascertained that the letter to General Gage was written in behalf of "*the town of Boston and Province of Massachusetts Bay*," the people of which were "considered by all America as suffering in the common cause for their noble and spirited opposition to oppressive acts of Parliament." The avowed object was "to entreat his Excellency, from the assurance we have of the peaceable disposition of *the inhabitants of the town of Boston and the Province of Massachusetts Bay*, to discontinue his fortifications." These were the "people" referred to by the Congress; and the children of the Pilgrims, who occupied at that period the town of Boston and Province of Massachusetts Bay, would have been not a little astonished to be reckoned as "one people," in any other respect than that of the "common cause," with the Roman Catholics of Maryland, the Episcopalians of Virginia, the Quakers of Pennsylvania, or the Baptists of Rhode Island.

The other citation of Mr. Everett is from the first sentence of the Declaration of Independence: "When in the course of human events it becomes necessary for *one people* to dissolve the political bands which have connected them with another," etc., etc. This, he says, characterizes "the good people" of the colonies as "one people."

Plainly, it does no such thing. The misconception is so palpable as scarcely to admit of serious answer. The Declaration of Independence opens with a general proposition. "One people" is equivalent to saying "*any* people." The use of the correlatives "one" and "another" was the simple and natural way of stating this general proposition. "One people" applies, and was obviously intended to apply, to all cases of the same category – to that of New Hampshire, or Delaware, or South Carolina, or of any other people existing or to exist, and whether acting separately or in concert. It applies to any case, and all cases, of dissolution of political bands, as well as to the case of the British colonies. It does not, either directly or by implication, assert their unification, and has no bearing whatever upon the question. [24]

As is evident from the outlandish contentions put forward by Edward Everett, the Consolidating School of Thought can sustain its main propositions only by advocating interpretations of historical facts and state papers that sometimes cross over the border of absurdity to enter the domain of the ludicrous. That school is even willing to stoop to the level of quoting expressions out of context to sustain their spurious theories. The subversive nature of this mode of misinterpretation of commonly used expressions is of significance to our under-

---

[24] Jefferson Davis, *Op. cit.*, Volume 1, pp. 116-118.

standing of the lack of veracity of the consolidating school. For this reason, we should consider some examples that will highlight the extent to which such a practice is capable of distorting even the most innocent of expressions.

Let us consider, by way of example, an expression that could readily be asserted in complete innocence by a Christian to emphasize the brotherhood of mankind, such as, "We are all brethren in the eye's of God." Should that be interpreted as meaning that we are all brothers in the literal, familial sense? "America is a great nation," is an expression that could readily be asserted by patriotic Americans. Should it be construed as a didactic treatise on the Constitution and as a political statement that the American people constitute a consolidated State of America? If other examples were necessary, then we may consider a statement typical of what a patriotic American might say about the United Nations Organization: "We must never surrender our national sovereignty to a World Government." Should such a statement be construed as a denial of the sovereignty of the States of our Federal Union? Or should such an expression be considered merely as a warning against surrendering American sovereignty – *irrespective of where it may be vested in our political system* – to any instrument of the New World Order?

We note with interest that even Satan has been known to cite Scripture when it suits his evil objectives. To cite colloquial and loose expressions in a vain attempt to sustain a lie is the hallmark of the Consolidating School of Thought, a deceptive theory of government born of corruption with a mission to cloak fraud in the garb of respectability and legality.

A Construing Supreme Court

The Supreme Court of the United States, throughout the history of our Republic, has a long and notorious record of undermining the Federal Constitution, subverting the principles of federalism, and assailing States' Rights. With the exception of that period in which Roger B. Taney was the Chief Justice of the United States, the U.S. Supreme Court has repeatedly demonstrated that it is thoroughly dedicated to consolidation of the government and the transfer of sovereignty from the peoples of the several States to the Federal Government. That the Federal Supreme Court could and would be a key instrument in the consolidating conspiracy against the American people became abundantly obvious when Chief Justice John Marshall was its guiding light.

Typical of the Supreme Court's ongoing contribution to the cause of consolidation is the historically famous case of *McCulloch vs. Maryland*, which was tried in 1819 and involved the State of Maryland and an agent of the Second Bank of the United States. The dispute was initiated when the State of

Maryland levied a tax against the Baltimore branch of the National Bank, the private banking system established as a monopoly by Congress as part of the Hamiltonian System. Mr. McCulloch, the cashier of the bank, refused to pay the tax, asserting that no State could tax an instrument of the Federal Government. The attorney for Maryland responded by truthfully claiming that Congress was not constitutionally empowered to incorporate a federal banking system, but even if it did, a sovereign State had the power to tax it.

Among the distinguished attorneys representing the State of Maryland before the U.S. Supreme Court was Luther Martin, who had been a delegate to the Constitutional Convention, in which he had been an ardent champion of federalism and republican government. Mr. Martin based the case of the State of Maryland on the argument that the Constitution did not delegate the power to charter a bank to the Federal Government. The distinguished Maryland attorney correctly explained that Article I, Section 8, Clause 18 of the Federal Constitution – often referred to as the *Necessary and Proper Clause* – was not a sweeping grant of implied powers, but merely authorized Congress to pass those laws necessary and proper for carrying into execution the expressly enumerated powers. Because the power to incorporate was not delegated to the Federal Government, he concluded, Congress could not pass a law to charter a bank. As to the power of a State government to tax the bank, Mr. Martin noted that such power had indeed been reserved to the States by the Federal Constitution.

Among those representing the Second Bank of the United States was Daniel Webster, who readily conceded that the Constitution did not expressly delegate to the Federal Government the power to incorporate a bank. But Mr. Webster claimed that the Necessary and Proper Clause must be interpreted loosely or liberally, so that the words *necessary and proper* may be interpreted to mean *convenient and useful*. By such a loose construction, he insisted, the power to incorporate a bank should be considered convenient and useful for collecting taxes, borrowing money, and maintaining the public property of the United States.

By such a mode of construction as advocated by Daniel Webster, it hardly needs to be mentioned, Congress could lay claim to a boundless field of power. In fact, by means of his *loose construction* mode of interpreting the Constitution, Mr. Webster was able to conjure up a power that the Constitutional Convention had deliberately withheld from the Government of the United States. Within the Philadelphia Convention of 1787, a proposal had been made to delegate to Congress the power to incorporate. But an objection was made that such a power could be used to incorporate a National Bank. Thus, that Convention resolved *not* to add the power to incorporate to the list of powers delegated to Congress.

However, the Supreme Court of the United States unanimously rejected every one of Maryland's claims and sustained the arguments of Daniel Webster. Speaking for the Court, Chief Justice Marshall endorsed the loose construction mode of constitutional interpretation, which served greatly to provide a cloak of legality to usurpation of power by the Federal Government:

> Let the end be legitimate, let it be within the scope of the Constitution, and all means which are appropriate, which are plainly adapted to that end, which are not prohibited, but consist with the letter and spirit of the Constitution, are constitutional. [25]

If we may construe the Chief Justice's words loosely, then what John Marshall was saying is that, in construing the Constitution, the principle that *the end justifies the means* should be the guiding light. Since the *end* for which the Federal Government exists is specified in the loose expression, *general welfare of the United States*, that government may assume whatever *means* or *powers* it deems convenient to fulfill that great end. Such a mode of construction, needless to say, could only result in a government of unlimited power – a sovereign government. As the authors of the political science textbook, *Government by the People*, have observed, "The long-range significance of *McCulloch* v. *Maryland* in providing support for the developing forces of nationalism can hardly be overstated." [26]

"One of the People"

The stronghold of the Consolidating School of Thought, as previously indicated, has traditionally been the Northern States of the Union, especially the New England States. The stronghold of the States' Rights School of Thought, on the other hand, has traditionally been the Southern States of the Federal Union. This is not to imply, however, that all Northern politicians and commentators have been the apostles of consolidation, or that all Southerners have been devoted to States' Rights and State sovereignty.

There have been a number of Northern statesmen, such as Franklin Pierce of New Hampshire, the fourteenth President of the United States, who have advocated principles and policies that sustained our federal system of government. Indeed, one of the textbooks on constitutional government used for teaching purposes at the Military Academy at West Point, published in 1829

---

[25] James MacGregor Burns, J.W. Peltason, and Thomas E. Cronin, *Government by the People*, Eleventh Edition, Prentice-Hall, Inc., Englewood Cliffs, 1981, quoted on p. 60.

[26] *Ibid.*, p. 60.

under the title of *A View of the Constitution of the United States of America*, positively asserted the right of the sovereign States to secede from the Union if they chose to do so. Its author, William Rawle, was a Northerner.

In similar fashion, there have been Southern politicians and commentators who have been enthusiastic advocates for the Consolidating School of Thought. Perhaps the most notorious of this latter class of politicians was George McDuffie of South Carolina, who, in 1821, penned a series of essays for a Georgia newspaper that were subsequently circulated widely in pamphlet form. Singing himself "One of the People," the South Carolina politician audaciously assailed the States' Rights School of Thought and denied the existence of sovereign States. Among his arguments were ideas that would later be used by Daniel Webster in his famous debates with Robert Y. Hayne and John C. Calhoun.

Within his series of 1821 essays, George McDuffie of South Carolina advanced the following ideas:

> The general government is as truly the government of the whole people, as a State government is of part of the people. Its Constitution, in the language of its Preamble, was ordained and established by "*the people of the United States.*"...For the moment the people met in Convention, all the elements of political power returned to them to receive a new modification and distribution by their sovereign will....It appears, then, that the "*people*"...created the whole mass of political powers that constitute the general government, reserving to *themselves*, by the elective franchise, the *immediate control* over the whole mass of delegated powers. What security, then, did the Convention, or in other words, "the People of the United States," provide to restrain their functionaries from usurping powers not delegated, and from abusing those with which they are invested? Was it by the discordant clamors and lawless resistance of the State *rulers*, that they intended to "insure domestic tranquility, and form a more perfect Union?" Was it by the officious interference of their *inferior agents*, appointed for no other purposes than those indicated by the State Constitutions, that they intended to "insure a salutary control over their *superior agents*?" No; the Constitution will tell you what is the real security they have provided. It is the responsibility of the officers of the general government, not to the State authorities, but to themselves, the people....
>
> The States, as political bodies, have no original, inherent rights. That they have such rights is a false, dangerous, and anti-republican assumption, which lurks at the bottom of all reasoning in favor of State Rights....As to those imaginary rights, they are by some supposed to exist in the States, in contradistinction to the people of the States, I neither understand nor regard them. They are mere sounds, used by misguided or designing men, for the advancement of their popularity in particular sections of the Union....I think they are to be ascribed to...men whose ambition exceeds their talents....Ambitious men of inferior talents, finding they have no hope to be

distinguished in the councils of the National Government, naturally wish to increase the power and consequences of the State governments, the theatres in which they expect to acquire distinction....

Let us now consider the principles of construction which ought to prevail on ascertaining the extent of the powers delegated by the Constitution to the National Government; and of the means provided for the application of those principles. As far as I can collect any distinct propositions from the medley of unconnected quotations you have made on these very important subjects, I understand you to affirm, that in expounding the Federal Constitution we should be "tied down to the strict" letter of that instrument; and that the general government "was not made the exclusive or final judge of the extent of the powers delegated to itself; but that, as in all other cases of compact among parties having no common judge, *each party has a right to judge for itself.*" As these may be considered the concentrated essence of all the wild and destructive principles that have ever been advanced, in relation to the subjects under consideration, and as they constitute the basis of a contemplated revolution in the administration of the general government, I have been particular in using your very language....Nothing is more clearly demonstrable than that your rule of construction would paralyze every living energy of the Constitution, and absolutely annihilate the government. Without implied and incidental powers, almost the entire mass of means by which the machine of government is kept in motion could not be wielded a single moment....To enumerate the various and detailed operations of a government for centuries to come, and the infinite variety of means that shall be employed, is not therefore the object of a Constitution. Its true object is to distribute the great political powers amongst the several departments of the government, giving a liberal discretion to public agents, in selecting the means by which those powers shall be carried into effect, but providing at the same time, by their responsibility to the people, the only adequate security against the abuse of that discretion....

You assert that when any conflict shall occur between the general and State governments, as to the extent of their respective powers, "*each party has a right to judge for itself.*"...No climax of political heresies can be imagined, in which this might not fairly claim the most prominent place. It resolves the government, at once, into the elements of physical force; and introduces us directly into a scene of anarchy and blood. There is not a single power delegated to the general government, which it would not be in the power of every State government to destroy, under the authority of this licentious principle. It would be only necessary for a State Legislature to pass a law forbidding that which the Federal Legislature enjoins or enjoining what the Federal Legislature forbids, and the work is accomplished. Perhaps you would require the State Judiciary to pronounce the State Law constitutional....

Suppose Congress should pass a law to "lay and collect Taxes, duties, imposts, and excises," and that a State Legislature should pass another declaring the objects for which the revenue was intended, *unconstitutional*, and therefore prohibiting the officers of the general government, by severe penalties, from collecting the "taxes, duties, imposts and excises."...You might, then, behold a revenue officer of the United States confined in a State dun-

> geon for obeying the revenue laws of Congress....In all governments there must be some *one* supreme power...or force must be the inevitable consequence....
>
> It is not less evident that it belongs to the *national judiciary* to pronounce upon the constitutionality or unconstitutionality of the laws of the national legislature. Its jurisdiction extends to "all cases" arising under them; and it is hard to conceive how in any possible case a federal Judge can decide a case arising under a law, without pronouncing upon the constitutionality of that law....I should suppose, therefore, that no professional man could hesitate in saying, that a forcible opposition to the judgment of the Federal Court, founded upon an act of Congress, by whatever State authority might be authorized, would be the very case which the Convention had in view, when they made provision for "calling forth the militia to execute the laws of the Union." But I sincerely hope that your licentious doctrines will never have the effect of misleading the State authorities so far as to render this terrible resort unavoidable. [27]

Within these passages, we see the main tenets of the Consolidating School of Thought expressed in cold, harsh, unmistakable terms. George McDuffie boldly asserted the corrupt thesis that the American people, acting independently of any State associations, framed and ratified the Federal Constitution, despite the plain language of the compact itself which states that it would exist *between the States* who ratified it. According to "One of the People," a mythological State of America adopted the Constitution *over* the States, which have *no inherent rights* as States. That Constitution supposedly established a supreme National Government, even though the Convention that framed the compact specifically rejected a supreme National Government, deliberately removing the word "national" from the evolving compact. Nonetheless, the Federal Government is ostensibly *supreme* over the *inferior* State governments, which is staffed by men of *inferior ambitions*. Therefore, the Government of the United States must be the exclusive judge of the limits of its own powers. And should any State dare to challenge the supreme National Government, that government will prove its supremacy in a blood sacrifice of the offending State.

"In all governments there must be some *one* supreme power," wrote George McDuffie. Therefore, he concluded that political supremacy or sovereignty must be vested in the Government of the United States, thereby rejecting the American Theory of Government, which is based on the concept that *no* government is vested with a *supreme power*. The American Theory of Government, as we have already demonstrated, is founded on the concept that sovereignty is vested in the people of the several States, and that their governments

---

[27] Charles Sellers (ed.), *Andrew Jackson, Nullification, and the State-Rights Tradition*, Rand McNally & Company, Chicago, 1963, pp. 31-33.

possess only *delegated powers*. The States, as sovereign bodies, are the sovereign *parties* to the federal compact. Therefore, they – and they alone – must make the final determination as to the extent of the powers to be exercised by their common agent. And only the sovereign States, as the parties to the compact, can determine, each for itself, in the last resort, if the common agent has exceeded its delegated powers.

According to Mr. McDuffie, however, the Constitution of the United States is whatever the Federal Supreme Court says it is, making it, in actual operation, the sovereign lord and master in the political kingdom. Yet, what would happen to his consolidating doctrine should the States resolve to add an amendment to the Federal Constitution that abolished the U.S. Supreme Court? Who would then become the final arbiter in questions of power? By elevating the *creature* to a position of greater importance than its *creators*, the consolidating doctrines of Mr. McDuffie bear a striking resemblance to a Frankenstein-like horror show of an out-of-control monster on the rampage, threatening to wreak violence and bloodshed on any who happen to confront it.

The Supreme Court of the United States, said George McDuffie, has jurisdiction in all cases arising under the powers delegated to the U.S. Government by the Federal Constitution. Accordingly, he asserted, that Court must be the final judge of the extent of powers delegated to the Federal Government. Yet, by the same line of reasoning, the Supreme Court of each State has final jurisdiction over all cases arising under the powers reserved to the States by the Tenth Amendment to the federal compact. Accordingly, each State Supreme Court must therefore be the final arbiter in regard to the powers reserved to the States by the Constitution of the United States. If the Federal Supreme Court can nullify an unconstitutional State law, should not a State Supreme Court have the right to nullify an unconstitutional federal law?

The answer to Mr. McDuffie's difficulty, of course, is the simple observation that determining the extent of powers that can be exercised by a government is a direct function of sovereignty. This issue must be decided, *in the final resort*, by the supreme *political* power, and not by the supreme *judicial* power. Only the peoples of the several States are vested with this supreme political power, and only they, as organized political communities, are parties to the federal compact. The State legislatures, directly representing the parties to the federal compact, may therefore rightfully act on behalf of their respective peoples to protect them from dangerous usurpations and abuses of power by the common agent of the Federal Union. To admit the right of the sovereign peoples of the several States to resist unconstitutional federal acts, but to deny to them the *practical means* of exercising such resistance, is a contradiction in logic that effectually nullifies this most fundamental right of self-defense and government-by-the-consent-of-the-governed.

According to the South Carolina consolidator, the Federal Government should not be tied to the strict letter of the Constitution, but must be allowed to assume and exercise *implied powers* that it might find convenient. By this same line of reasoning, the State governments should also be allowed to exercise implied powers that they find convenient. Such a mode of construction, needless to say, would soon result in both Federal and State governments attempting to claim possession of unlimited powers. The concept of strictly drawn and clearly defined demarcations between federal and State governmental powers is assuredly more preferable than the absurd mode of constitutional construction advocated by Mr. McDuffie.

The criticism of State Interposition and Nullification offered by "One of the People" could just as easily be applied to every other type of *checks and balances* within our system and form of government that is intended to serve as a *brake* against the abuse of power. His argument could also be applied, for example, to a Presidential veto of an act of Congress, as well as to a Presidential pardon of a party convicted in a federal court or to the Congressional override of a Presidential veto. Such *internal checks* are widely recognized and respected as necessary precautions to guard against despotism. Why, then, should not the same recognition and respect be extended to the *external check* on federal power that is afforded by State Interposition and Nullification? Whatever is lost in terms of efficiency in governmental operations by such checks on power will be more than compensated by the preservation of the liberties of the American people.

If the Federal Government may assume the powers not delegated, which would be inevitable if it is allowed to be the final judge as to the limits of its powers, what is to protect the people from eventual tyranny? On this question, George McDuffie fell back on the franchise. His contention was nothing short of advocacy for a revolutionary transformation of our constitutionally limited republican form of government into an unlimited majority rule democracy. Even if a supreme National Government should usurp powers right and left, thereby becoming a totalitarian government that enslaves the people by putting them in chains, all that would matter, Mr. McDuffie insisted, is that such a government is elective in nature. As long as the people could elect the rulers who held the ends of their chains, the masses would be happy and content. This, in the estimation of the Consolidating School of Thought, constitutes *good government* for the United States of America.

If further proof were required to illustrate the utter folly of relying solely on the franchise to safeguard the rights of man from invasions by the Government of the United States, then we may humbly offer an example to conclusively demonstrate it. Let us suppose, for purposes of illustration, that the Government of the United States should enact a law to confiscate all the property of every citizen in the State of Florida, with the proceeds of this wholesale plunder to be distributed among the other 49 States of the Union. Let us also suppose that this act received the enthusiastic support of the U.S. Representatives and Senators from all the States save Florida.

Such a federal act would unmistakably be unconstitutional, not to mention extremely subversive of liberty. We should expect that the internal system of checks and balances within the Federal Government would work to put a brake on the progress of the evil. Yet, continuing with our supposition, let us assume that the President refuses to veto the obnoxious act of Congress, and that the Supreme Court of the United States rules that the federal act is in perfect accord with its conception of the Federal Constitution. In a situation such as this, what recourse would the good people of the sovereign State of Florida have to prevent the progress of the evil?

According to "One of the People," the people of Florida would have no choice but to submit to despotism and allow themselves to be plundered. Their only hope would lie in the next federal election. Of course, the only federal officers accountable to the people of Florida are the two Senators and those Members of the Lower House of Congress elected by Florida. None of the other Senators and U.S. Representatives is accountable to the people of Florida, and the people being plundered would have no opportunity to vote them out of office. The victimized people of the Sunshine State would discover that the elective nature of the Federal Government offers no security whatsoever for the preservation of their most basic rights.

The security for fundamental human rights advocated by the States' Rights School of Thought, on the other hand, would offer real hope for the plundered Floridians in the scenario described above. The State Government of Florida, whose sole reason for existence is to protect the rights of the citizens of that State, would solemnly interpose its authority and nullify the obnoxious federal act. If the other States insisted on adding an amendment to the Federal Constitution specifically delegating the power to plunder Florida, the States' Rights School of Thought provides an answer for that threat as well. The State of Florida could rightfully and constitutionally secede from the Union.

By this illustration, we have demonstrated the practical effects of each school of thought. One places paramount importance on the smooth and efficient operation of the machinery of government, emphasizing that unchecked power must not be impeded by concerns for human rights. The other places a premium on the preservation of the inalienable rights of man, emphasizing that whenever power and liberty are in conflict, power must ever yield to liberty. The fundamental issue may be crystallized into a contest between uninterrupted power and enduring freedom. Which one matters most to the reader?

It is true, of course, that the governments of the States can themselves usurp and abuse powers and thereby threaten the rights and liberties of their respective populations. The same may be said of the governments at the county, city, and township levels. Yet, the entire history of the human race provides ample testimony that the closer a government is to the governed, the less potential danger it poses to liberty. Conversely, the farther from the people that a government is, the greater the number of people that it governs, the greater the diversity of the population under its jurisdiction, and the greater the territory within its control, the greater is the potential for abuse of power and, consequently, the more insecure are the rights of the people. All of these considerations point to the inescapable conclusion that the potential threat to the liberties of the American people posed by the Government of the United States is at least fifty times greater than the threat posed by any State government.

Men of Lofty Ambitions

"The assumption of State authorities will appear still more glaring and unwarrantable," wrote George McDuffie, "when we reflect, that whatever is assumed as a State right, pertains equally to every State in the Union, separately and individually." [28] If this is a valid argument against States' Rights, then it must also be a valid argument against the natural rights of man, because human rights pertain equally to every individual in society, separately and individually. But does that fact prove that individual human rights do not or should not exist? Should the separateness of States' Rights prove that the reserved rights and sovereignty of the several States do not or should not exist?

But the States have no need to fear for the safety of their reserved rights and powers, asserted "One of the People," because those officers chosen to administer the Federal Government are more intelligent, more patriotic, and more enlightened than the narrow-minded politicians who are elected to State offices. Having more lofty ambitions than chauvinistic State officials, the officers of the Federal Government would not wish to stoop to the level of pilfering powers from the States or of robbing the people of their liberties. Lofty ambition, Mr. McDuffie assured the American people, looks to higher and more noble pursuits.

As "One of the People" insisted:

> As long as we (the people,) continue the officers of the *general* government in office, their acts are ours; as their business is of greater impor-

---

[28] John Taylor, *New Views of the Constitution of the United States, Op. cit.*, quoted on p. 200.

> tance than yours, (the business of the State governments,) we of course select the most intelligent men to perform it, and your attempt to control them is therefore peculiarly unbecoming and arrogant. [29]

Those officers of our State governments, said Mr. McDuffie, must understand their position of inferiority within our system of government. Not only are their powers more inferior and their services offered to the people less important, but their intellects are obviously far less than the those of the politicians who fill federal offices. Any attempt to control these men of superior talents and ambitions, therefore, is unbecoming and arrogant. All officers of State and local governments must learn to act humbly toward their superiors in the Federal Government.

"Ambitious men of inferior talents," wrote George McDuffie, "finding they have no hope to be distinguished in the councils of the National Government, naturally wish to increase the power and consequence of the State governments, the theatres in which they expect to acquire distinction." "The powers of the State governments," he assured his readers, "constitute precisely that class of political powers that has the least attractions for ambition. They establish the rules of property, and fix and define the rights of persons."[30]

Continuing in this same vein, "One of the People" wrote:

> Ambition holds a loftier career. The States are excluded from all the pride, pomp, and circumstance of glorious war. When, therefore, we consider the nature of ambition, when we reflect that it is desirous of performing those actions only which history records with her brightest and most enduring colours, and nations behold with the highest admiration, the folly of the apprehension that the general government will subvert the State governments, is most strikingly apparent.
>
> Upon the discretion of Congress in laying and collecting taxes, and in raising and supporting armies, there are no restrictions except those imposed by nature. Congress may draw from the people (of the States too,) the utmost farthing that can be spread from their suffering families, to fill the national coffers; and call out the last man that can be spared from raising the necessaries of life, to fill the national armies, and fight the battles of ambitious rulers. These tremendous engines are harmless to the people, and will not be depredators upon the more peaceful, inefficient, and unattractive powers of the State governments. We are called upon to believe that our federal rulers will use with moderation the very powers by which ambitious men, have, in all ages, built up the monuments of their own aggrandizement; and yet that these rulers will consummate their ambitious purposes, and subvert our liberties, by the paltry and petit larceny process of pilfering little fragments from the temple of sovereignty. It is not in the course of ambition

[29] *Ibid.*, quoted on p. 198.
[30] *Ibid.*, quoted on p. 200-201.

> to descend, for in its proper motion it ascends. Abstractly considered, power has no allurements. It is only desirable from its imposing restrictions. [31]

The American people, "One of the People" assured his readers, have nothing to fear from a sovereign National Government that has no restrictions except those imposed by nature. The proud and pompous officers of such a government will be too busy pursuing the more lofty and imperial ambitions of glorious wars of conquest and building a socialistic New World Order to stoop to petit larceny of the rights of the people and the reserved powers of the States. The people of the United States have nothing to fear from politicians with great ambitions and great powers, despite all the lessons of history which dictate that great ambitions and great powers invariably beget despotism.

George McDuffie claimed that, should the consolidating school succeed in subverting the Constitution and erecting a supreme National Government, federal politicians and bureaucrats would not trouble themselves with the trivial affairs of American society. The Federal Government, under the control of highly ambitious politicians, would not attempt to meddle in the affairs of the marketplace, impose draconian regulations on American businesses, establish standards for public education, concern itself with urban renewal, establish racial quotas for hiring standards, attempt to regulate the environment, force the people to wear seatbelts in their automobiles, or involve itself in any other manner in the American way of life. Such affairs as these, "One of the People" proclaimed, are simply too trivial and mundane to tempt the pompous, proud, and intellectually superior federal politicians of superior talents and ambitions. All of these internal or domestic matters our ambitious federal rulers of the consolidating stripe would gladly leave to the State governments, whose inferior talents, ambitions, and intellects are more aptly suited to them.

We now have the advantage of hindsight to assist us in forming an assessment of these bold assurances given by "One of the People." When we look upon our modern Welfare State, in which the Government of the United States attempts to control everything and dictate to everyone without limitation, do we discover that scheming and ambitious federal politicians are content with merely conquering the world? Or are they also guilty of the grand theft of States' Rights and the invasion of the natural rights of the American people?

What we have discovered with the passage of time is that our ambitious federal rulers are not content with the petit larcenies of the reserved rights of the States, but seek to carry off the very temple of liberty – lock, stock, and barrel – by flatly denying the existence of the sovereignty of the States. And we have discovered that a government that does not acknowledge and respect the

---

[31] *Ibid.*, quoted on p. 201-202.

political rights of the people also refuses to acknowledge and respect their individual natural rights to life, liberty, and property.

The Tenth Amendment

As the brilliant constitutionalist, Jefferson Davis, noted in his great work, *The Rise and Fall of the Confederate Government*, the principle of the sovereignty of the States within our Federal Union is enshrined in the Tenth Amendment to the Constitution:

> If any lingering doubt could have existed as to the reservation of their entire sovereignty by the people of the respective States, when they organized the Federal Union, it would have been removed by the adoption of the Tenth Amendment to the Constitution, which was not only one of the amendments proposed by various States when ratifying that instrument, but the particular one which they substantially agreed, and upon which they most urgently insisted. Indeed, it is quite certain that the Constitution would never have received the assent and ratification of Massachusetts, New Hampshire, New York, North Carolina, and perhaps other States, but for a well-grounded assurance that the substance of this amendment would be adopted as soon as the requisite formalities could be complied with.... [32]

Amendment Ten to the Federal Constitution, which summarizes our entire federal system of government, is part of the cherished set of amendments known as the *Bill of Rights*. Only when the Federalists had agreed to the addition of a Bill of Rights to the Constitution were they able to secure the ratification of our present federal compact. Once the Constitution of 1787 went into effect, the promise was kept, and the new Congress compiled a list of twelve amendments, which were submitted to the States for ratification. Of those twelve proposed amendments in the Bill of Rights, ten were successfully ratified and incorporated into the supreme law of the land.

The cherished Tenth Amendment reads as follows: "The powers not delegated to the United States by the Constitution, nor prohibited by it to the States, are reserved to the States respectively, or to the people." [33]

This amendment constitutes a crucial cornerstone of the States' Rights School of Thought, for it contains a summary of the foundations of our system of constitutionally limited government. Its significance perhaps may be better understood by comparing and contrasting the opinions of Thomas Jefferson and Alexander Hamilton regarding the constitutionality of the bill to incorpo-

---

[32] Jefferson Davis, *Op. cit.*, Volume 1, p. 146.

[33] Harold C. Syrett (ed.), *American Historical Documents*, Barnes & Noble, Inc., New York, 1960, p. 117.

rate the First Bank of the United States during the Administration of President George Washington.

The power to incorporate, as we have previously noted, had been deliberately withheld from the Federal Government by the Philadelphia Convention of 1787 precisely because it was feared that such a power might be used to incorporate a National Bank. Yet, as a significant part of the Hamiltonian System of plunder and corruption, a National Bank was considered by the consolidators to be indispensable. For this reason, Mr. Hamilton, as Secretary of the Treasury, proposed to Congress the creation of the First Bank of the United States on December 14, 1790. When the bill was introduced in Congress, however, James Madison and others arose to declare the proposition unconstitutional. And when the bill eventually reached him, President Washington expressed reservations about its constitutionality and requested the opinions of his Cabinet members.

Needless to say, Alexander Hamilton, responding to President Washington's request, asserted that a National Bank was quite proper and constitutional. "Hamilton," noted Harold C. Syrett, "wrote what is generally recognized as a classic statement of the so-called broad or loose interpretation of the Constitution." [34] Thomas Jefferson, on the other hand, wrote a powerful indictment highlighting the measure's unconstitutionality. "Although Jefferson's opinion was rejected by Washington," wrote Mr. Syrett, "it still stands as one of the most penetrating arguments ever written for a strict interpretation of the Constitution." [35]

Within his opinion to President Washington, Alexander Hamilton laid the foundation of Consolidating School of Thought in regard to *interpreting* the Federal Constitution and introduced the subversive concept of *implied* or *inherent* powers supposedly possessed by the Government of the United States:

> Now it appears to the Secretary of the Treasury that this *general principle* is *inherent* in the very *definition* of government, and *essential* to every step of the progress to be made by that of the United States, namely: That every power vested in the government is in its nature *sovereign*, and includes, by *force* of the *term* a right to employ all the *means* requisite and fairly applicable to the attainment of the *ends* of such power, and which are not precluded by restrictions and exceptions specified in the Constitution, or not immoral, or not contrary to the *essential ends* of political society.... [36]

Here we see the practical application of the Consolidating School of Thought to the powers of the Federal Government. Because the Federal Gov-

---

[34] *Ibid.*, p. 134.
[35] *Ibid.*, p. 131.
[36] *Ibid.*, p. 134.

ernment is a *government,* Mr. Hamilton insisted, it was automatically sovereign, a concept that could only be supported by an acceptance of the Divine Rights of Kings theory of government. Because that government is sovereign, he insisted, it possesses the natural right to assume any powers it pleases, unless the power in question has been explicitly prohibited to it. The ends justify the means, according to the Consolidating School of Thought. The Necessary and Proper Clause, for example, when coupled with the General Welfare Clause, may be misinterpreted as a sweeping grant of implied power to pass all laws that the Congress may believe, or pretend to believe, are convenient for providing for whatever Congress proclaims to be the general welfare of the United States. By such interpretations as this, the entire concept of constitutionally limited government can be subverted and the Federal Government may be replaced with a supreme, sovereign National Government possessing unlimited powers.

In his opinion to President Washington, Thomas Jefferson laid the cornerstone for the States' Rights School of Thought in regard to interpreting the Federal Constitution:

> I consider the foundation of the Constitution as laid on this ground: that all powers not delegated to the United States, by the Constitution, nor prohibited by it to the States, are reserved to the States, or to the people....To take a single step beyond the boundaries thus specially drawn around the powers of Congress, is to take possession of a boundless field of power, no longer susceptible of any definition. [37]

In writing and adopting the Federal Constitution, the States carefully specified what powers had been delegated to the Federal Government. Inasmuch as the States are sovereign within our Union, it was automatically understood that they are the source of all political powers, and that all powers not delegated to the Federal Government, nor prohibited by the Constitution to the States, are reserved to the States, either to be exercised by the State governments or to be held in reserve by the people, who might wish to withhold some powers even from their own State governments.

As we have observed, the two great schools of thought – that of States' Rights and that of consolidation – are diametrically opposed in regard to the powers that can be rightfully exercised by the Government of the United States. In advocating a sovereign, supreme National Government, the Consolidating School of Thought bases its case on a claim for inherent or implied powers. The States' Rights School of Thought, on the hand, has always regarded the Tenth Amendment to be the *foundation* of our system of constitu-

---

[37] *Ibid.*, p. 131.

tionally limited government.

Regarding this highly significant amendment, Jefferson Davis commented:

> The full meaning of this article may not be as clear to us as it was to the men of that period, on account of the confusion of ideas by which the term "people" – plain enough to them – has since been obscured, and also the ambiguity attendant upon the use of the little conjunction *or*, which has been said to be the most equivocal word in our language, and for that reason has been excluded from indictments in the English courts. The true intent and meaning of the provision, however, may be ascertained from an examination and comparison of the terms in which it was expressed by the various States which proposed it, and whose ideas it was intended to embody. [38]

The true and precise meaning of the Tenth Amendment to the Federal Constitution, as Mr. Davis indicated, may be ascertained by examining the ordinances of ratification of seven of the original thirteen States of the Union. The States of Massachusetts, South Carolina, North Carolina, New Hampshire, Rhode Island, Virginia, and New York all submitted proposals that were subsequently combined and condensed into what is now Amendment Ten of our present Federal Constitution. Below are listed the proposals submitted by these sovereign States:

- **Massachusetts:** "That it be explicitly declared that all powers not expressly delegated by the aforesaid Constitution are reserved to the several States, to be by them exercised." [39]
- **South Carolina:** "This convention doth also declare that no section or paragraph of the said Constitution warrants a construction that the States do not retain every power not expressly relinquished by them and vested in the general government of the Union." [40]
- **North Carolina:** "Each State in the Union shall respectively retain every power, jurisdiction, and right, which is not by this Constitution delegated to the Congress of the United States or to the departments of the general government." [41]
- **New Hampshire:** "That it be explicitly declared that all powers not expressly delegated by the aforesaid Constitution are reserved

[38] Jefferson David, *Op. cit.*, Volume 1, p. 146.
[39] *Ibid.*, Volume 1, quoted on p. 147.
[40] *Ibid.*, Volume 1, quoted on p. 147.
[41] *Ibid.*, Volume 1, quoted on p. 147.

to the several States, to be by them exercised." [42]

- **Rhode Island:** "That Congress shall guarantee to each State its sovereignty, freedom, and independence, and every power, jurisdiction, and right, which is not by this Constitution expressly delegated to the United States." [43]
- **Virginia:** "We, the Delegates of the people of Virginia, ...Do, in the name and in behalf of the people of Virginia, declare and make known, that the powers granted under the Constitution, being derived from the people of the United States, may be resumed by them, whensoever the same shall be perverted to their injury or oppression, and that every power not granted thereby remains with them, and at their will...." [44]
- **New York:** "That the powers of government may be reassumed by the people whenever it shall become necessary to their happiness; that every power, jurisdiction, and right, which is not by the said Constitution clearly delegated to the Congress of the United States, or the departments of the general government thereof, remains to the people of the several States, or to their respective State governments, to whom they may have granted the same; and that those clauses of the said Constitution, which declare that Congress shall not have or exercise certain powers, do not imply that Congress is entitled to any powers not given by the said Constitution, but such clauses are to be construed either as exceptions to certain specified powers or as inserted merely for greater caution." [45]

It was from these various proposals that Amendment Ten was finally written and submitted to the States for their assent and approval. Perhaps it would have been better had the Tenth Amendment been worded precisely as the State of New York recommended, or as Rhode Island proposed. Nonetheless, it is clear that the Tenth Amendment, as it is now worded, conveys the same principles as these seven proposals from the various State Ratifying Conventions.

Considering together the Ninth Amendment and the Tenth Amendment, the purpose of the Founding Fathers was to fully and completely safeguard the rights of the American people. While the **Ninth Amendment** was designed to be a sweeping protection of unspecified *individual human rights*,

[42] *Ibid.*, Volume 1, quoted on p. 147.
[43] *Ibid.*, Volume 1, quoted on p. 148.
[44] Alexander H. Stephens, *Op. cit.*, Volume 1, quoted on pp. 254-255.
[45] Jefferson Davis, *Op. cit.*, Volume 1, quoted on p. 147.

the **Tenth Amendment** was designed to be a sweeping protection of the rights of the people in their *politically organized capacities* as sovereign States. Of these two, the Tenth Amendment may be considered the most important part of the entire Bill of Rights, for it serves the purpose of reinforcing the concept that the powers of the Federal Government are restricted to those enumerated in the Constitution. If the Federal Government can be effectually restricted to its enumerated powers, the natural rights of individual citizens will be secured as a natural consequence.

Of course, the perceptive reader does not need to be reminded that the Tenth Amendment, like the rest of the Bill of Rights, is not really necessary, as many of our Founding Fathers realized at the time the Constitution was adopted. The principles contained in Amendment Ten are *inherent* in the American Theory of Government, which holds that all powers not delegated by the people to their government are reserved to them. But even with the addition of the Tenth Amendment to the federal compact, the consolidating school has consistently refused to acknowledge this most basic principle.

In his debate with Senator John C. Calhoun in 1833, for instance, Daniel Webster declared:

> There is no language in the whole Constitution applicable to a Confederation of States. If the States be parties, as States, what are their rights, and what their respective covenants and stipulations? And where are their rights, covenants, and stipulations expressed? In the Articles of Confederation they did make promises, and did enter into engagements, and did plight the faith of each State for their fulfillment; but in the Constitution there is nothing of that kind. The reason is that, in the Constitution, it is the people who speak and not the States. The people ordain the Constitution and therein address themselves to the States and to the Legislatures of the States in the language of injunction and prohibition. [46]

If there is one point on which most historians and political scientists agree, even among those who support the Consolidating School of Thought, it is that the Federal Constitution represents a *bundle of compromises* between the States composing the Federal Union, from the three-fifths compromise for counting slaves for taxation and representation purposes, to the manner of representation in the Congress based on the various populations of the several States for the lower house and on their sovereign equality in the upper house. Yet, Senator Webster claimed that he could not find those stipulations and covenants in the federal compact. Incredibly he dared to ask, in regard to the States, "what are their rights?" He further inquired, "where are their rights ...expressed?" He could not even find the Tenth Amendment to the Federal

---

[46] *Ibid.*, Volume 1, quoted on p. 152.

Constitution!

Another equally absurd illustration of how the Consolidating School of Thought ignores the Tenth Amendment is the book, *Reconstruction*, which was written by Charles G. Loring, a Radical Republican, and published in 1866. With respect to the right of representation in the Congress, this consolidator stated: "The people of the United States was the grantor, and the several States respectively were the grantees, of that right." [47] As to how the "people of the United States" *in the aggregate* could possibly grant anything is difficult to comprehend, inasmuch as the only peoples recognized by the Constitution are the peoples of the sovereign States. Even more nonsensical was Mr. Loring's assertion that, "State rights and powers are such, and such only, as were granted, defined, or recognized by the Constitution." [48]

Thus, the Consolidating School of Thought contends that the powers of the Federal Government are implied and inherent, and hence, unlimited, whereas the powers of the States are only those that the so-called Nation has granted to them. Such a contention, needless to say, is precisely the opposite of reality, as a plain reading of the Tenth Amendment reveals. But in the eyes of the consolidating school, the Tenth Amendment does not exist.

Let us suppose, for sake of argument, that the Founding Fathers had decided to write the Tenth Amendment in different words, so that it read: "The States of this Union retain their sovereignty." Such a positive assertion of State sovereignty, however, would undoubtedly have not prevented the rise of the Consolidating School of Thought. Had the Tenth Amendment been worded in this manner, the consolidators would undoubtedly have attempted to undermine its meaning by improperly defining sovereignty or by claiming that the concept of sovereignty was too mysterious to have any real meaning within our system of government. And in the event that those arguments failed to sway the general public, the consolidators would undoubtedly have simply ignored such a positive assertion of State sovereignty as though it did not exist. The Consolidating School of Thought, it must always be remembered, was never intended to present an honest theory of constitutional government, but to conceal the obvious illegality of the policies advocated by the consolidators of humanity.

Although the Tenth Amendment does not contain the word sovereignty, it is based upon the concept of sovereign States. According to the American Theory of Government, sovereignty is vested in the States, and therefore, the Federal Government created by those States may possess and exercise only delegated powers, while all powers not delegated, nor prohibited to the States by agreement, are reserved to the States. Amendment Ten focuses exclusively

---

[47] Jabez Lamar Monroe Curry, *The Southern States in the American Union*, G.P. Putnam's Sons, New York, 1895, quoted on p. 135.

[48] *Ibid.*, quoted on p. 135.

on the *practical application* of the concept of State sovereignty within our system of government, by explicitly declaring that the Federal Government is one of enumerated powers and that the States possess inherent, unspecified powers.

The powers not delegated to the United States, nor prohibited by the Federal Constitution to the States, declares Amendment Ten, are reserved "to the States respectively, or to the people." To determine precisely what this means, we should reflect upon some basic truths. The only people who existed at the time the Constitution of 1787 was adopted were the people of thirteen sovereign States. There was no other organized body of people, only the thirteen sovereign States. The only people who delegated powers to the Government of the United States in the federal compact, therefore, were the people of the States who ratified it. No other political body of people ratified the compact and thereby delegated powers to the Federal Government.

By logical conclusion, *only those peoples who delegated powers could reserve the powers not delegated.* The powers not delegated remained precisely where they were originally invested, in the peoples of the several States. With this proper understanding, the final words of the Tenth Amendment could be changed – from "to the States respectively, or to the people," to read, "to the peoples of the several States" – without changing its meaning.

One final observation is in order, regarding the Tenth Amendment to the Constitution of the United States. The opening words of this amendment bear close scrutiny: "The powers not delegated to the United States by the Constitution...." This tells us two things. Firstly, this section of Amendment Ten tells us that the powers delegated by the States are delegated *by the Constitution.* The States yielded nothing except what was delineated or expressly declared within the Federal Constitution.

Secondly, this section of the Tenth Amendment tells us that the powers delegated by the peoples of the States were delegated *to the United States.* The United States of America, of course, is the title of our Federal Union, which is a political association among the States. In and of itself, the Union – the United States – is merely an abstract concept. The only *entity* actually created by the Union of States is the *Federal Government.* This section of the Tenth Amendment could be re-worded as follows, without altering its meaning: "The powers not delegated to the *Federal Government* by the Constitution...."

Anything yielded by the States to the "United States" ends up in the hands of the Government of the United States. Nothing was delegated to an amalgamated, consolidated Nation of Americans. All delegated powers were delegated to the Federal Government. Thus, if the States lost any or all of their sovereignty by adopting the Federal Constitution, such sovereignty could go nowhere else except to the Government of the United States. The consolidating school understands this all too well, yet hopes that the American people can be tricked into thinking that, if the States are robbed of their sovereignty, such sovereignty will somehow be magically vested in a consolidated Nation of Americans that does not really exist.

Sovereign States Are Sovereign People

It is utterly impossible for the American people to be sovereign unless the States are sovereign, for the people are the States, and the States are the people. Reflection reveals that those who deny the sovereignty of the States, however *democratic* they may appear on the surface, are actually consigning the American people to slavery. Invariably, he who assails States' Rights is an advocate of sovereign government, and it matters not if State sovereignty is assailed in the name of the people or in the name of a monied aristocracy. The consequences are all that matters.

Whatever facts the consolidators cannot ignore, they pervert and distort. Judge Joseph Story, for instance, with his notorious *Commentaries on the Constitution*, was forced to admit that the people voted *as States* when they ratified the compact. Yet, rather than concede that this fact unmistakably proved that the States adopted the compact as sovereign bodies, he merely glossed over this historical fact by stating that such was the only way a consolidated Nation of Americans could have assembled to express their sovereign will. The States were already organized political societies, and voting by States, he averred, was done merely as a matter of convenience.

Regarding this attempt to distort reality, Jefferson Davis made the following remarks in his great work, *The Rise and Fall of the Confederate Government*:

> Judge Story, referring to the fact that the voters assembled in the several States, asks where else they could have assembled – a pertinent question in our theory, but the idea he evidently intended to convey was that the voting of "the people" by States was a mere matter of geographical necessity, or local convenience; just as the people of a State vote by counties; the people of a county by towns, "beats," or "precincts"; and the people of a city by wards. It is hardly necessary to say that, in all organized republican communities, majorities govern. When we speak of the will of the people of a community, we mean the will of a majority, which, when constitutionally expressed, is binding on any minority of the same community.
>
> If, then, we can conceive, and admit for a moment, the possibility that, when the Constitution was under consideration, the people of the United States were politically "one people" – a collective unit – two deductions are clearly inevitable: In the first place, each geographic division of this great community would have been entitled to vote according to its relative

population; and, in the second, the expressed will of the legal majority would have been binding upon the whole. A denial of the first proposition would be a denial of common justice and equal rights; a denial of the second would be to destroy all government and establish mere anarchy.

> Now, *neither* of these principles was practiced or proposed or even imagined in the case of the action of the people of the United States (if they were one political community) upon the proposed Constitution. On the contrary, seventy thousand people in the State of Delaware had precisely the same weight – one vote – in its ratification, as seven hundred thousand (and more) in Virginia, or four hundred thousand in Pennsylvania. Would not this have been an intolerable grievance and wrong – would no protest have been uttered against it – if these had been fractional parts of one community of people?
>
> Again, while the will of the consenting majority *within* any State was binding on the opposing minority in the same, no majority, or majorities, of the States or people had any control whatever upon the people of *another* State. The Constitution was established, not "*over* the States," as asserted by Motley, but "*between* the States," and only "between *the States so ratifying* the same." Little Rhode Island, with her seventy thousand inhabitants, was not a fractional part of "the people of the whole land," during the period for which she held aloof, but was as free, independent, and unmolested, as any other sovereign power, notwithstanding the majority or more than three millions of "the whole people" on the other side of the question. [49]

Echoing these same sentiments was James Madison, the Father of the Constitution, who wrote in the *Federalist*, No. 39:

> That it will be a Federal and not a National act, as these terms are understood by objectors – the act of the people, as forming so many independent States, *not as forming one aggregate nation* – is obvious from this single consideration, that it is to result neither from the decision of a majority of the people of the Union nor from that of a majority of the States. It must result from the *unanimous* assent of the several *States that are parties to it*, differing no otherwise from their ordinary assent than in its being expressed, not by the legislative authority, but by that of the people themselves. Were the people regarded in this transaction as forming one Nation, the will of the majority of the whole people of the United States would bind the minority, in the same manner as the majority in each State must bind the minority; and the will of the majority must be determined either by a comparison of the individual votes or by considering the will of the majority of the States as evidence of the will of a majority of the people of the United States. Neither of these has been adopted. Each State, in ratifying the Constitution, is considered as a sovereign body, independent of all others, and only to be bound by its own voluntary act. In this relation, then, the new Constitution will, if

[49] Jefferson Davis, *Op. cit.*, Volume 1, pp. 132-133.

established, be a Federal and not a National Constitution. [emphasis added][50]

An issue appertaining to the question of sovereignty involves the concept of *loyalty* and *allegiance.* Only a sovereign power can demand allegiance, and only a sovereign power can execute a citizen for committing *treason.* According to *Webster's II New Riverside University Dictionary*, treason is defined as: "1. Violation of allegiance toward one's country or sovereign, esp. the betrayal of one's own country by waging war against it or by consciously and purposely acting to aid its enemies. 2. Betrayal of confidence or trust." [51] Treason cannot be regarded as a crime committed again*st a government*, unless that government is considered sovereign. According to the American Theory of Government, sovereignty is vested in the people of each State, as States. Treason in the United States, therefore, can only consist in betraying the States, either jointly or individually.

Article III, Section 3 of the Federal Constitution declares that, "Treason against the United States, shall consist only in levying War against *them*, or in adhering to *their* Enemies, giving them Aid and Comfort." [emphasis added] [52]

This provision, it should be noted, does not attempt to define treason within our entire political system, but only "treason against the United States." *Treason against a particular State* may be punished by the State against whom the traitor acts. Perhaps the most historically famous case of treason against one State is that involving John Brown and his infamous attack on Harper's Ferry on the eve of the War Between the States. The fanatical abolitionist was tried and convicted of committing murder and treason against the State of Virginia and paid for his crimes on the gallows.

Within the constitutional provision cited above, attention should be given to the words italicized, "them" and "their." These two words merit particular consideration, for they reveal that treason against the United States is a crime committed against more than one sovereignty; it is a crime against the *States United*, or against all of the States jointly.

It is of more than mere passing interest to note that, throughout the Federal Constitution, the term "United States" is treated as a *plural* concept, as we might expect if the term were reversed to read, "States United." Article I, Section 9, Clause 8, for instance, declares that, "No title of nobility shall be granted by the United States: and no person holding any office of profit or trust under *them* shall, without the consent of Congress, accept...." [emphasis

---

[50] Alexander Hamilton, James Madison, and John Jay, *Op. cit.*, pp. 243-244.

[51] Anne H. Soukhanov (ed.), *Webster's II New Riverside University Dictionary*, The Riverside Publishing Company, Boston, 1984, p. 1230.

[52] Harold C. Syrett (ed.), *Op. cit.*, p. 113.

added] [53] Article II, Section 1, Clause 6 provides another excellent illustration of this concept: "The President...shall not receive within that period any other emolument from the United States, or any of *them.*" [emphasis added] [54] Within these clauses, the phrase "United States" could be replaced with the phrase "States United" without altering the meaning conveyed.

The Supremacy Clause

One of the most frequently cited sections of the Constitution among consolidators is Article VI, Section 2, which is popularly and generally known as the *Supremacy Clause.* The favor which this clause finds in the eyes of consolidators is not due to its true meaning, but to the distorted meaning which the consolidators claim for it.

As this Supremacy Clause declares:

> This Constitution, and the laws of the United States which shall be made in pursuance thereof, and all treaties made, or which shall be made, under the authority of the United States, shall be the supreme law of the land; and the judges in every State shall be bound thereby, any thing in the Constitution or laws of any State to the contrary notwithstanding. [55]

In the Consolidating School of Thought, this constitutional provision completely and totally subverts State sovereignty. John L. Motley, for example, gleefully asserted:

> Could language be more imperial? Could the claim to State "sovereignty" be more completely disposed of at a word? How can that be sovereign, acknowledging no superior, supreme, which has voluntarily accepted a supreme law from something which it acknowledges as superior? [56]

Such ideas, of course, are ludicrous in the extreme. When the sovereign States, assembled in Convention, labored intensely to craft a plan of government for their common Union, which would be based upon a number of compromises, it would be only natural that they should insist upon compliance from all members of the Union. It would have been absurd to have written and adopted a common plan of government, if any or all of the States could with impunity ignore or violate the agreements contained in their compact. The Su-

---

[53] *Ibid.*, p. 109.
[54] *Ibid.*, p. 111.
[55] *Ibid.*, p. 114.
[56] Jefferson Davis, *Op. cit.*, Volume 1, quoted on p. 150.

premacy Clause, therefore, is merely an understanding among the sovereign States that they will abide by the Constitution which they, themselves, wrote and adopted.

The ones who wrote, adopted, and authorized the supreme law of the land are the true sovereigns within our political system. The Constitution and all laws and treaties made in pursuance of it constitute the *supreme law of the land* only because the States have so declared, in their sovereign capacities, that such shall be the case. *Only a supreme power can authorize a supreme law.* The Supremacy Clause, so far from detracting from the sovereignty of the States, is actually one more item of evidence that proves that the States are indeed sovereign within our political system.

As Russell Hoover Quynn has noted in his book, *The Constitutions of Abraham Lincoln and Jefferson Davis*, which was published in 1959:

> Motley's error lies in not perceiving that the States which ordained and established the Constitution accepted nothing besides what they themselves prescribed; they acknowledged no superior. The supremacy, both in degree and in extent, is only that which they were delegating in the agreement between themselves – to which agreement the general government was not a party but was the result created by it.[57]

Explaining the purpose of the Supremacy Clause, Captain Quynn wrote:

> Each existing State already had its own Constitution and code of statute laws; it was undoubtedly primarily with reference to these that the provision was inserted – not in the expectation, as [Jefferson] Davis says, of future conflicts and discrepancies. It was in this light that Madison, in the *Federalist*, No. XLIV, considered it, in explanation and vindication. Hamilton similarly pointed out, "...the laws of the Confederacy [that is, the United States] as to the *enumerated* and *legitimate* objects of its jurisdiction, will become the supreme law of the land" – the State functionaries co-operating in their observance and enforcement with the general government "*as far as its just and constitutional authority extends.*" (Italics are Hamilton's.) Indeed, so crude and confused seem most of the ideas about the Constitution that lawyers, even judges (not to mention the present Justices of the United States Supreme Court), and particularly legislators might profit, and the country with them, by attendance once more at law school to refresh their minds on aspects of constitutional law and the Constitution. [58]

Regarding the notion of a "supreme law," Alexander Hamilton made the following remarks before the New York State Ratifying Convention:

> I maintain that the word *supreme* imports no more than this – that

---

[57] Russell Hoover Quynn, *Op. cit.*, pp. 23-24.
[58] *Ibid.*, p. 24.

> the Constitution and laws made in pursuance thereof cannot be controlled or defeated by any other law. The acts of the United States, therefore, will be absolutely obligatory as to all the proper objects and powers of the general government. The States, as well as individuals, are bound by these laws; but the laws of Congress are restricted to a certain sphere, and when they depart from this sphere, they are no longer supreme or binding. In the same manner the States have certain independent powers, in which their laws are supreme; for example, in making and executing laws concerning the punishment of certain crimes, such as murder, theft, etc., the States cannot be controlled. With respect to certain other objects, the powers of the two governments are concurrent yet supreme. [59]

Commenting on the Supremacy Clause, Russell Hoover Quynn made these additional observations:

> It is not the *Government* of the United States that is declared supreme but the *Constitution* and the laws and the treaties made in accordance with it. A proposal to endow and organize a government of "supreme Legislative, Executive, and Judicial powers" was not adopted at the 1787 convention, but was *deliberately rejected*; and that rejection is more significant than would be the fact that it had never been proposed. This is a fact that no student of constitutional law, no lawyer, legislator, or judge, can overlook or pass by as inconsequential – if he remembers that the intention of the lawmaker is the law, surely here it is.
>
> It should also be remembered that all officers, civil and judicial, State and federal, swear to support, not the government, but the Constitution of the United States. This is another fact that cannot be overlooked, ignored, or not recognized. [60]

When the Constitutional Convention of 1787 finally decided to reject the concept of a supreme National Government in preference of a Federal Government, the concept of supremacy was accordingly altered in the evolving plan of government. As originally envisioned in the Virginia Plan, which was introduced at the outset of the Philadelphia Convention, the concept of supremacy was associated with the government itself. This conception, however, was supplanted with the concept inherent in the New Jersey Plan, which associated supremacy with the Constitution. This concept accorded fully with the principles of States' Rights and State sovereignty, on which the evolving plan would ultimately be based. In fact, it was Luther Martin of Maryland – the staunchest advocate of State sovereignty at the Grand Convention – who actually wrote our federal Supremacy Clause.

---

[59] Richard B. Morris (ed.), *The Basic Ideas of Alexander Hamilton*, Washington Square Press, Inc., New York, 1956, pp. 225-226.

[60] Russell Hoover Quynn, *Op. cit.*, pp. 22-23.

The Supremacy Clause of our present Federal Constitution was derived from the Articles of Confederation, which declared in Article XIII that, "Every State shall abide by the determination of the United States in Congress assembled, on all questions which by this Confederation is submitted to them." Furthermore, this provision stipulated that, "the Articles of this Confederation shall be inviolably observed by every State." [61]

When properly construed, therefore, the Supremacy Clause of our present Federal Constitution means no more than that the Constitution and those federal laws and treaties made in pursuance of the compact constitute the supreme law of the land *in the federal sphere*. The State Constitutions and all State laws within the sphere of powers reserved to the States constitute a portion of the supreme law of the land *within the respective States*. If a State government should usurp a power delegated exclusively to the Federal Government, its action would be unconstitutional. Likewise, should the Government of the United States usurp a power reserved to the States, its action would be equally unconstitutional, null, void, and of no force.

The Supremacy Clause, we may conclude, is in complete accord with the States' Rights School of Thought. What the Consolidating School of Thought envisions, in its misinterpretations of this clause, is not a *supreme law*, but a *supreme government* ruling with a rod of iron from Washington, D.C., plundering the people on behalf of favored special interests, and creating within the United States a Leviathan State.

Abraham Lincoln, the Ultimate Consolidator

The practical and ideological warfare between the two schools of thought reached a climax with the election, in 1860, of Abraham Lincoln of Illinois to the Presidency. Mr. Lincoln became the first President elected to office based purely on a sectional victory in the Electoral College. After his election, but before his inauguration, the States of the Deep South, fearing for the safety, seceded from the Union and formed a new Federal Union for themselves styled the Confederate States of America. When President Lincoln indicated his intention to wage war on the seceded States, some of the border States promptly seceded and joined the Southern Confederacy.

The crisis which Alexander Hamilton had foreseen as a necessity to force a sovereign government upon the American people had finally arrived. The consolidating school had no intention of allowing the Southern States to escape from the planned reign of tyranny. Accordingly, President Lincoln, terming the

---

[61] Alexander H. Stephens, *Op. cit.*, Volume 1, p. 555.

seceded States to be combinations too powerful to be suppressed by the ordinary process of the law, raised an army to carry fire and sword into the Southern Confederacy and to subdue and conquer the seceded States by force of arms.

In a message delivered to a special session of Congress on July 4, 1861, Abraham Lincoln sought to blame the seceded States for the War Between the States and to assert a justification for the conquest of sovereign States. Within his message to Congress, President Lincoln presented the most extreme principles and ideologies of the Consolidating School of Thought to justify the assumption of sovereignty by the Government of the United States.

In his message to the Members of the House of Representatives and the Senate, President Abraham Lincoln declared that "this issue embraces more than the fate of these United States." "It presents to the whole family of man," he claimed, "the question whether a constitutional Republic or Democracy – a government of the people by the same people – can or cannot maintain its territorial integrity against its own domestic foes." [62] In making this statement, Mr. Lincoln, of course, was denying the existence of sovereign States and was basing his remarks on the assumption that the United States of America was a single body politic, in which the seceded States were but a fractional part.

Within his message to the joint session of Congress, President Lincoln stated:

> [The Southern leaders]...invented an ingenious sophism which, if conceded, was followed by perfectly logical steps, through all the incidents, to the complete destruction of the Union. The sophism itself is that any State of the Union may consistently with the National Constitution, and therefore lawfully and peacefully, withdraw from the Union without the consent of the Union or of any other State....
>
> This sophism deserves much, perhaps the whole, of its currency from the assumption that there is some omnipotent and sacred supremacy pertaining to a State – to each State of our Federal Union. Our States have neither more nor less power than that reserved to them in the Union by the Constitution – no one of them ever having been a State out of the Union. The original ones passed into the Union even before they cast off their British colonial dependence; and the new ones came into the Union directly from a condition of dependence, excepting Texas. And even Texas, in its temporary independence, was never designated a State. The new ones only took the designation of States on coming into the Union, while that name was first adopted for the old ones in and by the Declaration of Independence. Therein the "United Colonies" were declared to be "free and independent States"; but even then the object plainly was not to declare their independence of one an-

[62] Edwin C. Rozwenc (ed.), *The Causes of the American Civil War*, D.C. Heath and Company, Lexington, 1961, p. 40.

> other or of the Union, but directly the contrary, as their mutual pledge and their mutual action before, at the time, and afterward, abundantly show. The express plighting of faith by each and all of the original thirteen in the Articles of Confederation, two years later, that the Union shall be perpetual, is most conclusive. Having never been States either in substance or in name outside of the Union, whence this magical omnipotence of "State Rights," asserting a claim of power to lawfully destroy the Union itself? Much is said about the "sovereignty" of the States: but the word even is not in the National Constitution, nor, as is believed, in any of the State Constitutions. What is "sovereignty" in the political sense of the term? Would it be far wrong to define it "a political community without a political superior"? Tested by this, no one of our States except Texas ever was a sovereignty. And even Texas gave up the character on coming into the Union; by which act she acknowledged the Constitution of the United States, and the laws and treaties of the United States made in pursuance of the Constitution, to be for her the supreme law of the land. The States have their status in the Union, and they have no other legal status. If they break from this, they can only do so against law and by revolution. The Union, and not themselves separately, procured their independence and their liberty. By conquest or purchase the Union gave each of them whatever of independence or liberty it has. The Union is older than any of the States, and, in fact, it created them as States. Originally some dependent colonies made the Union, and, in turn, the Union threw off their old dependence for them, and made them States, such as they are. Not one of them ever had a State Constitution independent of the Union....
>
> What is now combated is the position that secession is consistent with the Constitution – is lawful and peaceful....
>
> The seceders insist that our Constitution admits of secession....
>
> ...These politicians are subtle and profound on the rights of minorities. They are not partial to that power which made the Constitution and speaks from the Preamble calling itself "We, the People."...
>
> This is essentially a people's contest.... [63]

It is plain to observe that it was not this message to Congress that qualified Mr. Lincoln for the dubious title of "Honest Abe." According to President Lincoln, none of the American States have ever "been a State out of the Union," with the possible exception of Texas, which won its independence from Mexico by itself and existed for nearly a decade as the Lone Star Republic before being admitted into the Union. But, according to Mr. Lincoln, Texas lost its sovereignty when it was admitted into the Union, because the Supremacy Clause of the Federal Constitution robs all the members of the Federal Union of their sovereignty and vests it in a mythical Nation of America.

Were his contentions correct? Is it true that the original thirteen States never existed as States out of the Union under our current Federal Constitu-

---

[63] *Ibid.*, pp. 44-47.

tion? Did they not exist before the adoption of the Constitution of 1787? Did they not exist in another Federal Union under the Articles of Confederation, which went into effect in 1781? And did not those States come into existence on July 4, 1776, five years prior to their first Federal Union under the Articles? Did not the States, within the Declaration of Independence, assert that, as States, they were free, independent, and sovereign, having all the rights and powers of other sovereign Nations? Did not the Treaty of Paris of 1783 explicitly recognize the sovereignty, freedom, and independence of each of those thirteen original American States? Did not the Articles of Confederation expressly declare that the States were sovereign and that the United States of America existed to protect and defend the sovereignty of the States?

Did not the States send delegates to a Convention of States to draft the Constitution of 1787 as States, with each State having one vote? Did not the States ratify the Constitution of 1787 as sovereign States, with each State having one vote in meeting the minimum requirement of nine assenting States and with each State bound only by its own consent? Did not the ratifying States insist upon adding Amendment Ten to the compact to safeguard their sovereignty and reserved rights? Did not some of those ratifying States assert that the powers delegated to the Federal Government could be resumed should such action be deemed necessary at a future date? Did not the Constitutional Convention design representation in the United States Senate based on the sovereign equality of the States? Did not that Convention insert into Article VII of the Constitution a statement that the Federal Union was to exist, not over, but between the States, who alone would be the parties to the compact? Did not that Federal Convention refrain from inserting into the Constitution a statement that the Union was to be perpetual, knowing that such a statement had existed in the Articles of Confederation and had proven to be an embarrassment, inasmuch as that Union had lasted less than a decade?

All of these facts were conveniently ignored by "Honest Abe" because historical facts, common sense, and a plain reading of the Constitution do not accord with the conclusions espoused by the Consolidating School of Thought. Instead of acknowledging the obvious truth regarding the development of our constitutional system of government, Abraham Lincoln insisted that, "The Union is older than any of the States, and, in fact, it created them as States."

By this novel theory, the colonies were united by shared *sentiments* against a common foe even before the issuance of their common Declaration of Independence and by formation of a *military alliance* to resist the aggressions of Great Britain. Such shared sentiments and military cooperation, he insisted, must be regarded as a formal political Union, even though the colonies, prior to becoming States, were not sovereign and could not formally create a political Union. But if President Lincoln's historical account is correct, then France must also be considered a member of our Federal Union, for that Nation formed a military alliance with the States against Great Britain during the American Revolutionary War.

That the Founding Fathers viewed matters very differently is evident from their actions. At the same time that the Second Continental Congress resolved to adopt the Virginia Resolution to declare the independence of the several States through a common Declaration, it also adopted another Virginia Resolution to draft a Constitution for a Federal Union to politically unite the newly independent States. Had the Founders of the Republic considered the peoples of the States already merged into one Nation, as Abraham Lincoln claimed, would they have bothered to draft and adopt the Articles of Confederation – a Constitution for a League of States – in which each State was recognized as a sovereign Nation?

But President Lincoln insisted that the thirteen colonies become one unified State before becoming separate States, and that, upon adopting the Constitution of 1787, those States continued to exist within the original unified State. Such a view is at discord with both logic and historical truth. In adopting the present Federal Constitution, the original thirteen States seceded from their first Federal Union, even though it had been declared to be *perpetual.* When the new Union was inaugurated in 1789, in fact, two of those original States were not even members. Both North Carolina and Rhode Island thus existed outside our present Union until fully assured that the Bill of Rights would be incorporated into the Constitution. How does this fact fit into the theory advocated by Mr. Lincoln? Since it does not fit, it was conveniently ignored.

The only assertion remotely resembling truth in President Lincoln's message to Congress was his statement that, "This is essentially a people's contest." Indeed it was. It was a great contest between the sovereignty of the people and the Government of the United States. Unfortunately for the American people, the government won that war.

Now that we have previewed the basic tenets of the States' Rights School of Thought and the Consolidating School of Thought, it becomes obvious why the apologists for the consolidating school are quick to point to the victory over the States realized in the War Between the States as supposed justification for their misdeeds. The Consolidating School of Thought is based on absurdities and palpably false historical facts that cannot stand under close examination and scrutiny. What choice have the consolidators and their apologists, but to point to the War Between the States and proclaim that the *verdict of history* proves them correct, and to rely on the assertion that *might makes right*?

As for Abraham Lincoln, the President who presided over that tragic conquest of the sovereign States, the Consolidating School of Thought has done everything within its power to deify him in the eyes of succeeding generations of Americans. So thoroughly has this objective been realized that a surprising number of modern Americans hold the belief that the *Battle Hymn of the Republic* is a song dedicated to the glorification of Abraham Lincoln, when, in fact, it is song written to glorify God!

Thus it is, that the consolidating school has taught us to worship the tyrant who successfully conquered the Southern States, robbed all of the States of their sovereignty, gave birth to a sovereign National Government, and baptized that unholy offspring in a sea of gore and blood.

Chapter Eight

The Webster-Hayne Debate

When Robert Young Hayne rose to address the United States Senate on January 19, 1830, little did he realize that he was entering into what many historians would later describe as the greatest debate in American history, one that would bring the States' Rights School of Thought in direct confrontation with the Consolidating School of Thought. Although this great debate quickly expanded into one encompassing the most fundamental differences between States' Rights and consolidation, it had started a day earlier as a controversy over the public land policy of the Government of the United States, in particular that government's policy of managing the Western Territories. Lasting for some nine days, the debate ended when Senate Daniel Webster arose on January 26, 1830, to give his two-day oration on behalf of consolidation, an oration which one writer has termed "the most famous speech in Senate history." [1]

The spark for the debate was provided by the Foot Resolution, which had been introduced in late 1829 by Senator Samuel Augustus Foot of Connecticut, who had proposed that the committee on public lands study the possibility of limiting the sale of Western lands. The undisguised objective of the consolidators in promoting this maneuver was to significantly discourage the peopling of the Western Territories. One reason for this consolidating objective was immediately obvious to Senator Thomas Hart Benton of Missouri, who condemned this attempt to thwart Westward migration as a scheme to ensure a captive, and thereby cheap, labor supply for the New England factories.

Another reason for this attempt to thwart the peopling of the Western Territories is that such a migration across the continent was essential to the formation of new States from those lands. A territory could not assume self-government and enter the Federal Union as a sovereign State until its population had grown to a specified size. The consolidating school, whose stronghold was in the New England States, had always opposed the expansion of the United States, especially in terms of new States added to the Federal Union. As early as 1803, for instance, the Federalist Party had bitterly opposed the Louisi-

---

[1] "U.S. Senate Historical Minutes: Daniel Webster, The Most Famous Speech, January 26, 1830," http://www.senate.gov/learning/min_2ff.html, United States Senate, September 12, 2002.

ana Purchase, fearing that the new States to be created from that vast land mass would weaken the power wielded in the Union by the New England States. By the middle of the ante-bellum period, this antipathy to the growth of the United States had induced the consolidating school to openly oppose the development and creation of the Western States.

The States' Rights school understood the true implications of this consolidating policy toward the public lands and sided with the Westerners against the machinations of the consolidating school. When Senator Robert Y. Hayne entered the debate, he asserted that the high prices for land desired by the consolidators would result in enriching the federal treasury with moneys to be used for the corrupt purposes of Henry Clay's American System, while draining wealth from the West. "At the heart of his argument," one historian noted, "Hayne asserted that States should have the power to control their own lands," insisting that the fundamental issue revolved around the immoral principles of consolidation and the constitutional principles of States' Rights. [2] It was the earnest hope of Senator Hayne and other Southern statesmen that the Westerners would recognize this fact and unite with them to turn the tide against the consolidating conspiracy.

The Sagebrush Rebellion

As the perceptive reader has undoubtedly deduced, the great contest between the consolidating school and the States' Rights school could not be considered a mere difference of opinion among honest statesmen. The great contest was a battle for power and control, a battle to determine whether the Federal Government would be used to promote the genuine general welfare of all the States, or would be subverted into an instrument of plunder and oppression for the benefit of certain monied interests. The specific issue that sparked the great Webster-Hayne Debate of 1830 clearly illustrates the true policy and motives of the consolidating school to hold great numbers of Americans in what amounts to vassalage and to reduce the States to the level of colonies.

Land is wealth, and wealth is power. The land is the essential ingredient for agricultural production, as well as for mining operations, oil exploration, and energy production. In addition, land is necessary to support growing populations and a thriving housing industry. And, needless to say, these essential economic interests that are dependent upon the land support and nourish a great variety of other economic activities that are requisite to the prosperity and progress of American civilization. In a free society, the wisest policy is based on

---

[2] *Ibid.*

private ownership of land. But if any land is to be held in common, as public land, then such land should be owned by the sovereign States and controlled by them for their own interests. As Senator Hayne declared during the course of the great debate with Senator Webster, *the States must have the power and the right to control their own lands*. In contrast to this sentiment, the unfaltering policy of the consolidating school has been that as much land as possible should be publicly controlled and preferably owned directly by the Government of the United States.

The question of how to admit new States into the Union presented itself to the American Republic at an early date, before the consolidating school had mustered the audacity to push for gross inequality among the States of the Union. Initially, it was agreed by all those of the generation of the Founding Fathers, in consideration of the federal and republican principles of our political institutions, that the United States should be allowed to own territories, and that such territories could be controlled by the Federal Government, *but only on a temporary basis*. Such lands could be held in trust only until the populations of the territories were sufficient to admit them into the Union as States. And such new States, upon entering the Union, were to be regarded as *equal* to the original States in terms of their freedom, sovereignty, and independence. This, it was clearly understood, was the only manner in which the United States could own vast tracts of public land without subverting our system of government and transforming the Federal Government into a supreme, sovereign, imperial government.

As time progressed, however, the consolidating school began the process of subverting this wise public land policy. By the time of the War Between States, which engulfed the continent in blood, the consolidating school had seized complete control of the Government of the United States, and it was able to dictate the public land policy without serious opposition. Although the consolidators undoubtedly would have preferred that the Western Territories should never become States, but should instead remain permanent colonies, such an obvious display of imperialism would have been difficult to explain to the American people. Thus, the consolidating school settled on the best alternative. The territories would be admitted as new States, but all of their public lands would forever remain in the possession of the United States, under the control of the Federal Government.

When the State of Nevada entered the Union in 1864, for example, the conditions for admission required that the people of that territory had to "forever disclaim all right and title to the unappropriated public lands lying within said Territory," and thereby allow the Government of the United States to hold such lands in perpetuity. [3] Other Western States faced a similar fate when they were admitted to the Federal Union, which by then was firmly dominated by the consolidating school. By 1912, with the admission of Arizona into the Union of States, the United States had grown to forty-eight States. And in 1959, with the admissions of Hawaii and Alaska into the Union, the United States grew to its present size of fifty States.

While most Americans are aware that the Federal Government controls some public lands in the form of National Parks, what is less well known is the true extent of the public lands still controlled by the Government of the United States. The numbers are truly shocking. The Federal Government currently holds title to approximately one-third of the entire land mass of the United States of America, and it wields draconian control over slightly more than half of the land in the American West. The Federal Government, for example, owns 36 percent of Colorado, 48 percent of Wyoming, 53 percent of Oregon, 64 percent of Idaho, 66 percent of Utah, and 81 percent of Nevada. Even more shocking, the Government of the United States owns an amazing 96 percent of Alaska!

By way of comparison, it is of interest to note, when considering these percentages, that most economists consider any one party who owns as much as three or four percent of the stock in a large corporation to own a *controlling* share in that company. Alaska, Utah, Idaho, Nevada, and the other Western Territories are supposed to be sovereign States in our Union by the terms of our Federal Constitution, which solemnly proclaims that the Union shall exist *between States*. Yet, the citizens of those States have discovered, much to their dismay, that their States are, in reality, little more than colonial possessions of an imperial government in Washington, D.C., which lords over them, violating their private property rights and stifling their economic opportunities on behalf a monied aristocracy based in the Eastern States.

That a rebellion was inevitable became obvious in the latter portion of the Twentieth Century, as Westerners battled meddling federal bureaucrats over every conceivable issue, from timber rights, water rights, farming rights, mineral rights, grazing rights, homestead rights, and environmental control rights, to the underlying issue of States' Rights in general. The Government of the United States, Westerners sensed, regards animals as having more rights than people.

Starting in the decade of the 1960s and accelerating in the ensuing decade, a full-scale rebellion in the West finally erupted. The focus of this *Sagebrush Rebellion* was ownership and control of the public lands in the Western

---

[3] Steve Miller, "Sagebrush Rebellion II – Nevada: The Permanent Colony," Second of a Series, Electric Nevada, http://www.zianet.com/wblase/endtimes/rebel1a.htm, 1996.

States by the Government of the United States. "This vast federal holding means we are not our own landlords," asserted Richard D. Lamm, the then Governor of Colorado. "We cannot control our own destiny." [4]

As the Sagebrush Revolution spread throughout the Western States, it was not uncommon to see large road signs posted along highways, stating, "Welcome to the West. Property: U.S. Govt." [5] In Nevada, the Sagebrush Rebellion received a strong impetus with the passage of legislation which asserted that all of the 49 million acres of land within the State being administered by the federal Bureau of Land Management should be returned to the State of Nevada.

Commenting on this law, Steve Miller, writing in 1996 for *Electric Nevada*, noted that the move was openly intended to assert and affirm that Nevada was a sovereign State:

> *The law was bold, anarchic.*
>
> *It reflected the maverick strain. Its rationale reached back 115 years to the date Nevada was battle-born. The public lands had never been intended to be held in perpetuity by the Federal Government, Nevada said. It had been brought into the Union on "unequal footing." Sovereign States were meant to control their own destinies – but without land they could not do it.*
>
> *"We're not just a bunch of wild-eyed cowboys out to lynch some federal officials," said [then-] Attorney General Richard Bryan. "We're serious people asking for a serious look at the unfair treatment the West is receiving." Said rebel Calvin Black, it was time to end "federal colonialism."*
>
> *Nevada, 1979. The revolt was born. The shot heard 'round the West.* [6]

The mood of the courageous Westerners was summarized in the December 1, 1980 issue of *U.S. News & World Report*:

> Tactics in the conflict range from legal challenges of Washington's authority to outright defiance of federal laws. Irate Alaskans burned an airplane belonging to the National Park Service. Legislatures in Nevada, New Mexico, Washington, Wyoming, Utah and Arizona have passed laws laying claim to millions of acres of federal land inside their borders. In one of the boldest actions, Alaskan voters approved a proposal setting up a special statehood commission to "reconsider and recommend appropriate changes," a move viewed as the start of a quixotic attempt to secede from the Union. [7]

---

[4] "The Sagebrush Rebellion," http://www.vcdh.virginia.edu/PVCC/mbase/docs/sagebrush.html, U.S. News & World Report, December 1, 1980.

[5] *Ibid.*

[6] Steve Miller, "Sagebrush Rebellion II – The East's 132-Year Fight Against Nevada's Ranchers," Third of a Series, Electric Nevada, http://www.zianet.com/wblase/endtimes/rebel2a.htm, 1996.

[7] "The Sagebrush Rebellion," *Op. cit.*

During the Presidential election of 1980, candidate Ronald Reagan of California openly supported the Sagebrush Rebellion, and with his election, Westerners thought that justice, at long last, would become a reality. But within the Reagan Administration, after it assumed power, the only voice to be heard supporting the Sagebrush Rebellion was that of the Secretary of the Interior, James Watt, and he was soon driven out of the Administration. In desperation, the Sagebrush Rebellion leaders looked to the federal judiciary to right a grievous injustice that had been suffered for more than a century. But in this, they were to be disappointed. A federal court solemnly ruled that the Government of the United States was sovereign, and therefore had a right to own and control huge chunks of land within the States of our Union. As a consequence of this ruling, the Sagebrush Rebellion lost momentum and faded out of the public eye.

Although the Sagebrush Rebellion met defeat at the hands of the federal judiciary, the very fact that it had occurred at all was a significant indicator that a growing number of Americans have come to realize that there truly is something fundamentally wrong with the policies of the Government of the United States -- that that government regards the States, not as sovereign body politics, but as colonial possessions to be governed by a highly centralized bureaucracy that does not allow Americans to control their own destiny. And as we have already observed, the movement toward an imperial domination of the States began to manifest itself as early as 1830, and was strongly opposed by the States' Rights school at that time. It was, in fact, this specific issue of public land policy that sparked the great Webster-Hayne Debate of that year.

The grand debate between Robert Y. Hayne and Daniel Webster consisted of two orations by each Senator, addressed to the upper chamber of Congress over the course of several days. As we have noted previously, when Senator Hayne, a low-country lawyer who had represented South Carolina in the U.S. Senate since 1823, gave his first oration, it was not his intent to inaugurate a debate between titans. But in his first speech, he touched upon a raw nerve, and the reaction of the consolidators was explosive. Senator Webster, in replying to the Senator from South Carolina, sought not only to undermine the concept of States' Rights, but also to divert attention away from the immorality of the American System and consolidation in general, by focusing attention instead on the subject of chattel slavery in the Southern States and the concept of State Interposition and Nullification.

In examining the two schools of thought presented in the debate, we certainly should assess the accuracy of the logic and historical facts with a critical eye. Yet, we also should allow, to the greatest extent possible, each Senator to present his views in his own words, so that we may assess the style, tenor, and subtleties of the debaters. This will necessitate some rather lengthy quotations, but an effort will be made for the sake of brevity to focus on the more significant parts of the addresses. By striking a proper balance between brevity and thoroughness, however, we should have no difficulty understanding the true natures of the States' Rights School of Thought and the opposing Consolidator School of Thought. For the complete text of the speeches given by Senators Webster and Hayne, the reader is referred to the book, *The Webster-Hayne Debate on the Nature of the Union*, which was edited by Herman Belz and published in 2000 by the Liberty Fund.

The style of the Webster-Hayne Debate, it should be noted, followed the generally accepted custom of the United States Senate, wherein the speakers did not directly address one another, but instead directly addressed the *President of the Senate*, a position chaired, by the terms of the Federal Constitution, by the Vice-President of the United States. In such a capacity, the Vice-President of the United States formally presides over that body, although he cannot participate in the debates or cast a vote on any measures considered by the Senate, except to break a tie. At the time of the great Webster-Hayne Debate of 1830, the Vice-President of the United States was John C. Calhoun, the acknowledged leader of the States' Rights School of Thought at that time. He listened attentively to the debate between Senator Hayne and the Orator of Consolidation, little realizing that, three years later, he himself would confront Senator Daniel Webster in another great debate.

Senator Hayne's First Speech

On January 19, 1830, Senator Robert Y. Hayne of South Carolina arose to address the Senate of the United States. In the course of his speech, which was published the following day in *Niles Register*, Senator Hayne said:

> The object of the remarks I am about to offer, is merely to call public attention to the question, to throw out a few crude and undigested thoughts, as food for reflection, in order to prepare the public mind for the adoption, at no distant day, of some fixed and settled policy in relation to the public lands. I believe that out of the Western country there is no subject in the whole range of our legislation less understood, and in relation to which there exist so many errors, and such unhappy prejudices and misconceptions.
>
> There may be said to be two great parties in this country, who entertain very opposite opinions in relation to the character of the policy which the government has heretofore pursued in relation to public lands, as well as to that which ought, hereafter to be pursued. I propose very briefly to examine these opinions, and to throw out for consideration a few ideas in connexion with them. Adverting, first, to the past policy of the government, we find that one party, embracing a very large portion, perhaps at this time a major-

ity, of the people of the United States, in all quarters of the Union, entertain the opinion, that, in the settlement of the new States and the disposition of the public lands, Congress has pursued not only a highly just and liberal course, but one of extraordinary kindness and indulgence....While the other party embracing the entire West, insist that we have treated them from the beginning, not like heirs of the estate, but in the spirit of a hard taskmaster, resolved to promote our selfish interests from the fruit of their labor. Now, sir, it is not my present purpose to investigate all the grounds on which these two opinions rest; I shall content myself with noticing one or two particulars, in relation to which it has long appeared to me that the West has some cause for complaint....

...[I]t...would seem...[that] the cardinal point of our policy [is], not to settle the country, and facilitate the formation of new States, but to fill our coffers by coining our lands into gold....

It is said, sir, that we learn from our own misfortunes how to feel for the sufferings of others; and perhaps the present condition of the Southern States has served to impress more deeply on my mind the grievous oppression of a system by which the wealth of a country is drained off to be expended elsewhere. In that devoted region, sir, in which my lot has been cast, it is our misfortune to stand in that relation to the Federal Government, which subjects us to a taxation, which it requires the utmost efforts of our industry to meet.

Nearly the whole amount of our contributions is expended abroad – we stand towards the United States in the relation of Ireland to England. The fruits of our labors are drawn from us to enrich other and more favored sections of the Union, while, with one of the finest climates and the richest products in the world, furnishing, with one-third of the population, two-thirds of the whole exports of the country, we exhibit the extraordinary, the wonderful and painful spectacle of a country, enriched by the bounty of God, but blasted by the cruel policy of man....

In coming to the consideration of the next great question – what ought to be the future policy of the government in relation to the public lands? we find the most opposite and irreconcilable opinions between the two parties which I have before described. On the one side, it is contended that the public land ought to be received as a *permanent fund* for *revenue* and future distribution among the States, while, on the other, it is insisted that the whole of these lands of right belong to, and ought to be relinquished to the States in which they lie....Sir I may be singular, perhaps I stand alone here in the opinion, but it is one I have long entertained, that one of the greatest safeguards of liberty is a jealous watchfulness, on the part of the people, over the collection and expenditure of the public money – a watchfulness that can only be secured where the money is drawn by taxation directly from the pockets of the people. Every scheme or contrivance by which rulers are able to procure the command of money, by means unknown to, unseen, or unfelt by, the people, destroys this security.

Even the revenue system of this country, by which the whole of our pecuniary resources are derived from *indirect taxation* – from duties upon imports – has done much to weaken the responsibility of our federal rulers to the people, and has made them, in some measure, careless of their rights, and regardless of the high trust committed to their care. Can any man believe sir, that if $23,000,000 per annum were now levied by direct taxation, or by an apportionment of the same among the States, instead of being raised by an indirect tax, of the severe effect of which few are aware, that the waste and extravagance, of the unauthorized imposition of duties, and appropriations of money for unconstitutional objects, would have been tolerated for a single year? My life upon it, sir, they would not. I distrust therefore sir, the policy of creating a great permanent *national treasury,* whether, to be derived from public lands or from any source. If I had, sir, the powers of a magician, and could, by a wave of my hand, convert this capitol into gold for such a purpose, I would not do it. If I could, by a mere act of my will, put at the disposal of the Federal Government any amount of treasure which I might think proper to name, I should limit the amount to the means necessary for the legitimate purposes of the government. Sir, an immense national treasury would be a *fund for corruption.* It would enable Congress and the executive to exercise a control over States, as well as over great interests in the country – nay, even over corporations and individuals, utterly destructive of the purity, and fatal to the duration of our institutions. It would be equally fatal to the sovereignty and independence of the States.

Sir, I am one of those who believe that the very life of our system is the independence of the States; and that there is no evil more to be deprecated than the *consolidation* of this government. It is only by a strict adherence to the limitations imposed by the Constitution on the Federal Government, that this system works well, and can answer the great ends for which it was instituted. I am opposed, therefore, in any shape, to all unnecessary extension of the powers or the influence of the legislature or executive of the Union of the States; and, most of all, I am opposed to those partial distributions of favors whether by *legislation* or *appropriation*, which has a direct and powerful tendency to spread corruption through the land – to create an abject spirit of dependence – to sow the seeds of dissolution – to produce jealousy among the different portions of the Union, and, finally, to sap the very foundations of the government itself.

But, sir, there is another purpose, to which it has been supposed the public lands can be applied still more objectionable. I mean that suggested in a report from the Treasury Department, under the late Administration, of so regulating the disposition of the public lands as to create and preserve in certain quarters of the Union a population suitable for conducting great manufacturing establishments. It is supposed, sir, by the advocates of the American System, that the great obstacle to the progress of manufactures in this country is the want of that low and degraded population which infest the cities and towns of Europe, who having no other means of subsistence, will work for the lowest wages, and be satisfied with the smallest possible share of human enjoyment. – And this difficulty it is proposed to overcome, by so regulating and limiting the sales of the public lands as to prevent the drawing off this portion of the population from the manufacturing States. Sir, it is bad enough that the government should presume to regulate the industry of man – it is sufficiently monstrous that they should attempt, by arbitrary legislation, artificially to adjust and balance the various pursuits of society, and to "organize the whole labor and capital of the country."

But what shall we say of the resort to such means for these purposes? What? create a manufactory of paupers in order to enable the rich proprietors of woollen and cotton factories to amass wealth? From the bottom of my soul do I abhor and detest the idea that the powers of the Federal Government should ever be prostituted for such purpose....

...I can easily conceive that it may be extremely inconvenient, nay highly injurious to a State, to have immense bodies of land within her chartered limits, locked up from sale and settlement, withdrawn from the power of taxation and contributing in no respect to her wealth and prosperity.

While...[Westerners] shall continue to ask and gratefully to receive...petty and partial appropriations, they will be kept for ever in a state of dependence. Never will the Federal Government, or rather those who control its operations, consent to emancipate the West by adopting a wise and just policy, looking to any final disposition of the public lands, while the people of the West can be kept in subjection and dependence by occasional donations of these lands; and never will the Western States themselves assume their just and equal station among their sisters of the Union, while they are constantly looking to Congress for favors and gratuities.

What, then, Mr. President, is our true policy on this important subject?...Without attempting to indicate precisely what our policy ought...to be, I will, in the same spirit which has induced me to throw out the desultory thoughts which I have not presented to the Senate, suggest for consideration, whether it will not be sound policy and true wisdom, to adopt a system of measures looking to the final relinquishment of these lands, on the part of the United States, to the States in which they lie, on such terms and conditions as may fully indemnify us for the cost of the original purchase, and all the trouble and expense to which we may have been put on their account. Giving up the plan of using these lands for ever as a fund either for revenue or distribution – ceasing to hug them as a great treasure – renouncing the idea of administering them with a view to regulate and control the industry and population of the States, or of keeping in subjection and dependence the States, or the people of any portion of the Union, the task will be comparatively easy of striking out a plan for the final adjustment of the land question on just and equitable principles....The relinquishment may be made by a sale to the State at a fixed price, which I will not say should be nominal; but certainly I should not be disposed to fix the amount so high as to keep the States for any length of time in the debt of the United States.

In short, Mr. President, our whole policy in relation to the public lands may perhaps be summed up in the declaration with which I set out, that they ought not to be kept and retained for ever as a great treasure, but that they should be administered chiefly with a view to the creation, within reasonable periods, of great and flourishing communities, to be formed into

> free and independent States – to be invested in due season with the control of all the lands within their respective limits. [8]

By broadening the discussion from a mere consideration of the Foot Resolution, it was Senator Hayne's objective to throw the light of inquiry on the entire gamut of policies being promulgated by the consolidating school. The objectionable public land policy advocated by that school, he pointed out, was just one of many policies designed to undermine the sovereignty of the States, subvert our system of constitutionally limited government, and provide the Federal Government with a vast treasure with which to enrich the special interests favored by the consolidators. The public land policy favored by the consolidators, the Senator observed, also seemed to be designed for the objective of hindering the settlement of the Western Territories and for preventing those territories from entering the Union as sovereign and independent States.

Senator Hayne's observations on the sources of revenue used to fund the corrupt American System are especially interesting. Had the consolidators advocated the *direct taxation* of the American people to inaugurate their system of patronage and internal improvements, the people would have been outraged, for they would then have been able to directly compare the true costs of maintaining such a socialistic system with its supposed benefits. But the consolidators were sufficiently cunning to understand that the true costs of their system could be concealed from the public by relying on *indirect taxation* – such as protective tariffs – for funding. Another way to conceal such costs, Senator Hayne noted, was to charge very high prices for land sales in the Western Territories. A vast treasure in the hands of the Federal Government, he noted, would invariably become a *fund for corruption* that would eventually destroy our constitutional system of government and rob the people of their liberties.

The heart of Senator Hayne's oration – and the heart of the great issue confronting the American people – lay in that portion of his speech in which he specifically uses the word "consolidation" to identify the evil confronting the United States. The concepts expressed by Senator Hayne in this section of his address form the central argument of the States' Rights School of Thought, and are so significant to our understanding of the American constitutional system of government that we should repeat his words of wisdom here:

> Sir, I am one of those who believe that the very life of our system is the independence of the States; and that there is no evil more to be deprecated than the *consolidation* of this government. It is only by a strict adherence to the limitations imposed by the Constitution on the Federal Govern-

[8] "Debate in the Senate – From *Niles Register*, Feb 20, 1830 [Hayne's First Speech, Delivered Jan. 19]," *Niles Register*, http://www.earlyrepublic.net/hayne1.htm, orig. pub. 1830.

ment, that this system works well, and can answer the great ends for which it was instituted. I am opposed, therefore, in any shape, to all unnecessary extension of the powers or the influence of the legislature or executive of the Union of the States; and, most of all, I am opposed to those partial distributions of favors whether by *legislation* or *appropriation*, which has a direct and powerful tendency to spread corruption through the land – to create an abject spirit of dependence – to sow the seeds of dissolution – to produce jealousy among the different portions of the Union, and, finally, to sap the very foundations of the government itself. [9]

Senator Webster's First Reply

On January 20, 1830, the day after Senator Hayne's first speech, Daniel Webster rose in the United States Senate to reply to the Senator from South Carolina. During the course of his speech, which was published in *Niles Register*, the Orator of Consolidation made the following statements:

> [S]ir, though I have felt quite indifferent about the passing of the [Foot] Resolution, yet opinions were expressed yesterday on the general subject of the public lands, and on some other subjects, by the gentleman from South Carolina, so widely different from my own, that I am not willing to let the occasion pass without some reply....
>
> ...The truth is, that rapidly as population has increased, the surveys have, nevertheless, out-ran our wants. There are more lands than purchasers. They are now sold at low prices, and taken up as fast as the increase of people furnishes hands to take them up. It is obvious, that no artificial regulation, no forcing of sales, no giving away of the lands even, can produce any great and sudden augmentation of population.... My own opinion has uniformly been, that the public lands should be offered freely, and at low prices, so as to encourage settlement and cultivation as rapidly as the increasing population of the country is competent to extend settlement and cultivation....
>
> I now procede, sir, to some of the opinions expressed by the gentleman from South Carolina. Two or three topics were touched by him, in regard to which he expressed sentiments in which I do not at all concur.
>
> In the first place, sir, the honorable gentleman spoke of the whole course and policy of the government, towards those who have purchased and settled the public lands; and seemed to think this policy wrong. He held it to have been, from the first, hard and rigorous; he was of opinion that the United States had acted towards those who subdued the Western wilderness, in the spirit of a step-mother; that the public domain, had been improperly regarded as a source of revenue; and that we had rigidly compelled payment for that which ought to have been given away....

---

[9] *Ibid.*

Now, sir, I deny, altogether, that there has been anything harsh or severe in the policy of the government towards the new States of the West. On the contrary, I maintain, that it has uniformly pursued, towards those States, a liberal and enlightened system, such as its own duty allowed and required; and such as their interests and welfare demanded. The government has been no step-mother to the new States. She has not been careless of their interests, nor deaf to their requests, but from the first moment, when the territories which now form those States were ceded to the Union, down to the time in which I am now speaking, it has been the invariable object of the government, to dispose of the soil, according to the true spirit of the obligation under which it received it; to hasten its settlement and cultivation, as far and as fast as practicable; and to rear the new communities into equal and independent States, at the earliest moment of their being able, by their numbers, to form a regular government....

...Congress...in September, 1780, recommended to the several States in the Union, having claims to Western territory, to make liberal cessions of a portion thereof to the United States; and on the 10th of October, 1780, Congress resolved, *that any lands so ceded in pursuance of their preceding recommendation, should be disposed of for the common benefit of the United States; should be settled and formed into distinct Republican States, to become members of the Federal Union, with the same rights of sovereignty, freedom, and independence as the other States; and that the lands should be granted, or settled, at such times, and under such regulations, as should be agreed on by Congress.*

Again, in September, 1783, Congress passed another resolution, expressing the conditions on which cessions from States should be received; and in October following, Virginia made her cession, reciting the resolution, or act, of September preceding, and then transferring her title to her North-Western Territory to the United States, upon the express condition, *that the lands, so ceded, should be considered as a common fund for the use and benefit of such of the United States, as had become or should become members of the Confederation, Virginia inclusive, and should be faithfully and bona fide disposed of for that purpose, and for no other use or purpose whatsoever.* The grants from other States were on similar conditions. Massachusetts and Connecticut both had claims to Western lands, and both relinquished them to the United States in the same manner. These grants were all made on three substantial conditions or trusts. First, that the ceded territories should be turned into States, and admitted in due time into the Union, with all the rights belonging to other States. Second, that the lands should form a common fund to be disposed of for the general benefit of all the States. Third, that they should be sold and settled, at such time and in such manner as Congress should direct....

...The government has performed all the conditions of the grant. – While it has regarded the public lands as a common fund, and has sought to make what reasonably could be made of them, as a source of revenue, it has also applied its best wisdom to sell and settle them, as fast and as happily as possible; and whensoever numbers would warrant it, each territory has been successively admitted into the Union, with all the rights of an independent State.

Is there then, sir, I ask, any well founded charge of hard dealing, any just accusation for negligence indifference, or parsimony which is capable of being sustained against the government of the country, in its conduct towards the new states? Sir, I think there is not.

But there was another observation of the hon. member, which, I confess, did not a little surprise me. As a reason for wishing to get rid of the public lands as soon as we could, and as we might, the hon. gentleman, said, he wanted no permanent source of income. He wished to see the time when the government should not possess a shilling of permanent revenue. If he could speak magical word and by that word convert the whole capitol into gold, the word would not be spoken. The administration of a fixed revenue, he said, only consolidates the government and corrupts the people! Sir, I confess I heard these sentiments uttered on this floor, not without deep regret and pain.

I am aware that these, and similar opinions, are espoused by certain persons out of the capitol, and out of this government, but I did not expect so soon to find them here. Consolidation! – that perpetual cry both of terror and delusion -- consolidation! Sir, when gentlemen speak of the effects of a common fund, belonging to all the States, as having a tendency to consolidation, what do they mean? Do they mean, or can they mean any thing more than that the Union of the States will be strengthened, by whatever continues or furnishes inducements to the people of the States to hold together? If they mean merely this, then no doubt, the public lands, as well as every thing else in which we have a common interest, tends to consolidation and to this species of consolidation every true American ought to be attached; it is neither more nor less than strengthening the Union itself. This is the sense in which the framers of the Constitution use the word consolidation and in which sense I adopt and cherish it. They tell us, in the letter submitting the Constitution to the consideration of the country, that "In all our deliberations on this subject, we kept steadily in our view that which appears to us the greatest interest of every true American, the consolidation of our Union, in which is involved our prosperity, felicity, safety, perhaps our national existence. This important consideration, seriously and deeply impressed on our minds led each State in the Convention to be less rigid on points of inferior magnitude, than might have been otherwise expected."

This, sir, is General Washington's consolidation. This is the true constitutional consolidation. I wish to see no new powers drawn to the general government; but I confess I rejoice in whatever tends to strengthen the bond that unites us; and encourages the hope that our Union may be perpetual. And, therefore, I cannot but feel regret at the expression of such opinions as the gentleman has avowed; because I think their obvious tendency is to weaken the bond of our connexion.

I know that there are some persons in the part of the country from which the hon. member comes, who habitually speak of the Union in terms of indifference, or even of disparagement. The hon. member himself is not, I trust, and can never be, one of these. They significantly declare, that it is time to calculate the value of the Union, and their aim seems to be to enumerate and to magnify all the evils real and imaginary, which the government under the Union produces.

The tendency of all these ideas and sentiments is obviously to bring the Union into discussion, as a mere question of present and temporary expediency – nothing more than a mere matter of profit and loss. The Union to be preserved while it suits local and temporary purposes to preserve it; and to be sundered whenever it shall be found to thwart such purposes. Union, of itself, is considered by the disciples of this school as hardly a good. It is only regarded as a possible means of good; or, on the other hand as a possible means of evil. They cherish no deep and fixed regard for it, flowing from a thorough conviction of its absolute and vital necessity to our welfare.

Sir, I deprecate and deplore this tone of thought and feeling. I deem far otherwise of the Union of the States, and so did the framers of the Constitution themselves. What they said I believe; fully and sincerely believe, that the Union of the States is essential to the prosperity and safety of the States. I am a Unionist, and in this sense, a National Republican. I would strengthen the ties that hold us together. Far, indeed, in my wishes, very far distant be the day, when our associated and fraternal stripes shall be severed asunder, and when that happy constellation under which we have risen to so much renown, shall be broken up and be seen sinking star after star, into obscurity and night!...

As I have already remarked sir, it was one among the reasons assigned by the honorable member for his wish to be rid of the public lands altogether, that the public disposition of them and the revenues derived from them tends to corrupt the people. This, sir, I confess, passes my comprehension. These lands are sold at public auction, or taken up at fixed prices, to form farms and freeholds. Whom does this corrupt?...

The gentleman proceeded, sir, to draw a frightful picture of the future. He spoke of the centuries that must elapse, before all the lands could be sold, and the great hardships that the States must suffer while the United States reserved to itself, within their limits such large portions of soil, not liable to taxation. Sir, this is all, mostly imagination....Sir, if in any case any State can shew that the policy of the United States retards her settlement, or prevents her from cultivating the land within her limits she shall have my vote to alter that policy.

...I am quite aware that the sums drawn annually from the Western States make a heavy drain upon them, but that is unavoidable. For that very reason, among others, I have always been inclined to pursue towards them a kind and most liberal policy. But I am not at liberty to forget at the same time, what is due to other States, and to the solemn engagements under which the government rests.

I come now, Mr. President, to that part of the gentleman's speech, which has been the main occasion of my addressing the Senate. The East! The obnoxious, the rebuked the always reproached East!! We have come in, sir, on this debate, for even more than a common share of accusation and attack. If the honorable member from South Carolina was not our original accuser, he has yet recited the indictment against us, with the air and tone of a public prosecutor. He has summoned us to plead on our arraignment; and he tells us we are charged with the crime of a narrow and selfish policy; of endeavoring to restrain emigration to the West, and, having that object in view, of maintaining a steady opposition to Western measures and Western interests. And the cause of all this narrow and selfish policy the gentleman finds in the tariff I think he called it the accursed policy of the tariff. This policy the gentleman tells us, requires multitudes of dependent laborers, a population of paupers, and that it is to secure these at home that the East opposes whatever may induce to Western emigration. Sir, I rise to defend the East. I rise to repel, both the charge itself, and the cause assigned for it. I deny that the East has, at any time, shown an illiberal policy towards the West. I pronounce the whole accusation to be without the least foundation in any facts, existing either now, or at any previous time. I deny it in the general, and I deny each and all its particulars. I deny the sum total, and I deny the detail. I deny that the East has ever manifested hostility to the West and I deny that she has adopted any policy that would naturally have led her in such a course.

But the tariff! The tariff!! Sir, I beg to say, in regard to the East that the original policy of the tariff is not hers whether it be wise or unwise. New England is not its author. If gentlemen will recur to the tariff of 1816, they will find that that was not carried by New England votes. It was truly more a Southern than an Eastern measure. And what votes carried the tariff of 1824? Certainly, not those of New England....

But leaving all conjectures about causes and motives, I go at once to the fact, and I meet it with one broad, comprehensive, and emphatic negative. I deny, that in any part of her history at any period of the government or in relation to any leading object, New England has manifested such hostility as is charged upon her. On the contrary, I maintain that, from the day of the cession of the territories by the States to Congress, no portion of the country has acted either with more liberality or more intelligence on the subject of the Western lands in the new States, than New England....What system for sale and disposition should be adopted? Two modes for conducting the sales presented themselves; the one Southern, and the other a Northern mode....That which was adopted, was the Northern system, and is that which we now see in successful operation in all the new States....New England gave this system to the West and while it remains, there will be spread over all the West, one monument of her intelligence in matters of government, and her practical good sense....

Leaving then, Mr. President, these two great and leading measures and coming down to our own times what is there in the history of recent measures of government that exposes New England to this accusation of hostility to Western interests?...What she has done has been consonant to her view of the general good, and therefore she has done it....Let me see sir, any one measure favorable to the West which has been opposed by New England since the government bestowed its attention to these Western improvements....Will you take the Cumberland road? Who has made that? Will you take the Portland canal, whose support carried that bill? Sir, at what period beyond the Greek Islands could these measures or measures like these, have been accomplished, had they depended on the votes of the Southern gentlemen? Why, sir, we know that we must have waited till the constitutional no-

> tions of those gentlemen had undergone an entire change. Generally speaking, they have done nothing and can do nothing. All that has been effected, has been done by the votes of reprobated New England. I undertake to say, that if you look to the votes on any one of these measures and strike out from the list of ayes the names of New England members it will be found that in every case, the South would then have voted down the West and the measure would have failed. I do not believe that any instance can be found where this is not strictly true. I do not believe that one dollar has been expended for these purposes beyond the mountains, which could have been obtained without cordial co-operation and support from New England....
>
> The gentleman alluded to a report of the late Secretary of the Treasury, which, according to his reading or construction of it, recommended what he calls the tariff policy, or a branch of that policy; that is, the restraining of emigration to the West, for the purpose of keeping hands at home, to carry on the manufactures. I think, sir, that the gentleman misapprehended the meaning of the Secretary in the interpretation given to his remarks. I understand him only as saying, that since the low price of lands at the West acts as a constant and standing bounty to agriculture, it is, on that account the more reasonable, to provide encouragement for manufactures. But, sir, even if the Secretary's observation were to be understood as the gentleman understands it, it would not be a sentiment borrowed from any New England source. – Whether it be right or wrong, it does not originate in that quarter....
>
> ...I have felt it my duty on this occasion to vindicate the State I represent from charges and imputations on her public character and conduct, which I know to be undeserved and unfounded. – If advanced elsewhere, they might be passed, perhaps, without notice. But whatever is said here, is supposed to be entitled to public regard, and to deserve public attention – it derives importance and dignity from the place where it is uttered. [10]

Senator Webster, in the course of his first reply to Senator Hayne, acknowledged that the only fair, honorable, and constitutional manner in which to manage the public lands in the Western Territories was to follow the course initially advocated by Congress, which resolved on October 10, 1780, that such lands "should be settled and formed into distinct Republican States, to become members of the Federal Union, *with the same rights of sovereignty, freedom, and independence as the other States*." And he insisted that this was the public land policy advocated by the consolidating school, a policy which he described as "a liberal and enlightened system." The new Western States, he averred, will someday stand as one great *monument* to the wisdom, fairness, and honorableness of the public land policy practiced by the Government of the United States.

Today, some 175 years after Daniel Webster spoke these words, the Fed-

---

[10] "Debate in the Senate – From *Niles Register* – Feb. 20, 1830, pp 435-440," *Niles Register*, http://www.earlyrepublic.net/webster1.htm, orig. pub. 1830.

eral Government still owns and directly controls some *one-third* of the entire land mass of the United States, and *more than half* of the land mass within the Western States. And Westerners have erected their own *monument* to this sordid land policy which Senator Webster thought so fair and wonderful. In big, bold words, as we have previously indicated, their monument declares: "Welcome to the West. Property: U.S. Govt." As the Sagebrush Rebellion proved, Daniel Webster was dead wrong in his assertion that the public land policy advocated by the consolidating school was based on the concept of a Union of sovereign and equal States. And that "step-mother" Federal Government that the States' Rights school warned against in the time of Daniel Webster has since evolved into a Big Brother, which asserts that the people of the States are too ignorant to manage their own public lands, but must have their affairs controlled by a supreme, sovereign, centralized regime in Washington, D.C.

Senator Hayne, said Daniel Webster, had drawn "a frightful picture of the future." The South Carolina Senator, declared Senator Webster, had spoken "of the centuries that must elapse, before all the lands could be sold, and the great hardships that the States must suffer while the United States reserved to itself, within their limits such large portions of soil, not liable to taxation." Solemnly addressing the Senate of United States, the Orator of Consolidation insisted that such a thing was a nightmare – a figment of the imagination – that could never become a reality: "Sir, this is all, mostly imagination." That very nightmare envisioned by Senator Hayne, however, proved to be foresight, not imagination. Today – some 175 years after Senator Webster spoke – the Government of the United States still refuses to dispose of the vast tracts of land it is hording. And all indications are that even more centuries must pass before the Federal Government's chokehold on the public lands in the United States will be broken.

"I rise to defend the East," the Senator from Massachusetts asserted. "I deny that the East has, at any time, shown an illiberal policy towards the West. I pronounce the whole accusation to be without the least foundation in any facts, existing either now, or at any previous time." Such a denial, he claimed, was absolute and without limitation. "I deny it in the general, and I deny each and all its particulars," Senator Webster insisted. "I deny the sum total, and I deny the detail."

In making this sweeping denial, however, the Orator of Consolidation evidently forgot, or at least pretended to forget, the Report and Resolutions of the Hartford Convention of 1814. At that Convention, delegates from the New England wing of the Federalist Party, of which Senator Webster had been a member at the time, adopted a number of resolutions on January 4, 1815, that clarified the position of the consolidating school on a number of issues, including the embryonic Western States.

"The admission of new States into the Union formed at pleasure in the Western region," declared the Report and Resolutions of the Hartford Convention, "has destroyed the balance of power which existed among the original States, and deeply affected their interest." [11] Therefore, the Federalists in Convention assembled solemnly resolved that certain amendments should be added to the Federal Constitution, including one which would declare that, "No new State shall be admitted into the Union...without the concurrence of two thirds of both houses." [12]

Despite such obvious hostility toward the admission of new States into the Union, Senator Webster claimed that the Eastern States – the stronghold of the consolidating school – were the true friends of the Western States, and indeed, greater friends than the States' Rights school. For proof of this, the Massachusetts Senator referred to the votes taken in the Congress on internal improvements and other aspects of the corrupt and corrupting American System. The socialistic policies advocated by the consolidating school were thus offered as *proof* of the benevolence and fairness of the consolidators. Socialism, redistribution of wealth, taxing all for the benefit of favored interests, consolidation, and centralization of power – these were the very essence of the American way of governance, insisted Daniel Webster.

Senator Hayne's Second Speech

When Senator Webster concluded his first reply to Senator Hayne, Senator Benton of Missouri took the floor to offer some remarks in reply to the Senator from Massachusetts. On the following day – January 21, 1830 – Robert Y. Hayne again took the floor to offer his second, more lengthy, speech to the Senate of the United States. Within the course of this second oration, which was published in *Webster and Hayne's Speeches in the United States Senate, on Mr. Foot's Resolution of January, 1830*, Senator Hayne declared:

> Mr. HAYNE said, when he took occasion, two days ago, to throw out some ideas with respect to the policy of the government, in relation to the public lands, nothing certainly could have been further from his thoughts, than that he should have been compelled again to throw himself upon the indulgence of the Senate....
>
> The gentleman from Massachusetts, in reply to my remarks on the injurious operations of our land system on the prosperity of the West, pronounced an extravagant eulogium on the paternal care which the government had extended towards the West, to which he attributed all that was great and

---

[11] Harold C. Syrett (ed.), *American Historical Documents*, Barnes & Noble, Inc., New York, 1960, p. 161.
[12] *Ibid.*, p. 162.

excellent in the present condition of the new States. The language of the gentleman on this topic fell upon my ears like the almost forgotten tones of the Tory leaders of the British Parliament, at the commencement of the American Revolution. They, too, discovered that the colonies had grown great under the fostering care of the mother country; and I must confess, while listening to the gentleman, I thought the appropriate reply to his argument was to be found in the remark of a celebrated orator, made on that occasion: "They have grown great in spite of your protection."...

I contended that the public lands ought not to be treated merely as "a fund for revenue;" that they ought not to be hoarded "as a great treasure."...

In 1825, the gentleman [Senator Webster] told the world that the public lands "ought not to be treated as a treasure." He now tells us that "they must be treated as so much treasure."...If in the deeds of cession it has been declared that the grants were intended for "the common benefit of all the states," it is clear, from other provisions, that they were not intended merely as *so much property;* for it is expressly declared, that the object of the grants is the erection of new States; and the United States, in accepting this trust, bind themselves to facilitate the foundation of these States, to be admitted into the Union with all the rights and privileges of the original States. This, sir, was the great end to which all parties looked, and it is by the fulfillment of this high trust that "the common benefit of all the States" is to be best promoted....

But, sir, if we are bound to act on the narrow principles contended for by the gentleman, I am wholly at a loss to conceive how he can reconcile his principles with his own practice. The lands are, it seems, to be treated "as so much treasure," and must be applied to the "common benefit of all the States." Now, if this be so, whence does he derive the right to appropriate them for partial and local objects? How can the gentleman consent to vote away immense bodies of these lands, for canals in Indiana and Illinois, to the Louisville and Portland Canal, to Kenyon College in Ohio, to Schools for the Deaf and Dumb, and other objects of a similar description? If grants of this character can fairly be considered as made "for the common benefit of all the States," it can only be, because all the States are interested in the welfare of each, a principle which, carried to the full extent, destroys all distinction between local and national objects, and is certainly *broad enough* to embrace the principles for which I have ventured to contend. Sir, the true difference between us I take to be this; the gentleman wishes to treat the public lands as a great treasure, just as so much money in the treasury, to be applied to all objects, constitutional and unconstitutional to which the public money is constantly applied. I consider it as a sacred trust which we ought to fulfill on the principles for which I have contended.

The Senator from Massachusetts has thought proper to present, in strong contrast, the friendly feelings of the East towards the West, with sentiments of an opposite character displayed by the South in relation to appropriations for *internal improvements*....[T]he gentleman from Massachusetts, while he vaunts over his own personal devotion to Western interests,...claim[s] for the entire section of country to which he belongs an ardent friendship for the West, as manifested by their support of the system of internal improvement, while he casts in our teeth the reproach that the South has manifested hostility to Western interests in opposing appropriations for such objects. That gentleman, at the same time, acknowledged that the South entertains *constitutional scruples* on this subject. Are we then, sir, to understand that the gentleman considers it a just subject of reproach that we respect our oaths, by which we are bound "to preserve, protect, and defend the Constitution of the U. States?" Would the gentleman have us manifest our love to the West by trampling under foot our constitutional scruples....

In the session of 1824 and '25, however, (a memorable era in the history of this country,) a wonderful change took place in New England, in relation to Western interests. Sir, an extraordinary union of sympathies and of interests was then effected, which brought the East and the West into close alliance....Then it was, that that happy union between the members of the celebrated *coalition* was consummated, whose immediate issue was a President from *one quarter of the Union,* with the succession (as it was supposed) *secured to another.* The "American System," before a rude, disjointed, and misshapen mass, now assumed form and consistency. Then it was that it became "the settled policy of the government," that this system should be so administered as to create a reciprocity of interests and a reciprocal distribution of government favors, East and West, (the tariff and internal improvements,) while the South yes, sir, the impracticable South was to be "out of your protection."...Before I leave this topic, I must be permitted to say that the true character of the policy now pursued by the gentleman from Massachusetts and his friends, in relation to appropriations of land and money, for the benefit of the West, is in my estimation very similar to that pursued by Jacob of old towards his brother Esau: "It robs them of their birthright for a mess of pottage."...

Sir, let me tell that gentleman, that the South repudiates the idea that *pecuniary dependence* on the Federal Government is one of the legitimate means of holding the States together. A moneyed interest in the government is essentially a base interest; and just so far as it operates to bind the feelings of those who are subjected to it to the government, just so far as it operates in creating sympathies and interests that would not otherwise exist, is it opposed to all the principles of free government, and at war with virtue and patriotism. Sir, the link which binds the public creditors, *as such,* to their country, binds them equally to all governments, whether arbitrary or free. In a free government, this principle of abject dependence, if extended through all the ramifications of society, must be fatal to liberty. Already have we made alarming strides in that direction. The entire class of manufacturers, the holders of stocks, with their hundreds of millions of capital, are held to the government by the strong link of *pecuniary interests;* millions of people – entire sections of country, interested, or believing themselves to be so, in the public lands, and the public treasure are bound to the government by the expectation of *pecuniary favors.* If this system is carried much further no man can fail to see that every generous motive of attachment to the country will be destroyed, and in its place will spring up those low groveling, base, and selfish feelings which bind men to the footstool of a despot by bonds as strong and enduring as those which attach them to free institutions. Sir, I would lay the foundation of this government in the affections of the people – I would teach them to cling to it by dispensing equal justice, and above all, by securing the "blessings of liberty" to "themselves and to their posterity."

... Mr. President, the impression which has gone abroad of the *weakness of the South,* as connected with the *slave question,* exposes us to such constant attacks, has done us so much injury, and is calculated to produce such infinite mischiefs, that I embrace the occasion presented by the remarks of the gentleman of Massachusetts, to declare that we are ready to meet the question promptly and fearlessly. It is one from which we are not disposed to shrink, in whatever form or under whatever circumstances it may be pressed upon us....

...We deal in no *abstractions.* We will not look back to inquire whether our fathers were guiltless in introducing slaves into this country. If an inquiry should ever be instituted in these matters, however, it will be found that the profits of the slave trade were not confined to the South. Southern ships and Southern sailors were not the instruments of bringing slaves to the shores of America, nor did our merchants reap the profits of that "accursed traffic." But, sir, we will pass over all this. If slavery, as it now exists in this country, be an evil, we of the present day *found it readymade to our hands.* Finding our lot cast among a people whom God had manifestly committed to our care, we did not sit down to speculate on abstract questions of theoretical liberty. We met it as a practical question of *obligation and duty.* We resolved to make the best of the situation in which Providence had placed us, and to fulfill the high trusts which had devolved upon us as the owners of slaves, in the only way in which such a trust could be fulfilled, without spreading misery and ruin throughout the land....

...Shedding weak tears over sufferings which had existence in their own sickly imaginations, these "friends of humanity" set themselves systematically to work to seduce the slaves of the South from their masters....

...Sir, I have seen in the neighborhood of one of the most moral, religious, and refined cities of the North, a family of free blacks, driven to the caves of the rocks and there obtaining a precarious subsistence from charity and plunder....

Sir, on this subject I will quote an authority, which will, I doubt not, be considered by the Senator from Massachusetts as entitled to high respect. It is from the great father of the "American System," *honest Matthew Carey* – no great friend, it is true, at this time, to Southern rights and Southern interests, but not the worst authority on that account, *on the point in question.* Speaking of the *relative importance to the Union* of the SOUTHERN and the EASTERN STATES, Matthew Carey, in the sixth edition of his Olive Branch, (p. 278,) after exhibiting a number of statistical tables to show the declared superiority of the former, thus proceeds: –

"But I am tired of this investigation I sicken for the honor of the human species. What idea must the world form of the arrogance of the pretensions on the one side, [the East,] and of the folly and weakness of the rest of the Union, to have so long suffered them to pass without exposure and detection. The naked fact is, that the demagogues in the Eastern States, not satisfied *with deriving all the benefit from the Southern section of the Union that they would from so many wealthy colonies* – with making princely fortunes *they would from so many wealthy colonies* – with making princely fortunes by the carriage and exportation of its bulky and valuable productions, and *supplying it with their own manufacture,* and the productions of Europe and the East and West Indies, to an enormous amount, and at an immense profit, have uniformly treated it with outrage, insult, and injury.

"And, regardless of their vital interests, the Eastern States were lately *courting their own destruction,* by allowing a few restless turbulent men to lead them blindfolded *to a separation* which was *pregnant with their certain ruin.* Whenever *that* event takes place, they sink into insignificance. If a separation were desirable to any part of the Union, it would be to the Middle and Southern States, particularly the latter, who have been so long harassed with the complaints, the restlessness, the turbulence, and the ingratitude of the Eastern States, that their patience has been tried almost beyond endurance. Jeshurun run *waxed fat* and *kicked' – and* he will be severely punished for his kicking, in the event of a dissolution of the Union."

Sir, I wish it to be distinctly understood that I do not adopt these sentiments as my own. I quote them to show that very different sentiments have prevailed in former times as to the weakness of the slaveholding States from those which now seem to have become fashionable in certain quarters.

I know it has been supposed by certain ill-informed persons, that the South exists only by the countenance and protection of the North....

On this subject as in all others, we ask nothing of our Northern brethren but to "let us alone." Leave us to the undisturbed management of our domestic concerns, and the direction of our own industry, and we will ask no more....

There is a spirit, which, like the father of evil, is constantly "walking to and fro about the earth, seeking whom it may devour:" it is the spirit of FALSE PHILANTHROPY. The persons whom it possesses do not indeed throw themselves into the flames, but they are employed in lighting up the torches of discord throughout the community. Their first principle of action is to leave their own affairs, and neglect their own duties, to regulate the affairs and duties of others. Theirs is the task to feed the hungry, and clothe the naked, of other lands, while they thrust the naked, famished, and shivering beggar from their own doors; to instruct the heathen while their own children want the bread of life. When this spirit infuses itself into the bosom of a statesman, (if one so possessed can be called a statesman,) it converts him at once into a visionary enthusiast. Then it is that he indulges in golden dreams of national greatness and prosperity. He discovers that "liberty is power," and not content with fat schemes of improvement at home, which it would bankrupt the treasure of the world to execute, he flies to foreign lands, to fulfill obligations to "the human race" by inculcating the principles of "political and religious liberty," and promoting the "general welfare" of the whole human race.

It is a spirit which has long been busy with the *slaves of the South*; and is even now displaying itself in vain efforts to drive the government from its wise policy in relation to the *Indian.* It is this spirit which has filled the Land with thousands of wild and visionary projects, which can have no effect but to waste the energies and dissipate the resources of the country. It is the spirit of which the aspiring politician dexterously avails himself, when, by inscribing on his banner the magical words LIBERTY and Philanthropy he draws to his support that Class of persons who are ready to bow down at the very name of their idols.

But, sir, whatever difference of opinion may exist as to the effect of slavery on national wealth and prosperity, if we may trust to experience, there can be no doubt that it has never yet produced any injurious effect on *individual or national character.* Look through the whole history of the country, from the commencement of the revolution down to the present hour; where are there to be found brighter examples of intellectual and moral greatness than have been exhibited by the sons of the South? From the FATHER OF HIS COUNTRY down to the DISTINGUISHED CHIEFTAIN who has been elevated by a grateful people to the highest office in their gift, the interval is filled up by a long line of orators, of statesmen, and of heroes, justly entitled to rank among the ornaments of their country, and the benefactors of mankind. Look at the "Old Dominion," great and magnanimous Virginia, "whose jewels are her sons." Is there any State in this Union which has contributed so much to the honor and welfare of the country? Sir, I will yield the whole question – I will acknowledge the fatal effects of slavery upon character, if any one can say, that for noble disinterestedness, ardent love of country, exalted virtue, and a pure and holy devotion to liberty, the people of the Southern States have ever been surpassed by any in the world....

In the course of my former remarks, Mr. President, I took occasion to deprecate, as one of the greatest evils, *the consolidation of this government.* The gentleman takes alarm at the sound. "*Consolidation,*" like the *tariff* grates upon his ear. He tells us, "we have heard much of late about consolidation; that it is the rallying word of all who are endeavoring to *weaken the Union,* by adding to the power of the States." But consolidation (says the gentleman) was the very object for which the Union was formed; and, in support of that opinion, he read a passage from the address of the President of the Convention to Congress, which he assumes to be authority on his side of the question. But, sir, the gentleman is mistaken. The object of the framers of the Constitution, as disclosed in that address, was not the *consolidation of the government,* but "the consolidation of the Union." It was not to draw power from the States, in order to transfer it to a great National Government, but, in the language of the Constitution itself, "to form a more perfect Union;" – and by what means? By "establishing justice, promoting domestic tranquility, and securing the blessings of liberty to ourselves and our posterity." This is the true reading of the Constitution. But, according, to the gentleman's reading, the object of the Constitution was, to *consolidate the government,* and the means would seem to be, the promotion of injustice, causing domestic *discord,* and depriving the States and the people "of the blessings of liberty" forever.

The gentleman boasts of belonging to the party of NATIONAL REPUBLICANs. National Republicans! A new name, sir, for a very old thing. The National Republicans of the present day were the *Federalists* of '98, who became *Federal Republicans* during the War of 1812, and were *manufactured* into *National Republicans* somewhere about the year 1825.

As a party, (by whatever name distinguished,) they have always been animated by the same principles, and have kept steadily in view a common object, the consolidation of the government. Sir, the party to which am proud of having belonged, from the very commencement of my political life to the present day, were the *Democrats of* '98, *(Anarchists, Anti-Federalists, Revolutionists,* I think they were sometimes called.) They assumed the name of *Democratic Republicans* in 1822, and have retained their name and principles up to the present hour. True to their political faith, they have always, as a party, been in favor of limitations of power; they have insisted that all powers not delegated to the Federal Government are reserved, and have been constantly struggling, as they now are, to preserve the rights of the States, and to prevent them from being drawn into the vortex, and swallowed up by one great consolidated government.

Sir, any one acquainted with the history of parties in this country will recognize in the points now in dispute between the Senator from Massachusetts and myself the very grounds which have, from the beginning, divided the two great parties in this country, and which (call these parties by what names you will, and *amalgamate* them as you may) will divide them forever.

The true distinction between those parties is laid down in a celebrated manifesto, issued by the Convention of the Federalists of Massachusetts, assembled in Boston, in February, 1824, on the occasion of organizing a party opposition to the reelection of Governor Eustis. The gentleman will recognize this as "the canonical book of political scripture;" and it instructs us that, when the American colonies redeemed themselves from British bondage, and became so many *independent nations* they proposed to form a NATIONAL UNION, (not a Federal UNION, sir but a National Union.) Those who were in favor of *Union of the States in this form* became known by the name *of Federalists;* those who wanted no Union of the States or disliked the proposed form of union, became known by the name of *Anti-Federalists.*

By means which need not be enumerated, the *Anti-Federalists* became (after the expiration of twelve years) our national rulers, and for a period of sixteen years, until the close of Mr. Madison's administration, in 1817, continued to exercise the exclusive direction of our public affairs. Here, sir, is the true history of the origin, rise, and progress of the party of *National Republicans,* who date back to the very origin of the government, and who, then, as now, chose to consider the Constitution as having created, not a *Federal,* but a *National* Union; who regarded "consolidation" as no evil, and who doubtless consider it "a consummation devoutly to be wished" to build up a great central government, "one and indivisible." Sir, there have existed, in every age and every country, two distinct orders of men -- the lovers of freedom, and the devoted *advocates of power.*

...The people whom I represent, Mr. President, are the descendants of those who brought with them to this country, as the most precious of their possessions, "an ardent love of liberty;" and while that shall be preserved, they will always be found manfully struggling against the *consolidation of the Government* – THE WORST OF EVILS.

The senator from Massachusetts, in alluding to the tariff, becomes quite facetious. He tells us that "he hears of nothing but *tariff, tariff, tariff*; and, if a word could be found to rhyme with it, he presumes it would be celebrated in verse, and set to music." Sir, perhaps the gentleman, *in mockery of our complaints,* may be himself disposed to sing the praises of the tariff, in doggerel verse, to the tune of "Old Hundred." I am not at all surprised, however, at the aversion of the gentleman to the very name of *tariff.* I doubt not that it must always bring up some very unpleasant recollections to his mind.

If I am not greatly mistaken, the Senator from Massachusetts was a leading actor at a great meeting got up in Boston, in 1820, *against the tariff.* It has generally been supposed that he drew up the resolutions adopted by that meeting, denouncing the tariff system as unequal, oppressive, and unjust, and if I am not much mistaken, *denying its constitutionality.* Certain it is, that the gentleman made a speech on that occasion in support of those resolutions, denouncing the system in no very measured terms; and, if my memory serves me, *calling its constitutionality in question*....At that time, sir, the Senator from Massachusetts entertained the very sentiments in relation to the tariff which the South now entertains.

We next find the Senator from Massachusetts expressing his opinion on the tariff, as a member of the House of Representatives from the city of Boston, in 1824. On that occasion, sir, the gentleman assumed a position which commanded the respect and admiration of his country. He stood forth the powerful and fearless champion of *free trade*....

Mr. President, it is with pain and regret that I now go forward to the next great era in the political life of that gentleman, when he was found on this door, supporting, advocating, and finally voting for the Tariff of 1828 – that "bill of abominations." By that act, sir, the Senator from Massachusetts has destroyed the labors of his whole life, and given a wound to the cause of free trade never to be healed. Sir, when I recollect the position which that gentleman once occupied, and that which he now holds in public estimation, in relation to this subject, it is not at all surprising that the tariff should be hateful to his ears....

But, Mr. President,...what are we of the South to think of what we have heard this day? The Senator from Massachusetts tells us, that the tariff is not an Eastern measure, and treats it as if the East had no interest in it. The Senator from Missouri insists it is not a Western measure, and that it has done no good to the West. The South comes in, and, in the most earnest manner, represents to you that this measure which we are told "is of no value to the East or the West," is "utterly destructive of our interests." We represent to you that it has spread ruin and devastation through the land and prostrated our hopes in the dust. We solemnly declare that we believe the system to be wholly unconstitutional, and a violation of the compact between the States and the Union, and our brethren turn *a deaf ear to our complaints,* and refuse to relieve us from a system "which not enriches them, but makes us poor indeed."

Good God! Mr. President, *has it come to this.* Do gentlemen hold the feelings and wishes of their brethren at so cheap a rate, that they refuse to gratify them at so small a price? Do gentlemen value so lightly the peace and harmony of the country, that they will not yield a measure of this description to the affectionate entreaties and earnest remonstrances of their friends? Do gentlemen estimate the value of the Union at so low a price, that they will not even make one effort to bind the States together with the cords of affections And has it come to this? Is this the spirit in which this government is to be administered? If so, let me tell gentlemen, the seeds of dissolution are already sown, and our children will reap the bitter fruit....

...[T]he Senator from Massachusetts...has crossed the border, he has invaded the State of South Carolina, is making war upon her citizens, and endeavoring to overthrow her principles and her institutions.

...If the gentleman provokes the war, he shall have war. Sir, I will not stop at the border; I will carry the war into the enemy's territory, and not consent to lay down my arms until I have obtained "indemnity for the past and security for the future."...

...The Revolution of '98 restored the Constitution, rescued the liberty of the citizen from the grasp of these who were aiming at its life, and in the emphatic language of Mr. Jefferson, "saved the Constitution at its last gasp." And by whom was it achieved? By the South, sir, aided only by the democracy of the North and West.

I come now to the War of 1812 – a war which, I well remember was called in derision (while its event was doubtful) the Southern war, and sometimes the Carolina war; but which is now universally acknowledged to have done more for the honor and prosperity of the country than all other events in our history put together. What, sir, were the objects of that war? "Free trade and sailors' rights!" It was for the protection of Northern shipping and New England seamen that the country flew to arms. What interest had the South in that contest? If they had sat down coldly to calculate the value of their interests involved in it, they would have found that they had every thing to lose, and nothing to gain....

Such, sir, was the conduct of the South – such the conduct of my own State in that dark hour "which tried men's souls."

When I look back and contemplate the spectacle exhibited at that time in another quarter of the Union – when I think of the conduct of certain portions of New England, and remember the part which was acted on that memorable occasion by the political associates of the gentleman from Massachusetts – nay, when I follow that gentleman into the councils of the Nation, and listen to his voice during the darkest period of the war, I am indeed astonished that he should venture to touch upon the topics which he has introduced into this debate. South Carolina reproached by Massachusetts! And from whom does the accusation come? Not from the democracy of New England; for they have been in times past, as they are now, the friends and allies of the South. No, sir, the accusation comes from that party whose acts, during the most trying and eventful period of our national history, were of such a character, that their own legislature, but a few years ago, actually blotted them out from their records, as a stain upon the honor of the country. But how can they ever be blotted out from the recollection of any one who had a heart to feel, a mind to comprehend, and a memory to retain, the events of that day! Sir, I shall not attempt to write the history of the party in

New England to which I have alluded – the war party in peace, and the peace party in war....

[In one memorial prior to the War of 1812] from Boston, after stating the alarming and extensive condemnation of our vessels by Great Britain, which threatened "to sweep our commerce from the face of the ocean," and "to involve our merchants in bankruptcy," they call upon the government "to assert our rights and to adopt such measures as will support the dignity and honor of the United States."

From Salem we heard a language still more decisive; they call explicitly for "an appeal to arms," and pledge their lives and property in support of any measures which Congress might adopt....

In other quarters the common language of that day was, that our commerce and our seamen were entitled to protection; and that it was the duty of the government to afford it at every hazard. The conduct of Great Britain, we were then told was "an outrage upon our national independence." These clamors, which commenced as early as January, 1806, were continued up to 1812. In a message from the Governor of one of the New England States as late as the 10th October, 1811, this language is held: "A manly and decisive course has become indispensable; a course to satisfy foreign Nations, that, while we desire peace, we have the means and the spirit to repel aggression. We are false to ourselves when our commerce or our territory is invaded with impunity."...

Well, sir, the war at length came, and what did we behold? The very men who had been for six years clamorous for war, and for whose protection it was waged, became at once equally clamorous against it....And so far did this spirit extend, that a committee of the Massachusetts legislature actually fell to calculation, and discovered, to their infinite satisfaction, but to the astonishment of all the world besides, that only eleven Massachusetts sailors had ever been impressed.

Never shall I forget the appeals that had been made to the sympathies of the South in behalf of the "thousands of impressed Americans," who had been torn from their families and friends, and "immured in the floating dungeons of Britain." The most touching pictures were drawn of the hard condition of the American sailor, "treated like a slave...."

But let us look a little further into the conduct of the peace party of New England at that important crisis. Whatever difference of opinion might have existed as to the causes of the war, the country had a right to expect, that, when once involved in the contest, all America would have cordially united in its support. Sir, the war effected, in its progress, a union of all parties at the South. But not so in New England; there great efforts were made to stir up the minds of the people to oppose it. Nothing was left undone to embarrass the financial operations of the government, to prevent the enlistment of troops, to keep back the men and money of New England from the service of the Union to force the President from his seat....

...Yes, sir, those who cannot endure the thought that we should insist on a free trade, in time of profound peace, could, without scruple, claim and exercise the right of carrying on a free trade with the enemy in a time of war; and finally by getting up the renowned "Hartford Convention," and preparing the way for an open resistance to the government, and a separation of the States....

...I read, sir, from the Olive Branch of Matthew Carey, in which are collected "the actings and doings" of the peace party of New England during the continuance of the embargo and the war. I know the Senator from Massachusetts will respect the high authority of his political friend and fellow-laborer in the great cause of domestic industry.

In p. 301, et seq., 309 of this work, is a detailed account of the measures adopted in Massachusetts during the war, for the express purpose of embarrassing the financial operations of the government, by preventing loans and thereby driving our rulers from their seats, and forcing the country into a dishonorable peace. It appears that the Boston banks commenced an operation, by which a run was to be made upon all the banks to the South; at the same time stopping their own discounts; the effect of which was to produce a sudden and most alarming diminution of the circulating medium, and universal distress over the whole country – a distress which they failed not to attribute to the "unholy war."

...Sir, the author of the *Olive Branch*, with a holy indignation, denounces these acts as "treasonable!", "giving aid and comfort to the enemy." I shall not follow his example. But I will ask, With what justice or propriety can the South be accused of disloyalty from that quarter? If we had any evidence that the Senator from Massachusetts had admonished his brethren then, he might, with a better grace, assume the office of admonishing us now.

When I look at the measures adopted in Boston, at that day, to deprive the government of the necessary means for carrying on the war and think of the success and the consequences of these measures, I feel my pride, as an American, humbled in the dust. Hear, sir, the language of that day. I read from pages 301 and 302 of the Olive Branch. "Let no man who wishes to continue the war, by active means, by vote, or lending money, dare to prostrate himself at the altar on the fast day." "Will Federalists subscribe to the loan? Will they lend money to our national rulers? It is impossible. First, because of principle, and secondly, because of principal and interest." "Do not prevent the abusers of their trust from becoming bankrupt. Do not prevent them from becoming odious to the public, and being replaced by better men." "Any Federalist who lends money to government must go and shake hands with James Madison, and claim fellowship with Felix Grundy."...Let him no more "call himself a Federalist, and a friend to his country: he will be called by others infamous," &c.

...Of the same character with these measures was the conduct of Massachusetts in withholding her militia from the service of the United States, and devising measures for withdrawing her quota of the taxes, thereby attempting, not merely to cripple the resources of the country, but actually depriving the government (as far as depended upon her) of all the means of carrying on the war – of the bone, and muscle, and sinews of war – "of man and steel – the soldier and his sword." But it seems Massachusetts was to reserve her resources for herself – she was to defend and protect her own shores. And how was that duty performed? In some places on the coast neutrality was declared, and the enemy was suffered to invade the soil of Massachusetts, and allowed to occupy her territory until the peace, without one effort to rescue it from his grasp. Nay, more – while our own government and our rulers were considered as enemies, the troops of the enemy were treated like friends – the most intimate commercial relations were established with them, and maintained up to the peace. At this dark period of our national affairs where was the Senator from Massachusetts? How were his political associates employed? "Calculating the value of the Union?"...

"If you do not wish," said a reverend clergyman, in a sermon preached in Boston, on the 23d July, 1812, "to become the slaves of those who own slaves, and who are themselves the slaves of French slaves, you must either, in *the language of the day,* CUT THE CONNECTION, or so far alter the national compact as to insure to yourselves a due share in the government," (Olive Branch p 319.) "The Union," says the same writer, (p. 320,) "has been long since virtually dissolved, and it is full time that this part of the disunited States should take care of itself."...

One or two more quotations, sir, and I shall have done. A reverend doctor of divinity, the pastor of a church at Byfield, Massachusetts, on the 7th of April, 1814, thus addresses his flock, (p. 321:) "The Israelites became weary of yielding the fruit of their labor to pamper their splendid tyrants. They left their political woes. THEY SEPARATED; where is our Moses? Where the rod of his miracles? Where is our Aaron? Alas! No voice from the burning bush has directed them here."

"We must trample on the mandates of despotism, or remain slaves forever,"(p. 322.) "You must drag the chains of Virginian despotism, unless you discover some other mode of escape. Those Western States which have been violent for this abominable war – those States which have thirsted for blood – God has given them blood to drink," (p. 323.) Mr. President, I can go no further. The records of the day are full of such sentiments, issued from the press, spoken in public assemblies, poured out from the sacred desk....

The sentiments I have read were the sentiments of a party embracing the political associates of the gentleman from Massachusetts. If they could only be found in the columns of a newspaper, in a few occasional pamphlets, issued by men of intemperate feeling, I should not consider them as affording any evidence of the opinions even of the peace party of New England. But, sir, they were the common language of that day; they pervaded the whole land; they were issued from the legislative hall, from the pulpit, and the press. Our books are full of them; and there is no man who now hears me but knows that they were the sentiments of a party, by whose members they were promulgated. Indeed, no evidence of this would seem to be required beyond the fact that such sentiments found their way even into the pulpits of New England. What must be the state of public opinion, where any respectable clergyman would venture to preach, and to print, sermons containing the sentiments I have quoted?...

As soon as the public mind was sufficiently prepared for the measure, the celebrated Hartford Convention was got up; not as the act of a few unauthorized individuals, but by authority of the legislature of Massachusetts; and, as has been shown by the able historian of that convention, in accordance with the views and wishes of the party of which it was the organ....It will be recollected that...[the Federal Government's] credit was nearly gone, Washington had fallen, the whole coast was blockaded, and an immense force, collected in the West Indies, was about to make a descent, which it was supposed we had no means of resisting. In this awful state of our public affairs, when the government seemed almost to be tottering on its base, when Great Britain, relieved from all her other enemies, had proclaimed her purpose of "reducing us to unconditional submission," we beheld the peace party of New England (in the language of the work before us) "pursuing a course calculated to do more injury to their country, and to render England more effective service than all her armies."...Such were the dark and portentous signs of the times, which ushered into being the renowned Hartford Convention. That convention met, and, from their proceedings, it appears that their chief object was to keep back the men and money of New England from the service of the Union, and to effect radical changes in the government – changes that can never be effected without a dissolution of the Union....

...In the fourth volume of...[Thomas Jefferson's] Memoirs, which has just issued from the press, we have the following history of disunion from the pen of that illustrious statesman: "Mr. Adams called on me pending the embargo, and while endeavors were making to obtain its repeal: he spoke of the dissatisfaction of the Eastern portion of our Confederacy with the restraints of the embargo then existing, and their restlessness under it; that there was nothing which might not be attempted to rid themselves of it; that he had information of the most unquestionable authority, that certain citizens of the Eastern States (I think he named Massachusetts particularly) were in negotiation with agents of the British Government, the object of which was an agreement that the New England States should take no further part in the war (the commercial war, the 'war of restrictions,' as it was called) then going on, and that, without formally declaring their separation from the Union, they should withdraw from all aid and obedience to them, &c. From that moment," Says Mr. J., "I saw the necessity of abandoning it, [the embargo,] and, instead of effecting our purpose by this peaceful measure, we must fight it out or break the Union." In another letter, Mr. Jefferson adds, "I doubt whether a single fact known to the world will carry as clear conviction to it of the correctness of our knowledge of the treasonable views of the Federal Party of that day, as that disclosed by this, the most nefarious and daring attempt to dissever the Union, of which the Hartford Convention was a subsequent chapter; and both of these having failed, consolidation becomes the fourth chapter of the next book of their history. But this opens with a vast accession of strength, from their younger recruits, who, having nothing in them of the feelings and principles of '76, now look to a single and splendid government, &c., riding and ruling over the plundered ploughman and beggared yeomanry." (vol. iv. pp. 419, 422.)

The last chapter, says Mr. Jefferson, of that history, is to be found in the conduct of those who are endeavoring to bring about consolidation; ay, sir, that very consolidation for which the gentleman from Massachusetts is contending – the exercise by the Federal Government of powers not delegated in relation to "internal improvements" and "the protection of manufactures." And why, sir, does Mr. Jefferson consider consolidation as leading directly to disunion? Because be knew that the exercise, by the Federal Government, of the powers contended for, would make this "a government without limitation of powers," the submission to which he considered as a greater evil than disunion itself.

There is one chapter in this history however, which Mr. Jefferson has not filled up; and I must therefore supply the deficiency. It is to be found in the protests made by New England against the acquisition of Louisiana. In relation to that subject, the New England doctrine is thus laid down by one of her learned doctors of that day, now a doctor of laws, at the head of the great literary institution of the East; I mean Josiah Quincy, President of Harvard College. I quote from the speech delivered by that gentleman on the floor of Congress, on the occasion of the admission of Louisiana into the Union.

"Mr. Quincy repeated and justified a remark he had made, which, to save all misapprehension, he had committed to writing, in the following words: If this bill passes, it is my deliberate opinion that it is virtually a dissolution of the Union; that it will free the States from their moral obligation; and as it will be the right of all, so it will be the duty of some, to prepare for a separation, amicably if they can, violently if they must."

Mr. President, I wish it to be distinctly understood, that all the remarks I have made on this subject are intended to be exclusively applied to a party, which I have described as the "peace party of New England" embracing, the political associates of the Senator from Massachusetts – a party which controlled the operations of that State during the embargo and the war, and who are justly chargeable with all the measures I have reprobated. Sir, nothing has been further from my thoughts than to impeach the character or conduct of the people of New England....

Who, then, Mr. President, are the true friends of the Union? Those who would confine the Federal Government strictly within the limits prescribed by the Constitution; who would preserve to the States and the people all powers not expressly delegated; who would make this a Federal and not a National Union, and who, administering the government in spirit of equal justice, would make it a blessing, and not a curse. And who are its enemies? Those who are in favor of consolidation; who are constantly stealing power from the States, and adding strength to the Federal Government; who, assuming an unwarrantable Jurisdiction over the States and the people, undertake to regulate the whole industry and capital of the country. But, sir, of all descriptions of men, I consider those as the worst enemies of the Union, who sacrifice the equal rights which belong to every member of the Confederacy to combinations of interested majorities, for personal or political objects. But the gentleman apprehends no evil from the dependence of the States on the Federal Government; he can see no danger of corruption from the influence of money or of patronage. Sir, I know that it is supposed to be a wise saying that "patronage is a source of weakness;" and in support of that maxim, it has been said, that "every ten appointments make a hundred enemies."

But I am rather inclined to think, with the eloquent and sagacious orator now reposing on his laurels on the banks of the Roanoke [John Randolph] that "the power of conferring favors creates a crowd of dependents," he gave a forcible illustration of the truth of the remark, when he told us of the effect of holding up the savory morsel to the eager eyes of the hungry hounds gathered around his door. It mattered not whether the gift was bestowed on Towzer or Sweetlips, "Tray, Blanch, or Sweetheart," while held in suspense, they were all governed by a nod, and when the morsel was bestowed, the expectation of the favors of to-morrow kept up the subjection of to-day.

The Senator from Massachusetts, in denouncing what he is pleased to call the Carolina doctrine, has attempted to throw ridicule upon the idea that a State has any constitutional remedy, by the exercise of its sovereign authority, against "a gross, palpable, and deliberate violation of the Constitution." He calls it "an idle" or "a ridiculous notion," or something to that effect, and added, that it would make the Union a "mere rope of sand." Now, sir, as the gentleman has not condescended to enter into any examination of the question, and has been satisfied with throwing the weight of his authority into the scale, I do not deem it necessary to do more than to throw into the opposite scale the authority on which South Carolina relies; and there, for the present, I am perfectly willing to leave the controversy. The South Carolina doctrine, that is to say, the doctrine contained in an exposition reported by a committee of the legislature in December, 1828, and published by their authority, is the good old Republican Doctrine of '98 – the doctrine of the celebrated "Virginia Resolutions" of that year, and of "Madison's Report" of '99. It will be recollected that the legislature of Virginia, in December, 98, took into consideration the Alien and Sedition Laws, then considered by all Republicans as a gross violation of the Constitution of the United States, and on that day passed, among others, the following resolutions: –

"The General Assembly doth explicitly and peremptorily declare, that it views the powers of the Federal Government, as resulting from the compact to which the States are parties, as limited by the plain sense and intention of the instrument constituting that compact, as no further valid than they are authorized by the grants enumerated in that compact; and that in case of a deliberate, palpable, and dangerous exercise of other powers not granted by the said compact, the States who are parties thereto have the right, and are in duty bound, to interpose for arresting the progress of the evil, and for maintaining, within their respective limits, the authorities, rights, and liberties appertaining to them."

In addition to the above resolution, the General Assembly of Virginia "appealed to the other States, in the confidence that they would concur with that commonwealth, that the acts aforesaid [the Alien and Sedition Laws] are unconstitutional, and that the necessary and proper measures would be taken by each for cooperating with Virginia in maintaining unimpaired the authorities, rights, and liberties reserved to the States respectively, or to the people."

The legislatures of several of the New England States, having, contrary to the expectation of the legislature of Virginia, expressed their dissent from these doctrines, the subject came up again for consideration during the session of 1799, 1800, when it was referred to a select committee, by whom was made that celebrated report which is familiarly known as "Madison's Report," and which deserves to last as long as the Constitution itself. In that report, which was subsequently adopted by the legislature, the whole subject was deliberately reexamined, and the objections urged against the Virginia Doctrines carefully considered. The result was, that the legislature of Virginia reaffirmed all the principles laid down in the Resolutions of 1798, and issued to the world that admirable report which has stamped the character of Mr. Madison as the preserver of that Constitution which he had contributed so largely to create and establish. I will here quote from Mr. Madison's report one or two passages which bear more immediately on the point in controversy.

"The Resolutions, having taken this view of the federal compact, proceed to infer 'that in case of a deliberate, palpable, and dangerous exercise of other powers, not granted by the said compact, the States who are parties thereto have the right, and are in duty bound, to interpose for arresting the progress of the evil, and for maintaining, within their respective limits, the authorities, rights, and liberties appertaining to them.'"

"It appears to your committee to be a plain principle, founded in common sense, illustrated by common practice, and essential to the nature of compacts, that, where resort can be had to no tribunal superior to the authority of the parties, the parties themselves must be the rightful judges in the last resort, whether the bargain made has been pursued or violated.

"The Constitution of the United States was formed by the sanction of the States, given by each in its sovereign capacity. It adds to the stability and dignity, as well as to the authority, of the Constitution, that it rests upon this legitimate and solid foundation. The States, then, being the parties to the constitutional compact, and in their sovereign capacity, it follows of necessity that there can be no tribunal above their authority to decide, in the last resort, whether the compact made by them be violated and consequently that, as the parties to it, they must themselves decide, in the last resort, such questions as may be of sufficient magnitude to require their interposition."

"The Resolution has guarded against any misapprehension of its object by expressly requiring for such an interposition 'the case of a deliberate, palpable, and dangerous breach of the Constitution, by the exercise of powers not granted by it.' It must be a case, not of a light and transient nature, but of a nature dangerous to the great purposes for which the Constitution was established.

"But the Resolution has done more than guard against misconstruction, by expressly referring to cases of a deliberate, palpable, and dangerous attire. It specifies the object of the interposition, which it contemplates, be solely that of arresting the progress of the evil of usurpation, and of maintaining the authorities, rights, and liberties appertaining to the States, as parties to the Constitution.

"From this view of the Resolution, it would seem inconceivable that it can incur any just disapprobation from those who, laying aside all momentary impressions, and recollecting the genuine source and object of the Federal Constitution, shall candidly and accurately interpret the meaning of the General Assembly. If the deliberate exercise of dangerous powers, palpably withheld by the Constitution, could not justify the parties to it in interposing even so far as to arrest the progress of the evil, and thereby to preserve the Constitution itself, as well as to provide for the safety of the parties to it, there would be an end to all relief from usurped power, and a direct subversion of the rights specified or recognized under all the State Constitutions, as well as a plain denial of the fundamental principles on which our independence itself was declared."

But sir, our authorities do not stop here. The State of Kentucky responded to Virginia, and on the 10th of November, 1798, adopted those celebrated resolutions, well known to have been penned by the author of the Declaration of American Independence. In those Resolutions, the legislature of Kentucky declare, "that the government created by this compact was not made the exclusive or final judge of the extent of the powers delegated to itself, since that would have made its discretion, and not the Constitution, the measure of its powers; but that, as in all other cases of compact among parties having no common judge, each party has an equal right to judge, for itself, as well of infractions as of the mode and measure of redress."

At the ensuing session of the legislature, the subject was reexamined, and on the 14th of November, 1799, the Resolutions of the preceding year were deliberately reaffirmed, and it was, among other things, solemnly declared, -

"That, if those who administer the general government be permitted to transgress the limits fixed by that compact, by a total disregard to the special delegations of power therein contained, an annihilation of the State governments, and the erection upon their ruins of a general consolidated government, will be the inevitable consequence.

"That the principles of construction contended for by sundry of the State legislatures, that the general government is the exclusive judge of the extent of the powers delegated to it, stop nothing short of despotism; since the discretion of those who administer the government, and not the Constitution, would be the measure of their powers. That the several States who formed that instrument, being sovereign and independent, have the unquestionable right to judge of its infraction, and that a nullification by those sovereignties, of all unauthorized acts done under color of that instrument is the rightful remedy."

Time and experience confirmed Mr. Jefferson's opinion on this all important point. In the year 1821, he expressed himself in this emphatic manner: "It is a fatal heresy to suppose that either our State governments are superior to the federal, or the federal to the State; neither is authorized literally to decide which belongs to itself or its copartner in government; in differences of opinion, between their different sets of public servants, the appeal is to neither, but to their employers peaceably assembled by their representatives in convention." The opinion of Mr. Jefferson on this subject has been so repeatedly and so solemnly expressed, that they may be said to have been among the most fixed and settled convictions of his mind.

In the protest prepared by him for the legislature of Virginia, in December, 1825, in respect to the powers exercised by the Federal Government in relation to the tariff and internal improvements, which he declares to be "usurpations of the powers retained by the States, mere interpolations into the compact, and direct infractions of it," he solemnly reasserts all the principles of the Virginia Resolutions of '98, protests against these acts of the federal branch of the government as null and void, and declares that, although Virginia would consider a dissolution of the Union as among the greatest calamities that could befall them, yet it is not the greatest. There is one yet greater – submission to a government of unlimited powers. It is only when the hope of this shall become absolutely desperate, that further forbearance could not be indulged.

In his letter to Mr. Giles, written about the same time, he says, –

"I see as you do, and with the deepest affliction, the rapid strides with which the federal branch of our government is advancing towards the usurpation of all the rights reserved to the States, and the consolidation in itself of all powers, foreign and domestic, and that too by constructions which leave no limits to their powers, &c. Under the power to regulate commerce, they assume, indefinitely, that also over agriculture and manufactures, &c. Under the authority to establish post roads, they claim that of cutting down mountains for the construction of roads, and digging canals, &c. And what is our resource for the preservation of the Constitution. Reason and argument? You might as well reason and argue with the marble columns encircling them, &c. Are we then to stand to our arms with the hot-headed Georgian? No; [and I say no, and South Carolina has said no;] that must be the last resource. We must have patience and long endurance with our brethren, &c., and separate from our companions only when the sole alternatives left are a dissolution of our Union with them, or submission to a government without limitation of powers. Between these two evils, when we must make a choice, there can be no hesitation."

Such, sir, are the high and imposing authorities in support of "the Carolina Doctrine," which is, in fact, the Doctrine of the Virginia Resolutions of 1798.

Sir, at that day the whole country was divided on this very question. It formed the line of demarcation between the Federal and Republican Parties; and the great political revolution which then took place turned upon the very questions involved in these Resolutions. That question was decided by the people, and by that decision the Constitution was, in the emphatic language of Mr. Jefferson, "saved at its last gasp." I should suppose, sir, it would require more self-respect than any gentleman here would be willing to assume, to treat lightly doctrines derived from such high resources.

Resting on authority like this, I will ask gentlemen whether South Carolina has not manifested a high regard for the Union, when under a tyranny ten times more grievous than the Alien and Sedition Laws, she has hitherto gone no further than to petition, remonstrate, and to solemnly protest against a series of measures which she believes to be wholly unconstitutional and utterly destructive of her interests. Sir, South Carolina has not gone one step further than Mr. Jefferson himself was disposed to go, in relation to the present subject of our present complaints – not a step further than the statesmen from New England were disposed to go, under similar circumstances; no further than the Senator from Massachusetts himself once considered as within "the limits of a constitutional opposition." The doctrine that it is the right of a State to judge of the violations of the Constitution on the part of the Federal Government, and to protect her citizens from the operations of unconstitutional laws, was held by the enlightened citizens of Boston, who assembled in Faneuil Hall, on the 25th of January, 1809. They state in that celebrated memorial, that "they looked only to the State legislature, who were competent to devise relief against the unconstitutional acts of the general government. That your power (say they) is adequate to that object, is evident from the organization of the Confederacy."

A distinguished Senator from one of the New England States, (Mr. Hillhouse,) in a speech delivered here, on a bill for enforcing the embargo; declared, "I feel myself bound in conscience to declare, (lest the blood of those who shall fall in the execution of this measure shall be on my head,) that I consider this to be an act which directs a mortal blow at the liberties of my country – an act containing unconstitutional provisions, to which the people are not bound to submit, and to which, in my opinion, they will not submit."

And the Senator from Massachusetts himself, in a speech delivered on the same subject in the other house, said, "This opposition is constitutional and legal; it is also conscientious. It rests on settled and sober conviction, that such policy is destructive to the interests of the people, and dangerous to the being of government. The experience of every day confirms these sentiments. Men who act from such motives are not to be discouraged by trifling obstacles, nor awed by any dangers. They know the limit of constitutional opposition; up to that limit, at their the discretion, they will walk, and walk fearlessly."...

Thus it will be seen, Mr. President, that the South Carolina Doctrine is the Republican Doctrine of '98 – that it was promulgated by the fathers of the faith – that it was maintained by Virginia and Kentucky in the worst of times – that it constituted the very pivot on which the political revolution of that day turned – that it embraces the very principles, the triumph of which, at that time, saved the Constitution at its last gasp, and which New England statesmen were not unwilling to adopt, when they believed themselves to be the victims of unconstitutional legislation. Sir, as to the doctrine that the Federal Government is the exclusive judge of the extent as well as the limitations of its powers, it seems to me to be utterly subversive of the sovereignty and independence of the States. It makes but little difference, in my estimation, whether Congress or Supreme Court are invested with this power. If the Federal Government, in all, or any, of its departments, is to prescribe the limits of its own authority, and the States are bound to submit to the decision, and are not to be allowed to examine and decide for themselves, when the barriers of the Constitution shall be overleaped, this is practically "government without limitation of powers." The States are at once reduced to mere petty corporations and the people are entirely at your mercy. I have but one word more to add.

> In all the efforts that have been made by South Carolina to resist the unconstitutional laws which Congress has extended over them, she has kept steadily in view the preservation of the Union, by the only means by which she believes it can belong preserved – a firm, manly, and steady resistance against usurpation. The measures of the Federal Government have, it is true, prostrated her interests, and will soon involve the whole South in irretrievable ruin. But even this evil, great as it is, is not the chief ground of our complaints. It is the principle involved in the contest – a principle which, substituting the discretion of Congress for the limitations of the Constitution, brings the States and the people to the feet of the Federal Government, and leaves them nothing they can call their own. Sir, if the measures of the Federal Government were less oppressive, we should still strive against this usurpation. The South is acting on a principle she has always held sacred – resistance to unauthorized taxation....Sir, if acting on these high motives – if animated by that ardent love of liberty which has always been the most prominent trait in the Southern character – we should be hurried beyond the bounds of a cold and calculating prudence, who is there, with one *noble* and generous sentiment in his bosom, that would not be disposed, in the language of Burke, to exclaim, "You must pardon something to the spirit of liberty"? [13]

With this appeal to the *spirit of liberty*, Senator Hayne concluded his second oration in the great debate with Daniel Webster in the Senate of the United States. And now that we have presented the very words of the Senator from South Carolina, let us examine and analyze the ideas and principles he presented.

Analysis of Senator Hayne's Speech

New States admitted into the Union, said Senator Hayne, might achieve some level of greatness, but such success would be in spite of, not because of, the meddling interference in their domestic affairs by a Big Brother Government in Washington, D.C. While the public lands in the Western Territories are indeed a great treasure for the United States, the Senator acknowledged, such a treasure should not be hoarded by the Federal Government, but should be turned over to the ownership of individual citizens, so that those treasures can be properly enjoyed and used to create even greater wealth and prosperity. "I contended that the public lands ought not to be treated merely as 'a fund for revenue,'" Senator Hayne concluded, adding that, "they ought not to be

---

[13] "Hayne's Second Speech on Foot's Resolution," *Webster and Hayne's Speeches in the United States Senate, on Mr. Foot's Resolution of January, 1830,* T.B. Peterson & Brothers, Philadelphia, http://www.earlyrepublic.net/hayne2a.htm, http://www.earlyrepublic.net/hayne2b.htm, http://www. earlyrepublic.net/hayne2c.htm.

hoarded 'as a great treasure.'" Not only would the hoarding of such a treasure be economically unsound, but such a policy would also be subversive of the concept of free government.

The consolidating school, noted the South Carolina Senator, was determined to blur the distinction between local objects and federal objects. Their American System was grounded on the unconstitutional contention that the Federal Government's powers extended to all affairs, domestic and foreign. By doling out public monies as subsidies for local internal improvements, the consolidationalists were using the money thus taken from all the people to buy votes and patronage. Within such a system, a cunning politician could assure himself of a successful political career by stating to the special interest groups: "You feed my political ambition, and I will feed your avarice."

But such a sweeping system of corruption comes with a heavy price. Not only were the American people forced to pay a great tribute for this socialistic system, in terms of taxation, but the people were also destined to live under a government that had escaped from the confining chains of the Constitution. Under such a system of corruption and redistribution of wealth, candidates for public office would no longer be elected based on their love of country or their devotion to the maintenance of the Constitution in the true spirit in which it had been adopted by the States. Instead, politicians would be elected to office based on their abilities to secure largess from the public treasury, and such candidates might even be required to explain to their constituents why they had failed to acquire more subsidies for their districts. To Senator Hayne and the States' Rights school, such a political system was the very definition of *corruption*. To Senator Webster and the consolidating school, such an immoral political system was the very essence of their *un-American* American System.

The Western States, in particular, would pay a hefty price should they support such an unconstitutional and corrupt system. In exchange for losing control of their own lands, they would receive a few scraps of largess in the form of subsidies for internal improvements. Robert Y. Hayne likened this to the biblical account of Esau selling his birthright to his brother for a mess of pottage.

Senator Hayne's critique of the corrupt and corrupting American System was summarized in these words:

> [T]he South repudiates the idea that *pecuniary dependence* on the Federal Government is one of the legitimate means of holding the States together. A moneyed interest in the government is essentially a base interest; and just so far as it operates to bind the feelings of those who are subjected to it to the government, just so far as it operates in creating sympathies and interests that would not otherwise exist, is it opposed to all the principles of free government, and at war with virtue and patriotism....[M]illions of peo-

> ple – entire sections of country, interested, or believing themselves to be so, in the public lands, and the public treasure are bound to the government by the expectation of *pecuniary favors*. If this system is carried much further no man can fail to see that every generous motive of attachment to the country will be destroyed, and in its place will spring up those low groveling, base, and selfish feelings which bind men to the footstool of a despot by bonds as strong and enduring as those which attach them to free institutions.

The true theory of our Constitution, the Senator noted, was not difficult to comprehend or to effect. "On this subject as in all others," Senator Hayne stated, "we ask nothing of our Northern brethren but to 'let us alone.' Leave us to the undisturbed management of our domestic concerns, and the direction of our own industry, and we will ask no more."

Regarding the fanatical abolitionists, most zealous where least informed, Robert Y. Hayne stated that they were animated by a *pseudo-philanthropy*. While ignoring the plight of the free Blacks living in poverty in the Northern cities, they ranted and railed against the conditions of those Blacks on the Plantations of the Old South. Today, we would use such terminology as *double standards* and *hypocrisy* to describe those abolitionists. Senator Hayne preferred the term "false philanthropy" to describe those hypocrites of his day known as abolitionists.

It is of interest to note that Senator Hayne, within his second speech of the debate, alluded to the efforts of the consolidating school to alter the Federal Government's Indian policy. Was he referring to the policy of the Jackson Administration in regard to the Cherokee Indians, a policy that forced them out of North Carolina along a *Trail of Tears* to Oklahoma? Or had he perhaps caught a glimpse of the cruel treatment of the American Indians that would later become the official policy of the Government of the United States? After the War Between the States, with the consolidating school in firm control of our federal affairs, the Federal Government inaugurated a virtual war of extermination against our native Indian tribes, forcing them off of their ancestral lands and herding them onto Reservations, where that government could watch and manage them as a rancher might corral his livestock.

Senator Hayne's lengthy account of the history of political parties in the United States, and especially his account of the conduct of the Federalists during the War of 1812, highlighted a significant difference between the States' Rights school and the consolidating school. The former school correctly understood that the purpose of the Federal Union was to unite the States in their *foreign affairs*, while leaving them independent in their *domestic affairs*. When the United States is at war, and when the enemy is invading American soil and burning our cities, that is the time for all Americans to set aside their local and sectional feelings and to rally to the common defense of the Federal Republic.

That, said the South Carolina Senator, constitutes genuine *patriotism*. True patriotism also requires that the States jealously safeguard their own rights in times of peace to prevent the Federal Government from usurping powers and attempting to steal control over their domestic affairs. These were the true principles upon which the Federal Constitution was founded, and upon which the States' Rights school was established.

The consolidating school, noted Senator Hayne, seemed to be based on the opposite principles. During peacetime, when the Southern States sought to thwart the unconstitutional practices of the Federal Government's socialistic redistribution of wealth, the consolidating school proclaimed that such jealousy for State interests was somehow unpatriotic. Yet, that same school thought nothing of crippling the defensive efforts of the United States in the War of 1812, even going so far as to openly welcome the invasion of American soil by enemy troops. Such conduct might well be regarded as *treason*, the Senator from South Carolina noted. The consolidating school's concept of patriotism seemed to be limited to regarding the Union as little more than a tool or means to rob and plunder others for the aggrandizement of its favored special interest groups. And whenever a significant body of Americans should raise a cry of protest against such a system of exploitation, the consolidating school dared to condemn the protesters as unpatriotic.

The fact that this immoral and wicked system of plunder had a sectional bias in terms of beneficiaries and victims was actually a coincident. The true victims of socialistic exploitation are *the American people as a whole*, North, South, East, and West. Yet, by coincidence, the South, during the ante-bellum years of the Republic, was almost entirely agrarian. Therefore, the Southerners of that time period were not corrupted by the system based on avarice, and resistance to the unconstitutional system accordingly partook the nature of a great sectional conflict.

At one point in his second speech of the debate, Senator Hayne went so far as to speak of the great battle between the States' Rights school and the consolidation school as a War Between the States. Daniel Webster, said Senator Hayne, "had crossed the border" and "invaded the State of South Carolina," in order to make "war upon her citizens" and "to overthrow her principles and her institutions." "If the gentleman provokes the war," Senator Hayne asserted, "he shall have war." The Southern States, he warned, would not tamely submit to such an invasion, but would fight to maintain their rights and their freedoms. The Senator's comments demonstrated that, even by 1830, it was readily apparent that a War Between the States was inevitable, unless the consolidating school could be defeated by peaceful means.

"Who, then, Mr. President," asked Senator Hayne, "are the true friends of the Union?" The answer was self-evident: "Those who would confine the

Federal Government strictly within the limits prescribed by the Constitution; who would preserve to the States and the people all powers not expressly delegated; who would make this a Federal and not a National Union, and who, administering the government in spirit of equal justice, would make it a blessing, and not a curse."

"And who are its enemies?" was the logical next question. Again, the answer was self-evident: "Those who are in favor of consolidation; who are constantly stealing power from the States, and adding strength to the Federal Government; who, assuming an unwarrantable Jurisdiction over the States and the people, undertake to regulate the whole industry and capital of the country."

In regard to the "danger of corruption from the influence of money or of patronage," Robert Y. Hayne quoted John Randolph of Roanoke as saying that "the power of conferring favors creates a crowd of dependents." The Senator also alluded to an analogy offered by that distinguished Virginian, who was one of the early leaders in the States' Rights school and a contemporary of Thomas Jefferson and John Taylor of Carolina. Mr. Randolph had compared the effects of the corrupt policy advocated by the consolidating school with those of a master who has trained his dogs to salivate at the mere thought of being fed a scrap of meat.

This analogy referred to by Senator Hayne is of special significance, for it highlights several pernicious effects of the system of plunder and redistribution of wealth advocated by the consolidating school. By offering "free" money to the States and their peoples, the consolidating school hoped to corrupt the morals of the recipients and to train them to look to the Government of the United States as the means of obtaining wealth and prosperity. Such recipients of federal subsidization would naturally look to that government for their wants and needs and would zealously support those politicians who promised to loot the public treasury for the personal gains of their constituents. Such extravagance, ultimately, would bankrupt the United States, destroy the independence of the States and their peoples, and render meaningless the concept of a government of constitutionally limited powers.

Another consequence of such a corrupting system may be ascertained from the wise maxim that *money is power, and power is control.* Whatever the Government of the United States subsidizes, it controls. The champions of States' Rights understood all too well that the so-called American System advocated by the consolidating school would work to subvert the independence of individuals and States alike. The Federal Government, under such a system, was destined to become the master of all, the controller of everything, and the true possessor of sovereignty in the United States of America.

In time, such a system of corruption would result in the creation of *voting blocks,* defined by groups of citizens united to promote their own special interests at the expense of other Americans. Under such a system, the people could truthfully say that they had the best politicians that money could buy. In turn, a politician could say that his supporters constituted the best voting blocks that money could buy.

Under such a system, a politician who supported its corrupt nature would be deemed an enlightened statesman instilled with great compassion for the people. Of course, if that same politician attempted to buy votes with his own money, he would be considered a criminal and could expect to spend time in a federal penitentiary. But by using public funds for same purpose, he could expect to be sent to Washington, D.C. as the people's representative. And as the system of plunder and redistribution became widespread, affecting the entire body of the people, virtually no one would be spared from its corrupting influence, until the entire population of the United States would be divided into voting blocks, perhaps even in competition with one another to secure a larger share of the limited federal funds in the treasury. Then, indeed, would begin *the war of all against all.* Such are the ultimate consequences of the socialistic system of plunder and redistribution of wealth advocated by the Consolidating School of Thought.

Toward the end of his second speech, Senator Robert Y. Hayne directed his attention toward a *remedy* for the corrupting, immoral policies being advocated by the consolidating school. Two possible solutions presented themselves, assuming that the Government of the United States continued to pursue its course of usurpation and subversion of the Federal Constitution. One such remedy was *secession from the Union,* a remedy that every State possessed by virtue of its sovereignty, to be used as a remedy of last resort.

Secession was the ultimate States' Right. The Declaration of Independence had made each of the original thirteen States sovereign. The War of Independence had been fought to defend that sovereignty, and the Treaty of Paris of 1783 had formally established international recognition of the sovereignty of the States. Within the Articles of Confederation, State sovereignty was expressly acknowledged, and the purpose of a Union between the States was identified as being the security of that State sovereignty. In adopting the Constitution of 1787, the thirteen original States were regarded as sovereign body politics, with each State bound to the new Union only by its own consent. And the new Federal Union was to be established, not over, but *between,* the States in the Union. Furthermore, any new States admitted to the Union after the adoption of our present federal compact were to be admitted on the same footing as the original thirteen States, in regard to their freedom, independence, and sovereignty.

According to the American Theory of Government, our constitutional system is founded upon the sovereignty of the peoples of the several States, who, by virtue of their sovereignty, are entitled to govern themselves. This concept of self-government, or government-by-the-consent-of-the-governed, is based on the right of the sovereign peoples of each State to establish political institutions for themselves and to alter or abolish any political institution if such a course is deemed necessary for their welfare and happiness. If the sovereign people of a State can resolve to join a Federal Union with other sovereign States, then they must, of necessity, possess the right to withdraw from that same Union should they deem such an action to be in their best interests. To deny the right of secession to a member of the Federal Union would be to deny the sovereignty of its people and to reduce those people to political prisoners, unable to rightfully escape from impending tyranny.

There is, however, another remedy available to a sovereign State, short of secession. That remedy is generally known by the name of *State Interposition and Nullification*. Again, this remedy is based upon the sovereignty of the several States, which dictates the order of superiority within our political system. According to the American Theory of Government, the Federal Government is whatever the Constitution says it is, while the Constitution is whatever the States say it is. The States wrote the federal compact and gave it life by their acts of ratification. Only the States can change the Constitution through the amendment process. The Federal Government played no role at all in drafting and adopting the Constitution. And while Congress may suggest changes to the compact, the Government of the United States cannot lawfully change a single word in that instrument.

Should the Federal Government assume powers dangerous to the lives, liberties, and properties of the American people, such an exercise of power is clearly unconstitutional, and hence illegal. The States, in adopting the federal compact, never consented to unite under a government of undefined, and hence unlimited, powers. Whenever the Federal Government usurps power, therefore, a sovereign State may interpose its authority and declare the federal act to be null and void. In such a case of contested power, the proper resolution of the matter would be for an amendment to the Constitution to be proposed that would delegate to the Federal Government, in clear and unmistakable terms, the power in question. Should such an amendment be adopted by the requisite number of States, then the exercise of such a power by the Federal Government would clearly be constitutional. But unless such an amendment was adopted, the Government of the United States should not exercise the power in question.

The States themselves are clearly to be considered as the *final arbiters* in questions of power, simply because they are sovereign. Determining the extent of powers to be exercised by a government – any government – is one of the highest functions of sovereignty. Whoever possesses that right to be the final arbiter in questions of power is clearly and without question the sovereign master within the political system.

The Federal Government, needless to say, cannot be considered the final arbiter of its own powers because that would make it, not the peoples of the States, sovereign. While the Supreme Court of the United States, for example, may claim final jurisdiction in all *judicial* questions arising *under* the Federal Constitution, that does not mean that it is the final arbiter on *political* questions involving the *extent of powers* delegated to the United States by the Constitution. To assert otherwise would be to summarily transfer sovereignty or political supremacy from the peoples of the several States to the Government of the United States.

As one final observation on this issue, it must be noted that the States, by the amendment process, can constitutionally abolish the Supreme Court of the United States. Can the Supreme Court constitutionally abolish the States? It is clear that the Federal Government exists at the sufferance of the several States. That observation, in and of itself, should be sufficient to determine who is sovereign and who should be considered the true final arbiter in questions of power.

These concepts of State Interposition and Nullification, as well as the right of a State to secede from the Union, were fully presented by Thomas Jefferson and James Madison in the celebrated Kentucky and Virginia Resolutions of 1798. The Author of the Declaration of Independence subsequently reaffirmed these basic States' Rights principles in the Kentucky Resolution of 1799. In that same year, the Father of the Constitution reaffirmed these fundamental principles within a lengthy Report for the State of Virginia that bears his name.

In advocating these very same fundamental principles, Robert Y. Hayne, John C. Calhoun, and others of the States' Rights School of Thought in the middle years of the ante-bellum period of our history took great pains to demonstrate the intellectual connection of the ideas they advocated with the principles espoused by Thomas Jefferson and James Madison. The consolidating school, however, endeavored to deny the existence of such continuity, insisting upon labeling the notion of State Interposition and Nullification as the *Carolina Doctrine*. Proving that an intellection with Mr. Jefferson and Mr. Madison existed, however, was easily accomplished, as Senator Hayne demonstrated in his second speech of the debate.

"Such, sir, are the high and imposing authorities in support of 'the Carolina Doctrine,'" stated Senator Hayne, "which is, in fact, the Doctrine of the Virginia Resolutions of 1798." As to the consolidating school's assertion that the Federal Government should decide for itself the extent of its powers,

Robert Y. Hayne considered this to be a major revolution in the American Theory of Government and utterly subversive of the Federal Constitution.

Senator Hayne's words on this matter are worth repeating:

> Sir, as to the doctrine that the Federal Government is the exclusive judge of the extent as well as the limitations of its powers, it seems to me to be utterly subversive of the sovereignty and independence of the States. It makes but little difference, in my estimation, whether Congress or Supreme Court are invested with this power. If the Federal Government, in all, or any, of its departments, is to prescribe the limits of its own authority, and the States are bound to submit to the decision, and are not to be allowed to examine and decide for themselves, when the barriers of the Constitution shall be overleaped, this is practically "government without limitation of powers." The States are at once reduced to mere petty corporations and the people are entirely at your mercy.

The Senator from South Carolina concluded his great speech by quoting Edmund Burke, who stated, "You must pardon something to the spirit of liberty." As we shall soon discover, this parting sentiment is the precise opposite of the sentiment that Daniel Webster imparted at the close of his second reply to Senator Hayne. To the States' Rights School of Thought, *liberty* was paramount to all else. All levels of government – from the federal level down to the State and county level – exist merely to serve the interests of the people and to safeguard their natural rights. What mattered most was not the permanency of any government, nor the permanency of any political Union, but the permanency of *freedom*. And if there should ever be a conflict between government and freedom – or between any political Union and freedom – all those who champion the inalienable rights of man should have no difficulty in determining which must yield to the other.

Senator Robert Y. Hayne's second speech constituted a powerful defense for States' Rights and a damning indictment of consolidation and its zealous advocates. The South Carolina Senator had thrown down the gauntlet at the feet of the consolidators and challenged Daniel Webster to answer him, if he could. That challenge was promptly met when Senator Webster rose to give his reply to Senator Hayne's second speech in the debate. Let us turn, now, and see how the Orator of Consolidation responded to this great challenge from the States' Rights School of Thought.

Chapter Nine

The Orator of Consolidation

Following Senator Robert Y. Hayne's second speech in the great Webster-Hayne Debate of 1830, all eyes turned to Daniel Webster of Massachusetts to answer on behalf of the Consolidating School of Thought. Within his second oration, Senator Hayne had clearly stressed that the great contest between States' Rights and consolidation in the United States was not merely a matter of an honest difference of opinion between well-meaning statesmen. The great contest, the South Carolina Senator had asserted, was between the honest advocates of constitutionally limited government and the sovereignty of the peoples of the States on the one side, and those dishonest schemers who strove to subvert the Federal Constitution, usurp the reserved powers of the States, and rob the American people of their sovereignty on the other side.

Although the great debate had begun over the issue of the public land policy of the Federal Government, it had quickly escalated to encompass the treasonous actions of the consolidating school's Federalist Party during the War of 1812, the false philanthropy of the fanatical abolitionists, the socialistic policies of the consolidators that were based on Northern aggrandizement and redistribution of wealth, and the very nature of the Federal Union itself. The historical analysis and constitutional reasoning that Senator Hayne presented to the Senate of the United States had been well grounded on facts and sound reason.

Would Senator Webster be able to meet the challenge presented to him? On Monday, January 25, 1830, the same day that Senator Hayne concluded his second speech, the Senator from Massachusetts rose to give his response, but yielded the floor for a motion for adjournment. The following day, Daniel Webster began his second reply to Senator Hayne, delivering a speech considerably longer than his first response in the debate. Senator Webster's second reply, which took two days to present, was the one which endeared him forever to the consolidating school, and it inspired one admirer to paint a romantic portrait showing the Senator majestically addressing the Senate chamber as John C. Calhoun and Robert Y. Hayne listened intently. According to modern-day admirers of Daniel Webster, this was not only his greatest speech, but was also the greatest speech ever delivered in the Senate of the United States. Undeniably, it was this speech that established Daniel Webster's fame as the Orator of Consolidation.

Evasive Eloquence

On January 26, 1830, Senator Daniel Webster of Massachusetts rose in the Senate of the United States to deliver his famous second reply to Senator Hayne, a speech that was published in Edwin P. Whipple's book, *The Speeches and Orations of Daniel Webster, with an Essay on Daniel Webster as a Master of English Style.* During the course of his speech, Senator Webster stated:

> Every topic in the wide range of our public affairs, whether past or present, – every thing, general or local, whether belonging to national politics or party politics, – seems to have attracted more or less of the honorable member's attention, save only the resolution before the Senate. He has spoken of every thing but the public lands; they have escaped his notice. To that subject, in all his excursions, he has not paid even the cold respect of a passing glance....
>
> ...I paid the honorable member the attention of listening with respect to his first speech; and when he sat down, though surprised, and I must even say astonished, at some of his opinions, nothing was farther from my intention than to commence any personal warfare....
>
> ...I did sleep on the gentleman's speech, and slept soundly. And I slept equally well on his speech of yesterday, to which I am now replying. It is quite possible that in this respect, also, I possess some advantage over the honorable member, attributable, doubtless, to a cooler temperament on my part; for, in truth, I slept upon his speeches remarkably well.
>
> ...Sir, I shall not allow myself, on this occasion, I hope on no occasion, to be betrayed into any loss of temper; but if provoked, as I trust I never shall be, into crimination and recrimination, the honorable member may perhaps find, that, in that contest, there will be blows to take as well as blows to give; that others can state comparisons as significant, at least, as his own, and that his impunity may possibly demand of him whatever powers of taunt and sarcasm he may possess. I commend him to a prudent husbandry of his resources....
>
> I spoke, Sir, of the Ordinance of 1787, which prohibits slavery, in all future times, northwest of the Ohio, as a measure of great wisdom and foresight, and one which had been attended with highly beneficial and permanent consequences. I supposed that, on this point, no two gentlemen in the Senate could entertain different opinions. But the simple expression of this sentiment has led the gentleman, not only into labored defence of slavery, in the abstract, and on principle, but also into a warm accusation against me, as having attacked the system of domestic slavery now existing in the Southern

States....

And yet, Sir, the gentleman's optics have discovered, even in the mere expression of this sentiment, what he calls the very spirit of the Missouri question! He represents me as making an onset on the whole South, and manifesting a spirit which would interfere with, and disturb, their domestic condition!

...There is not, and never has been, a disposition in the North to interfere with these interests of the South. Such interference has never been supposed to be within the power of government; nor has it been in any way attempted. The slavery of the South has always been regarded as a matter of domestic policy, left with the States themselves, and with which the Federal Government had nothing to do. Certainly, Sir, I am, and ever have been, of that opinion....I regard domestic slavery as one of the greatest evils, both moral and political. But whether it be a malady, and whether it be curable, and if so, by what means; or, on the other hand, whether it be the *vulvas immedicabile* of the social system, I leave it to those whose right and duty it is to inquire and to decide. And this I believe, Sir, is, and uniformly has been, the sentiment of the North....

...[I]t has never been maintained or contended at the North, that Congress had any authority to regulate or interfere with the condition of slaves in the several States. No Northern gentleman, to my knowledge, has moved any such question in either House of Congress.

...When it became necessary, or was thought so, by some political persons, to find an unvarying ground for the exclusion of Northern men from confidence and from lead in the affairs of the Republic, then, and not till then, the cry was raised, and the feeling industriously excited, that the influence of Northern men in the public counsels would endanger the relation of master and slave. For myself, I claim no other merit than that this gross and enormous injustice towards the whole North has not wrought upon me to change my opinions or my political conduct. I hope I am above violating my principles, even under the smart of injury and false imputations. Unjust suspicions and undeserved reproach, whatever pain I may experience from them, will not induce me, I trust, to overstep the limits of constitutional duty, or to encroach on the rights of others. The domestic slavery of the Southern States I leave where I find it, – in the hands of their own governments. It is their affair, not mine....I go for the Constitution as it is, and for the Union as it is.... [1]

Senator Webster had much more to say in the course of his second response to Senator Hayne, and we shall allow him to continue shortly. But at this point, we should pause to make a few observations on what the Massachusetts Senator has thus far stated in his address. It is apparent, from this initial sampling from Daniel Webster's second reply to Senator Hayne that the Senator from the Bay State was a master of evasive eloquence.

[1] Edwin P. Whipple, *The Speeches and Orations of Daniel Webster, with an Essay on Daniel Webster as a Master of English Style*, Little, Brown and Co., Boston, 1879, http://www.earlyrepublic.net/webstr2a. htm.

After falsely accusing Senator Hayne of completely avoiding the topic of the Federal Government's public land policy, Senator Webster proceeded to eloquently dodge the real issue involved in the subject of slavery. Aside from the fanatical abolitionists, no one seriously considered that the Government of the United States had the power to interfere with the institution of slavery in those States that already existed. The real issue was the unconstitutional Missouri Compromise of 1820 and the illegal division of the Federal Union into two sub-confederacies based on "Free States" and "Slave States."

The Western Territories supposedly belonged to the States in common as a "common treasure" to be shared by all, and in theory even Senator Webster conceded as much. Yet, by means of the unconstitutional efforts to maintain a "balance of power" between the two sub-confederacies, the consolidating school was determined to win that struggle for supremacy by preventing the people of the Southern States from migrating to and settling in all of the Western Territories. By prohibiting slavery in the territories north of the Mason-Dixon Line, it was the intent of the consolidating school to isolate the Southern States and to prevent them, as much as possible, from sharing in the fruits of the spirit of Manifest Destiny.

Although Daniel Webster conveniently evaded the real issue involved in the slavery controversy, he did manage to falsely accuse the Southern statesmen of being responsible for the growth of sectional politics in the United States, as though they, and not the consolidating school, had been the ones who had introduced the subject of slavery in the federal arena. "I go for the Constitution as it is," said Senator Webster, "and for the Union as it is." In making such an assertion, the Senator was affecting total ignorance of the struggle for a "balance of power" thrust upon the Union by his own Federalist Party before it met its just fate. Had he really been for the Union as intended by the Federal Constitution, he would have joined with the Southern statesmen and demanded an end to discrimination in the settlement of the Western Territories.

Let us now return to Senator Webster's second reply to Senator Hayne in the great Webster-Hayne Debate of 1830:

> But as to the Hartford Convention, Sir, allow me to say, that the proceedings of that body seem now to be less read and studied in New England than farther South. They appear to be looked to, not in New England, but elsewhere, for the purpose of seeing how far they may serve as a precedent....I have nothing to do, Sir, with the Hartford Convention. Its journal, which the gentleman has quoted, I never read. So far as the honorable member may discover in its proceedings a spirit in any degree resembling that which was avowed and justified in those other conventions to which I have alluded, or so far as those proceedings can be shown to be disloyal to the Constitution, or tending to disunion, so far I shall be as ready as any one to

> bestow on them reprehension and censure.
>
> Having dwelt long on this convention, and other occurrences of that day, in the hope, probably, (which will not be gratified,) that I should leave the course of this debate to follow him at length in those excursions, the honorable member returned, and attempted another object. He referred to a speech of mine in the other house, the same which I had occasion to allude to myself, the other day; and has quoted a passage or two from it, with a bold, though uneasy and laboring air of confidence, as if he had detected in me an inconsistency.... There is not only no contradiction, no difference, but, in truth, too exact a similarity, both in thought and language, to be entirely in just taste....
>
> I need not repeat at large the general topics of the honorable gentleman's speech. When he said yesterday that he did not attack the Eastern States, he certainly must have forgotten, not only particular remarks, but the whole drift and tenor of his speech; unless he means by not attacking, that he did not commence hostilities....He, in the first place, disapproved of the whole course of the government, for forty years, in regard to its disposition of the public lands; and then, turning Northward and Eastward, and fancying he had found a cause for alleged narrowness and niggardliness in the "accursed policy" of the tariff, to which he represented the people of New England as wedded, he went on for a full hour with remarks, the whole scope of which was to exhibit the results of this policy, in feelings and in measures unfavorable to the West. I thought his opinions unfounded and erroneous, as to the general course of the government, and ventured to reply to them....
>
> The real question between me and him is, Has the doctrine been advanced at the South or the East, that the population of the West should be retarded, or at least need not be hastened, on account of its effect to drain off the people from the Atlantic States? Is this doctrine, as has been alleged, of Eastern origin? That is the question. Has the gentleman found any thing by which he can make good his accusation? I submit to the Senate, that he has entirely failed....
>
> So then, Sir, New England is guiltless of the policy of retarding Western population, and of all envy and jealousy of the growth of the new States. Whatever there be of that policy in the country, no part of it is hers.... [2]

Within his second speech in the debate, Robert Y. Hayne had dwelt at length on demonstrating that the consolidating school had a history of treasonous conduct and certainly had no claim to lofty patriotism and love of country. So damning had been Senator Hayne's indictment of Senator Webster's old Federalist Party that the Massachusetts Senator could not altogether avoid mentioning the subject. And mention it he did. After mentioning it, however, he dismissed the subject as being one the consolidating school would prefer that everyone would forget. It was an eloquent way of conceding defeat on that

---

[2] *Ibid.*, http://www.earlyrepublic.net/webstr2a.htm and http://www.earlyrepublic.net/webstr2b.htm.

issue without actually conceding defeat.

Senator Webster again asserted that the public land policy of the Federal Government, which was supported by the consolidating school, in no way worked toward restricting settlement of the Western States or toward inhibiting new Western States from exercising sovereign control over their own lands. Viewed from the vantage point of hindsight, we now know that such a claim on his part was simply untrue. The States' Rights school had detected the inauguration of a conspiracy against the future Western States at an early date, and the test of time has proven them to be correct.

A Defense of Internal Improvements

Whereas Senator Webster's early remarks had been characterized by evasive eloquence, when he reached the subject of federal funding for internal improvements, the Senator became much more candid:

> We approach, at length, Sir, to a more important part of the honorable gentleman's observations. Since it does not accord with my views of justice and policy to give away the public lands altogether, as a mere matter of gratuity, I am asked by the honorable gentleman on what ground it is that I consent to vote them away in particular instances. How, he inquires, do I reconcile with these professed sentiments, my support of measures appropriating portions of the lands to particular roads, particular canals, particular rivers, and particular institutions of education in the West? This leads, Sir, to the real and wide difference in political opinion between the honorable gentleman and myself. On my part, I look upon all these objects as connected with the common good, fairly embraced in its object and its terms; he, on the contrary, deems them all, if good at all, only local good. This is our difference. The interrogatory which he proceeded to put at once explains this difference. "What interest," asks he, "has South Carolina in a canal in Ohio?" Sir, this very question is full of significance. It develops the gentleman's whole political system; and its answer expounds mine. Here we differ. I look upon a road over the Alleghenies, a canal round the falls of the Ohio, or a canal or railway from the Atlantic to the Western waters, as being an object large and extensive enough to be fairly said to be for the common benefit. The gentleman thinks otherwise, and this is the key to his construction of the powers of the government. He may well ask what interest has South Carolina in a canal in Ohio. On his system, it is true, she has no interest. On that system, Ohio and Carolina are different governments, and different countries; connected here, it is true, by some slight and ill-defined bond of union, but in all main respects separate and diverse. On that system, Carolina has no more interest in a canal in Ohio than in Mexico. The gentleman, therefore, only follows out his own principles; he does no more than arrive at the natural conclusions of his own doctrines; he only announces the true results of

that creed which he has adopted himself, and would persuade others to adopt, when he thus declares that South Carolina has no interest in a public work in Ohio.

Sir, we narrow-minded people of New England do not reason thus. Our *notion* of things is entirely different. We look upon the States, not as separated, but as united. We love to dwell on that Union, and on the mutual happiness which it has so much promoted, and the common renown which it has so greatly contributed to acquire. In our contemplation, Carolina and Ohio are parts of the same country; States, united under the same general government, having interests, common, associated, intermingled. In whatever is within the proper sphere of the constitutional power of this government, we look upon the States as one. We do not impose geographical limits to our patriotic feeling or regard; we do not follow rivers and mountains, and lines of latitude, to find boundaries, beyond which public improvements do not benefit us. We who come here, as agents, and representatives of these narrow-minded and selfish men of New England, consider ourselves as bound to regard with an equal eye the good of the whole, in whatever is within our powers of legislation. Sir, if a railroad or canal, beginning in South Carolina and ending in South Carolina, appeared to me to be of national importance and national magnitude, believing, as I do, that the power of government extends to the encouragement of works of that description, if I were to stand up here and ask, What interest has Massachusetts in a railroad in South Carolina? I should not be willing to face my constituents. These same narrow-minded men would tell me, that they had sent me to act for the whole country, and that one who possessed too little comprehension either of intellect or feeling, one who was not large enough, both in mind and in heart, to embrace the whole, was not fit to be intrusted with the interest of any part.

Sir, I do not desire to enlarge the powers of the government by unjustifiable construction, nor to exercise any not within a fair interpretation. But when it is believed that a power does exist, then it is, in my judgment, to be exercised for the general benefit of the whole. So far as respects the exercise of such a power, the States are one. It was the very object of the Constitution to create unity of interests to the extent of the powers of the general government. In war and peace we are one; in commerce, one; because the authority of the general government reaches to war and peace, and to the regulation of commerce. I have never seen any more difficulty in erecting lighthouses on the lakes, than on the ocean; in improving the harbors of inland seas, than if they were within the ebb and flow of the tide; or in removing obstructions in the vast streams of the West, more than in any work to facilitate commerce on the Atlantic coast. If there be any power for one, there is power also for the other; and they are all and equally for the common good of the country.

There are other objects, apparently more local, or the benefit of which is less general, towards which, nevertheless, I have concurred with others, to give aid by donations of land. It is proposed to construct a road, in or through one of the new States, in which this government possesses large quantities of land. Have the United States no right, or, as a great and untaxed proprietor, are they under no obligation to contribute to an object thus calculated to promote the common good of all the proprietors, themselves included? And even with respect to education, which is the extreme case, let the question be considered. In the first place, as we have seen, it was made matter of compact with these States, that they should do their part to promote education. In the next place, our whole system of land laws proceeds on the idea that education is for the common good; because, in every division, a certain portion is uniformly reserved and appropriated for the use of schools. And, finally, have not these new States singularly strong claims, founded on the ground already stated, that the government is a great untaxed proprietor, in the ownership of the soil? It is a consideration of great importance, that probably there is in no part of the country, or of the world, so great call for the means of education, as in these new States, owing to the vast numbers of persons within these ages in which education and instruction are usually received, if received at all.... Whatever the government can fairly do towards these objects, in my opinion, ought to be done.

...[R]easons like these, I presume, have influenced the votes of other gentlemen from New England. Those who have a different view of the powers of the government, of course, come to different conclusions, on these, as on other questions.

I observed, when speaking on this subject before, that if we looked to any measure, whether for a road, a canal, or anything else, intended for the improvement of the West, it would be found that, if the New England *ayes* were struck out of the lists of votes, the Southern *noes* would always have rejected the measure. The truth of this has not been denied, and cannot be denied. In stating this, I thought it just to ascribe it to the constitutional scruples of the South, rather than to any other less favorable or less charitable cause....

...I have endeavored to prove that every thing of this kind, designed for Western improvement, has depended on the votes of New England; all this is true beyond the power of contradiction....

...[I]mprovement, -- how was it to be accomplished, and who was to accomplish it? We were ten or twelve millions of people, spread over almost half a world. We were more than twenty States, some stretching along the same seaboard, some along the same line of inland frontier, and others on opposite banks of the same vast rivers. Two considerations at once presented themselves with great force, in looking at this state of things. One was, that that great branch of improvement which consisted in furnishing new facilities of intercourse necessarily ran into different States in every leading instance, and would benefit the citizens of all such States. No one State, therefore, in such eases, would assume the whole expense, nor was the co-operation of several States to be expected. Take the instance of the Delaware breakwater. It will cost several millions of money. Would Pennsylvania alone ever have constructed it? Certainly never, while this Union lasts, because it is not for her sole benefit. Would Pennsylvania, New Jersey, and Delaware have united to accomplish it at their joint expense? Certainly not, for the same reason. It could not be done, therefore, but by the general government. The same may be said of the large inland undertakings, except that, in them, government, instead of bearing the whole expense, co-operates with others who

> bear a part. The other consideration is, that the United States have the means. They enjoy the revenues derived from commerce and the States have no abundant and easy sources of public income. The custom-houses fill the general treasury, while the States have scanty resources, except by resort to heavy direct taxes. [3]

Within this section of his speech, Daniel Webster candidly confessed that one significant difference between the States' Rights School of Thought and the Consolidating School of Thought was a difference of opinion as to which economic system was mandated by the Federal Constitution, and even which economic system was most desirable. The States' Rights school asserted that not only was *free enterprise*, or *laissez-faire*, the best economic system for the United States, but that such an economic system was mandated by the federal compact. The Federal Constitution does not delegate any powers to the Government of the United States to manipulate the marketplace, to promote favored industries, or to inhibit disfavored enterprises.

It is true, of course, that the *Commerce Clause* of the Constitution states that the Federal Government may *regulate* commerce, but no specific powers to control the marketplace was delegated for that purpose, because the intent of the Commerce Clause was negative in nature. At the time the Philadelphia Convention of 1787 convened, many States were separately regulating interstate commerce by imposing tariffs on goods that crossed their State lines. The purpose of the Commerce Clause was to promote *free trade* internally in the United States by transferring the regulation of commerce to the Federal Government. Such a *purpose* explains why no specific powers to manipulate the marketplace were delegated to the Federal Government.

Nonetheless, Senator Webster insisted that the Government of the United States had a constitutional right to actively manipulate the marketplace, promote favored industries, and by logical deduction, to inhibit or retard disfavored industries. The economic system described by the Massachusetts Senator is nothing short of *socialism*. According to this system, all Americans are taxed by the Federal Government, and that government then selects favored local enterprises and private business ventures that it wishes to subsidize for the benefit of local interests. It is of interest to note that the Senator made no attempt to justify the constitutionality of this socialistic system. Not once did he point to any particular phrase of the Federal Constitution in support of his contention that socialism is compatible with the federal compact.

Clearly, none of the specific delegations of power to Congress could justify the internal improvements advocated by Senator Webster and the consolidating school. Not one delegated power, for example, authorizes Congress to

---

[3] *Ibid.*, http://www.earlyrepublic.net/webstr2b.htm.

fund the building of a canal or to subsidize the establishment of a school for the education of children. Yet, the Senator from Massachusetts claimed that these projects are for the "general welfare" and therefore can be considered within the sphere of powers delegated to the Federal Government.

The Commerce Clause, as we have already observed, does not warrant such a construction. Nor do the specific delegations of powers listed in the Federal Constitution. There is, of course, what has been called the *Necessary and Proper Clause,* which provides that Congress may enact laws necessary and proper *to carry into effect the delegated powers.* This, however, in and of itself, conveys no power whatsoever to the Federal Government. It merely states that the Congress may create laws to carry into effect those specific powers that have been delegated to it.

Undoubtedly, the clause in the federal compact that Senator Webster was relying upon to supposedly justify his contention for sweeping federal powers is what is generally termed the *General Welfare Clause,* which provides that the tax-and-spend powers delegated to Congress are to be used to promote the general welfare of the United States. This expression, however, was copied from the Articles of Confederation and, in and of itself, delegates no power at all to the Congress. It merely explains the *reason* why the delegated powers were delegated to Congress and actually serves to provide a *limitation* on the delegated powers by *restricting* the actions of Congress to the general welfare, as opposed to the local or person welfare of favored interests.

Although Daniel Webster acknowledged in the course of his second reply to Senator Hayne that the powers of the Federal Government were limited to those delegated by the Constitution of the United States, such an acknowledgement was rendered meaningless by his claim for unlimited powers for the Federal Government. Based on the Senator's claim for sweeping federal powers, we would expect to see some clause in the Federal Constitution that asserted, "The Congress is hereby vested with all powers which it deems proper to provide for whatever it deems to be the general welfare of the United States." After asserting that the Constitution has delegated such a sweeping power to the Federal Government, it was quite easy for a consolidator like Daniel Webster to humbly claim that the Government of the United States should be confined to its delegated powers.

Before leaving this topic, it is of interest to note that the differences between the consolidating school and the States' Rights school go deeper on this subject than a difference of opinion as to the limits of federal power. There are some powers that no government at any level – federal, State, or local – should possess, because they are inherently dangerous to the liberties of the people. The sweeping powers for which Senator Webster contended represented more than wholesale usurpations of the powers reserved to the States; they were, in some cases, powers that no government should rightfully exercise. Commerce and the intricacies of the marketplace are best governed by the laws of nature, as dictated by the free enterprise economic system. Whenever government actively intervenes to disrupt natural law, the results inevitably are an infringement upon the inalienable rights of the people and the creation of a system based on avarice, greed, corruption, and patronage.

Counter Charges of Switching Sides

Continuing with his second reply to Senator Hayne, Daniel Webster focused attention on Senator Hayne's contention that Senator Webster and other consolidators were supporting socialistic schemes which they had earlier denounced as unconstitutional. In response, the Massachusetts Senator pointed out that some of those in the States' Rights school had earlier supported those very socialistic schemes. As Senator Webster stated:

> Under this view of things, I thought it necessary to settle, at least for myself, some definite notions with respect to the powers of the government in regard to internal affairs. It may not savor too much of self-commendation to remark, that, with this object, I considered the Constitution, its judicial construction, its contemporaneous exposition, and the whole history of the legislation of Congress under it; and I arrived at the conclusion, that government had power to accomplish sundry objects, or aid in their accomplishment, which are now commonly spoken of as INTERNAL IMPROVEMENTS. That conclusion, Sir, may have been right, or it may have been wrong. I am not about to argue the grounds of it at large. I say only, that it was adopted and acted on even so early as in 1816....
>
> ...A strong party had arisen in the South hostile to the doctrine of internal improvements. Anti-consolidation was the flag under which this party fought; and its supporters inveighed against internal improvements, much after the manner in which the honorable gentleman has now inveighed against them, as part and parcel of the system of consolidation. Whether this party arose in South Carolina itself, or in the neighborhood, is more than I know. I think the latter....
>
> ...I hold in my hand, Sir, a printed speech of...[a] distinguished gentleman, *(Ed: Mr. McDuffie)* "INTERNAL IMPROVEMENTS," delivered about the period to which I now refer, and printed with a few introductory remarks upon *consolidation;* in which, Sir, I think he quite consolidated the arguments of his opponents, the Radicals, if *to crush* be to consolidate. I give you a short but significant quotation from these remarks. He is speaking of a pamphlet, then recently published, entitled "Consolidation"; and, having alluded to the question of renewing the charter of the former Bank of the United States, he says: -
>
> "Moreover, in the early history of parties, and when Mr. Crawford

advocated a renewal of the old charter, it was considered a Federal measure; which internal improvement *never was,* as this author erroneously states. This latter measure originated in the administration of Mr. Jefferson, with the appropriation for the Cumberland Road; and was first proposed, as *a system,* by Mr. Calhoun, and carried through the House of Representatives by a large majority of the Republicans, including almost every one of the leading men who carried us through the late war."

So, then, internal improvement is not one of the Federal heresies. One paragraph more, Sir: -

"The author in question, not content with denouncing as Federalists, General Jackson, Mr. Adams, Mr. Calhoun, and the majority of the South Carolina delegation in Congress, modestly extends the denunciation to Mr. Monroe and the whole Republican party. Here are his words: 'During the administration of Mr. Monroe much has passed which the Republican party would be glad to approve if they could! But the principal feature, and that which has chiefly elicited these observations, is the renewal of the SYSTEM OF INTERNAL IMPROVEMENTS. Now this measure was adopted by vote of 115 to 86 of a Republican Congress, and sanctioned by a Republican President. Who, then, is this author, who assumes the high prerogative of denouncing, in the name of the Republican Party, the Republican administration of the country? A denunciation including within its sweep *Calhoun, Lowndes, and Cheves,* men who will be regarded as the brightest ornaments of South Carolina, and the strongest pillars of the Republican Party, as long as the late war shall be remembered, and talents and patriotism shall be regarded as the proper objects of the admiration and gratitude of a free people!"

Such are the opinions, Sir, which were maintained by South Carolina gentlemen, in the House of Representatives, on the subject of internal improvements, when I took my seat there as a member from Massachusetts in 1823....

The tariff, which South Carolina had an efficient hand in establishing, in 1816, and this asserted power of internal improvement, advanced by her in the same year, and, as we have seen, approved and sanctioned by her Representatives in 1824, – these two measures are the great grounds on which she is now thought to be justified in breaking up the Union, if she sees fit to break it up!

Here the Vice-President [John C. Calhoun] said, *"Does the chair understand the gentleman from Massachusetts to say that the person now occupying the chair of the Senate has changed his opinions on the subject of internal improvements?"*

From nothing ever said to me, Sir, have I had reason to know of any change in the opinions of the person filling the chair of the Senate. If such change has taken place, I regret it. I speak generally of the State of South Carolina....

On yet another point, I was still more unaccountably misunderstood. The gentleman had harangued against "consolidation." I told him, in reply, that there was one kind of consolidation to which I was attached, and that was the consolidation of our Union; that this was precisely that consolidation

> to which I feared others were not attached, and that such consolidation was the very end of the Constitution, the leading object, as they had informed us themselves, which its framers had kept in view....I said, in terms, that I wished not in the slightest degree to augment the powers of this government; that my object was to preserve, not to enlarge; and that by consolidating the Union I understood no more than the strengthening of the Union, and perpetuating it....[I]t passes comprehension how any man could understand me as contending for an extension of the powers of the government, or for consolidation in that odious sense in which it means an accumulation, in the Federal Government, of the powers properly belonging to the States.
>
> ...The gentleman had said that he wished for no fixed revenue, –not a shilling. If by a word he could convert the Capitol into gold, he would not do it. Why all this fear of revenue? Why, Sir, because, as the gentleman told us, it tends to consolidation....
>
> ...The strenuous toil of the gentleman has been to raise an inconsistency between my dissent to the tariff in 1824, and my vote in 1828. It is labor lost....It was a change of position to meet new circumstances, but on the same level....I said then, and say now, that, as an original question, the authority of Congress to exercise the revenue power, with direct reference to the protection of manufactures, is a questionable authority, far more questionable, in my judgment, than the power of internal improvements....
>
> Sir, as to the general subject of the tariff, I have little now to say....No more of the tariff. [4]

If Senator Webster and his fellow consolidators had been embarrassed by the exposure of their inconsistency, then certain members of the States' Rights school could share in that embarrassment. In denying his own inconsistency, Daniel Webster was not telling the truth. But in accusing certain members of the States' Rights school of being equally inconsistent, he was telling the truth.

During the War of 1812, the consolidating school so hated the Federal Union that their chief thoughts centered on helping the enemy win the war and on contemplating the possibility of secession. Not until Henry Clay had packaged the various socialistic measures into his American System and the consolidators had succeeded in infiltrating the Democratic-Republican Party, thereby ensuring the election of John Quincy Adams to the Presidency, did the consolidating school suddenly attach great value to the Union as the means of unfairly enriching their favored interest groups.

Some leaders in the States' Rights school – including Thomas Jefferson, John Taylor of Caroline, and John Randolph of Roanoke – maintained a high degree of consistency in principles throughout this entire period, for they clear understood the true consequences of protective tariffs and federal funding for internal improvements. Yet, some members of the next generation – including John C. Calhoun of South Carolina – who would later become leaders in the

---

[4] *Ibid.*, http://www.earlyrepublic.net.webstr2b.htm and http://www.earlyrepublic.net.webstr2c.htm.

States' Rights school, initially failed to comprehend the inherent dangers of such policies. Shortly after the American System was introduced, however, such men quickly saw the dangers posed by the socialistic schemes and switched sides to firmly oppose such measures.

It is clear that *switching sides* on the great issue of consolidating policies was not confined to any one politician. And here we must raise the pertinent question of which group of politicians was the worse: Those who, upon recognizing the unconstitutionality and corrupting effects of the consolidating system, switched sides to *oppose* it; or those who, upon recognizing how such a corrupt system could be used to enrich favored interest groups, switched sides to *support* such an unconstitutional system? The reader is left to provide his own answer.

"It passes comprehension how any man could understand me as contending for an extension of the powers of the government," said Senator Webster, "or for consolidation in that odious sense in which it means an accumulation, in the Federal Government, of the powers properly belonging to the States." Such a profession of innocence could hardly have been calculated to pacify those wishing to preserve constitutionally limited government, inasmuch as the Senator had already stated his opinion that the powers delegated to the Federal Government were so broad that they encompassed everything that might be proclaimed to be for the general welfare of the United States. After contending that the Government of the United States possessed unlimited powers, this claim to oppose consolidation by Senator Webster merely demonstrated the low esteem he placed on the intelligence of those he was addressing.

More Eloquence and More Evasion

Continuing in his speech, Senator Webster once again focused his attention on Senator Hayne's account of the sordid history of the Federalist Party of New England. And once again, the Massachusetts Senator demonstrated that he could be both evasive and eloquent at the same time. As Senator Webster stated:

> Professing to be provoked by what he chose to consider a charge made by me against South Carolina, the honorable member, Mr. President, has taken up a new crusade against New England. Leaving altogether the subject of the public lands, in which his success, perhaps, had been neither distinguished nor satisfactory, and letting go, also, of the topic of the tariff, he sallied forth in a general assault on the opinions, polities, and parties of New England, as they have been exhibited in the last thirty years....The politics of New England became his theme... Has he maintained his own

charges? Has he proved what he alleged? Has he sustained himself in his attack on the government, and on the history of the North, in the matter of the public lands?...Why, Sir, he has stretched a drag-net over the whole surface of perished pamphlets, indiscreet sermons, frothy paragraphs, and fuming popular addresses, – over whatever the pulpit in its moments of alarm, the press in its heats, and parties in their extravagance, have severally thrown off in times of general excitement and violence....This is his war. This it is to carry war into the enemy's country....

Mr. President, I shall not, it will not, I trust, be expected that I should, either now or at any time, separate this farrago into parts, and answer and examine its components. I shall barely bestow upon it all a general remark or two. In the run of forty years, Sir, under this Constitution, we have experienced sundry successive violent party contests. Party arose, indeed, with the Constitution itself, and, in some form or other, has attended it through the greater part of its history....In all these conflicts there was, no doubt, much of violence on both and all sides. It would be impossible, if one had a fancy for such employment, to adjust the relative quantum of violence between these contending parties. There was enough in each, as must always be expected in popular governments....For myself, Sir, I shall not rake among the rubbish of bygone times, to see what I can find, or whether I cannot find something by which I can fix a blot on the escutcheon of any State, any party, or any part of the country....I see enough of the violence of our own times, to be no way anxious to rescue from forgetfulness the extravagances of times past....

...This, Sir, is an abstract of the gentleman's history of Federalism. I am not about to controvert it. It is not, at present, worth the pains of refutation; because, Sir, if at this day any one feels the sin of Federalism lying heavily on his conscience, he can easily procure remission....A man now-a-days is at liberty to choose his political parentage. He may elect his own father. Federalist or not, he may, if he choose, claim to belong to the favored stock, and his claim will be allowed....We all know a process, Sir, by which the whole Essex Junto could, in one hour, be all washed white from their ancient Federalism, and come out, every one of them, original Democrats, dyed in the wool! Some of them have actually undergone the operation, and they say it is quite easy....

...He referred...to the Hartford Convention. Did he do this for authority or for a topic of reproach? Apparently for both, for he told us that he should find no fault with the mere fact of holding such a convention, and considering and discussing such questions as he supposes were then and there discussed; but what rendered it obnoxious was its being held at the time, and under the circumstances of the country then existing. We were in a war, he said, and the country needed all our aid; the hand of government required to be strengthened, not weakened; and patriotism should have postponed such proceedings to another day. The thing itself, then, is a precedent; the time and manner of it only, a subject of censure. Now, Sir, I go much further, on this point, than the honorable member. Supposing, as the gentleman seems to do, that the Hartford Convention assembled for any such purpose as breaking up the Union, because they thought unconstitutional laws had been

> passed, or to consult on that subject, or *to calculate the value of the Union*; supposing this to be their purpose, or any part of it, then I say the meeting itself was disloyal, and was obnoxious to censure, whether held in time of peace or time of war, or under whatever circumstances. The material question is the *object*. Is dissolution the *object*? If it be, external circumstances may make it a more or less aggravated case, but cannot affect the principle. I do not hold, therefore, Sir, that the Hartford Convention was pardonable, even to the extent of the gentleman's admission, if its objects were really such as have been imputed to it.... [5]

The purpose of the Federal Union is to unite the States in their foreign affairs, while leaving them independent in their domestic affairs, and the Union was intended to be a fraternal Union in which membership is voluntary. The original thirteen States had been united in a *perpetual Union* under the Articles of Confederation. Yet, no one considered it unpatriotic or treasonous when those States *calculated the value* of that Union and then resolved to secede from that original Federal Union and to form a new voluntary Union under the Constitution of 1787. Yet, Senator Webster insinuated that the mere contemplation of secession was the equivalent of treason!

The horrible crime that the Federalist Party leaders committed during the War of 1812, stated the Senator, was not their support for the enemy in that conflict, but their possible consideration of secession from the Union. This stands in stark contrast to what Senator Hayne had cited as the great crime of Daniel Webster's old party. Secession from the Union is a right inherent in the sovereignty of the peoples of the several States. But treason is not a constitutional right of anyone. It is a crime. By confounding the issue, Senator Webster undoubtedly hoped to equate States' Rights and treason in the public mind.

It is especially disturbing to note how often Senator Webster employed the word *violence* in his speech. In this section of his speech, he referred to "times of general excitement of violence," to "sundry successive violent party contests," to "much violence on both and all sides," to "the relative quantum of violence between these contending parties," and to "the violence of our own times." As we shall discover, such references to *violence* and *anarchy* would be employed often in the remainder of Senator Webster's second reply to Senator Hayne. So often was the metaphor employed, in fact, that the *violence of free government*, in contrast to the peaceful repose of a sovereign government ruling imperially without challenge or opposition, might be considered an underlying theme of his speech. One cannot help but to be reminded of the similar argument made centuries earlier by Thomas Hobbes, who justified his *Leviathan State* by claiming that the only alternative to the violence and anarchy of free-

---

[5] *Ibid.*, http://www.earlyrepublic.net.webstr2c.htm.

dom was a totalitarian dictatorship.

The Nature of the Federal Union

After dismissing these preliminary topics and introducing the theme of violence as a prelude for the main portion of his speech, Daniel Webster turned his attention to the critical topics of States' Rights, State Interposition and Nullification, and the very nature of the Federal Union. To ensure that his ideas are properly understood, we will cite the remainder of his speech before offering further critical analysis.

As the great Orator of Consolidation stated:

> Then, Sir, the gentleman has no fault to find with these recently promulgated South Carolina opinions. And certainly he need have none; for his own sentiments, as now advanced, and advanced on reflection, as far as I have been able to comprehend them, go the full length of all these opinions. I propose, Sir, to say something on these, and to consider how far they are just and constitutional....
>
> There yet remains to be performed, Mr. President, by far the most grave and important duty, which I feel to be devolved on me by this occasion. It is to state, and to defend, what I conceive to be the true principles of the Constitution under which we are here assembled. I might well have desired that so weighty a task should have fallen into other and abler hands. I could have wished that it should have been executed by those whose character and experience give weight and influence to their opinions, such as cannot possibly belong to mine. But, Sir, I have met the occasion, not sought it; and I shall proceed to state my own sentiments, without challenging for them any particular regard, with studied plainness, and as much precision as possible.
>
> I understand the honorable gentleman from South Carolina to maintain, that it is a right of the State legislatures to interfere, whenever, in their judgment, this government transcends its constitutional limits, and to arrest the operation of its laws.
>
> I understand him to maintain this right, as a right existing *under* the Constitution, not as a right to overthrow it on the ground of extreme necessity, such as would justify violent revolution.
>
> I understand him to maintain an authority, on the part of the States, thus to interfere, for the purpose of correcting the exercise of power by the general government, of checking it, and of compelling it to conform to their opinion of the extent of its powers.
>
> I understand him to maintain, that the ultimate power of judging of the constitutional extent of its own authority is not lodged exclusively in the general government, or any branch of it; but that, on the contrary, the States may lawfully decide for themselves, and each State for itself, whether, in a

given case, the act of the general government transcends its power.

I understand him to insist, that, if the exigency of the case, in the opinion of any State government, requires it, such State government may, by its own sovereign authority, annul an act of the general government which it deems plainly and palpably unconstitutional.

This is the sum of what I understand from him to be the South Carolina Doctrine, and the doctrine which he maintains. I propose to consider it, and compare it with the Constitution. Allow me to say, as a preliminary remark, that I call this the South Carolina Doctrine only because the gentleman himself has so denominated it. I do not feel at liberty to say that South Carolina, as a State, has ever advanced these sentiments. I hope she has not, and never may....

That there are individuals besides the honorable gentleman who do maintain these opinions, is quite certain. I recollect the recent expression of a sentiment, which circumstances attending its utterance and publication justify us in supposing was not unpremeditated. "The sovereignty of the State, – never to be controlled, construed, or decided on, but by her own feelings of honorable justice."

Mr. Hayne here rose and said, that, for the purpose of being clearly understood, he would state that his proposition was in the words of the Virginia resolution, as follows: –

"That assembly doth explicitly and peremptorily declare, that it views the power of the Federal Government as resulting from the compact to which the States are parties, as limited by the plain sense and intention of the instrument constituting that compact, as no farther valid than they are authorized by the grants enumerated in that compact; and that, in ease of a deliberate, palpable, and dangerous exercise of other powers not granted by the said compact, the States who are parties thereto have the right, and are in duty bound, to interpose, for arresting the progress of the evil, and for maintaining within their respective limits the authorities, rights, and liberties appertaining to them."

Mr. Webster resumed: –

I am quite aware, Mr. President, of the existence of the Resolution which the gentleman read, and has now repeated and that be relies on it as his authority. I know the source, too, from which it is understood to have proceeded. I need not say that I have much respect for the constitutional opinions of Mr. Madison; they would weigh greatly with me always. But before the authority of his opinion be vouched for the gentleman's proposition, it will be proper to consider what is the fair interpretation of that Resolution, to which Mr. Madison is understood to have given his sanction. As the gentleman construes it, it is an authority for him. Possibly he may not have adopted the right construction. That resolution declares, that, *in the case of the dangerous exercise of powers not granted by the general government, the States may interpose to arrest the progress of the evil.* But how interpose, and what does this declaration purport? Does it mean no more than that there may be extreme cases, in which the people, in any mode of assembling, may resist usurpation, and relieve themselves from a tyrannical government? No one will deny this. Such resistance is not only acknowledged to be just in America, but in England also. Blackstone admits as much, in the theory, and practice, too, of the English Constitution. We, Sir, who oppose the Carolina Doctrine, do not deny that the people may, if they choose, throw off any government when it becomes oppressive and intolerable, and erect a better in its stead. We all know that civil institutions are established for the public benefit, and that when they cease to answer the ends of their existence they may be changed.

But I do not understand the doctrine now contended for to be that, which, for the sake of distinction, we may call the right of revolution. I understand the gentleman to maintain, that, without revolution, without civil commotion, without rebellion, a remedy for supposed abuse and transgression of the powers of the general government lies in a direct appeal to the interference of the State governments.

[Mr. Hayne here rose and raid: He did not contend for the mere right of revolution, but for the right of constitutional resistance. What he maintained was, that in case of a plain, palpable violation of the Constitution by the general government, a State may interpose; and that this interposition is constitutional.]

Mr. Webster resumed: –

So, Sir, I understood the gentleman, and am happy to find that I did not misunderstand him. What he contends for is, that it is constitutional to interrupt the administration of the Constitution itself, in the hands of those who are chosen and sworn to administer it, by the direct interference, in form of law, of the States, in virtue of their sovereign capacity. The inherent right in the people to reform their government I do not deny; and they have another right, and that is, to resist unconstitutional laws, without overturning the government. It is no doctrine of mine that unconstitutional laws bind the people. The great question is, Whose prerogative is it to decide on the constitutionality or unconstitutionality of the laws? On that, the main debate hinges. The proposition, that, in case of a supposed violation of the Constitution by Congress, the States have a constitutional right to interfere and annul the law of Congress, is the proposition of the gentleman.

I do not admit it. If the gentleman had intended no more than to assert the right of revolution for justifiable cause, he would have said only what all agree to. But I cannot conceive that there can be a middle course, between submission to the laws, when regularly pronounced constitutional, on the one hand, and open resistance, which is revolution or rebellion, on the other. I say, the right of a State to annul a law of Congress cannot be maintained, but on the ground of the inalienable right of man to resist oppression; that is to say, upon the ground of revolution. I admit that there is an ultimate violent remedy, above the Constitution and in defiance of the Constitution, which may be resorted to when a revolution is to be justified. But I do not admit, that, under the Constitution and in conformity with it, there is any mode in which a State government, as a member of the Union, can interfere and stop the progress of the general government, by force of her own laws, under any circumstances whatever.

This leads us to inquire into the origin of this government and the source of its power. Whose agent is it? Is it the creature of the State legislatures, or the creature of the people? If the government of the United States be the agent of the State governments, then they may control it, provided they can agree in the manner of controlling it; if it be the agent of the people, then the people alone can control it, restrain it, modify, or reform it. It is observable enough, that the doctrine for which the honorable gentleman contends leads him to the necessity of maintaining, not only that this general government is the creature of the States, but that it is the creature of each of the States severally, so that each may assert the power for itself of determining whether it acts within the limits of its authority. It is the servant of four-and-twenty masters, of different wills and different purposes, and yet bound to obey all. This absurdity (for it seems no less) arises from a misconception as to the origin of this government and its true character. It is, Sir, the people's Constitution, the people's government, made for the people, made by the people, and answerable to the people. The people of the United States have declared that this Constitution shall be the supreme law. We must either admit the proposition, or dispute their authority. The States are, unquestionably, sovereign, so far as their sovereignty is not affected by this supreme law. But the State legislatures, as political bodies, however sovereign, are yet not sovereign over the people. So far as the people have given power to the general government, so far the grant is unquestionably good, and the government holds of the people, and not of the State governments. We are all agents of the same supreme power, the people. The general government and the State governments derive their authority from the same source. Neither can, in relation to the other, be called primary, though one is definite and restricted, and the other general and residuary. The National Government possesses those powers which it can be shown the people have conferred on it, and no more. All the rest belongs to the State governments, or to the people themselves. So far as the people have restrained State sovereignty, by the expression of their will, in the Constitution of the United States, so far, it must be admitted, State sovereignty is effectually controlled. I do not contend that it is, or ought to be, controlled farther.

The sentiment to which I have referred propounds that State sovereignty is only to be controlled by its own "feeling of justice"; that is to say, it is not to be controlled at all, for one who is to follow his own feelings is under no legal control. Now, however men may think this ought to be, the fact is, that the people of the United States have chosen to impose control on State sovereignties. There are those, doubtless, who wish they had been left without restraint; but the Constitution has ordered the matter differently. To make war, for instance, is an exercise of sovereignty; but the Constitution declares that no State shall make war. To coin money is another exercise of sovereign power; but no State is at liberty to coin money. Again, the Constitution says that no sovereign State shall be so sovereign as to make a treaty. These prohibitions, it must be confessed, are a control on the State sovereignty of South Carolina, as well as of the other States, which does not arise "from her own feelings of honorable justice." The opinion referred to, therefore, is in defiance of the plainest provisions of the Constitution....

...[Let us suppose that there] is such a usurpation, therefore, as calls upon the States to exercise their right of interference. Here is a case, then, within the gentleman's principles, and all his qualifications of his principles.

It is a case for action. The Constitution is plainly, dangerously, palpably, and deliberately violated; and the States must interpose their own authority to arrest the law. Let us suppose the State of South Carolina to express this same opinion, by the voice of her legislature. That would be very imposing; but what then? Is the voice of one State conclusive? It so happens that, at the very moment when South Carolina resolves that the tariff laws are unconstitutional, Pennsylvania and Kentucky resolve exactly the reverse. *They* hold those laws to he both highly proper and strictly constitutional. And now, Sir, how does the honorable member propose to deal with this case? How does he relieve us from this difficulty, upon any principle of his? His construction gets us into it; how does be propose to get us out?

In Carolina, the tariff is a palpable, deliberate usurpation; Carolina, therefore, may nullify it, and refuse to pay the duties. In Pennsylvania, it is both clearly constitutional and highly expedient; and there the duties are to be paid. And yet we live under a government of uniform laws, and under a Constitution too, which contains an express provision, as it happens, that all duties shall be equal in all the States. Does not this approach absurdity?

If there be no power to settle such questions, independent of either of the States, is not the whole Union a rope of sand? Are we not thrown back again, precisely, upon the old Confederation?

It is too plain to be argued. Four-and-twenty interpreters of constitutional law, each with a power to decide for itself, and none with authority to bind anybody else, and this constitutional law the only bond of their union! What is such a state of things but a mere connection during pleasure, or, to use the phraseology of the times, *during feeling*? And that feeling, too, not the feeling of the people, who established the Constitution, but the feeling of the State governments.

...Open resistance to the laws, then, is the constitutional remedy, the conservative power of the State, which the South Carolina Doctrines teach for the redress of political evils, real or imaginary. And its authors further say, that, appealing with confidence to the Constitution itself, to justify their opinions, they cannot consent to try their accuracy by the courts of justice. In one sense, indeed, Sir, this is assuming an attitude of open resistance in favor of liberty. But what sort of liberty? The liberty of establishing their own opinions, in defiance of the opinions of all others; the liberty of judging and of deciding exclusively themselves, in a matter in which others have as much right to judge and decide as they; the liberty of placing their own opinions above the judgment of all others, above the laws, and above the Constitution. This is their liberty, and this is the fair result of the proposition contended for by the honorable gentleman. Or, it may be more properly said, it is identical with it, rather than a result from it....

Resolutions, Sir, have been recently passed by the legislature of South Carolina. I need not refer to them; they go no farther than the honorable gentleman himself has gone, and I hope not so far. I content myself, therefore, with debating the matter with him.

And now, Sir, what I have first to say on this subject is, that at no time, and under no circumstances, has New England, or any State in New England, or any respectable body of persons in New England, or any public man of standing in New England, put forth such a doctrine as this Carolina Doctrine.

The gentleman has found no case, he can find none, to support his own opinions by New England authority. New England has studied the Constitution in other schools, and under other teachers. She looks upon it with other regards, and deems more highly and reverently both of its just authority and its utility and excellence....She rejects it now; she always did reject it; and till she loses her senses, she always will reject it. The honorable member has referred to expressions on the subject of the embargo law, made in this place, by an honorable and venerable gentleman (Mr. Hillhouse, of Connecticut), now favoring us with his presence. He quotes that distinguished Senator as saying, that, in his judgment, the embargo law was unconstitutional, and that therefore, in his opinion, the people were not bound to obey it. That, Sir, is perfectly constitutional language. An unconstitutional law is not binding; *but then it does not rest with a resolution or a law of a State legislature to decide whether an act of Congress be or be not constitutional....*

...Who is to decide this? Who is to judge between the people and the government? And, Sir, it is quite plain, that the Constitution of the United States confers on the government itself, to be exercised by its appropriate department, and under its own responsibility to the people, this power of deciding ultimately and conclusively upon the just extent of its own authority. If this had not been done, we should not have advanced a single step beyond the old Confederation.

...[T]he question...must be decided by the judicial tribunals of the United States....

...I maintain, that between submission to the decision of the constituted tribunals, and revolution, or disunion, there is no middle ground; there is no ambiguous condition, half allegiance and half rebellion.

And, Sir, how futile, how very futile it is, to admit the right of State interference, and then attempt to save it from the character of unlawful resistance, by adding terms of qualification to the causes and occasions, leaving all these qualifications, like the case itself, in the discretion of the State governments. It must be a clear case, it is said, a deliberate case, a palpable case, a dangerous case. But then the State is still left at liberty to decide for herself what is clear, what is deliberate, what is palpable, what is dangerous. Do adjectives and epithets avail any thing?

Sir, the human mind is so constituted, that the merits of both sides of a controversy appear very clear, and very palpable, to those who respectively espouse them; and both sides usually grow clearer as the controversy advances....I was forcibly struck, Sir, with one reflection, as the gentleman went on in his speech. He quoted Mr. Madison's Resolutions, to prove that a State may interfere, in a case of deliberate, palpable, and dangerous exercise of a power not granted. The honorable member supposes the tariff law to be such an exercise of power; and that consequently a case has arisen in which the State may, if it see fit, interfere by its own law. Now it so happens, nevertheless, that Mr. Madison deems this same tariff law quite constitutional. Instead of a clear and palpable violation, it is, in his judgment, no violation at all. So that, while they use his authority for a hypothetical case, they reject it in the very case before them. All this, Sir, shows the inherent futility, I had almost used a stronger word, of conceding this power of interference to the State, and then attempting to secure it from abuse by imposing qualifications of which the States themselves are to judge. One of two things is true; either the laws of the Union are beyond the discretion and beyond the control of the States; or else we have no constitution of general government, and are thrust back again to the days of the Confederation.

...Sir, I deny the whole doctrine. It has not a foot of ground in the Constitution to stand on. No public man of reputation ever advanced it in Massachusetts in the warmest times, or could maintain himself upon it there at any time.

I wish now, Sir, to make a remark upon the Virginia Resolutions of 1798. I cannot undertake to say how these resolutions were understood by those who passed them. Their language is not a little indefinite. In the case of the exercise by Congress of a dangerous power not granted to them, the resolutions assert the right, on the part of the State, to interfere and arrest the progress of the evil. This is susceptible of more than one interpretation. It may mean no more than that the States may interfere by complaint and remonstrance, or by proposing to the people an alteration of the Federal Constitution. This would all be quite unobjectionable. Or it may be that no more is meant than to assert the general right of revolution, as against all governments in cases of intolerable oppression. This no one doubts, and this, in my opinion, is all that he who framed the resolutions could have meant by it; for I shall not readily believe that he was ever of opinion that a State, under the Constitution and in conformity with it, could upon the ground of her own opinion of its unconstitutionality however clear and palpable she might think the case, annul a law of Congress, so far as it should operate on herself by her own legislative power.

I must now beg to ask, Sir, Whence is this supposed right of the States derived? Where do they find the power to interfere with the laws of the Union? Sir, the opinion which the honorable gentleman maintains is a notion founded in a total misapprehension, in my judgment, of the origin of this government, and of the foundation on which it stands. I hold it to be a popular government, erected by the people; those who administer it, responsible to the people; and itself capable of being amended and modified, just as the people may choose it should be. It is as popular, just as truly emanating from the people, as the State governments. It is created for one purpose; the State governments for another. It has its own powers; they have theirs. There is no more authority with them to arrest the operation of a law of Congress, than with Congress to arrest the operation of their laws. We are here to administer a Constitution emanating immediately from the people, and trusted by them to our administration. It is not the creature of the State governments. It is of no moment to the argument, that certain acts of the State legislatures are necessary to fill our seats in this body. That is not one of their original State powers, a part of the sovereignty of the State. It is a duty which the people, by the Constitution itself, have imposed on the State legislatures; and which they might have left to be performed elsewhere, if they had seen fit. So they have left the choice of President with electors; but all this does not affect the proposition that this whole government, President, Senate, and House of Representatives, is a popular government. It leaves it still all its popular character....This government, Sir, is the independent offspring of the popular will. It is not the creature of State legislatures; nay, more, if the whole truth must be told, the people brought it into existence, established it, and have hitherto supported it, for the very purpose, amongst others, of imposing certain salutary restraints on State sovereignties. The States cannot now make war; they cannot contract alliances; they cannot make, each for itself, separate regulations of commerce; they cannot lay imposts; they cannot coin money. If this Constitution, Sir, be the creature of State legislatures, it must be admitted that it has obtained a strange control over the volitions of its creators.

The people, then, Sir, erected this government. They gave it a Constitution, and in that Constitution they have enumerated the powers which they bestow on it. They have made it a limited government. They have defined its authority. They have restrained it to the exercise of such powers as are granted; and all others, they declare, are reserved to the States or the people. But, Sir, they have not stopped here. If they had, they would have accomplished but half their work. No definition can be so clear, as to avoid possibility of doubt; no limitation so precise as to exclude all uncertainty. Who, then, shall construe this grant of the people? Who shall interpret their will, where it may be supposed they have left it doubtful? With whom do they repose this ultimate right of deciding on the powers of the government? Sir, they have settled all this in the fullest manner. They have left it with the government itself, in its appropriate branches. Sir, the very chief end, the main design, for which the whole Constitution was framed and adopted, was to establish a government that should not be obliged to act through State agency, or depend on State opinion and State discretion. The people had had quite enough of that kind of government under the Confederation. Under that system, the legal action, the application of law to individuals, belonged exclusively to the States. Congress could only recommend; their acts were not of binding force, till the States had adopted and sanctioned them. Are we in that condition still? Are we yet at the mercy of State discretion and State construction? Sir, if we are, then vain will be our attempt to maintain the Constitution under which we sit.

But, Sir, the people have wisely provided, in the Constitution itself, a proper, suitable mode and tribunal for settling questions of constitutional law. There are in the Constitution grants of powers to Congress, and restrictions on these powers. There are, also, prohibitions on the States. Some authority must, therefore, necessarily exist, having the ultimate jurisdiction to fix and ascertain the interpretation of these grants, restrictions, and prohibitions. The Constitution has itself pointed out, ordained, and established that authority. How has it accomplished this great and essential end? By declaring, Sir, that *"the Constitution, and the laws of the United States made in pursuance thereof, shall be the supreme law of the land, any thing in the constitution or laws of any State to the contrary notwithstanding."*

This, Sir, was the first great step. By this the supremacy of the Constitution and laws of the United States is declared. The people so will it. No

State law is to be valid which comes in conflict with the Constitution, or any law of the United States passed in pursuance of it. But who shall decide this question of interference? To whom lies the last appeal? This, Sir, the Constitution itself decides also, by declaring, *"that the judicial power shall extend to all cases arising under the Constitution and laws of the United States."* These two provisions cover the whole ground. They are, in truth, the keystone of the arch! With these it is a government; without them it is a confederation....Having constituted the government, and declared its powers, the people have further said, that, since somebody must decide on the extent of these powers, the government shall itself decide; subject, always, like other popular governments, to its responsibility to the people. And now, Sir, I repeat, how is it that a State legislature acquires any power to interfere? Who, or what, gives them the right to say to the people, "We, who are your agents and servants for one purpose, will undertake to decide, that your other agents and servants, appointed by you for another purpose, have transcended the authority you gave them!" The reply would be, I think, not impertinent, "Who made you a judge over another's servants? To their own masters they stand or fall."

Sir, I deny this power of State legislatures altogether. It cannot stand the test of examination. Gentlemen may say, that, in an extreme case, a State government might protect the people from intolerable oppression. Sir, in such a case, the people might protect themselves, without the aid of the State governments. Such a case warrants revolution. It must make, when it comes, a law for itself. A nullifying act of a State legislature cannot alter the case, nor make resistance any more lawful. In maintaining these sentiments, Sir, I am but asserting the rights of the people. I state what they have declared, and insist on their right to declare it. They have chosen to repose this power in the general government, and I think it my duty to support it, like other constitutional powers.

...And, Sir, if we look to the general nature of the case, could any thing have been more preposterous, than to make a government for the whole Union, and yet leave its powers subject, not to one interpretation, but to thirteen or twenty-four interpretations? Instead of one tribunal, established by all, responsible to all, with power to decide for all, shall constitutional questions be left to four-and-twenty popular bodies, each at liberty to decide for itself, and none bound to respect the decisions of others, – and each at liberty, too, to give a new construction on every new election of its own members? Would any thing, with such a principle in it, or rather with such a destitution of all principle, be fit to be called a government? No, Sir. It should not be denominated a Constitution....It would not be a government. It would not be adequate to any practical good, or fit for any country to live under.

To avoid all possibility of being misunderstood, allow me to repeat again, in the fullest manner, that I claim no powers for the government by forced or unfair construction. I admit that it is a government of strictly limited powers; of enumerated, specified, and particularized powers; and that whatsoever is not granted, is withheld. But notwithstanding all this, and however the grant of powers may be expressed, its limit and extent may yet, in some cases, admit of doubt; and the general government would be good for nothing, it would be incapable of long existing, if some mode had not been provided in which those doubts, as they should arise, might be peaceably, but authoritatively, solved.

...If a thing can be done, an ingenious man can tell *how* it is to be done and I wish to be informed *how* this State interference is to be put in practice, without violence, bloodshed, and rebellion....The militia of the State will be called out to sustain the nullifying act. They will march, Sir, under a very gallant leader; for I believe the honorable member himself commands the militia of that part of the State. He will raise the NULLIFYING ACT on his standard, and spread it out as his banner! It will have a preamble, setting forth that the tariff laws are palpable, deliberate, and dangerous violations of the Constitution!...

..."South Carolina is a sovereign State," he would reply. That is true; but would the judge admit our plea? "These tariff laws," he would repeat, "are unconstitutional, palpably, deliberately, dangerously." That may all be so; but if the tribunal should not happen to be of that opinion, shall we swing for it? We are ready to die for our country, but it is rather an awkward business, this dying without touching the ground! After all, that is a sort of hemp tax worse than any part of the tariff.

Mr. President, the honorable gentleman would be in a dilemma, like that of another great general. He would have a knot before him which he could not untie. He must cut it with his sword. He must say to his followers, "Defend yourselves with your bayonets"; and this is war, – civil war.

Direct collision, therefore, between force and force, is the unavoidable result of that remedy for the revision of unconstitutional laws which the gentleman contends for. It must happen in the very first case to which it is applied. Is not this the plain result? To resist by force the execution of a law, generally is treason. Can the courts of the United States take notice of the indulgence of a State to commit treason? The common saying, that a State cannot commit treason herself, is nothing to the purpose. Can she authorize others to do it?...Talk about it as we will, these doctrines go the length of revolution. They are incompatible with any peaceable administration of the government. They lead directly to disunion and civil commotion; and therefore it is, that at their commencement, when they are first found to be maintained by respectable men, and in a tangible form, I enter my public protest against them all.

The honorable gentleman argues, that, if this government be the sole judge of the extent of its own powers, whether that right of judging be in Congress or the Supreme Court, it equally subverts State sovereignty....The gentleman's opinion may be, that the right *ought not* to have been lodged with the general government; he may like better such a constitution as we should have under the right of State interference; but I ask him to meet me on the plain matter of fact. I ask him to meet me on the Constitution itself. I ask him if the power is not found there, clearly and visibly found there?...

If any thing be found in the National Constitution, either by original provision or subsequent interpretation, which ought not to be in it, the people know how to get rid of it. If any construction, unacceptable to them, be

> established, so as to become practically a part of the Constitution, they will amend it, at their own sovereign pleasure....Gentlemen do not seem to recollect that the people have any power to do any thing for themselves. They imagine there is no safety for them, any longer than they are under the close guardianship of the State legislatures....
>
> Mr. President, I have thus stated the reasons of my dissent to the doctrines which have been advanced and maintained....I profess, Sir, in my career hitherto, to have kept steadily in view the prosperity and honor of the whole country, and the preservation of our Federal Union. It is to that Union we owe our safety at home, and our consideration and dignity abroad. It is to that Union that we are chiefly indebted for whatever makes us most proud of our country....
>
> ...While the Union lasts, we have high, exciting, gratifying prospects spread out before us, for us and our children. Beyond that I seek not to penetrate the veil. God grant that, in my day, at least, that curtain may not rise! God grant that on my vision never may be opened what lies behind!...When my eyes shall be turned to behold for the last time the sun in heaven, may I not see him shining on the broken and dishonored fragments of a once glorious Union; on States dissevered, discordant, belligerent; on a land rent with civil feuds, or drenched, it may be, in fraternal blood! Let their last feeble and lingering glance rather behold the gorgeous ensign of the Republic, now known and honored throughout the earth, still full high advanced, its arms and trophies streaming in their original lustre, not a stripe erased or polluted, nor a single Star obscured, bearing for its motto, no such miserable interrogatory as "What is all this worth?" nor those other words of delusion and folly, "Liberty first and Union afterwards"; but everywhere, spread all over in characters of living light, blazing on all its ample folds, as they float over the sea and over the land, and in every wind under the whole heavens, that other sentiment, dear to every true American heart, – Liberty *and* Union, now and for ever, one and inseparable! [6]

Assessment of Senator Webster's Oration

We have quoted Daniel Webster's speech at some length so that his constitutional principles, as expressed in his own words, may be fully understood. This speech, as attested by the Consolidating School of Thought, represents the best argument that has ever been made in support of the contention for a supreme, sovereign National Government. Now that we have presented the Senator's actual words, let us put his conception of the nature of our Federal Union to the ultimate test of constitutionality. As we shall discover, his principles do not pass that test.

Our analysis should begin by noting the *reason* why Senator Webster ex-

---

[6] *Ibid.*

pounded the Constitution in the manner he did. "This leads, Sir, to the real and wide difference in political opinions between the honorable gentleman and myself," stated the Senator. "On my part, I look upon all these objects" of a domestic concern "as connected with the common good, fairly embraced in its objects and its terms; he, on the contrary, deems them all, if good at all, only local good. This is our difference."

Thus, Daniel Webster's leading object was to undermine our federal system of constitutionally limited government, to usurp the reserved rights of the States, to transform the Federal Government into a National Government, and to invest that government with sovereignty and unlimited powers. This, of course, is the very definition of consolidation. The concept of a federation of sovereign States is alien to this consolidating scheme of government. "In our contemplation," said the Senator, "Carolina and Ohio are parts of the same country," just as the counties within a State are merely parts of the whole State.

To effect his consolidating goal required a complete denial of the existence of sovereign States and all that is implied by the word sovereignty. "This leads us to inquire into the origin of this government and the source of its power," he stated. "Whose agent is it? Is it the creature of the State legislatures, or the creature of the people?"

According to the Orator of Consolidation, our political system was created by the American people, and not by the States, implying that the people and the States are two entirely different concepts in our system of government. He deemed it sufficient to establish his contention by showing that the State *governments* did not establish the Federal Constitution, a contention, incidentally, that no one had ever advocated. By stating that the federal compact was not created by the State governments, he suggested by implication that it had been created by a single, amalgamated American Nation of people. He therefore denied the validity of any concept asserting that the States had, in any way, created the Constitution of the United States.

"Now, however men may think this ought to be," claimed Daniel Webster, "the fact is, that the people of the United States have chosen to impose control on State sovereignties." If the "people of the United States" chose to impose control on State sovereignties, that would make the people of the United States *more* sovereign than the sovereign people of the States. Is it possible for one political body of people to be *more* sovereign than another sovereign political body of people? Is it possible for one *supreme* authority to be *more supreme* than another *supreme* authority?

If the States are sovereign, as even Senator Webster was willing to admit, then how could anyone else "impose control" over them? Imposing control in the political sense is the essence of sovereignty. The only conclusion consistent with logic is that the "people of the United States" to which the Senator referred do not really exist, but was merely a figment of his imagination. To be sure, the American people do exist. But they exist in their sovereign political capacities only as States of the Union, not as an amalgamated single Nation.

The restrictions on the exercise of certain specified powers by the States contained in the Federal Constitution were not controls *externally* placed over the States, as the Orator of Consolidation claimed. Everything in the Constitution represents the will, not of a Nation of people independent of the States, but of the States themselves. The Constitution of the United States is a compact – *a bundle of compromises and agreements* – among the States themselves, who voluntarily accepted the terms of the compact when ratifying the Constitution.

The people whose voice is heard speaking through the Federal Constitution are the peoples of the several States, not a mythological people of a consolidated American Nation that did not and could not possibly have existed at the time the federal compact was adopted. By conjuring up this mythical Nation of people, Senator Webster's objective was to transfer sovereignty from the real peoples of the several States to the Government of the United States. Flattering appeals to a mythical Nation of Americans was merely offered as an excuse to rob the real peoples of the States of their sovereignty.

The Massachusetts politician stated that, "the doctrine for which the honorable gentleman contends leads him to the necessity of maintaining, not only that this general government is the creature of the States, but that it is the creature of each of the States severally." That doctrine, however, was not merely Senator Hayne's contention, for it was an historical fact. Even more, such a contention was expressly declared within the text of the Federal Constitution, which provided that each State must ratify the compact separately from the others and could be bound only by its own consent. No consolidated State of America, as a single body politic, adopted the Federal Constitution.

Senator Webster, however, was not one to allow historical facts or the plain words of the Constitution to deter him, no matter how absurd were the theories he espoused. "This absurdity (for it seems no less) arises from a misconception as to the origin of this government and its true character," he declared. "It is, Sir, the people's Constitution, the people's government, made for the people, made by the people, and answerable to the people. The people of the United States have declared that this Constitution shall be the supreme law." "The States are," the Senator added, "unquestionably, sovereign, so far as their sovereignty is not affected by this supreme law. But the State legislatures, as political bodies, however sovereign, are not yet sovereign over the people."

To use the Senator's own term, these views presented by him are grossly absurd. The *people* he referred to have never existed. The only people recognized by the Federal Constitution are the people of the several States, either as individual citizens or as sovereign political bodies styled States. In this regard, it is of interest to note that those in olden days who espoused a sovereign government by virtue of the Divine Rights of Kings actually had a better case to argue than the one offered by Daniel Webster. At least God exists and really is the source of Political Sovereignty for all mankind, which is more than we can say for the mythical people that Senator Webster claimed was the source of authority for his sovereign National Government.

Constitutionally speaking, the terms "State" or "States" could be substituted for "people" in his statement, so that it declares: "It is, Sir, the States' Constitution, the States' government, made for the States, made by the States, and answerable to the States. The States of the Union have declared that this Constitution shall be the supreme law."

It is significant to note that, while admitting the existence of State sovereignty, Senator Webster claimed that such sovereignty was vested in the State governments. Yet, such State governments, he stated, although sovereign, are not sovereign over the people. A State government, thus, is *supreme*, but the people are *more supreme*. We can readily ascertain why those who adore power have ever regarded Daniel Webster as a great master of the spoken word!

According to Daniel Webster, "One of two things is true; either the laws of the Union are beyond the discretion and beyond the control of the States; or else we have no Constitution of general government." The *people*, in their sovereign capacities, are the *States*, and the *States* are the *people*. Let us, therefore, substitute the equivalent word "people" for the word "States" and see how his contention really stands: "One of two things is true; either the laws of the Union are beyond the discretion and beyond the control of the people; or else we have no Constitution of general government." Stated thusly, Senator Webster's true principles become more obvious, and more alarming.

Establishing a government, delegating powers to it, drafting its constitution, and determining the extent and ends of its powers, all constitute the highest function or attribute of sovereignty. *Whoever is sovereign determines the limits of powers to be exercised by a government.* If the people make this determination, they are sovereign; but if the government itself may decide its own limits of power, then that government is clearly sovereign. The American Theory of Government clearly rests upon the former seat of sovereignty; the consolidating school, however, contends for the latter seat of sovereignty.

As Senator Webster asserted, "The people, then, Sir, erected this government. They gave it a Constitution, and in that Constitution they have enumerated the powers which they bestow on it. They have made it a limited government. They have defined its authority." Although we may certainly disagree with regard to *which* people performed these acts – the real people of the States, or a mythical people of a non-existent American Nation – there can be no doubt that the Senator is here contending for the sovereignty of the people. If the people created the Federal Government, whether as States or as a single Nation, should not those same people have the *ultimate* or *final* say in regard to the limits of power exercised by their Federal Government?

"Who, then, shall construe this grant of the people?" asked Senator Webster. "Who shall interpret their will, where it may be supposed they have left it doubtful? With whom do they leave this *ultimate* right of deciding on the powers of the government?" Senator Webster, who preferred to portray himself as a great champion of the people, answered thusly: "They have left it, with the government itself, in its appropriate branches." Hence, while claiming affinity to the near-sacred concept of the sovereignty of the people, the Massachusetts Senator categorically concluded that, in the final analysis, the Government of the United States is empowered to be the *final* or *ultimate* judge of the extent of its own powers. Such a conclusion at once subverts the political supremacy of the people, transfers sovereignty to the Federal Government, and establishes the right of that government to lay claim to an unlimited field of powers.

Senator Daniel Webster correctly noted that, "Some authority must...necessarily exist, having the ultimate jurisdiction to fix and ascertain the interpretations of these grants, restrictions, and prohibitions" contained in the Federal Constitution. He then asked, "But who shall decide this question of interference? To whom lies the *last appeal*?" He then proclaimed that the Supreme Court of the United States was empowered with the sovereign right of altering and amending the Federal Constitution. Of the three branches of government, he selected the one that is the most removed from any responsibility to the American people!

How far different is Senator Webster's concept of sovereignty from the Divine Rights of Kings theory of Sir Robert Filmer or the notions of tyranny proclaimed by Thomas Hobbes for his Leviathan State? Would it make any real difference whether this sovereignty was wielded by one monarch in the form of a King, or by nine monarchs seated on the bench of the U.S. Supreme Court? Is a majority of nine monarchs preferable to a single monarch? The system advocated by Senator Webster was certainly not based on the republican principles of popular government, in spite of his pretended devotion to the people of the United States.

To support his contention that "all questions of constitutional power" should be brought "to the final decision of the Supreme Court," Senator Daniel Webster relied on two sections of the Federal Constitution, one relating to the judicial power and the other to the supremacy of the Constitution. Neither of these clauses, however, sustains his contention. The judicial power of the United States, as expressed in Article III, Section 2 of the Constitution, extends to all cases, *in law and equity*, arising *under* the Constitution and laws of the United States. The jurisdiction of the Federal Supreme Court, therefore, is *limited* to the federal sphere of authority and is *under*, not *over*, the Constitution. By way of comparison, Article VII of the Constitution states that the compact shall exist *between* the States of the Federal Union.

According to the American Theory of Government, the Supreme Court of the United States is whatever the Federal Constitution says it is, and that Constitution is whatever the States say it is. Senator Webster reversed this order of superiority. According to him, the Constitution and the States are whatever the Supreme Court says they are. By claiming that the supreme law of the land must conform to the personal constitutions of a majority on the U.S. Supreme Court, Senator Webster advocated the replacement of the *rule of law* with the *rule of men*, a contention calculated to subvert the very republican nature of our form of government.

The other clause that Senator Webster cited was the Supremacy Clause, stating that, "the supremacy of the Constitution and laws of the United States is declared. The people so will it." The people who so willed it, of course, were the peoples of the States, acting in their sovereign capacities *as States*. And they who may rightfully decree a supreme law are certainly the supreme masters in the political system. Yet, what exactly is it that is declared by the States in their Federal Constitution to be supreme? The Supremacy Clause asserts the supremacy of the *Constitution* and all laws and treaties *made in pursuance of it*. According to this clause, not all laws passed by Congress become a part of the supreme law of the land, but only those that are made in pursuance of the Constitution. Those laws not made in pursuance of the Constitution are no laws at all, but are null, void, and of no force.

The real issue, of course, is encompassed by the question, Who shall have the final or ultimate say in this regard? Whose voice and whose opinion should be regarded as the most commanding, the highest in the land, beyond which there can be no appeal on this earth? Clearly, whoever possesses that ultimate authority is the sovereign lord and master in the political kingdom. Senator Webster made it clear who his lord and master was, when he stated that, "the people have...said, that, since somebody must decide on the extent of these powers, the government shall itself decide."

Ironically, the Orator of Consolidation attacked the States' Rights School of Thought because its adherents asserted that the State governments, acting as the shields of the peoples of the States, could rightfully protect the people from a power-mad Federal Government. He denied that such a right of State Interposition and Nullification existed, for the State governments did not create the Federal Government. Instead, he proclaimed, the right to be the final arbiter of power belonged to the U.S. Supreme Court. Of these two entities – the State governments and the U.S. Supreme Court – which one played a greater role in creating our present system of government?

The State governments commissioned delegates to attend the Philadelphia Convention of 1787. How many delegates to that Convention were commissioned by the U.S. Supreme Court? The State governments authorized the State Ratifying Conventions that adopted our present Federal Constitution. What role did the Federal Supreme Court play in ratifying the Constitution. At the time of the Webster-Hayne Debate of 1830, the State governments each elected two Senators to the upper house of Congress. How many could the Supreme Court elect?

The State governments are empowered by the Federal Constitution to ratify amendments to it. Does the Constitution delegate to the U.S. Supreme Court the power to amend the Constitution? The legislators of each State are elected by the people of the State and are accountable to them. Which people elect the Justices of the U.S. Supreme Court? By the amendment process, the State governments can abolish the Supreme Court of the United States. Can that Court constitutionally abolish a State government?

Admittedly, the State governments are not sovereign. The people of each State are sovereign. The State governments are thus one step removed from the seat of sovereignty in the United States. The Federal Government, on the other hand, is two steps removed from the seat of sovereignty. And since the Supreme Court of the United States is not responsible directly to the people, it is actually three steps removed from the seat of sovereignty. The people, as individual citizens, are not sovereign. As organized body politics, or States, however, they are sovereign. How, in their sovereign capacity, can they possibly check or halt the exercise of dangerous and unconstitutional powers by their Federal Government?

Clearly, the American people, as individuals, cannot resist the enforcement of federal laws, even unconstitutional federal laws, without resorting to the right of revolution, because the American people are not sovereign as individuals. Senator Webster acknowledged that the people, as individuals, had a right to revolution. Yet, he also stated that, "To resist by force the execution of a law, generally, is treason." Thus, according to the Consolidating School of Thought, the American people, as individuals, have a right to rebel against the Federal Government, although that same government has the right to execute the rebels for treason.

This highlights another facet of Senator Webster's stated doctrines. We cannot fail to notice how the theme of *violence* runs like a refrain through his second reply to Senator Hayne. Everything associated with free and popular government is portrayed as anarchic and violent, from the workings of political parties to the efforts of States to interpose their authority and nullify dangerous federal laws. Checks and balances between independent levels of government, and any form of opposition to the workings of the Federal Government in general, are characterized as lawless and inherently violent. The only alternative to this violent anarchy, it would appear, is for the States and their peoples to tamely submit to a sovereign National Government that supremely decides for itself the extent of its own powers.

Let us examine Senator Webster's acknowledgement of the *right of revolution* a bit further. Although he emphatically denies the right of State Interposition and Nullification, he admits that the American people have a natural right to rebel against tyranny, but insists that the people can resist despotism only as individuals, not as sovereign States. Of course, the efforts of any individual American citizen to resist the awesome power of the Federal Government can have only one outcome. And the consolidating school understands this perfectly well. No one man can resist the organized power of a government, and to offer this as the only alternative to submission to federal tyranny is to offer no protection at all for the liberties of the American people.

But let us inquire; if the American people, as Senator Webster admitted, have the *right* as individuals to resist federal tyranny, do they not also have a corresponding right to *unite* their efforts to form a united front against Leviathan? To admit the first right while denying the second right would be illogical. In fact, the American people are already united and organized in political bodies called States for the very purpose of protecting their rights from unjust invasions. Thus, the peoples of the several States, *as States*, have the right to self-defense against federal despotism, and to expect that their State governments will intervene, when necessary, to protect them from dangerous and unconstitutional actions by the Government of the United States.

Senator Webster acknowledged that questions of contested power could be resolved by amending the Federal Constitution. In advocating that, he was in agreement with the States' Rights School of Thought. Yet, the Senator from Massachusetts used reversed logic in presenting this method for resolving disputed power. The States' Rights School of Thought contended that, whenever a State interposed its authority and nullified a federal act, those who advocated the contested power should propose an amendment to the federal compact specifically delegating the power in question to the Federal Government. If such an amendment were ratified, then the Federal Government could exercise the power. This logic was based upon the American Theory of Government, which holds that the Federal Government can only exercise expressly delegated powers.

Senator Webster reversed this logic. The burden of amending the federal compact, under his conception, fell on those who denied the legitimacy of the power in contention. To prevent the Federal Government from exercising such the contested power, under this concept, an amendment should be adopted that specifically *denied* the power to the Government of the United States. Such a concept accorded with the Senator's previous claim that the Federal Government had power to pass any law that was proclaimed to be for the general welfare of the United States. Although this concept accorded with the theory of government advocated by the Consolidating School of Thought, it was utterly subversive of the true principles of the Federal Constitution.

It should be remembered that the proponents of the Constitution of 1787, during the period of ratification, repeatedly assured the American people that their State governments would act as shields for their liberties, and that a State government would constitute the *arm of resistance* to any dangerous acts perpetrated by the Government of the United States.

By all considerations, therefore, the weight of logic and historical fact rests on the side of the advocates of States' Rights. The Supreme Court of the United States is not, as Senator Webster contended, the final arbiter in questions of contended power. Such a right springs directly from sovereignty, which the States alone possess. And each State government, being the political organization *closest* to the seat of sovereignty, provides the most logical and constitutional means to interpose and nullify an unconstitutional federal act on behalf the sovereign people it represents.

The key to understanding the threat posed by Senator Webster's theory of government lies in his definition of *treason*. "To resist by force the execution of a law, generally, is treason," he declared. Is this true? Is this how the Constitution of the United States defines treason? Article III, Section 3, Clause 1 of the Federal Constitution defines the crime in these words: "Treason against the United States, shall consist only in levying war against them, on in adhering to their enemies, giving them aid and comfort." [7]

According to Senator Webster, treason is the refusal to obey federal laws, whether just or unjust. According to the Federal Constitution, treason is the waging of war against the sovereign States, either severally or individually, for an attack upon one State is considered an attack upon all. Why did Senator Webster offer an unconstitutional definition of the serious crime of treason? According to the Federal Constitution, it is possible for the officers of the Government of the United States – even the President of the United States – to commit treason by waging war against one or more States. According to Senator Webster and the Consolidating School of Thought, anyone, whether an individual citizen or a sovereign State, who refuses to submit to federal tyranny is committing treason.

The difference between Senator Webster's concept of treason and that of

[7] Alexander H. Stephens, *A Constitutional View of the Late War Between the States; Its Causes, Character, Conduct and Results*, Volume 1, Kraus Reprint Co., New York, 1970 (orig. pub. 1868), p. 565.

the Constitution may be explained by the different concepts of where sovereignty is vested. If the States are sovereign, then treason is disloyalty to the States. But if the Federal Government is sovereign, then treason is disloyalty to that government. Since Senator Webster advocated a sovereign National Government, it was logical in his theory for resistance to the will of that dread lord sovereign to be regarded as treason.

According to the Federal Constitution, only to uphold the laws of a sovereign State and to ensure the survival of its republican form of government may the Government of the United States employ martial force against the citizens of a State, and even then only when such federal coercive assistance is specifically requested by a State government. If the Federal Government waged war against and conquered a sovereign State, would that not violate the constitutional guarantee to the States of a republican form of government? *Such an act of war and conquest would constitute the very definition of treason.*

The States are sovereign; they are supreme; they are the masters within our political system. A master cannot betray himself, but the servant can betray the master. Despite all of Senator Webster's eloquent appeals to lofty sentiments and patriotic spirit, the doctrines that he advocated in his second reply to Senator Hayne were utterly subversive of the Constitution of the United States and dangerous to the liberties of the American people.

Additional Statements by the Debaters

Following Daniel Webster's second reply in the great debate, Robert Y. Hayne rose on January 27, 1830, to address the Senate once again and provide some additional remarks on behalf of the States' Rights School of Thought, which were published in the Fourth Volume of *Elliot's Debates*. As the Senator from South Carolina stated:

> The gentleman insists that the States have no right to decide whether the Constitution has been violated by acts of Congress or not; but that the Federal Government is the exclusive judge of the extent of its own powers....Having thus distinctly stated the points in dispute between the gentleman and myself, I proceed to examine them. And here it will be necessary to go back to the origin of the Federal Government. It cannot be doubted, and is not denied, that before the Constitution, each State was an independent sovereignty, possessing all the rights and powers appertaining to independent Nations; nor can it be denied, that, after the Constitution was formed, they remained equally sovereign and independent, as to all powers not expressly delegated to the Federal Government. This would have been the case even if no positive provisions to that effect had been inserted in that instrument. But

to remove all doubt, it is expressly declared, by the 10th article of the amendment of the Constitution, "that the powers not delegated to the United States, by the Constitution, nor prohibited by it to the States, are reserved to the States respectively, or to the people." The true nature of the Federal Constitution, therefore, is (in the language of Mr. Madison) "a compact to which the States are parties," – a compact by which each State, acting in its sovereign capacity, has entered into an agreement with the other States, by which they have consented that certain delegated powers shall be exercised by the United States, in the manner prescribed in the instrument. Nothing can be clearer than that, under such a system, the Federal Government, exercising strictly delegated powers, can have no right to act beyond the pale of its authority, and that all such acts are void. A State, on the contrary, retaining all powers not expressly given away, may lawfully act in all cases where she has not voluntarily imposed restrictions on herself. Here, then, is a case of a compact between sovereigns....When it is insisted by the gentleman that one of the parties "has the power of deciding ultimately and conclusively upon the extent of its own authority," I ask for the grant of such a power. I call upon the gentleman to show it to me in the Constitution. It is not to be found there....

Here, however, we are met by the argument that the Constitution was not formed by *the States* in their sovereign capacity, but by *the people*; and it is therefore inferred that the Federal Government, being created by all the people, must be supreme; and though it is not contended that the Constitution may be rightfully violated, yet it is insisted that from the decision of the Federal Government there can be no appeal.

I deny that the Constitution was framed by the people *in the sense in which that word is used on the other side*, and insist that it was framed by the States, acting in their sovereign capacity. When, in the Preamble of the Constitution, we find the words, "We, the people of the United States," it is clear they can only relate to the people as citizens of the several States, because the Federal Government was not then in existence.

We accordingly find, in every part of that instrument, that the people are always spoken of in that sense. Thus, in the 2d section of the 1st article, it is declared, "that the House of Representatives shall be composed of members chosen every second year by the people of the several States." To show that, in entering into this compact, the States acted in their sovereign capacity, and not merely as parts of one great community, what can be more conclusive than the historical fact, that when every State had consented to it except one, she was not held to be bound. A majority of the people in any State bound that State; but nine tenths of all the people of the United States could not bind the people of Rhode Island, until Rhode Island, as a State, had consented to the compact. [8]

In response, Daniel Webster of Massachusetts rose to make some closing

---

[8] Jonathan Elliot (ed.), *The Debates in the Several State Conventions, on the Adoption of the Federal Constitution, as Recommended by the General Convention at Philadelphia, in 1787*, Volume 4, Second Edition, Published under the Sanction of Congress, Washington, 1836, pp. 509-510.

remarks in the great debate:

> His argument consists of two propositions and an inference. His propositions are, –
>
> 1. That the Constitution is a compact between the States.
>
> 2. That a compact between two, with authority reserved to one to interpret its terms, would be a surrender to that one of all power whatever.
>
> 3. Therefore, (such is his inference,) the general government does not possess the authority to construe its own powers.
>
> Now, Sir, who does not see, without the aid of exposition or detection, the utter confusion of ideas involved in this so elaborate and systematic argument.
>
> The Constitution, it is said, is a compact *between States*; the States, then, and the States only, *are parties* to the compact. How comes the general government itself a *party*? Upon the honorable gentleman's hypothesis, the general government is the result of the compact, the creature of the compact, not one of the parties to it. Yet the argument, as the gentleman has now stated it, makes the government itself one of its own creators. It makes it a party to that compact to which it owes its own existence.
>
> For the purpose of erecting the Constitution on the basis of a compact, the gentleman considers the States as parties to that compact; but as soon as his compact is made, then he chooses to consider the general government, which is the offspring of that compact, not its offspring, but one of its parties; and so, being a party, without the power of judging on the terms of compact. Pray, Sir, in what school is such reasoning as this taught?
>
> If the whole of the gentleman's main proposition were conceded to him, – that is to say, if I admit, for the sake of the argument, that the Constitution is a compact between States, – the inferences which he draws from that proposition are warranted by no just reasoning. If the Constitution be a compact between States, still that Constitution, or that compact, has established a government, with certain powers; and whether it be one of those powers, that it shall construe and interpret for itself the terms of the compact, in doubtful cases, is a question which can only be decided by looking to the compact, and inquiring what provisions it contains on this point. Without any inconsistency with natural reason, the government even thus created might be trusted with this power of construction. The extent of its powers, therefore, must still be sought for in the instrument itself.
>
> If the old Confederation had contained a clause, declaring that resolutions of the Congress should be the supreme law of the land, any State law or constitution to the contrary notwithstanding, and that a committee of Congress, or any other body created by it, should possess judicial powers, extending to all cases arising under resolutions of Congress, then the power of ultimate decision would have been vested in Congress under the Confederation, although that Confederation was a compact between States; and for this plain reason, – that it would have been competent to the States, who alone were parties to the compact, to agree who should decide in cases of dispute arising on the construction of the compact.

For the same reason, Sir, if I were now to concede to the gentleman his principal proposition, namely, that the Constitution is a compact between States, the question would still be, What provision is made, in this compact to settle points of disputed construction, or contested power, that shall come into controversy? And this question would still be answered, and conclusively answered, by the Constitution itself.

While the gentleman is contending against construction, he himself is setting up the most loose and dangerous construction. The Constitution declares, that *the laws of Congress passed in pursuance of the Constitution shall be the supreme law of the land.* No construction is necessary here. It declares, also with equal plainness and precision, that *the judicial power of the United States shall extend to every case arising under the laws of Congress.* This needs no construction. Here is a law, then, which is declared to be supreme; and here is a power established, which is to interpret that law. Now, Sir, how has the gentleman met this? Suppose the Constitution to be a compact, yet here are its terms; and how does the gentleman get rid of them? He cannot argue the *seal off the bond,* nor the words out of the instrument. Here they are; what answer does he give to them? None in the world, Sir, except, that the effect of this would be to place the States in a condition of inferiority; and that it results from the very nature of things, there being no superior, that the parties must be their own judges! Thus closely and cogently does the honorable gentleman reason on the words of the Constitution. The gentleman says, if there be such a power of final decision in the general government, he asks for the grant of that power. Well, Sir, I show him the grant. I turn him to the very words. I show him that the laws of Congress are made supreme; and that the judicial power extends, by express words, to the interpretation of these laws. Instead of answering this, he retreats into the general reflection, that it must result *from the nature of things,* that the States, being parties, must judge for themselves.

I have admitted, that, if the Constitution were to be considered as the creature of the State governments, it might be modified, interpreted, or construed according to their pleasure. But, even in that case, it would be necessary that they should *agree.* One alone could not interpret it conclusively; one alone could not construe it; one alone could not modify it. Yet the gentleman's doctrine is, that Carolina alone may construe and interpret that compact which equally binds all, and gives equal rights to all.

So, then, Sir, even supposing the Constitution to be a compact between the States, the gentleman's doctrine, nevertheless, is not maintainable; because, first, the general government is not a party to that compact, but a *government* established by it, and vested by it with the powers of trying and deciding doubtful questions; and secondly, because, if the Constitution be regarded as a compact, not one State only, but all the States, are parties to that compact, and one can have no right to fix upon it her own peculiar construction.

So much, Sir, for the argument, even if the premises of the gentleman were granted, or could be proved. But, Sir, the gentleman has failed to maintain his leading proposition. He has not shown, it cannot be shown, that the Constitution is a compact between State governments. The Constitution itself, in its very front, refutes that idea; it, declares that it is ordained and established *by the people of the United States*. So far from saying that it is established by the governments of the several States, it does not even say that it is established by the people *of the several States*; but it pronounces that it is established by the people of the United States, in the aggregate. The gentleman says, it must mean no more than the people of the several States. Doubtless, the people of the several States, taken collectively, constitute the people of the United States; but it is in this, their collective capacity, it is as all the people of the United States, that they establish the Constitution. So they declare; and words cannot be plainer than the words used.

When the gentleman says the Constitution is a compact between the States, he uses language exactly applicable to the old Confederation. He speaks as if he were in Congress before 1789. He describes fully that old state of things then existing. The Confederation was, in strictness, a compact; the States, as States, were parties to it. We had no other general government. But that was found insufficient, and inadequate to the public exigencies. The people were not satisfied with it, and undertook to establish a better. They undertook to form a general government, which should stand on a new basis; not a confederacy, not a league, not a compact between States, but a *Constitution*; a popular government, founded in popular election, directly responsible to the people themselves, and divided into branches with prescribed limits of power, and prescribed duties. They ordained such a government, they gave it the name of a *Constitution*, therein they established a distribution of powers between this, their general government, and their several State governments. When they shall become dissatisfied with this distribution, they can alter it. Their own power over their own instrument remains. But until they shall alter it, it must stand as their will, and is equally binding on the general government and on the States.

The gentleman, Sir, finds analogy where I see none. He likens it to the case of a treaty, in which, there being no common superior, each party must interpret for itself, under its own obligation of good faith. But this is not a treaty, but a constitution of government, with powers to execute itself, and fulfill its duties.

I admit, Sir, that this government is a government of checks and balances; that is, the House of Representatives is a check on the Senate, and the Senate is a check on the House, and the President a check on both. But I cannot comprehend him, or, if I do, I totally differ from him, when he applies the notion of checks and balances to the interference of different governments. He argues, that, if we transgress our constitutional limits, each State, as a State, has a right to check us. Does he admit the converse of the proposition, that we have a right to check the States? The gentleman's doctrines would give us a strange jumble of authorities and powers, instead of governments of separate and defined powers. It is the part of wisdom, I think, to avoid this; and to keep the general government and the State government each in its proper sphere, avoiding as carefully as possible every kind of interference.

Finally, Sir, the honorable gentleman says, that the States will only interfere, by their power, to preserve the Constitution. They will not destroy

> it, they will not impair it; they will only save, they will only preserve, they will only strengthen it! Ah! Sir, this is but the old story. All regulated governments, all free governments, have been broken by similar disinterested and well-disposed interference. It is the common pretence. But I take leave of the subject. [9]

Within these closing remarks, Senator Daniel Webster concisely summarized the foundations of the Consolidating School of Thought. According to him, the Founding Fathers made a terrible mistake when they retained the title of the old Confederation – "United States of America" – for the new Federal Union. Instead, the new Union should have been style the "Amalgamated People of America," or the "Consolidated State of America," or even the "Sovereign State of America." According to the Consolidating School of Thought, the States played no real role at all in the formation of the Federal Union and the adoption of the Federal Constitution of 1787.

The Orator of Consolidation conceded that the States were sovereign under the Articles of Confederation, and that the people were thus equivalent to the States. Yet, in forming our present Federal Constitution, the people somehow removed themselves from their States and proceeded to act as one sovereign Nation in the creation of our present system of government. As to how such a fantastic maneuver was performed was a mystery so deep that the Senator from Massachusetts could not even offer a hint.

In support of his thesis for a sovereign National Government, Senator Webster again cited the Supremacy Clause of the Federal Constitution, claiming that a declaration of the *supremacy of the Constitution* was equivalent to asserting that the government itself is supreme. The Massachusetts politician also claimed that deciding the limits of powers of the Federal Government *in the last resort* is a judicial power delegated by the Constitution to the Supreme Court of the United States, completely obscuring the distinction between the *judicial power* and the *political power* in the United States.

The judicial power delegated by the Constitution of the United States to the federal judiciary is merely a power to apply the Federal Constitution and federal statutory laws to specific cases that come before it. In fulfilling its obligations, the U.S. Supreme Court, of necessity, must interpret the Constitution and apply its interpretations to the cases that arise under its jurisdiction. The judicial power is not, however, a power to determine, *in the last resort*, the extent of powers that are delegated to the Government of the United States. *That is a political power, the power of sovereignty.* Our republican *form of government* dictates that only the *people* – not the U.S. Supreme Court – can possess this power of sovereignty. And our federal *system of government* dictates that those

[9] Edwin P. Whipple, http://www.earlyrepublic.net/webstr2c.htm, *Op. cit.*

sovereign peoples are the *States*.

The consolidator from Massachusetts also cited the Preamble of the Federal Constitution as supposed justification for his contention for a *national* sovereignty. This Preamble, he exulted, proved that the States are meaningless entities within our system of government. That Preamble, he insisted, proved that the American people, acting independently of the States, ordained and established the Federal Constitution over the States. In stating this thesis, however, the Senator failed to reconcile his construction of the Preamble with the plain words of Article VII, which declare that the Constitution was to go into effect *between the States* that ratified it.

Senator Webster's explanation of which people established our present Federal Constitution stands in stark contrast to what James Madison, the Father of the Constitution, stated in the Virginia State Ratifying Convention:

> Who are the parties to it [the Constitution]? The people – *but not the people as composing one great body*; but the people *as composing thirteen sovereignties*.... [W]ere it such a government as is suggested, it would be now binding on the people of this State, without having the privilege of deliberating upon it; but, Sir, no State is bound by it, as it is, *without its own consent*.... [emphasis added] [10]

And in the *Federalist*, No. 40, Mr. Madison explained the basic principles of the Constitution of 1787 in these words:

> I ask, What are these principles? Do they require that in the establishment of the Constitution the States should be regarded as distinct and independent sovereigns? They are so regarded by the Constitution proposed....
>
> The truth is that the great principles of the Constitution proposed by the Convention may be considered less as absolutely new than as the expansion of principles which are found in the Articles of Confederation. [11]

Parting Thoughts

Setting aside the additional remarks made by each debater at the conclusion of the great debate, the Webster-Hayne Debate of 1830 consisted to two main speeches by each of the two primary debaters. At the end of the second speeches made by Robert Y. Hayne and Daniel Webster, each Senator con-

[10] Warren L. McFerran, "States' Rights: Foundation of the Federal Republic," *The New American*, June 6, 1988, quoted on p. 32.
[11] *Ibid.*, quoted on p. 32.

cluded with a parting thought. As these parting thoughts are illustrative of the real differences between the two schools of thought, we should conclude our analysis of this great debate by comparing and contrasting the final sentiments expressed by each debater.

Senator Hayne ended his second speech with a quotation from Burke that emphasized the primary importance of the rights of man: "You must pardon something to the spirit of liberty." Senator Webster concluded his second reply by emphasizing the equivalence of liberty and government: "Liberty *and* Union, now and for ever, one and inseparable!"

It is of interest to note that, just a few months after the Webster-Hayne Debate, on April 13, 1830, the Democratic Party held its Jefferson Day dinner. At that function, President Andrew Jackson proposed a toast: "Our Federal Union – it must be preserved." [12] In response, John C. Calhoun proposed another toast: "The Union – next to our liberty, the most dear." [13]

What we see in these four expressions of sentiment are two opposing and clashing conceptions that go to the very *ends* and *means* of American civilization. According to the American Theory of Government, the reason why mankind left the State of Nature and joined together in body politics or sovereign States, was to provide greater security for their inalienable rights to life, liberty, and property. The primary *means* to accomplish that great *end* of civilization was the institution of government. Stated concisely, the chief end of civil society is the perpetuation of liberty, and the chief means to accomplish that objective is government. And whenever that government fails to achieve the objective, or becomes itself a threat to liberty, that government can and should be abolished and replaced by another political institution that will more effectively accomplish the great end of civilization. This, as the reader undoubtedly perceives, is precisely the concept maintained in the very opening passages of the Declaration of Independence.

The thirteen original sovereign States initially united under the Articles of Confederation, in which the Union was formally declared to be *perpetual*. That "perpetual" Union lasted less than a decade. Determining that the then-existing Federal Union did not fulfill their needs, the States resolved to terminate that Union and establish a new Union under a new Federal Constitution. But this time, they wisely refrained from proclaiming the new Union to be perpetual within the new compact.

Both Senator Hayne, in the parting sentiment of his second speech, and Vice President Calhoun, at the 1830 Jefferson Day dinner, expressed the true American Theory of Government, which declares that it is *liberty* that must be

---

[12] William D. Crane, *Patriotic Rebel: John C. Calhoun*, Julian Messner, New York, 1972, quoted on p. 87.

[13] *Ibid.*, quoted on p. 87.

perpetuated at all costs, not *government*. Senator Webster, in his parting sentiment, and President Jackson, in his toast, reversed the concept and declared that, in essence, it was the perpetuation of the Government of the United States that must be considered the great end of American civilization.

Daniel Webster, it is true, did include liberty in his concept of the great end of American civilization, but by also including the perpetuation of the Government of the United States as an identical end, he nullified liberty. Had the Senator said something to this effect – "Liberty *and* Union, now and forever, let us hope that they shall be one and inseparable!" or "Long may the Union be the safeguard of our liberty" – then his expressed sentiment would have accorded with the American Theory of Government. But he did not express such a sentiment. He stated that liberty and government are identical, that liberty was a captive of the Federal Government, and that the only thing that mattered was the perpetual existence of the Federal Union and its supremely magnificent government. When President Andrew Jackson made his toast a few months later, he dropped liberty from the sentiment altogether.

As is apparent, the States' Rights School of Thought was established on sentiments that properly regard the preservation of the natural rights of man as the great and chief end of American civilization, while assigning to government its proper role as merely a means to that end. The Consolidating School of Thought, on the other hand, has ever espoused the principle that the Federal Union and the Federal Government are ends unto themselves, and that they must be perpetuated even at the expense of liberty itself. From such poisoned waters as these flow despotism and tyranny.

From the moment the great Webster-Hayne Debate of 1830 ended, those who adore power sought to immortalize the concluding sentiment espoused by Daniel Webster. American school children recited his words as though his parting sentiment was a thing of wondrous beauty. It would perhaps be a public service were we to offer a counter sentiment in the name of liberty. We therefore conclude our analysis of the Webster-Hayne Debate with these words of wisdom, written by the Father of the States' Rights School, Thomas Jefferson:

> *Resolved,* That...it would be a dangerous delusion were a confidence in the men of our choice to silence our fears for the safety of our rights; that confidence is everywhere the parent of despotism – free government is founded in jealousy, and not in confidence; it is jealousy and not confidence which prescribes limited Constitutions, to bind down those whom we are obliged to trust with power; that our Constitution has accordingly fixed the limits to which, and no further, our confidence may go....In questions of power, then, let no more be heard of confidence in man, but bind him down

from mischief by the chains of the Constitution. [14]

[14] Alexander H. Stephens, *Op. cit.*, Volume 1, p. 573.

Chapter Ten

The Webster-Calhoun Debate

Three years after the famous Webster-Hayne Debate of 1830, another great debate occurred within the Senate of the United States that explored in depth the organic nature of the Federal Union. Although the two leading debaters in the second great debate represented the same States as in the previous one – Massachusetts and South Carolina – only one of the debaters remained unchanged. As before, Senator Daniel Webster spoke on behalf of the Consolidating School of Thought. Representing the States' Rights School of Thought was John Caldwell Calhoun, one of the most brilliant political theorists the United States has ever produced.

We have already introduced Daniel Webster, who was originally from New Hampshire and, after entering politics, relocated to Massachusetts. The Massachusetts politician had been a diehard supporter of Alexander Hamilton's Federalist Party until it finally expired, then supported the election of John Quincy Adams to the Presidency, and subsequently helped to form the Whig Party. Although Mr. Webster aspired to the Presidency himself, it was an ambition that was never realized. It was as a United States Senator that the Massachusetts politician achieved his greatest claim to fame, and his idolization as the Orator of Consolidation resulted from his role in the Webster-Hayne Debate of 1830.

Senator Webster's personal life was as unethical as the constitutional theories he advocated, and his willingness to accept financial rewards for his votes and political support is a matter of historical record. From the moment he entered politics, Daniel Webster was a thoroughgoing "sectional man," always considering the concerns of influential special interest groups in his section of the Union above the interests of the United States in general. It was his stated view and practice that the powers of the Government of the United States should be substantially enlarged by usurpation and false constructions of the Constitution, and that those powers should be used to pilfer the pockets of the American people for the benefit of favored special interests. He was an enthusiastic supporter of Henry Clay's *un-American* American System, the socialist system of redistribution of wealth based on protective tariffs and federal subsidies for internal improvements. And through his unethical association with and support of the Second Bank of the United States, the Massachusetts politician was closely linked with the monied aristocracy.

As an orator, Daniel Webster was a dynamic speaker who was especially gifted at uttering generalized statements that rang patriotic to the uniformed ear. But he always encountered difficulty whenever he attempted to descend from lofty generalities into specific details. The historical facts required to sustain his contentions simply did not exist, and the theories he espoused lacked sufficient logic to withstand close scrutiny. The fallacies of his espoused theories, although evident in the 1830 debate with Senator Hayne, became even more apparent in the Webster-Calhoun Debate of 1833, which focused greater attention on the nature of the Federal Union. As historian Richard N. Current noted in his book, *John C. Calhoun*, "though less colorful and less celebrated than the Webster-Hayne Debate three years earlier," the Webster-Calhoun Debate of 1833 "exposed the issues far more thoroughly." [1]

The Orator of States' Rights

In his biography of the statesman from South Carolina, Professor Richard N. Current observed:

> For approximately the first third of his career he was a nationalist who urged the bold use of governmental powers to develop and strengthen the country as a whole. For the remaining two-thirds, he was a State-rights man and a sectionalist who strove to limit the powers of the Federal Government and thus protect the interests of the South. [2]

Like his counterpart in the consolidating school, Daniel Webster, John C. Calhoun began his career in politics as an advocate of principles and causes he would later come to oppose. This fact is much more than a mere coincidence, for the reversal of the political views of both Mr. Webster and Mr. Calhoun reveals much about their guiding motivations.

As we have observed previously, Daniel Webster entered politics at a time when the States' Rights school held a controlling influence over the Government of the United States. Like the other Federalists of New England at the time, Mr. Webster was an ardent sectionalist, advocating a strong jealousy toward nearly every act of the Federal Government, and was guided by the *pecuniary* interests based in his quarter of the Union. When the interests of this monied aristocracy changed to favor an all-powerful Federal Government, Mr.

---

[1] Richard N. Current, *John C. Calhoun*, Washington Square Press, Inc., New York, 1963, p. 17.

[2] *Ibid.*, p. 4.

Webster underwent a quick change of "principles" to sustain the desires of that pecuniary interest.

John C. Calhoun also entered politics when the States' Rights school held the reins of power in Washington, D.C. Since the Southern States were not threatened at the time, Mr. Calhoun quickly developed a "nationalistic" outlook, eager to always promote what he regarded as the welfare and good of the United States as a whole. His desire was never to enrich his own section of the Union at the expense of another section, but only to promote the interests of all sections. Whereas Mr. Webster had supported the treasonous elements in New England during the War of 1812, Mr. Calhoun was a patriotic supporter of America's rights in the world. And as Professor Current noted, "After the return of peace, Calhoun rose to be majority leader of the Jeffersonian Republicans in the House." [3]

The South Carolina statesman rose higher and higher within the offices of the Federal Government. He served as the Secretary of War in the Cabinet of President James Monroe, and served as Vice-President in the Administration of President John Quincy Adams. He was also Vice-President of the United States during the Administration of President Andrew Jackson, although he resigned from that office to assume a seat in the Senate of the United States, where his voice could be better heard on behalf of the States' Rights School of Thought.

Due to his patriotic desires in the early years of his political career, Mr. Calhoun failed to comprehend the potential dangers of an energetic government. And while some highly principled members of the States' Rights School of Thought, such as John Randolph of Roanoke, continuously warned against the dangerous trend toward consolidation, Mr. Calhoun initially failed to share their foresight. It was only when the consolidating school introduced their American System that he realized the dangers inherent in consolidation and terminated the nationalistic phase of his career.

As Richard N. Current noted in his biography of the South Carolina statesman:

> While Southerners were turning against the tariff (and internal improvements as well), New Englanders were coming to its support. Among New Englanders, as among Southerners, ideas changed with changing interests. A majority of New England representatives, including Daniel Webster, had voted against the Tariff of 1816, because the predominant interest of their region then lay in the shipping business, in the import trade. [4]

---

[3] *Ibid.*, p. 7.
[4] *Ibid.*, p. 11.

John C. Calhoun's conversion to the States' Rights School of Thought, as noted previously, began during the Administration of President John Quincy Adams, when the American System of Henry Clay was first introduced. With the adoption of the *Tariff of Abominations* in 1828, Mr. Calhoun, like nearly all Southerners, became greatly alarmed at the rapid strides being made to convert the Federal Government into an instrument for the socialistic redistribution of wealth. In that same year, he anonymously authored the South Carolina *Exposition* to protest against the corrupt and unconstitutional economic system of the Federal Government.

During the Webster-Hayne Debate of 1830, Vice-President Calhoun was serving as the President of the Senate. Occupying that chair, he could merely listen to the debaters espouse their respective theories of government, for the procedural rules of the Senate did not allow the Senate President to enter into the debate. A few months later, at the Jefferson Day dinner held by the Democratic Party, Mr. Calhoun proposed his famous alternative toast in support of the need to perpetuate liberty in response to President Jackson's toast on the need to perpetuate the Union.

By 1832, John C. Calhoun had become the universally acknowledged leader of the States' Rights School of Thought, following in the footsteps of his predecessor, Thomas Jefferson, who had died six years earlier. In December of that year, the South Carolina statesman resigned from the Vice-Presidency and was elected to the United States Senate to fill the seat vacated by Robert Y. Hayne, who had left the Senate to become Governor of South Carolina.

Following Mr. Calhoun's election to the U.S. Senate, it was inevitable that a great debate between him and Senator Webster would occur. The controversy over protective tariffs had reached a climax. South Carolina had just issued a Proclamation of Nullification, and President Andrew Jackson was entertaining the idea of using federal coercion to force that sovereign State to submit to the Federal Government. It was this contemplated use of federal force against a sovereign State that provided the background for the great Webster-Calhoun Debate of 1833. And it was the masterful expounding of the Federal Constitution by John C. Calhoun during that debate that established his reputation as the great *Orator of States' Rights*.

Although the principles espoused by Senator Calhoun during the debate, as we shall discover, were found upon the everlasting rock of truth, there are those who are willing to dismiss everything he said simply because the Southern States were subsequently defeated in the War Between the States. This is a view shared even by his biographer, Richard N. Current, who asserted that, "After the Civil War the reputation of Calhoun declined....His theories, it seemed, had been put to the test of battle, and they had failed the test." [5]

It scarcely needs to be mentioned that this excuse for summarily dismissing the great principles of States' Rights espoused by Senator Calhoun is palpably shallow and devoid of moral substance. Stating the matter bluntly, the idea that *might makes right* is the reasoning of savages, not of civilized men. Any "test of battle," if battle can ever be considered a test of anything, is decided by the *military might* and *military strategy* of the contending forces, not by their moral values or constitutional principles. To those who adore power, the *test of battle* will always be conclusive in the affairs of man. But to those who cherish truth, the *test of reason* is the only true guide for deciding right.

The Calhoun Resolutions

By 1832, the Federal Union faced a dire crisis. The sovereign State of South Carolina had solemnly resolved to interpose its authority and nullify an abominable protective tariff act of the Federal Government. Other Southern States, although generally supportive of States' Rights and cognizant of the unfair effects of the American System, reacted with an overabundance of caution and refused to openly support their sister State. In Washington, D.C., rumors abounded that President Andrew Jackson would order the arrest of John C. Calhoun. Another rumor circulated that the President wanted to invade South Carolina with an army to crush the nullifiers and conquer that sovereign State, thereby inaugurating a War Between the States and the destruction of both our republican form of government and our federal system. Adding to the general alarm throughout the Union, Congress entertained legislation, generally referred to as the *Force Bill*, which would supposedly justify precisely such drastic actions.

The people of South Carolina, however, courageously refused to be intimidated by such threats of invasion and conquest, and patriotically held their ground. In the Senate of the United States, all eyes turned toward John C. Calhoun, the universally recognized intellectual behind the resistance offered to federal usurpations of power by the sovereign State of South Carolina. The Senate did not have long to wait for Senator Calhoun to make his move.

On January 22, 1833, just one day after the despotic Force Bill had been enacted, John C. Calhoun introduced a set of Resolutions in the United States Senate. During the course of the general proceedings of the Senate, Daniel Webster called for a reading of the Calhoun Resolutions on February 16th of that year, clearly indicating that he wished to challenge the principles espoused

---

[5] *Ibid.*, pp. 136-137.

by those resolutions.

These Calhoun Resolutions of 1833 declared:

> *Resolved*, That the people of the several States, composing these United States, are united as Parties to a Constitutional Compact, to which the people of each State acceded as a separate sovereign community, each binding itself by its own particular ratification; and that the Union, of which the said compact is the bond, is a Union *between the States* ratifying the same.
>
> *Resolved*, That the people of the several States, thus united by the Constitutional Compact, in forming that instrument, and in creating a general government to carry into effect the objects for which they were formed, delegated to that government, for that purpose, certain definite powers, to be exercised jointly, reserving, at the same time, each State to itself, the residuary mass of powers, to be exercised by its own separate government; and that whenever the general government assumes the exercise of powers not delegated by the compact, its acts are unauthorized, and are of no effect; and that the same government is not made the final judge of the powers delegated to it, since that would make its discretion, and not the Constitution, the measure of its powers; but that, as in all other cases of compact among sovereign parties, without any common judge, each has an equal right to judge for itself, as well of the infraction as of the mode and measure of redress.
>
> *Resolved*, That the assertions, that the people of these United States, taken collectively as individuals, are now, or ever have been, united on the principle of the social compact, and, as such, are now formed into one Nation or people, or that they have ever been so united in any one stage of their political existence; that the people of the several States composing the Union have not, as members thereof, retained their sovereignty; that the allegiance of their citizens has been transferred to the general government; that they have parted with the right of punishing treason through their respective State governments; and that they have not the right of judging in the last resort as to the extent of the powers reserved, and of consequence of those delegated, – are not only without foundation in truth, but are contrary to the most certain and plain historical facts, and the clearest deductions of reason; and that all exercise of power on the part of the general government, or any of its departments, claiming authority from such erroneous assumptions, must of necessity be unconstitutional, – must tend, directly and inevitably, to subvert the sovereignty of the States, to destroy the federal character of the Union, and to rear on its ruins a consolidated government, without Constitutional check or limitation, and which must necessarily terminate in the loss of liberty itself. [6]

All the principles contained within these Calhoun Resolutions of 1833 are undeniably true, for they are based on proven historical facts and sound reason. Yet, the Consolidating School of Thought had no intention of acknowl-

[6] Alexander H. Stephens, *A Constitutional View of the Late War Between the States; Its Causes, Character, Conduct and Results*, Volume 1, Kraus Reprint Co., New York, 1970 (orig. pub. 1868), quoted on pp. 299-300.

edging the truth or of allowing the truth to go unchallenged. To have allowed the Calhoun Resolutions of 1833 to go unchallenged would have been to forfeit their own so-called principles and theories of government. Daniel Webster of Massachusetts therefore arose in the United States Senate to call into question the very foundation of these resolutions. Thus began the famous Webster-Calhoun Debate of 1833, which was, in truth, the most significant debate ever held in the Senate of the United States, a debate that fully explored the very nature of the American system of government.

Initial Remarks by Senator Webster

In his initial remarks on the Calhoun Resolutions, Daniel Webster made these observations:

> The Resolutions introduced by the Gentleman, were apparently drawn up with care, and brought forward upon deliberation. I shall not be in danger, therefore, of misunderstanding him, or those who agree with him, if I proceed at once to these Resolutions, and consider them as an authentic statement of those opinions upon which the great Constitutional question, by which the proceedings in South Carolina are attempted to be justified.
>
> These Resolutions are three in number.
>
> The third seems intended to enumerate, and to deny, the several opinions expressed in the President's proclamation, respecting the nature and powers of this government. On this third Resolution, I purpose, to take no particular notice.
>
> The first two Resolutions of the honorable member affirm these positions, viz.: –
>
> 1. That the political system under which we live, and under which Congress is now assembled, is a Compact, to which the people of the several States, as separate and sovereign communities, are the parties.
>
> 2. That these sovereign parties have a right to judge, each for itself, of any alleged violation of the Constitution by Congress; and in case of such violation, to choose, each for itself, its own mode and measure of redress.
>
> It is true, Sir, that the honorable member calls this a "Constitutional" Compact; but still he affirms it to be a Compact between sovereign States. What precise meaning, then, does he attach to the term *Constitutional*? When applied to Compacts between sovereign States, the term *Constitutional* affixes to the word *Compact* no definite idea. Were we to hear of a Constitutional league or treaty between England and France, or a Constitutional Convention between Austria and Russia, we should not understand what could be intended by such a league, such a treaty, or such a Convention. In these connections, the word is void of all meaning; and yet, sir, it is easy, quite easy, to see why the Honorable Gentleman has used it in these Resolutions. He cannot open the book, and look upon our written frame of gov-

ernment, without seeing that it is called a *Constitution*. This may be appalling to him. It threatens his whole doctrine of Compact....Because, if he admits our instrument of government to be a *Constitution*, then, for that very reason, it is not a Compact between sovereigns; a Constitution of government and a Compact between sovereign powers being things essentially unlike in their very natures, and incapable of ever being the same. Yet the word Constitution is on the very front of the instrument. He cannot overlook it....He introduces a new word of his own, viz., Compact, as importing the principal idea, and designed to play the principal part, and degrades *Constitution* into an insignificant, idle epithet, attached to *Compact*. The whole then stands as a *"Constitutional Compact!"*...Sir, we reject this new rules of syntax altogether....By the Constitution, we mean, not a "Constitutional Compact," but, simply and directly, the Constitution, the fundamental law; and if there be one word in the language which the people of the United States understand, this is that word....

...The proposition still is, that our system of government is but a Compact between the people of separate and sovereign States.

...[A] just conclusion is often avoided, or a false one reached, by the adroit substitution of one phrase, or one word, for another. Of this, we have, I think, another example in the Resolutions before us.

The first Resolution declares that the people of the several States "acceded" to the Constitution, or to the Constitutional Compact, as it is called. This word "accede," not found in either the Constitution itself, or in the ratification of it by any one of the States, has been chosen for use here, doubtless, not without a well-considered purpose.

The natural converse of *accession* is *secession*; and, therefore, when it is stated that the people of the States acceded to the Union, it may be more plausibly argued that they may secede from it. If, in adopting the Constitution, nothing was done but acceding to a Compact, nothing would seem necessary, to break it up, but to secede from the same Compact. But the term is wholly out of place. Accession, as a word applied to political associations, implies coming into a league, treaty, or confederacy, by one hitherto a stranger to it; and secession implies departing from such league or confederacy. The people of the United States have used no such form of expression in establishing the present government. They do not say that they *accede* to a league, but they declare that they *ordain and establish* a Constitution. Such are the very words of the instrument itself; and in all the States, without an exception, the language used by their Convention was, that they "*ratified the* Constitution;" some of them employing the additional words "assented to" and "adopted," but all of them "ratifying."

There is more importance than may, at first sight, appear, in the introduction of this new word by the honorable mover of these Resolutions. Its adoption and use are indispensable to maintain those premises from which his main conclusion is to be afterwards drawn. But before showing that, allow me to remark, that this phraseology tends to keep out of sight the just view of a previous political history, as well as to suggest wrong ideas as to what was actually done when the present Constitution was agreed to....[A]s far back as the meeting of the first Congress, in 1774, they had been, in some

> measure, and for some National purposes, united together. Before the Confederation of 1781, they had declared independence jointly, and had carried on the war jointly, both by sea and land; and this not as separate States, but as one people. When, therefore, they formed that Confederation, and adopted its articles as articles of perpetual Union, they did not come together for the first time; and, therefore, they did not speak of the States as *acceding* to the Confederation, although it was a league, and rested on nothing but plighted faith for its performance....
>
> Having thus used the terms *ratify* and *confirm*, even in regard to the old Confederation, it would have been strange, indeed, if the people of the United States, after its formation, and when they came to establish the present Constitution, had spoken of the States, or the people of the States, as *acceding* to this Constitution....
>
> Therefore, Sir, since any State, before she can prove her right to dissolve the Union, must show her authority to undo what has been done; no State is at liberty to *secede*, on the ground that she and other States have done nothing but *accede*....
>
> If, Mr. President, in drawing these Resolutions, the honorable member had confined himself to the use of Constitutional language, there would have been a wide and awful *hiatus* between his premises and his conclusion. Leaving out the two words *Compact* and *accession*, which are not Constitutional modes of expression, and stating the matter precisely as the truth is, his first Resolution would have affirmed that *the people of the several States ratified this Constitution, or form of government*. These are the very words of South Carolina herself, in her act of ratification. Let, then his first Resolution tell the exact truth; let it state the fact precisely as it exists; let it say that the people of the several States ratified a Constitution, or form of government, and then, Sir, what will become of his inference in his second Resolution, which is in these words, viz.: "That, as in all other cases of Compact among sovereign parties, each has an equal right to judge for itself, as well of the infraction as of the mode and measure of redress?" It is obvious, is it not, Sir? that this conclusion requires for its support quite other premises; it requires premises which speak of *accession* and of *Compact* between sovereign powers; and, without such premises, it is altogether unmeaning....
>
> ...This is the reason, Sir, which makes it necessary to abandon the use of Constitutional language for a new vocabulary, and to substitute, in the place of plain historical facts, a series of assumptions. This is the reason why it is necessary to give new names to things, to speak of the Constitution, not as a Constitution, but as a Compact, and of the ratifications by the people, not as ratifications, but as acts of accession. [7]

Daniel Webster had more to say in his speech on the Calhoun Resolutions, but at this point we should pause to give due reflection upon the points raised in his initial remarks. The Orator of Consolidation called into question the use of such terms as *compact* and *accede* in reference to the Federal Consti-

---

[7] *Ibid.*, Volume 1, quoted on pp. 301-308.

tution, stating that such terminology was invented by Senator Calhoun and wholly inapplicable to our federal compact. Of course, the notion that the Constitution of the United States is a compact to which the States are *parties* is inherent in the theory of State sovereignty. But in their zeal to deny the existence of sovereign States, the consolidating school – as exemplified by the Senator from Massachusetts – has ever insisted that such a notion, while applicable under the Articles of Confederation, is nonsense under our present U.S. Constitution.

Senator Webster's argument against the compact nature of our constitutional federation was not limited to the Webster-Calhoun Debate of 1833. In his rebuttal to Senator Robert Y. Hayne on January 27, 1830, the Senator from Massachusetts had made a similar argument:

> So much, Sir, for the argument, even if the premises of the gentleman were granted, or could be proved. But, Sir, the gentleman has failed to maintain his leading proposition. He has not shown – it cannot be shown – that the Constitution is a *Compact*....The Constitution itself, in its very front, refutes the proposition; it declares that it is ordained and established by the people of the United States....[I]t does not even say that it is established by the people of the several States; but it pronounces that it is established by the people of the United States, *in the aggregate*. The gentleman says, it must mean no more than that the people of the several States, taken collectively, constitute the people of the United States....[I]t is as all the people of the United States that they establish the Constitution....
>
> When the gentleman says, the Constitution is a *Compact between the States*, he uses language exactly applicable to the old Confederation. He speaks as if he were in Congress before 1789. He describes fully that old state of things then existing. The Confederation was, in strictness, a *Compact*; the States, as States, *were parties to it*. We had no other general government. But that was found insufficient and inadequate to the public exigencies. The people were not satisfied with it, and undertook to establish a better. They undertook to form a general government, *which should stand on a new basis – not a Confederacy, not a league, not a Compact between States*, but a Constitution. [emphasis added] [8]

Three years later – in 1833 – in his debate with Senator John C. Calhoun of South Carolina, Daniel Webster again denied that the Federal Constitution was a compact between the States, and that the States were the parties to that compact or agreement:

> *Does it call itself a Compact?* Certainly not. It uses the word "Compact" but once, and that when it declares that the States shall enter into no

[8] Jonathan Elliot (ed.), *Elliot's Debates*, Volume 4, Published under the Sanction of Congress, Washington, 1836, p. 518.

> Compact. Does it call itself a league, a confederacy, a subsisting treaty between the States? Certainly not. There is not a particle of such language in all its pages. [emphasis added] [9]

Is this a valid argument? Is it a requirement that, before we may utilize a term to refer to or describe anything, that the item being referred to must have that term stamped upon it? Is a book still a book if it fails to expressly identify itself as such by stating, "This is a book"? Is it improper to refer to a car as an automobile unless it has etched on its side in chrome letters, "This is an automobile"? How is it possible for us to refer to a horse as a horse, unless it has the words, "This is a horse," branded on its hide? How can we refer to the *Iliad* and the *Aeneid* as "epic poems," when they nowhere term themselves to be such? Simply because the Federal Constitution does not describe itself or the Federal Union by such terms as *compact*, *confederacy*, or *league of States*, does not mean that it is not a compact that established a Confederacy for a league of sovereign States.

The concept of the Federal Constitution being a compact, or pact, is derived from the fact that it is a solemn *agreement* or *understanding* between the sovereign States, who are the parties to it. The Constitution, as many historians rightly attest, represents a *bundle of compromises* between the original thirteen States. The Constitutional Convention *could* have worded the Preamble of the Constitution, as follows, without altering either fact or theory, for such a statement would have been explicitly truthful: "We the peoples of the several States comprising the United States of America hereby establish this Constitution for ourselves and our posterity, and this Constitution constitutes an agreement amongst ourselves on the structure of the Federal Government established by it, and on the powers delegated by it to that government." This is the idea behind references to the Federal Constitution as a *compact* between the States.

In addition to the term compact, Senator Daniel Webster attacked the usage of the term "accede" in his address on the Calhoun Resolutions of 1833:

> This word "accede," not found either in the Constitution itself or in the ratification of it by any one of the States, has been chosen for use here, doubtless not without a well-considered purpose. *The natural converse of accession is secession*; and therefore, when it is stated that the people of the States *acceded* to the Union, it may be more plausibly argued that *they may secede from it.* If, in adopting the Constitution, nothing more was done but *acceding to a Compact*, nothing would seem necessary, in order to break it up, but to secede from the same *Compact. But the term is wholly out of place. Accession*, as

[9] Jefferson Davis, *The Rise and Fall of the Confederate Government*, Volume 1, Thomas Yoseloff, New York, 1958 (orig. pub. 1881), quoted on p. 135.

> a word applied to political associations, *implies coming into a league, treaty, or confederacy*. The people of the United States have used no such forms of expression in establishing the present government. [emphasis added] [10]

Thus, concluded Senator Webster:

> This is the reason, Sir, which makes it necessary to abandon the use of constitutional language for *a new vocabulary*, and to substitute, in the place of plain, historical facts, *a series of assumptions*. This is the reason why it is necessary to give *new names* to things; to speak of the Constitution, not as a constitution, but as a *Compact*; and of the ratifications by the people, not as ratifications, but as *acts of accession*. [emphasis added] [11]

Is there really a difference in meaning between the terms *ratify*, *assent*, and *accede*, as claimed by Daniel Webster? Were the two terms in question – compact and accede – used by our Founding Fathers in reference to our present Federal Constitution? Or were those terms, as Senator Webster insisted, the invention of John C. Calhoun, thus constituting a *new vocabulary*?

According to *Webster's II New Riverside University Dictionary*, which was published in 1984, the word *ratify* means, "To give formal sanction or approval to and thereby validate." [12] The same dictionary defines the intransitive verb *assent* as meaning, "To express agreement: CONCUR." [13] The Constitution itself employs the former verb, and Daniel Webster acknowledged that the State acts of ratification contained, in some instances, both of these verbs.

Does the word "accede" convey a meaning different from the ones conveyed by the other two words? According to the same dictionary, *accede* means, "1. To give consent. 2. To come into an office or dignity. 3. To become a party to an agreement or treaty." [14] The third definition is especially applicable to our Federal Constitution *if it truly is a compact between sovereign States*. As Senator Webster correctly noted, the terms *compact* and *accede* are quite compatible with one another.

The Third Edition of *Roget's International Thesaurus* associates the word "assent" with the following synonyms: *acquiesce*, *accede*, *agree*, *accept*, *subscribe to*, *say yes to*, *consent*, *concur*, *go along with*, *shake hands on*, *ratify*, *endorse*, *validate*, *accept*, *approve*, *pass*, and *grant*. [15] Thus, the words "ratify," "assent," and "accede" may be regarded as synonymous. The latter term would apply to the adoption of our present Federal Constitution with great significance if the

---

[10] *Ibid.*, Volume 1, quoted on pp. 136-137.
[11] *Ibid.*, Volume 1, quoted on p. 137.
[12] *Webster's II New Riverside University Dictionary*, The Riverside Publishing Company, Boston, 1984, p. 976.
[13] *Ibid.*, p. 131.
[14] *Ibid.*, p. 70.
[15] *Roget's International Thesaurus*, Third Edition, Thomas Y. Crowell Company, New York, 1962, p. 339.

Founding Fathers understood that instrument to be a compact among sovereign States.

The Constitution of the United States provides for its own adoption by the States in the following language: "The *ratification* of the Conventions of nine States shall be sufficient for the establishment of this Constitution between the States so *ratifying* the same." [16] The two words herein italicized must be connected and associated with the concept of establishing the compact *between the States*. The very nature of the Federal Union established by the Constitution reveals that the acts of ratification on the part of the States were truly acts of accession. We might also add that the term in question – ratification – was also employed in the Articles of Confederation, which even Daniel Webster conceded was a compact between the sovereign States who acceded to it.

An examination of the papers of our Founding Fathers reveals that they certainly understood the words "compact" and "accede" to be applicable to our present Federal Constitution. Elbridge Gerry of Massachusetts, for example, said before the Philadelphia Convention of 1787 that, "If nine out of thirteen States can dissolve the *compact*, six out of nine will be just as able to dissolve *the new one* hereafter." [17] James Madison, widely regarded as the Father of the Constitution, declared that, "In the case of a union of people under one Constitution, the nature of *the pact* has always been understood." [18] Even Alexander Hamilton, the founder of the Consolidating School of Thought, spoke of the Federal Constitution as a "compact" in the *Federalist*, Nos. 9 and 85.

Gouverneur Morris of Pennsylvania, a strong advocate of consolidation at the Federal Convention, is recorded in James Madison's records of the Convention's proceedings as having said:

> He came here to form a *compact* for the good of Americans. He was ready to do so with all the States. He hoped and believed all would enter into such a *compact*. If they would not, he would be ready to join with any States that would. But, as the *compact* was to be voluntary, it is in vain for the Eastern States to insist on what the Southern States will never agree to. [19]

In the Constitutional Convention of 1787, Luther Martin of Maryland stated: "Will you tell us we ought to trust you because you now enter into a solemn *compact* with us?...Will you now make an appeal to the Supreme Being, and call on Him to guarantee your observance of this *compact*?" [20]

Both George Washington and Thomas Jefferson considered the Federal

---

[16] Alexander H. Stephens, *Op. cit.*, Volume 1, p. 566,

[17] Jefferson Davis, *Op. cit.*, Volume 1, quoted on p. 137.

[18] *Ibid.*, Volume 1, quoted on p. 138.

[19] *Ibid.*, Volume 1, quoted on pp. 137-138.

[20] *Ibid.*, Volume 1, quoted on p. 138,

Constitution to be a *compact* between sovereign States. In his correspondence during the period of ratification, the Father of His Country repeatedly used the terms "accede" and "accession," and once used the term "secession." With regard to the great struggle in Virginia over ratification, for instance, George Washington inquired as to what course his own State would pursue "if nine other States should *accede* to the Constitution." [21]

In the famous Kentucky Resolutions of 1798, written by Thomas Jefferson on behalf of that sovereign State, Mr. Jefferson asserted:

> ...[T]he several States composing the United States of America, are not united on the principle of unlimited submission to their general government; but that by *compact* under the style and title of the Constitution of the United States and of amendments thereto, they constituted a general government for special purposes, *delegated* to that government certain definite powers, reserving each State to itself, the residuary mass of right to their own self-government.... [22]

The views of the Father of the States' Rights School never altered, and in 1825 – some 27 years after penning the Kentucky Resolutions cited above – he wrote a stirring protest on behalf of the State of Virginia in an effort to warn against the evils of consolidation. This protest was entitled, "The Solemn Declaration and Protest of the Commonwealth of Virginia, on the Principles of the Constitution of the United States of America, and on the Violations of Them."

Within this official document, Thomas Jefferson declared:

> The States in North America which confederated to establish their independence of the government of Great Britain, of which Virginia was one, became, on that acquisition, *free and independent States*, and as such, authorized to constitute governments, each for itself, in such form as it thought best.
>
> They entered into a *compact* (which is called the Constitution of the United States of America), by which they agreed to unite in a single government as to their relations with each other, and with foreign nations, and as to certain other articles particularly specified. They retained at the same time, each to itself, the other rights of *independent* government, comprehending mainly their domestic interests. [23]

Just five years after Thomas Jefferson had penned this declaration for the State of Virginia, Daniel Webster – in his debate with Senator Robert Y. Hayne – arose in the United States Senate to declare:

---

[21] *Ibid.*, Volume 1, quoted on p. 138.

[22] Harold C. Syrett (ed.), *American Historical Documents*, Barnes & Noble, Inc., New York, 1960, p. 148.

[23] Warren L. McFerran, *The Constitutional Principles of Thomas Jefferson*, Southern Liberty Press, 1976, quoted on p. 23.

> So much, Sir, for the argument, even if the premises of the gentleman were granted, or could be proved. But, Sir, the gentleman has failed to maintain his leading proposition. He has not shown – *it cannot be shown* – that the Constitution is a *compact*.... [24]

Three years later – during the Webster-Calhoun Debate – Senator Webster inquired, "Does it call itself a *compact*?" His own answer was, "Certainly not." Terms such as *compact* and *accession*, he proclaimed, comprised "new names" and a "new vocabulary." "The people of the United States have used no such form of expression in establishing the present government," he solemnly insisted. Although he willingly admitted that such terms implied the "coming into a league, treaty, or confederation," he staunchly asserted that such terminology had never been employed by the Founding Fathers of the United States.

Either the Senator from Massachusetts was ignorant – which hardly seems likely, considering his prominence as a lawyer – or else he did not consider the Father of His Country, the Author of the Declaration of Independence, the Father of the Constitution, the authors of the *Federalist Papers*, the delegates to the Constitutional Convention of 1787, and the members of the various State Ratifying Conventions to be among the Founding Fathers of the United States!

We have two more items of proof from the Ratification Period that will further refute the arguments made by Daniel Webster in his debate on the Calhoun Resolutions of 1833. One is the official act of ratification of the Constitution by his State of nativity, New Hampshire. The other is the official act of ratification by his adopted State of Massachusetts. In both acts, the term "compact" was employed!

The official ratification of our present Federal Constitution by the State of Massachusetts is in the following words:

> The Convention, having impartially discussed and fully considered a Constitution for the United States of America, reported to Congress by the Convention of delegates from the United States of America, and submitted to us by a resolution of the General Court of the said Commonwealth, passed the 25th day of October last past, and acknowledging with grateful hearts the goodness of the Supreme Ruler of the universe, in affording the people of the United States, in the course of his Providence, an opportunity, deliberately and peaceably, without fraud or surprise, of entering into an explicit and solemn *compact* with each other, by assenting to and ratifying a new Constitution, in order to form a more perfect Union, establish justice, insure domestic tranquillity, provide for the common defense, promote the

---

[24] Jonathan Elliot (ed.), *Op. cit.*, Volume 4, pp. 516-518.

> general welfare, and secure the blessings of liberty to themselves and their posterity – do, in the name and in behalf of the people of the Commonwealth of Massachusetts, assent to and ratify the said Constitution for the United States of America. [25]

Thus, it was clearly understood by Daniel Webster's own State – at least by the generation that adopted the federal compact – that the States were entering into a "compact with each other" upon their decision to "assent to" the Federal Constitution. And Senator Webster's State of nativity, New Hampshire, acceded to the compact in *precisely* the same language as Massachusetts, with the only difference being the date of accession and the use of the term "State" instead of "Commonwealth."

Further Remarks by Senator Webster

During the course of his speech in the Webster-Calhoun Debate on the Calhoun Resolutions of 1833, Senator Daniel Webster made these additional remarks:

> Allow me, now, Mr. President, to inquire further into the extent of the propositions contained in the Resolutions, and their necessary consequences.
>
> Where sovereign communities are parties, there is no essential difference between a Compact, a Confederation, and a League. They all equally rest on the plighted faith of the sovereign party. A League, or Confederacy, is but a subsisting or continuing treaty.
>
> The Gentleman's Resolutions, then, affirm, in effect, that these twenty-four United States are held together only by a subsisting treaty, resting for its fulfillment and continuance on no inherent power of its own, but on the plighted faith of each State, or, in other words, that our Union is but a league....
>
> The necessary import of the Resolution, therefore, is, that the United States are connected only by a League....The result of the whole is, that any State may secede at pleasure; that any State may resist a law which she herself may choose to say exceeds the power of Congress; and that, as a sovereign power, she may redress her own grievances, by her own arms, at her own discretion....
>
> If, Sir, this be our political condition, it is time the people of the United States understood it....
>
> ...If one State may secede, ten may do so, twenty may do so, twenty-three may do so....
>
> ...The Gentleman seems not conscious of the direction or the rapid-

[25] Jefferson Davis, *Op. cit.*, Volume 1, quoted on p. 139.

> ity of his own course. The current of his opinions sweeps him along, he knows not whither....
>
> ...Sir, the Constitution of the United States was received as a whole, and for the whole country....
>
> Such, Sir, are the inevitable results of this doctrine. Beginning with the original error, that the Constitution of the United States is nothing but a Compact between sovereign States; asserting, in the next step, that each State has a right to be its own sole judge of the extent of its own obligations, and, consequently, of the Constitutionality of laws of Congress....However, it seeks to protect itself against these plain inferences, by saying that an unconstitutional law is no law, and that it only opposes such laws as are unconstitutional, yet, this does not, in the slightest degree, vary the result; since it insists on deciding this question for itself....
>
> And now, Sir, against all these theories and opinions, I maintain: –
>
> 1. That the Constitution of the United States is not a League, Confederacy or Compact, between the people of the several States in their sovereign capacities; but a government proper, founded on the adoption of the people, and creating direct relations between itself and individuals.
>
> 2. That no State authority has power to dissolve these relations; that nothing can dissolve them but revolution; and that, consequently, there can be no such thing as secession without revolution.
>
> 3. That there is a supreme law, consisting of the Constitution of the United States, and Acts of Congress, passed in pursuance of it, and treaties; and that, in cases not capable of assuming the character of a suit in law or equity, Congress must judge of, and, finally, interpret, the supreme law, so often as it has occasion to pass acts of legislation; and, in cases capable of assuming, and actually assuming, the character of a suit, the Supreme Court of the United States is the final interpreter.
>
> 4. That an attempt by a State to abrogate, annul, or nullify an Act of Congress, or to arrest its operation within her limits, on the ground that, in her opinion, such law is unconstitutional, is a direct usurpation on the just powers of the general government, and on the equal rights of other States; a plain violation of the Constitution, and a proceeding essentially Revolutionary in its character and tendency. [26]

Regarding these four consolidating doctrines enumerated by the Senator from Massachusetts, several observations are in order. The first Webster Doctrine is utterly false and groundless. His insistence that the Constitution is not a compact "between the people of the several States in their sovereign capacities," but is instead a Constitution "founded on the adoption of the people," is contradictory to plain historical fact and to the specific words of the Constitution itself. The only people who existed at the time our present Federal Constitution was adopted, and therefore the only people who could have adopted it, were the peoples of the several States. And the only manner in which those people

[26] Alexander H. Stephens, *Op. cit.*, Volume 1, quoted on pp. 308-311, 313-314, and 317-319.

could have adopted the federal compact was in their *sovereign capacities* as States. If the American people did *not* act in their sovereign capacities *as States* when adopting the Federal Constitution, then that instrument does *not* rest upon a valid foundation.

As we have previously observed, however, Article VII of the Constitution expressly declares that it was indeed adopted by the American people in their sovereign capacities as States. Furthermore, that constitutional provision asserts that the compact shall exist *between the States* that ratified it. And, by agreement among those of the generation of our Founding Fathers, all new States admitted into the Federal Union after its establishment could only be admitted on terms of sovereign equality with the original thirteen States.

The second Webster Doctrine is equally groundless and devoid of merit. Senator Webster had already conceded that, if the States *acceded* to the compact, then the obvious implication was that they had the right to *secede* from the Union. And as we have already determined, the States did in fact accede to the Constitution when they ratified it. The *right of secession* can also be logically deduced from the mere fact that the States within the Federal Union are sovereign. Furthermore, it must be remembered that some of the original States, upon ratifying the present Federal Constitution, specifically asserted the constitutional right of secession from the Union within their acts of ratification. If a State has a *right* to perform an act, then its action cannot be considered *revolutionary*.

The third Webster Doctrine is quite frankly an undisguised assertion or plea for a supreme, sovereign National Government. If any branch of the Federal Government is allowed to be the final arbiter in questions of power, then that government would usurp the sovereignty of the people. And that would truly be a *revolution* within our system of government, for it would at once subvert the very foundations of the American Theory of Government. If the Government of the United States is allowed to be the final judge as to the extent of its own powers, it would render meaningless the concept of constitutionally limited government and would allow that government to assume a boundless field of power.

Finally, the fourth Webster Doctrine asserts that, since the States are supposedly not sovereign, they have no inherent right to resist any federal act, even if such an act is dangerously unconstitutional. A mythical Nation of Americans adopted the Federal Constitution for the purpose of subduing the States, the Senator insisted, and those States have no choice but to submit to anything that the Federal Government does. Resistance to federal tyranny is revolution, and while the people, as individuals, have the right to revolt, the Government of the United States has an equal right to hang the rebels for treason. Such a doctrine as this, it hardly needs to be said, is profoundly absurd and extremely dangerous to the liberties of the American people.

Continuing with his address to the United States Senate during the course of the Webster-Calhoun Debate of 1833, the Orator of Consolidation declared:

> Whether the Constitution be a Compact between States in their sovereign capacities, is a question which must be mainly argued from what is contained in the instrument itself. We all agree that it is an instrument which has in some way been clothed with power. We all admit that it speaks with authority. The first question then is, what does it say of itself? What does it purport to be? Does it style itself a League, Confederacy, or Compact between sovereign States?...What the Constitution says of itself, therefore, is as conclusive as what it says on any other point. Does it call itself a "Compact?" Certainly not. It uses the word *Compact* but once, and that is when it declares that the States shall enter into no Compact. Does it call itself a "League," a "Confederacy," a "subsisting Treaty between the States?" Certainly not. There is not a particle of such language in all its pages. But it declares itself a Constitution....
>
> This, then, Sir, is declared to be a *Constitution*....It is as if the people had said, "We prescribe this fundamental law," or "this supreme law," for they do say that they establish this Constitution, and that it shall be the supreme law. They say that they *ordain* and *establish* it. Now, Sir, what is the common application of these words? We do not speak of *ordaining* Leagues and Compacts. If this was intended to be a Compact or League, and the States to be parties to it, why was it not so said? Why is there found no one expression, in the whole instrument, indicating such intent?...
>
> Again, Sir, the Constitution speaks of that political system which is established as "the Government of the United States." Is it not doing a strange violence to language to call a League or a Compact between sovereign powers a *government*?...The broad and clear difference between a Government and a League or Compact is, that a Government is a body politic; it has a will of its own; and it possesses powers and faculties to execute its own purposes....[A] Government executes its decisions by its own supreme authority....
>
> ...I do not agree that the Constitution is a Compact between States in their sovereign capacities. I do not agree, that, in strictness of language, it is a Compact at all....
>
> It appears to me, Mr. President, that the plainest account of the establishment of this government presents the most just and philosophical view of its foundations. The people of the several States had their separate State governments; and between the States there also existed a Confederation. With this condition of things the people were not satisfied, as the Confederation had been found not to fulfill its intended objects. It was proposed, therefore, to erect a new, common government, which should possess certain definite powers, such as regarded the prosperity of the people of all the States, and to be formed upon the general model of American Constitutions. This proposal was assented to, and an instrument was presented to the peo-

> ple of the several States for their consideration. They approved it, and agreed to adopt it, as a Constitution....Now, Sir, is not this the truth of the whole matter? And is not all that we have heard of Compact between sovereign States the mere theoretical and artificial mode of reasoning upon the subject? A mode of reasoning which disregards plain facts for the sake of hypothesis?
>
> Mr. President, the nature of sovereignty, or sovereign power, has been extensively discussed by gentlemen on this occasion, as it generally is when the origin of our government is debated....The Sovereignty of Government is an idea belonging to the other side of the Atlantic. No such thing is known in North America. Our governments are all limited....[W]ith us, all power is with the people. They alone are sovereign; and they erect what governments they please, and confer on them such powers as they please. None of these governments is sovereign, in the European sense of the word, all being restrained by Constitutions. It seems to me, therefore, that we only perplex ourselves when we attempt to explain the relations existing between the general government and the several State governments, according to those ideas of sovereignty which prevail under systems essentially different from our own.
>
> ...The maintenance of this Constitution does not depend on the plighted faith of the States, as States, to support it; and this again shows that it is not a League. It relies on individual duty and obligation.
>
> The Constitution of the United States creates direct relations between this government and individuals....Nothing, certainly, can more clearly distinguish a Government from a Confederation of States than the possession of these powers. No closer relations can exist between individuals and any government. [27]

The political views expressed by the Orator of Consolidation constitute grotesque perversions of plain historical facts and logical reasoning. The Massachusetts Senator rhetorically asked if the Constitution styled itself a league, confederacy, or compact between sovereign States. Such a contention, however, ignored the Preamble of the Constitution of the United States, which proclaimed that the federal compact was ordained and established *for* a league of sovereign body politics named the *United States of America*. That, of course, was identical to the name given to the federation of sovereign States under the Articles of Confederation, our first Federal Constitution, which defined the United States of America as a league of States whose purpose was to protect and defend the sovereignty of the several States. And as we have already observed, Article VII of our present Federal Constitution asserts that it shall exist as a compact *between the States* in the Federal Union.

Daniel Webster rhetorically asked, "Is it not doing a strange violence to language to call a League or a Compact between sovereign powers a *government*?" But even he acknowledged that the Articles of Confederation had been

---

[27] *Ibid.*, Volume 1, quoted on pp. 319-325.

a compact, forming a political league or Union between sovereign States. Thus, by his reasoning, it is a strange violence to language to refer to the Federal Government created by those Articles as a *government*. The Founding Fathers of the United States, however, thought differently. They repeatedly made reference to the "Federal Government" existing under the Articles of Confederation, proof that *they* did not deem it to be a "strange violence to language" to call the administrative authority created by a league or compact between sovereign States a government.

Senator Webster stated that the Constitution of 1787 "was presented to the people of the several States for their consideration." Furthermore, he stated that, "They approved it, and agreed to adopt it, as a Constitution." Why was the proposed Constitution submitted to the *people of the several States* for their consideration, unless those people were sovereign? Why was the proposed plan of government not submitted to an amalgamated Nation of Americans for its consideration and approval? The answer, of course, is that the proposed Constitution could not be submitted to a consolidated State of America, because no such people existed. Only the people of the several States existed, and the proposed Constitution was submitted to them because they, and they alone, were sovereign.

Daniel Webster insisted that, "No closer relations can exist between individuals and any government," than those that exist between the American people and their Federal Government. Such a concept would have astonished the Founding Fathers, for it was, beyond dispute, their intention that the State governments should be the *primary governments* within our political system. The chief duty of the Government of the United States, as established by the Federal Constitution, is to conduct the foreign affairs of the Federal Republic, a duty that has little to do with individual citizens in their daily lives. The State governments, on the other hand, are empowered with the basic duty of conducting the domestic affairs of the States, a duty that, of necessity, involves the citizenry in their individual capacities. Traffic laws, health care, welfare policies, policing the streets, marriage and family matters, education of children, human and civil rights issues, and every other concern of a personal or individual matter were all reserved to the several States by the Constitution.

At one point in his speech, the Orator of Consolidation correctly noted that, "The sovereignty of Government is an idea belonging to the other side of the Atlantic. No such thing is known in North America. Our governments are all limited." Sovereignty, he stressed was vested in the people, and not in any government. Such principles, of course, accord completely with the American Theory of Government. Yet, while admitting this truth, *as a general principle*, the Senator from Massachusetts nonetheless advocated, *in actual practice*, a supreme, sovereign National Government for the United States of America.

Within his oration, Daniel Webster asserted a very alarming concept that completely negated his general statements on behalf of the sovereignty of the people. "The broad and clear difference between a Government and a League or Compact," he proclaimed, "is, that *a Government is a body politic*; *it has a will of its own*; and it possesses powers and faculties to execute *its own powers.*" Furthermore, he insisted, "a Government executes its decisions by *its own supreme authority.*"

These statements frankly, openly, and without reservation vest sovereignty within not only the Government of the United States, but also within all other governments within our political system. By this line of reasoning, even the State governments, the county governments, and the city and town governments are sovereign, and we thus have a system of thousands of supreme governments, each one vested with sovereignty and thereby authorized to claim unlimited powers. Yet, is it true that, under the American Theory of Government, a government may execute its decisions by *its own supreme authority*? Or are those decisions executed under the *authority of the Constitution*? If the latter, then whose voice of authority speaks through the Constitution, if not the people of the sovereign States, acting in their capacities as States?

What the Orator of Consolidation was really contending for is a supreme, sovereign National Government that is, within itself, a sovereign State, and as such, empowered by *natural right* to decide for itself the extent of the powers it will exercise. Such a supremely sovereign government could lay claim to the right to control all aspects of the lives of the American people, and could demand their undivided loyalty and allegiance. Submission to such a government would be mandatory, and resistance would be revolution and treason. Such a theory goes even beyond the absurd theory of the Divine Rights of Kings in terms of absolutism and totalitarianism. What Senator Webster was espousing was no less than a Leviathan State for the American people.

The central fallacy of Daniel Webster's theory lies in his assertion that "a Government is a *body politic.*" By this fallacy, he equates *government* and *people*, and equation that makes it easy to sing praises to the general concept of the sovereignty of the people while really arguing on behalf of a sovereign government. A "body politic" is defined by *Webster's II New Riverside University Dictionary* as, "The people as a group of a politically organized unit, as a Nation or State." [28]

Here, then, is the fundamental flaw in Daniel Webster's conception of the nature of our Federal Union. A *body politic* is the *people* of a State, who are sovereign. Senator Webster claimed that the *Government of the United States* is a *body politic*, and as such should be considered sovereign. Only such a false

[28] *Webster's II New Riverside University Dictionary, Op. cit.*, p. 187.

premise could justify his revolutionary and un-American conclusion that "a Government executes its decisions by its own supreme authority."

Concluding Remarks by Senator Webster

Continuing in his address on the Calhoun Resolutions of 1833, Daniel Webster remarked:

> There is no language in the whole Constitution applicable to a Confederation of States. If the States be parties, as States, what are their rights, and what their respective covenants and stipulations? And where are their rights, covenants, and stipulations expressed? The States engage for nothing, they promise nothing. In the Articles of Confederation, they did make promises, and did enter into engagements, and did plight the faith of each State for their fulfillment; but in the Constitution there is nothing of that kind. The reason is, that, in the Constitution, it is the *people* who speak, and not the States. The people ordain the Constitution, and therein address themselves to the States, and to the Legislatures of the States, in the language of injunction and prohibition. The Constitution utters its behests in the name and by authority of the people, and it does not exact from States any plighted public faith to maintain it. On the contrary, it makes its own preservation depend on individual duty and individual obligation....
>
> Looking still further to the provisions of the Constitution itself, in order to learn its true character, we find its great apparent purpose to be, to unite the people of all the States under one general government, for certain definite objects, and, to the extent of the Union, to restrain the separate authority of the States....
>
> The truth is, Mr. President, and no ingenuity of argument, no subtlety of distinction, can evade it, that, as to certain purposes, the people of the United States are one people....The very end and purpose of the Constitution was to make them one people in [certain]...particulars; and it has effectually accomplished its object. All this is apparent on the face of the Constitution itself....
>
> But, Sir, let us go to the actual formation of the Constitution; let us open the Journal of the Convention itself; and we shall see that the very first resolution which the Convention adopted, was, "That a National Government ought to be established, consisting of a supreme legislature, judiciary, and executive."
>
> This, itself, completely negatives all idea of League, and Compact, and Confederation. Terms could not be chosen more fit to express an intention to establish a National Government, and to banish forever all notion of a Compact between Sovereign States.
>
> This resolution was adopted on the 30th of May, 1787. Afterwards, the style was altered; and instead of being called a National Government, it was called the Government of the United States; but the substance of this resolu-

> tion was retained, and was at the head of that list of resolutions which was afterwards sent to the Committee who were to frame the instrument.
>
> It is true, there were gentlemen in the Convention, who were for retaining the Confederation, and amending its Articles; but the majority was against this, and was for a National Government. Mr. Paterson's propositions, which were for continuing the Articles of Confederation, with additional powers, were submitted in the Convention, on the 15th of June, and referred to the Committee of the Whole. The resolutions forming the basis of a National Government, which had once been agreed to in the Committee of the Whole, and reported, were recommitted to the same Committee of the Whole, on the 19th of June, had both these plans before them; that is to say, the plan of a Confederacy, or Compact, *between the States*, and the plan of a National Government. Both these plans were considered and debated, and the Committee reported, "That they do not agree to the propositions offered by the Honorable Mr. Paterson, but that they again submit the resolutions formerly reported." If, Sir, any historical fact in the world be plain and undeniable, it is that the Convention, with some amendments, rejected that scheme, and adopted the plan of a National Government, with a Legislature, an Executive and a Judiciary of its own. They were asked to preserve the League; they rejected the proposition. They were asked to continue the existing Compact *between States*; they rejected it. They rejected Compact, League, and Confederation, and set themselves about framing the Constitution of a National Government; and they accomplished what they undertook. [29]

Senator Daniel Webster's account of the proceedings of the Philadelphia Convention of 1787 were calculated to mystify the workings of that Convention in the hope of resurrecting what that Convention rejected. His account of those proceedings was at discord with the accounts given by those who actually attended the Constitutional Convention. It is true, of course, that a *supreme National Government* was proposed in the Federal Convention by Edmund Randolph of Virginia that would have subverted the sovereignty of the States and reduced them to a subordinate role in a new Union. The concept of a supreme National Government, however, was ultimately rejected by the Constitutional Convention. For that reason, the word "national" was deliberately stricken out of the evolving federal compact. And, it should be added, the word "supreme" was removed as a descriptive adjective for the Government of the United States. A Supreme Court, it is true, did remain in the language of the Constitution, but that merely referred to the *superiority* of that high court over *inferior* federal courts that Congress might establish.

Rather than a supreme National Government, the Philadelphia Convention of 1787 drafted a plan for a Federal Government. Instead of a *supreme government*, they provided for a *supreme law*. Other powers that would be consis-

[29] Alexander H. Stephens, *Op. cit.*, Volume 1, quoted on pp. 326-330.

tent with a supreme National Government, but not with a Federal Government – such as power to veto a State law – were likewise removed from the evolving Constitution by the Grand Convention.

During the Ratification Period, the advocates of ratification styled themselves *Federalists* in an effort to assure the American people that the Constitution of 1787 provided for a federal system of government resting on the pillars of State sovereignty. According to Daniel Webster, the friends of the Constitution, during this period, were lying to the American people and were attempting to perpetrate a gigantic fraud. Was he correct? Were the Founding Fathers guilty of deception? Or was it Daniel Webster himself who was guilty of trying to deceive the Senate and general public with his fraudulent theories of government?

Senator Webster admitted that the word "national" had been deliberately omitted from the Federal Constitution, although he insisted that this was merely a matter of style. In fact, it was a matter of *style and substance*. Not only did the advocates of federalism in the Federal Convention succeed in removing the term "national" from the federal compact, but they also secured the key, decisive victory over nationalism with the creation of the Senate of the United States. Representation in the Senate was to be based upon equal representation among the States, regardless of differences in population, and it was acknowledged by all the Founding Fathers that *the Senate would forever stand as a monument to the sovereignty of the States*. To further emphasize the importance of this living monument to State sovereignty, the framers inserted into the Constitution a statement that no amendment can deny to any State its equal representation in the U.S. Senate. It was truly ironic that, in contending for a consolidated, supreme National Government during the Webster-Calhoun Debate of 1833, Daniel Webster should make his plea while standing within the very monument to federalism and State sovereignty!

According to the Orator of Consolidation, the Philadelphia Convention of 1787 had to choose between two different systems of government, "the plan of a Confederacy, or Compact, *between the States*, and the plan of a National Government." The Federal Convention was "asked to continue the existing *Compact between States*," but that Convention "rejected it," and gave us instead the supreme National Government. Yet, the very words of the Constitution of the United States reject Daniel Webster's conclusion. In Article VII of that compact, the Federal Constitution states that it shall exist as a compact *between the States*. Senator Webster said that the supreme National Government was chosen by the Federal Convention instead of the compact between the States. But the Constitution states categorically that the compact between the States was chosen instead of the supreme National Government.

Concluding his speech on the Calhoun Resolutions of 1833, Daniel

Webster said:

> You will observe, Sir, that it is the people, and not the States, who have entered into this Compact; and it is the *people of all the United States*....This consent of the people has been called, by European writers, the *social Compact*; and, in conformity to this common mode of expression, [the Constitution may be regarded as a Compact]..., not which the States had entered into with each other, but which the *people* of the United States had entered into.
>
> Finally, Sir, how can any man get over the words of the Constitution itself? "We, the people of the United States, do ordain and establish this Constitution." These words must cease to be a part of the Constitution, they must be obliterated from the parchment on which they are written, before any human ingenuity or human argument can remove the popular basis on which that Constitution rests, and turn the instrument into a mere Compact between Sovereign States! [emphasis added] [30]

Senator Webster's fantastic oration thus ended with his incredible analysis of the theory of a *social contract* as applied to the United States of America. According to his conception, the Federal Constitution is much more of a "compact" than had ever been advocated by the States' Rights School of Thought. Daniel Webster was asserting that the American people, as a whole, had seceded from the States under the Articles of Confederation, had assumed places as sovereign individuals in the State of Nature, had reunited once more in the form of a single body politic through a social contract, had thereby created an entirely new State of America, and had adopted a supreme National Government. And they had done all of this while retaining their old State governments and State boundary lines, perhaps for sentimental reasons.

This was the only way in which the Orator of Consolidation was able to separate the American people from their States. Only in this manner could he claim that the people, acting as a consolidated Nation rather than as States, created the Constitution. Rather than acknowledging that the people, in their sovereign capacity, and the States are equivalent, Senator Webster advocated a philosophy that equated the people of a mythical American Nation with the Government of the United States. The inevitable result of his tortured reasoning was a supreme, sovereign government.

Yet, no matter how hard he tried to sustain his principles, he could never get around the plain words of the Federal Constitution. Regardless of who established the federal compact, the Preamble of the Constitution clearly stated that the instrument had been ordained and established on behalf of the *United States of America*, which the Articles of Confederation had previously defined as

---

[30] *Ibid.*, Volume 1, quoted on p. 335.

a league of sovereign States. Then there was Article VII of the Federal Constitution, which plainly identified the instrument as a compact *between the States*. No tortured reasoning, and no distortion of historical facts, could ever obscure the true meaning of the language of the Constitution itself.

Regarding Daniel Webster's speech on the Calhoun Resolutions of 1833, Alexander H. Stephens had this to say in his book, *A Constitutional View of the Late War Between the States*:

> [I]t is true that I ever regarded Mr. Webster as one of the ablest of our statesmen....In mental power, in grasp of thought, and in that force and manner of expression which constitute eloquence, he had no superior. Intellectually he was a man of huge proportions....Such was and is my estimation of him....[His speech on the Calhoun Resolutions of 1833] is the embodiment of all that can be said upon [the consolidating school's]...side of the question. It was the characteristic of Mr. Webster to leave nothing unsaid, on his side of any subject he spoke on, that could be said to strengthen it, and all that could be said, he always said better than any body else....But it is not the lot of any man to be perfect. I am far from believing Mr. Webster free from political errors. And this speech of his, which, by many..., is considered the greatest of his life, you will allow me to say, contains more errors of this sort than any he ever made. His premises being erroneous, his conclusions must be of the same character. The super-structure is grand. It is the work of a master genius. But the foundations are not solid. It was this speech, by the by, which gave him the appellation of the "Great Expounder of the Constitution," with the Consolidators of that day. In it he did throw all the might of his Gigantic and Titan powers. But the subject was an overmatch for him; the undertaking was too great even for him. Facts were too stubborn. His whole soul was in the subject, and he strove to establish what he wished rather than what actually existed. His effort was to make facts bend to theory. That could not be done. His speech, I readily admit, is the best and ablest that ever was made upon that side of the question. It stands as a monument of genius and eloquence. As such it may well take its place by the side of the great argument of Hume in defence of the Prerogatives of the Crown, claimed by the Stuarts, or of Sir Robert Filmer's famous productions in favor of the Divine Right of Kings, or Sir George McKenzie's "*Jus Regium*." [31]

Initial Remarks of Senator Calhoun

We have now examined what may be considered the greatest speech ever delivered on behalf of the Consolidating School of Thought. Following Daniel Webster's erroneous expounding of the Federal Constitution, John C. Calhoun of South Carolina addressed the Senate of the United States to offer a penetrat-

[31] *Ibid.*, Volume 1, p. 336-337.

ing and thorough rebuttal of the doctrines espoused by the Senator from Massachusetts. Senator Calhoun's reply to Senator Webster constitutes one of the most penetrating arguments ever made on behalf of the States' Rights School of Thought.

Before presenting Senator Calhoun's response to Senator Webster, however, we should first pause to reflect that the topic of the debate was truly fundamental, in that it examined the organic structure of the United States, the foundation of our system of government, and the principles on which the Federal Republic was built. Of necessity, such an examination required a thorough examination of principles and theories, as well as historical facts. One tactic of the consolidators, however, was to criticize John C. Calhoun's reasoning as being too theoretical, logical, and even metaphysical. Several days before the South Carolina Senator gave his reply to Senator Webster, he arose in the Senate to answer the criticism that he was too metaphysical in his reasoning.

Speaking before the Senate of the United States, John C. Calhoun declared:

> The Senator from Delaware (Mr. Clayton) calls this metaphysical reasoning, which, he says, he cannot comprehend. If, by metaphysics, he means that scholastic refinement which makes distinctions without difference, no one can hold it in a more utter contempt than he [Mr. Calhoun]; but if, on the contrary, he means the power of analysis and combination – that power which reduces the most complex ideas into its elements, which traces causes to their first principles, and by the power of generalization and combination, unites the whole into one harmonious system; then, so far from deserving contempt, it is the highest attribute of the human mind. It is the power which raises man above the brute – which distinguishes his faculties from mere sagacity, which he holds in common with inferior animals. It is this power which has raised the astronomer, from being a mere gazer at the stars, to the high intellectual eminence of a Newton or a La Place; and astronomy itself, from a mere observation of insulated facts, into that noble science which displays to our admiration the system of the universe. And shall this high power of the mind, which has effected such wonders, when directed to the laws which control the material world, be forever prohibited, under a senseless cry of metaphysics, from being applied to the high purpose of political science and legislation. He held them to be subject to laws as fixed as matter itself, and to be as fit a subject for the application of the highest intellectual power. Denunciation may, indeed, fall upon the philosophical inquirer into these first principles, as it did upon Galileo and Bacon, when they first unfolded the great discoveries which have immortalized their names; but the time will come, when truth will prevail in spite of prejudice and denunciation; and when politics and legislation will be considered as much a science as astronomy and chemistry. [32]

[32] *Ibid.*, Volume 1, quoted on pp. 341-342.

In response to the radical doctrines espoused by Daniel Webster on the Calhoun Resolutions of 1833, Senator John C. Calhoun addressed the U.S. Senate on February 26, 1833, and declared:

> The Senator from Massachusetts, in his argument against the Resolutions, directed his attack almost exclusively against the first; on the ground, I suppose, that it was the basis of the other two, and that, unless the first could be demolished, the others would follow of course. In this he was right. As plain and as simple as the facts contained in the first are, they cannot be admitted to be true without admitting the doctrines for which I, and the State I represent, contend. He commenced his attack with a verbal criticism on the Resolution, in the course of which he objected strongly to two words, "Constitutional" and "accede." To the former, on the ground that the word, as used (Constitutional Compact), was obscure – that it conveyed no definite meaning – and that Constitution was a noun-substantive, and not an adjective. I regret that I have exposed myself to the criticism of the Senator. I certainly did not intend to use any expression of doubtful sense, and if I have done so, the Senator must attribute it to the poverty of my language, and not to design....
>
> ...It will be seen by this extract [from the debate on the Foot Resolution in 1830, in which Daniel Webster had used the term "Constitutional Compact" in a speech], that the Senator not only used the phrase "Constitutional Compact," which he now so much condemns, but, what is still more important, he calls the Constitution a Compact – a bargain – which contains important admissions, having a direct and powerful bearing on the main issue, involved in the discussion, as will appear in the sequel. But, strong as his objection is to the word "Constitutional," it is still stronger to the word "accede," which, he thinks, has been introduced into the Resolution with some deep design, as I suppose, to entrap the Senate into an admission of the doctrine of State Rights. Here, again, I must shelter myself under authority. But I suspect the Senator, by a sort of instinct (for our instincts often strangely run before our knowledge), had a prescience, which would account for his aversion for the word, that this authority was no less than Thomas Jefferson himself, the great apostle of the doctrines of State Rights. The word was borrowed from him. It was taken from the Kentucky Resolution, as well as the substance of the resolution itself. But I trust I may neutralize whatever aversion the authorship of this word may have excited in the mind of the Senator, by the introduction of another authority – that of Washington, himself – who, in his speech to Congress, speaking of the admission of North Carolina into the Union, uses this very term, which was repeated by the Senate in their reply. Yet, in order to narrow the ground between the Senator and myself as much as possible, I will accommodate myself to his strange antipathy against the two unfortunate words, by striking them out of the Resolution, and substituting, in their place, those very words which the Senator himself has designated as Constitutional phrases. In the place of that abhorred adjective "Constitutional," I will insert the very noun substantive "Constitution;" and, in the place of the word "accede," I will insert the word "ratify," which

he designates as the proper term to be used.

As proposed to be amended, the Resolution would read: –

"*Resolved*, That the people of the several States composing these United States are united as parties to a Compact, under the title of the Constitution of the United States, which the people of each State ratified as a separate and sovereign community, each binding itself by its own particular ratification; and that the Union of which the said Compact is the bond, is a Union *between* the States ratifying the same."

Where, Sir, I ask, is that plain case of revolution? Where that hiatus, as wide as the globe, between the premises and the conclusion, which the Senator proclaimed would be apparent, if the Resolution was reduced into Constitutional language? For my part, with my poor powers of conception, I cannot perceive the slightest difference between the Resolution, as first introduced, and as it is proposed to be amended in conformity to the views of the Senator. And, instead of that hiatus between the premises and conclusion, which seems to startle the imagination of the Senator, I can perceive nothing but a continuous and solid surface, sufficient to sustain the magnificent superstructure of State Rights. Indeed, it seems to me that the Senator's vision is distorted by the medium through which he views every thing connected with the subject; and that the same distortion which has presented to his imagination this hiatus, as wide as the globe, where not even a fissure exists, also presented that beautiful and classical image of a strong man struggling in a bog, without the power of extricating himself, and incapable of being aided by any friendly hand; while, instead of struggling in a bog, he stands on the everlasting rock of truth.

Having now noticed the criticisms of the Senator, I shall proceed to meet and repel the main assault on the Resolution. He directed his attack against the strong point, the very horn of the citadel of State Rights. The Senator clearly perceived that, if the Constitution be a Compact, it was impossible to deny the assertions contained in the Resolutions, or to resist the consequences which I had drawn from them, and, accordingly, directed his whole fire against that point; but, after so vast an expenditure of ammunition, not the slightest impression, so far as I can perceive, has been made. But to drop a simile, after a careful examination of the notes which I took of what the Senator said, I am now at a loss to know whether, in the opinion of the Senator, our Constitution is a Compact or not, though almost the entire argument of the Senator was directed to that point. At one time he would seem to deny directly and positively that it was a Compact, while at another he would appear, in language no less strong, to admit that it was.

I have collated all that the Senator has said upon this point; and, that what I have stated may not appear exaggerated, I will read his remarks in juxtaposition. He said that:

"The Constitution means a Government, not a Compact." "Not a Constitutional Compact, but a Government." "If a Compact, it rests on plighted faith, and the mode of redress would be to declare the whole void." "States may secede, if a League or Compact."

I thank the Senator for these admissions, which I intend to use hereafter.

"The States agreed that each should participate in the sovereignty of the other."

Certainly, a very correct conception of the Constitution; but where did they make that agreement but by the Constitution, and how could they agree but by Compact?

"The system, not a Compact between States in their sovereign capacity, but a Government proper, founded on the adoption of the people, and creating individual relations between itself and the citizens."

This, the Senator lays down as a leading, fundamental principle to sustain his doctrine, and, I must say, with strange confusion and uncertainty of language; not, certainly, to be explained by any want of command of the most appropriate words on his part.

"It does not call itself a Compact, but a Constitution. The Constitution rests on Compact, but it is no longer a Compact."

I would ask, to what Compact does the Senator refer, as that on which the Constitution rests? Before the adoption of the present Constitution, the States had formed but one Compact, and that was the old Confederation; and, certainly, the Gentleman does not intend to assert that the present Constitution rests upon that. What, then, is his meaning? What can it be, but that the Constitution itself is a Compact? And how will his language read, when fairly interpreted, but that the Constitution was a Compact, but is no longer a Compact? It had, by some means or another, changed its nature, or become defunct.

He next states that –

"A man is almost untrue to his country who calls the Constitution a Compact."

I fear the Senator, in calling it a "Compact, a bargain," has called down this heavy denunciation on his own head. He finally states that –

"It is founded on Compact, but not a Compact." "It is the result of a Compact."

To what are we to attribute this strange confusion of words? The Senator has a mind of high order, and perfectly trained to the most exact use of language. No man knows better the precise import of the words he uses. The difficulty is not in him, but in his subject. He who undertakes to prove that this Constitution is not a Compact, undertakes a task which, be his strength ever so great, must oppress him by its weight. Taking the whole of the argument of the Senator together, I would say that it is his impression that the Constitution is not a Compact....

He thinks there is an incompatibility between Constitution and Compact. To prove this, he adduces the words "ordain and establish," contained in the Preamble of the Constitution. I confess I am not capable of perceiving in what manner these words are incompatible with the idea that the Constitution is a Compact. The Senator will admit that a single State may ordain a Constitution; and where is the difficulty, where the incompatibility, of two States concurring in ordaining and establishing a Constitution? As between the States themselves, the instrument would be a Compact; but in reference to the government, and those on whom it operates, it would be ordained and established – ordained and established by the joint authority of two, instead of the single authority of one.

The next argument which the Senator advances to show that the language of the Constitution is irreconcilable with the idea of its being a Compact, is taken from that portion of the instrument which imposes prohibitions on the authority of the States. He said that the language used, in imposing the prohibitions, is the language of a superior to an inferior; and that, therefore, it was not the language of a Compact, which implies the equality of the parties. As a proof, the Senator cited several clauses of the Constitution which provide that no State shall enter into treaties of alliance and confederation, lay imposts, etc., without the assent of Congress. If he had turned to the Articles of the old Confederation, which he acknowledges to have been a Compact, he would have found that those very prohibitory Articles of the Constitution were borrowed from that instrument; that the language, which he now considers as implying superiority, was taken *verbatim* from it. If he had extended his researches still further, he would have found that it is the habitual language used in treaties, whenever a stipulation is made against the performance of any act. Among many instances, which I could cite, if it were necessary, I refer the Senator to the celebrated treaty negotiated by Mr. Jay with Great Britain, in 1793, in which the very language used in the Constitution is employed.

To prove that the Constitution is not a Compact, the Senator next observes that it stipulates nothing, and asks, with an air of triumph, "Where are the evidences of the stipulations between the States?" I must express my surprise at this interrogatory, coming from so intelligent a source....

So far from regarding it in the light in which the Senator regards it, I consider the whole instrument but a mass of stipulations. What is that but a stipulation to which the Senator refers when he states, in the course of his argument, that each State had agreed to participate in the sovereignty of the others.

But the principal argument on which the Senator relied to show that the Constitution is not a Compact, rests on the provision, in that instrument, which declares that "this Constitution, and laws made in pursuance thereof, and treaties made under their authority, are the supreme law of the land." He asked, with marked emphasis, "Can a Compact be the supreme law of the land?" His argument, in fact, as conclusively proves that treaties are not Compacts as that the Constitution is not a Compact. I might rest the issue on this decisive answer; but, as I desire to leave not a shadow of doubt on this important point, I shall follow the Gentleman in the course of his reasoning.

He defines a Constitution to be a fundamental law, which organizes the Government, and points out the mode of its actions. I will not object to the definition, though, in my opinion, a more appropriate one, or, at least, one better adapted to American ideas, could be given. My objection is not to the definition, but to the attempt to prove that the fundamental laws of a State cannot be a Compact, as the Senator seems to suppose. I hold the reverse to be the case; and that, according to the most approved writers on the subject of government, these very fundamental laws which are now stated not only not to be Compacts, but inconsistent with the very idea of Compacts, are held invariably to be Compacts; and, in that character, are distinguished from the ordinary laws of the country....

A reference to the Constitution of Great Britain, with which we are better acquainted than with that of any other European government, will show that that is a Compact....

But why should I refer to writers upon the subject of government, or inquire into the Constitution of foreign States, when there are such decisive proofs that our Constitution is a Compact? On this point the Senator is estopped. I borrow from the Gentleman, and thank him for the word. His adopted State, which he so ably represents on this floor, and his native State, the States of Massachusetts and New Hampshire, both declared, in their ratification of the Constitution, that it was a Compact....

...But proof, if possible, still more decisive, may be found in the celebrated resolutions of Virginia on the Alien and Sedition Law, in 1798, and the responses of Massachusetts and the other States. These resolutions expressly assert that the Constitution is a Compact between the States, in the following language:

"That this Assembly doth explicitly and peremptorily declare, that it views the powers of the Federal Government, as resulting from the Compact, to which the States are parties, as limited by the plain sense and intention of the instrument constituting that Compact, as no farther valid than they are authorized by the grants enumerated in that Compact; and that in case of a deliberate, palpable, and dangerous exercise of other powers not granted by the said Compact, the States who are parties thereto have the right, and are in duty bound, to interpose for arresting the progress of the evil, and for maintaining within their respective limits the authorities, rights, and liberties appertaining to them.

"That the General Assembly doth also express its deep regret that a spirit has, in sundry instances, been manifested by the Federal Government to enlarge its powers by forced constructions of the Constitutional Charter, which defines them; and that indications have appeared of a design to expound certain general phrases (which, having been copied from the very limited grant of powers in the former Articles of Confederation, were less liable to be misconstrued), so as to destroy the meaning and effect of the particular enumeration which necessarily explains and limits the general phrases, and so as *to consolidate the States, by degrees, into one sovereignty, the obvious tendency and inevitable result of which would be, to transform the present Republican system of the United States into an absolute, or, at best, a mixed monarchy*!" [emphasis added]

They were sent to the several States. We have the replies of Delaware, New York, Connecticut, New Hampshire, Vermont, and Massachusetts, not one of which contradicts this important assertion on the part of Virginia; and, by their silence, they all acquiesce in its truth. The case is still stronger against Massachusetts, which expressly recognizes the fact that the Constitution is a Compact.

[Here Senator Calhoun read from the answer of Massachusetts, in which the Constitution is called a *solemn Compact*.]

Now, I ask the Senator himself – I put it to his candor to

> say,...whether he and Massachusetts, after this clear, full, and solemn recognition that the Constitution is a Compact (both on his part and that of his State), be not forever estopped on this important point?
>
> There remains one more of the Senator's arguments, to prove that the Constitution is not a Compact, to be considered. He says it is not a Compact, because it is a Government; which he defines to be an organized body, possessed of the will and power to execute its purposes by its own proper authority; and which, he says, bears not the slightest resemblance to a Compact. But I would ask the Senator, Whoever considered a Government, when spoken of as the agent to execute the powers of the Constitution, and distinct from the Constitution itself, as a Compact? In that light it would be a perfect absurdity. It is true, in general and loose language, it is often said that the Government is a Compact, meaning the Constitution which created it, and vested it with authority to execute the powers contained in the instrument; but when the distinction is drawn between the Constitution and the Government, as the Senator has done, it would be as ridiculous to call the Government a Compact, as to call an individual, appointed to execute the provisions of a contract, a contract; and not less so to suppose that there could be the slightest resemblance between them....
>
> I have examined all of the arguments of the Senator intended to prove that the Constitution is not a Compact; and I trust I have shown, by the clearest demonstration, that his arguments are perfectly inconclusive, and that this assertion is against the clearest and most solemn evidence – evidence of record, and of such a character that it ought to close his lips forever.[33]

John C. Calhoun had more to say in his reply to Daniel Webster in the great Webster-Calhoun Debate of 1833, and we shall soon resume his speech. But first, we should pause to comment on a point that was raised by the South Carolina Senator that deserves closer scrutiny. And this key point is that there is a definite difference between the Constitution of the United States and the Federal Government established by it. The people of the United States, acting in their capacities as sovereign States, "ordained and established" the Federal Constitution, not the Government of the United States. The Constitution, and not the government, therefore, is the *compact* between the States.

The federal compact established the Federal Government, delegated powers to it, and limits its powers to only those enumerated in the pact. The sole objective of the Government of the United States is to execute the will of the sovereign States, as expressed in their compact. For this reason, it is the Federal Constitution which is supreme – the supreme law of the land – and not the Federal Government. The Federal Government is *inferior* to the compact, or Constitution, and cannot lawfully alter a single provision in it. The States, however, are *superior* to the compact, in that they made it and may alter its provisions whenever they please. The *order of superiority* within the Federal Un-

[33] *Ibid.*, Volume 1, quoted on pp. 343-351 and 353-356.

ion is as follows: sovereign States are the supreme masters, the Federal Government is the servant of the States, and the Constitution is the supreme command of the States to their joint servant.

Further Remarks by Senator Calhoun

In the course of his brilliant reply to Daniel Webster during the historical Webster-Calhoun Debate of 1833, the Orator of States' Rights asserted:

> I turn now to consider the other, and, apparently, contradictory aspect in which the Senator presented this part of the subject: I mean that in which he states that the government is founded in Compact, but is no longer a Compact. I have already remarked, that no other interpretation could be given to this assertion, except that the Constitution was once a Compact, but is no longer so. There was a vagueness and indistinctness in this part of the Senator's argument, which left me altogether uncertain as to its real meaning. If he meant, as I presume he did, that the Compact is an executed, and not an executory one – that its object was to create a government, and to invest it with proper authority – and that, having executed this office, it had performed its functions, and, with it, had ceased to exist, then we have the extraordinary avowal that the Constitution is a dead letter – that it had ceased to have any binding effect, or any practical influence or operation.
>
> It has, indeed, often been charged that the Constitution has become a dead letter; that it is continually violated, and has lost all its control over the government; but no one has ever before been bold enough to advance a theory on the avowed basis that it was an executed, and, therefore, an extinct instrument. I will not seriously attempt to refute an argument, which, to me, appears so extravagant. I had thought that the Constitution was to endure forever....
>
> I will now return to the first Resolution, to see how the issue stands between the Senator from Massachusetts and myself. It contains three propositions. First, that the Constitution is a Compact; second, that it was formed by the States, constituting distinct communities; and, lastly, that it is a subsisting and binding Compact between the States. How do these three propositions now stand? The first, I trust, has been satisfactorily established; the second, the Senator has admitted, faintly, indeed, but still he has admitted it to be true. This admission is something. It is so much gained by discussion. Three years ago even this was a contested point. But I cannot say that I thank him for the admission; we owe it to the force of truth. The fact that these States were declared to be free and independent States at the time of their independence; that they were acknowledged to be so by Great Britain in the treaty which terminated the war of the Revolution, and secured their independence; that they were recognized in the same character in the old Articles of the Confederation; and, finally, that the present Constitution was formed by a Convention of the several States; afterwards submitted to them for their respective ratifications, and was ratified by them separately, each for itself, and each, by its own act, binding its citizens, – formed a body of facts

and each, by its own act, binding its citizens, – formed a body of facts too clear to be denied, and too strong to be resisted.

It now remains to consider the third and last proposition contained in the [first] Resolution, – that it is a binding and a subsisting Compact between the States. The Senator was not explicit on this point. I understood him, however, as asserting that, though formed by the States, the Constitution was not binding between the States as distinct communities, but between the American people in the aggregate; who, in consequence of the adoption of the Constitution, according to the opinion of the Senator, became one people, at least to the extent of the delegated powers. This would, indeed, be a great change. All acknowledge that, previous to the adoption of the Constitution, the States constituted distinct and independent communities, in full possession of their sovereignty; and, surely, if the adoption of the Constitution was intended to effect the great and important change in their condition which the theory of the Senator supposes, some evidence of it ought to be found in the instrument itself. It professes to be a careful and full enumeration of all the powers which the States delegated, and of every modification of their political condition. The Senator said that he looked to the Constitution in order to ascertain its real character....But, with the exception of "We, the people of the United States," in the Preamble, he has not pointed out a single indication in the Constitution, of the great change which as he conceives, has been effected in this respect.

Now, Sir, I intend to prove, that the only argument on which the Gentleman relies on this point, must utterly fail him. I do not intend to go into a critical examination of the expression of the Preamble to which I have referred. I do not deem it necessary. But if it were, it might be easily shown that it is at least as applicable to my view of the Constitution as to that of the Senator....[T]he people of the United States may mean *all* the people living within these limits, without reference to the States or Territories in which they may reside, or of which they may be citizens; and it is in this sense only, that the expression gives the least countenance to the argument of the Senator.

But it may also, *the States united,* which inversion alone, without further explanation, removes the ambiguity to which I have referred. The expression in this sense, obviously means no more than to speak of the people of the several States in their united and confederated capacity; and, if it were requisite, it might be shown that it is only in this sense that the expression is used in the Constitution....

But I intend not to leave this important point, the last refuge of those who advocate consolidation....On this point there is a very important part of the Constitution entirely and strangely overlooked by the Senator in this debate, as it is expressed in the first Resolution, which furnishes conclusive evidence not only that the Constitution is a Compact, but a subsisting Compact, binding between the States. I allude to the Seventh Article, which provides that the ratification of the conventions of nine States shall be sufficient for the establishment of this Constitution "*between the States* so ratifying the same." These little words mean a volume. Compacts, not laws, bind *between* States; and it here binds, not as between individuals, but between *the States*:

the States *ratifying*; implying, as strong as language can make it, that the Constitution is what I have asserted it to be – a Compact, ratified by the States, and a subsisting Compact, binding the States ratifying it.

But, Sir, I will not leave this point, all-important in establishing the true theory of our government, on this argument alone, as demonstrative and conclusive as I hold it to be. Another, not much less powerful, but of a different character, may be drawn from the tenth amended Article, which provides that the powers not delegated to the United States by the Constitution, nor prohibited by it to the States, are reserved to the States respectively or to the people. The Article of Ratification, which I have just cited, informs us that the Constitution, which delegates powers, was ratified by the States, and is binding between them. This informs us to whom the powers are delegated, – a most important fact in determining the point immediately at issue between the Senator and myself. According to his views, the Constitution created a Union between individuals, if the solecism may be allowed, and that it formed, at least to the extent of the powers delegated, one people, and not a Federal Union of the States, as I contend; or, to express the same idea differently, that the delegation of powers was to the American people in the aggregate (for it is only by such delegation that they could be constituted one people), and not to the *United States*, – directly contrary to the Article just cited, which declares that the powers are delegated to the United States. And here it is worthy of notice, that the Senator cannot shelter himself under the ambiguous phrase, "to the people of the United States," under which he would certainly have taken refuge, had the Constitution so expressed it; but fortunately for the cause of truth and the great principles of Constitutional liberty for which I am contending, "people," is omitted: thus making the delegation of power clear and unequivocal to the *United States*, as distinct political communities, and conclusively proving that all the powers are reciprocally delegated by the States to each other, as distinct political communities.

So much for the delegated powers. Now, as all admit, and as it is expressly provided for in the Constitution, the *reserved* powers are reserved "to the States *respectively*, or to the people." None will pretend that, as far as they are concerned, we are one people, though the argument to prove it, however absurd, would be far more plausible than that which goes to show that we are one people to the extent of the delegated powers. This reservation "to the people" might, in the hands of subtle and trained logicians, be a peg to hang a doubt upon....

I have now established, I hope, beyond the power of controversy, every allegation contained in the first Resolution – that the Constitution is a Compact formed by the people of the several States, as distinct political communities, and subsisting and binding between the States in the same character; which brings me to the consideration of the consequences which may be fairly deduced, in reference to the character of our political system, from these established facts.

The first and most important is, they conclusively establish that ours is a Federal System – a system of States arranged in a Federal Union, each retaining its distinct existence and sovereignty. Ours has every attribute which belongs to a Federative System. It is founded on Compact; it is formed by sovereign communities, and is binding between them in their sovereign capacity. I might appeal, in confirmation of this assertion, to all elementary writers on the subject of government, but will consent myself with citing one only. Burlamaqui, quoted with approbation by Judge Tucker, in his Commentary on Blackstone, himself a high authority, says:

[Here Mr. Calhoun quotes from Tucker's Blackstone as follows]:

"Political bodies, whether great or small, if they are constituted by a people formerly independent, and under no civil subjection, or by those who justly claim independence from any civil power they were formerly subject to, have the civil supremacy in themselves, and are in a State of equal right and liberty with respect to all other States, whether great or small. No regard is to be had in this matter to names, whether the body-politic be called a kingdom, an empire, a principality, a dukedom, a country, a republic, or free town. If it can exercise justly all the essential parts of civil power within itself, independently of any other person or body-politic, – and no other has any right to rescind or annul its acts, – it has the civil supremacy, how small soever its territory may be, or the number of its people, and has all the rights of an independent State.

"This independence of States, and their being distinct political bodies from each other, is not obstructed by any alliance or confederacies whatsoever, about exercising jointly any parts of the supreme powers, such as those of peace and war, in league offensive and defensive. Two States, notwithstanding such treaties, are separate bodies, and independent.

"These are, then, only deemed politically united, when some one person or council is constituted with a right to exercise some essential powers for both, and to hinder either from exercising them separately....

"...[W]hen only a portion of the supreme civil power is vested in one person or council for both, such as that of peace and war, or of deciding controversies between different States, or their subjects, while each, within itself, exercises other parts of the supreme power, independently of all the others – in this case they are called *Systems of States*, which Burlamaqui defines to be an assemblage of perfect governments, strictly united by some common bond, so that they seem to make but a single body with respect to those affairs which interest them in common, though each preserves its sovereignty, full and entire, independently of all others. And in this case, he adds, the Confederate States engage to each other only to exercise, with common consent, certain parts of the sovereignty, especially that which relates to their mutual defence against foreign enemies. But each of the Confederates retains an entire liberty of exercising, as it thinks proper, those parts of the sovereignty which are not mentioned in the treaty of Union, as parts that ought to be exercised in common. And of this nature is the American Confederacy, in which each State has regained the exercise of certain parts of the supreme civil power which they possessed before (except in common with the other States included in the Confederacy), reserving to themselves all their former powers, which are not delegated to the United States by the common bond of Union.

"...In the United States of America,...each State retains its own antecedent form of government; its own laws, subject to the alteration and con-

> trol of its own legislature only; its own executive officers and council of State; its own courts of Judicature, its own judges, its own magistrates, civil officers, and officers of the militia; and, in short, its own civil State, or body politic, in every respect whatsoever. And by the express declaration of the 12th article of the amendment [Amendment Ten] to the Constitution, the powers not delegated to the United States by the Constitution, nor prohibited by it to the States, are reserved to the States respectively, or to the people....[I]n the American States, a general *Federal* council and administration is provided, for the joint exercise of such of their several powers as can be more conveniently exercised in that mode than any other, leaving their *civil State* unaltered; and all the other powers, which the States antecedently possessed, to be exercised by them respectively, as if no Union or connection were established between them....
>
> "These Confederacies, by which several States are united together by a perpetual league or alliance, are chiefly founded upon this circumstance, that each particular people choose to remain their own masters, and yet are not strong enough to make head against a common enemy. The purport of such an agreement usually is, that they shall not exercise some part of the sovereignty, there specified, without the general consent of each other....We observed before that these Unions submit only some certain parts of the sovereignty to mutual direction; for it seems hardly possible that the affairs of different States should have so close a connection, as that all and each of them should look on it as their interest to have no part of the chief government exercised without the general concurrence. The most convenient method, therefore, seems to be, that the particular States reserve to themselves all those branches of the supreme authority, the management of which can have little or no influence in the affairs of the rest." [34]

As the Senator from South Carolina noted in the course of his speech, the Tenth Amendment to the Federal Constitution forms the cornerstone of the States' Rights School of Thought. That amendment is phrased as follows: "The powers not delegated to the United States by the Constitution, nor prohibited by it to the States, are reserved to the States respectively, or to the people." [35]

Within the phraseology of this part of the supreme law of the land lies the answer to the whole question of sovereignty in the United States, for it encompasses *the sum total of all political powers appertaining to sovereignty*. This amendment speaks of *delegated powers* and of *reserved powers*, and it tells us how the delegation of enumerated powers was made. Specifically, it tells us that the powers of the Federal Government are delegated to it by the Constitution of the United States, and that they are delegated to the United States.

All powers not delegated are reserved to the States. Careful attention

---

[34] *Ibid.*, Volume 1, quoted on pp. 357-367 and 369.
[35] *Ibid.*, Volume 1, p. 569.

should be paid to the positioning of the word "people" in Amendment Ten. The people are considered the equivalent of the States, *possessing the powers not delegated*, while the Federal Government is considered the equivalent of the United States, at least in terms of the delegated powers, for it possesses the powers delegated by the Federal Constitution.

A simple exercise in logic is conducive to our better understanding of the Tenth Amendment to the Constitution of the United States. The following proposition is offered for the reader's consideration: *Only those who delegated powers to the United States – to the Federal Government – could have reserved the powers not delegated.* This statement is grounded in logic and reason, and should be undeniable. The powers *not* delegated, of course, would remain precisely where they where vested before the Constitution was adopted.

Who delegated the powers enumerated in the U.S. Constitution to the Federal Government? The answer is, the States – not the State governments, but the peoples of the several States, acting in their sovereign capacities through State Ratifying Conventions. Since they, and they alone, delegated the powers to the Federal Government, they, and they alone, reserve all the powers not delegated to the Federal Government. This is simple logic, and this is precisely the meaning conveyed by the Tenth Amendment of the federal compact. According to that amendment, the reserved powers are possessed by "the States respectively," or by "the people." Here, "States" and "people" are synonymous, and the "or" contained in the amendment should be regarded as a conjunction connecting expressions with the same meaning.

Admittedly, the Tenth Amendment, construed separately, without regard to our political history and the rest of the compact, and with a fuzzy eye, could be misconstrued. Uninformed interpreters could, and indeed have, misinterpreted the word "States" to mean the State governments, and the word "people" to mean the people in their capacities as individual citizens. But these two interpretations are totally false for one very basic and irrefutable reason: *Only those who delegated powers to the United States – to the Federal Government – could have reserved the powers not delegated.*

Did the State governments delegate any powers to the Federal Government? Did the American people, as individual citizens, delegate powers to the Government of the United States? Or were those powers delegated to the Federal Government by the people in their status as sovereign States, with each State acting through its own ratifying conventions? If there could possibly be any doubt as to the answer, then we may refer to Article VII of the federal compact, which explicitly identifies the source of the delegated powers to be the State Ratifying Conventions.

The American people, it is true, possess inalienable human rights which the Federal Government may not invade. But these were addressed in the first eight articles of the Bill of Rights. And the Ninth Amendment contains a sweeping summary of all the natural rights possessed by individual citizens: "The enumeration in the Constitution, of certain rights, shall not be construed to deny or disparage others retained by the people." [36] This amendment is patterned on the one that follows it, but it deals exclusively with the rights of the American people *as individual citizens*. Amendment Ten, on the other hand, is concerned with the reserved powers and rights of the American people *in their sovereign capacities*, as organized into States of the Union.

Amendment Ten clearly reveals who is sovereign within our federal system. Only those who are sovereign can delegate and reserve political powers, and only the peoples of the several States possess that supremacy. The United States, considered as the *recipient* of the delegated powers – meaning, in this consideration, the Federal Government – is on the receiving end of the delegation of powers, while the States – meaning the peoples of those States – are on the delegating end, and thereby reserve what is not delegated. This is further proof that the States are sovereign and that the United States, either its government or the political Union, is not sovereign.

This particular amendment to the federal compact also tells us that the "United States" is, *in terms of powers delegated*, the equivalent of the Government of the United States. In practical terms, everything delegated by the States to the Federal Union is vested in the Federal Government, and nothing is vested in any mythical, consolidated Nation of Americans. Whatever is reserved to the States, however, is not necessarily vested in the State governments. The peoples of the several States have wisely resolved to limit the powers of their respective State governments, as well as those of their joint government in Washington, D.C. Thus, there are some powers that have not been delegated to any sphere of government.

The Tenth Amendment clearly reveals that there is not any single Nation or State of America, but that the people of America exist as sovereign States who delegated certain powers to the Federal Government, while reserving to themselves all powers not delegated. As Thomas Jefferson once observed, Amendment Ten forms the foundation on which the Federal Constitution is based.

Concluding Remarks by Senator Calhoun

In the concluding portion of his speech in the Webster-Calhoun Debate of 1833, Senator John C. Calhoun said:

---

[36] *Ibid.*, Volume 1, p. 569.

If we compare our present system with the old Confederation, which all acknowledge to have been *Federal* in its character, we shall find that it possesses all the attributes which belong to that form of government as fully and completely as that did. In fact, *in this particular*, there is but a single difference, and that not essential, as regards the point immediately under consideration, though very important in other respects. The Confederation was the act of the State governments, and formed a Union of governments. The present Constitution is the act of the States themselves, or, which is the same thing, of the people of the several States, and forms a Union of them as sovereign communities. The States, previous to the adoption of the Constitution, were as separate and distinct political bodies as the governments which represent them, and there is nothing in the nature of things to prevent them from uniting under a Compact, in a Federal Union, without being blended in one mass, any more than uniting the governments themselves, in like manner, without merging them in a single government. To illustrate what I have stated by reference to ordinary transactions, the Confederation was a contract between agents – the present Constitution a contract between the principals themselves; or, to take a more analogous case, one is a League made by ambassadors; the other, a League made by sovereigns – the latter no more tending to unite the parties into a single sovereignty than the former. The only difference is in the solemnity of the act and the force of the obligation....

We will now proceed to consider some of the conclusions which necessarily follow from the facts and positions already established. They enable us to decide a question of vital importance under our system: Where does Sovereignty reside? If I have succeeded in establishing the fact that ours is a federal system, as I conceive I conclusively have, that fact of itself determines the question which I have proposed. It is of the very essence of such a system, that the sovereignty is in the parts, and not in the whole....Ours, then, is a government of twenty-four Sovereignties, united by a Constitutional Compact, for the purpose of exercising certain powers through a common government as their joint agent, and not a Union of the twenty-four Sovereignties into one, which, according to the language of the Virginia Resolutions, already cited, would form a Consolidation....

Another consequence is equally clear, that, whatever modifications were made in the condition of the States under the present Constitution, they extended only to the exercise of their powers by Compact, and not to the Sovereignty itself, and are such as Sovereigns are competent to make: it being a conceded point, that it is competent to them to stipulate to exercise their powers in a particular manner, or to abstain altogether from their exercise, or to delegate them to agents, without in any degree impairing sovereignty itself. The plain state of the facts, as regards our government, is, that these States have agreed by Compact to exercise their sovereign powers jointly, as already stated; and that, for this purpose, they have ratified the Compact in their sovereign capacity, thereby making it the Constitution of each State, in nowise distinguished from their own separate Constitutions, but in the super-added obligation of Compact – of faith mutually pledged to each other. In this Compact, they have stipulated, among other things, that it may be amended by three fourths of the States: that is, they have conceded to each other by Compact the right to add new powers or to subtract old, by the consent of that proportion of the States, without requiring, as otherwise would have been the case, the consent of all: a modification no more inconsistent, as has been supposed, with their sovereignty, than any other contained in the Compact. In fact, the provision to which I allude furnishes strong evidence that the sovereignty is, as I contend, in the States severally, as the amendments are effected, not by any one three fourths, but by any three fourths of the States, indicating that the sovereignty is in each of the States.

If these views be correct, it follows, as a matter of course, that the allegiance of the people is to their several States, and that treason consists in resistance to the joint authority of the *States* united, not, as has been absurdly contended, in resistance to the Government of the United States, which, by the provision of the Constitution, has only the right of punishing....

The Senator,...in order to sustain his main position,...fell back on that clause of the Constitution which provides that "this Constitution, and the laws made in pursuance thereof, shall be the supreme law of the land."

This is admitted; no one has ever denied that the Constitution, and the laws made in *pursuance* of it, are of Paramount authority. But it is equally undeniable that laws *not* made in pursuance are not only not of Paramount authority, but are of no authority whatever, being of themselves null and void; which presents the question, who are to judge whether the laws be or be not pursuant to the Constitution?...This the Senator also felt, and has attempted to overcome, by setting up, on the part of Congress and the judiciary, the final and exclusive right of judging, both for the Federal Government and the States, as to the extent of their respective powers....

Now, passing over this vague and loose phraseology [of Mr. Webster's assertion that the federal legislature and judiciary should be the final judges on questions of power], I would ask the Senator upon what principle can he concede this extensive power to the Legislative and Judicial departments, but withhold it entirely from the Executive? If one has the right it cannot be withheld from the other. I would also ask him on what principle – if the departments of the general government are to possess the right of judging, finally and conclusively, of their respective powers – on what principle can the same right be withheld from the State governments, which, as well as the general government, properly considered, are but departments of the same general system, and form together, properly speaking, but one government?...

But I contend that the States have a far clearer right to the sole construction of their powers than any of the departments of the Federal Government can have....

...To establish the opposite, the Senator relies upon the authority of Mr. Madison, in the *Federalist*, to prove that it was intended to invest the Court with the power in question. In reply, I will meet Mr. Madison with his own opinion, given on a most solemn occasion, and backed by the sagacious Commonwealth of Virginia. The opinion to which I allude will be found in the celebrated Report of 1799, of which Mr. Madison was the author. It says:

"But it is objected, that the judicial authority is to be regarded as *the sole expositor of the Constitution in the last resort*; and it may be asked for what reason the declaration by the General Assembly, supposing it to be theoretically true, could be required at the present day, and in so solemn a manner.

"On this objection it might be observed, *first*, that there may be instances of usurped power, which the forms of the Constitution would never draw within the control of the Judicial department; *secondly*, that, if the decision of the judiciary be raised above the authority of the Sovereign parties to the Constitution, the decisions of the other departments, not carried by the forms of the Constitution before the judiciary, must be equally authoritative and final as the decisions of this department....[Yet,] dangerous powers, not delegated, may not only be usurped and executed by the other departments, but that the Judicial department, also, may exercise or sanction dangerous powers beyond the grant of the Constitution; and, consequently, that the ultimate right of the parties to the Constitution to judge whether the Compact was dangerously violated, must extend to violations by one delegated authority as well as by another; by the judiciary as well as by the executive or the legislature."

But why should I waste words in reply to these or any other authorities, when it has been so clearly established that the rights of the States are reserved against each and every department of the [Federal] Government, and no authority in opposition can possibly shake a position so well established?...

I have now, I trust, shown satisfactorily, that there is no provision in the Constitution to authorize the general government, through any of its departments, to control the action of a State within the sphere of its reserved powers, and that, of course, according to the principle laid down by the Senator from Massachusetts himself, the government of the States, as well as the general government, has the right to determine the extent of their respective powers, without the right on the part of either to control the other....If the object had been to get clear of the veto of the States, as the Senator states, the Convention, certainly, performed their work in a most bungling manner. There was, unquestionably, a large party in that body, headed by men of distinguished talents and influence, who commenced early and worked earnestly to the last, to deprive the States – not directly, for that would have been too bold an attempt, but indirectly – of the veto. The good sense of the Convention, however put down every effort, however disguised and perseveringly made. I do not deem it necessary to give, from the journals, the history of these various and unsuccessful attempts – though it would afford a very instructive lesson. It is sufficient to say that it was attempted, by proposing to give to Congress power to annul the acts of the States which they might deem inconsistent with the Constitution; to give to the President the power of appointing the Governors of the States, with a view of vetoing State laws through his authority; and, finally, to give the judiciary the power to decide controversies between the States and the general government; all of which failed – fortunately for the liberty of the country – utterly and entirely failed; and in this failure we have the strongest evidence, that it was not the intention of the Convention to deprive the States of the veto power....I know that there is a diversity of opinion among the friends of State Rights in regard to this power, which I regret, as I cannot but consider it as a power essential to the protection of the minor and local interests of the community, and the liberty of the Union of the country. It is the very shield of State Rights, and the only power by which that system of injustice against which we have contended for more than thirteen years can be arrested; a system of hostile legislation – of plundering by law, which must necessarily lead to a conflict of arms, if not prevented.

But I rest the right of a State to judge of the extent of its reserved powers, in the last resort, on higher grounds – that the Constitution is a Compact, to which the States are parties in their sovereign capacity; and that, as in all other cases of Compact between parties having no common umpire, each has a right to judge for itself....Having established this point, I now claim, as I stated I would do, in the course of the discussion, the admissions of the Senator, and, among them, the right of Secession and Nullification, which he conceded would necessarily follow if the Constitution be, indeed, a Compact.

I have now replied to the arguments of the Senator from Massachusetts so far as they directly apply to the Resolutions, and will, in conclusion, notice some of his general and detached remarks....

It is...objected by the Senator from Massachusetts, and others, against the doctrine of State Rights, as maintained in this debate, that, if it should prevail, the peace of the country would be destroyed. But what if it should not prevail? Would there be peace? Yes, the peace of despotism; that peace which is enforced by the bayonet and the sword; the peace of death, where all the vital functions of liberty have ceased. It is this peace which the doctrine of State Sovereignty may disturb by that conflict, which, in every free State, if properly organized, necessarily exists between liberty and power; but which, if restrained within proper limits, gives a salutary exercise to our moral and intellectual faculties.... [37]

Regarding the impact of John C. Calhoun's speech, Alexander H. Stephens remarked:

On these points [covered by Senator Calhoun] never was a man more completely answered than Mr. Webster was. The argument is a crusher, an extinguisher, an annihilator!

[Mr. Webster made no rejoinder.]...He followed with a few remarks only, disavowing any personal unkind feelings to Mr. Calhoun, explaining how he had used the term "Constitutional Compact," in 1830; and attempting to parry one or two of the blows, but he never made any regular set reply or rejoinder. He never came back at his opponent at all on the real questions at issue. Mr. Calhoun stood master of the arena. This speech of his was not answered then, it has not been answered since, and in my judgment never will be, or can be answered while truth has its legitimate influence, and reason controls the judgment of men!

---

[37] *Ibid.*, Volume 1, quoted on pp. 369-375, 377-381, and 383.

> The power and force of this speech must have been felt by Mr. Webster himself. He was a man of too much reason and logic not to have felt it. This opinion I am the more inclined to from the fact, that he not only did not attempt a general reply to it at the time, but from the further fact, that in after life he certainly, to say the least of it, greatly modified the opinions held by him in that debate. [38]

Not only did Senator John C. Calhoun win the debate by sheer force of reasoning and presentation of historical facts, but the sovereign State of South Carolina also realized a victory through its Interposition and Nullification action. President Jackson resolved not to attempt the use of military coercion to force that State to submit, thus avoiding bloodshed. And Congress resolved to reduce the obnoxious tariff rates to a more reasonable level of taxation.

As for the two debaters, it is of significance to note that, when John C. Calhoun died in 1850, it was Daniel Webster who gave the eulogy at the funeral. And shortly before his own death two years later, Mr. Webster defied his own Whig Party and acknowledged in unmistakable terms that the Federal Constitution truly was a *compact* between sovereign States. He reprimanded his fellow consolidators by informing them that, if the Northern States refused to uphold the Fugitive Slave act, which was based on a specific provision in the Constitution, the Southern States would no longer be bound by the compact and would be constitutionally justified in seceding from the Union.

Such expressed views by Mr. Webster in the final days of his life, however, are conveniently overlooked and ignored by the consolidating school, which prefers to remember the giant from Massachusetts as the great advocate of consolidation. As for John C. Calhoun, that same school has dismissed any need to answer his logic and reasoning by claiming that he was sufficiently answered by the Federal Government's conquest of the States in the War Between the States. For them, the proper response to superior logic and reason is superior brute force, and thus, the so-called *verdict of history* should be sufficient in itself to summarily dismiss every word ever uttered by the Orator of States' Rights. But for those who champion the cause of States' Rights, the sovereignty of the people, and constitutionally limited government, the great principles espoused by John C. Calhoun will forever stand as words of wisdom and truth.

[38] *Ibid.*, Volume 1, p. 387.

Chapter Eleven

"We the People"

Despite historical facts, common sense, logic, and reason, which all dictate that the American Federal Union is a league of sovereign States, many eminent personalities have arisen to declare that the Union was ordained and established by "the people" *in their aggregate capacity* – not by the people as politically organized into States, but by the people as constituting a single, amalgamated, sovereign American Nation. The entire Consolidating School of Thought, in fact, ultimately rests upon that fallacious foundation.

The favorite argument of the consolidators and their apologists to support this theory, as we have already observed, is to simply refer to the victory of the Government of the United States on the field of battle during the War Between the States. The *arbitrament of the sword*, the *test of battle*, and the *verdict of history* are often used expressions to dispense with the need to offer proof for their theories of government.

Yet, whenever the need arises to offer actual proof – not mere meaningless expressions based on the notion that might makes right – the Consolidating School of Thought invariably turns to one portion of the Constitution of the United States. This particular section of the compact constitutes their ultimate refuge, on which they are willing to stake their bottom dollar and make their final stand. Perhaps it was Daniel Webster who best presented the creed of the consolidating school in regard to this portion of the Federal Constitution during the famous Webster-Hayne Debate of 1830.

As the Massachusetts Senator declared on January 27, 1830:

> The Constitution itself, *in its very front*...declares that it is ordained and established by *the people of the United States*. So far from saying that it is established by the governments of the several States, *it does not even say that it is established by the people of the several States*; but it pronounces that it is established by the people of the United States, *in the aggregate*....[I]t is in this their *collective capacity*, it is as *all the people of the United States*, that they establish the Constitution. So they declare; and words cannot be plainer than the words used. [emphasis added] [1]

---

[1] Jonathan Elliot (ed.), *Elliot's Debates*, Volume 4, Published under the Sanction of Congress, Washington, 1836, p. 518.

The "plain words" to which Daniel Webster referred, of course, are those contained in the *Preamble* of the Federal Constitution. No words in the entire Constitution have been more misunderstood, perverted, confused, and distorted than those of the Preamble, especially its first seven words. Considering the great significance placed upon the Preamble by the Consolidating School of Thought, it would be of benefit to our general understanding of constitutional government to consider this opening statement of the Federal Constitution in more detail.

The Preamble of the Constitution

The Preamble of the Constitution of the United States contains fifty-two words and reads as follows:

> We the People of the United States, in order to form a more perfect Union, establish Justice, insure domestic Tranquillity, provide for the common defence, promote the general Welfare, and secure the Blessings of Liberty to ourselves and our Posterity, do ordain and establish this CONSTITUTION for the United States of America. [2]

From this Preamble, several very important facts may be ascertained as to the nature of the Federal Union that was established by the Constitution, and the Preamble itself can be divided into four logical sections. The first section tells us *whose voice speaks through the compact*, namely, "We the people of the United States." This, it should be noted, is the true *voice of sovereignty* in the United States of America.

The third section of the Preamble tells us what the people of the United States *did* or accomplished, namely, they acted to "ordain and establish this Constitution." Once again, we are reminded of the fact that the ordination and establishment of a Constitution of Government is *an act of sovereignty*. The second section of the Preamble tells us *why* the people of the United States ordained and established the Federal Constitution, and six specific reasons are given, as follows:

1. To form a more perfect Union;
2. To establish justice;
3. To ensure domestic tranquility;
4. To provide for the common defense;

[2] Alexander H. Stephens, *A Constitutional View of the Late War Between the States; Its Causes, Character, Conduct and Results*, Volume 1, Kraus Reprint Co., New York, 1970 (orig. pub. 1868), p. 557.

5. To promote the general welfare;
6. To secure the blessings of liberty for generations to come.

Finally, the fourth section of the Preamble tells us who is the *beneficiary* of this act of the people of the United States. In other words, it tells us *for whom* the Constitution was ordained and established. In the words of the Preamble, the Federal Constitution was ordained and established "for the United States of America." That, of course, was the very same title applied to the League of States under the old Articles of Confederation, in which each State was explicitly recognized as sovereign and in which the objective of the Federal Union was declared to be the preservation of the sovereignties of the several States.

But there is one thing that the Preamble, by itself, does not tell us. It does not tell us *how*, or *in what manner*, or *in what capacity*, the people of the United States ordained and established the Federal Constitution. Based merely on the Preamble, it is possible to derive two very different interpretations of exactly how the Constitution was ordained and established by the American people. It could, for instance, be interpreted to mean, "We the people of the United States, *acting as a consolidated and sovereign American Nation*,...do ordain and establish this Constitution for the United States of America." On the other hand, the Preamble could be interpreted to mean, "We the people of the United States, *acting in our capacities as sovereign States, each State bound only by its own consent*,...do ordain and establish this Constitution for the United States of America."

While the Consolidating School of Thought contends that the former construction of the Preamble is the only one possible, all historical facts, not to mention the remainder of the Constitution itself, sustain the latter construction. While the Preamble vaguely tells us *who* ordained and established the Constitution, Article VII of that compact tells us *how* – or in what capacity – the American people established the instrument. As Article VII states, "The Ratification of the Conventions of nine States, shall be sufficient for the Establishment of this Constitution between the States so ratifying the Same." [3]

For an interpretation of the Preamble to be valid, therefore, the construction of it must conform to Article VII of the Constitution, so that the notion of, "We the people of the United States,...do ordain and establish this Constitution," is properly joined with the act of the "establishment of this Constitution between the States so ratifying the same." In ordaining and establishing the compact, "We the people of the United States" acted as separate and distinct sovereign body politics.

[3] *Ibid.*, Volume 1, p. 566.

A Confusion of Terms

Before proceeding further with our inquiry into the true construction of the Preamble of the Federal Constitution, a reminder of the correct meaning of the term "State" might be helpful. Considerable misunderstanding about the nature of our Federal Union may be attributed to the erroneous equation of the term *State* with the term *government*. Admittedly, the word "State" may possess three different meanings, depending on how it is employed. Reduced to its most basic elements, a State consists of three entities: people, government, and territory. Depending on how it is used, the word in question might refer to any one of these entities.

By way of example, let us consider three sentences. "The State of Mississippi has scenic beaches." "The State of Mississippi enacted no new legislation yesterday." "The State of Mississippi is sovereign." Clearly, within each of these sentences, we are referring to the three different essentials of Statehood: geography, government, and people, respectively. But if we wish to narrow the definition of a State even further, then it should be noted that a State is strictly defined as a body politic, or a Nation of sovereign people.

Under the Articles of Confederation, the Federal Government was clearly the creation of the State *governments*, and those governments were the parties to the original federal compact. On the other hand, under our present Federal Constitution, the Government of the United States was clearly *not* the creation of the State governments. Consolidators thus conclude, quite erroneously, that, based upon this observation, the Constitution must have been established by an amalgamated, sovereign Nation of Americans. The idea that the States contain people as well as governments seems to be beyond their comprehension.

The Founding Fathers of the United States, by employing the terminology of the Preamble, intended to convey the message that it was the people of the States, and not the State governments, who ordained and established the Federal Constitution. The first seven letters of the Preamble, thus, are to be interpreted only as a distinction between the people and the governments of the several States.

The concept herein presented is highly significant for a proper understanding of the Preamble, so we will repeat the illustration. We have stated positively that the current Constitution of the United States was established, ordained, and ratified by the States. It was not ordained and established by the State governments, but it was ordained and established by the people of the States. There were no other people in the United States of America except those peoples of the several States. The "people of the United States," therefore, could only have been the people of the States. Simple logic and reasoning dictates that the "people of the United States" is an expression equivalent to the "people of the States," and that the Preamble could be altered – without changing its meaning – to read as follows: "We the people of the States,...do ordain and establish this Constitution for the United States of America."

John Taylor of Caroline, in his book, *Construction Construed and Constitutions Vindicated,* which was originally published in 1820, presented a case which should forever put an end to the fallacious notion that the words "State" and "government" are invariably equivalent. As this noted author observed:

> Nevertheless, to take away the pretext, however unsubstantial, for a different construction of the Constitution, on account of the capacity or title under which the people acted in its establishment, it is material to ascertain the meaning of the phrase "We the people of the United States;" towards which, let us run over most of the State Constitutions.
>
> *New Hampshire.* "The people of this State have *the sole and exclusive* right of governing themselves as a free, *sovereign* and independent *State.* Every subject of this *State.* In the government of this *State.* The people inhabiting the territory formerly called the province of New Hampshire, do hereby solemnly and *mutually agree with each other* to form themselves into a free, *sovereign* and independent *body politick or State.* That the *State may be equally represented.* I do swear that I will bear faith and true *allegiance to the State* of New Hampshire."
>
> *Massachusetts.* "The body politick is formed by voluntary *association of individuals.* The people of this commonwealth have the sole right of governing themselves as a free, *sovereign* and independent *State.* The people do hereby *mutually agree with each other,* to form themselves into a free, *sovereign* and independent body politick *or State.*"
>
> *New York.* "This convention, in the name and by the authority of the good *people of this State.* The legislature of this *State.* No member of this *State* shall be disfranchised. Delegates to represent this *State* in the general Congress of the *United States.* Be it enacted by the people of the *State.*"
>
> *Pennsylvania.* "*We the people* of the commonwealth of Pennsylvania ordain. The legislature of a free *State.* All government originates from the people and is found in compact only."
>
> *Delaware.* "The people of this *State.* The government shall be called the Delaware *State.* The legislature of this *State.* The general assembly of this *State.* There shall be no establishment of any one religious sect in this *State.*"
>
> *Maryland.* "The *people of this State* ought to have the sole and exclusive right of regulating the *internal government* thereof. The *legislature of this State.* The delegates to Congress from this *State* shall be chosen by joint ballot of both houses of assembly. I will be faithful and bear true allegiance to the *State.*"
>
> *Virginia.* "All power is derived from the people. Magistrates are their trustees or servants. A well regulated militia is the proper defence of a *free State.*"
>
> *North Carolina.* "The *people of this State* have the sole and exclusive

right of regulating the *internal government* thereof. Monopolies are contrary to the genius of a free *State*. All commissions shall be run in the name of the *State* of North Carolina. The legislature of this *State*. The Constitution of this *State*."

South Carolina. "The legislative authority of this *State*. The several election districts in this *State* shall elect. The style of process shall be 'The *State* of South Carolina, and conclude against the peace and dignity of the *State*.' I swear to preserve the Constitution of this *State* and of the *United States*."

Georgia. "Members of the legislature shall swear to promote the good of the *State*, to bear true allegiance to the same, and to observe the Constitution. To make laws necessary for the good of the State. Citizens and inhabitants of this *State*."

Vermont. "The people are the sole source of power. They have the exclusive right of *internal government*. All officers of government are their servants. Legislative and executive business of this *State*. The people have a right to exact from their legislators and magistrates the good government of the *State*. The legislature of a free and *sovereign State*. Every officer shall swear to be faithful to the *State* of Vermont, and to do nothing injurious to the Constitution or *government* thereof."

Without further quotations, let us demonstrate the force of these, extracted from a majority of the State Constitutions, to fix the meaning of the term "State" according to the publick judgment, by substituting the word "government" for it. They would read as follows:

"The people of this *government* have the sole and exclusive right of governing themselves as a free, *sovereign* and independent *government*."

"In the government of this *government*."

"That the *government* may be equally represented."

"The people of this *government* ought to have the sole and exclusive right of regulating the *internal government thereof*."

"The legislature of this *government*."

"I will be faithful and bear true allegiance to the *government*."

"The several election districts in this *government* shall elect."

"Members of the legislature shall swear to promote the good of the *government* and to make laws for the good of the *government*."

"Citizens and inhabitants of this *government*."

"The people have a right to exact from their legislators and magistrates the good government of the *government*."

"Commissions shall be in the name of the freemen of the *government*."

It would be an incivility to the reader, to subjoin to these quotations, many arguments, to prove, that the term "State" is not in any one instance used in reference to all the people of the United States, either as composing a single State, or as being about to compose a single State. Used geographically, it refers to State territory; used politically, it refers to the inhabitants of this territory, united by mutual consent into a civil society. The sovereignty of this association, the allegiance due to it, and its right to internal government,

> are all positively asserted. The terms "State and government" far from being synonimous, are used to convey different ideas; and the latter is never recognised as possessing any species of sovereignty. [4]

To repeat what we have before observed, the American people are politically organized into sovereign States. The Constitution recognizes that the people, in their sovereign capacity, are the States, and that the States are the people. By this logical mode of reasoning, "We the people of the United States" could only refer to the peoples of the *States United* in a Federal Union by the Constitution.

The Original Preamble

It would facilitate our understanding of the Preamble if we should consider its evolution in the Constitutional Convention of 1787. From the records of the proceedings of that Convention, it is apparent that the Preamble was first drafted on August 6, 1787, and was tentatively approved by the Convention on the next day. This Preamble, in its original form, was strikingly different in language from the one that finally emerged from the Federal Convention in September of that year.

The Preamble of our present Federal Constitution was originally expressed in the following words:

> We, the *people of the States* of New-Hampshire, Massachusetts, Rhode-Island and Providence Plantations, Connecticut, New-York, New-Jersey, Pennsylvania, Delaware, Maryland, Virginia, North-Carolina, South-Carolina, and Georgia, do ordain, declare and establish the following Constitution for the Government of Ourselves and our Posterity. [emphasis added][5]

This Preamble, as originally written, clearly indicated that the Federal Constitution, and the Federal Union and Federal Government to be established by it, would be the creations of the peoples of the several States, and not the creations of a consolidated Nation of Americans. As originally phrased, the Preamble contained no doubtful phrases and was not susceptible to misconceptions and false constructions.

This original Preamble was approved by the Grand Convention on August 7, 1787. Then, on September 8th, near the conclusion of the Convention,

---

[4] John Taylor, *Construction Construed and Constitutions Vindicated*, Da Capo Press, New York, 1970 (orig. pub. 1820), pp. 40-42.

[5] Charles A. Beard, *The Republic: Conversations on Fundamentals*, The Viking Press, New York, 1944, quoted on p. 2.

a Committee of Style was appointed, headed by Gouverneur Morris of Pennsylvania and charged with writing the Constitution in its final and polished verse. The purpose of the Committee, as its name indicated, was not to alter the *meaning* of any portion of the Constitution, but only to write the instrument in polished style and to ensure conformity in all its parts. By September 12th, the Committee of Style had completed its task, and the Constitution was then in its final verse, with the Preamble reading as it does today.

Why did the Committee of Style deem it necessary to change the wording of the Preamble? The answer lies in two facts that dictated a change in wording. First of all, Article VII of the compact stipulated that as few as nine States would be sufficient to establish the new Constitution between themselves. It was quite possible, therefore, that not all of the States mentioned in the original Preamble would actually join the new Federal Union. And if less than all the thirteen States joined the new Union, it was impossible to predict which combination of States would unite to form the new United States of America. A second consideration that necessitated a change in the Preamble was that new States might later join the Union, and it was clearly impossible to know how many States would eventually comprise the United States or to know their names.

Under these considerations, the Committee of Style correctly determined that the Preamble would need a revision in its phraseology to remove all reference to specific States. Without changing the meaning of the Preamble, the Committee of Style changed the opening words of the Preamble to read, "We the people of the United States," which was understood by all the delegates to mean the people of States of the Union. This new phraseology was subsequently received and approved by the Convention as a whole.

The change in the wording of the Preamble, in summary, was necessitated by the fact that, in adopting the Constitution, the States were regarded as sovereign body politics, to be bound only by the determination of each State separately. Considering the reason why the wording of the Preamble was changed by the Convention, it is quite ironic that the Consolidating School of Thought should later claim that the phraseology of the Preamble supposedly proves that the Constitution was adopted by a consolidated Nation of Americans.

The framers of the Constitution, it is true, did list each and every one of the thirteen original States by name in another part of the Constitution in order to assign the number of Representatives from each State until the 1790 census could be taken. This listing of the States by name for representation in the House of Representatives was left unchanged by the Committee of Style because such an enumeration was unavoidable.

From the records of the proceedings of the Philadelphia Convention of

1787, there can be no doubt whatsoever as to the true and obvious meaning of the Preamble. It should be interpreted *as if* to say:

> *We the people of the several States of the Federal Union*, in order to form a more perfect Union, establish justice, insure domestic tranquility, provide for the common defense, promote the general welfare, and secure the blessings of liberty to ourselves and our posterity, do ordain and establish this Constitution for the United States of America.

Unfortunately, the meaning of the opening words of the final version of the Preamble can be easily distorted and perverted by deceitful constructions. The very fact that the States are not specifically listed in the Preamble has actually been offered to supposedly sustain the theory of a National Government and a national sovereignty.

As Jefferson Davis of Mississippi noted in his book, *The Rise and Fall of the Confederate Government*:

> The phraseology of this Preamble has been generally regarded as the stronghold of the advocates of consolidation. It has been interpreted as meaning that "We, the people of the United States," as a collective body, or as a "nation," in our aggregate capacity, had "ordained and established" the Constitution *over* the States. [6]

We have already witnessed how Daniel Webster sought refuge in the Preamble in support of his consolidating principles. He was but one of many consolidators to utilize that tactic. On July 4, 1861, for instance, Edward Everett of Massachusetts addressed the Academy of Music in New York, declaring:

> That instrument does not purport to be a "compact," but a Constitution of government. It appears, in its first sentence, not to have been entered into by the States, but to have been ordained and established by the people of the United States for themselves and their "posterity." *The States are not named in it*; nearly all the characteristic powers of *sovereignty* are expressly granted to the general government and expressly prohibited to the States. [emphasis added] [7]

In another part of his address, Mr. Everett again stressed the fact that, "*The States are not named in it.*" [8] This, in fact, seemed to be the foundation of

---

[6] Jefferson Davis, *The Rise and Fall of the Confederate Government*, Volume 1, Thomas Yoseloff, New York, 1958 (orig. pub. 1881), p. 121.
[7] *Ibid.*, Volume 1, quoted on p. 129.
[8] *Ibid.*, Volume 1, quoted on p. 129.

his entire philosophy of the nature of the Federal Union – since the States are not specifically named in the Preamble, sovereignty must have been transferred to the Government of the United States. Once again, we note the irony of such a contention, considering that the reason why the States could not be listed in the Preamble was owing to the fact that they are sovereign.

If Edward Everett's comments seem ridiculous, then the views expressed by John Lothrop Motley will appear fantastically absurd. Destined to become Minister to the Court of St. James, this Radical Republican wrote a letter to the London *Times* that was published in 1861 under the title, "Causes of the Civil War." His letter was a masterpiece of deception, and in just two paragraphs he succeeded in squeezing more outrageous notions of our political system than perhaps anyone, before or since, has been able to do in the same amount of space.

As Mr. Motley boldly asserted:

> It was not a compact. Who ever heard of a compact to which there were no parties? Or who ever heard of a compact made by a single party with himself? Yet *the name of no State is mentioned in the whole document*; the States themselves are only mentioned to receive commands or prohibitions; and the "people of the United States" is the single party by whom alone the instrument is executed.
>
> The Constitution was not drawn up by the States, it was not promulgated in the name of the States, it was not ratified by the States. The States never acceded to it, and possess no power to secede from it. It was "ordained and established" *over* the States by a power *superior to the States*; by the people of the *whole land* in their *aggregate capacity*.... [emphasis added] [9]

The honor of exposing the foolish notions of Edward Everett and John Lothrop Motley fell to Jefferson Davis, the former President of the Confederate States of America, who wrote in 1881:

> It would be very hard to condense a more amazing account of audacious and reckless falsehood in the same space. In all Mr. Motley's array of bold assertions, there is not one single truth – unless it be, perhaps, that "the Constitution was not drawn up by the States." Yet it was drawn up by their delegates, and it is of such material as this, derived from writers whose reputation gives a semblance of the authenticity to their statements, that history is constructed and transmitted.
>
> One of the most remarkable – though, perhaps, the least important – of these misstatements is that which is also twice repeated by Mr. Everett – that the name of no State is mentioned in the whole document, or, as he puts it, "the States are not named in it." Very little careful examination would

[9] *Ibid.*, Volume 1, quoted on p. 129.

> have sufficed to find, in the second section of the very first article of the Constitution, the names of every one of the thirteen then existent States distinctly mentioned with the number of representatives to which each would be entitled, in case of acceding to the Constitution, until a census of their population could be taken. The mention there made of the States by name is of no special significance; it has no bearing upon any question of principle; and the denial of it is a purely gratuitous illustration of the recklessness of those from whom it proceeds, and the low estimate put on the intelligence of those addressed. It serves, however, to show how much credence is to be given to their authority as interpreters and expounders.
>
> The reason why the names of the ratifying States were not mentioned has already been given: it was simply because it was not known which States would ratify. But, as regards mention of "the several States," "each State," "any State," "particular States," and the like, the Constitution is full of it. I am informed, by one who has taken the pains to examine carefully that document with reference to this very point, that – without including any mention of "the United States" or of "foreign States," and excluding also the amendments – the Constitution, in its original draft, makes mention of the States, *as* States, no less than *seventy* times; and of these seventy times, only *three* times in the way of prohibition of the exercise of a power. In fact, it is full of statehood. Leave out all mention of the States – I make no mere verbal point or quibble, but mean the States in their separate, several, distinct capacity – and what would remain would be of less account than the play of the Prince of Denmark with the part of *Hamlet* omitted. [10]

It is actually no mere grammatical quibble to assert that the United States would truly be the *United Nothing* without the States, as States. The fallacious philosophy which asserts that the Constitution was established by the American people in their aggregate capacity over the States only serves to reflect upon the deceitfulness of its promoters and the ignorance of those who believe such a concept. The records of the proceedings of the Philadelphia Convention of 1787 were published at a relatively early date in American history, and it would seem inexcusable for any political theorist, who professes to be literate, to expound views of the Constitution radically different from those professed by the Founding Fathers. To excuse the advocates of national sovereignty on the grounds of illiteracy, however, would be more generous than the situation warrants. Those seeking to sacrifice States' Rights on the altar of Big Government do not act from misguided religious zeal, but from a desire to sustain a totalitarian system based on plunder, corruption, and fraud. The Preamble has been seized upon merely as a convenient vehicle to effect their goal of consolidation.

In his book, *The Southern States in the American Union*, Dr. Jabez Lamar Monroe Curry noted:

---

[10] *Ibid.*, Volume 1, pp. 129-131.

"The people of His Majesty' Colonies," "the people of the United Colonies," "the people of the United States," are modes of expression which frequently occurred, without intending in any wise to deny or surrender the separateness of the several Colonies or States. The people of the several Colonies were never a unit in a political sense, neither before nor after the Declaration of Independence. They were never a Nation, nor an entire community, contradistinguished from the people of the several States, having, as such, community rights and powers of a political character. The Revolutionary Government, as has been amply shown, was emphatically a Government of the States, through Congress, as their agent, with very limited powers. The phrase of the Preamble is the most common reliance of those who claim the nationality and sovereignty of the general government, and it is confidently quoted as tantamount to the lodging in the hands of the [Federal] Government all the powers that belong to any other government *qua* government. [11]

As the noted commentator, James J. Kilpatrick, wrote in his book, *The Sovereign States*:

Was it ever intended that the States should be reduced to the weakling role thrust upon them in our own time? We must inquire whether this proud possession of State sovereignty, so eloquently proclaimed in 1776, so resolutely affirmed in the Articles of 1781, so clearly recognized in the events of the time, somehow vanished, died, turned to dust, totally ceased to exist in the period of the next six years.

Now, the argument here advanced is this – it is the argument of John Taylor of Caroline and John Randolph of Roanoke – that sovereignty, like chastity, cannot be surrendered "in part." This was the argument also of Calhoun: "I maintain that sovereignty is in its nature indivisible. It is the supreme power in a State, and we might just as well speak of half a square, or half a triangle, as of half a sovereignty." This was the position, too, of the bellicose George Troup of Georgia, of Alexander H. Stephens, of Jefferson Davis. It is the position of plain common sense: Supreme and ultimate power must be precisely that....And so it is with the States of the American Union. In the last resort, it is *their* prerogative alone (not that of Congress, not that of the Supreme Court, not that of the "whole people") to make or unmake our fundamental law. The argument here is that the States, in forming a new perpetual Union to replace their old perpetual Union, remained in essence what they had been before: Separate, free, and independent States. They *surrendered* nothing to the Federal Government they created. *Some of their powers they delegated; all of their sovereignty they retained.*

...Sovereignty is the essence, the life spirit, the soul: And in this Republic, sovereignty remains today where it was vested in 1776, in the people. But in the people as a whole? No. In the *people-as-States.*

---

[11] Jabez Lamar Monroe Curry, *The Southern States in the American Union*, G.P. Putnam's Sons, New York, 1895, pp. 98-99.

> The delusion that sovereignty is vested in the whole people of the United States is one of the strangest misconceptions of our public life. This hallucination has been encouraged, if not directly espoused, by such eminent figures as Marshall, Story, and Andrew Jackson. It is still embraced by excessively literal and unthinking fellows who read "we the people" in the Preamble to the Constitution, and cry triumphantly, "that means everybody." It does not; it never did. [12]

The Foresight of Patrick Henry

As if by foresight, many distinguished leaders in the various States during the Ratification Period, who had not attended the Philadelphia Convention of 1787, recognized that a misconstruction of the Preamble's first seven words could subvert the Constitution and undermine the federal system. Writing to Richard Henry Lee, for example, the great Boston patriot Samuel Adams professed that, upon his first reading of the new Constitution, he had "stumbled at the threshold." [13]

A number of others also stumbled at the threshold of the new federal compact. In Virginia, a great struggle – perhaps the greatest among all the States – arose over the question of ratification of the Federal Constitution. Many were skeptical of the proposed plan of government and a bit suspicious of the motives of some of the Federalists who urged its adoption. Accordingly, these Antifederalists were determined to accurately ascertain and note on the public record the true meaning of each and every doubtful phrase and clause in the Constitution of the United States.

Among the more skillful and articulate of the Virginia Antifederalists was the renowned Patrick Henry of Revolutionary fame. In the course of his inquiries within the Virginia State Ratifying Convention, Mr. Henry devoted particular attention to the Preamble, especially to its first seven words. As he saw it, the words, "We the people of the United States," were so vague and ambiguous as to require a detailed explanation.

As Patrick Henry stated before the Virginia State Ratifying Convention:

> I would make this inquiry of those worthy characters who composed a part of the late Federal Convention. I am sure they were fully impressed with the necessity of forming a great consolidated government, instead of a Confederation. That this is a consolidated government is demonstrably clear; and the danger of such a government is, to my mind, very striking. I have the highest veneration for those gentlemen; but, Sir, give me leave to demand,

---

[12] James J. Kilpatrick, *The Sovereign States*, Henry Regnery Company, Chicago, 1957, pp. 14-15.
[13] Jefferson Davis, *Op. cit.*, Volume 1, quoted on p. 121.

> What right had they to say, *We, the people*? My political curiosity, exclusive of my anxious solicitude for the public welfare, leads me to ask, Who authorized them to speak the language of "*We, the people*," instead of *We, the States*? States are the characteristics and soul of a Confederation. If the States be not the agents of the compact, it must be one great consolidated National Government of all the people of all the States. [14]

Mr. Henry's address was not to state a fact that the Constitution would establish a consolidated national system. His intention in making these statements was to draw from the Federalists a statement of the true meaning of the Preamble. Of course, proponents of ratification had attempted to allay such fears of consolidation with the name in which they had styled themselves – *Federalists*. The Antifederalists, however, intended to leave nothing to implication, not even the very threshold – the Preamble – of the new compact.

Patiently, Patrick Henry waited for an answer to his inquiry from the Federalists. When the proponents of ratification failed to provide a satisfactory explanation for the Preamble, Mr. Henry arose in the Virginia State Ratifying Convention the following day to once again press for an answer to his question:

> When I asked that question, I thought the meaning of my interrogation was obvious. The fate of this question and of America may depend on this. Have they said, We, the States? Have they made a proposal of a compact between States? If they had, this would be a Confederation: it is otherwise most clearly a consolidated government. The question turns, Sir, on that poor little thing – the expression, "We, the people," instead of the States of America. [15]

Patrick Henry was determined to publicly establish the true meaning of the Preamble and to record its construction beyond doubt for the benefit of future generations of Americans. His determination was finally rewarded when the leading Federalist in the Virginia State Ratifying Convention – James Madison – arose to answer Mr. Henry's query.

The Father of the Constitution informed the ratifying convention:

> Who are the parties to it? *The people – but not the people as composing one great body; but the people as composing thirteen sovereignties*: were it, as the gentleman asserts, a consolidated government, the assent of a majority of the people would be sufficient for its establishment, and as a majority have adopted it already, the remaining States would be bound by the act of the majority, even if they unanimously reprobated it: were it such a government as is suggested, it would be now binding on the people of this State, without

[14] Jonathan Elliot (ed.), *Elliot's Debates*, Volume 3, Published under the Sanction of Congress, Washington, 1836, p. 54.

[15] *Ibid.*, Volume 3, p. 72.

> having had the privilege of deliberating upon it; but, Sir, no State is bound by it, as it is, without its own consent. Should all the States adopt it, it will be then *a government established by the thirteen States of America*, not through the intervention of the legislature, but by the people at large. In this particular respect the distinction between the existing and proposed governments is very material. The existing system has been derived from the dependent, derivative authority of the legislatures of the States, whereas this is derived from the superior power of the people. [emphasis added] [16]

As Mr. Madison thus explained, the key to properly interpreting the first seven words in the Preamble lies in Article VII of the Constitution of the United States, which specifies the mode of ratification. One of the most basic rules of proper construction of the Constitution is that every part of that instrument must be interpreted so as to be in harmony with the remainder of the compact. Should a construction of any part of the Constitution result in a contradiction with any other part of the instrument, this is a clear indicator that the interpretation offered is incorrect. If the Preamble is to be properly interpreted, its construed meaning must be consistent with the meaning of Article VII, which states that the compact shall exist *between the States* of the Federal Union.

The Virginia State Ratifying Convention was not the only one to explore and explicitly establish the true meaning of the Preamble. Throughout the States, during the Ratification Period, there were a number of Antifederalists who shared the concerns of Patrick Henry, and who had the foresight to demand that the construction of the Preamble be settled at the time of the Constitution's adoption. Proponents of ratification in the various States were required to address this issue, and their responses mirrored the one offered by James Madison before the Virginia State Ratifying Convention.

Typical of the explanations being echoed throughout the States during the struggle for ratification was that presented by Trench Coxe to the Pennsylvania State Ratifying Convention:

> If the Federal Convention had meant to exclude the idea of "union" – that is, of several and separate sovereignties joining in a Confederacy – they would have said, "We, the people of America"; for union necessarily involves the idea of competent States, which complete consolidation excludes. [17]

Commenting on the Preamble and the misconstructions of it by the consolidating school, Dr. J.L.M. Curry has written:

---

[16] *Ibid.*, Volume 3, p. 114-115.

[17] Jefferson Davis, *Op. cit.*, Volume 1, quoted on p. 128.

> If the Constitution had been made by "the people" of the United States, "in their collective capacity," a certain portion, *prima facie* the majority, would have had that right. Did such a majority ever act? Can the time or the occasion be specified when power was visibly exercised by others than those personally delegated by the organized political peoples of the several States? Was there any mode prescribed by which the majority might act; or, if acting, by which their will could be, or was, ascertained? It is possible that the Constitution became the fundamental law by the suffrages of a minority, for we know that it was laid before the conventions of several States and by them ratified and adopted, each State acting for itself, without reference to any other State, and that the government was put into operation, when the necessary number was obtained, without counting the aggregate vote, or waiting to inquire whether a majority of the people had assented. The "people of the United States," in the sense held by the Nationalists, were not the authors of the Constitution, and could not have formed it, since they did not appoint the Convention, nor ratify their act, nor in any way adopt it as obligatory upon them. It was voted for by States in the Convention, submitted to the people of each State separately, and became the Constitution only of the States adopting it. "The people of the United States," as a political organism, never had an existence; in the aggregate, never performed a single political act, never was entrusted with any civil function, never was appealed to for sanction to any proceeding, and never can do what a National Government might do, without an entire radical revolution of our system of constitutional, representative, confederated Republics. It seems conclusive of controversy to say that the Government of the United States has no *inherent* powers whatever, none by virtue of the fact that it is a government. Its powers are all derivative, nominated in the bond, specifically granted, and what is not granted was reserved to the States respectively, or to the people thereof. [18]

James Fenimore Cooper, the noted early American author, in his book, *The American Democrat,* which was published in 1838, made the following observations on the Preamble and the term *people*:

> The term "people," like most other substantives, has its general and its specific significations. In its general signification, the people of a country, means the population of a country; as the population of a country includes the women and children, nothing can be clearer than that the "people," in this signification did not form the American Constitution. The specific significations of this word are numerous, as rich, poor, wise, silly, good and bad people. In a political sense, the people means whose who are vested with political rights, and, in this particular instance, the people vested with political rights, were the constituencies of the several States, under their various laws, modifications and Constitutions, which is but another name for the governments of the States themselves. "We the *people,*" as used in the Preamble of the Constitution, means merely, "We the *constituencies* of the several States."

---

[18] Jabez Lamar Monroe Curry, *Op. cit.*, pp. 99-100.

> It follows, that the Constitution of the United States was formed by the States, and not by the people of the entire country, as contended; the term used in the Preamble being used in contra-distinction to the old divine right of sovereigns, and as a mode of expressing the general republican character of the government. The States, by a prescribed majority, can also amend the Constitution, altering any of its provisions, with the exception of that which guaranties the equal representation of the States in the Senate. It might be shown, that States possessing a minority of all the people of the Union can alter the Constitution, a fact, in itself, which proves that the Government of the United States, though a Republick, is not necessarily a popular government, in the broadest meaning of the word. The Constitution leaves the real character of the institutions of the country, with the exception that it prohibits monarchies, to be settled by the several States themselves. [19]

The simple truth is that the expression, "We the people of the United States," as used in the Preamble, means only, "*We the States.*" Any other construction can only serve to subvert the Constitution, undermine the sovereignty of the people, and establish the means of usurping the reserved powers of the States. No matter what clever constructions of the Preamble are offered by the consolidating school, what decisions are rendered by the United States Supreme Court, what decrees are made by the Chief Executive, or what laws are enacted by Congress, no interpretation, opinion, decree, or law can alter the truth.

As the noted writer and historian, Albert T. Bledsoe, observed:

> "I remember," says Mr. Webster, "to have heard Chief-Justice Marshall ask counsel, who was insisting upon the authority of an act of legislation, *if he thought an act of legislation could create or destroy a fact, or change the truth of history*? 'Would it alter the fact,' said he, 'if a legislature should solemnly enact that Mr. Hume never wrote the History of England?' A legislature may alter the law," continues Mr. Webster, "but no power can reverse a fact." Hence, if the Constitution of 1787 had expressly declared that the Constitution was ordained by "the people of the United States *in the aggregate*," or by the people of America as one Nation, this would not have destroyed the fact that it was ratified by each State for itself, and that each State was bound only by "its own voluntary act." [20]

People Versus Peoples

Perhaps the meaning of the first seven words of the Preamble would have been less liable to misconstruction had the framers of the Constitution

[19] Peter Witonski (ed.), *The Wisdom of Conservatism*, Volume 3, New Rochelle, N.Y., 1971, p. 1841.
[20] Jefferson Davis, *Op. cit.*, Volume 1, quoted on p. 134.

phrased it in different words. However, in their defense, it must be acknowledged that the term "people" was freely used in their time, as it is in modern times, to refer to the peoples of various political communities either in the singular or in the plural form of the word. When referring to inhabitants of the countries of Asia, for example, we could use either of two expressions – "the *people* of Asia" or "the *peoples* of Asia" – and it should still be understood that the people of the continent of Asia are politically divided into separate countries. Using the former expression, with its singular form of the word *people*, does not inherently imply that the inhabitants of Asia constitute a single Nation. The same principle applies to such expressions as "the people of the States," "the peoples of the States," "the people of the United States," and "the peoples of the United States."

Commenting on the singular and plural usage of the term *people*, Jefferson Davis observed:

> Could the authors of the Constitution have foreseen the perversion to be made of their obvious meaning, it might have been prevented by an easy periphrasis – such as, "We, the people of the States hereby united," or something to the same effect. The word "people" in 1787, as in 1880, was, as it is, a collective noun, employed indiscriminately, either as a unit in such expressions as "this people," "a free people," etc., or in a distributive sense, as applied to the citizens or inhabitants of one state or country or a number of states or countries. When the Convention of the colony of Virginia, in 1774, instructed their delegates to the Congress that was to meet in Philadelphia, "to obtain a redress of those grievances, without which the *people of America* can neither be safe, free, nor happy," it was certainly not intended to convey the idea that the people of the American Continent, or even of the British colonies in America, constituted one political community. Nor did Edmund Burke have any such meaning when he said, in his celebrated speech in Parliament, in 1775, "The people of the colonies are descendants of Englishmen."
>
> We need go no further than the familiar language of King James' translation of the Bible for multiple illustrations of this indiscriminate use of the term, both in its collective and distributive senses. For example, King Solomon prays at the dedication of the temple:
>
> "That thine eyes may be open unto the supplication...of thy *people* Israel, to hearken unto them in all that they call for unto thee. For thou didst separate them from among *all the people* of the earth, to be thine inheritance." (1 Kings viii, 52, 53.)
>
> Here we have both the singular and plural sense of the same word – *one people*, Israel, and *all the people of the earth* – in two consecutive sentences. In "the people of the earth," the word *people* is used precisely as it is in the expression "the people of the United States" in the Preamble of the Constitution, and has exactly the same force and effect. If in the latter case it implies that the people of Massachusetts and those of Virginia were mere

> fractional parts of one political community, it must in the former imply a like unity among the Philistines, the Egyptians, the Assyrians, Babylonians, and Persians, and all other "people of the earth," except the Israelites. Scores of examples of the same sort might be cited if it were necessary.
>
> In the Declaration of Independence we find precisely analogous instances of the employment of the singular form for both singular and plural senses – "one people," "a free people," in the former, and "the good people of these colonies" in the latter. Judge Story, in the excess of his zeal in behalf of a theory of consolidation, bases upon this last expression the conclusion that the assertion of independence was the act of "*the whole people* of the United Colonies" as a unit; overlooking or suppressing the fact that, in the very same sentence, the colonies declare themselves "free and independent *States*" – not a free and independent *State* – repeating the words "independent States" three times.
>
> If, however, the Declaration of Independence constituted one "*whole people*" of the colonies, then that geographical section of it, formerly known as the colony of Maryland, was in a state of revolt or "rebellion" against the others, as well as against Great Britain, from 1778 to 1781, during which period Maryland refused to ratify or be bound by the Articles of Confederation, which, according to this theory, was binding upon her, as a majority of the "whole people" had adopted it. *A fortiori*, North Carolina and Rhode Island were in a state of rebellion in 1789-'90 while they declined to ratify and recognize the Constitution adopted by the other eleven fractions of this united people. Yet no hint of any such pretension – of any claim of authority over them by the majority – of any assertion of "the supremacy of the Union" – is to be found in any of the records of that period.
>
> It might have been unnecessary to bestow so much time and attention in exposing the absurdity of the deductions from a theory so false, but for the fact that it has been specious enough to secure the countenance of men of such distinction as Webster, Story, and Everett; and that it has been made the plea to justify a bloody war against that principle of State sovereignty and independence, which was regarded by the fathers of the Union as the cornerstone of the structure and the basis of the hope for its perpetuity. [21]

The word "people," like the word "fish," has both a singular and a plural *meaning* as well as a singular and a plural *form*. In its singular form – *fish* – the word can have either a singular or a plural sense, referring to either one fish or many fish. In its plural form – *fishes* – the word has only a plural sense, always referring to more than one fish. Consider, by way of example, the following sentence: "Yesterday, I caught three *fish*, but today I caught only one *fish*." The word *fishes* could be substituted for the word fish in the first instance, but not in the second instance.

When referring to more than one fish, it is acceptable to use either the singular or the plural form of the word. Yet, the form of choice will depend on

[21] *Ibid.*, Volume 1, pp. 125-127.

what emphasis is desired, especially if emphasis on the different characteristics of the whole is preferred. When emphasizing the common characteristics of more than one fish, for example, the singular form of the word fish is generally used. On the other hand, when emphasizing that fish are divided into different groups or sets of fish, the plural form of the term is generally utilized. Marine biologists, for example, often prefer to say that the ocean is full of *fishes* – emphasizing the various species of fish – rather than to say that the ocean is full of *fish*.

In similar fashion, the word "people" has both a plural and a singular *form* as well as a plural and a singular *sense*. And, needless to say, we are here interested in this word only as it applies to *political* usage. The *Webster's II New Riverside University Dictionary* provides two acceptable definitions of the word people in its singular form and singular sense: "A body or persons living in the same country under one government: NATIONALITY," and, "The citizens of a political unit, as a Nation or State: ELECTORATE." [22]

Thus, in its singular form, the word *people*, when used in a political sense, is best employed in reference to the citizens or inhabitants of a sovereign State or Nation. When referring to more than one State or Nation, the plural form – *peoples* – is the choice of preference, for it underscores the fact that the people in question are divided into separate body politics. Unfortunately, mankind does not always follow this rule of wisdom, and the singular form of the word people is frequently employed in its plural sense, making the word identical in its import to the word peoples.

To illustrate the concept here presented, let us offer a practical example: "The people of Mississippi are the brethren of the rest of the people of the United States." In both instances, the word "people" is used in its singular form, although the sense is different in each case. The plural form of the word – peoples – may be substituted for "people" in the second instance, but not in the first.

Based on what has been presented, the following expressions may be considered as conveying identical meanings:

- The people of the United States
- The peoples of the United States
- The people of the States
- The peoples of the States
- The people of the several States
- The peoples of the several States

---

[22] *Webster's II New Riverside University Dictionary*, The Riverside Publishing Company, 1984, p. 871.

Those expressions that utilize the more precise terminology of "peoples," needless to say, are more preferable precisely because the term used is more precise in its import. The usage of the singular form of "people," however, cannot be interpreted to imply a single, consolidated Nation of Americans, because a proper interpretation of such expressions must conform with historical reality and those provisions of the Federal Constitution which clearly identify our system of government as a Federal Union between sovereign States.

The usage of the term "several" before the word "States" in the sample expressions listed above illustrate another device employed for greater precision of comprehension, for its usage further emphasizes the fact that each State of our Union is a separate, sovereign Nation. But no matter which of the above expressions are employed, none of them should be interpreted as robbing the States of their sovereignty. No mere grammatical quibble – or matter of simple semantics – should form the basis of conquering sovereign States and reducing them to colonial status.

If more examples were necessary to demonstrate the singular and plural sense of the word "people" in its singular form, then we may refer to the King James Version of the Bible, which contains many such illustrations. Verses 6 and 7 of the seventh chapter of Deuteronomy offer an excellent example:

> For thou art an holy *people* unto the Lord thy God: the Lord thy God hath chosen thee to be a special *people* unto himself, above all *people* that are upon the face of the earth.
>
> The Lord did not set his love upon you, nor choose you, because ye were more in number than any *people*; for ye were the fewest of all *people*. [emphasis added] [23]

In these two verses of the Holy Bible, the word "people" is employed five times, always in the singular form, but not always in the singular sense. The first two usages of the term – "an holy people" and "a special people" – the sense in which the word is used is singular, referring solely to the Israelites. In the third instance – "all people" – the word is clearly used in its plural sense. In the fourth usage of the word – "any people" – it's meaning is singular, for the expression is used in reference to any *one* people. Finally, in the last usage of the term – "all people" – the sense is plural.

Now let us apply this understanding of the term "people" to the first seven words of the Preamble of our present Federal Constitution: "We the *people* of the United States." The word in question is here used in its singular form. But is it used in its singular or its plural sense? Clearly, the form is singular, but the sense is plural. The plural form of the word – peoples – could be

[23] C.I. Scofield (ed.), *The New Scofield Reference Bible*, Oxford University Press, New York, 1967, p. 226.

substituted for the singular form of the word in the Preamble without altering its true meaning: "We the *peoples* of the United States." This substitution accords completely with the idea expressed by James Madison before the Virginia State Ratifying Convention: "Who are the parties to it? The people – but not the people as composing one great body; but the *people* as composing thirteen sovereignties." [24]

Distorting the Obvious

While differing from the Articles of Confederation in one significant aspect – that the people themselves, not the State governments, established the Constitution of 1787 – it was clearly understood by the generation that adopted the compact that it was not created by the American people in their aggregate capacity. The very mode of its ratification made it obvious to the generation of the Founding Fathers that the Constitution rested on the foundation of sovereign States. Yet, a mere generation later, the Preamble was being misconstrued by the consolidating school in an effort to distort the obvious.

By 1830, Daniel Webster of Massachusetts could dare to arise in the Senate of the United States and boldly proclaim:

> The Constitution itself, in its very front...declares that it is ordained and established by the people of the United States. So far from saying that it is established by the governments of the several States, it does not even say it is established by the people of the several States; but pronounced that it is established by the people of the United States, in the aggregate. The Gentleman says, it must mean no more than that the people of the several States, taken collectively, constitute the people of the United States....[But] it is as all the people of the United States, that they establish the Constitution. So they declare; and words cannot be plainer than the words used. [25]

The objective of such denials of basic truths, of course, was to transform our federal system of government into a national system, and to convert our republican form of government into a form based on unlimited and unrestrained majority rule. Such a conversion of our form and system of government, needless to say, would result in a consolidated National Government, the centralization of all powers in Washington, and the eventual transformation of our free enterprise economic system into a socialistic despotism. This is the inevitable result to be expected from a sovereign government, which has ever been the goal of the consolidating school.

---

[24] Jonathan Elliot (ed.), *Op. cit.*, Volume 3, p. 114.
[25] Jonathan Elliot (ed.), *Op. cit.*, Volume 4, p. 518.

As Dr. Jabez L.M. Curry has observed:

> The Constitution is federative in the power which framed it, in the power which adopted and ratified it, in the power which sustains and keeps it alive, in the power by which alone it can be altered or amended, and is federative in the structure of all its departments. In no sense is our Federal Government a democracy, or do the people rule *en masse*. The doctrine of State co-operation, or concurrent majorities, or restraints upon mere popular will, of checks and balances, runs through and dominates the whole system. The Government of the Union is the creature of the States. It is not a party to the Constitution, but the result of it, as made by the constituent States, and cannot, as originally formed and designed, exist independently of it, or of the States, its creators. The Union, so much lauded and so beneficial and necessary, is not a self-existing thing. It is a consequence, a creation, and whatever powers it possesses or can exercise, whatever authority it can use, whatever allegiance it can claim, grow out of the voluntary and separate acts of the separate States. The States are united to the extent of the delegated powers; beyond those the States are not in a Union....The Federal theory of our Government made the party which has sedulously guarded the States against encroachment or usurpation, and has construed the Constitution strictly in its grants and limitations. Standing over in antagonism to this is the opposing view as to the extent of the powers conferred upon the Government, – a view which makes the Government a creature of national sovereignty, and in its machinery of administration independent of, and superior to, the weal of State governments. This theory makes the National Government the ultimate and sole interpreter of its own powers, with no remedy except revolution against usurpation; for there can be no difference between a government having originally all powers, and one having the right to take what powers it pleases. At one time, in the progress of framing the Constitution, the words "National Government" were inserted, but after debate, on motion of Mr. Ellsworth of Connecticut, were stricken out unanimously, thus showing that the Convention intended the Government to be Federal, not National. Mr. Calhoun, in 1811, used this clear and terse language: "The chief object for which the Constitution was formed was to give the general government power, security, and respectability abroad. In our relations with foreign countries, where strength of government and national security were most required, the powers of government are undivided. In those exterior relations abroad, this Government is the sole and exclusive representative of the united majority, sovereignty, and power of the States constituting this great and glorious Union. To the rest of the world, we are one. Neither State nor State government is known beyond our borders....It is only at home, in their internal relations that they are many." [26]

It is of interest to compare the Preamble of our present Federal Constitution with the Preamble of the Charter of the United Nations Organization.

---

[26] Jabez Lamar Monroe Curry, *Op. cit.*, pp. 101-104.

This Preamble of United Nations Charter begins by stating that, "*We the Peoples of the United Nations,*" to effect a number of specified global objectives, "*Have Resolved to Combine our Efforts to Accomplish These Aims.*" [27]

The Preamble of the U.N. Charter then concludes with these words:

> Accordingly, our respective Governments, through representatives assembled in the city of San Francisco, who have exhibited their full powers found to be in good and due form, have agreed to the present Charter of the United Nations and do hereby establish an international organization to be known as the United Nations. [28]

Despite the fact that the Charter of the United Nations was ordained and established by the *governments* of those Nations that adopted it, the Preamble of that Charter for World Government begins with the words, "We the peoples of the United Nations." And here the question must be raised: Do these first seven words of the Preamble of the U.N. Charter automatically rob the various States belonging to the United Nations of their sovereignty?

Let us place the two Preambles in question next to one another for better comparison:

U.S. Constitution: "We the people of the United States...."
U.N. Charter: "We the peoples of the United Nations...."

If the first expression robs the several States of the American Union of their sovereignty, then the second expression must rob the member Nations of the Global Union of their sovereignty. Yet, the very text of the United Nations Charter denies such a construction. Article 2, Section 1 of the U.N. Charter categorically states that, "The Organization is based on the principle of the sovereign equality of all its Members." [29] Thus, if the opening words of the U.N. Charter do not rob the several Nations of the World Union of their sovereignty, how, then, could the opening words of the Constitution of 1787 rob the States of the American Union of their sovereignty?

Would it have made any difference had the singular form of the word "people," rather than its plural form, been utilized in the Charter of the United Nations? Would it not have been automatically understood that, had the singular form been employed, the word would have been used in its plural sense? Is it not likewise understood by all who have common sense that the plural form of the word "people" could have been used in the Preamble of the U.S. Consti-

---

[27] Bradford Chambers, *Vest-Pocket Handbook of the United Nations*, Follett Publishing Company, Chicago, 1965, pp. 276-277.
[28] *Ibid.*, p. 277.
[29] *Ibid.*, p. 278.

tution without altering, in any degree, its true meaning and import?

Just 31 years after the Constitution of the United States had been adopted by the States, the clairvoyant theorist from Virginia, John Taylor of Caroline, recognized the beginning of a trend to misconstrue the Preamble for ulterior motives. Writing in 1820 – a full decade before Daniel Webster delivered his famous speech in the Webster-Hayne Debate, in which he cited the Preamble as "proof" that a consolidated Nation of people had created the Constitution – John Taylor of Caroline presented a brilliant refutation of this absurd theory in his book, *Construction Construed and Constitutions Vindicated.*

As Mr. Taylor observed:

> Who made it [*i.e.*, the Union]? "We, the people of the United States." But who were they? The associated inhabitants of each State, or the unassociated inhabitants of all the States. The question is an exposition, either of the ignorance or the design of construction. If there is no difficulty in answering it, construction ought to be laughed at for playing the fool; but if it gives the wrong answer, as supposing it to furnish contrary inferences to the right one, it ought to be suspected of playing the knave. At least an attempt to construe away a fact, known to everybody, is a fine specimen of its character when aiming at an accession of power. It has been imagined, that by considering the Union as the act of the people, in their natural, and not in their political associated capacity, some aspect of consolidation might be shed over the country, and the Federal Government might thereby acquire more power. [30]

The true objective of the consolidating school is the acquisition of a boundless field of power – to consolidate all power in the hands of the Government of the United States of America. The means to attain that nefarious end is to bestow upon the Federal Government the exclusive right to determine the limits of its own power. This, in turn, is to be accomplished through the artifice of a mythical State of America supposedly vested with a "national sovereignty." Standing squarely in the way of such schemes, however, and serving as a roadblock to the centralization of all power in Washington, is the sovereignty of each State in our Federal Union.

To achieve their objectives, the Consolidating School of Thought must wage war upon States' Rights in an effort to steal sovereignty from the States and vest it in the hands of the Federal Government, while paying lip service to a non-existent Nation of Americans. This warfare has produced a host of subterfuges, omissions and distortions of facts, and complete falsehoods designed to deny the existence of sovereign States. And there has been no greater deception propagated by the consolidators than that involving their misconstruction

---

[30] John Taylor, *Op. cit.*, p. 39.

of the Preamble.

The whole issue of misconstruing the Preamble to effect evil ends was brilliantly and succinctly exposed by James Madison in the celebrated Virginia Resolutions of 1798:

> Had the States been despoiled of their sovereignty by the generality of the Preamble, had the Federal Government been endowed with whatever they should judge to be instrumental towards justice, tranquillity, common defence, general welfare, and the preservation of liberty, nothing could have been more frivolous than an enumeration of powers. [31]

---

[31] Jabez Lamar Monroe Curry, *Op. cit.*, quoted on pp. 100-101.

Chapter Twelve

Some Common Misconceptions

Considerable ground has been covered in the preceding chapters in our inquiry into the nature of sovereignty in the United States of America. During the course of our inquiry, we have examined the issue of exactly where political supremacy is and should be invested within our political system. Stated more precisely, we have determined whether such sovereignty is constitutionally vested in the government or in the people. And if in the people, we have ascertained which people are and should be sovereign, either the peoples of the several States, or the people of a consolidated American Nation.

Based upon historical fact, the words of the Federal Constitution, and sound reason and logic, it has been conclusively demonstrated that the American Theory of Government is founded upon the concept that sovereignty is vested in the people, and not in any government. Furthermore, it has been conclusively shown that, in the United States, such political supremacy is vested by natural right in the peoples of the several States composing the Federal Union. And during the course of our inquiry, it has been demonstrated that the American people exist politically as the States, for there is no such political community as the State of America. To steal sovereignty from the States for the supposed purpose of vesting it in a non-existent American Nation is nothing more than a clever scheme to rob the people of their supremacy and to vest such sovereignty in the Government of the United States.

Despite the undeniable truth of these principles, however, there are at least six common misconceptions regarding the development and progress of our political institutions that serve to generate reluctance to acknowledge the true American Theory of Government or, when acknowledged, to fully comprehend the significance of maintaining – or, more precisely, of restoring – the true sovereignty of the people, States' Rights, and the federal system of government. For this reason, we should focus attention on these common misconceptions, which are listed below:

1. States' Rights and the sovereignty of the peoples of the States might be historically accurate and constitutionally valid principles; yet such concepts somehow seem unpatriotic. As patriotic Americans, we should heed the words of our Pledge of Allegiance and give our loyalty and allegiance to the flag and to the Republic for which

that flag stands, one Nation under God and indivisible. The concept of State sovereignty seems to violate our Pledge of Allegiance.

2. Irrespective of the conquest of the sovereign States as a result of the War Between the States, our political system retains its elective nature. And what matters most in any political system is that the people elect those who are to administer the powers of the government. As long as the Government of the United States remains elective in nature, the people can express their supremacy – their sovereignty – at the ballot box. And as long as they have the right to vote, their freedoms are safe and secure.
3. Regardless of the historical and constitutional basis for States' Rights and State sovereignty, the federal system is highly inefficient, with a total of 51 governments instead of one National Government. The United States can be best governed by a centralized administration in Washington, D.C., that meets the local needs as well as the general needs of the American people. The Government of the United States is also the best guarantor of our natural and civil rights, protecting the people from abusive and potentially abusive State governments.
4. Even if considerable power has been centralized in the United States, our Federal Constitution still exists as the supreme law of the land. And the States, although no longer sovereign, still exist. As long as the Constitution and the States continue to exist, we have no need to be concerned. The system may be bent, so to speak, but it is not broken.
5. The true American Theory of Government may rest upon the pillars of sovereign States, but the true greatness of America has been realized only since the War Between the States converted the United States into a Nation. And for this, we have the consolidating school to thank.
6. Although the Government of the United States conquered the States and robbed them of their sovereignty, we Americans have no real need to be concerned. The great struggle over sovereignty ended long ago in favor of nationalism. Whether we have State sovereignty or a national sovereignty, we are still an independent country empowered to control and shape our own destiny. And that is what really matters the most.

It must be acknowledged that these misconceptions are shared by a number of Americans, who fail to understand either the true extent of the damage already wrought by consolidation on the character of our institutions or the tendency of the ongoing consolidating conspiracy to destroy – not merely in practice, but literally – not only the Constitution and the States, but the United States of America. It would, therefore, be a public service to demonstrate the fallacies associated with these common misconceptions, which constitute obstacles to a full acknowledgment of both the rightfulness of the sovereignty of the States and the great danger to liberty posed by a sovereign Government of the United States. States' Rights and federalism, as we shall conclusively demonstrate, are not merely dictated by the Constitution of the United States, but they constitute the greatest bulwark that could ever be devised to safeguard the United States from the forces determined to terminate its existence.

The Pledge of Allegiance

The first common misconception that serves as an obstacle to the acceptance of the true American Theory of Government and to an acknowledgment of the importance of maintaining – or, more precisely, of resurrecting – State sovereignty and the federal system within the United States is as follows:

> States' Rights and the sovereignty of the peoples of the States might be historically accurate and constitutionally valid principles; yet such concepts somehow seem unpatriotic. As patriotic Americans, we should heed the words of our Pledge of Allegiance and give our loyalty and allegiance to the flag and to the Republic for which that flag stands, one Nation under God and indivisible. The concept of State sovereignty seems to violate our Pledge of Allegiance.

There is indeed an incompatibility between the Pledge of Allegiance and the genuine American Theory of Government, but the problem lies with the Pledge, and not with the true principles of our constitutional system. None of the Founding Fathers of the United States would recognize the Pledge of Allegiance, for it was not introduced to the general public until 1892, and most of the Founders of our Republic, had they survived to that date, would have considered it anything but patriotic.

The Pledge of Allegiance was first published in the September 8, 1892 issue of *The Youth's Companion*, which has been described as the *Reader's Digest* of its day, and was simultaneously distributed widely throughout the United States in leaflet form. In its original form, this Pledge of Allegiance read as follows: "I pledge allegiance to my Flag, and the Republic for which it stands: one Nation indivisible, with Liberty and Justice for all." [1] A month later – in October of 1892 – the word "to" was added before the expression "the Republic." In that same month, the revised Pledge was given tremendous publicity through an official program of the National Public School Celebration of Columbus Day, in which more than twelve million children in public schools in every State of the Union recited it as part of a flag ceremony.

Following this initial introduction of the Pledge of Allegiance to the general public, a concerted effort was made to give the Pledge a place of permanency in the public school systems of the United States. The undisguised objective was to make the Pledge of Allegiance, the American Flag, and Patriotism equivalent concepts in the minds of the American people. And since the first recital by some twelve million American schoolchildren, the wording of the Pledge has been modified three times.

---

[1] "The Story of the Pledge," http://www.flagday.org/Pages/StoryofPledge.html.

At the First National Flag Conference held in Washington, D.C., on June 14, 1923, the expression "my Flag" in the Pledge was replaced with the words "the Flag of the United States." And in 1924, the words "of America" were added after the expression "the Flag of the United States." Finally, on June 14, 1954 – Flag Day – the words "under God" were added, so that the Pledge of Allegiance was finally worded as follows: "I pledge allegiance to the Flag of the United States of America and to the Republic for which it stands, one Nation under God, indivisible, with liberty and justice for all." [2]

Although the Pledge of Allegiance gained wide circulation almost immediately after it had been first published in 1892, it was not until June 22, 1942, that the Pledge assumed the status of an official pledge or oath for citizens of the United States. Congress, on that date, included the Pledge in the United States Flag Code (title 36), and three years later the formerly unofficial *Pledge to the Flag* received its official title of *The Pledge of Allegiance*.

For a number of years after it was incorporated into public school systems throughout the Union, schoolchildren were taught to recite their pledge or oath with one arm extended, palm up. This official salute, however, bore a close resemblance to a Nazi salute, and after World War II it was decided to replace the extended-arm salute with a gesture of placing one hand over the heart.

Based upon what has thus far been presented, the perceptive reader has undoubtedly detected three problems with the Pledge of Allegiance. The first problem is the very nature of any type of pledge of loyalty or allegiance by the American people. If the people of the United States are sovereign, why should they recite any pledge of allegiance? If any pledge or oath is to be recited, should not those pledges and oaths be recited by those who administer the government, who are the servants of the people? A pledge of allegiance given by the citizens of the United States is what we would expect if the Government of the United States had robbed the people of their sovereignty. There is certainly nothing patriotic about that.

The second problem associated with our Pledge of Allegiance is its inherent concept of loyalty or allegiance to the *Flag of the United States* and to the *Republic for which it stands*. If interpreted literally, this Pledge directs the allegiance of the American people to a piece of cloth. While the *Stars and Stripes* is indeed a beautiful flag and should be treated with respect as a political symbol, it is, in truth, merely a symbol. Its stripes represent the original thirteen States, and its fifty stars represent the present States of the Federal Union. That flag is a symbol of American Statehood, and, as such, merits our respect and admiration. Yet, the American Flag is not, of itself, a sovereign power to which we

---

[2] *Ibid.*

should pledge our allegiance.

According to the Pledge of Allegiance, allegiance is also owed to *the Republic* for which the American flag represents. Loyalty would indeed be owed to the Federal Republic if it were a consolidated sovereign Nation. However, as has been conclusively demonstrated, sovereignty in the United States is by natural right vested in the several States. A denial of State sovereignty does not result in transferring supremacy to a consolidated Nation of Americans, for no such Nation exists. Denying the sovereignty of the States can only result in a sovereign Government of the United States. This is precisely the effect and intention of the Pledge of Allegiance. Once again, there is nothing patriotic about the theft of sovereignty from the people of the United States.

The third problem connected with the Pledge of Allegiance lies in the phrase "one Nation under God, indivisible." Although the words "under God" have come under heavy attack from atheists in recent years, those are probably the only words in the Pledge that are unobjectionable. Yet, the notion that the United States is *one indivisible Nation* throws a blaze of light of the true intent of the Pledge of Allegiance. This pledge, far from being patriotic, is clearly intended to reinforce the morally debased contention that, inasmuch as the Government of the United States conquered the sovereign States in the War Between the States, the *verdict of history* dictates that we are now one Nation, and no State can escape from the clutches of Big Government in Washington, D.C. There is nothing patriotic about that idea, and there is nothing patriotic about the Pledge of Allegiance.

The true extent of the subversive nature of the Pledge of Allegiance can be better appreciated by understanding the character and intent of its original author. At the time the Pledge was originally published in *The Youth's Companion* in 1892, Francis Bellamy of Rome, New York, and James Upham of Malden, Massachusetts, were both members of its staff, and in later years the families of each man claimed that his was the authorship. To resolve the dispute, the United States Flag Association appointed a three-man committee to investigate the claims made by each family. On the committee were Professor Charles C. Tansill, Professor W. Reed West, and Professor Bernard Mayo. This committee unanimously decided in favor of Francis Bellamy, and that decision has been widely accepted ever since.

The author of the original Pledge of Allegiance, Francis Bellamy, was a Baptist minister who described himself as a "Christian Socialist" and who preached from the pulpit that "Jesus was a socialist." [3] Eventually, Mr. Bellamy was dismissed from his ministerial position due to his incessant habit of preach-

[3] Thomas J. DiLorenzo, "Pledging Allegiance to the Omnipotent Lincolnian State," LewRockwell.com, http://www.lewrockwell.com/dilorenzo54.html, October 17, 2003.

ing the Gospel of Marx instead of the Gospel of Christ.

As Professor Thomas J. DiLorenzo has noted:

> [Francis] Bellamy was the cousin of Edward Bellamy, author of the extremely popular 1888 socialist fantasy, *Looking Backward*. In this novel the main character, Julian West, falls asleep in 1887 and awakens in the year 2000 when the socialist "utopia" has been achieved: All industry is state owned, Soviet style; everyone is an employee of the state who is conscripted at age 21 and retires at age 45; and all workers earn the same income. [4]

Regarding Francis Bellamy's cousin, one writer has noted that, "Edward Bellamy, after the appearance of 'Looking Backward,' became the recognized leader of the Nationalistic or Marxian Socialistic movement in the Republic." [5] Both Edward Bellamy and his cousin Francis were part and parcel of the socialist and nationalist movements that sprang to life in the aftermath of the War Between the States and Radical Reconstruction. The consolidation of the government and the inauguration of the process of centralization of power that resulted from those tragedies contributed significantly toward the creation of a *monopoly of power* which socialism requires in order to regiment and control society. Accordingly, both Bellamy cousins, as avid socialists, became enthusiastic promoters of the concept of a consolidated *Nationalism* – including a National Government vested with national sovereignty. Before long, the Bellamy cousins were promoting a growing number of *Nationalist Clubs* and celebrating the publication of *The Nationalist Magazine*, in which the principles of socialism and nationalism mingled freely.

The Pledge of Allegiance was merely one part of a concerted effort to ensure a victory of the Consolidating School of Thought over the minds of the American people, as Professor DiLorenzo noted:

> Francis Bellamy said that one purpose of the Pledge of Allegiance was to help accomplish his lifelong goal of making his cousin's socialist fantasy a reality in America. He further stated that the "true reason for allegiance to the Flag" was to indoctrinate American school children in the false history of the American founding that was espoused first by Daniel Webster and, later, by Abraham Lincoln. [6]

Francis Bellamy himself confessed that the purpose of the Pledge of Allegiance was to celebrate the triumph of the Government of the United States over the sovereign States in the bloody War Between the States:

---

[4] *Ibid.*

[5] Jim Zwick (ed.), "Edward Bellamy and the Nationalistic and Socialistic Movement in America," http://www.boondocksnet.com/editions/progressive/pmwm08.html.

[6] Thomas J. DiLorenzo, *Op. cit.*

> The true reason for allegiance to the Flag is the "Republic for which it stands."...And what does that vast thing, the Republic mean? It is the concise political word for the Nation – the One Nation which the Civil War was fought to prove. To make that One Nation idea clear, we must specify that it is indivisible, as Webster and Lincoln used to repeat in their great speeches. [7]

The Pledge of Allegiance is part and parcel of the consolidating conspiracy against the American people. The reader is again reminded that there is nothing patriotic about the conquest of a sovereign American State. For that very reason, there is nothing patriotic about the Pledge of Allegiance. Allegiance and loyalty are owed to the sovereign, which, in our constitutional system, consists of the peoples of the several States.

The Guardian State

As the perceptive reader has detected, there is more than a mere coincidental relationship between the *consolidating conspiracy* and the *socialist conspiracy* in the United States of America, a relationship which the Marxist enthusiasts have readily acknowledged. And the reason for this close relationship is not difficult to understand. Consolidation of the government is, by definition, the centralization of power in one set of hands, thereby creating a *monopoly of power*. It is precisely that centralization of power which is a prerequisite for the conversion of the United States into a Socialist State.

The great issues that divided the consolidating school and the States' Rights school in the ante-bellum period of our Republic, as we have already observed, extended to the redistribution of wealth by the Federal Government's exercise of its tax-and-spend powers for unconstitutional purposes. It was only a few short steps to go from the planned economy of the American System of Henry Clay and Daniel Webster to the economic planning of Franklin D. Roosevelt's Welfare State. In principle, both systems were based on the same unconstitutional methods and goals.

In his book, *Horace Greeley and Other Pioneers of American Socialism*, which was published in 1915, Charles Sotheran acknowledged the indebtedness of the Twentieth Century Socialists to the Nineteenth Century Consolidating School of Thought:

> The theory of the commercial power inherent in the Constitution, as enunciated on various occasions by Alexander Hamilton, Daniel Webster, Abraham Lincoln, and Charles Sumner, as well as the right of eminent do-

---

[7] *Ibid.*, quoted in article.

> main, have simplified long years ago the future carrying into action of Socialist political and economic demands. [8]

This will serve as an introduction to the second common misconception that serves as an obstacle to the acceptance of the true American Theory of Government and to an acknowledgment of the importance of maintaining – or, more precisely, of resurrecting – State sovereignty and the federal system within the United States, which is as follows:

> Irrespective of the conquest of the sovereign States as a result of the War Between the States, our political system retains its elective nature. And what matters most in any political system is that the people elect those who are to administer the powers of the government. As long as the Government of the United States remains elective in nature, the people can express their supremacy – their sovereignty – at the ballot box. And as long as they have the right to vote, their freedoms are safe and secure.

As has been conclusively demonstrated in the course of our inquiry into sovereignty in the United States, the American people, in their sovereign capacities, are the States of the Federal Union. It has long been a ploy of the Consolidating School of Thought to disguise their efforts to establish a sovereign National Government by pretending that such sovereignty is vested in a non-existent American Nation, and that the American people, in their sovereign capacity, are identical with the Government of the United States. Under this pretension, it has been claimed that, to limit the powers of that government is tantamount to limiting the power of the whole people of the United States. In lieu of controlling the government by limitation of powers, therefore, the consolidating school has long assured us that the elective nature of the government alone is sufficient to ensure the control of the people over those who are chosen as the rulers of America.

The best answer ever offered to refute this argument was provided by Alexis Charles Henri Clerel de Tocqueville. Within the second volume of his great work, *Democracy in America*, which was published in 1840, this young Frenchman devoted an entire chapter to an analysis of "What Sort of Despotism Democratic Nations Have to Fear," with an emphasis on the type of despotism to which the United States of America was especially susceptible. The amazing description that he offered of a future *Guardian State*, based on a totalitarian government controlled only by periodic elections, bears a striking resemblance to the modern Welfare State.

Commenting on the potential of a Guardian State, Alexis de Tocqueville

---

[8] Charles Sotheran, *Horace Greeley and Other Pioneers of American Socialism*, Mitchell Kennerley, New York, 1915, p. 16.

noted:

> When I consider the petty passions of our contemporaries, the mildness of their manners, the extent of their education, the purity of their religion, the gentleness of their morality, their regular and industrious habits, and the restraint which they almost all observe in their vices no less than in their virtues, I have no fear that they will meet with tyranny in their rulers, but rather with guardians.
>
> I think, then, that the species of oppression by which democratic Nations are menaced is unlike anything that ever before existed in the world; our contemporaries will find no prototype of it in their memories. I seek in vain for an expression that will accurately convey the whole of the idea I have formed of it; the old words *despotism* and *tyranny* are inappropriate; the thing itself is new, and since I cannot name, I must attempt to define it. [9]

Mr. Tocqueville then proceeded to offer the following definition of the Guardian State:

> Above this race of men stands an immense and tutelary power, which takes upon itself alone to secure their gratifications and to watch over their fate. That power is absolute, minute, regular, provident, and mild. It would be like the authority of a parent if, like that authority, its object was to prepare men for manhood; but it seeks, on the contrary, to keep them in perpetual childhood: it is well content that the people should rejoice, provided they think of nothing but rejoicing. For their happiness such a government willingly labors, but it chooses to be the sole agent and the only arbiter of that happiness; it provides for their security, foresees and supplies their necessities, facilitates their pleasures, manages their principal concerns, directs their industry, regulates the descent of property, and subdivides their inheritances: what remains, but to spare them all the care of thinking and all the trouble of living?
>
> Thus it every day renders the exercise of the free agency of man less useful and less frequent; it circumscribes the will within a narrower range and gradually robs a man of all the uses of himself. The principle of equality has prepared men for these things; it has predisposed men to endure them and often to look on them as benefits.
>
> After having thus successively taken each member of the community in its powerful grasp and fashioned him at will, the supreme power then extends its arm over the whole community. It covers the surface of society with a network of small complicated rules, minute and uniform, through which the most original minds and the most energetic characters cannot penetrate, to rise above the crowd. The will of man is not shattered, but softened, bent, and guided; men are seldom forced by it to act, but they are constantly restrained from acting. Such a power does not destroy, but it prevents exis-

[9] Alexis de Tocqueville, *Democracy in America*, Volume II, Vintage Books, New York, 1945 (orig. pub. 1840), pp. 335-336.

> tence; it does not tyrannize, but it compresses, enervates, extinguishes, and stupefies a people, till each Nation is reduced to nothing better than a flock of timid and industrious animals, of which the government is the shepherd.
>
> I have always thought that servitude of the regular, quiet, and gentle kind which I have just described might be combined more easily than is commonly believed with some of the outward forms of freedom, and that it might even establish itself under the wing of the sovereignty of the people.
>
> Our contemporaries are constantly excited by the two conflicting passions: they want to be led, and they wish to remain free. As they cannot destroy either the one or the other of these contrary propensities, they strive to satisfy them both at once. They devise a sole, tutelary, and all-powerful form of government, but elected by the people. They combine the principle of centralization and that of popular sovereignty; this gives them a respite: they console themselves for being in tutelage by the reflection that they have chosen their own guardians. Every man allows himself to be put in leading-strings, because he sees that it is not a person or a class of persons, but the people at large who hold the end of his chain.
>
> By this system the people shake off their state of dependence just long enough to select their master and then relapse into it again. [10]

Although the totalitarian government within this corrupt and unnatural state – call it by whatever name we please, the Guardian State, the Welfare State, or the Socialist State – is not outwardly despotic, it is nonetheless tyrannical at its core. Within such a Guardian State, the chief political ruler of the society would hardly consider presenting himself to the masses as an undisguised dictator, addressing them with such words as, "I am your imperial ruler. Hear me and obey!" On the contrary, the leader of such a State could be expected to convey such sentiments as, "I want to take care of you. Trust me. I love you, and I want you to love me, too."

Such a system would seldom display the outward signs of a Police State, such as goose-steeping soldiers marching down the streets, or police armed with machine guns stationed at every corner, or public displays of book burnings. Yet, such an all-powerful government would insist upon regulating everything and controlling everybody. It would control the air breathed by the people, assure the quality of their drinking water, and guarantee the safety of the food they eat. Such a government would supervise the health care of the people from cradle to grave, control and regulate the education of their children, provide them with unemployment compensation, establish minimum wage laws, and even encourage the masses to wear their automobile seat belts with gentle but coercive methods. There would be nothing too minute or personal within the lives of individuals that this all-powerful Big Brother Government would not wish to supervise, regulate, and control. And yet, in spite of its benevolent as-

---

[10] *Ibid.*, pp. 336-337.

surances, the all-powerful government itself would be the sole judge of what is best for the people.

Within such a Totalitarian State, those who never stray from the herd or dare to contemplate an independent thought may never realize how circumscribed their freedoms are. Even when the vast restrictions on their liberties are pointed out to them, they may fail to recognize that they are essentially living in slavery. But the true nature of such a State will be readily apparent to all who prefer to be self-reliant and to think for themselves.

An ironic aspect of this Guardian State is that its greatest appeal to the weaker and baser nature of man is precisely what makes it so dangerous to liberty. The reason why any man would consider such a State beneficial is that it spares him from the responsibility of self-reliance and rugged individualism, by allowing the State to provide for his personal wants and needs. Yet, as Alexis de Tocqueville noted, "It must not be forgotten that it is especially dangerous to enslave men in the minor details of life."[11] *Tyranny at the personal level is the worst type of tyranny.*

It might be inquired if the people within such a Guardian State, in which they develop such a dependent mentality, could truly muster the independence of thought necessary to intelligently and wisely select their masters at periodic elections. Is it realistic to expect that a people who are deemed incapable of governing their own lives, should possess the wisdom to select the best rulers to govern the entire Nation?

This was an issue raised by Mr. Tocqueville in his book, *Democracy in America*:

> Subjection in minor affairs breaks out every day and is felt by the whole community indiscriminately. It does not drive men to resistance, but it crosses them at every turn, till they are led to surrender the exercise of their own will. Thus their spirit is gradually broken and their character enervated; whereas that obedience which is exacted on a few important but rare occasions only exhibits servitude at certain intervals and throws the burden of it upon a small number of men. It is in vain to summon a people who have been rendered so dependent on the central power to choose from time to time the representatives of that power; this rare and brief exercise of their free choice, however important it may be, will not prevent them from gradually losing the faculties of thinking, feeling, and acting for themselves, and thus gradually falling below the level of humanity.
>
> I add that they will soon become incapable of exercising the great and only privilege which remains to them. The democratic notions that have introduced freedom into their political constitution at the very time when they were augmenting the despotism of their administrative constitution have been led into strange paradoxes. To manage those minor affairs in which

[11] *Ibid.*, p. 338.

> good sense is all that is wanted, the people are held to be unequal to the task; but when the government of the country is at stake, the people are invested with immense powers; they are alternately made the playthings of their ruler, and his masters, more than kings and less than men. After having exhausted all the different modes of election without finding one to suit their purpose, they are still amazed and still bent on seeking further; as if the evil they notice did not originate in the constitution of the country far more than in that of the electoral body.
>
> It is indeed difficult to conceive how men who have entirely given up the habit of self-government should succeed in making a proper choice of those by whom they are to be governed; and no one will ever believe that a liberal, wise, and energetic government can spring from the suffrages of a subservient people. [12]

The elective nature of a government is undeniably an important feature that allows a *free and independent people* to ensure that the government is held accountable for its acts and deeds. Yet, this tool to ensure accountability should never be relied upon as the *only* means of controlling a government. *The primary means of controlling government is to limit its powers to only those necessary for providing for the common good.* A government confined to wise limitations of power poses only a minimal danger to the liberties of the people. The franchise, within such a properly constituted system, would be required only to ensure that those chosen to administer the government fulfill their duties honestly and faithfully observe the constitutional mandates prescribed by the people.

A totalitarian government, regardless of whether or not it is elective in nature, is a despotic government. If a government has the power to tyrannize, it can and it will tyrannize the people. This is true regardless of whether the government is an oligarchy, an aristocracy, or a popular government elected by the majority of the people. The brunt of tyranny always falls upon the people as individual citizens, and despotism may exist under any form of government. The *tyranny of the majority* is just as dangerous to the rights and welfare of the individual as the *tyranny of the minority*.

The very nature of the Guardian State or Welfare State – whichever term the reader prefers – requires that it will be characterized by an oppressive bureaucracy and by extravagance. If such a government is to provide for the wants and needs of the people and to care for their well being, it must necessarily establish rules and regulations, as well as administer benefits, by means of *unelected and unaccountable bureaucracies*. If the government is to provide for and manage the health care of the citizenry, for example, a bureaucracy staffed by a veritable army of health care professionals will be required. And what is true for health care would hold true for housing, agriculture, industry, commerce, ur-

---

[12] *Ibid.*, pp. 338-339.

ban development, education, and every other sphere of human activity that is to be supervised, regulated, and controlled by the government. Yet, the very existence of these unelected bureaucracies serves to greatly minimize the control over the government that the franchise might provide.

Another consideration that tends to minimize or even negate the effectiveness of the franchise as the solitary control of the people over their government is the very nature of man. As James Madison noted, if men were angels, there would be no need for government; and since our rulers are not angels, there is need to limit their powers. *Politicians lie!* That is a truth that no one would dare to deny. In a recent poll that asked Americans to rate various categories of professionals based on how trustworthy they were, respondents ranked politicians at the very bottom of the list, even lower than used car salesmen.

If the only control the people have over those they elect are periodic elections, then they will always risk being the victims of lying politicians, who will promise anything in order to get elected, but upon assuming office will act according to their dishonest natures. And should the people discover that they have been deceived into electing a lying politician, what consolation do they have? Within a system of constitutionally limited government, they may be assured that the liar does not immediately have access to the powers necessary to oppress them. But in the Guardian State, the lying knave, upon assuming public office, has immediate access to unlimited powers.

In the United States, few Americans realize how truly limited is their control over the government by means of the franchise. One entire branch of the Federal Government – the judicial branch – is in no wise controlled by or responsible directly to the people. Even the executive branch is significantly less influenced by the franchise than many realize, and we are here referring to much more than merely the Electoral College system, by which the people of the States indirectly elect the President and Vice-President of the United States.

Under the influence of the Consolidating School of Thought, the executive branch has been transformed into the *dominant branch* of the Federal Government. Not only is a large percentage of the laws enacted by Congress initiated by the White House, but the President of the United States, in modern times, is even allowed to usurp the power of the legislature to declare war. Although the President and Vice-President of the United States are indirectly elected by the people through the Electoral College system, the executive branch of government is, in fact, staffed by a number of powerful individuals who are not directly accountable to the people.

In addition to the Cabinet, there are key advisers to the President, sometimes referred to as a *Brains Trust*, who exert a tremendous influence over public affairs. For these reasons, those elected by the people in Presidential elections are not necessarily the ones who will actually control the executive branch of Government of the United States. All too often, an elected President spends much of his time playing golf, taking lengthy vacations, or performing public relations work, while the real affairs of the executive branch are coordinated and managed by the Cabinet, bureaucrats, and an appointed Brains Trust.

An excellent illustration to demonstrate this principle is the Administration of President Woodrow Wilson, who was elected as a "Progressive" pledged to curtail the power and influence of the monied aristocracy. Yet, in the book, *Woodrow Wilson: The Unforgettable Figure Who Has Returned to Haunt Us*, Gerald W. Johnson wrote that, "Little by little it became apparent that there should be one boss of industry as there was one of the army. The man Wilson chose for this post was Bernard Mannes Baruch…, New York businessman and financier." [13] When the American people elected the candidate pledged to curtail the power and political influence of Wall Street, how many realized that, once elected, that President would appoint a Wall Street luminary to be the *Boss of American Industry*?

Continuing with our example of President Woodrow Wilson's inner circle of advisers, strategists, and policy makers, this is how Gerald W. Johnson described the President's closest adviser and confidant:

> Not all his advisers were equally popular. There was, for example, Wilson's diplomatic agent, Edward Mandell House, usually known as "Colonel" House. Nobody knew much about him, but he was everywhere, and the President had great confidence in him. He became one of the most famous, if one of the most mysterious, men in America. [14]

Regarding the *most mysterious man in America* who secretly controlled the Wilson Administration, Alexander L. George and Juliette L. George have noted:

> A clue to the nature and scope of House's ambition is a novel, *Philip Dru: Administrator*, which he wrote anonymously during the winter of 1911-12, shortly after meeting Wilson. Philip Dru, barred by ill health from the military career for which he has been trained, becomes leader of an insurrection against an incompetent administration, and subsequently dictator of the United States. Dispensing with constitutional government, he institutes a series of sweeping reforms by executive decree and then benevolently relinquishes his dictatorial powers in order to re-establish a democratic government under the terms of a new and improved constitution.
>
> The reader will wonder in how far House identified himself with Philip Dru. A letter he wrote in 1915, at a time when he was still trying to

[13] Gerald W. Johnson, *Woodrow Wilson: The Unforgettable Figure Who Has Returned to Haunt Us*, Harper & Brothers Publishers, New York, 1944, p. 157.
[14] *Ibid.*, p. 154.

> conceal his authorship of the book, is revealing: "I am sending you the book of which I spoke," wrote House. "...It was written by a man I know....My friend – whose name is not to be mentioned – told me...that Philip *was all that he himself would like to be but was not.*" Philip Dru was handsome, dashing – and dictator of the United States.[15]

Edward Mandell House noted on the dedication page of his book that, "This book is dedicated to the unhappy many who have lived and died lacking opportunity, because, in the starting, the world-wide social structure was wrongly begun." [16] And within the chapter entitled, "The Prophet of a New Day," Philip Dru is presented as an example of the future leaders of America, dedicated to "Socialism as dreamed of by Karl Marx." [17]

Thus it was that the American people, who elected Woodrow Wilson to the Presidency, ended up with an executive branch dominated by a Wall Street luminary and a megalomaniac whose fondest dream was to conquer the United States by the sword, establish himself as the Communist Dictator of America, and replace the Constitution with a new, socialist instrument of government.

The example of the Wilson Administration illustrates all too well why the United States remains in constant danger as long as it is governed by an all-powerful centralized regime controlled only by the elective principle. The evils that lurk in the hearts of ambitious politicians can only be checked by binding them down from mischief by the chains of the Constitution and by restoring that wise division of powers between independent levels of government that is mandated by the principles of our federal system of government.

Within a system based on an absolute government controlled only by the franchise, those seeking to gratify their ambitions by seeking public office will invariably appeal to the lowest and most base passions of the electorate, corrupting both the political system and the morals of society in general. Vote buying, patronage, the socialistic redistribution of wealth, voting blocks, greed, and avarice would soon become the hallmarks of such a Guardian State. Over time, the demands made on the government for pecuniary and other benefits would exceed the ability of those forced to bear the costs of government to support the corrupt and immoral system. But those accustomed to receiving substantial benefits from the government within this State would have a tendency to view such benefits as a *right*, not a mere privilege, and any attempt to curtail such supposed rights could result in civil strife and violent upheaval, propelling the society toward complete disintegration.

Inherent within this Guardian State is the principle of *collectivism*, as the

---

[15] Alexander L. George and Juliette L. George, *Woodrow Wilson and Colonel House: A Personality Study*, Dover Publications, Inc., New York, 1956, p. 131.
[16] Edward Mandell House, *Philip Dru: Administrator – A Story of Tomorrow, 1920-1935*, New York, 1912, iv.
[17] *Ibid.*, p. 45.

notion of the "greater good" replaces the principle of individual natural rights. Alexis de Tocqueville commented on this tendency in his book:

> Another tendency which is extremely natural to democratic Nations and extremely dangerous is that which leads them to despise and undervalue the rights of private persons. The attachment that men feel to a right and the respect that they display for it are generally proportioned to its importance or to the length of time during which they have enjoyed it. The rights of private persons among democratic Nations are commonly of small importance, of recent growth, and extremely precarious; the consequence is that they are often sacrificed without regret and almost always violated without remorse.
>
> But it happens that, at the same period and among the same Nations in which men conceive a natural contempt for the rights of private persons, the rights of society at large are naturally extended and consolidated; in other words, men become less attached to private rights just when it is most necessary to retain and defend what little remains of them. It is therefore most especially in the present democratic times, that the true friends of the liberty and the greatness of man ought constantly to be on the alert to prevent the power of government from lightly sacrificing the private rights of individuals to the general execution of its designs. At such times no citizen is so obscure that it is not very dangerous to allow him to be oppressed; no private rights are so unimportant that they can be surrendered with impunity to the caprices of a government. The reason is plain: if the private right of an individual is violated at a time when the human mind is fully impressed with the importance and the sanctity of such rights, the injury done is confined to the individual whose right is infringed; but to violate such a right at the present day is deeply to corrupt the manners of the Nation and to put the whole community in jeopardy, because the very notion of this kind of right constantly tends among us to be impaired and lost. [18]

Even in societies which have a tradition of regarding individual rights with great respect, the practical effect of the Guardian State will be to overcome any impediment to the efficiency of the machinery of government. Obstacles to the unlimited exercise of power, such as a regard for the inalienable rights of each citizen, will be minimized and ultimately ignored by a totalitarian government intolerant of any restraints on its actions. In such cases, noted Mr. Tocqueville, "the principle of public utility is called in, the doctrine of political necessity is conjured up, and men accustom themselves to sacrifice private interests without scruple and to trample on the rights of individuals in order to more speedily accomplish any public purpose." [19]

Such a Guardian State is the inevitable consequence of a supreme, sovereign National Government that is controlled only by the franchise. And such is

---

[18] Alexis de Tocqueville, *Op. cit.*, Volume 2, pp. 344-345.

[19] *Ibid.*, p. 346.

the political system that the consolidating school has forced upon the United States following its victory in the War Between the States. Such a system is *totalitarianism* masquerading as popular government. It is *despotism* with feigned compassion. It is *tyranny* with a friendly smile. It is the *Leviathan State* disguised as Big Brother.

The Myth of Centralized Efficiency

The third common misconception that serves as an obstacle to the acceptance of the true American Theory of Government and to an acknowledgment of the importance of maintaining – or, more precisely, of resurrecting – State sovereignty and the federal system within the United States is as follows:

> Regardless of the historical and constitutional basis for States' Rights and State sovereignty, the federal system is highly inefficient, with a total of 51 governments instead of one National Government. The United States can be best governed by a centralized administration in Washington, D.C., that meets the local needs as well as the general needs of the American people. The Government of the United States is also the best guarantor of our natural and civil rights, protecting the people from abusive and potentially abusive State governments.

This sentiment, unfortunately, has dominated American politics since the tragic conquest of the sovereign States in the War Between the States. Rarely are the words *States' Rights* heard in the Halls of Government since that time, except in derision and contempt. Even on those occasions when a politician actually acknowledges that the States should play a vital role in our system of government, such expressions are often little more than lip service to the principles of the old Federal Republic.

A speech delivered by President Calvin Coolidge at the College of William and Mary in Williamsburg, Virginia, on May 15, 1926, illustrates how modern-day politicians can make glowing tributes to the true American Theory of Government, but then render such tributes devoid of substance by asserting a national dominance over the States. Referring to the State of Virginia as a "sovereign Commonwealth," President Coolidge said:

> [T]he States are the sheet anchors of our institutions. If the Federal Government should go out of existence, the common run of people would not detect the difference in the affairs of their daily life for a considerable length of time. But if the authority of the States were struck down disorder approaching chaos would be upon us within twenty-four hours. No method of procedure has ever been devised by which liberty could be divorced from

> local self-government. No plan of centralization has ever been adopted which did not result in bureaucracy, tyranny, inflexibility, reaction, and decline. Of all forms of government, those administered by bureaus are about the least satisfactory to an enlightened and progressive people. Being irresponsible they become autocratic, and being autocratic they resist all development....
>
> While we ought to glory in the Union and remember that it is the source from which the States derive their chief title to fame, we must also recognize that the national administration is not and can not be adjusted to the needs of local government. It is too far away to be informed of local needs, too inaccessible to be responsive to local conditions. The States should not be induced by coercion or by favor to surrender the management of their own affairs. The Federal Government ought to resist the tendency to be loaded up with duties which the States should perform.... [20]

Within this section of his speech, Calvin Coolidge truly, concisely, and brilliantly defined our constitutional system of government. Had he ended his speech on this note, his address might have stood as one of the greatest speeches ever delivered by a Twentieth-Century President on behalf of the genuine American Theory of Government. Unfortunately, Mr. Coolidge did not stop speaking at this point of his speech, but proceeded to utter sentiments that served only to nullify his previously expressed praises for States' Rights.

As Mr. Coolidge said:

> [O]n the other hand, when the great body of *public opinion* of the *Nation* requires action the States ought to understand that unless they are responsive to such sentiment the *national authority* will be *compelled to intervene*. The doctrine of State Right is not a *privilege* to continue in wrong-doing but a *privilege* to be free from interference in well-doing....Unless the States meet these requirements, the *National Government* reluctantly will be crowded into the position of *enlarging its own authority at their expense*. [emphasis added] [21]

These latter sentiments, it scarcely needs to be mentioned, completely nullify the previous lofty utterances of praise for the constitutionally reserved rights of the States. The *reserved rights* of the sovereign States, said President Coolidge, are merely *privileges* that can be trampled upon by the Federal Government whenever that government, listening with its impartial ear, hears the voice of *public opinion* cry out for some action that the State governments refuse to undertake. Such a theory of government, however, can only be sustained by the concept that the Constitution of the United States is merely a set of guidelines or suggestions, to be heeded or ignored, at the sole discretion of

---

[20] Calvin Coolidge, *Foundations of the Republic: Speeches and Addresses*, Charles Scribner's Sons, New York, 1926, pp. 410-411.

[21] *Ibid.*, p. 411.

the Federal Government.

Yet, as the Federal Constitution declares in unmistakable language, it is not a set of guidelines or suggestions, but rather the *supreme law of the land.* To obey or disobey this supreme law is not the prerogative of the Federal Government. Either it obeys the sovereign will of the people, whose voice speaks through the Constitution, or else it utterly subverts the sovereignty of the people and assumes the character of a lawless regime.

If the Tenth Amendment to the Federal Constitution were rewritten to conform to the theory of government espoused by Calvin Coolidge, it would read as follows: "The powers not delegated to the United States by the Constitution, nor prohibited by it to the States, are reserved to the States respectively, unless the Federal Government disapproves of the manner in which the States exercise or refrain from exercising their reserved powers, in which case the Federal Government may usurp the said reserved powers." Such a revised Tenth Amendment would accord fully with the principles of the Consolidating School of Thought.

When evaluating the merits of our constitutional system of government, administrative efficiency is certainly desirable, inasmuch as efficiency is preferable to inefficiency, waste, and ineptitude. However, efficiency is not the *primary consideration* by which we should judge the merits of any governmental system. *What matters most is how well the political system balances power and liberty.* Such a system should provide sufficient power to the government to fulfill its legitimate ends, yet sufficiently restrain power to preserve the inalienable rights of man.

To establish this proper balance, the American constitutional system wisely provides for independent spheres of power between the Federal and State governments, delegating the management of foreign affairs to the former, while reserving the management of domestic affairs to the latter governments. And within the Federal Government, an internal system of *checks and balances* was established to prevent an abuse of power by any one branch of the government. Such divisions of power and checks and balances accomplish their purpose of protecting liberty by serving as restraints or brakes on the otherwise unimpeded exercise of power. To shift the emphasis toward *efficiency in government* would be to undermine these established safeguards for the liberties of the people.

Even if we were to set aside considerations of the effects of centralized power on the liberties of the people, the fact remains that a centralized authority in the United States cannot provide for the domestic or local concerns of the people as efficiently as State and local governments are able to do. As Thomas Jefferson noted, even in his time, the United States was *too large* to have all of its affairs directed by a single government. Such a concentration of power in

Washington, he contended, would establish conditions where politicians and their votes could be more easily bought and sold, as if at market. And such a consolidated system, even if honestly administered, could not adequately provide for the needs of a country the size of the United States. Since his time, the United States has grown considerably in both population and territory, and Mr. Jefferson's conclusion applies with even greater force today than it did in his time.

While all States' Rights advocates acknowledge this truism, what is surprising is that even some extreme Socialists have admitted the truthfulness of this proposition. Perhaps the most eminent Socialist to acknowledge the truthfulness of this Jeffersonian principle was Harold Laski, a Professor of Political Science at the London School of Economics and a leading light in the British Labour Party in the first half of the Twentieth Century, during which time he established a reputation for being an uncompromising Marxist.

In his book, *Studies in the Problem of Sovereignty*, which was originally published in 1917 by Yale University Press, Mr. Laski wrote:

> It can never be too thoroughly emphasized that the Founders of the American Constitution did not intend to create a complete system of government. They took the States for granted, and it was upon their complex foundation that they attempted to build. [22]

Elsewhere in his book, Harold Laski noted:

> Federal government, we are therefore told, is notoriously weak government, since in it there is no final arbiter. The legislature of the United States...is a non-sovereign lawmaking body. It derives its powers...from a written document, which simultaneously limits them. Federalism, Professor Dicey notes further, tends to produce Conservatism. For the Constitution is written and rigid. It acquires a kind of sacrosanct character in the eyes of the people. Change of any kind becomes difficult because it almost seems irreligious. It is condemned before it is attempted. [23]

Still elsewhere in his book, Mr. Laski noted that consolidation or nationalism had triumphed over federalism in the United States, much to the detriment of the true interests of the American people:

> Nationalism, then, is triumphant....But there is...[an] aspect of this unified sovereignty about which certain doubts may be expressed. It stands for centralization; that is to say, changes the whole character of the federal

---

[22] Harold Laski, *Studies in the Problem of Sovereignty*, Howard Fertig, New York, 1968 (orig. pub. 1917), p. 277.

[23] *Ibid.*, p. 268.

> idea....Yet even an observer handicapped, as I am, by an alien tradition, can not help but realize that there is in America a certain fundamental disunity of circumstance. When I am in Kansas, I know that I am not in New York. The problems, even the thoughts and the desires, are different and affect people differently. Is it wise to make Washington a kind of Hegelian harmonization of these differences and say that Congress can transcend them in a federal statue? In the result, as every statesman must know, what are called the "interests of the Republic" in New York will probably be called "discrimination against the Middle West" in Kansas....
>
> The growth of National Government, with the consequent strengthening of its sovereign character, leads, as I have urged, to its increasing centralization. This is true not of America alone. [24]

The conclusion arrived at by Harold Laski was that, "Congress, of a certainty, can not give proper attention to local problems." [25] He even warned his readers that, "We seem in genuine danger of going back to an ancient and false worship of unity, to a trust in an undivided sovereignty as the panacea for our ills." [26] Considering that Mr. Laski was a deeply committed Socialist, his words are all the more remarkable and should serve as a warning to all those who cannot see the dangers inherent in a sovereign Government of the United States.

If examples were required to demonstrate the inability of a consolidated government to properly and adequately govern all the affairs of the United States, then we have many from which to choose. But one should serve well to illustrate this fact. In the immediate wake of the catastrophic damage sustained by New Orleans, Louisiana, and the Mississippi Gulf Coast during Hurricane Katrina in late August of 2005, all eyes desperately turned to the Federal Government to provide disaster relief. That government was supposedly ready and prepared to respond to such disasters through its agency, the Federal Emergency Management Agency (FEMA). Yet, the utter chaos created of the relief efforts by FEMA in that emergency will forever stand as a monument to the inefficiency of the bloated federal bureaucracies.

A glimpse of the utter confusion and mismanagement of FEMA's response to Hurricane Katrina may be ascertained from the results of an NBC investigation that was published on September 16, 2005, under the title, "The FEMA Ice Follies." The investigation, which focused solely on how FEMA mismanaged the simple task of getting ice to the hurricane victims, discovered that the bureaucracy had ordered a sufficient supply of frozen water, but mismanaged the shipment of the ice to the Gulf Coast regions devastated by the hurricane.

---

[24] *Ibid.*, pp. 278-279.
[25] *Ibid.*, p. 280.
[26] *Ibid.*, p. 284.

"NBC News located hundreds of trucks full of ice sitting around the country," this report stated, noting that FEMA had shipped the ice to Maryland, Missouri, Georgia, Tennessee, Mississippi, and Louisiana. "Some had been on trips to nowhere for the past two weeks." One truck driver was quoted as saying that, "We really don't understand why FEMA is sending to all these different locations and just putting us in cold storage." [27]

As this NBC News report noted:

> Dan Wessels' Cool Express ice company has worked with FEMA for years. He says he's never seen anything like it – only one-third of his trucks have actually unloaded the ice that FEMA ordered.
>
> "The left hand doesn't know what the right hand is doing," said Wessels. "The right hand is telling us to go to the left hand. We get to the left hand, they tell us to go back."
>
> For example, one truck of ice left Oshkosh, Wis., on Sept. 6, and went to Louisiana. Then it was sent by FEMA to Georgia but was rerouted before it arrived to South Carolina, then to Cumberland, Md., where it has been sitting for three days at an added cost to taxpayers so far of $9,000.
>
> Multiplied by hundreds of trucks, this sort of dispatching could mean millions of dollars are being wasted.
>
> "From a trucking aspect, I'm happy. Keep it coming," said Wessels. "From a taxpayer aspect, it's sick."
>
> A FEMA official says, in the rush to respond to Katrina, the agency ordered too much ice. Rather than let it melt, they sent it to other parts of the country to be ready for the next hurricane.
>
> But Wessels says FEMA just ordered more ice and re-routed some of his trucks again – to Idaho. [28]

Although the disaster relief provided by the Federal Government in the wake of Hurricane Katrina underscored the palpable inefficiency of centralized bureaucratic administration, it must be noted that the Government of the United States did display *a disturbing efficiency* in the one area where efficiency is the least desirable. With impressive efficiency, that government seized control of the City of New Orleans and blocked all independent relief efforts, forcing the hurricane victims to rely solely on the Federal Government for relief. Obtaining and maintaining a monopoly of power and control is what the Federal Government does best.

It is claimed, however, that the Government of the United States is our greatest guardian of human and civil rights, protecting the basic freedoms of the American people from the wicked State governments. This form of attack

[27] Lisa Myers & the NBC Investigative Unit, "The FEMA Ice Follies," MSNBC.com, September, 16, 2005, http://www.msnbc.com/id/9369937/print/displaymode/1098.
[28] *Ibid.*

on States' Rights was inaugurated by the Radical Republicans in the wake of the War Between the States, and was renewed when Hubert Horatio Humphrey uttered in 1948 that it was time for the Democratic Party to stop walking in the dark shadows of States' Rights and to walk instead in the bright sunshine of human rights. The Republican Party, it should be noted, has joined its sister party in trampling States' Rights underfoot. But rather than expand civil and human rights, or even ensure the their preservation, this crusade against States' Rights has done nothing more than replace genuine human rights with the Federal Government's phony definition of civil rights.

Under this new assault by the Federal Government, the United States has witnessed that spectacular travesty of justice known as *forced* racial integration, which has produced everything from the *busing* of schoolchildren to achieve racial quotas in public schools, to *White Flight* from the inner cities by those fearful for the safety of their children, to *racial quotas* in admissions to institutions of higher learning and in job hiring and promotions, to the promotion of collective *White Guilt* for all of the ills of society, to the sharp curtailment of genuine property rights, to the creation of *voting blocks* based solely on skin color. *Reverse Discrimination* is now the official racist policy of the Government of the United States, as it seeks to openly oppress the bulwark of the American middle class by mandating discrimination against the White race in every sphere of human activity.

To drive the point home, we have been informed by an official no less authoritative than Mary Frances Berry, a former Chairman of the U.S. Commission on Civil Rights, that the anti-discrimination laws of the Federal Government are not intended to apply to, and cannot be used to protect the rights of, White Americans. And yet, the Government of the United States has the audacity to proclaim that its policies are designed to ensure *equal justice under the law* and to guarantee *equal opportunities* for all Americans!

If further proof were required to demonstrate that the State governments are better guardians of human rights than the Federal Government, we need look no farther than the protections afforded to the most fundamental right of our most vulnerable citizens – the *Right to Life* of the unborn. Prior to 1973, the States, with only a few exceptions, guaranteed the sanctity of life for unborn babies. Then the U.S. Supreme Court intervened and, in the infamous case of *Roe* v. *Wade*, imperially decreed that the State governments could no longer protect the lives of innocent unborn babies.

So important is the continued sanctioning of the murder of the innocents that support for *Roe* v. *Wade* has become a litmus test to determine the acceptability of any nominee to the U.S. Supreme Court. Support by Supreme Court nominees for the "law" established by the 1973 Court decision is now considered by many politicians to be more important than support for the

Constitution itself.

And how many millions of innocent human beings have been murdered in cold blood since 1973, under the protective sanction of the Government of the United States? Forty million? Fifty million? Could the State governments possibly display a more wanton disregard for the genuine rights of the American people than this?

Is the Constitution Obsolete?

The fourth common misconception that serves as an obstacle to the acceptance of the true American Theory of Government and to an acknowledgment of the importance of maintaining – or, more precisely, of resurrecting – State sovereignty and the federal system within the United States is as follows:

> Even if considerable power has been centralized in the United States, our Federal Constitution still exists as the supreme law of the land. And the States, although no longer sovereign, still exist. As long as the Constitution and the States continue to exist, we have no need to be concerned. The system may be bent, so to speak, but it is not broken.

Advocates of constitutionally limited government, federalism, States' Rights, and the sovereignty of the people may indeed take heart that, in spite of the damage wrought to our system of government by the consolidating school, the Federal Constitution still survives and the States still exist. And as long as they exist, the American people can still hold hope for the restoration of the true American Theory of Government. But the question must be raised as to how much longer the Constitution, and even the States, will be allowed to exist?

That many eminent and respectable men have always, and will always, abhor the very existence of our Constitution and even the existence of the States, is a fact that cannot be denied. As ambition, greed, and avarice know no limits, so the lust for power is limitless, and anything that even remotely serves as an obstacle to the acquisition of unbounded power will be regarded, sooner or later, as an obstacle to overcome.

As we have already observed, this lust for power was evident as early as the Philadelphia Convention of 1787, in which certain individuals, under a veil of secrecy, candidly acknowledged a desire to totally abolish the States and establish a plan of Union compatible only with a government of unlimited powers. Following the failure of the consolidating school within that Constitutional Convention, the consolidators resolved to effect their goal by *false constructions* of the Constitution, asserting that the General Welfare Clause and the Necessary and Proper Clause authorized Congress to pass any law that was convenient to promoting what the federal legislators considered to be the general welfare of the United States.

The War Between the States was followed by Radical Reconstruction, during which the consolidating school illegally incorporated the *Fourteenth Amendment* into the federal compact. For a number of years, that illegal and vaguely phrased amendment provided the Supreme Court of the United States with a convenient excuse to justify the vast expansion of power on the part of the Federal Government.

Following the excesses of the New Deal of President Franklin D. Roosevelt, the consolidating school began to search for new ways to justify the continued growth of the Government of the United States. The result was a new concept styled *the living Constitution*, which asserted that pretensions of fidelity to the *original intent* of the Founding Fathers were no longer required. Rather than rely on false constructions of the Constitution dishonestly claimed to be the true and original intent of the compact, future interpretations would be made that openly and unpretentiously defied the original intent of the Framers of the Constitution. As a consequence, the American people beheld the Supreme Court of the United States interpreting the Federal Constitution, not in light of the intent of those who made and adopted it, but in light of such *modern authorities* as psychologists, sociologists, politicians, and even the courts of foreign Nations!

Through each phase of consolidation, the Consolidating School of Thought succeeded in advancing their goal of expanding the power and sphere of influence of the Government of the United States. Despite these successes, however, that school has ever been cognizant of the fact that the States continue to exist, and that the original Federal Constitution, with only a few modifications, remains the official supreme law of the land. *Officially, the United States of America continues to exist as a Federal Union between sovereign States.* As long as that situation exists, the consolidating school will never be content.

Undoubtedly, the consolidating school during the ante-bellum period of the Republic would have preferred to totally abolish the Federal Constitution and replace it with one more suited to their conceptualization of proper government for a consolidated State of America. But, undoubtedly realizing the futility of such an endeavor, they wisely selected the tool of false constructions of the existing compact to further their goals and ambitions. There can also be little doubt that the Radical Republicans, rather than basing their hopes on the illegal Fourteenth Amendment, would have preferred to tear the Constitution to pieces and replace it with a wholly new one more suitable to their black hearts.

The fanatical abolitionists had openly displayed their utter contempt for the Constitution of the United States at a surprisingly early date, placing their curses upon it, tearing it to pieces before audiences, and publicly committing it to flames. Certainly, no other group in the United States was as ready as they were to replace the Federal Constitution with an entirely new plan of government. When the abolitionist and terrorist leader John Brown, for example, invaded the State of Virginia just prior to the War Between the States, his intention was not merely to incite an armed slave revolt, but also to overthrow the Constitution of the United States. The terrorist, in conjunction with others of a like mind, had previously created a new Constitution for America, which included the establishment of Communist-style neighborhood spy committees that would closely monitor the activities of every citizen in every community in the United States.

After the start of the Twentieth Century, even ambitious men with respectable credentials began proposing new constitutions of government for the American people. As we have already demonstrated, Edward Mandell House, the man who secretly controlled the Administration of President Woodrow Wilson, fantasized about conquering the United States by the sword and imposing a Communist Constitution on the people of America. Others shared Mr. House's fantasy, including Rexford Guy Tugwell, a member of President Franklin D. Roosevelt's notorious *Brains Trust.* Mr. Tugwell, a Senior Fellow at the Center for the Study of Democratic Institutions who was funded by the Ford Foundation's Fund for the Republic, actually published a version of a new plan of government for the United States in 1970, under the title *Model for a New Constitution*. Among other things, his proposed plan called for the abolition of the existing States, the centralization of all power in a supreme National Government, the establishment of a Regulatory Branch and a Planning Branch of government, and the creation of official *Overseers* and *Watchdogs* to lord over and closely monitor the activities of the people of the United States.

Other proposals for a new plan of government to replace our present Federal Constitution have included one calling for a Parliamentary form of government, in which the majority party in the legislative branch would elect and control the executive branch of the government. This type of government, which ensures consistent unity and conformity of policies between those two branches of government, was promoted with an appeal to its efficiency. Such efficiency was openly contrasted with the American System of Government, in which the legislative and executive branches are independent and serve as checks on one another. Checks and balances, it was asserted, reduce the efficiency of government and retard the unimpeded and absolute rule of the majority, and are therefore bad.

Perhaps the most recent proposal for revising or replacing our current Federal Constitution is the book, *How Democratic Is the American Constitu-*

tion?, which was originally published in 2002, with a second edition published the following year. This book has received unqualified praise from those who hate the Constitution of the United States. "An admirable, even inspiring blend of normative and analytical, citizenly and scholarly, generous and disinterested," is how George Scialabba described it in *American Prospect.* [29]

"The author argues that we should not be afraid to examine [the Constitution] and to consider other options for achieving a more democratic society," proclaimed a review in the *Washington Post Book World.* [30] Gordon S. Wood, writing for the *New York Review of Books*, described the book as, "A devastating attack on the undemocratic character of the American Constitution." [31]

The book's author is Robert A. Dahl, a Sterling Professor Emeritus of Political Science at Yale University, whose credentials indicate clearly that he is someone whose ideas must be seriously considered even by those who might strongly disagree with him. Professor Dahl is a Senior Research Scientist in Sociology, with membership in the National Academy of Sciences, the American Philosophical Society, and the American Academy of Arts and Sciences. In addition, he is a corresponding member of the British Academy and the past President of the American Political Science Association. The professor has a number of publications to his credit, and portions of his book, *How Democratic Is the American Constitution?*, were originally presented as a series of Castle Lectures in Yale University's Program in Ethics, Politics, and Economics that were delivered by him at Yale in 2000.

The book opens with Professor Dahl's assertion that, "My aim in this brief book is not to propose changes in the American Constitution but to suggest changes in the way we *think* about our Constitution." [32] Although it is clear from a reading of the book that Professor Dahl prefers a complete replacement of our existing Federal Constitution, he understands that such a goal might not be realistic due to the high regard in which the American people hold the Constitution of 1787.

As Professor Dahl noted:

> I am well aware that in expressing reservations about the Constitution, as I have in these essays, I may be judged guilty of casting stones at a national icon. "From the time of the Founding Fathers," a historian has recently remarked, "there [has] been a sacred aura about the Constitution, manifest in holiday political rhetoric." During the years between the two World Wars, worship of the Constitution "acquired the trappings of a reli-

---

[29] Robert A. Dahl, *How Democratic Is the American Constitution?*, Second Edition, Yale University Press, New Haven, 2003, back cover.
[30] *Ibid.*, back cover.
[31] *Ibid.*, front cover.
[32] *Ibid.*, p. 1.

> gious cult." This reverential attitude continues. In a telephone survey of one thousand adult U.S. citizens in 1997, 71 percent said they strongly agreed with the statement that they were proud of the Constitution; another 20 percent somewhat agreed. In a 1999 survey, 85 percent said they thought the Constitution is a major reason why "America has been successful during this past century." [33]

Inasmuch as the American people, even in modern times, overwhelmingly hold the Constitution of the United States in very high regard, the desires of its enemies to radically alter or even abolish it are frustrated. If the Federal Constitution is to be replaced by a Socialist Constitution, the attitudes and thinking of the American people toward their Constitution must first be changed. For this reason, Professor Dahl stated that the objective of his book was to change how the American people *think* about their present Federal Constitution.

As the professor wrote:

> Yet the question remains: if our Constitution is in some important ways defective by democratic standards, should we change it, and how? As I said, my aim here is not so much to suggest changes in the existing Constitution as to encourage us to change the way we *think* about it, whether it be the existing one, an amended version of it, or a new and more democratic constitution. [34]

Professor Dahl is certainly correct in stating that a blind and meaningless worship of anything, including the Constitution of the United States, is not a practice that merits commendation. If the American people are to continue to hold their Constitution in high regard, their esteem should be based on the *merits* of that compact. Where Professor Dahl makes his fundamental mistake is that he fails to understand the true merits of the plan of government established by the Founding Fathers of the United States. The very things that he regards as flaws in the Federal Constitution are, in fact, its greatest virtues.

Robert A. Dahl establishes the groundwork for his entire line of argument within the following passage in his book: "By what *standards* does our Constitution serve us well? In particular, how well does our constitutional system meet *democratic* standards of the present day?" [35] Indeed, the very title of his book indicates that his purpose was to evaluate the merits of the Federal Constitution with only one standard in mind – how *democratic* is the Constitution of the United States?

---

[33] *Ibid.*, pp. 121-122.
[34] *Ibid.*, p. 4.
[35] *Ibid.*, p. 3.

The Founders of the American Republic, it should be remembered, sought to safeguard the American people from both types of despotism – the *tyranny of the minority* and the *tyranny of the majority*. To prevent the former, they based our political institutions on the principle of *majority rule*. To guard against the latter, they divided powers between two independent levels of government – State and Federal – and established a federal system based on the pillars of State sovereignty. The Founders were especially fearful of centralized power, and they therefore based the exercise of power at the federal level on a principle known as the *Concurrent Majority*.

The principle of the Concurrent Majority acknowledges the propriety of majority rule, but seeks to minimize the negative impact of majority rule on the rights of the minority. This is accomplished within the Constitution by providing checks and restraints on majority rule. The first and primary restraint, of course, consists of the limitations placed on the powers to be exercised by the Government of the United States. That government's powers are limited to those delegated to it by the Federal Constitution, with all other powers being reserved to the several States.

Majority rule is further restrained by the Federal Constitution in the composition of the two Houses of Congress. Representation in the House of Representatives is based on the *populations* of the States, whereas representation in the Senate is based on the *sovereign equality* of the States. Thus, a majority of representatives of the population of the States in the House is checked and restrained by a majority of the representatives of the equality of the States in the Senate. Even Presidential elections are based on the concept of the Concurrent Majority, in which voting is done by States, with each State having a number of votes equal to its number of Representatives and Senators. The purpose of the principle of the Concurrent Majority, like federalism itself, is to allow majority rule, but at the same time to provide safeguards to the rights of the minority and to foster the spirit of consensus.

Professor Dahl despises the Constitution of the United States precisely because it establishes limitations and restraints on majority rule, which he considers undemocratic in nature. He regards the Electoral College system as absurd, cannot understand why each State should have equal representation in the Senate, fails to comprehend that the Constitution is based on the concept of sovereign States, disdains States' Rights and the Tenth Amendment to the Constitution, and considers federalism to be the bane of our Republic.

Within his book, Robert A. Dahl anticipated criticism based on the fact that the Founders of the United States established a Federal *Republic* and guaranteed to each State a *republican* form of government, rather than a *Democracy*. He attempted to defuse this criticism in an appendix, in which he quoted James Madison and Montesquieu and provided his own insights to arrive at a conclusion that a proper definition of a Republic was too difficult to accomplish and that, therefore, a Democracy and a Republic may be regarded as essentially equivalent forms of government. For this reason, he asserts that the American Form of Government is or at least should be a Democracy.

In truth, there is a profound difference between a Republic and a Democracy, and the key difference was one that the professor never mentioned, much less considered. Although both a Republic and a Democracy are based upon the concept of the sovereignty of the people and the principle of majority rule, the term Democracy literally means the *rule of the people*, whereas the term Republic literally means the *public thing – the law*, or, in other words, the *rule of law*. In actual practice, a Democracy is characterized by *unlimited majority rule*, whereas a Republic is characterized by *constitutionally limited majority rule*. This explains why a Democracy is compatible with totalitarianism, while a Republic is inimical to absolute government.

Although Professor Dahl's most fervent wish appears to be the replacement of our constitutionally limited Federal Republic with an unlimited majority rule National Democracy, it is of interest to note that even he is willing to acknowledge the fallacies of unrestrained numerical majority rule. A system in which the majority wins and the minority loses, he concedes, is not as good as a political system based on *consensus* or *proportionality*.

As Professor Dahl observed:

> What is more, proportionality can strengthen consensus not just for politics but for democracy as well. The reason appears to be that proportionality results in fewer losers. To clarify this point let me overstate it: In a majoritarian system the only winners in elections are the citizens who happen to be in the majority; all the other citizens, being in the defeated minority, are losers. By contrast, in proportional systems with consensus governments, everyone – well, almost everyone – can win, not everything they hoped for perhaps but enough to leave them basically satisfied with their government. [36]

The professor probably never realized that, in making these statements, he was stating the true merits of the system of government established by the Constitution of the United States. States' Rights, federalism, and the republican form of government are all based on the type of consensus or proportionality majority rule of which the professor wrote, wherein the principle of majority rule is tempered by considerations for the rights of minorities. Why, therefore, should America abolish its existing Constitution for one based on absolute majority rule?

If the United States should replace its present Federal Constitution, with

---

[36] *Ibid.*, pp. 107-108.

its cherished Bill of Rights, what would exist to protect the liberties of the people from a government established by a different type of constitution? Within his book, Professor Dahl curiously states that, "in the end a democratic country cannot depend on its constitutional systems for the preservation of its liberties," an idea that would have shocked the Founding Fathers of the United States. Instead of relying on a constitution of government to secure human rights, the professor insists that Americans should instead rely on the good will and benevolence of the elites within society. "It can only depend," he writes, "on the beliefs and cultures shared by its political, legal, and cultural elites and by the citizens to whom these elites are responsive." [37]

This would appear to be an open and alarming endorsement of the elitist Guardian State, against which Alexis de Tocqueville warned. This perhaps explains why Robert A. Dahl found it necessary to criticize the views espoused by the Frenchman in the book, *Democracy in America*. Such sentiments as those expressed by Professor Dahl raise the question of which type of government he really prefers – a Democracy or an Aristocracy of the Elite? Such sentiments also raise the pertinent question of whether the American people are willing to abolish their present Federal Constitution and replace it with one that officially establishes a Guardian State, in which their liberties are protected by little more than the benevolence of the social and political elites. Professor Dahl candidly admits that, at the present time, they are not willing to make that fatal leap. But he hopes to change the way that Americans think about the Constitution, so that someday they can be persuaded to commit political suicide.

Shall We Abolish the States?

Another modern-day writer who advocates the abolition of our existing constitutional system of government is Michael Kinsley, an eminent journalist whose credentials are sufficient to ensure that his views must be taken seriously. Mr. Kinsley graduated from Harvard College in 1972, attended Oxford University, and graduated from Harvard Law School in 1977. But it has been in the field of journalism, not law, where Mr. Kinsley has achieved significant success. He served as a moderator for William F. Buckley's "Firing Line" debates and co-hosted CNN's "Crossfire." In addition, he was editor-in-chief of *Harper's*, editor of the American Survey section at *The Economist*, and was managing editor of *The Washington Monthly*. For two decades, Mr. Kinsley was associated with *The New Republic*, and in 1995 he founded Slate, the internet-based magazine published by Microsoft. He has also been associated with the

---

[37] *Ibid.*, p. 99.

Los Angeles Times, and has written numerous articles for *The New Republic*, *The Wall Street Journal*, the *Times of London*, *The New Yorker*, *The Reader's Digest*, *Vanity Fair*, and other publications.

In its March 28, 1981 issue, *The New Republic* featured an article by Michael Kinsley, entitled "The Withering Away of the States." The front cover illustration of the magazine captured the spirit of the article quite well, portraying a graveyard, with the Capitol in the background. In the cemetery were fifty tombstones, each one bearing the name of one of the American States. In large letters the magazine cover bore the words: "Abolish the States." Judging from the magazine cover alone, it was obvious that Mr. Kinsley shared the dream of Alexander Hamilton and the extreme wing of the Consolidating School of Thought to abolish, not merely subdue, the sovereign States of our Federal Union.

In bold letters, the thrust of Michael Kinsley's argument was summarized with the statement: "Reviving federalism is no way to get the government off our backs." The election of Ronald Reagan to the Presidency caused Mr. Kinsley to believe that States' Rights might actually be restored in the United States, and the very thought of that caused him great anxiety. To counter such a restoration of constitutionally limited government, Mr. Kinsley offered the clever argument that federalism meant fifty times as much government as nationalism, because there are fifty times as many State governments as there are Federal governments in the United States. Therefore, his argument contended, Americans concerned about Big Government should rally to nationalism, rather than urge the restoration of the constitutionally mandated federal system.

The absurdity of this line of reasoning is so obvious that its erroneous foundation scarcely needs to be pointed out. Considering the eminence of Michael Kinsley as a journalist, however, we will stoop to the level of acknowledging his argument and provide an answer. It is simply not true that the State governments represent fifty times more government than the Federal Government, inasmuch as the jurisdictions of the State governments are confined to the boundaries of the respective States. For each citizen, there are only *two levels of government* – State and Federal. Each citizen therefore has but two governments – *one* Federal Government and *one* State government. What matters is how the powers of government are distributed between those two levels of government.

The exercise of powers by a State government can be more easily checked and monitored by the citizens of that State, inasmuch as the State government is closer to them and more directly accountable to them. The Federal Government, on the other hand, is more distant and remote, and it is therefore more difficult for the people of a State to monitor and control that government or to hold it directly accountable to them. When the federal authority assumes greater powers, whether by constitutional amendment or by usurpation, the people of a State are left with less control over how those powers are exercised. Even if we set aside the requirements established by the Constitution, common sense dictates that as much power as possible should remain in each State, to be controlled by the people in each State to their own advantage.

In terms of the *total quantity of government*, the federal system again offers an advantage over a national system. If all the powers usurped over the years by the Federal Government were returned to the States, this would not alter or change the quantity of government, despite Mr. Kinsley's pretension that this would increase total government by fifty times. For each citizen, the *amount of government* would be the same, should the usurped powers claimed by the federal head be returned to the respective State governments. In fact, a good case could be made showing that the restoration to the States of the powers stolen from them by the Federal Government would result in a *reduction* in the total quantity of government, inasmuch as local government can more efficiently serve the local needs of Americans than can a highly centralized regime, which must instead rely on costly and bloated bureaucracies.

Within his article, Michael Kinsley labors to illustrate the "nuisance of living in a federal system," by claiming:

> In this country there are 51 independent court systems, and the relationship among them is one of infinite complexity and beautiful subtlety of doctrine, weaved by legal artisans over 200 years....
>
> ...[W]e all suffer the nuisance of living in a federal system. Now President Reagan wants to reverse the trend of 200 years and give the States a larger role in governing our lives. He hasn't yet explained why. It's clear he wants less government *in toto*, but how will shifting function between levels of government achieve this? Some see racist intent in Reagan's revival of the term "States Rights." Others argue that transferring social services "back" to the States, which never provided them in the first place, is just a sneaky way of canceling them. [38]

It is ironic that Michael Kinsley should question how the restoration of States' Rights could possibly result in less government *in toto*, and then proceed to answer the question himself. Transferring "social services" back to the States, he notes, could well be "a sneaky way of canceling them," for such costly and extravagant welfare programs were conceived by the Federal Government, not by the States, in an effort to buy votes and create voting blocks as a way to convert the franchise from a means of holding the government accountable into a means of patronizing politicians who are generous with the monies of the tax-

---

[38] Michael Kinsley, "The Withering Away of the States," *The New Republic*, March 28, 1981, p. 18.

payers. Transferring control of these welfare programs back to the States would, as Mr. Kinsley understood perfectly well, result in a genuine reduction in the overall quantity of government control over the lives of the American people, because the State governments are less inclined than the Federal Government to use the money of taxpayers to buy votes. That, in and of itself, should be sufficient reason to resurrect the federal system of government!

Elsewhere in his article, Michael Kinsley asserted:

> Anyone truly concerned about making America more productive, more democratic, less wasteful, less bureaucratic, would want to hasten the withering away of the States as quickly as possible.
>
> Everyone knows, for example, that America fritters away far too much brainpower on legal matters while the Japanese are inventing computers that design robots that build automobiles and so on. One main reason is federalism. Half of the standard three-year legal education could be wiped out if we had a single government with a single set of courts administering a single set of laws. Almost that many lawyers could be wiped out, too. There are elaborate constitutional doctrines about what the States can and cannot do because they are joined in a Nation, and what the central government can and cannot do because we are 50 sovereign States. [39]

The necessity for a division of powers and a system of checks and balances seems to have eluded Mr. Kinsley's grasp, as it does for many of those of the Consolidating School of Thought. Divisions of and limitations on the powers of government, although essential for the preservation of liberty, serve as obstacles to unrestrained majority rule, and as such are supposedly costly and needless relics of outmoded and antiquated notions of government. Yet, if we wish to follow Mr. Kinsley's example and dispense with the need to safeguard liberty, why not take his argument even farther? We could reduce the Constitution to a single sentence: "The Government of the United States has unlimited power to do whatever it pleases." The beauty of such a constitution, of course, is that there would be no need for any law schools or lawyers, for neither the States nor individual citizens would have any rights to defend. Such a system would therefore spare us the *nuisance* of living with lawyers. Perhaps someday a consolidator will actually make a case based on this argument, in an effort to persuade us of the wondrous beauty of absolute consolidation.

Mr. Kinsley insists that our federal system results in extravagance and wastefulness. But if the goal is to reduce bureaucracy and extravagance, as he suggested, then the question must be asked, which level of government has been the most extravagant and bureaucratic over the years, the State governments or the Federal Government? If any doubt could possibly exist, then let

---

[39] *Ibid.*, p. 18.

the candid reader look at the Government of the United States and acknowledge that no government could possibly exhibit a more bloated and extravagant bureaucracy than it does. And in regard to extravagance, let it also be noted that the Federal Government is farther in debt than all the other governments of the world combined. The annual Federal Budget is so often characterized by such profound deficit spending that it stands as one of the most shameful acts ever committed by the Government of the United States. If we are to abolish one level of government in order to simplify our political system and restore fiscal sanity, honesty compels us to assert that the government to be eliminated should be the Government of the United States, and not the State governments.

After lamenting that, "On most important matters, each State makes its own laws and settles its own arguments," Michael Kinsley declared:

> Mr. Reagan...probably believes in equal justice under the law. Federalism makes this impossible in the United States. A recent survey by the *National Law Journal* found that an American will spend more time in prison for robbery in South Carolina than for willful homicide in half a dozen other States; that the average felony conviction leads to 13 months of jail in South Dakota and 58 months in Massachusetts; and so on. The biggest disparity is that some States have capital punishment and others don't. [40]

This argument is utterly devoid of substance and could, with equal force, be applied to all the Nations of the world. Within some African countries, it is perfectly acceptable for a husband to beat his wife. In some Middle Eastern countries, a thief is punished by amputating his hand. If we are to overlook the fact that the world consists of sovereign and independent Nations, does not the concept of *equal justice* demand that all Nations administer the same punishment for the same crimes? Perhaps, to satisfy the consolidating school, we should accept wife beating as legal and adopt limb amputation as lawful punishment for theft. The answer to Mr. Kinsley, of course, is that the American States, like other Nations of the world, are sovereign. Consequently, each has a right to adopt its own system of equal justice under the law.

Continuing with his critique of our constitutional system of government, Mr. Kinsley asserted:

> Anyone who believes that enhancing federalism is a sensible way to reduce the cost of government should look up "national" and "State" in that great political science treatise, the Washington, D.C., telephone book. The Founding Fathers thought that the Senate could adequately represent the interests of the States to one another and the central government. Reagan may

---

[40] *Ibid.*, p. 19.

think that's still how it works. In fact, untold millions are spent every year in the attempt to coordinate 50 sovereignties within a single Nation.

Thirty-two State governments, at last count, have offices in Washington. Many of these are located in the "Hall of the States," an office building on Capitol Hill that also houses the National Governors Association and the National Conference of State Legislatures. But that's just the beginning. The State of California has 21 separate governmental offices in Washington. They include the State office itself, with a dozen staff members ("middle-sized," says one of them), and offices for Alameda County, Los Angeles County, San Bernadino County, San Diego County, Santa Clara County, Inglewood County, the California County Supervisors Association, Los Angeles City, six other cities and city groupings, the League of California Cities, the California university, State college, and community college systems, the California Department of Education, and the California legislature.

Besides the Governors and State legislatures, there are separate National Associations (or "Assemblies" or "Conferences" or "Centers" or "Leagues") of (or "for" or "on"): Community Arts Agencies, State Art Agencies, State Units on Aging, Conservation Districts, Consumer Justice Planning Directors, Government Communicators, Regional Councils, State Alcohol and Drug Abuse Directors, State Aviation Officials, State Boards of Education, State Boating Law Administrators, State Budget Officers, State Credit Union Supervisors, State Departments of Agriculture, State Development Agencies, State Directors of Special Education, State Lotteries, State Mental Health Program Directors, State Mental Retardation Program Directors, State Savings and Loan Supervisors, State Universities and Land Grant Colleges, Tax Administrators, Town and Township Officials, Urban Flood Management Agencies, City Councilmen, State Courts, and so on. And then there is the Advisory Commission on Intergovernmental Relations, a creation of the Federal Government itself, with a staff of 37 dedicated to grinding out fat reports on federalish topics. It may be expected to survive the Stockman ax.

Well, this is a big and complicated country, federalism or no. But these offices don't replace the coordinating function of a single central government. Most of them duplicate a whole hierarchy of federal offices on matters like historic preservation, mental health, criminal justice, and so on. These State offices generally perform two functions. One is to deal with the special problems created by federalism: 50 separate building codes, professional licensing procedures, criminal records systems. A more important function is to lobby the Federal Government.

Reagan and his people seem vividly aware of how "special interest groups" thwart the functioning of democracy, clog the wheels of government, and subvert the assertion of the general will. But they seem unaware of how much federalism aggravates this problem. It turns lower levels of government from units on an established hierarchy into independent duchies, free to join with or join battle with all the other special interests. [41]

---

[41] *Ibid.*, p. 19.

If this was intended to be an argument against genuine federalism, then Mr. Kinsley failed miserably in his presentation. The horrible picture he presented is indeed a portrait in political ugliness, but the ugly system that he described was not federalism. It is not the spirit of federalism that attempts "to coordinate 50 sovereignties within a single Nation," but rather the spirit of nationalism. What Mr. Kinsley described was *nationalistic colonialism*, a system in which the once-sovereign States have been reduced to mere provinces within a greater national system and are forced – even encouraged – to beg for handouts at the feet of Big Brother in Washington, D.C.

The Government of the United States, within our modern and corrupted political system, is the center of all significant political decisions and the source of most revenue for all major spending projects, at the federal, State, and local levels. The formerly sovereign States, therefore, are thus reduced by this corrupt system into little more than one of the many *interest groups* that lobby for federal funding, seeking their "fair share" of the largesse.

What Mr. Kinsley failed to note is that such a morally bankrupt system is not the one established by the Constitution, but was forced upon the United States by the consolidating school as part of its grand objective to buy votes and patronage with handouts from the federal treasury. Such a system was deliberately designed to convert the State and local governments into beggars on Capitol Hill, with full knowledge that federal funds come with strings attached. In return for federal cash, the State and local governments are thus forced to sell their independence to the politicians in Washington, D.C. The ugly system described by Mr. Kinsley is, in fact, a consolidated nationalist system built upon the ruins of a federal system. Rather than urge the restoration of genuine constitutional federalism, Michael Kinsley claimed that we should completely obliterate the federal system, ruins and all.

Mr. Kinsley's confusion as to what constitutes federalism led him to write:

> Millions of your State tax dollars are being spent every day in efforts to affect how your federal tax dollars are spent, while millions of your federal tax dollars are spent fending them off. This is efficient government?
>
> Speaking of your taxes, federalism makes a mess of them. Having different levels of government raising revenues independently not only makes life needlessly complicated. Taxation depends on the government having a monopoly. A rational and fair tax system is impossible when governments must compete with one another. The growth of multinational corporations made this an insoluble problem among Nations. The Balkanization of our tax system creates a perfectly needless problem in this country. [42]

---

[42] *Ibid.*, pp. 19-20.

Making reference to taxation is a poor strategy for the Consolidating School of Thought, for most taxpayers know all too well that it is *federal* taxes that threaten to rob them of their last farthing. Most taxpayers, therefore, would ill brook any suggestion that we should abolish the State governments so that the Federal Government can have a *monopoly* of power and control over their pocketbooks.

What Mr. Kinsley failed to mention is that the Government of the United States already has more of a *monopoly on taxation* than most Americans realize, for a considerable amount of State taxation is levied in order to qualify for federal "matching" funds or to fulfill the stipulations specified by the Federal Government. The foolish *No Child Left Behind Act*, for example, is an extravagant and wasteful federal law, but the waste and extravagance must be borne largely by the State governments. Another recent example of this trend is the Federal Government's very costly *Prescription Drug Benefit Plan*, whose cost was cleverly shifted to the State governments. For this reason, the true extravagance of the Federal Government can only be calculated by considering a significant portion of the budgets of the several States, as well as the hefty Federal Budget.

Continuing with his assault on the American constitutional system of government, Michael Kinsley wrote:

> [F]ederalism makes sensible regulations impossible to apply and enforce. There are two reasons for this. First, we do have open State borders, for the moment, and air and water currents remain unimpressed by the doctrine of States Rights. This means that matters like gun control and pollution standards simply cannot be addressed on the State level....Second, regulation, like taxation, must be a monopoly to work right. This may sound undemocratic, but it's actually the essence of democracy. Almost everybody in the country might agree that a certain degree of regulation is desirable, but no State will be able to pass it for fear of losing business. [43]

Federalism, asserted Mr. Kinsley, protects the American people from the draconian rules and regulations of Big Government in Washington, D.C. Were it not for federalism, he lamented, the Government of the United States would hold a *monopoly* on power and could rule over the people without restraint, even disarming them and leaving them defenseless in the face of tyranny. His argument is the probably the best one that could ever be made on why we need to maintain – or, more accurately, to restore – our federal system of government. Nothing could better serve the cause of freedom than to thwart the creation of that monopoly of power which Mr. Kinsley advocates.

---

[43] *Ibid.*, p. 20.

Elsewhere in his article, this consolidator made the following bold claim:

> Federalism makes the government a much better deal for some people than for others. This is not a question of letting local areas decide how much government they want. Government Balkanization lets some people get more services for less money. This can be seen most clearly in metropolitan areas, where rich suburbs are able to have lower tax rates but higher per-capita expenditures than central cities, which often must support area-wide services like museums and zoos. [44]

This attempt to associate *tax rates* with *per-capita expenditures* reveals the low estimate that its author placed on the intelligence of those he was addressing. The average resident of those "rich suburbs" he referred to, for example, could earn ten times as much money as the average resident of the inner city, but pay only five times as much in taxation. In turn, the local government could spend twice as much per person for the residents of the suburbs as it does for those in the inner city. This scenario would certainly qualify for Mr. Kinsley's criteria of a lower tax rate associated with a higher per-capita spending level by local government.

But this point actually has little bearing on the main issue. Under federalism, in which each State government taxes the citizens of the State and spends the money for their benefit, there is less likelihood that the tax-and-spend power of government will be used to favor special interest groups, than would be the case under a national system, in which the Federal Government spent money for local purposes. Under a national system, it is quite possible that entire States, and even entire regions of the country, could be unfairly taxed for the benefit of more favored sections of the United States. It is nationalism, not federalism, which breeds a system of unfair taxation.

Another argument raised by Michael Kinsley is that States' Rights create "a dangerous growth in geographical chauvinism," and erode "our feeling of national community." [45] That is certainly a weighty argument, but we must humbly observe that nationalism creates its own kind of arrogant *geographical chauvinism* that is hostile to local interests. Under federalism, the local interests of the American people would remain under their local control, and there could not exist any conflicts of interest, as would be the case should the domestic affairs of the States be *nationalized* and managed centrally by the Federal Government. By respecting the right of each State to govern itself, and by confining the Federal Government to its proper role of conducting foreign affairs, the American people can achieve the desired objective of *unity in common con-*

---

[44] *Ibid.*, p. 20.
[45] *Ibid.*, p. 21.

cerns and *separateness in separate concerns*. It is nationalism, or consolidation, which throws everything – domestic, as well as foreign, affairs – into the sphere of common concern, that breeds sectional jealousies and conflict.

Michael Kinsley ridicules those who believe that, "to the extent we must have government, State government is inherently more efficient than the Federal Government, and less prone to the dreaded waste, fraud, and abuse." He insisted that, "There is no evidence to support this belief." [46] For evidence to support this well-founded belief, we offer Exhibit A: The Federal Budget of the Government of the United States of America. Anyone who troubles himself to read the annual Federal Budget will have a new appreciation for the words extravagant and wasteful. And anyone who knows the full extent of the indebtedness of the Federal Government and the size of its shameful deficits will conclude that its fiscal management is nothing short of criminal. Could our State governments possibly be more reckless and extravagant?

Mr. Kinsley concluded his assault upon federalism with these words:

> [P]erhaps we should drop it. Federalism, I mean. It was great fun, but it was just one of those things. We don't need to do anything so drastic as abolishing the States. They could remain as reservoirs of sentiment and employers of last resort for people's brothers-in-law. But billions could be saved by both the government and the private sector if we were to nationalize huge chunks of the law such as negligence, incorporation and business regulation, and professional licensing. Justice and economy would be served by unifying the court system and the punishment of crime. A single national taxing authority would put thousands of lawyers and accountants out of work. (States could still set their own tax rates, but Uncle Sam would make the rules and do the collecting for everybody.) National authority over social concerns like welfare and environmental rules would assure that society as a whole makes rational, democratic decisions about issues that affect society as a whole.
>
> ...It will be no triumph for freedom to get the Federal Government off our backs only to have 50 State governments climb back on. [47]

With this bold plea on behalf of total centralization and consolidation to create a monopoly of power in the Government of the United States, Michael Kinsley's article deserves to take its ideological place alongside Sir Robert Filmer's assertions for the Divine Rights of Kings and Thomas Hobbes' argument for a Leviathan State. And Mr. Kinsley's article should serve as a warning to all Americans that, while our Federal Constitution still exists, it may not exist much longer, for the Consolidating School of Thought will never be truly satisfied until our Federal Constitution has been officially replaced with a Constitution for the People's Socialist Republic of America. When that day arrives, the

[46] *Ibid.*, p. 21.
[47] *Ibid.*, p. 21.

people of the United States will discover that all hope for reform has passed.

The Greatness of America

The fifth common misconception that serves as an obstacle to the acceptance of the true American Theory of Government and to an acknowledgment of the importance of maintaining – or, more precisely, of resurrecting – State sovereignty and the federal system within the United States is as follows:

> The true American Theory of Government may rest upon the pillars of sovereign States, but the true greatness of America has been realized only since the War Between the States converted the United States into a Nation. And for this, we have the consolidating school to thank.

This, of course, depends entirely on how we are to define *greatness*. If that term is employed to describe the threat or actual use of marital force to intimidate, bully, and dictate to the States of the Federal Union and to foreign Nations, then there can be little doubt that the consolidating school has contributed mightily to that type of "greatness." But if, by that term, it is meant the attainment of material prosperity, sufficient strength to repel any foreign attack, and respect for the liberties of the people, then it may be truthfully stated that America is great *in spite of*, not because of, the machinations of the consolidating school.

Nearly every attribute that truly makes America great was either established or inaugurated during the ante-bellum period of American civilization, the period of our history *before* the consolidating school had seized firm control of the United States. It was during this significant period of time that the United States achieved remarkable growth, both in terms of economic prosperity and in geographical territory.

Beginning as thirteen States situated along the Atlantic seaboard in 1776, the spirit of Manifest Destiny spurred the rapid Westward migration of American civilization. By 1850, with the admission of California into the Union, the United States of America literally stretched from the Atlantic Ocean to the Pacific Ocean. And the strength, power, and prestige of the United States grew as rapidly as the territorial expansion of the Republic. By the time of the War of 1812, for example, the United States was able to defeat Great Britain, considered at the time to be the most powerful Nation on earth, without the assistance of allies. And by 1848, even Abraham Lincoln was willing to concede that the American Confederacy had attained such greatness and prestige in the world that no other Nation on earth would dare to attack and invade the

United States.

By the middle of the ante-bellum period, the United States of America had become the envy of the entire world, which marveled at the prosperity of the American people, the American spirit of rugged individualism, and the American system of constitutionally limited government. Alexis de Tocqueville was but one of many Europeans who visited the United States during that period of our development to look for the secret to America's greatness. As he and other visitors discovered, *America had attained greatness because America was good.* And should America ever cease to be good, they rightfully concluded, America would cease to be great.

Whatever further progress was made by the United States to augment the greatness of American civilization since the War Between the States has been realized in spite of the intrigues of the consolidating school. The primary "gifts" bestowed upon America by that school after its conquest of the American States have been the incessant growth of the power and size of the Federal Government, the increasing collectivization of the American economy, and imperialistic wars of conquest. Rather than contributing to the further greatness of America, however, these contributions have proven to be a curse upon the happiness and welfare of the people of the United States.

The American people were led to believe, for example, that the Federal Government thrust the United States into World War I to make the world safe for Democracy. Under that conviction, thousands of young Americans were sent overseas to fight and die on the battlefields of Europe. The sobering truth about U.S. involvement in that war, however, was not disclosed until nearly two decades later when the Senate's Nye Committee demonstrated that President Woodrow Wilson went to war, not to make the world safe for Democracy, but to make the world safe for the monied aristocracy.

As the authors of the history textbook, *The National Experience*, point out:

> Who had drawn the United States in and why? The new disillusion was clinched in 1934 and 1935 by the work of a Senate committee set up under the chairmanship of Gerald P. Nye of North Dakota to investigate the munitions industry. The Nye Committee unearthed a wealth of documentation purporting to show that the United States had been shoved into war when international bankers, especially the House of Morgan, saw no other way to guarantee repayment of the vast credits they had granted to the western Allies. To demonstrate that no President could be trusted with discretionary power in matters of war and peace, Nye charged Wilson with duplicity in pretending to be ignorant of the secret treaties.
>
> The Nye Committee completed the work of consolidating the isolationist philosophy....These views summed up the prevailing opinion of the

American people.[48]

Just a few years after the Nye Committee had completed its work, the United States was manipulated into World War II. Once again, thousands of young Americans were sent overseas to fight and die for obscure reasons. Although that war did end the Fascist and Nazi threat to Europe, it also established the Soviet Union as a superpower and created a worldwide menace in the form of the Communist Conspiracy.

For nearly half a century, as a consequence of this disaster of global proportions, the United States found itself engaged in a Cold War, with hot wars fought in Korean and Vietnam. Not only were Americans fighting and dying for obscure purposes in distant lands, but the American people beheld the alarming growth of the executive branch of their Federal Government, as the President of the United States usurped the power of Congress to declare war and declared himself to be, in essence, the King of the World.

On the home front, the American people witnessed the spectacle of the Government of the United States assuming a *permanent war status*, as it waged endless and relentless domestic wars, from a War on Drugs to a War on Poverty to a War on Racism. All of these presents to America were gifts from the Consolidating School of Thought, which also gave the people of the United States the Welfare State, the American version of Alexis de Tocqueville's Guardian State.

The Cold War had scarcely ended when the United States found itself involved in yet another war that had no end in sight – the War on Terrorism – with its escalating warfare in the Middle East, the creation of countless new enemies who hate America, and the infamous Patriot Act, which confers tyrannical powers on the executive branch of government. Under its provisions, any American can be accused of supporting terrorism, made to disappear, secretly held indefinitely in a military prison, and even sent to some foreign country that specializes in torturing suspects.

In 2005, President George W. Bush declared war on every single Nation on earth whose form of government did not measure up to the consolidating school's standard of Democracy. As a consequence, Americans can now expect to spend considerably more money supporting imperialistic adventures, to shed more of the blood of their sons in wars waged in obscure corners of the globe for mysterious purposes, to sacrifice more of their freedoms in the hope of obtaining greater security, and to suffer more terrorist attacks from those seeking revenge and retribution for U.S. meddling in the internal affairs of other Nations.

---

[48] John M. Blum, Bruce Catton, Edmund S. Morgan, *et. al.*, *The National Experience: A History of the United States*, Harcourt, Brace & World, Inc., New York, 1963, p. 681.

These are but a few of the "contributions" made to the United States by the advocates of a supreme, sovereign, imperial National Government. Such contributions have added to the strength and greatness of America in the same manner that a tapeworm or other parasite contributes strength and health to the human body. For the true greatness of America, we have the States' Rights school to thank. The consolidating school has been nothing but a curse upon American civilization.

The New World Order

The final common misconception that serves as an obstacle to the acceptance of the true American Theory of Government and to an acknowledgment of the importance of maintaining – or, more precisely, of resurrecting – State sovereignty and the federal system within the United States is as follows:

> Although the Government of the United States conquered the States and robbed them of their sovereignty, we Americans have no real need to be concerned. The great struggle over sovereignty ended long ago in favor of nationalism. Whether we have State sovereignty or a national sovereignty, we are still an independent country empowered to control and shape our own destiny. And that is what really matters the most.

In one respect, George McDuffie, writing under the pseudonym of "One of the People," was correct when he asserted that the ambitious consolidators seeking a monopoly of control over the Government of the United States would never be content by merely usurping the reserved rights of the States. Since their ambitions were boundless, they would invariably seek to *ascend* to more lofty levels of conquest, and *such grander conquests would be naturally accompanied by a desire to move the seat of sovereignty to grander heights*. But after conquering and subduing the American States, what higher level of conquest would tempt these ambitious men with superior talents, having at their disposal natural resources never before enjoyed by men of great ambition? Only one forbidden fruit remained to tempt them – the entire world!

It appears to be the nature of uncontrolled ambition and lust for power to amalgamate and centralize both sovereignty and power to the greatest extent possible. Following the triumph of the consolidating conspiracy in the War Between the States, the remainder of the Nineteenth Century witnessed the consolidation of the victory over the American States. But with the dawn of the Twentieth Century came new desires, new ambitions, and new quests. Moved by such ambitions, the *nationalists* of the previous century evolved into *interna-*

tionalists, and the lust to conquer the American States quickly grew into a lust to conquer the world.

That such an evolution could transpire should come as no surprise to those who understand the nature of man and the influence of ambition. The motives of the consolidating school have ever been anything but patriotic. It was not a love for any mythological American Nation, but a lust for power and control, that inspired that school to seek to rob the American States of their sovereignty. Only the naïve and uninformed would expect that those who justify the theft of sovereignty from the peoples of the several States can be trusted to safeguard the sovereignty of any American Nation of people, whether real or pretended. To those seeking to conquer the human race, American sovereignty – whether State or national – is merely an obstacle to be overcome and ultimately destroyed.

With the failure of the United States to join the League of Nations following World War I, the Internationalist Conspiracy of the consolidating school received a temporary setback. Following World War II, however, the internationalist dream received a tremendous boost with the creation of the *United Nations Organization*. The U.N., the American people were assured, was essential to achieve universal peace by ensuring an end to all war. That organization, its advocates proclaimed with religious fervor, was the world's last, best hope – indeed, the world's only hope.

What few Americans at the time realized was that the Founding Fathers of the United States had also considered proposals to participate in the creation of a World Government, but had wisely rejected such proposals because the very concept of a World Government was hostile to the freedom of mankind. When one such proposal was made by the French philosopher, Jean Jacques Rousseau, the danger inherent in internationalism was exposed by James Madison, who wrote the following in the February 2, 1792 issue of the *National Gazette*:

> Among the various reforms which have been offered to the world, the projects for universal peace have done the greatest honor to the hearts, though they seem to have done very little to the heads of their authors. Rousseau, the most distinguished of these philanthropists, has recommended a Confederation of Sovereigns, under a council of deputies, for the double purpose of arbitrating external controversies among Nations, and of guaranteeing their respective governments against internal revolutions. He was aware, neither of the impossibility of executing his pacific plan among governments which feel so many allurements to war, nor, what is more extraordinary, of the tendency of his plan to perpetuate arbitrary power wherever it existed; and, by extinguishing the hope of one day seeing an end of oppression, to cut off the only source of consolation remaining to the oppressed.
>
> A universal and perpetual peace, it is to be feared, is in the catalogue

> of events, which will never exist but in the imaginations of visionary philosophers, or in the breasts of benevolent enthusiasts. [49]

A World Government, as Mr. Madison pointed out, could not possibly offer any real benefits to the human race, simply because it could never accomplish its proposed objective of universal peace. On the contrary, a World Government, he indicated, poses a serious threat to the inalienable rights of man by allowing a concert of Nations to suppress liberty on a global scale. While this constitutes sufficient reason for honest advocates to firmly oppose any and all proposals for World Government, it is precisely for this reason that the consolidating internationalists promote World Government under the style of a *New World Order*. Whether that World Government will be established by a frontal assault on national sovereignty – either by means of the United Nations or a newly created superstructure – or by an end run around national sovereignty, by means of regional pacts, remains to be seen. But either way, those seeking to terminate the existence of the United States are determined to establish a Reign of Tyranny over all mankind.

The strategies employed to conquer and subdue the sovereign Nations of the earth, which were inaugurated in the Twentieth Century, bear a striking similarity to the strategies inaugurated in the Nineteenth Century to conquer and subdue the American States of our Federal Union. Whereas the consolidating nationalists sought to convince the people of the States to think of themselves as citizens of a consolidated Nation, so the consolidating internationalists seek to convince the people of America to regard themselves as *Citizens of the World*. To facilitate this process, books have been published under that very title, and a number of *Declarations of Interdependence* have been promulgated in an attempt indoctrinate the people of the United States with the concepts of internationalism.

As with the Pledge of Allegiance, a primary target of the internationalist indoctrinate campaign has been schoolchildren, as exemplified by the 241-page National Education Association book of "suggestions and recommendations" to teachers, which asserted that pupils should become "world-minded." "The world-minded American," the book stated, "knows that unlimited national sovereignty is a threat to world peace." [50]

As early as 1945, a group styled the Student Federalists adopted a statement of purposes, which declared that its aim was, "To educate the rising generation in the principles of democracy and world federal union and to prepare

---

[49] Saul K. Padover (ed.), *The Complete Madison: His Basic Writings*, Kraus Reprint Co., New York, 1971, p. 260.

[50] Joseph P. Kamp, *We Must Abolish the United States: The Hidden Facts Behind the Crusade for World Government*, Hallmark Publishers, New York, 1950, quoted on p. 70.

youth for world citizenship." [51] The extent of the influence of such ideas became apparent in 1949, when Garry Davis, a youthful member of the United World Federalist organization, tore up his American passport, renounced his U.S. citizenship, and declared that he had become a "citizen of the world." [52]

Another similarity of strategies between the consolidating conspiracy against the American States and that directed against the sovereign Nations of the world may be found in the desire to subvert the supreme law. The supreme law in the United States, of course, is the Federal Constitution, which the consolidating school has long sought to undermine as part of its war against the sovereignty of the States of the American Union. The corresponding supreme law among the Nations of the world has traditionally been referred to as the *Law of Nations*, which has also been referred to as *International Law*, the *Laws of Nature*, the *Laws of God*, and the *Law of Right and Wrong*. The Law of Nations is not statutory law, or law legislated by man, but exists naturally and may be deduced by common sense, logic, and reason. One of the key objectives of the internationalists, however, is to subvert the traditional Law of Nations by replacing it with *man-made International Law*, such as the resolutions, edicts, and codifications promulgated by the United Nations, as though the internationalists were somehow wiser than God.

An integral part of this strategy to subvert the genuine Law of Nations involves replacing the great historical works that are based on the Laws of Nature and have long guided Nations in treating with one another, such as the works of Hugo Grotius and Emmerich de Vattel, with modernistic works on International Law that define a new International Law based on the codifications of the United Nations. Nowhere was this strategy more plainly stated than in the book, *A Modern Law of Nations*, which was published in 1952 and written by Philip C. Jessup, the internationalist whose affinity for the color Red drew the attention of Senator Joseph R. McCarthy of Wisconsin.

As Dr. Jessup noted in the Preface of his book: "The General Assembly of the United Nations has begun its task of initiating studies and making recommendations for the purpose of 'encouraging the progressive development of International Law and its codification' as required by Article 13 of the Charter." [53]

This project, stated Philip C. Jessup, was of paramount importance to all those involved in the Internationalist Conspiracy:

> It is natural that some minds seek a complete change through the

---

[51] *Ibid.*, quoted on p. 71.
[52] *Ibid.*, quoted on p. 71.
[53] Philip C. Jessup, *A Modern Law of Nations: An Introduction*, The Macmillan Company, New York, 1952, p. vii.

> immediate creation of a World Government. Others would prefer to build more slowly through the medium of what is generally called international organization or administration, now typified by the United Nations. One point of agreement may be found in all plans and proposals, whether they come from statesmen or from laymen, from experts or from novices. That common point is the necessity for an adequate International Law. [54]

Although the Charter of the United Nations Organization expressly declares that the world organization is founded on the recognition of the *sovereign equality* of its member States, such assurances were intended only to deceive the unwary. As Dr. Jessup indicated in his book, it has ever been the intention of the internationalists to sacrifice the "national sovereignty" of the United States and other Nations on the altar of World Government: "Unlimited sovereignty is no longer automatically accepted as the most prized possession or even as a desirable attribute of States." [55]

This idea was echoed by Bernard M. Baruch, who wrote in 1960:

> Every treaty involves some diminution of sovereignty. For myself, I believed it was time to start freeing ourselves from the *fetish of national sovereignty*. Just as the doctrine of unbridled *laissez-faire* is no longer application to Twentieth-Century America and the world, so the *extreme dogma of national sovereignty* is no longer applicable in an age when the lives and destinies of Nations are inextricably bound together. Naturally, the international control of atomic energy involves the *surrender* of some portion of sovereignty to *a higher sovereignty* – to an instrument of world order. [emphasis added] [56]

As Mr. Baruch indicated, it is a contention of the Consolidating School of Thought that not only is it desirable for the Federal Government to surrender the sovereignty of the people of the United States to a World Government, but that, by treaty, the Government of the United States can legitimately effect that transfer of sovereignty. Both the expressed desire for a sovereign World Government and the claim made for the treaty power of the Federal Government, however, are glaringly incorrect. The *treaty-making power* of the Federal Government, like all the other powers delegated to that government, is *limited* to the ends prescribed by the Constitution of the United States, and those ends are compatible only with the continued existence of sovereign States. The Federal Government can no more legally rob the people of the States of their sovereignty by a treaty, than it can legally accomplish that objective by passing a statutory law.

Writing in 1801, Thomas Jefferson said:

---

[54] *Ibid.*, p. 1.
[55] *Ibid.*, p. 1.
[56] Bernard M. Baruch, *Baruch: The Public Years*, Pocket Books, Inc., New York, 1960, p. 352.

> By the general power to make treaties, the Constitution must have intended to comprehend only those objects which are usually regulated by treaties, and cannot be otherwise regulated. It must have been meant to except out all those rights reserved to the States; for surely the President and the Senate cannot do by treaty what the whole government is interdicted from doing in any way. [57]

The sovereignty of the American people is constitutionally reserved to the States, and the Government of the United States cannot by law or treaty transfer that sovereignty to any World Government. But the Consolidating School of Thought rests upon the concept that constitutionally established restraints on power can be ignored and therefore contends that the Federal Government can indeed transfer, by law and treaty, the sovereignty of the American people to an instrument of world order. And the ongoing crusade on behalf of a sovereign World Government has been in continuous operation for the past half century in utter violation of the Constitution of the United States.

In the January/February, 2004, issue of *Foreign Affairs*, for example, Robert A. Pastor asserted the sustained "New Vision" of internationalism to render the sovereignty of the people of the United States "obsolete." [58] Writing in the July/August, 2004, issue of that official Journal of the Council on Foreign Relations, Senator Chuck Hagel of Nebraska insisted that, despite the ability of the United States to defend itself, Americans must continue to advance the cause of the New World Order:

> [T]he United States' long-term security interests are connected to alliances, coalitions, and international institutions....No single country, including the United States with all its vast military and economic power, can successfully meet the challenges of the Twenty-First Century alone. Winning the War on Terrorism, for example, will require a seamless network of relationships.
>
> The United States must therefore help strengthen global institutions and alliances, beginning with the United Nations and NATO. [59]

Another similarity of strategies between the consolidating conspiracy of the Nineteenth Century and that of the Twentieth Century and beyond is the reliance on tax-supported subsidies from the Federal Government to purchase patronage. Under the old American System of Henry Clay, the consolidating school discovered that it was possible to use funds obtained by taxing all Americans to secure the patronage of favored interest groups by appealing to

---

[57] G. Edward Griffin, *The Fearful Master: A Second Look at the United Nations*, Western Islands, Boston, 1964, quoted on p. 190.

[58] Robert A. Pastor, "North America's Second Decade," *Foreign Affairs*, January/February 2004, p. 134.

[59] Chuck Hagel, "A Republican Foreign Policy," *Foreign Affairs*, July/August 2004, p. 68.

the greed and avarice inherent in human nature. In similar fashion, modern-day *foreign aid* is utilized by the Government of the United States to establish and maintain socialistic regimes in the Third World Nations and to ensure the continued cooperation of those foreign regimes in the creation of the New World Order.

Should any Third World Nation dare to assert a spirit of independence, however, then the internationalists borrow another strategy utilized by the consolidators of old – the use of *physical coercion*, including *economic sanctions* and, if required to ensure obedience, *military invasion* and the *overthrow of the independent-minded government*. To facilitate this coercive process, the internationalists adopted another strategy that has proved effective in robbing the American States of their sovereignty – the claim that concerns for *human rights* must trump any concerns for the sovereignty of the Nation being targeted for conquest.

Accordingly, the United Nations and associated organs for world control bristle with Declarations on the Rights of the Child and other such assertions of a similar nature. Even within the United States Department of State, a Bureau of Democracy, Human Rights, and Labor has been created, with the defined objective to "promote democracy as a means to achieve security, stability, and prosperity for the entire world" and to "identify and denounce regimes that deny their citizens the right to choose their leaders in elections that are free, fair, and transparent." [60]

In vain do we search the Constitution of the United States to find any provision that delegates such a power to the Federal Government. But, thanks to the Consolidating School of Thought, the Government of the United States is no longer restrained by the federal compact, and may assume any powers it pleases, including the power to interfere in the internal affairs of any Nation on earth. Such a power, it hardly needs to be pointed out, can only be claimed by a *sovereign government.* Such is the type of National Government that the consolidating nationalists have imposed on the United States, and such is the type of World Government which the consolidating internationalists are striving to impose on humanity.

Long ago, the U.N. World Court decreed that the United Nations is a World Government vested with *unlimited powers*, and is, therefore, a sovereign government:

> Under International Law, the organization [United Nations] must be deemed to have those powers which, though not expressly provided in the Charter are conferred upon it by necessary implication as being essential to

---

[60] John B. Judis, "Putting Liberty First: The Case Against Democracy," *Foreign Affairs*, May/June 2003, quoted on p. 128.

the performance of its duties.[61]

Thus it is that the ultimate conspiracy of consolidation seeks to achieve the ultimate degree of centralization, by transferring all sovereignty on the planet to a Socialist World Government that will wield unlimited powers over the entire human race, including the people of the United States. We are again reminded of the sober assessment given by G. Edward Griffin in his book, *The Fearful Master: A Second Look at the United Nations*:

> The next time you hear someone speak lightly about sovereignty or national independence, remember that this was the one single accomplishment of the American Revolution. Our present involvement in the United Nations has put us right back where the shooting began in 1775.[62]

[61] G. Edward Griffin, *Op. cit.*, quoted on p. 198.
[62] *Ibid.*, p. 234.

Chapter Thirteen

Conclusions

Within the course of our inquiry into the nature of sovereignty in the United States of America, we have examined a number of historical facts, concepts, principles, and theories relative to the character of the Government of the United States and the American Union of States. Considering the significance of the subject of sovereignty, we should summarize the main points which have been raised in the course of our inquiry. At this point, the following concepts and principles should be conclusively established as forming the basis of the American constitutional system of government.

1. God is the true Sovereign of the Universe, and inasmuch as He made all men equally in His image, no one has any authority to rule over another unless such authorization has been granted by the Creator. The Supreme Ruler of the Universe, as revealed in the Holy Bible, has delegated four distinct types of sovereignty to the human race. Personal Sovereignty is that species of authority that authorizes every man to be the master of his own destiny and to assume full responsibility for his own welfare and advancement. Patriarchal Sovereignty is that type of authority delegated by God to every husband to rule over his wife and act as the head of his own household. Parental Sovereignty is the God-ordained authority that every mother and father have to govern the rearing of their own children. Finally, Political Sovereignty is the supreme authority delegated to mankind to enforce an observance of the Laws of Nature and to punish criminals. Inasmuch as our inquiry deals exclusively with Political Sovereignty, we have referred to it simply as sovereignty, with the understanding that we are referring to the supreme political authority.

2. Although many modern-day Americans do not fully comprehend the nature and significance of sovereignty, its importance in the history of all human government is undeniable. In any civil society in which sovereignty is truly vested in the people, they are the masters and the their government is their servant. But should the government succeed in stealing supremacy from the people, then it becomes their master and they become its slaves. Much of the history of the human race has been characterized by a struggle between people and government to determine who should posses and exercise that political supremacy. By definition, a sovereign government is a government of unlimited pow-

ers, which constitutes the very foundation of tyranny.

3. The theory of governmental supremacy reached its pinnacle when Sir Robert Filmer penned his famous defense of the so-called Divine Rights of Kings, and when Thomas Hobbes presented a defense for the Leviathan State, ruled by an absolute government. According to Sir Robert, Kings are naturally invested with sovereignty and, therefore, have a natural claim upon unlimited powers over their subjects. Mr. Hobbes, on the other hand, claimed that a totalitarian government was the only alternative to the chaos and lawlessness of anarchy.

4. The honor of refuting the theories of both Sir Robert Filmer and Thomas Hobbes fell upon John Locke, the renowned English philosopher whose principles provided the intellectual framework for Britain's Glorious Revolution. In the *First Treatise of Government*, Mr. Locke exposed the fallacies and inconsistencies in the Divine Rights of Kings theory of government. And in the *Second Treatise of Government*, he offered an enlightened alternative philosophy to the Leviathan State mentality, by asserting that civil society and government should be based on consent. In advocating this concept, John Locke contributed greatly to the rise of the Age of Reason and significantly influenced the Western World's concepts of government in favor of modern-day middle class values of individualism, private property rights, limited government, the trustee nature of government, and government-by-the-consent-of-the-government.

5. In advocating the proper development of civil society and human government, John Locke offered some historical examples that demonstrated his concepts. His primary objective, however, was not to explain the foundations of civil society from an historical perspective, but rather, to state the concepts of the proper foundation of civil society from a moral perspective based on the irrefutable values of right and wrong. From an historical perspective, however, the foundations of American civilization – from the Mayflower Compact, to the Declaration of Independence, to the Constitution of 1787 – represent the closest approximation of actual historical facts to the enlightened theories espoused by the Father of the Age of Reason.

6. According to the Lockean Theory of Government, when God vested sovereignty in mankind, the delegation was made to all men equally as individuals. God did not directly institute human government, but merely delegated supreme political authority to every human being. Prior to the creation of human government, men lived in a State of Nature, which was also a State of Perfect Freedom, in which each man was his own King, vested with all the powers we normally associate with government.

7. While the State of Nature was a State of Perfect Freedom, the Lockean Theory of Government asserts that it was also a State of Insecurity, in

which no man's life, liberty, and property were safe from invasion by others. To provide greater security for their inalienable rights, mankind resolved to create a number of separate civil societies and to pool their individual sovereignty into separate body politics known as Nations or States. Theoretically, the initial creation of a sovereign State occurred as the result of a Social Contract, which should have been established by the unanimous consent of every member of the society. After the creation of such a civil society, its affairs could be conducted on behalf of the whole by the consent of the majority.

8. Those who are born into an existing body politic are not born into a State of Nature and, therefore, do not individually possess sovereignty. As they are nurtured into adulthood, they receive the benefits of the existing society, which exists to safeguard the rights of all innocent persons to life, liberty, and property. Upon reaching adulthood, those born into an existing State have the alternative of either migrating elsewhere or remaining within that society, thereby giving what amounts to their tacit consent to that society.

9. Sovereignty, within a properly founded civil society, is vested in the whole people of the State. By its very nature, sovereignty is the supreme, unlimited political power, the power from which all the other powers of government are derived. Once a sovereign State has been established by unanimous consent, the majority of the people of that State may constitute a government by establishing its organs and offices, and by delegating some powers to it. The powers of such a properly constituted government are limited to those expressly delegated to it, and it holds those powers as a trust. Sovereignty, however, remains vested in the people of that State, who remain the masters over their government. The people may decide to delegate additional powers to their government at a later date, or to remove some powers from that government. The people may even resolve to completely abolish the existing government and to replace it with a new government. This they have a natural right to do, because they, and not the government, are vested with sovereignty.

10. Sovereignty must not be confused with the ordinary powers exercised by government, which are merely derived from the supreme political power. Sovereignty is the power to create a government, delegate powers to it, limit its powers by means of a constitution, and dictate that all powers not delegated are prohibited to that government. As long as the government thus created confines its exercise of powers to the constitutionally defined ends and means, the people remain sovereign over their government. But whenever that government embarks on a course of usurpation of power or assumes the right to determine the extent of its own powers, it effectively robs the people of their sovereignty and becomes, in theory and, ultimately, in reality, a government of unlimited powers, or a sovereign government.

11. The Lockean Theory of Government had a more profound impact

on the minds of the American people than on the minds of Englishmen, as may be demonstrated by the arguments presented by the colonists to protest the abusive practices of the British Government prior to the American Revolution. When applied to the American form and system of government, which are based on the foundation of sovereign States, the Lockean Theory of Government becomes a uniquely American Theory of Government.

12. According to the American Theory of Government, the thirteen American colonies became sovereign States with the publication of their unanimous Declaration of Independence on July 4, 1776. Within that Declaration, written by Thomas Jefferson, the Lockean concept of government-by-the-consent-of-the-governed is presented in its first section, in which the purpose of government is defined as the safeguarding of the inalienable rights of man. In the second section of the Declaration, Mr. Jefferson listed the specific grievances of the colonies against King George III. And the third and final section of the Declaration, Thomas Jefferson penned the actual Birth Certificate of the American States, by declaring that each of the thirteen original colonies was thenceforth a sovereign State, on a footing equal to the State of Great Britain, and empowered as any other sovereign State or Nation on earth.

13. Each one of the original thirteen American States fought the War of Independence to secure its own sovereignty, although, recognizing the value of alliances, aligned itself with the others to form a unified front against the common enemy. At the same time the States resolved to declare their independence, they also resolved to form a political association with each other. To emphasize their military alliance and their anticipated political Union, the term "United States of America" was utilized within the Declaration of Independence. But that Declaration, in itself, did not create any political Union. Thus, the newly independent States promptly set about the task of formally adopting a compact of government amongst themselves, styled the Articles of Confederation.

14. By 1781, the Articles of Confederation had finally been adopted by all thirteen States, and this first Federal Constitution for the United States created a Federal Union between the States. The style of the League of States was the "United States of America," which was defined as a firm league of friendship amongst the American States, and the purpose or reason why the United States was created was declared by the Articles to be the preservation of the sovereignties of the member States, who were expressly declared to be sovereign. This Union styled the United States of America was commonly referred to as a Federal Republic.

15. When the War of Independence ended with an American victory, the American peace negotiators secured from the British Government specific recognition for the sovereignty and independence of each of the former thirteen

colonies. As a consequence, within the Treaty of Paris of 1783, King George III specifically acknowledged, not the freedom and sovereignty and independence of the United States, but the freedom and sovereignty and independence of each one of the thirteen American States.

16. The most widely acknowledged and influential book in the history of the world delineating the proper Natural Laws governing Nations was Vattel's *Law of Nations*, a treatise with which the Founding Fathers of the United States were intimately familiar. Within his celebrated book, Mr. Vattel explained that sovereign States may unite together to constitute a Federal Republic without each State losing its individual sovereignty. Simply because such States might voluntarily agree to refrain from the full exercise of their sovereignty within the Federal Union, he explained, does not imply that such States are no longer sovereign.

17. When a Convention of States was called to convene in Philadelphia, Pennsylvania, in the summer of 1787, for the purpose of revising the Articles of Confederation, all of the States save Rhode Island sent delegates. As soon as that Philadelphia Convention convened, however, the delegates resolved that a new plan of government should be proposed to replace the then existing Federal Constitution. The only issue that remained was to determine the nature of the new plan of government. And on this issue, the Constitutional Convention was deeply divided.

18. Luther Martin, a delegate to that Federal Convention from Maryland, and a staunch advocate of the sovereignty of the States, noted that no less than three discernable factions existed within the Convention. The largest faction, comprising nearly half of the delegates, advocated the republican form and the federal system of government, on which the Articles had been based. A smaller faction described by Mr. Martin also advocated the republican form of government, but strove to replace the federal system with a national system of government. The smallest faction was devoted to nationalism and monarchy. But, realizing that neither the Convention nor the American people would accept a Monarchy, this last faction ended up forming an alliance with the other nationalists in an effort to hold sway over the advocates of federalism.

19. Each faction within the Grand Convention introduced its own Plan of Government. On behalf of the National Monarchists, Alexander Hamilton introduced the Hamiltonian Plan of Government, which represented extreme consolidation and centralization of power. This plan openly established a sovereign National Government vested with the right to enact any law it pleased, and with authority to appoint the State Governors, who would wield a national veto over any State laws. Mr. Hamilton's proposal pleased a few delegates but frightened even more. Although the Convention never seriously considered his proposed Plan of Government, it is of interest to note that Alexander Hamilton

became the Father of the Consolidating School in the United States after the adoption of our present Federal Constitution.

20. Acting on behalf of the Federal Republicans within the Constitutional Convention, William Paterson introduced the New Jersey Plan. When put to a vote, the Convention rejected this early effort by the advocates of federalism. Instead, the Convention, in its early stages, resolved to adopt the Virginia Plan, which had been first introduced by Edmund Randolph and strongly supported by James Madison. Although decidedly more republican in nature than Mr. Hamilton's Plan, the Virginia Plan called for the creation of a *supreme National Government* that would subordinate the States. Among other things, such a National Government would have a veto power over the laws of the several States.

21. Although initially defeated in the Federal Convention, the Federal Republicans adopted a new strategy that was to prove ultimately successful. Little by little, they assailed the nationalistic features of the Virginia Plan until they had converted it into a plan for a Federal Government. One key victory for federalism occurred when the Convention was moved to strike out the words "National Government" from the evolving compact and to substitute the words "Government of the United States." As a consequence, the word "national" appears nowhere in our present Constitution. Another key victory for federalism occurred when the supremacy of the government was converted into the supremacy of the Constitution, thereby ensuring that it would be the people, not their government, which was regarded as sovereign. Yet another victory for federalism occurred when the veto power over State laws was removed from the evolving plan of government. The decisive turning point, however, occurred after a bitter battle over representation in the Senate of the United States. When the Convention finally decided that the Senate should represent the *sovereign equality of the States*, the nationalists fully understood that they had been beaten. Such a government as this, the delegates generally conceded, could only be considered a Federal Government, not a National Government.

22. During the Ratification Period, the advocates of the new Constitution styled themselves Federalists and called their opponents Antifederalists, in an effort to assure the American people that the proposed Constitution was truly federal in nature. And Alexander Hamilton, James Madison, and John Jay, in an effort to persuade New York to adopt the new compact, penned a series of essays that have since been published under the name of *The Federalist Papers* – not *The Nationalist Papers*, but *The Federalist Papers*. And within each State Ratifying Convention, the Federalists repeatedly assured the respective Ratifying Conventions that the new compact was truly federal and did not threaten the sovereignty of the States. These repeated assurances, coupled with a promise to add a Bill of Rights to the new Constitution, enabled the success-

ful ratification of the new Plan of Union.

23. Each State, in ratifying our present Federal Constitution, was bound only by its own act of ratification, and several States, within their official acts of ratification, asserted the right of any sovereign State to secede from the new Union. Those assertions of the right of secession were accepted by the other States, and by the new Government of the United States, without objection. At the time the new government was organized under the Constitution of 1787, only eleven States belonged to the new Federal Union. North Carolina and Rhode Island did not join their sister States in the new Union until after it had been established. And by agreement among the Founding Fathers, any new States admitted into the Union could only be admitted with the same status as the original States, in regard to their sovereignty, freedom, and independence.

24. The Preamble of our present Federal Constitution begins with the words, "We the people of the United States." That expression has historically been the stronghold of the consolidating school, which seeks to justify centralization of power by asserting that the people of the United States, in the aggregate – as a consolidated, single, sovereign American Nation – ordained and established the Federal Constitution over the States. Such an interpretation, however, is at discord with both common sense and the remainder of the federal compact. Article VII, for example, asserts that the Constitution shall exist as a compact between the States, which utterly demolishes the idea of a single State of America. The purpose of the first seven words of the Preamble is only to emphasize that the source of the powers of the Federal Government are the people of the States, not the State governments.

25. Within the Constitutional Convention, the Preamble had originally read, "We the people of the States of," followed by the names of each of the thirteen original States. Yet, the Convention realized that the wording of the Preamble had to be changed. Only nine States were required to adopt the new compact, and no one knew whether all or only nine States would ratify it. And if only nine, which nine? To avoid potential embarrassment, the Committee of Style changed the style – not the meaning – of the Preamble to read as it does today. The Convention accepted the new wording of the Preamble without debate. Thus, the true meaning of the first seven words of the Preamble is as follows: "We the peoples of the several States comprising the Federal Union styled the United States of America…."

26. The foundation of the Constitution of the United States is the Tenth Amendment to that compact, which asserts that all powers not delegated to the United States, nor prohibited to the States, are reserved to the respective States or to the people. This amendment tells us that everything delegated to the United States ends up in the hands of the Federal Government. It also tells us that the people are associated with the reserved powers, not with the dele-

gated powers. And common sense dictates that only those who delegated powers could reserve the powers not delegated. The only ones who delegated powers to the Federal Government were the peoples of the several States. They are the ones who retain all the powers not delegated.

27. In terms of sovereignty, the people of the United States are politically organized as States. Thus, the States are the people in their sovereign capacities, and the people are the States. The American people, acting as sovereign States, ordained and established the Federal Constitution. The people, as States, reserved the powers not delegated by the Constitution. And only the people, as sovereign States, may amend the federal compact.

28. The Constitution of the United States does not recognize the existence of a single, consolidated State of America. It recognizes the American people only as individual citizens and as sovereign States. In the House of Representatives, the States are represented based on population. In the Senate, the States are represented as equal sovereigns. In Presidential elections, each State has a total number of votes equal to the sum of its Representatives and Senators. And, as noted previously, only the States can ratify an amendment to the Constitution. The State of America is nowhere represented in the Federal Government, cannot vote in federal elections, cannot amend the federal compact, and has no reserved powers. The reason lies in the fact that the State of America does not exist. The only politically associated peoples constitutionally recognized in the United States are the peoples of the sovereign States.

29. The intention of the Founding Fathers, in establishing our federal system of government, was that the Federal Government would conduct the foreign affairs of the several States of the Federal Union, while each State would conduct and manage its own domestic or internal affairs. By this division of powers, coupled with the internal system of checks and balances between the departments of the Federal Government, the objective was to safeguard liberty by preventing a monopoly of power. Limitations on the powers of government, combined with the concept of the Concurrent Majority, serve to protect individual citizens from both the tyranny of the minority and the tyranny of the majority.

30. Although the adoption of our present Federal Constitution should have conclusively resolved the dispute between the advocates of federalism and those of nationalism, history and human nature plainly reveal that there has always been, and always will be, eminent individuals who are determined to transform our system of government into a consolidated system headed by a supreme, sovereign National Government. Almost immediately after the adoption of our Federal Constitution, advocates of consolidation rallied under the leadership of Alexander Hamilton and formed the Federalist Party, whose stronghold was in the New England States. The objective of this party was to

consolidate power in the United States in Washington, D.C., to give to the Federal Government a boundless field of power, and to pervert the ends of that government by using the tax-and-spend powers for the benefit of special interest groups, particularly an interest group generally referred to as the monied aristocracy. The advocates of such consolidation and centralization of power may be termed the Consolidating School of Thought, a school that has persisted through every change of political parties in American history. Some of its leading advocates in the ante-bellum period of our history have included, in addition to Mr. Hamilton, George McDuffie, Joseph Story, John Marshall, Henry Clay, Daniel Webster, John Motley, Edward Everett, and Abraham Lincoln.

31. Opposed to the consolidating conspiracy were the advocates of what may be termed the States' Rights School of Thought, which was founded by Thomas Jefferson, with its stronghold being centered in the Southern quarter of the Union. Initially, the States' Rights school organized the Democratic-Republican Party under the leadership of Mr. Jefferson. Other key leaders and advocates of the States' Rights school in the ante-bellum era of the Republic included James Madison, John Taylor of Caroline, John Randolph of Roanoke, Robert Y. Hayne, John C. Calhoun, and Jefferson Davis. After the War Between the States, Alexander H. Stephens contributed greatly to this school of thought.

32. Henry Clay made a significant contribution to the consolidating conspiracy by introducing his American System, which was based upon a socialistic redistribution of wealth by the Government of the United States. Under this unconstitutional and un-American system, the Federal Government was encouraged to levy taxes on all Americans, most notably the unconstitutional protective tariff, and to then bestow pecuniary favors on selected interest groups under a policy named Internal Improvements. The corrupting effects of such a system upon the character of our institutions was profound, for it taught the American people to look upon the Government of the United States as the source of "free" money. And the more debased and unprincipled a politician was, the more popular he was among those receiving handouts from the federal treasury. The Consolidating School of Thought was an enthusiastic supporter of this socialistic scheme. The States' Rights School of Thought, on the other hand, provided the bulwark of support for the constitutionally mandated economic system of free enterprise.

33. In opposing the consolidating conspiracy, the States' Rights school advocated that, as the States were sovereign, they were not required to tamely submit to unconstitutional usurpations and dangerous abuses of power by the Government of the United States. As sovereign States, each one had the natural right to secede from the Federal Union. Yet, each State also had a right of resistance short of secession. By means of Interposition and Nullification, a sover-

eign State could interpose its authority and nullify an illegal act of the Federal Government to prevent the progress of evil. In such an eventuality, the States should resolve to settle the matter by the amendment process. Only if an amendment were added to the Constitution specifically delegating the power in question could the Federal Government rightfully exercise the power.

34. The consolidating school has always advocated its own theory as to who should be the final arbiter in questions of power. That school has steadfastly insisted that the Government of the United States should possess that ultimate authority, usually insisting that the final arbiter ought to be the U.S. Supreme Court. Yet, such a power is not a judicial power, but a political power – it is the sovereign power! If the right to act as the final arbiter in questions of power is wielded by the Government of the United States, then it may delegate to itself any powers that it pleases. And if it may do that, then it truly is a sovereign government.

35. The consolidating school, recognizing that the American people distrusted in general the concept of an all-powerful National Government, sought to divert the attention of the people of the United States by introducing the subject of chattel slavery as an emotional issue. They succeed in 1820 in dividing the Federal Union into two unconstitutional sub-confederacies, styled "Free States" and "Slave States," and thereby inaugurated the concept of a *Balance of Power*. In time, that balance tipped in favor of the numerical majority in the Northern States. By 1860, the Radical Republican Party, which was openly hostile to the Southern States, succeeded in capturing the White House. Fearful for their continued safety, the Southern States reacted by seceding from the Federal Union, and what followed was the most disastrous period of strife and bloodshed in American history.

36. Before his death, Alexander Hamilton had concluded that only by means of a fratricidal War Between the States could a sovereign, supreme National Government be forced upon the American people. His prophecy was fulfilled under the leadership of President Abraham Lincoln. As a consequence of the tragic War Between the States and Radical Reconstruction, the consolidating school succeeded in subduing the States and thereafter would always proclaim that State sovereignty had been defeated when General Robert E. Lee surrendered at Appomattox.

37. Ever since that tragic era of American history, the consolidating school and its apologists have claimed that the Verdict of History somehow proves that the States are not sovereign, but that sovereignty is supposedly invested in a consolidated State of America. That, of course, is merely a polite way of saying that sovereignty is now vested in the Government of the United States, while pretending that it is vested in a mythical Nation of Americans. Yet, as might does not make right, future generations of Americans should not

consider themselves the political prisoners of past misdeeds and tragedies. Although the Federal Government has clearly usurped tremendous powers and has undeniably subdued the States, it must be noted that the States still exist, and that the Federal Constitution still exists. If the American people ever decide that they want to restore constitutionally limited government, they do not need to look far to find the solution.

38. This is not to deny that considerable damage has already been done to our Federal Republic by the consolidating school since seizing a monopoly of control over the Government of the United States as a result of the War Between the States. Under that school's leadership, the United States has witnessed the incessant growth of a Big Brother type of government in the United States, based on a Welfare State that bears a striking resemblance to the Guardian State described so alarmingly by Alexis de Tocqueville. And the consolidators of America have led the American people into one foreign, imperialistic war after another, at great expense in both blood and treasure.

39. Unfortunately, there are eminent individuals today who desire to facilitate the complete abolition of the American States and the replacement of our existing Federal Constitution with a Constitution for a People's Socialist Republic of America. The ambitions that induced the consolidators to centralize sovereignty in the United States have, in modern times, given rise to inducements to transfer that sovereignty to an instrument of World Government. If these conspiratorial Internationalists succeed in their mission, the United States of America will simply cease to exist. Needless to say, should that ever occur, all hope for reform will vanish forever.

The Lost Cause Revisited

Although the Consolidating School of Thought and its apologists are fond of reminding the American people that the sovereign States were conquered and subdued in the War Between the States, this cannot and should not be an excuse to forever condemn the people of the United States to live under a supremely arrogant Big Brother Government in Washington, D.C. Might does not make right, and the so-called Verdict of History holds no moral superiority over the Verdict of Truth. And the undeniable truth is that the American Theory of Government rests upon the pillars of sovereign States.

The Government of the United States may have stolen sovereignty from the States, but it must never be forgotten that, as long as the States exist and the Constitution survives, the United States of America is officially, legally, and constitutionally a League of Sovereign States. And what matters most is how we *think* about our constitutional system of government. The so-called *Lost Cause* of States' Rights and State sovereignty can be resurrected to once again serve as the foundations for the American political system if enough patriotic Americans resolve to demand the restoration of constitutionally limited government to the United States.

In his book, *The Rise and Fall of the Confederate Government*, Jefferson Davis soberly acknowledged the considerable damage done to the United States by the War Between the States. Yet, he also observed that the great struggle for liberty, the federal system, States' Rights, and the sovereignty of the people would never die as long as the desire for freedom lived in the hearts of the American people.

As this distinguished advocate of the genuine American Theory of Government wrote:

> It must be manifest to every one that there has been a fatal subversion of the Constitution of the United States. In estimating the results of the war, this is one of the most deplorable; because it is self-evident that, when a constitutional government once oversteps the limits fixed for the exercise of its powers, there is nothing beyond to check its further aggression, no place where it will voluntarily halt until it reaches the subjugation of all who resist the usurpation. This was the sole issue involved in the conflict of the United States Government with the Confederate States; and every other issue, whether pretended or real, partook of its nature, and was subordinate to this one. Let us repeat an illustration: In strict observance of their inalienable rights, in abundant caution reserved, when they formed the compact or Constitution – whichever the reader pleases to call it – of the United States, the Confederate States sought to withdraw from the Union they had assisted to create, and to form a new and independent one among themselves. Then the Government of the United States broke through all the limits fixed for the exercise of the powers with which it had been endowed, and, to accomplish its own will, assumed, under the plea of necessity, powers unwritten and unknown in the Constitution, that it might thereby proceed to the extremity of subjugation. Thus it will be perceived that the question still lives. Although the Confederate armies may have left the field, although the citizen soldiers may have retired to the pursuits of peaceful life, although the Confederate States may have renounced their new Union, they have proved their indestructibility by resuming their former places in the old one, where, by the organic law, they could only be admitted as republican, equal, and sovereign States of the Union. And, although the Confederacy as an organization may have ceased to exist as unquestionably as though it had never been formed, the fundamental principles, the eternal truths, uttered when our colonies in 1776 declared their independence, on which the Confederation of 1781 and the Union of 1788 were formed, and which animated and guided in the organization of the Confederacy of 1861, yet live, and will survive, however crushed they may be by despotic force, however deep they may be buried under the *debris* of crumbling States, however they may be disavowed by the time-serving and the faint-hearted; yet I believe they have the eternity of

truth, and that in God's appointed time and place they will prevail.

The contest is not over, the strife is not ended. It has only entered on a new and enlarged arena. The champions of constitutional liberty must spring to the struggle, like the armed men from the seminated dragon's teeth, until the Government of the United States is brought back to its constitutional limits, and the tyrant's plea of "necessity" is bound in chains strong as adamant:

"For Freedom's battle once begun,
Bequeathed by bleeding sire to son,
Though baffled oft, is ever won."

When the war closed, who were the victors? Perhaps it is too soon to answer that question. Nevertheless, every day, as time rolls on, we look with increasing pride upon the struggle our people made for constitutional liberty. The war was one in which fundamental principles were involved; and, as force decides no truth, hence the issue is still undetermined, as has been already shown. We have laid aside our swords; we have ceased our hostility; we have conceded the physical strength of the Northern States. But the question still lives, and all Nations and peoples that adopt a confederated agent of government will become champions of our cause. While contemplating the Northern States – with their Federal Constitution gone, ruthlessly destroyed under the tyrant's plea of "necessity," their State sovereignty made a byword, and their people absorbed in an aggregated mass, no longer, as their fathers left them, protected by reserved rights against usurpation – the question naturally arises: On which side was the victory? Let the verdict of mankind decide. [1]

The Conscience of a Conservative

Although the consolidating school incessantly insists that the people of the United States must forever accept as permanent the disastrous consequences of the War Between the States, the torch of liberty has always burned deeply in the American soul. By the decade of the 1950s, a revival of interest in States' Rights aroused the patriotic fervor of many Americans. By 1957, James J. Kilpatrick's influential book, *The Sovereign States: Notes of a Citizen of Virginia*, had been published. Three years later, *The Conscience of a Conservative*, by Senator Barry Goldwater of Arizona, was published and served as the inspiration for a grassroots campaign to restore constitutionally limited government to the United States.

In the Presidential election of 1964, which pitted Republican Barry Goldwater against Democratic Lyndon B. Johnson, the American people had before them, for the first time in many years, *a choice, not an echo*. So funda-

---

[1] Jefferson Davis, *The Rise and Fall of the Confederate Government*, Volume II, Thomas Yoseloff, New York, 1958 (orig. pub. 1881), pp. 293-295.

mental were the principles at stake in that great contest that they transcended ordinary party politics. States with a long history of voting Democratic switched to vote, in mass, in favor of Senator Goldwater, while some powerful figures entrenched in the Republican Party worked to subvert and undermine the campaign of the nominee of their own party.

Although Senator Goldwater lost that momentous Presidential election, the record bequeathed to future generations by the Arizona statesman in his book, *The Conscience of a Conservative*, adds yet another contribution to the illustrious and sound States' Rights School of Thought. The third chapter of Senator Goldwater's book, in particular, constitutes one of the most succinct and brilliant arguments made in the Twentieth Century on behalf of our constitutionally established federal system of government. The argument presented within this significant chapter, entitled "States' Rights," may still serve to provide inspiration even as the United States begins its journey into the Twenty-First Century, and with that hope in mind, let us here recite Senator Goldwater's words of wisdom.

As Barry Goldwater wrote:

> The Governor of New York, in 1930, pointed out that the Constitution does not empower the Congress to deal with "a great number of...vital problems of government, such as the conduct of public utilities, of banks, of insurance, of business, of agriculture, of education, of social welfare, and a dozen other important features." And he added that "Washington must not be encouraged to interfere" in these areas.
>
> Franklin Roosevelt's rapid conversion from Constitutionalism to the doctrine of unlimited government is an oft-told story. But I am here concerned not so much by the abandonment of States' Rights by the national Democratic Party – an event that occurred some years ago when that party was captured by the Socialist ideologues in and about the labor movement – as by the unmistakable tendency of the Republican Party to adopt the same course. The result is that today *neither* of our two parties maintains a meaningful commitment to the principle of States' Rights. Thus, the cornerstone of the Republic, our chief bulwark against the encroachment of individual freedom by Big Government, is fast disappearing under the piling sands of absolutism.
>
> ...In recent years the Federal Government has continued, and in many cases has increased, federal "grants-in-aid" to the States in a number of areas in which the Constitution recognizes the exclusive jurisdiction of the States. These grants are called "matching funds" and are designed to "stimulate" State spending in health, education, welfare, conservation or any other area in which the Federal Government decides there is a need for national action....
>
> There are two things to note about these programs. The first is that they are *federal* programs – they are conceived by the Federal Government both as to purpose and as to extent. The second is that the "stimulative"

grants are, in effect, a mixture of blackmail and bribery. The States are told to go along with the program "or else." Once the Federal Government has offered matching funds, it is unlikely, as a practical matter, that a member of a State Legislature will turn down his State's fair share of revenue collected from all of the States. Understandably, many legislators feel that to refuse aid would be political suicide. This is an indirect form of coercion, but it is effective nonetheless.

A more direct method of coercion is for the Federal Government to *threaten* to move in unless State governments take action that Washington deems appropriate. Not so long ago, for example, the Secretary of Labor gave the States a lecture on the wisdom of enacting "up-to-date" unemployment compensation laws. He made no effort to disguise the alternative: if the States failed to act, the Federal Government would....

We can best understand our error, I think, by examining the theory behind it. I have already alluded to the book, *A Republican Looks at His Party*, which is an elaborate rationalization of the "Modern Republican" approach to current problems. (It does the job just as well, I might add, for the Democrats' approach.) Mr. Larson devotes a good deal of space to the question of States' Rights. He contends that while there is "a general presumption" in favor of States' Rights, thanks to the Tenth Amendment, this presumption must give way whenever it appears to the federal authorities that the States are not responding satisfactorily to "the needs of the people." This is a paraphrase of his position but not, I think, an unjust one. And if this approach appears to be a high-handed way of dealing with an explicit constitutional provision, Mr. Larson justifies the argument by summoning the concept that "for every right there is a corresponding duty." "When we speak of States' Rights," he writes, "we should never forget to add that there go with those rights the corresponding States' responsibilities." Therefore, he concludes, if the States fail to do their duty, they have only themselves to blame when the Federal Government intervenes.

The trouble with this argument is that it treats the Constitution of the United States as a kind of handbook in political theory, to be heeded or ignored depending on how it fits the plans of contemporary federal officials. The Tenth Amendment is *not* "a general assumption," but a prohibitory rule of law. The Tenth Amendment recognizes the States' *jurisdiction* in certain areas. States' Rights means that the States have a right to act or *not to act*, as they see fit, in the areas reserved to them. The States may have duties corresponding to those rights, but the duties are owed to the people of the States, not to the Federal Government. Therefore, the recourse lies not with the Federal Government, which is not sovereign, but with the people who are, and who have full power to take disciplinary action....The Constitution, I repeat, draws a sharp and clear line between federal jurisdiction and State jurisdiction. The Federal Government's failure to recognize that line has been a crushing blow to the principle of limited government.

But again, I caution against a defensive, or apologetic, appeal to the Constitution. There is a *reason* for its reservation of States' Rights. Not only does it prevent the accumulation of power in a central government that is remote from the people and relatively immune from popular restraints; it also recognizes the principle that essentially local problems are best dealt with by the people most directly concerned. Who knows better than New Yorkers how much and what kind of publicly-financed slum clearance in New York City is needed and can be afforded? Who knows better than Nebraskans whether that State has an adequate nursing program? Who knows better than Arizonans the kind of school program that is needed to educate their children? The people of my own State – and I am confident that I speak for the majority of them – have long since seen through the spurious suggestion that federal aid comes "free." They know that the money comes out of their own pockets, and that it is returned to them minus a broker's fee taken by the federal bureaucracy. They know, too, that the power to decide how that money shall be spent is withdrawn from them and exercised by some planning board deep in the caverns of one of the federal agencies. They understand this represents a great and perhaps irreparable loss – not only in their wealth, but in their priceless liberty.

Nothing could so far advance the cause of freedom as for State officials throughout the land to assert their rightful claims to lost State power; and for the Federal Government to withdraw promptly and totally from every jurisdiction which the Constitution reserved to the States. [2]

Education and Political Action

If constitutionally limited government is ever to be restored to the United States, there are two keys that are required to unlock the door to success. One key is *education* – to educate the American people in the principles of the true American Theory of Government. While most modern Americans can recite the Pledge of Allegiance from memory, for example, only a relatively few are capable of explaining why that Pledge is subversive of our constitutionally mandated federal system of government. And if most Americans do not understand the basic principles on which our constitutional system is founded, there obviously can be little hope that such a system can ever be restored to the United States. As the wise old aphorism states, *ignorant and free can never be.*

It scarcely needs to be pointed out that required education cannot be acquired from the public educational system in the United States, for the Federal Government long ago seized control of the public schools and converted them into government indoctrination centers. In fact, public education in the United States must be regarded as part of the problem, not as part of the solution. As John Locke noted hundreds of years ago, no greater harm can possibly be done to any Nation than the teaching of false theories concerning government.

What is required is for patriotic Americans to pen books, write magazine

---

[2] Barry Goldwater, *The Conscience of a Conservative*, A Macfadden Capitol Hill Book, New York, 1960, pp. 25-31.

articles, and submit letters to the editors of local newspapers that challenge the constitutionality of the illegal acts and misdeeds of the Government of the United States and that expound the genuine principles of our Federal Constitution. When sufficient numbers of Americans begin to *think* differently about their Constitution and their criminal Big Brother Government in Washington, D.C., meaningful reform will become possible.

The second key to successfully restoring constitutionally limited government to the United States is *political action*. But in pursuing this objective, the friends of the Constitution must avoid the temptation to focus immediately on the big prize. While it would certainly be most gratifying to elect a constitutional-minded, principled statesman to occupy the White House, initial efforts would undoubtedly prove more successful if focused on electing principled statesmen to fill seats in the United States Senate and House of Representatives.

Political action must also be applied to State and local governments. Perhaps nothing paints a more tragic picture than to witness officers of a State government bowing to their federal masters in Washington and selling their patronage in return for subsidies for local purposes from the federal treasury. Such spineless politicians must be replaced by principled statesmen who are willing to assert the genuine independence of the State governments and to resist federal encroachments upon the reserved rights of the States.

In pursuing this worthy objective, we must adopt a practical perspective on the value of political parties. Political parties are not ends in themselves, but exist merely as a means to an end. If existing parties – whether the two major parties or existing third parties – cannot be used to attain the desired end, then they should be abandoned without further thought or consideration. If necessary, a new political party dedicated to restoring federalism should be created.

By this combination of education and political action, the advocates of constitutionally liberty may successfully restore the Constitution of the United States as the supreme law of the land. And as a consequence of this reformation, sovereignty may be returned to the people of the States, where it rightfully belongs, and the Government of the United States may once again be bound by the confining chains of the Constitution.

Appendix A
The Declaration of Independence

The Unanimous Declaration of the Thirteen United States of America

When, in the course of human events, it becomes necessary for one people to dissolve the political bands which have connected them with another, and to assume among the powers of the earth, the separate and equal station to which the Laws of Nature and of nature's God entitle them, a decent respect to the opinions of mankind requires that they should declare the causes which impel them to the separation.

We hold these truths to be self-evident, that all men are created equal, that they are endowed by their Creator with certain unalienable rights, that among these are life, liberty and the pursuit of happiness. That to secure these rights, governments are instituted among men, deriving their just powers from the consent of the governed. That whenever any form of government becomes destructive to these ends, it is the right of the people to alter or to abolish it, and to institute new government, laying its foundation on such principles and organizing its powers in such form, as to them shall seem most likely to effect their safety and happiness. Prudence, indeed, will dictate that governments long established should not be changed for light and transient causes; and accordingly all experience hath shown that mankind are more disposed to suffer, while evils are sufferable, than to right themselves by abolishing the forms to which they are accustomed. But when a long train of abuses and usurpations, pursuing invariably the same object evinces a design to reduce them under absolute despotism, it is their right, it is their duty, to throw off such government, and to provide new guards for their future security. – Such has been the patient sufferance of these colonies; and such is now the necessity which constrains them to alter their former systems of government. The history of the present King of Great Britain is a history of repeated injuries and usurpations, all having in direct object the establishment of an absolute tyranny over these States. To prove this, let facts be submitted to a candid world.

He has refused his assent to laws, the most wholesome and necessary for the public good.

He has forbidden his Governors to pass laws of immediate and pressing importance, unless suspended in their operation till his assent should be obtained; and when so suspended, he has utterly neglected to attend to them.

He has refused to pass other laws for the accommodation of large districts of people, unless those people would relinquish the right of representation in the legislature, a right inestimable to them and formidable to tyrants only.

He has called together legislative bodies at places unusual, uncomfortable, and distant from the depository of their public records, for the sole purpose of fatiguing them into compliance with his measures.

He has dissolved representative houses repeatedly, for opposing with manly firmness his invasions on the rights of the people.

He has refused for a long time, after such dissolutions, to cause others to be elected; whereby the legislative powers, incapable of annihilation, have returned to the people at large for their exercise; the State remaining in the meantime exposed to all the dangers of invasion from without, and convulsions within.

He has endeavored to prevent the population of these States; for that purpose obstructing the laws for naturalization of foreigners; refusing to pass others to encourage their migration hither, and raising the conditions of new appropriations of lands.

He has obstructed the administration of justice, by refusing his assent to laws for establishing judiciary powers.

He has made judges dependent on his will alone, for the tenure of their offices, and the amount and payment of their salaries.

He has erected a multitude of new offices, and sent hither swarms of officers to harass our people, and eat out their substance.

He has kept among us, in times of peace, standing armies without the consent of our legislature.

He has affected to render the military independent of and superior to civil power.

He has combined with others to subject us to a jurisdiction foreign to our constitution, and unacknowledged by our laws; giving his assent to their acts of pretended legislation:

For quartering large bodies of armed troops among us:

For protecting them, by mock trial, from punishment for any murders which they should commit on the inhabitants of these States:

For cutting off our trade with all parts of the world:

For imposing taxes on us without our consent:

For depriving us in many cases, of the benefits of trial by jury:

For transporting us beyond seas to be tried for pretended offenses:

For abolishing the free system of English laws in a neighboring province, establishing therein an arbitrary government, and enlarging its boundaries so as to render it at once an example and fit instrument for introducing the same absolute rule in these colonies:

For taking away our charters, abolishing our most valuable laws, and altering fundamentally the forms of our governments:

For suspending our own legislatures, and declaring themselves invested with power to legislate for us in all cases whatsoever.

He has abdicated government here, by declaring us out of his protection and waging war against us.

He has plundered our seas, ravaged our coasts, burned our towns, and destroyed the lives of our people.

He is at this time transporting large armies of foreign mercenaries to complete the works of death, desolation and tyranny, already begun with circumstances of cruelty and perfidy scarcely paralleled in the most barbarous ages, and totally unworthy of the head of a civilized nation.

He has constrained our fellow citizens taken captive on the high seas to bear arms against their country, to become the executioners of their friends and brethren, or to fall themselves by their hands.

He has excited domestic insurrections amongst us, and has endeavored to bring on the inhabitants of our frontiers, the merciless Indian savages, whose known rule of warfare, is undistinguished destruction of all ages, sexes and conditions.

In every stage of these oppressions we have petitioned for redress in the most humble terms: our repeated petitions have been answered only by repeated injury. A prince, whose character is thus marked by every act which may define a tyrant, is unfit to be the ruler of a free people.

Nor have we been wanting in attention to our British brethren. We have warned them from time to time of attempts by their legislature to extend an unwarrantable jurisdiction over us. We have reminded them of the circumstances of our emigration and settlement here. We have appealed to their native justice and magnanimity, and we have conjured them by the ties of our common kindred to disavow these usurpations, which, would inevitably interrupt our connections and correspondence. We must, therefore, acquiesce in the necessity, which denounces our separation, and hold them, as we hold the rest of mankind, enemies in war, in peace friends.

We, therefore, the representatives of the United States of America, in General Congress, assembled, appealing to the Supreme Judge of the world for the rectitude of our intentions, do, in the name, and by the authority of the good people of these colonies, solemnly publish and declare, that these United Colonies are, and of right ought to be free and independent States; that they are absolved from all allegiance to the British Crown, and that all political connection between them and the State of Great Britain, is and ought to be totally dissolved; and that as free and independent States, they have full power to levy war, conclude peace, contract alliances, establish commerce, and to do all other acts and things which independent States may of right do. And for the support of this Declaration, with a firm reliance on the protection of Divine Providence, we mutually pledge to each other our lives, our fortunes and our sacred honor.

John Hancock
Button Gwinnett
Lyman Hall
Geo. Walton
Wm. Hooper
Joseph Hewes
John Penn
Edward Rutledge
Thos. Heyward, Junr.
Thomas Lynch, Junr.
Arthur Middleton
Samuel Chase
Wm. Paca
Thos. Stone
Charles Carroll of
Carrollton
George Wythe
Richard Henry Lee
Th. Jefferson
Benja. Harrison
Thos. Nelson, Jr.
Francis Lightfoot Lee
Carter Braxton
Robt. Morris
Benjamin Rush
Benja. Franklin
John Morton
Geo. Clymer
Jas. Smith
Geo. Taylor
James Wilson
Geo. Ross
Caesar Rodney
Geo. Read
Tho. Mckean
Wm. Floyd
Phil. Livingston
Frans. Lewis
Lewis Morris
Richd. Stockton
Jno. Witherspoon
Fras. Hopkinson
John Hart
Abra. Clark
Josiah Bartlett
Wm. Whipple
Saml. Adams
John Adams
Robt. Treat Paine
Elbridge Gerry
Step. Hopkins
William Ellery
Roger Sherman
Samuel Huntington
Wm. Williams
Oliver Wolcott
Matthew Thornton

Appendix B

The Articles of Confederation

Preamble

To all to whom these Presents shall come, we the undersigned Delegates of the States affixed to our Names send greeting.

Articles of Confederation and perpetual Union between the States of New Hampshire, Massachusetts-bay Rhode Island and Providence Plantations, Connecticut, New York, New Jersey, Pennsylvania, Delaware, Maryland, Virginia, North Carolina, South Carolina and Georgia.

Article I

The Stile of this Confederacy shall be "The United States of America."

Article II

Each State retains its sovereignty, freedom, and independence, and every power, jurisdiction, and right, which is not by this Confederation expressly delegated to the United States, in Congress assembled.

Article III

The said States hereby severally enter into a firm league of friendship with each other, for their common defense, the security of their liberties, and their mutual and general welfare, binding themselves to assist each other, against all force offered to, or attacks made upon them, or any of them, on account of religion, sovereignty, trade, or any other pretense whatever.

Article IV

The better to secure and perpetuate mutual friendship and intercourse among the people of the different States in this Union, the free inhabitants of each of these States, paupers, vagabonds, and fugitives from justice excepted, shall be entitled to all privileges and immunities of free citizens in the several States; and the people of each State shall free ingress and regress to and from any other State, and shall enjoy therein all the privileges of trade and commerce, subject to the same duties, impositions, and restrictions as the inhabitants thereof respectively, provided that such restrictions shall not extend so far as to prevent the removal of property imported into any State, to any other State, of which the owner is an inhabitant; provided also that no imposition, duties or restriction shall be laid by any State, on the property of the United States, or either of them.

If any person guilty of, or charged with, treason, felony, or other high misdemeanor in any State, shall flee from justice, and be found in any of the United States, he shall, upon demand of the Governor or executive power of the State from which he fled, be delivered up and removed to the State having jurisdiction of his offense.

Full faith and credit shall be given in each of these States to the records, acts, and judicial proceedings of the courts and magistrates of every other State.

Article V

For the most convenient management of the general interests of the United States, delegates shall be annually appointed in such manner as the legislatures of each State shall direct, to meet in Congress on the first Monday in November, in every year, with a power reserved to each State to recall its delegates, or any of them, at any time within the year, and to send others in their stead for the remainder of the year.

No State shall be represented in Congress by less than two, nor more than seven members; and no person shall be capable of being a delegate for more than three years in any term of six years; nor shall any person, being a delegate, be capable of holding any office under the United States, for which he, or another for his benefit, receives any salary, fees or emolument of any kind.

Each State shall maintain its own delegates in a meeting of the States, and while they act as members of the committee of the States.

In determining questions in the United States in Congress assembled, each State shall have one vote.

Freedom of speech and debate in Congress shall not be impeached or questioned in any court or place out of Congress, and the members of Congress shall be protected in their persons from arrests or imprisonments, during the time of their going to and from, and attendance on Congress, except for treason, felony, or breach of the peace.

Article VI

No State, without the consent of the United States in Congress assembled, shall send any embassy to, or receive any embassy from, or enter into any conference, agreement, alliance or treaty with any King, Prince or State; nor shall any person holding any office of profit or trust under the United States, or any of them, accept any present, emolument, office or title of any kind whatever from any King, Prince or foreign State; nor shall the United States in Congress assembled, or any of them, grant any title of nobility.

No two or more States shall enter into any treaty, confederation or alliance whatever between them, without the consent of the United States in Congress assembled, specifying accurately the purposes for which the same is to be entered into, and how long it shall continue.

No State shall lay any imposts or duties, which may interfere with any stipulations in treaties, entered into by the United States in Congress assembled, with any King, Prince or State, in pursuance of any treaties already proposed by Congress, to the courts of France and Spain.

No vessel of war shall be kept up in time of peace by any State, except such number only, as shall be deemed necessary by the United States in Congress assembled, for the defense of such State, or its trade; nor shall any body of forces be kept up by any State in time of peace, except such number only, as in the judgment of the United States in Congress assembled, shall be deemed requisite to garrison the forts necessary for the defense of such State; but every State shall always keep up a well-regulated and disciplined militia, sufficiently armed and accoutered, and shall provide and constantly have ready for use, in public stores, a due number of field pieces and tents, and a proper quantity of arms, ammunition and camp equipage.

No State shall engage in any war without the consent of the United States in Congress assembled, unless such State be actually invaded by enemies, or shall have received certain advice of a resolution being formed by some nation of Indians to invade such State, and the danger is so imminent as not to admit of a delay till the United States in Congress assembled can be consulted; nor shall any State grant commissions to any ships or vessels of war, nor letters of marque or reprisal, except it be after a declaration of war by the United States in Congress assembled, and then only against the Kingdom or State and the subjects thereof, against which war has been so declared, and under such regulations as shall be established by the United States in Congress assembled, unless such State be infested by pirates, in which case vessels of war may be fitted out for that occasion, and kept so long as the danger shall continue, or until the United States in Congress assembled shall determine otherwise.

Article VII

When land forces are raised by any State for the common defense, all officers of or under the rank of colonel, shall be appointed by the legislature of each State respectively, by whom such forces shall be raised, or in such manner as such State shall direct, and all vacancies shall be filled up by the State which first made the appointment.

Article VIII

All charges of war, and all other expenses that shall be incurred for the common defense or general welfare, and allowed by the United States in Congress assembled, shall be defrayed out of a common treasury, which shall be supplied by the several States in proportion to the value of all land within each State, granted or surveyed for any person, as such land and the buildings and improvements thereon shall be estimated according to such mode as the United States in Congress assembled, shall from time to time direct and appoint.

The taxes for paying that proportion shall be laid and levied by the authority and direction of the legislatures of the several States within the time agreed upon by the United States in Congress assembled.

Article IX

The United States in Congress assembled, shall have the sole and exclusive right and power of determining on peace and war, except in the cases mentioned in the sixth article – of sending and receiving ambassadors – entering into treaties and alliances, provided that no treaty of commerce shall be made whereby the legislative power of the respective States shall be restrained from imposing such imposts and duties on foreigners, as their own people are subjected to, or from prohibiting the exportation or importation of any species of goods or commodities whatsoever – of establishing rules for deciding in all cases, what captures on land or water shall be legal, and in what manner prizes taken by land or naval forces in the service of the United States shall be divided or appropriated – of granting letters of marque and reprisal in times of peace – appointing courts for the trial of piracies and felonies committed on the high seas and establishing courts for receiving and determining finally appeals in all cases of captures, provided that no member of Congress shall be appointed a judge of any of the said courts.

The United States in Congress assembled shall also be the last resort on appeal in all disputes and differences now subsisting or that hereafter may arise between two or more States concerning boundary, jurisdiction or any other causes whatever; which authority shall always be exercised in the manner following. Whenever the legislative or executive authority or lawful agent of any State in controversy with another shall present a petition to Congress stating the matter in question and praying for a hearing, notice thereof shall be given by order of Congress to the legislative or executive authority of the other State in controversy, and a day assigned for the appearance of the parties by their lawful agents, who shall then be directed to appoint by joint consent, commissioners or judges to constitute a court for hearing and determining the matter in question: but if they cannot agree, Congress shall name three persons out of each of the United States, and from the list of such persons each party shall alternately strike out one, the petitioners beginning, until the number shall be reduced to thirteen; and from that number not less than seven, nor more than nine names as Congress shall direct, shall in the presence of Congress be drawn out by lot, and the persons whose names shall be so drawn or any five of them, shall be commissioners or judges, to hear and finally determine the controversy, so always as a major part of the judges who shall hear the cause shall agree in the determination: and if either party shall neglect to attend at the day appointed, without showing reasons, which Congress shall judge sufficient, or being present shall refuse to strike, the Congress shall proceed to nominate three persons out of each State, and the secretary of Congress shall strike in behalf of such party absent or refusing; and the judgment and sentence of the court to be appointed, in the manner before prescribed, shall be final and conclusive; and if any of the parties shall refuse to submit to the authority of such court, or to appear or defend their claim or cause, the court shall nevertheless proceed to pronounce sentence, or judgment, which shall in like manner be final and decisive, the judgment or sentence and other proceedings being in either case transmitted to Congress, and lodged among the acts of Congress for the security of the parties concerned: provided that every commissioner, before he sits in judgment, shall take an oath to be administered by one of the judges of the supreme or superior court of the State, where the cause shall be tried, "well and truly to hear and determine the matter in question, according to the best of his judgment, without favor, affection or hope of reward": provided also, that no State shall be deprived of territory for the benefit of the United States.

All controversies concerning the private right of soil claimed under different grants of two or more States, whose jurisdictions as they may respect such lands, and the States which passed such grants are adjusted, the said grants or either of them being at the same time claimed to have originated antecedent to such settlement of jurisdiction, shall on the petition of either party to the Congress of the United States, be finally determined as near as may be in the same manner as is before prescribed for deciding disputes respecting territorial jurisdiction between different States.

The United States in Congress assembled shall also have the sole and exclusive right and power of regulating the alloy and value of coin struck by their own authority, or by that of the respective States – fixing the standards of weights and measures throughout the United States – regulating the trade and managing all affairs with the Indians, not members of any of the States, provided that the legislative right of any State within its own limits be not infringed or violated – establishing or regulating post offices from one State to another, throughout all the United States, and exacting such postage on the papers passing through the same as may be requisite to defray the expenses of the said office – appointing all officers of the land forces, in the service of the United States, excepting regimental officers – appointing all the officers of the naval forces, and commissioning all officers whatever in the service of the United States – making rules for the government and regulation of the said land and naval forces, and directing their operations.

The United States in Congress assembled shall have authority to appoint a committee, to sit in the recess of Congress, to be denominated "A Committee of the States," and to consist of one delegate from each State; and to appoint such other committees and civil officers as may be necessary for managing the general affairs of the United States under their direction – to appoint one of their members to preside, provided that no person be allowed to serve in the office of President more than one year in any term of three years; to ascertain the necessary sums of money to be raised for the service of the United States, and to appropriate and apply the same for defraying the public expenses – to borrow money, or emit bills on the credit of the United States, transmitting every half-year to the respective States an account of the sums of money so borrowed or emitted – to build and equip a navy – to agree upon the number of land forces, and to make requisitions from each State for its quota, in proportion to the number of white inhabitants in such State; which requisition shall be binding, and thereupon the legislature of each State shall appoint the regimental officers, raise the men and cloath, arm and equip them in a solid-like manner, at the expense of the United States; and the officers and men so cloathed, armed and equipped shall march to the place appointed, and within the time agreed on by the United States in Congress assembled. But if the United States in Congress assembled shall, on consideration of circumstances judge proper that any State should not raise men, or should raise a smaller number of men than the quota thereof, such extra number shall be raised, officered, cloathed, armed and equipped in the same manner as the quota of each State, unless the legislature of such State shall judge that such extra number cannot be safely spread out in the same, in which case they shall raise, officer, cloath, arm and equip as many of such extra number as they judge can be safely spared. And the officers and men so cloathed, armed, and equipped, shall march to the place appointed, and within the time agreed on by the United States in Congress assembled.

The United States in Congress assembled shall never engage in a war, nor grant letters of marque or reprisal in time of peace, nor enter into any treaties or alliances, nor coin money, nor regulate the value thereof, nor ascertain the sums and expenses necessary for the defense and welfare of the United States, or any of them, nor emit bills, nor borrow money on the credit of the United States, nor appropriate money, nor agree upon the number of vessels of war, to be built or purchased, or the number of land or sea forces to be raised, nor appoint a commander in chief of the army or navy, unless nine States assent to the same: nor shall a question on any other point, except for adjourning from day to day be determined, unless by the votes of the majority of the United States in Congress assembled.

The Congress of the United States shall have power to adjourn to any time within the year, and to any place within the United States, so that no period of adjournment be for a longer duration than the space of six months, and shall publish the journal of their proceedings monthly, except such parts thereof relating to treaties, alliances or military operations, as in their judgment require secrecy; and the yeas and nays of the delegates of each State on any question shall be entered on the journal, when it is desired by any delegates of a State, or any of them, at his or their request shall be furnished with a transcript of the said journal, except such parts as are above excepted, to lay before the legislatures of the several States.

Article X

The Committee of the States, or any nine of them, shall be authorized to execute, in the recess of Congress, such of the powers of Congress as the United States in Congress assembled, by the consent of the nine States, shall from time to time think expedient to vest them with; provided that no power be delegated to the said Committee, for the exercise of which, by the Articles of Confederation, the voice of nine States in the Congress of the United States assembled be requisite.

Article XI

Canada acceding to this Confederation, and adjoining in the measures of the United States, shall be admitted into, and entitled to all the advantages of this Union; but no other colony shall be admitted into the same, unless such admission be agreed to by nine States.

Article XII

All bills of credit emitted, monies borrowed, and debts contracted by, or under the authority of Congress, before the assembling of the United States, in pursuance of the present Confederation, shall be deemed and considered as a charge against the United States, for payment and satisfaction whereof the said United States, and the public faith are hereby solemnly pledged.

Article XIII

Every State shall abide by the determination of the United States in Congress assembled, on all questions which by this Confederation are submitted to them. And the Articles of this Confederation shall be inviolably observed by every State, and the Union shall be perpetual; nor shall any alteration at any time hereafter be made in any of them; unless such alteration be agreed to in a Congress of the United States, and be afterwards confirmed by the legislatures of every State.

And Whereas it hath pleased the Great Governor of the World to incline the hearts of the legislatures we respectively represent in Congress, to approve of, and to authorize us to ratify the said Articles of Confederation and perpetual Union. Know Ye that we the undersigned delegates, by virtue of the power and authority to us given for that purpose, do by these presents, in the name and in behalf of our respective constituents, fully and entirely ratify and confirm each and every of the said Articles of Confederation and perpetual Union, and all and singular the matters and things therein contained: And we do further solemnly plight and engage the faith of our respective constituents, that they shall abide by the determinations of the United States in Congress assembled, on all questions, which by the said Confederation are submitted to them. And that the Articles thereof shall be inviolably observed by the States we respectively represent, and that the Union shall be perpetual.

In Witness whereof we have hereunto set our hands in Congress. Done at Philadelphia in the State of Pennsylvania the ninth day of July in the Year of our Lord One Thousand Seven Hundred and Seventy-Eight, and in the Third Year of the independence of America.

On the part and behalf of the State of New Hampshire:
Josiah Bartlett
John Wentworth Junr.
August 8th 1778

On the part and behalf of The State of Massachusetts Bay:
John Hancock
Francis Dana
Samuel Adams
James Lovell
Elbridge Gerry
Samuel Holten

On the part and behalf of the State of Rhode Island and Providence Plantations:
William Ellery
John Collins
Henry Marchant

On the part and behalf of the State of Connecticut:
Roger Sherman
Titus Hosmer
Samuel Huntington
Andrew Adams
Oliver Wolcott

On the Part and Behalf of the State of New York:
James Duane
Wm Duer
Francis Lewis
Gouv Morris

On the Part and in Behalf of the State of New Jersey, November 26, 1778.
Jno Witherspoon
Nathaniel Scudder

On the part and behalf of the State of Pennsylvania:
Robt Morris
William Clingan
Daniel Roberdeau
Joseph Reed
John Bayard Smith
22nd July 1778

On the part and behalf of the State of Delaware:
Tho Mckean February 12, 1779
John Dickinson May 5th 1779
Nicholas Van Dyke

On the part and behalf of the State of Maryland:
John Hanson March 1 1781
Daniel Carroll Do

On the Part and Behalf of the State of Virginia:
Richard Henry Lee
Jno Harvie
John Banister
Francis Lightfoot Lee
Thomas Adams

On the part and Behalf of the State of No Carolina:
John Penn July 21St 1778
Corns Harnett
Jno Williams

On the part and behalf of the State of South Carolina:
Henry Laurens
Richd Hutson
William Henry Drayton
Thos Heyward Junr
Jno Mathews

On the part and behalf of the State of Georgia:
Jno Walton 24th July 1778
Edwd Telfair
Edwd Langworthy

Appendix C

The Constitution of the United States

Preamble

We the People of the United States, in Order to form a more perfect Union, establish Justice, insure domestic Tranquility, provide for the common defence, promote the general Welfare, and secure the Blessings of Liberty to ourselves and our Posterity, do ordain and establish this Constitution for the United States of America.

Article I

Section 1

All legislative Powers herein granted shall be vested in a Congress of the United States, which shall consist of a Senate and House of Representatives.

Section 2

[Clause 1] The House of Representatives shall be composed of Members chosen every second Year by the People of the several States, and the Electors in each State shall have the Qualifications requisite for Electors of the most numerous Branch of the State Legislature.

[Clause 2] No Person shall be a Representative who shall not have attained to the Age of twenty five Years, and been seven Years a Citizen of the United States, and who shall not, when elected, be an Inhabitant of that State in which he shall be chosen.

[Clause 3] Representatives and direct Taxes shall be apportioned among the several States which may be included within this Union, according to their respective Numbers, which shall be determined by adding to the whole Number of free Persons, including those bound to Service for a Term of Years, and excluding Indians not taxed, three fifths of all other Persons. [*The part of this Clause relating to the mode of apportionment of representatives among the several States has been affected by Section 2 of amendment XIV, and as to taxes on incomes without apportionment by amendment XVI.*] The actual Enumeration shall be made within three Years after the first Meeting of the Congress of the United States, and within every subsequent Term of ten Years, in such Manner as they shall by Law direct. The Number of Representatives shall not exceed one for every thirty Thousand, but each State shall have at Least one Representative; and until such enumeration shall be made, the State of New Hampshire shall be entitled to chuse three, Massachusetts eight, Rhode-Island and Providence Plantations one, Connecticut five, New-York six, New Jersey four, Pennsylvania eight, Delaware one, Maryland six, Virginia ten, North Carolina five, South Carolina five, and Georgia three.

[Clause 4] When vacancies happen in the Representation from any State, the Executive Authority thereof shall issue Writs of Election to fill such Vacancies.

[Clause 5] The House of Representatives shall chuse their Speaker and other Officers; and shall have the sole Power of Impeachment.

Section 3

[Clause 1] The Senate of the United States shall be composed of two Senators from each State, chosen by the Legislature thereof, for six Years; and each Senator shall have one Vote. [*This Clause has been affected by Clause 1 of Amendment XVII.*]

[Clause 2] Immediately after they shall be assembled in Consequence of the first Election, they shall be divided as equally as may be into three Classes. The Seats of the Senators of the first Class shall be vacated at the Expiration of the second Year, of the second Class at the Expiration of the fourth Year, and of the third Class at the Expiration of the sixth Year, so that one third may be chosen every second Year; and if Vacancies happen by Resignation, or otherwise, during the Recess of the Legislature of any State, the Executive thereof may make temporary Appointments until the next Meeting of the Legislature, which shall then fill such Vacancies. [*This Clause has been affected by Clause 2 of Amendment XVIII.*]

[Clause 3] No Person shall be a Senator who shall not have attained to the Age of thirty Years, and been nine Years a Citizen of the United States, and who shall not, when elected, be an Inhabitant of that State for which he shall be chosen.

[Clause 4] The Vice President of the United States shall be President of the Senate, but shall have no Vote, unless they be equally divided.

[Clause 5] The Senate shall chuse their other Officers, and also a President pro tempore, in the Absence of the Vice President, or when he shall exercise the Office of President of the United States.

[Clause 6] The Senate shall have the sole Power to try all Impeachments. When sitting for that Purpose, they shall be on Oath or Affirmation. When the President of the United States is tried, the Chief Justice shall preside: And no Person shall be convicted without the Concurrence of two thirds of the Members present.

[Clause 7] Judgment in Cases of Impeachment shall not extend further than to removal from Office, and disqualification to hold and enjoy any Office of honor, Trust or Profit under the United States: but the Party convicted shall nevertheless be liable and subject to Indictment, Trial, Judgment and Punishment, according to Law.

Section 4

[Clause 1] The Times, Places and Manner of holding Elections for Senators and Representatives, shall be prescribed in each State by the Legislature thereof; but the Congress may at any time by Law make or alter such Regulations, except as to the Places of chusing Senators.

[Clause 2] The Congress shall assemble at least once in every Year, and such Meeting shall be on the first Monday in December, unless they shall by Law appoint a different Day. [*This Clause has been affected by Amendment XX.*]

Section 5

[Clause 1] Each House shall be the Judge of the Elections, Returns and Qualifications of its own Members, and a Majority of each shall constitute a Quorum to do Business; but a smaller Number may adjourn from day to day, and may be authorized to compel the Attendance of absent Members, in such Manner, and under such Penalties as each House may provide.

[Clause 2] Each House may determine the Rules of its Proceedings, punish its Members for disorderly Behaviour, and, with the Concurrence of two thirds, expel a Member.

[Clause 3] Each House shall keep a Journal of its Proceedings, and from time to time publish the same, excepting such Parts as may in their Judgment require Secrecy; and the Yeas and Nays of the Members of either House on any question shall, at the Desire of one fifth of those Present, be entered on the Journal.

[Clause 4] Neither House, during the Session of Congress, shall, without the Consent of the other, adjourn for more than three days, nor to any other Place than that in which the two Houses shall be sitting.

Section 6

[Clause 1] The Senators and Representatives shall receive a Compensation for their Services, to be ascertained by Law, and paid out of the Treasury of the United States. [*This Clause has been affected by Amendment XXVII.*] They shall in all Cases, except Treason, Felony and Breach of the Peace, be privileged from Arrest during their Attendance at the Session of their respective Houses, and in going to and returning from the same; and for any Speech or Debate in either House, they shall not be questioned in any other Place.

[Clause 2] No Senator or Representative shall, during the Time for which he was elected, be appointed to any civil Office under the Authority of the United States, which shall have been created, or the Emoluments whereof shall have been increased during such time; and no Person holding any Office under the United States, shall be a Member of either House during his Continuance in Office.

Section 7

[Clause 1] All Bills for raising Revenue shall originate in the House of Representatives; but the Senate may propose or concur with Amendments as on other Bills.

[Clause 2] Every Bill which shall have passed the House of Representatives and the Senate, shall, before it become a Law, be presented to the President of the United States; If he approve he shall sign it, but if not he shall return it, with his Objections to that House in which it shall have originated, who shall enter the Objections at large on their Journal, and proceed to reconsider it. If after such Reconsideration two thirds of that House shall agree to pass the Bill, it shall be sent, together with the Objections, to the other House, by which it shall likewise be reconsidered, and if approved by two thirds of that House, it shall become a Law. But in all such Cases the Votes of both Houses shall be determined by yeas and Nays, and the Names of the Persons voting for and against the Bill shall be entered on the Journal of each House respectively. If any Bill shall not be returned by the President within ten Days (Sundays excepted) after it shall have been presented to him, the Same shall be a Law, in like Manner as if he had signed it, unless the Congress by their Adjournment prevent its Return, in which Case it shall not be a Law.

[Clause 3] Every Order, Resolution, or Vote to which the Concurrence of the Senate and House of Representatives may be necessary (except on a question of Adjournment) shall be presented to the President of the United States; and before the Same shall take Effect, shall be approved by him, or being disapproved by him, shall be repassed by two thirds of the Senate and House of Representatives, according to the Rules and Limitations prescribed in the Case of a Bill.

Section 8

[Clause 1] The Congress shall have Power To lay and collect Taxes, Duties, Imposts and Excises, to pay the Debts and provide for the common Defence and general Welfare of the United States; but all Duties, Imposts and Excises shall be uniform throughout the United States;

[Clause 2] To borrow Money on the credit of the United States;

[Clause 3] To regulate Commerce with foreign Nations, and among the several States, and with the Indian Tribes;

[Clause 4] To establish an uniform Rule of Naturalization, and uniform Laws on the subject of Bankruptcies throughout the United States;

[Clause 5] To coin Money, regulate the Value thereof, and of foreign Coin, and fix the

Standard of Weights and Measures;

[Clause 6] To provide for the Punishment of counterfeiting the Securities and current Coin of the United States;

[Clause 7] To establish Post Offices and post Roads;

[Clause 8] To promote the Progress of Science and useful Arts, by securing for limited Times to Authors and Inventors the exclusive Right to their respective Writings and Discoveries;

[Clause 9] To constitute Tribunals inferior to the Supreme Court;

[Clause 10] To define and punish Piracies and Felonies committed on the high Seas, and Offences against the Law of Nations;

[Clause 11] To declare War, grant Letters of Marque and Reprisal, and make Rules concerning Captures on Land and Water;

[Clause 12] To raise and support Armies, but no Appropriation of Money to that Use shall be for a longer Term than two Years;

[Clause 13] To provide and maintain a Navy;

[Clause 14] To make Rules for the Government and Regulation of the land and naval Forces;

[Clause 15] To provide for calling forth the Militia to execute the Laws of the Union, suppress Insurrections and repel Invasions;

[Clause 16] To provide for organizing, arming, and disciplining, the Militia, and for governing such Part of them as may be employed in the Service of the United States, reserving to the States respectively, the Appointment of the Officers, and the Authority of training the Militia according to the discipline prescribed by Congress;

[Clause 17] To exercise exclusive Legislation in all Cases whatsoever, over such District (not exceeding ten Miles square) as may, by Cession of particular States, and the Acceptance of Congress, become the Seat of the Government of the United States, and to exercise like Authority over all Places purchased by the Consent of the Legislature of the State in which the Same shall be, for the Erection of Forts, Magazines, Arsenals, dock-Yards, and other needful Buildings; – And

[Clause 18] To make all Laws which shall be necessary and proper for carrying into Execution the foregoing Powers, and all other Powers vested by this Constitution in the Government of the United States, or in any Department or Officer thereof.

Section 9

[Clause 1] The Migration or Importation of such Persons as any of the States now existing shall think proper to admit, shall not be prohibited by the Congress prior to the Year one thousand eight hundred and eight, but a Tax or duty may be imposed on such Importation, not exceeding ten dollars for each Person.

[Clause 2] The Privilege of the Writ of Habeas Corpus shall not be suspended, unless when in Cases of Rebellion or Invasion the public Safety may require it.

[Clause 3] No Bill of Attainder or ex post facto Law shall be passed.

[Clause 4] No Capitation, or other direct, Tax shall be laid, unless in Proportion to the Census or Enumeration herein before directed to be taken. [*This Clause has been affected by Amendment XVI.*]

[Clause 5] No Tax or Duty shall be laid on Articles exported from any State.

[Clause 6] No Preference shall be given by any Regulation of Commerce or Revenue to the Ports of one State over those of another: nor shall Vessels bound to, or from, one State, be obliged to enter, clear, or pay Duties in another.

[Clause 7] No Money shall be drawn from the Treasury, but in Consequence of Appropriations made by Law; and a regular Statement and Account of the Receipts and Expenditures of all public Money shall be published from time to time.

[Clause 8] No Title of Nobility shall be granted by the United States: And no Person holding any Office of Profit or Trust under them, shall, without the Consent of the Congress, accept of any present, Emolument, Office, or Title, of any kind whatever, from any King, Prince, or foreign State.

Section 10

[Clause 1] No State shall enter into any Treaty, Alliance, or Confederation; grant Letters of Marque and Reprisal; coin Money; emit Bills of Credit; make any Thing but gold and silver Coin a Tender in Payment of Debts; pass any Bill of Attainder, ex post facto Law, or Law impairing the Obligation of Contracts, or grant any Title of Nobility.

[Clause 2] No State shall, without the Consent of the Congress, lay any Imposts or Duties on Imports or Exports, except what may be absolutely necessary for executing its inspection Laws: and the net Produce of all Duties and Imposts, laid by any State on Imports or Exports, shall be for the Use of the Treasury of the United States; and all such Laws shall be subject to the Revision and Controul of the Congress.

[Clause 3] No State shall, without the Consent of Congress, lay any Duty of Tonnage, keep Troops, or Ships of War in time of Peace, enter into any Agreement or Compact with another State, or with a foreign Power, or engage in War, unless actually invaded, or in such imminent Danger as will not admit of delay.

Article II

Section 1

[Clause 1] The executive Power shall be vested in a President of the United States of America. He shall hold his Office during the Term of four Years, and, together with the Vice President, chosen for the same Term, be elected, as follows

[Clause 2] Each State shall appoint, in such Manner as the Legislature thereof may direct, a Number of Electors, equal to the whole Number of Senators and Representatives to which the State may be entitled in the Congress: but no Senator or Representative, or Person holding an Office of Trust or Profit under the United States, shall be appointed an Elector.

[Clause 3] The Electors shall meet in their respective States, and vote by Ballot for two Persons, of whom one at least shall not be an Inhabitant of the same State with themselves. And they shall make a List of all the Persons voted for, and of the Number of Votes for each; which List they shall sign and certify, and transmit sealed to the Seat of the Government of the United States, directed to the President of the Senate. The President of the Senate shall, in the Presence of the Senate and House of Representatives, open all the Certificates, and the Votes shall then be counted. The Person having the greatest Number of Votes shall be the President, if such Number be a Majority of the whole Number of Electors appointed; and if there be more than one who have such Majority, and have an equal Number of Votes, then the House of Representatives shall immediately chuse by Ballot one of them for President; and if no Person have a Majority, then from the five highest on the List the said House shall in like Manner chuse the President. But in chusing the President, the Votes shall be taken by States, the Representation from each State having one Vote; A quorum for this Purpose shall consist of a Member or Members from two thirds of the States, and a Majority of all the States shall be necessary to a Choice. In every Case, after the Choice of the President, the Person having the greatest Number of Votes of the Electors shall be the Vice President. But if there should remain two or more who have equal Votes, the Senate shall chuse from them by Ballot the Vice President. [*This Clause has been superseded by Amendment XII.*]

[Clause 4] The Congress may determine the Time of chusing the Electors, and the Day on which they shall give their Votes; which Day shall be the same throughout the United States.

[Clause 5] No Person except a natural born Citizen, or a Citizen of the United States, at the time of the Adoption of this Constitution, shall be eligible to the Office of President; neither shall any Person be eligible to that Office who shall not have attained to the Age of thirty five Years, and been fourteen Years a Resident within the United States.

[Clause 6] In Case of the Removal of the President from Office, or of his Death, Resignation, or Inability to discharge the Powers and Duties of the said Office, the Same shall devolve on the Vice President, and the Congress may by Law provide for the Case of Removal, Death, Resignation or Inability, both of the President and Vice President, declaring what Officer shall then act as President, and such Officer shall act accordingly, until the Disability be removed, or a President shall be elected. [*This Clause has been affected by Amendment XXV.*]

[Clause 7] The President shall, at stated Times, receive for his Services, a Compensation, which shall neither be increased nor diminished during the Period for which he shall have been elected, and he shall not receive within that Period any other Emolument from the United States, or any of them.

[Clause 8] Before he enter on the Execution of his Office, he shall take the following Oath or Affirmation: – "I do solemnly swear (or affirm) that I will faithfully execute the Office of President of the United States, and will to the best of my Ability, preserve, protect and defend the Constitution of the United States."

Section 2

[Clause 1] The President shall be Commander in Chief of the Army and Navy of the United States, and of the Militia of the several States, when called into the actual Service of the United States; he may require the Opinion, in writing, of the principal Officer in each of the executive Departments, upon any Subject relating to the Duties of their respective Offices, and he shall have Power to grant Reprieves and Pardons for Offences against the United States, except in Cases of Impeachment.

[Clause 2] He shall have Power, by and with the Advice and Consent of the Senate, to make Treaties, provided two thirds of the Senators present concur; and he shall nominate, and by and with the Advice and Consent of the Senate, shall appoint Ambassadors, other public Ministers and Consuls, Judges of the Supreme Court, and all other Officers of the United States, whose Appointments are not herein otherwise provided for, and which shall be established by Law: but the Congress may by Law vest the Appointment of such inferior Officers, as they think proper, in the President alone, in the Courts of Law, or in the Heads of Departments.

[Clause 3] The President shall have Power to fill up all Vacancies that may happen during the Recess of the Senate, by granting Commissions which shall expire at the End of their next Session.

Section 3

He shall from time to time give to the Congress Information of the State of the Union, and recommend to their Consideration such Measures as he shall judge necessary and expedient; he may, on extraordinary Occasions, convene both Houses, or either of them, and in Case of Disagreement between them, with Respect to the Time of Adjournment, he may adjourn them to such Time as he shall think proper; he shall receive Ambassadors and other public Ministers; he shall take Care that the Laws be faithfully executed, and shall Commission all the Officers of the United States.

Section 4

The President, Vice President and all civil Officers of the United States, shall be removed from Office on Impeachment for, and Conviction of, Treason, Bribery, or other high Crimes and Misdemeanors.

Article III

Section 1

The judicial Power of the United States, shall be vested in one Supreme Court, and in such inferior Courts as the Congress may from time to time ordain and establish. The Judges, both of the supreme and inferior Courts, shall hold their Offices during good Behaviour, and shall, at stated Times, receive for their Services, a Compensation, which shall not be diminished during their Continuance in Office.

Section 2

[Clause 1] The judicial Power shall extend to all Cases, in Law and Equity, arising under this Constitution, the Laws of the United States, and Treaties made, or which shall be made, under their Authority; – to all Cases affecting Ambassadors, other public Ministers and Consuls; – to all Cases of admiralty and maritime Jurisdiction; – to Controversies to which the United States shall be a Party; – to Controversies between two or more States; – between a State and Citizens of another State; – between Citizens of different States, –between Citizens of the same State claiming Lands under Grants of different States, and between a State, or the Citizens thereof, and foreign States, Citizens or Subjects. [*This Clause has been affected by Amendment XI.*]

[Clause 2] In all Cases affecting Ambassadors, other public Ministers and Consuls, and those in which a State shall be Party, the Supreme Court shall have original Jurisdiction. In all the other Cases before mentioned, the Supreme Court shall have appellate Jurisdiction, both as to Law and Fact, with such Exceptions, and under such Regulations as the Congress shall make.

[Clause 3] The Trial of all Crimes, except in Cases of Impeachment, shall be by Jury; and such Trial shall be held in the State where the said Crimes shall have been committed; but when not committed within any State, the Trial shall be at such Place or Places as the Congress may by Law have directed.

Section 3

[Clause 1] Treason against the United States, shall consist only in levying War against them, or in adhering to their Enemies, giving them Aid and Comfort. No Person shall be convicted of Treason unless on the Testimony of two Witnesses to the same overt Act, or on Confession in open Court.

[Clause 2] The Congress shall have Power to declare the Punishment of Treason, but no Attainder of Treason shall work Corruption of Blood, or Forfeiture except during the Life of the Person attainted.

Article IV

Section 1

Full Faith and Credit shall be given in each State to the public Acts, Records, and judicial Proceedings of every other State. And the Congress may by general Laws prescribe the Manner in which such Acts, Records and Proceedings shall be proved, and the Effect thereof.

Section 2

[Clause 1] The Citizens of each State shall be entitled to all Privileges and Immunities of Citizens in the several States.

[Clause 2] A Person charged in any State with Treason, Felony, or other Crime, who shall flee from Justice, and be found in another State, shall on Demand of the executive Authority of the State from which he fled, be delivered up, to be removed to the State having Jurisdiction of the Crime.

[Clause 3] No Person held to Service or Labour in one State, under the Laws thereof, escaping into another, shall, in Consequence of any Law or Regulation therein, be discharged from such Service or Labour, but shall be delivered up on Claim of the Party to whom such Service or Labour may be due. [*This Clause has been affected by Amendment XIII.*]

Section 3

[Clause 1] New States may be admitted by the Congress into this Union; but no new State shall be formed or erected within the Jurisdiction of any other State; nor any State be formed by the Junction of two or more States, or Parts of States, without the Consent of the Legislatures of the States concerned as well as of the Congress.

[Clause 2] The Congress shall have Power to dispose of and make all needful Rules and Regulations respecting the Territory or other Property belonging to the United States; and nothing in this Constitution shall be so construed as to Prejudice any Claims of the United States, or of any particular State.

Section 4

The United States shall guarantee to every State in this Union a Republican Form of Government, and shall protect each of them against Invasion; and on Application of the Legislature, or of the Executive (when the Legislature cannot be convened) against domestic Violence.

Article V

The Congress, whenever two thirds of both Houses shall deem it necessary, shall propose Amendments to this Constitution, or, on the Application of the Legislatures of two thirds of the several States, shall call a Convention for proposing Amendments, which, in either Case, shall be valid to all Intents and Purposes, as Part of this Constitution, when ratified by the Legislatures of three fourths of the several States, or by Conventions in three fourths thereof, as the one or the other Mode of Ratification may be proposed by the Congress; Provided that no Amendment which may be made prior to the Year One thousand eight hundred and eight shall in any Manner affect the first and fourth Clauses in the Ninth Section of the first Article; and that no State, without its Consent, shall be deprived of its equal Suffrage in the Senate.

Article VI

[Clause 1] All Debts contracted and Engagements entered into, before the Adoption of this Constitution, shall be as valid against the United States under this Constitution, as under the Confederation.

[Clause 2] This Constitution, and the Laws of the United States which shall be made in Pursuance thereof; and all Treaties made, or which shall be made, under the Authority of the United States, shall be the supreme Law of the Land; and the Judges in every State shall be bound thereby, any Thing in the Constitution or Laws of any State to the Contrary notwithstanding.

[Clause 3] The Senators and Representatives before mentioned, and the Members of the several State Legislatures, and all executive and judicial Officers, both of the United States and of the several States, shall be bound by Oath or Affirmation, to support this Constitution; but no religious Test shall ever be required as a Qualification to any Office or public Trust under the United States.

Article VII

The Ratification of the Conventions of nine States, shall be sufficient for the Establishment of this Constitution between the States so ratifying the Same.

Done in Convention by the Unanimous Consent of the States present the Seventeenth Day of September in the Year of our Lord one thousand seven hundred and Eighty seven and of the Independence of the United States of America the Twelfth In witness whereof We have hereunto subscribed our Names,

GO WASHINGTON--Presidt. and deputy from Virginia

Delaware
Geo: Read
Gunning Bedford jun
John Dickinson
Richard Bassett
Jaco: Broom

Maryland
James MCHenry
Dan of ST ThoS. Jenifer
DanL Carroll.

Virginia
John Blair--
James Madison Jr.
North Carolina
WM Blount
RichD. Dobbs Spaight.
Hu Williamson

South Carolina
J. Rutledge
Charles 1ACotesworth Pinckney
Charles Pinckney
Pierce Butler.

Georgia
William Few
Abr Baldwin

New Hampshire
John Langdon
Nicholas Gilman

Massachusetts

Nathaniel Gorham
Rufus King

Connecticut
Wm. SamL. Johnson
Roger Sherman

New York
Alexander Hamilton

New Jersey
Wil: Livingston
David Brearley.
WM. Paterson.
Jona: Dayton

Pennsylvania
B Franklin
Thomas Mifflin
RobT Morris
Geo. Clymer
ThoS. FitzSimons
Jared Ingersoll
James Wilson.
Gouv Morris

Attest William Jackson Secretary

Amendment I

Congress shall make no law respecting an establishment of religion, or prohibiting the free exercise thereof; or abridging the freedom of speech, or of the press; or the right of the people peaceably to assemble, and to petition the Government for a redress of grievances.

Amendment II

A well regulated Militia, being necessary to the security of a free State, the right of the people to keep and bear Arms, shall not be infringed.

Amendment III

No Soldier shall, in time of peace be quartered in any house, without the consent of the Owner, nor in time of war, but in a manner to be prescribed by law.

Amendment IV

The right of the people to be secure in their persons, houses, papers, and effects, against unreasonable searches and seizures, shall not be violated, and no Warrants shall issue, but upon probable cause, supported by Oath or affirmation, and particularly describing the place to be searched, and the persons or things to be seized.

Amendment V

No person shall be held to answer for a capital, or otherwise infamous crime, unless on a presentment or indictment of a Grand Jury, except in cases arising in the land or naval forces, or in the Militia, when in actual service in time of War or public danger; nor shall any person be subject for the same offence to be twice put in jeopardy of life or limb; nor shall be compelled in any criminal case to be a witness against himself, nor be deprived of life, liberty, or property, without due process of law; nor shall private property be taken for public use, without just compensation.

Amendment VI

In all criminal prosecutions, the accused shall enjoy the right to a speedy and public trial, by an impartial jury of the State and district wherein the crime shall have been committed, which district shall have been previously ascertained by law, and to be informed of the nature and cause of the accusation; to be confronted with the witnesses against him; to have compulsory process for obtaining witnesses in his favor, and to have the Assistance of Counsel for his defence.

Amendment VII

In Suits at common law, where the value in controversy shall exceed twenty dollars, the right of trial by jury shall be preserved, and no fact tried by a jury, shall be otherwise re-examined in any Court of the United States, than according to the rules of the common law.

Amendment VIII

Excessive bail shall not be required, nor excessive fines imposed, nor cruel and unusual punishments inflicted.

Amendment IX

The enumeration in the Constitution, of certain rights, shall not be construed to deny or disparage others retained by the people.

Amendment X

The powers not delegated to the United States by the Constitution, nor prohibited by it to the States, are reserved to the States respectively, or to the people.

Amendment XI

The Judicial power of the United States shall not be construed to extend to any suit in law or equity, commenced or prosecuted against one of the United States by Citizens of another State, or by Citizens or Subjects of any Foreign State.

Amendment XII

The Electors shall meet in their respective States, and vote by ballot for President and Vice-President, one of whom, at least, shall not be an inhabitant of the same State with themselves; they shall name in their ballots the person voted for as President, and in distinct ballots the person voted for as Vice-President, and they shall make distinct lists of all persons voted for as President, and of all persons voted for as Vice-President, and of the number of votes for each, which lists they shall sign and certify, and transmit sealed to the seat of the government of the United States, directed to the President of the Senate; –The President of the Senate shall, in the presence of the Senate and House of Representatives, open all the certificates and the votes shall then be counted; –The person having the greatest number of votes for President, shall be the President, if such number be a majority of the whole number of Electors appointed; and if no person have such majority, then from the persons having the highest numbers not exceeding three on the list of those voted for as President, the House of Representatives shall choose immediately, by ballot, the President. But in choosing the President, the votes shall be taken by States, the representation from each State having one vote; a quorum for this purpose shall consist of a member or members from two-thirds of the States, and a majority of all the States shall be necessary to a choice. And if the House of Representatives shall not choose a President whenever the right of choice shall devolve upon them, before the fourth day of March next following, then the Vice-President shall act as President, as in the case of the death or other constitutional disability of the President. [*This sentence has been superseded by section 3 of Amendment XX*] – The person having the greatest number of votes as Vice-President, shall be the Vice-President, if such number be a majority of the whole number of Electors appointed, and if no person have a majority, then from the two highest numbers on the list, the Senate shall choose the Vice-President; a quorum for the purpose shall consist of two-thirds of the whole number of Senators, and a majority of the whole number shall be necessary to a choice. But no person constitutionally ineligible to the office of President shall be eligible to that of Vice-President of the United States.

Amendment XIII

Section 1. Neither slavery nor involuntary servitude, except as a punishment for crime whereof the party shall have been duly convicted, shall exist within the United States, or any place subject to their jurisdiction.

Section 2. Congress shall have power to enforce this article by appropriate legislation.

Amendment XIV

[*Not Lawfully Ratified*]

Section 1. All persons born or naturalized in the United States, and subject to the jurisdiction thereof, are citizens of the United States and of the State wherein they reside. No State shall make or enforce any law which shall abridge the privileges or immunities of citizens of the United States; nor shall any State deprive any person of life, liberty, or property, without due process of law; nor deny to any person within its jurisdiction the equal protection of the laws.

Section 2. Representatives shall be apportioned among the several States according to their respective numbers, counting the whole number of persons in each State, excluding Indians not taxed. But when the right to vote at any election for the choice of electors for President and Vice President of the United States, Representatives in Congress, the Executive and Judicial officers of a State, or the members of the Legislature thereof, is denied to any of the male inhabitants of such State, being twenty-one years of age, [*See amendment XIX and section 1 of amendment XXVI.*] and citizens of the United States, or in any way abridged, except for participation in rebellion, or other crime, the basis of representation therein shall be reduced in the proportion which the number of such male citizens shall bear to the whole number of male citizens twenty-one years of age in such State.

Section 3. No person shall be a Senator or Representative in Congress, or elector of President and Vice President, or hold any office, civil or military, under the United States, or under any State, who, having previously taken an oath, as a member of Congress, or as an officer of the United States, or as a member of any State legislature, or as an executive or judicial officer of any State, to support the Constitution of the United States, shall have engaged in insurrection or rebellion against the same, or given aid or comfort to the enemies thereof. But Congress may by a vote of two-thirds of each House, remove such disability.

Section 4. The validity of the public debt of the United States, authorized by law, including debts incurred for payment of pensions and bounties for services in suppressing insurrection or rebellion, shall not be questioned. But neither the United States nor any State shall assume or pay any debt or obligation incurred in aid of insurrection or rebellion against the United States, or any claim for the loss or emancipation of any slave; but all such debts, obligations and claims shall be held illegal and void.

Section 5. The Congress shall have power to enforce, by appropriate legislation, the provisions of this article.

Amendment XV

Section 1. The right of citizens of the United States to vote shall not be denied or abridged by the United States or by any State on account of race, color, or previous condition of servitude.

Section 2. The Congress shall have power to enforce this article by appropriate legislation.

Amendment XVI

The Congress shall have power to lay and collect taxes on incomes, from whatever source derived, without apportionment among the several States, and without regard to any census or enumeration.

Amendment XVII

The Senate of the United States shall be composed of two Senators from each State, elected by the people thereof, for six years; and each Senator shall have one vote. The electors in each State shall have the qualifications requisite for electors of the most numerous branch of the State legislatures.

When vacancies happen in the representation of any State in the Senate, the executive authority of such State shall issue writs of election to fill such vacancies: Provided, That the legislature of any State may empower the executive thereof to make temporary appointments until the people fill the vacancies by election as the legislature may direct.

This amendment shall not be so construed as to affect the election or term of any Senator chosen before it becomes valid as part of the Constitution.

Amendment XVIII

[*Repealed by Section 1 of Amendment XXI.*]

Section 1. After one year from the ratification of this article the manufacture, sale, or transportation of intoxicating liquors within, the importation thereof into, or the exportation thereof from the United States and all territory subject to the jurisdiction thereof for beverage purposes is hereby prohibited.

Section. 2. The Congress and the several States shall have concurrent power to enforce this article by appropriate legislation.

Section. 3. This article shall be inoperative unless it shall have been ratified as an amendment to the Constitution by the legislatures of the several States, as provided in the Constitution, within seven years from the date of the submission hereof to the States by the Congress.

Amendment XIX

The right of citizens of the United States to vote shall not be denied or abridged by the United States or by any State on account of sex.

Congress shall have power to enforce this article by appropriate legislation.

Amendment XX

Section 1. The terms of the President and Vice President shall end at noon on the 20th day of January, and the terms of Senators and Representatives at noon on the 3d day of January, of the years in which such terms would have ended if this article had not been ratified; and the terms of their successors shall then begin.

Section. 2. The Congress shall assemble at least once in every year, and such meeting shall begin at noon on the 3d day of January, unless they shall by law appoint a different day.

Section. 3. If, at the time fixed for the beginning of the term of the President, the President elect shall have died, the Vice President elect shall become President. If a President shall not have been chosen before the time fixed for the beginning of his term, or if the President elect shall have failed to qualify, then the Vice President elect shall act as President until a President shall have qualified; and the Congress may by law provide for the case wherein neither a President elect nor a Vice President elect shall have qualified, declaring who shall then act as President, or the manner in which one who is to act shall be selected, and such person shall act accordingly until a President or Vice President shall have qualified.

Section. 4. The Congress may by law provide for the case of the death of any of the persons from whom the House of Representatives may choose a President whenever the right of choice shall have devolved upon them, and for the case of the death of any of the persons from whom the Senate may choose a Vice President whenever the right of choice shall have devolved upon them.

Section. 5. Sections 1 and 2 shall take effect on the 15th day of October following the ratification of this article.

Section. 6. This article shall be inoperative unless it shall have been ratified as an amendment to the Constitution by the legislatures of three-fourths of the several States within seven years from the date of its submission.

Amendment XXI

Section 1. The eighteenth article of amendment to the Constitution of the United States is hereby repealed.

Section 2. The transportation or importation into any State, Territory, or possession of the United States for delivery or use therein of intoxicating liquors, in violation of the laws thereof, is hereby prohibited.

Section 3. This article shall be inoperative unless it shall have been ratified as an amendment to the Constitution by conventions in the several States, as provided in the Constitution, within seven years from the date of the submission hereof to the States by the Congress.

Amendment XXII

Section 1. No person shall be elected to the office of the President more than twice, and no person who has held the office of President, or acted as President, for more than two years of a term to which some other person was elected President shall be elected to the office of the President more than once. But this article shall not apply to any person holding the office of President when this article was proposed by the Congress, and shall not prevent any person who may be holding the office of President, or acting as President, during the term within which this article becomes operative from holding the office of President or acting as President during the remainder of such term.

Section 2. This article shall be inoperative unless it shall have been ratified as an amendment to the Constitution by the legislatures of three-fourths of the several states within seven years from the date of its submission to the states by the Congress.

Amendment XXIII

Section 1. The District constituting the seat of government of the United States shall appoint in such manner as the Congress may direct:

A number of electors of President and Vice President equal to the whole number of Senators and Representatives in Congress to which the District would be entitled if it were a state, but in no event more than the least populous State; they shall be in addition to those appointed by the States, but they shall be considered, for the purposes of the election of President and Vice President, to be electors appointed by a State; and they shall meet in the District and perform such duties as provided by the twelfth article of amendment.

Section 2. The Congress shall have power to enforce this article by appropriate legislation.

Amendment XXIV

Section 1. The right of citizens of the United States to vote in any primary or other election for President or Vice President, for electors for President or Vice President, or for Senator or Representative in Congress, shall not be denied or abridged by the United States or any state by reason of failure to pay any poll tax or other tax.

Section 2. The Congress shall have power to enforce this article by appropriate legislation.

Amendment XXV

Section 1. In case of the removal of the President from office or of his death or resignation, the Vice President shall become President.

Section 2. Whenever there is a vacancy in the office of the Vice President, the President shall nominate a Vice President who shall take office upon confirmation by a majority vote of both Houses of Congress.

Section 3. Whenever the President transmits to the President pro tempore of the Senate and the Speaker of the House of Representatives his written declaration that he is unable to discharge the powers and duties of his office, and until he transmits to them a written declaration to the contrary, such powers and duties shall be discharged by the Vice President as Acting President.

Section 4. Whenever the Vice President and a majority of either the principal officers of the executive departments or of such other body as Congress may by law provide, transmit to the President pro tempore of the Senate and the Speaker of the House of Representatives their written declaration that the President is unable to discharge the powers and duties of his office, the Vice President shall immediately assume the powers and duties of the office as Acting President.

Thereafter, when the President transmits to the President pro tempore of the Senate and the Speaker of the House of Representatives his written declaration that no inability exists, he shall resume the powers and duties of his office unless the Vice President and a majority of either the principal officers of the executive department or of such other body as Congress may by law provide, transmit within four days to the President pro tempore of the Senate and the Speaker of the House of Representatives their written declaration that the President is unable to discharge the powers and duties of his office. Thereupon Congress shall decide the issue, assembling within forty-eight hours for that purpose if not in session. If the Congress, within twenty-one days after receipt of the latter written declaration, or, if Congress is not in session, within twenty-one days after Congress is required to assemble, determines by two-thirds vote of both Houses that the President is unable to discharge the powers and duties of his office, the Vice President shall continue to discharge the same as Acting President; otherwise, the President shall resume the powers and duties of his office.

Amendment XXVI

Section 1. The right of citizens of the United States, who are 18 years of age or older, to vote, shall not be denied or abridged by the United States or any State on account of age.

Section 2. The Congress shall have the power to enforce this article by appropriate legislation.

Amendment XXVII

No law varying the compensation for the services of the Senators and Representatives shall take effect until an election of Representatives shall have intervened.

Index